The Elements of Statistics
with Applications to Economics and the Social Sciences

James B. Ramsey
New York University

with Labs by

H. Joseph Newton
Texas A&M University

Jane Harvill
Mississippi State University

Contributors

DUXBURY
™
THOMSON LEARNING

Australia • Canada • Mexico • Singapore • Spain • United Kingdom • United States

DUXBURY

THOMSON LEARNING

Statistics Editor: Curt Hinrichs
Editorial Assistant: Nathan Day
Technology Project Manager: Burke Taft
Marketing Manager: Tom Ziolkowski
Print/Media Buyer: Karen Hunt
Permissions Editor: Stephanie Keough-Hedges
Production: Greg Hubit Bookworks

Text Designer: Harry Voigt
Copy Editor: Lura Harrison
Illustrator: Publication Services
Cover Designer: Lisa Langhoff
Cover Illustrator: Gary Eldridge/The Stock Illustration Source
Compositor: Publication Services
Printer: Transcontinental Printing

Included on the accompanying CD are StatConcepts laboratories by H. Joseph Newton of Texas A&M University and Jane Harvill of Mississippi State University. StatConcepts contains visual demonstrations of important statistical concepts in an interactive learning environment. For more extensive study and full documentation of StatConcepts, we recommend you purchase StatConcepts (ISBN 0-534-26552-9) from your local bookseller.

ISBN 0-534-37111-6

Wadsworth Group/Thomson Learning
10 Davis Drive
Belmont, CA 94002-3098
USA

For more information about our products, contact us:
Thomson Learning Academic Resource Center
1-800-423-0563
http://www.duxbury.com

International Headquarters
Thomson Learning
International Division
290 Harbor Drive, 2nd Floor
Stamford, CT 06902-7477
USA

UK/Europe/Middle East/South Africa
Thomson Learning
Berkshire House
168-173 High Holborn
London WC1V 7AA
United Kingdom

Asia
Thomson Learning
60 Albert Street, #15-01
Albert Complex
Singapore 189969

Canada
Nelson Thomson Learning
1120 Birchmount Road
Toronto, Ontario M1K 5G4
Canada

Brief Contents

*On CD only.

Detailed Contents

Part Four   Basic Principles of Inference   313

*On CD only.

Preface

This Preface is useful for explaining to both the reader and the instructor my objectives in presenting the material in this text as I did. I begin by defining the intended readership and the organization of the text. This leads to a discussion of the innovations in the text and the reasons for including them. Next, I discuss the careful design that underlies the Exercises; mere "numbers" are not enough. I then summarize the required level of mathematical reasoning in the last section.

Because my objectives for the reader of this text differ from those in conventional texts, some students may require guidance to use the text most effectively. This is especially true of the Exercises. Consequently, at the end of Chapter 1, I have provided an "Addendum for the Reader," which every student is strongly encouraged to read.

The Intended Audience

This is intended as an introduction to statistical reasoning for undergraduates at the sophomore level who have an inquiring mind. By this, I mean the type of student who, if presented with a challenge, will attempt to respond and, if encouraged and aided to do so, will enjoy experimenting with new ideas.

Because I am an economist who teaches in a faculty of arts and science department as well as in a business school, my initial tendency was to use economic and business examples. But I soon recognized in the early stages of teaching my course that students were more interested in and receptive to examples to which they could relate personally. Consequently, as my objective was to engage students' minds, I decided that I had to show them that "statistical reasoning" is everywhere, and that they could not escape having to deal with statistical concepts. Statistical concepts were important in their personal lives, not just as a tool in their professional careers. The result is a book that is intended for an audience much broader than what is traditionally regarded as "economics and business." The intended audience is restricted only by the inquisitiveness of the student and the acceptance of innovation by the instructor. This book may be a challenge for some undergraduates, but a little perseverance will be highly rewarded. However, it is also true that the book's approach and use of computers means that for such a student learning statistics can actually be intellectually fun.

Later, I will discuss the level of mathematical reasoning this text involves, but first I want to define the text's objectives. The limited objective is to produce statistically literate people who will have acquired enough background to be taught specific tools in a work environment and who can read the popular press with new insight. By no means do I think that two quarters of instruction, or even two semesters of statistics, is enough to produce a "statistician"—someone able to work on his or her own within any organization. Further, I suspect no other instructor does either. Consequently, the task that I set myself was to produce a book that would enable a student to gain sufficient insight into statistical reasoning and practice to be able to understand the major strengths and weaknesses of the statistical approach and to appreciate what it is that statistical methods can and cannot achieve. In this connection and for the business school student in particular, it is my objective to produce someone who has sufficient theoretical background to be able to learn quickly and efficiently what specifically has to be mastered within any organization. Firms, agencies, and nonprofits all want to train their own people using their own methods. At the entry level, they are not hiring Ph.D.'s in statistics. What is wanted in the real world is the ability to learn fast. This text attempts to provide this facility in the context of statistical reasoning.

This perspective marks a substantial difference from the spirit that pervades many contemporary texts. The contemporary view seems to be to give the student as extensive an exposure to statistical procedures as possible, presumably with a view to providing someone who can enter a firm and begin applications immediately. But in one semester, such an extensive exposure comes at the cost of the intensive margin; the student gets a lot without much depth. The philosophy underlying this text is that given a reasonable level of depth in the analysis, students can later acquire a much more extensive, and even more intensive, exposure to statistics on their own, or in the context of the work environment. This text is not intended to be an encyclopedia of statistical techniques.

For the mathematically prepared student, the entire book can be covered comfortably in one semester, with classes meeting for 1 hour and 15 minutes. Students who are not well prepared mathematically also can complete the text (with the exception of Chapters 12 and 14 and the sections labeled "For the Student Comfortable with Calculus") within this time frame.

Some words about pacing are useful. The first two chapters in particular are fairly easy for students to grasp their own; two lectures will suffice, and the instructor can leave the details to the text. The next three chapters are more challenging but less so than Chapters 6 on. The book is designed so that the pace begins easily but quickly builds up. This is to help students build confidence in a course of study that has a reputation for opacity and difficulty. During the earlier "easier" period, students should ensure they have mastery over the basic algebra that will be used intensively throughout the remainder of the course; I use the first few "lab sessions" for this purpose.

The most challenging chapters that require the most time are Chapters 6 through 8 and 12. These chapters develop the basic theory, and students always have difficulty in mastering theoretical concepts. Once these have been mastered the remainder can be handled by students with equanimity, in part, because from their perspective the later material is much more concerned with practical issues.

The Organization of This Text

The basic outline of the material covered in the text is simple. The text begins with descriptive statistics. This beginning is motivated by the notion that given data that are presumed to be *acausal,* either through ignorance of the model underlying the data-generating mechanism, or because there are no causal links, one has to develop new specific tools to analyze such a unique type of data. The first two parts of the text do far more than merely list descriptive statistics. Students will see by numerous examples that large numbers of repetitions of an experiment give rise to uniquely shaped histograms. These insights are extended to bivariate data in Chapter 5. These early chapters stress the importance of the shape of histograms and the connection between shape and the experiment generating the data. Including a discussion of the description of bivariate data so early in the course is unusual but is pedagogically reasonable given my approach. Students are encouraged in the context of descriptive statistics to extend the ideas of the previous chapters to bivariate data.

By this stage in the text, students will realize that observations on random data involve regularities that are to be explained by some "theory of statistics," and that these regularities involve the shapes of bivariate histograms or scatter diagrams as well.

In Part Three, Probability theory is introduced as the theory of statistics and, more precisely, as the theory of histograms. Distributions enable students to see in detail the theoretical analysis underlying the idea of a probability distribution as an analogue of sample histograms.

Chapter 9, Elementary Sampling Theory, opens Part Four and provides the bridge between probability and distribution theory in Part Three and the observations discussed in Parts One and Two. The link between theory and observation culminates in Chapters 10 and 11, on estimation and hypothesis testing, respectively. Part Five opens with a discussion of the theory of regression in Chapter 13 and the analysis of variance in Chapter 14; this discussion complements the purely descriptive analysis contained in Chapter 5. Chapter 15 offers a retrospective on the major lessons of the text.

The Innovations in This Text

A basic feature of the style of exposition of this text is one of discovery for students. Each new step poses new questions that require answers, and students are guided in discovering the answers. Each new step provides a reasonable solution to a practical problem; results are not presented as *obiter dicta,* or incidental observations, to be remembered and not questioned. Consequently, the exposition explores the alternative solutions to a problem and then settles on a reasonable resolution as a useful procedure until a better idea comes up. Statistical procedures are presented as practical attempts to solve practical problems—not as arbitrary rules to be blindly followed by the uninitiated.

The approach taken in this text is *process* oriented, not *fact* oriented. For example, I want students to be aware of the process of convergence, not just the existence of such a property. I am more concerned that students have some intuitive feel for the process involved in the central limit theorem than that they merely know of the existence of such a phenomenon.

One key feature is to get students to realize the unique aspects of statistical theory. The first of the two most important aspects is that statistics *per se* deal with random phenomena, phenomena which by their definition are not causally related. Such phenomena are very different from all that students have been exposed to during their prior academic careers. Statistics are in essence *acausal*. Keeping this fact firmly in mind helps students to deal later in the text with the subtle issues of how to use statistical analysis to evaluate scientific hypotheses. For example, knowing that statistics are *acausal* enables students to recognize that correlation is neither necessary nor sufficient for causality. Causality can only have meaning in the context of the theory of physical phenomena, or the theory of economic phenomena, or the theory of political phenomena, and so on.

Consequently, the text begins by considering data for which we have no explanation at all; no model; and no ability to predict values, either from observing other variables or from observing the past. Having no theory, no model, we are forced to consider what we can learn from such phenomena. From performing calculations of descriptive statistics and then observing the histograms of a large number of observations on a variety of phenomena, or different experiments, students learn pragmatically several lessons. They discover from the examples that for continuous variables the histograms become smooth; that the same experiment repeated gives rise to the same shape of histogram, or relative frequency distribution for discrete data; and that different experiments give rise to different shapes of histograms, or relative frequency plots. A wide variety of examples of distributions are presented. In each case, the observed shape of a distribution is linked to the conditions of the experiment that generated it. And this is, of course, the key to statistical analysis. Students, having begun with the idea that when observing random data there was nothing to explain, now see that there are a lot of regularities and that a theory is needed to explain them. The stage is set for the development of probability theory and the derivation of density functions that is to come in the second part of the text.

Within the first two parts of the text, the first four moments play a substantial role in formalizing the ideas of the shape of a histogram and a distribution function. The focus is on enabling students to relate the shape of histograms to the values of standardized moments. Thus, students should be able to provide a reasonable guess as to the values of the first four moments from observing a smooth histogram and, in turn, provide a reasonable approximation of a smooth histogram from a given set of moments. This experience in calculating the first four sample moments and in interpreting the results provides a natural introduction to the analysis of distributions that is to come in the theoretical part of the text.

In Chapter 5, I introduce bivariate data and correlation as a *descriptive* measure of linear "association." The correlation coefficient is developed as the "first cross product moment," and as such is a natural extension of the moments discussed in Chapter 4. Further, the correlation coefficient is another measure of shape, in this case of the distribution of bivariate data. This material provides the summary statistics explained by the theory developed later in the text. The analogy between the development of descriptive bivariate statistics and the descriptive statistics developed in prior chapters is strongly emphasized; this analogy continues to apply to the corresponding development of the theory in the chapters on bivariate distributions, ANOVA, and regression.

All distributions are derived while emphasizing the relationship between experiment and the shape of the distribution. These results mirror the observed empirical results from Chapter 3. Students are led through "labs" that enable them to experiment with generating alternative distributions and comparing outcomes to sample histograms. After deriving the theoretical moments of a probability distribution and relating them to the parameters of the distribution, students will perceive a triangle involving, for a given distributional class, the shape of the distribution, the parameters, and the four moments. This analysis provides a clear link between the lessons learned in Part Two on sample moments and the later chapters on inference in Part Four. In Chapter 7, I introduce expectation as a generalization of the calculation of theoretical moments and explore many of its interesting properties.

Chapter 9, Elementary Sampling Theory, provides the essential link between the theory developed in Part Three and the actual observations discussed in Parts One and Two. Sampling theory is the mechanism by which theory is used to provide the necessary interpretation of observed data, and it provides the rationale for the inferences drawn in Chapters 10 and 11 on estimation and hypotheses testing, respectively.

Chapters 10 and 11 focus on the properties of estimators and the principles of hypothesis testing. These chapters contain a few unique features. One, for example, is to discuss why the 10%, 5%, and 1% test sizes in tables were chosen in the first place and that with modern computers we do not need to be bound by such conventions. Indeed, this text contains no formal tables, except as examples, because all the information normally contained in the numerous tables can more easily be obtained from computer algorithms. Another unique subject is the trade-off between Type I and II errors and the role of one's preferences in making these decisions. Experiments enable readers on their own to observe the relationship between the size of a hypothesized difference, the sample size, the chosen α level, the power, and the size of the error variance in formulating hypotheses tests.

Chapters 13 and 14, which discuss regression and ANOVA, respectively, are prefaced by a unique discussion on the generation of bivariate and conditional distributions in Chapter 12. Conditional probability is given a lot of weight because it provides the basis for the theory of regression and ANOVA. The insights provided in Chapter 12 facilitate understanding the principles of regression and the nebulous connection between regression and causality. It is at this stage that the more conventional view of statistics as a way of modeling "models observed with error" comes to the forefront. The role of the model in the analysis and the effect it has on drawing inferences from the data are emphasized. At this stage, students can begin to appreciate through simple examples the intimate interaction between probability theory and the formulation of scientific models.

The last chapter, "Retrospective," is novel. Its objective is to review in broad terms the basic concepts of the text and to readdress the issues raised in the first two chapters concerning the role of statistics in decision making, policy implementation, and science. Chapter 15 attempts to enable students to begin to appreciate the enormous gains in understanding that derive from applying the theory of statistics to observations of data. Interpretation is the key to understanding, and interpretation comes from our mastery of the underlying principles of inference.

A single case study is carried throughout the text; every chapter contains a reference to the case study and indicates how the contents of the chapter relate to the problem posed. I hope by this device to provide for students a motivating example, a unifying framework, and the ability to observe within a single context the development of the tools discussed in the text. This device also will enable students to observe the growth in their knowledge and understanding.

The Roles of the Exercises

The Exercises play several distinct roles in this text. Much material, useful insights, and interesting applications are in these exercises. If you do not see a favorite procedure in the main body of the text, look in the index and you may well find it in one of the exercise problems. The Exercises challenge better prepared students, leading them to investigate developments of the material and examine the ideas with greater rigor.

Learning is facilitated by including worked examples in the Exercises. Each worked example is headed by a statement of its objective. These exercises extend and illustrate the material and enable students to experiment on their own. Statistics can only be learned through doing and examining the repetition of exercises that exemplify stochastic variation in all its forms. This is achieved in a seamless manner in this text.

The exercises contain a far greater number of worked examples than is customary. These worked examples provide students with a detailed set of instructions for carrying out a procedure; a set of examples for answering the various types of questions normally placed in the text; and the tools for enabling them to experiment with the concepts. When assigning exercises, look for the nearest worked example that will provide a "blueprint" for doing the exercise that you have assigned. Routinely assigning the worked examples is a good practice; there is much to be learned in them. In Section 1.7, I have instructed students to pay particular attention to the worked examples. Indeed, if no other exercises are done, these should be. The benefits from working through them cannot be exaggerated. In this connection, the instructor is recommended to bring Section 1.7 to his or her students' attention, because it will aid their study efforts dramatically; my own students declare that it is "a must read again and again" section.

The exercises attached to each chapter are in three sections: Calculation Practice, Exploring the Tools, and Applications. Each section provides training in a different skill.

Calculation Practice

The first section, "Calculation Practice," contains problems designed to give students manipulative skills and facility in calculation. The initial exercises in this first set involve very simple numbers so that students can easily carry out the calculations by hand. It is only after gaining some feel for the calculations that the exercises move to using the computer and more "realistic" numbers. The idea is that to understand what is involved in statistical calculations students must have some manipulative practice themselves before they can understand what the computer is doing when used with more realistic data.

The numbers are kept very simple at first, so that "arithmetic" is no barrier to understanding the objective. The computer is next introduced with easy-to-use menu commands to facilitate using more realistic numbers. The next stage for more complicated formulae, such as that for the correlation coefficient, is to pull together the individual terms in the correlation coefficient "by hand." This is done before allowing students to use a packaged computer routine and then not until they have verified that the packaged routine does indeed produce the same numerical result as their own calculations.

The text contains an easy-to-use program on a CD that is a simplified student version of S-Plus. S-Plus comes with a series of laboratory routines as well as a fully developed statistical analysis package with extensive graphing capabilities. Almost all of the calculations, graphing, and routines needed by students can be accessed through a menu-driven GUI interface. S-Plus has been chosen as the main vehicle for using the computer to carry out the calculations because it provides excellent graphics; students can generate their own distributions and histograms; and they can be taught very easily how to *use only those tools that are needed at the moment that they are needed.* Some summary instructions for using S-Plus are contained in Appendix B.

That I chose to use S-Plus as the vehicle for the programming should be irrelevant to the instructor and the student. I have set up the computer procedures so that readers can quickly and effortlessly carry out the exercises with a minimum of instruction. In no sense must students spend time "learning some computer program" that they may never see again, even though S-Plus is a superb tool for the professional statistician as well as for the neophyte.

I have tried to prevent the use of the computer being a barrier to understanding and a source of both complexity and frustration, as is so often the case. I also wanted to make sure that if students perform any calculation *exactly* as I have done, they are guaranteed to obtain *precisely* the same result as that indicated in the text. I have restricted the use of the available algorithms to a very limited set because I am reluctant to expose students to the use of packaged computer programs to perform complex operations, such as regression analysis or ANOVA, until they have done it by hand a few times. Black boxes of any type are to be avoided because they lead the student into mindless manipulations of data with no intuition for what is involved. The manner in which the computer algorithmns have been implemented means that neither the instructor nor the student need be aware of what the underlying routines are; the computer has become an extension of the student's analysis and merely provides shortcuts to tedious routine calculations, each of which is thoroughly understood.

Exploring the Tools

The second set of questions, "Exploring the Tools," is designed to help students explore the properties and limitations of the statistical tools learned in each chapter. For example, students should acquire a feel for the effect from adding or deleting variable values on the calculation of sample moments or for when the distribution of values is special. This is the section in which the student is encouraged to experiment in trying to gain a deeper understanding of the concepts. "Labs" here provide an exceptional introduction to random variation and statistical analysis. Every distribution, statistic, and test discussed in the text can be simulated and its statistical properties examined by computer.

My intent is to provide a vehicle for engaging students' interest and enabling them to develop insight into statistical concepts. As it will be very easy for students to experiment with the labs on their own, I am confident that this is what they will do.

Applications

The last section of questions, "Applications," provides students with applications of the tools. There are some unique features here as well. For example, greater stress is placed in this section on the formulation of the problem, the questions that have to be answered to proceed with the analysis. Most of the questions concentrate on the *interpretation* of the results obtained from the statistical procedures, rather than the mere mechanical application of the procedures.

In large part, the questions posed here address the issues normally ignored, or assumed away, in the standard textbook question, which often restricts its attention to the mechanics of substituting numbers into formulae and reducing the resulting expression. The guiding principle in this text is something like "If you were employed as a statistician for a firm, or an agency, what sort of questions would your boss pose to you?" Most such questions would state the problem and ask what data we need to solve it and how we proceed. The real question is, "What is the statistical question?" To enhance this questioning attitude, questions are sometimes asked in the later chapters that do not require use of any of the tools in the current chapter; the idea is to encourage the student to think about the problem before writing down a formula.

Finally, the remaining exercises in the "Applications" section relate to the case study discussed at the end of every chapter. Students should be able to see the relevance of the chapter's contents to the case study and, by concentrating on a single case study throughout the text, recognize the context and the links to the concepts presented in other chapters. Students will quickly begin to perceive the growth in their knowledge of statistical thinking.

Why I Wrote the Text This Way

My reasons for developing the text in this way arose out of my frustration in observing the teaching of statistics with seemingly little long-term impact, even for students who obtained good grades. Examining the issue, I discovered that most students studied statistics by engaging in a sophisticated form of memorization; that is, they would memorize the formulae and create rules of thumb for the insertion of the formulae into word problems. This enabled them to earn a good grade in most statistics classes and without understanding very much at all. Within six weeks of the end of the course, the formulae are forgotten and the whole exercise has been a waste of everyone's time. Statistics is not the only discipline that tends to be taught in this manner for the non-major; much of mathematics is taught in the same way and with equally depressing results. For example, I have run experiments for years on the mathematical knowledge of students and found that while they can instantaneously shout out the formulae for common derivatives and integrals, the simplest problem defeats them if not put into the context that they had in their mathematics class.

I feel that many modern statistical texts encourage memorization and treat "the study of statistics" as a sequence of cookbook recipes. I appreciate the fact that for many instructors their chosen approach to teaching statistics is to provide a series of statistical recipes. The argument is that an introductory undergraduate course cannot do anything else because the students have neither the knowledge nor the skills to follow a more insightful course. Although I can appreciate the concerns and constraints of such instructors, whose constraints often include the stricture to "cover regression analysis at any cost," I believe that such an approach is ultimately neither challenging to the student nor rewarding to the instructor. The alternative approach is to be prepared to cover less material but to cover the material that is included more intensively.

This text is for those instructors who have been looking for a text that tries to stress the understanding of the basics and the development of "statistical intuition." This is a text for the instructor who is willing to give up covering a long list of "applied topics" in exchange for a greater appreciation by students of the elementary ideas and the fundamental logic underlying all the applications that they are ever likely to meet. Although it is true that in using a text of this type fewer applications will be covered, I trust that what is covered will be more intuitively appealing to students. I am hopeful that students will be encouraged not to memorize undigested formulae as the only way to pass statistics tests but to recognize that the material can be understood, and that there is a logical and understandable explanation for everything that is done.

A very simple example will illustrate my intent and explain an aspect of the text's organizational structure. In most texts, one statistic that is presented very early is the sample variance, s^2. Before s^2, the mean has been presented and, if other moments are mentioned later, they will be defined in terms of division by sample size, n, not $(n-1)$. The student is sometimes told, he "will learn the reason for this exception later," or there is a footnote to the effect that the problem has something to do with "degrees of freedom." But most students are unlikely to understand these comments. Here is yet another "mysterious formula" that has to be memorized, because its logic escapes the student.

In this text I take a different approach. Although I am developing sample moments as measures of properties of histograms, the second moment is no exception to the general rule of moments; $m_2(x)$ is defined by division by n, just as is the case for the first and all other moments. The pattern makes sense; there are no strange exceptions. But, when I get to Section 7.5 on expectations where the student learns that $m_2(x)$ is biased for σ^2, it is not only appropriate at that time to tell students about s^2, they can discover it for themselves.

The Mathematics Requirements for the Text

The formal mathematics required in the text are a little beyond basic algebra to begin and build from there. Calculus concepts are used, but little in the way of formalism. The intent is to build intuition about the relevant concepts, even without a careful explanation of the subtleties of mathematical analysis. I start with easy material and provide students with the facility to improve their manipulative skills. As students proceed through the text and gain confidence in their ability to handle the mathematical concepts and tools, the requirements are raised. To avoid letting students fall into the mindless manipulation of symbols without understanding, developing intuition into the mathematics used is stressed. Little is required beyond what a student should have on entering a first calculus course, and certainly no more than would be known by the end of a first calculus course. Currently, most students in economics or business statistics courses have had at least one calculus course.

The manner in which the mathematics are developed in the text reflects my observation that for the vast majority of students the weak link is algebra. In short, students have relatively less difficulty with calculus concepts than they do with algebraic concepts and procedures. Consequently, I have spent some considerable space in the text on the development of the algebraic tools that are needed and relatively less on the review of calculus concepts. Those with a strong mathematics background might feel that the text is too easy in the beginning relative to the level at which it ends. However, given the uneven nature of students' preparation—that is, too little familiarity with algebra—this is not so.

All the mathematics used in the text are explained in Appendix A. Exercises are provided on all the material both in the Exercises at the end of each chapter and in Appendix A. The introduction starts at a low level that should be easy for all students, although "Σ notation" seems to be a perennial difficulty. Further, there may be gaps in a particular student's training, so that beginning slowly with a comprehensive review should be an encouraging introduction. In addition, by beginning slowly, those who are likely to be mathematically challenged by the later portions of the text will have had the opportunity to gain some confidence before tackling the tougher sections. The material builds throughout the text in complexity to include basic ideas of *continuity*, *limit*, *differentiation*, and *integral*, mainly as the concept of the "area under a curve." Little formalism is invoked but intuition is stressed.

The rationale for this approach is that the material to be taught necessitates some calculus intuition. Some understanding of the concepts of limits, continuity, differentiability, and integration are essential for students to grasp the idea of a density function, the relationship between the density function and the probability function, the meaning of expectation, and so on. However, in contrast to some approaches to the study of statistics, this material can be made intelligible without a heavy reliance on "full mathematical rigor." If the student goes on to study statistics more seriously and therefore in greater depth, then at that time there will be a need for enhanced rigor. However, I believe that such a student will proceed much faster and with less difficulty in a more mathematically demanding course, having already obtained the basic insights that I try to inculcate in this text.

Acknowledgments

The author of any complex technical book inevitably owes a debt of gratitude to many people, and I am no exception. Numerous graduate students and undergraduates have contributed to the final form of the text to the ultimate benefit of the reader. To all of these, I owe my heartfelt thanks.

However, there are some key individuals who have contributed in special ways to the publication that has been so long in coming. A long-standing thanks is due to George Lobell, an editor of great talent, who originally urged me to write the text and who patiently waited for many years while research took precedence over completion. I hope that he feels that the wait has been adequately rewarded.

Clearly, we are all in the debt of Joe Newton and Jane Harvill, who wrote the labs that are such an important component of the development of the material.

It is customary to thank one's spouse, but in my case, my heartfelt thanks cannot adequately express the debt that I, and the reader, owe Kate Ramsey. Not only did she keep me focused on completion and alleviate my frequent disappointments, but she was also instrumental in creating the computer instructions for all the exercises. She pulled together and edited the numerous data sets and spent hours proofreading the text for accuracy and consistency of notation. She never let imprecise statements, especially in the exercises, go by without challenge. Quite literally, the text would not have been finished without her help and support.

Three graduate students in particular played a critical role in editing the text and creating many of the exercises and their solutions—Alannah Orrison, Enrique Schroth, and Guillermo Felices. I am deeply grateful for their imaginative contributions. Very special thanks also go to Eliane Catilina, an instructor at the University of Virginia, who made useful comments and was one of the first instructors to use the text in the classroom. Because of her great teaching talent, the student response to the text was a most successful experiment.

At a late stage in writing the manuscript I added the Bayesian supplement (on the accompanying CD) and was fortunate to persuade Arnold Zellner to read it through. The reader will benefit from Arnold's insightful comments, even though I was not able to incorporate all his excellent suggestions. My thanks to Arnold for his continuing support of my academic efforts over these many years. I am also grateful for insightful comments and the case study provided by Elias Grivoyannis.

I am highly indebted to the following reviewers who reviewed drafts of the manuscript and made many helpful suggestions: Hongshik Ahn, SUNY Stony Brook; Anthony D. Becker, St. Olaf College; Michael A. Boozer, Yale University; Bruce Cooil, Vanderbilt University; Jerry Dwyer, Clemson University; Mark Eakin, University of Texas, Arlington; Yongmiao Hong, Cornell University; James Stapleton, Michigan State University; Ebenge Usip, Youngstown State University; Keith Womer, University of Mississippi.

Lastly, but essential for publication, I would like to express my appreciation to my editor, Curt Hinrichs. Curt had the courage to support a book that was not designed for the mass market. He was instrumental in bringing together all the complex interactions between text, labs, computer instructions, data, computer software, supplemental chapters, web sites, and the creation and provision of compact discs bound with the text to a successful resolution; no mean feat.

I hope only that the efforts of all these talented people will be rewarded by the pedagogical success of the text.

PART ONE

Introduction and Fundamental Ideas

CHAPTER

1

Statistics as Science

1.1 What You Will Learn in This Chapter

The study of statistics is unique. It provides the methodology for decision making; it provides the methodology for the evaluation and advancement of science. Yet it is a science itself. We will see that the primitive notion of **randomness**, or unpredictability, is pervasive in the observable world. Examples of randomness include weather variations, changes in stock market prices and volumes, interest rates, the sex of offspring, roulette wheels, atomic decay, minor oscillations in the earth's orbit, and tidal flows. All these examples involve variations that to some extent are unpredictable; the unpredictable component is called *random*. The interaction between all the sciences and the study of statistics is fundamental because randomness is inherent in all science; this arises from the inherent presence of randomness, inevitable errors in observation and measurement, and lack of complete control of any experiment. Because randomness is universal, all practical decisions must in some fashion discover solutions to decision making under uncertainty. Will it rain, or not? Will interest rates rise, or not? Will I get prostate cancer? In each case, what do I do and how do I decide? In broad terms, decision making under uncertainty is the subject of this entire book.

1.2 Introduction

We all know how to make decisions. Or do we? What criteria do we use, what facts do we need, and how do we assess those facts? When your doctor tells you that the probability of your operation being successful is at least 90%, what does he mean and how do you interpret that information? In any case, where did the number *90%* come from, and can we trust it? What is the probability of getting cancer by sunbathing? How do I evaluate the answer when I get it? How does it compare to the probability of dying in an airplane crash or in an automobile accident? If the quoted probability is 1 in 100,000, is that big or small? How do I judge? Besides, what is this word *probability,* and what does it mean anyway?

When an atmospheric scientist tells us that there is global warming, that is an indisputable fact. Or is it? "Tax the millionaires," cries a political candidate, "and we can balance the budget and increase welfare payments." How plausible is that statement? Are there really enough millionaires to make this claim a feasible policy option? Aerosols and air conditioners are depleting the ozone layer, claims an environmental group; but how do they know and how accurate is that information? Democrats protest that under Reagan the rich got richer and the poor got poorer, whereas others with equal conviction claim the opposite. Why is this problem so difficult? Surely, this is a simple fact to determine. Or is it?

1.3   Statistics: A Framework for Decision Making

All these examples involve the making of decisions and the evaluating of claims by others. The decisions and evaluations all involve collecting and assessing data and determining their relevance to our problem. Data are the "facts" that we deal with in statistics. Data can be "official government statistics" that are produced by some governmental department or agency, such as measures of interest rates, price levels, or levels of productive activity. Data might be the information contained in surveys or opinion polls; or data might be observations on some experiment.

We might conclude from the tone of the previous two paragraphs that all data are not created equal. Some data may be more informative than others, some data may be less reliable than others; but how do we judge? What clues should we look for to discover that all may not be as stated, or that the data do not support the proponents as they claim? How much uncertainty can we tolerate; how much must we live with?

There is currently a raging debate about global warming; however, you may remember that only a little over a decade ago, we were being bombarded by fears of global cooling. Whatever is the truth of the hypothesized relationship between human activity and global warming, the debate, if it is to be decided on rational grounds, is an argument about atmospheric statistics and their interpretation. Without the concepts provided by probability and the theory of statistics, it would be difficult even to conceptualize the problem. Consider just one small example of this.

There is a positive association between the average temperature of the Pacific Ocean and the level of carbon dioxide in that region. Does this prove the claims of global warming? No; for the issues are more subtle than can be decided on the basis of casual empiricism. You will soon learn that empirically discovered patterns of association—*correlation* is the technical term—are not to be confused with causality. **Causality,** you will recall, is the concept that there is a logical link between two events that indicates that variation in one leads to changes in the values taken by the other. Although there are a number of hidden subtleties in this simple definition, the primitive notion is clear enough.

In our current example, we can immediately ask which of two plausible causal mechanisms is applicable. One claim is that high levels of carbon dioxide lead to warming; another is that the Pacific Ocean is an enormous carbon dioxide "sink"—the cooler the ocean the more carbon dioxide it can hold and the warmer the ocean the less it can hold. The former hypothesis claims that the direction of causality is from carbon dioxide levels to warming, and the other hypothesis is that the direction of causality is the opposite. Both involve a positive association between carbon dioxide levels and warming, but the policy implications are vastly different. To resolve even this question requires some fairly sophisticated statistical techniques.

But you may ask why should you have to worry about the matter, because that is why people hire statisticians anyway and you, for one, have absolutely no desire ever to become a statistician. Recognize however, that as a voter you are and will be asked to pass judgment on the matter by voting. In any event, the outcome is going to affect your income and lifestyle in a very significant manner. If the "global warmists" have their political way, you are going to be asked to pay a very heavy price in terms of lost income, lost freedom of choice, and a lower standard of living; "saving the environment" does not come cheap. If the global warmists are correct and we ignore the problem, we will also pay a heavy price in terms of lost income and a lower standard of living. Here is a difficult choice that will not go away with wishful thinking. Given the enormous potential costs, might not an investment in knowledge about the decision be helpful? But what knowledge and how should it be used? We will see that the field of statistics helps us to discuss this issue as well.

Continuing our example, let me illustrate the knowledge difficulty that someone wishing to vote responsibly has. In the following quote from the *Wall Street Journal* (July 11, 1996), Dr. Ellsaesser comments on the evidence cited by the Intergovernmental Panel on Climate Control (IPCC). Dr. Ellsaesser retired from the Air Force after 20 years as an air weather officer and from the Lawrence Livermore National Laboratory after 23 years in atmospheric and climate research. As you will observe, you will require a fair amount of understanding of statistical matters to be able to discern what the argument is about and who is likely to be more correct. Consider the quote:

> By concentrating on IPCC rules and procedures, IPCC writers and supporters have managed to avoid the more important scientific debate as to whether the balance of evidence suggests that there is a discernible human influence on global climate.
>
> Santer et al. attempted to identify this human influence by correlating year-by-year global patterns . . . of mean annual departures from the control run averaged over the last 20 years of each equilibrium experiment. An upward trend in the correlations of the annual means from about −0.2 ca. 1950 to about +0.4 ca. 1970 was uncritically accepted as confirming that the observed temperatures were evolving toward the temperature pattern predicted by the model. . . . Completely ignored were the facts that the annual correlations decreased from about 0.28 in 1910 to about −0.2 ca. 1950, and that while they remained relatively steady from 1970 to 1985, they decreased sharply after 1985, ending up in 1993 near 0.12, well below their starting point in 1910.

In first reading this quote, you can be forgiven for reacting that it is all unintelligible and you will never be able to fathom what is really being said. However, you should not be so pessimistic; after finishing this text you will be able to assess the statistical merits of this discussion and have a far better appreciation of what the debate is all about. You will also be able to recognize the inherent difficulties that are involved in such research, especially the subtle issue of what is, or is not, causing global warming, if indeed there is such warming.

AIDS has captured the public's attention as no other disease has done in nearly a century. The theory and practice of statistics permeates this debate, at least at the technical level and should at the policy level as well. Consider an example chosen for its seeming irrelevance to a statistical approach. Whether people who have tested HIV positive should be allowed to pursue jobs that bring them into intimate contact with the public is a thorny issue because it brings two "rights" into conflict. On the one hand, individuals seek the right to pursue their own goals, and the government has passed much legislation to facilitate a nondiscriminatory job market. On the other, people also have the right not to be needlessly exposed to life-threatening risks in the normal course of living, and the government has passed much legislation to support this right as well. The issue cannot be resolved in the absence of a knowledge of the risks and the relative costs that are involved, and this is a problem in statistics. If the risk of getting AIDS from one's dentist were zero, few would argue about restricting dentists with AIDS from practicing. But if it were absolutely certain that attending an AIDS-infected dentist led to getting AIDS, then few would object to preventing such dentists from practicing as usual. The reality is that the probability of getting AIDS from one's dentist is between these two extremes. The question now becomes how to trade off the cost of inhibiting the freedom of individuals to practice dentistry with the cost of infecting the population with AIDS. The theory of statistics provides not only the procedures but the very language for framing an answer to this question.

A related example that was posed in terms of medical ethics was debated in the *New York Times* (September 18, 1997). The ostensible issue was ethical, but the proper formulation of the problem requires some knowledge of statistical theory and practice as well as a good understanding of the rationale for experimental design. The National Institute for Health and the Centers for Disease Control and Prevention sponsored research on the transmission of AIDS by mothers to their children. The objective was to find an inexpensive method to prevent the transmission of HIV to babies that would be economically feasible in the developing world. The controversy arose because a very important part of the research strategy in trying to learn from experiments is the need to have a control group that does not receive the drug. This is important because in real experiments there are many other factors at play that can mislead researchers in measuring drug effectiveness. Further, it is imperative for a successful research design strategy that the recipients and the nonrecipients be chosen "at random"—that is, chosen so as to attempt to avoid unforeseen biases that might arise in the analysis.

The best strategy requires that not only the potential recipients do not know who gets the drug and who does not, but the monitors of the experiment do not know either. However, *if* the drug is successful and does not have severe deleterious side effects, the nonrecipients will have a higher incidence of HIV than the recipients. Please note the all important "ifs" in this premise. In analyzing this situation and passing judgment on its ethical status, one needs to understand the roles of controls and "randomization" in research; with them one can determine the effectiveness of a drug much more quickly and efficiently. Consequently, if the drug is in fact successful, the sooner we discover that fact, the sooner future babies will be saved. One needs to know how to balance the lives of future infants against those in the experiment. Of course, we have begged the question, because in these situations, we do not know whether the drug is effective, and we certainly will not know whether the drug has serious deleterious side effects. Imagine, for example, the reaction to this experiment if there were a substantial and horrifying side effect; one's position on the ethics of excluding some from receiving the drug might well be very different.

A tragic example of the need for the services of a competent statistician examining all the available data was provided by the explosion of the space shuttle *Challenger* in 1986. As we shall see later in the text, the available data clearly indicated a low-temperature problem with the O rings. The tragedy was that these data were not analyzed properly, and as a result the space shuttle exploded.

Enough of fire, famine, and pestilence, let us proceed to less-depressing subjects for statistical analysis. Your passion might be literature or art, so what can statistics do for you here? You may be thankful to know not much, at least directly, but the use of statistical procedures is creeping into the evaluation of art and literature. This is especially so in the detection of fraud and in the attempts to ascribe a text or work of art to a specific author or artist. The question is always, "How 'probable' is it that this book, or painting, was indeed the work of a particular person?" The statistical analysis of writer's styles is now an elaborate specialized field. Later, we will discuss the role of statistics in analyzing the sales and popularity of rock music; so even here the "most dismal of sciences" has a niche.

How about "lifestyle" decisions? Are they the proper subjects of statistical thinking? Where does statistics come in, for example, in your choice of profession? Certainly, one will want to weigh to some extent the anticipated future earnings, even if one claims not to be "money hungry." Other aspects involve the job's implied life expectancy. A miner must face a higher probability of death from accident and work-induced diseases, but what is the income trade-off and how do you calculate it? How risky is it really to be a policeman? Is it worth taking 2 years off to get an M.B.A.? If I want to become an actress, how do I decide when to quit trying? Or finally, can I live on my inheritance, or must I learn a profession?

Other decisions are more personal. As a woman, if you delay marriage and having children for your career development, how do the probabilities for birth defects change? Suppose that you are contemplating a second career after successfully completing a first; how much educational investment is it worth? You are contemplating an operation for the removal of a tumor; the decision hinges on the probabilities of whether the tumor is benign and whether you will be seriously debilitated by the operation itself. Of equal importance in this case is how reliable the probabilities are that you have been quoted and how you take such knowledge into account.

A recent article, "The Fat's in the Fire, Again," in the *New York Times* (January 11, 1998) illustrates the need to understand the process of statistical analysis. Researchers analyzed the behavior of 324,135 adult males over 12 years and concluded that the excess risk of dying associated with obesity was modest and declined with age! Given all the previous evidence this was a remarkable statement, and as you might expect it generated a storm of controversy. The article ended with the following statements:

> "The only disagreement is among people who don't know the facts and don't have the scientific evidence," Dr. Manson said in an interview.
>
> Not surprisingly, others disagree about the disagreement.

In the same article, other evidence was quoted that indicated that obesity was very highly correlated with diabetes, high blood pressure, and high levels of blood cholesterol—all potential killers. As you read this text, you will gain some insight into this controversy and recognize the impact of the vagueness of the research question, that correlation and causality are very different concepts, and that there are many questions about the experimental procedures that need to be asked before coming to the conclusion that obesity is a benign state.

You may worry about the safety of cars or other products; the levels of pollution, what is tolerable and how to decide; how much cholesterol you can consume; or the fact that your parents both had early heart attacks, the probability of your having a heart attack before 40, and how likely it is that your children will have early heart attacks. You are offered an insurance annuity; is it a good deal? You just bought a new appliance; should you also purchase the maintenance contract? Is it worth getting a cheap airfare before you are sure that you will use it?

Each of these examples requires the collection of facts. We are inundated by data and facts. Everyone who is pushing a cause, or fighting those who are, claims to have the "facts." But as we have already indicated, not all data are created equal. One of the tasks of statistics is to provide procedures for evaluating the value of any data. We have to ask whether the data that we are provided to buttress an argument really do buttress the argument. As we shall see, the way in which data are collected and processed for our purposes can change the meaning that we attach to the data and how we interpret the results of research.

These are just a few scattered examples of how a knowledge of statistical concepts will help you to pose the right questions and indicate to you the type of data that you might need to answer the questions. If nothing else, a knowledge of statistical reasoning will provide you with a framework within which you can analyze the problem you face.

1.4   Statistics and the Methodology of Science

All of this is interesting and fun perhaps, but the mass of the day-to-day use of statistics is in the sciences—physical, life, and social—and in engineering. We will discuss the science role of statistics in some detail later in the chapter, but at this stage the question arises whether a nonscientist needs to have any knowledge of these questions at all. If you are not a scientist of any type and have no interest in the subject at all, why should you worry about ostensible scientific debates in general and those about health and environmental issues in particular? Why should you concern yourself with the essential role that statistics plays in the debate?

We have already answered this; because the decisions that are being made will affect you and your children directly and indirectly. The decisions made for good or bad reasons, with knowledge of the facts or not, and with or without reasonable interpretations of the data, will affect your income, lifestyle, and freedom to choose, not to mention your health. Perhaps some knowledge of how statistics in the sciences are used and, much more important, abused in the evaluation of data will help you in your evaluation of the research that will alter your life. The interpretation and the misinterpretation of statistics are being used every day in ways that affect almost all aspects of your life, economic, political, and social. One should think this is reason enough to study statistics and probability.

The study of statistics is itself a science. But first, let us briefly and intuitively consider the role of statistics in the sciences. Sciences are unified by the scientific method; they are distinguished by their subject matter. Statistics is a science, but as we will see it plays a unique role and has a unique subject matter.

The unifying scientific method is best characterized as an approach to understanding data rather than as a formal universal procedure that is to be rigidly followed at all costs. Even the physical sciences are not that tidy. The basic concept is the continuous interplay of hypothesis, observation, and measurement. In the early stages of a science, observation and measurement dominate; theorizing comes later.

The first step in this process is to create categories of similar objects, so that one can compare and contrast the objects within similar groups and between different groups. Many of the life and social sciences are only just beginning to evolve from this stage. This part of the process involves measurement and the discovery of what characteristics to measure. The theory and practice of statistics is important even at this stage, because the central task is collecting and ordering information, or "statistics," relevant to the science's subject matter.

The second stage involves the proposal of hypotheses to explain whatever relationships or regularities are observed in the data. This is the stage involving the most use of imagination and insight and prepares the way for the third stage. The objective in this second stage of the development of the science is to create a story that provides a unifying framework into which most of the observations can be placed. More precisely, the objective is to provide a framework that allows us to interpret the observed relationships.

There are many ways, for example, to interpret the observed orbits of the stars and planets. We may invent a story about the Sun and the stars orbiting Earth as in the Greek myths or as in the religion of the ancient Britons who built Stonehenge in England, or we may postulate that the planets including Earth circle the Sun, or that planetary and Earth's orbits around the Sun are ellipses. Each of these stories purports to provide a unifying idea that links all the observed relationships.

This second stage involves "modeling" the data; **modeling** is the process of creating a hypothesis that purports to explain the data. Essentially, in creating a hypothesis we build a model of the presumed mechanism that is generating the observations. *Explanation* in this context means that the hypothesis provides a set of logical links between groups of observations. This process enables us to say that if we observe one set of observations, here is the reason why we will see a second set of observations as a consequence. Both the theories of Copernicus and Kepler explained planetary and star observations and provided links between observations that enabled early astronomers to forecast even such rare events as eclipses.

As another example, the theory of demand in the study of economics provides a reason why we should expect to see a decrease in the quantity of a product consumed when the price is raised. In this example, the two groups of observations are "quantity consumed of a good" and "price." The reason for the link between the two sets of observations is provided by the theory of demand based on the concept of maximization of individual utility. The process of specifying the causal link is the modeling of the data.

We now come to the crux of the scientific method: how to choose between competing hypotheses. The time-honored method is to choose the story that best matches the data, or provides "the best fit to the data." This is the third stage in the development of a science and the best known: the "testing of hypotheses" stage.

We now face two difficulties. The first is that none of the hypotheses fits any of the data precisely; there are known errors of observation, not to mention the fact that the hypotheses are at best idealized abstractions from reality. The second is that we have to decide how to determine which of the alternative stories provides the best fit to the data; indeed, we even have to decide what we mean by "the best fit." This is where the study of statistics and probability provides the whole of science with the basic methodology needed to answer these pervasive and vital questions. The development of these procedures is the central aim of this book.

In the previous few paragraphs we stated that the language of statistics provides the methodological tools that are needed by all the other sciences to evaluate their theories and to measure the advance of knowledge in the field. The process of rejecting some hypotheses against others requires both the language and the techniques of statistics to be implemented. It is not too strong a statement to make that the other sciences could not advance without statistical theory and practice. The language of statistics is said to provide a *metalanguage* for the evaluation of the methodology used in the sciences; a **metalanguage** is a language that is independent of the language used to formulate the theories of the discipline under review. The applicability of the procedures generated by the field of statistics does not depend on the correctness, or "truth-falsity," of the hypotheses under examination. This is a most useful property. If the validity of our testing procedures depended on the truth of the very hypothesis that we were trying to check, the results of any such test would be useless.

1.5　Statistics as a Science

The discipline of statistics is unique. Although the language of statistics provides a metalanguage for the analysis of any other discipline's methodology, there is no other language in which to analyze the methodology of statistics; it cannot evaluate itself. The sole criterion for the success of statistical theory is the pragmatic one of whether or not the theory works. The evidence so far is that it does.

But the study of statistics is unique in another respect. We have said that sciences are distinguished by their subject matter. The subject matter of physics is in the physical properties of matter and energy; the subject matter of chemistry is in the chemical properties; that of economics is in the class of economic properties—that is, those having to do with the value of goods in exchange; that of biology is in the physical and chemical processes involved in living organisms; and so on.

The Subject Matter of Statistics

But what is the subject of statistics? In one sense, it is the subject matter of all the other disciplines; and in another sense, it is none of these. The subject matter of statistics is randomness, or stochastic variation. But randomness may be present, indeed is likely to be present, in the observation of all the data of all the other disciplines. In this sense, the subject matter of statistics includes all types of data. The subject matter of statistics is unique in that randomness is a property peculiar to the study of statistics. Let us briefly and intuitively examine this notion of randomness and see how it distinguishes statistics from all other disciplines. The terms to be used below will be explained more fully in the next chapters, but for now let us try to get a basic understanding of the main ideas.

The explanations, or stories, that we hypothesized about the relationships that exist in other disciplines are mainly *causal*. By this we mean that the story, or explanation, purports to show how the variation in one set of variables affects the values taken by another set of variables. Newton used his theory of gravity to explain the orbits of the planets; Boyle defined the relationship between temperature, pressure, and the volume of a gas; and demand theory in economics relates levels of consumption to levels of income. The variables in each of these examples are, respectively, *planetary orbits; temperature, pressure,* and *volume;* and *consumption* and *income*. In all these examples, the relationships are expressed functionally; that is, the relationship is an "if, then" type. The values of one set of variables are being determined by, at least according to the theory, the other set of variables.

In the simplest of cases one variable is controlled and so is called **deterministic.** If the other variable is functionally related to our deterministic, or controlled, variable, then it is also called deterministic. If I pluck a taut string of fixed length and mass with a given degree of tension, I will produce a specific tone, or frequency of vibration. The tone is functionally determined by the circumstances of the experiment, such as the nature of the material of the string, the degree of tension, and the length of the string. If we alter the length of the string, which is a controlled variable and so is deterministic itself, the theory of harmonic oscillators provides a function that predicts the tone that will be heard; so the tone is by our definition a deterministic variable as well.

The variables that are the subject matter of statistics are not deterministic; they are said to be random. A naive definition of a **random variable** that will do for now is one for which there is no known causal explanation. Random variables are not predictable. If we had an explanation for the variable, we would use it and there would be no need for a concept of randomness. Random variables are variables that are not part of a simple "if, then" type of explanation. These really are a different type of data. You are familiar with examples of such data: the individual outcomes of the tossing of coins or dice, drawing cards from a well-shuffled deck, roulette numbers, lotteries, the timing of lightbulb burnouts, the sex of offspring, tire blowouts, the paths of gas molecules, and so on. What is common about all these examples is that, given our current level of understanding, we cannot predict individual outcomes. We cannot provide a causal explanation for the occurrences of any of these phenomena as we have discussed them. We cannot specify through a theory a functional relationship between some other deterministic variable, or some variable that we control, and that we are seeking to explain. Statistics is all about *acausal* data. This explanation is simplified, of course, to stress the distinction between the two types of variables, or data, that the sciences use.

If statistics is the science of variables with no explanation, no theory of causality, then we have to wonder what might be meant by "explanation" in the context of such data. We might also question the earlier claim that in one sense statistics has as subject matter all of science.

Let us tackle the "explanation" question first. Clearly, the explanation provided by statistics is not going to be the same as that used in the other sciences. We will spend a few chapters on this very topic; you cannot expect to get a full idea within a few paragraphs. The explanation provided by the theory of statistics is descriptive of properties of large collections of such data; that is, we eschew trying to provide specific statements about individual occurrences and content ourselves with statements about large collections of observations. The models in such a theory are called **distributions,** and they are used to characterize the statistical properties of large collections of the data. What sort of properties these are we have yet to discover. For the moment, some brief ideas that we could describe include where the data seem to be centered, to what extent they vary about the center, whether there is symmetry, whether there is a small number of very large observations, and so on.

Statistics and Science Intertwined

The link to the other sciences is now not as difficult as it appeared to be just a few paragraphs ago. We have already mentioned that real data—the data that are actually observed in experiments or in the real-time functioning of an economy, an ecological system, or the orbits of the planets and the stars—are all observed with error. These are errors of observation, errors of measurement, errors of recording, or errors of control over the external circumstances that can impinge upon the mechanism under inspection. This last example is very important in that our control over our experiment, or rather our lack of control, most often leads to false conclusions. Lack of control is exemplified by experiments that do not adequately allow for contamination of the results, by surveys that contain hidden biases to the responses, by collecting incomplete data on the experiment, and so on. Almost by their very nature, we can claim that such errors will have no causal explanation that would allow us to extend our "causal theory" to causal explanations of error. If there were such an explanation, then we could incorporate it into our theory; but experience teaches us that we will end up with an irreducible residue of acausal, or random, effects.

We can guess that for large numbers of measurements that the average error might not be so large. Almost instinctively, we all do this in our daily lives. Whenever the length is critical, we measure the curtains several times; we may not know where any specific tennis serve is going to land, but on average, we have a very good idea; our trip to the university never takes the same time, but on average we know what to do to avoid being late.

Even in the simplest of situations, observed data in the physical, biological, and social sciences contain two components (at least in theory): a deterministic part that is described directly by the theory and a random component that must be described by statistical reasoning. Consequently, the empirical validation of all sciences and the refutation of hypotheses requires a methodology that blends deterministically formulated relationships with a random component. This is in fact what happens in all science. The difficulty is to separate the two components and to discover how to "remove the stochastic veil," or the veil of randomness, to discover the actual relationship that is buried in *noise*, as the random variation is often called. Sometimes the level of noise is so great that the underlying signal is impossible to detect without very sophisticated tools, and often not even then. Atmospheric data are very noisy, which is why, in part, trying to detect small, long-run changes is so very difficult; such efforts are a real test of the power of statistical procedures.

If this were all there were to the matter, the science of statistics would be useful, but not very interesting in its own right. As it turns out, there are relationships in science that can only usefully be formulated in terms of random variables. We previously stated that the theory of statistics is embedded in the distributions of collections of data, so the explanations provided by statistical reasoning are in terms of the properties of these distributions. Many scientific relationships must be couched in terms of the distributions of the variables rather than in terms of the variables themselves. This approach is most clearly exemplified in terms of thermodynamics, in describing the dynamical processes involved in chemical reactions, and most likely in the whole of the social sciences. We do not try to predict what a particular individual will do in responding to a price change but what will happen with a large collection of people all facing the same circumstances. We do not try to predict where an individual gas molecule will be within a container but content ourselves with a macrodescription of an enormous collection of molecules, such as specifying the pressure of the gas at a given temperature.

The difference in the way theory is formulated with respect to "distributions, or large collections, of random variables" and the usual formulation in terms of "if, then" relationships is a very important one. The distinction changes the way in which a scientist views explanation and certainly changes the way in which one decides how to choose between alternative models of behavior. As we will see, a distribution is a way of describing collections of events and is itself modeled by a mathematical function. The change in viewpoint can now be characterized by a shift from simple causal relationships between deterministic variables to a relationship between a variable, random or deterministic, and a function; as the variable changes, so does the function that models the distribution of the other variable. If the size of a container of a gas is suddenly expanded, for example, the distribution of the gas molecules will shift over time in reaction to the new conditions; that is, we have to change our description of the collection of positions of the molecules. If the price of a commodity is lowered, the distribution of levels of consumption of that good by a group of consumers will shift to reflect the new circumstance; that is, our description of the collection of individual levels of consumption will change. If there is an increase in the demand for a product, the distribution of costs across firms in the industry will shift to reflect the change; or we restate the matter by saying that our description of the collection of costs changes in reaction to the change in demand.

We now see that an important contribution of statistical thinking is in the very formulation of some of the theories in all the other sciences. The introduction of random variables into scientific models shifts the concentration from trying to describe the specific paths of individual elements to the behavior of large collections, or "ensembles," of data and from simple "if, then" relationships to explaining the factors that change distributions of random variables. We now see that the theory of statistics and probability is inextricably linked to all the sciences. Not only does the study of statistics provide the methodology for the empirical evaluation of science, but it provides the basic concepts for the conceptualization of many of the relationships in the sciences.

Whatever you choose to study in science, whatever science that you need to use, whatever policy that requires the physical or social sciences as basic information, that choice will necessitate an understanding of the theory and practice of statistics. Now you understand why statistics is a part of almost any university curriculum, especially in the sciences (physical, life, and social as well as in engineering).

1.6   Summary

In this first chapter, we have introduced several new ideas and reviewed a few others.

Our first lesson is that the discipline of statistics is concerned with the problems generated by decision making and the need to evaluate data for either scientific or policy reasons. We presented examples to indicate the wide range of alternative situations in which a statistical approach was needed to tackle the problem. We claimed that the discipline of statistics provides the framework for analyzing decisions, although the precise formulation of such a framework is to be left to later chapters.

The case was made that statistics is a science in that it shares with all science the same methodology. Actually, the theory of statistics provides the methodology for evaluating data and for the testing of hypotheses that is used by all the sciences. The discipline of statistics involves the process of choosing between alternative explanations of observed data. In this regard statistics is unique.

The subject matter of statistics, narrowly defined, is also unique. The subject matter is random, or "acausal" data—that is, data for which there is no known causal explanation or prediction. Whereas the simplest theoretical models in the sciences involve "if, then" relationships between the observed values of the science's variables, the situation in statistics is more complex.

Because statistics deals with data for which there is no causal relationship, "explanation" in statistics means specifying a distribution for large collections, or ensembles, of random variables; such distributions become the models for an acausal science. We give up trying to predict the specific values of a particular observation for saying something about the properties of large collections of observations.

The connection with the sciences became clear when we first realized that all variables observed in science involve errors of observation, and that these errors are essentially acausal in nature. The empirical verification of any science involves statistics because the observed variables have two components: one that might be deterministic and one, due to error, that is random.

The next step in the development of our understanding led to the realization that the concepts of statistics often are involved in science at a more fundamental level. Some parts of the physical sciences—such as thermodynamics, and probably the whole of the social sciences—are best formulated as relationships between variables and those functions that we have called "distributions." This insight involves a fundamental shift in thinking about the meaning of both causality and the concept of explanation in science. In the expanded view, causality must be expressed in terms of shifts in distribution functions—that is, in terms of descriptions of collections of events rather than of naive "if, then" relationships between the levels of the variables of the system.

The next chapter will elaborate on these topics at greater length and clarify some of the terms that we are beginning to use.

Case Study

Was There Age Discrimination in a Public Utility?

A small public utility was facing the impact of new organizational structures within its industry. This necessitated regrouping production facilities and redetermining the use of its labor force to obtain the necessary gains in efficiency that would enable it to survive. An outside consulting firm was called in to advise it on setting up new procedures and to design new job descriptions.

The restructured firm's procedure to deal with this situation was to have everyone resign from the "old" firm and then reapply to the "new" firm along with other potential employees recruited through advertising for the "new" jobs with the new job descriptions. This change was imposed on all em-

ployees, including senior management. New employees were hired from the enlarged pool of applicants in three stages; the most senior managers were hired first, then intermediate level managers, then everyone else.

The union representing the old, lower-level employees promptly sued the new firm for age discrimination, claiming that the distribution of new hires in the new firm had a much younger average age of employees than was true for the old firm. Statistically trained economists were hired by both parties to aid the lawyers in resolving this problem.

In this text, we will explore this issue in depth using the tools that we shall develop. Our first task is to note the role played by statistical analysis in this court case. The amount of money involved was approximately $42 million and the number of

continues on next page

(Continued)

ex-employees involved in the suit was 52, so the issues involved were substantial.

Here are some of the questions that we might ask to deal with this issue. We might compare the age of those hired with those not hired and with the age of the original employees. How does the age of those employees rehired compare with that of the external candidates that were hired? How do the salaries before and after the restructuring compare, especially for those over 40 years of age, and how does this difference, if any, depend on the breakdown between hired and not hired, and internal versus external, candidates? The real issue is whether there was discrimination by age, and did that discrimination have an impact on the wages paid. But to answer these questions we will have to separate the effects of other factors that may be related to age and salary levels coincidentally.

We will carry this case forward through all the chapters of the book to show you how the analysis that you will learn applies to this real-life situation. We seek to show you how the study of statistics will guide you in recognizing the important is-

sues, how to determine a procedure for analyzing the data, and how to decide what data to collect and in what manner. Finally, we hope to be able to demonstrate both the strengths and limitations of statistical analysis in this and similar situations. But mainly, as you progress through each chapter, you will discover how much you will learn as you master more and more statistical analysis.

You should also recognize that the data set listed in the Xfiles is a real data set used in an actual court case. As such, there are inevitable errors, misstatements, and inconsistencies; look out for these difficulties. Being on guard for procedural and recording errors is also part of learning to be a statistician!

The key to what follows is not that "as a statistician" you will have more data available, but that you will be able to extract far more information from the data that you do have. The primary gain for decision making that a statistician contributes is his or her interpretation of the existing data—that is, the ability to determine the extent of the relevance, or the lack of relevance, of the available data to the solution of the problem at hand.

1.7 Addendum for the Reader

You will soon discover, if you have not done so already, that this text differs from others. This section indicates some of those ways and outlines the implications for how you read the book and address some of the exercises.

You may have already realized that in this text we focus much more on the understanding of *processes,* of discovering new ways of viewing the world, not just learning new terms and symbols. Together, we are trying to tackle a more difficult task than you may be used to considering: the discovery of a new way of thinking about the facts that you observe, a new way to organize data. Such a process is more challenging and requires more effort on your part than the simple acquisition of a sequence of facts. Although this might all sound obvious, it makes a considerable difference in the way you approach the text and particularly in how you interpret some of the questions in the exercises. Let me explain.

First, let us review the best way to read the text. I suggest that for each chapter, you begin by looking at the title, read the "What You Will Learn in This Chapter" section, look through the Introduction, note the section headings, and read the Summary.

This will give you an overview of what is in the chapter and some idea of the terms that will be introduced. It also will provide a rough goal to be achieved in mastering the chapter. This step will usually take only a few minutes and is soon well rewarded.

The second stage is to read through the whole chapter quite quickly. Your task at this stage is to note the sections that you find fairly easy to understand, note those where you have difficulties, and determine the terms and formulae that you will have to learn and remember. Most important, the second reading is to enable you to acquire a broad overview of the material in the text. Do not at this stage try to slog doggedly through each paragraph, one by one, mastering every detail as soon as it is met. Do pay attention to the graphs; switch back and forth between the texts and the graphs, integrating the two, and observe how the graphs illustrate and illuminate the text.

The third stage is to review the whole chapter, trying first to be sure that you do understand the easier sections. You can do this by querying yourself about what the text means and by summarizing the argument in your own words. More important, when you come to the difficult sections, you need to ask yourself some very important questions concerning your difficulties. Try to figure out *why* you are having trouble.

The simplest reason may be because the text is using notation, concepts, or mathematical tools with which you are unfamiliar. Before proceeding any further, make sure that you understand the terms and concepts that the text presumes you know. These may be ideas introduced earlier in the text that you did not master at that time, so go back and make sure of the earlier material. The difficult concepts may be mathematical ideas that you have forgotten, so review the mathematical appendix. Or you may decide that the idea being presented is one that you just do not understand.

If the last case is the situation, concentrate on the difficult passage. Reread it carefully, line by line, querying yourself about your understanding at each step. Try to formulate your own simple examples that attempt to illustrate the ideas being discussed. Look at the exercises that illustrate the idea, especially the worked exercises. Best, try to draw a picture of what is going on, and write down your own efforts to present the argument. If you like, pretend that you are trying to explain this concept to someone else; often the very attempt to do that will suddenly reveal to you what is involved. Talk to other students about the problem; what may be difficult for you in one situation may be easy for someone else. Later, you will be able to return the favor in a passage that you find easy and they find difficult. Remember that you are trying to understand a "process," the way in which statisticians view the world. This requires you to develop new skills and new ways of thinking. It is inevitable, if you are learning new ways of thinking, that there will be times when you will see the logic of the process only after some effort. If you have ever learned a new sport, say tennis, you will recognize that it took some time to learn how to process information on the ball's flight, the properties of the racket, and the mechanisms that you needed to develop to be able to control your strokes. Similarly, in this situation you are trying to discipline your brain to think in certain ways that may well be very novel to you. This will require practice and analysis of your mistakes.

Having worked your way through the chapter, reread it and write down your own summary of the chapter. Include all formulae that you may need to remember. Your notes should be sufficiently complete to enable you to answer any question about the material.

With respect to the problem of remembering formulae, note that the main task in the text is to *understand* the equations and formulae; the text is written to facilitate exactly that process. However, while you are learning, and especially during examinations, it is more efficient if you can remember the various formulae and equations without having to look them up every time. There is a painless way to master the required memorization. Obtain a set of $3'' \times 5''$ index cards. Every time you come across a formula, a definition, or an equation that you want to remember, write it down on the card; limit it to one per card. Carry these cards with you always. Then, when you are waiting for a bus, a plane, or a friend, or you are standing in line at the supermarket checkout counter, take out a few of these cards and refresh your memory. See how much you can remember without looking and then review the card. Very soon and with seemingly little effort, you will remember more concepts than you ever thought you could manage.

The exercises are somewhat different from what you may have experienced before. Beginning with Chapter 2, exercises in each chapter are divided into three sections. The ones in the first section, "Calculation Practice," will be fairly simple and are the closest to your normal experience. Even here, recognize that you are developing a new skill, the ability to perform calculations easily and without hesitation. The objective here is for you to reach a state in which you no longer have to think about the mechanics of your calculations. The skills that you will develop in this first section proceed in stages. The first stage will use very simple numbers to make you familiar with the calculations. The second stage introduces the computer as a device to relieve you of the tedium of adding up products of numbers. For more complicated formulae, after you have gained experience in pulling together all the components by hand, you will be able to use the computer to perform all the calculations. Do this only after having verified that the computer algorithm is in fact producing the same results that you have obtained for yourself.

The exercises in the "Exploring the Tools" sections do require you to think a lot more about what you are doing and why. You are trying to explore the meaning and proper use of the tools by considering their use and properties in unusual circumstances; you are being challenged to think about what you are doing, not just to perform repetitious calculations. Many of the questions require you to make a series of similar calculations and then ask you to compare your results. This is a request for you to think about your results to try to gain a better appreciation for what you are doing. Requiring you to consider the similarities and differences between a series of related calculations facilitates this process. When you are requested to compare results, look for the way in which the results are similar, or different, and how those similarities or differences vary as you vary the parameters under your control.

The exercises in the "Applications" sections require the most thinking. You will soon learn that the major question in Applications is, "What is the statistical question?" and the most important outcome from the analysis is, "What did I learn from the exercise?" Consequently, many of the questions in the Applications sections will be open ended with no simple formulaic response. Many of the questions ask for your evaluation of the results that you obtain. The more you learn and the better you understand statistical theory, the more sophisticated and useful will be your insights and interpretations of the data you observe. Indeed, the entire objective of any statistical analysis is to provide useful interpretations of the data. Many questions in the exercises ask you to compare results of two different calculations, or results of the same calculation on different data. Your answers here require your use of judgment, insight into the nature of the problem, and an ability to determine how to use the tools to address the essential issues involved. Indeed, determining the essential issues is itself a key part of the question. These questions are a far cry from the type of question exemplified by:

> If a train is traveling on a track at 50 miles per hour and left its station at 10:00 and another train left its station 300 miles away at 10:00 and is traveling at 40 miles per hour in the opposite direction, at what time will the trains meet?

There is no room here for having to determine what the question is, nor for deciding how to solve it, nor for deciding what data are needed to answer the question, nor for interpreting your answer. One merely carries out a calculation and quotes an answer that is either right or wrong. The problems that we begin to address in the Applications sections are not so simple. You will need to decide what the relevant question is, how you are going to solve it, what data you need, what procedures you should use, and how you interpret the results. But of course, this reflects the questions that you will have to deal with in real life.

In answering the questions in the exercises, especially in the Exploring the Tools and Applications sections, you will often have to return to the text to review what is written there and to reconsider what you thought you understood before you began to answer the question. Do not be discouraged by this process of repeatedly reviewing the text; this is part of the learning process. We only really learn when we are confronted with having to do something, to make a decision. It is then that we discover that what we thought we knew, we do not. This is the most important objective of the exercises, so do expect to reread the text along with the graphs and the exercises.

There are many "worked" exercises. These are examples of how to use statistical thinking to analyze a problem or guidance in how to learn more about the tools that you are trying to acquire. They also provide a blueprint for doing similar exercises on your own. These exercises, which are always introduced with a sentence that gives the objective of the exercise, are most important. If you do no other exercises, at least do these. If you are unsure how to answer a question that you have had assigned, look back to a worked exercise that is close to the question you are trying to answer. Work through the worked exercise, and then you should have no difficulty in doing the assigned exercise on your own.

I hope that the computer exercises will encourage you to explore the tools and concepts you are trying to master. Feel free to try anything you fancy in these exercises, especially anything that I have not already suggested. Be bold; you cannot damage anything.

I trust that you will enjoy reading the text and learning the basics of statistics from it. A mastery of elementary statistical reasoning is a major component of your training and one that you will use in all aspects of your life; so it is comforting if you can enjoy the process as well. No matter what you do in life, you will need to evaluate statistics and statistical reasoning on almost a daily basis; so a good working knowledge of statistical processes is important for success in your chosen career.

Exercises

Topics for Consideration

Before beginning the exercises, you should read the "Addendum to the Reader" at the end of Chapter 1 if you have not already done so.

It would be advantageous for you to keep your answers to these questions on file. In Chapter 15, you will be asked to reconsider these questions in light of the analysis that you will learn in the chapters to follow.

1.1 According to a *Wall Street Journal* (March 28, 2000) article:

> Most years, a majority of portfolio managers trail the market. A big reason is the drag from investment costs, including management fees and trading. But the pattern of stock returns also plays a role. The market average (which is a weighted mean) tends to be driven by a fistful of stocks that post huge gains, so that the median stock lags behind the market. Result? Each year, you end up with a minority of money managers who hold the year's hottest stocks and thus earn fabulous returns, while the rest miss out on the big winners and therefore trail the index.

Note the terms that you need to know to be able to follow the argument, *mean* and *median,* for example. Discuss this quote. Try to address the following issues:

■ What data would you collect to confirm or deny this claim?

■ What would constitute rejection of the author's claims, and how would you assess the matter?

■ Assess the impact of these statements on your own choice of investment portfolio.

1.2 According to a *Wall Street Journal* (January 18, 2000) article:

> Kyoto [conference on global warming] supporters cheer new findings that the Earth's surface temperature is probably rising. But this trend isn't recent and isn't man made. (Arthur and Noah Robinson)

The authors point out that the current warming trend began about 300 years ago after the bottom of the Little Ice Age and that current temperatures are far below those of about a thousand years ago. Further, an average increase in temperature will increase the growing seasons and extend their geographical limits. *Scientific American* (August 2000) counters that diseases common to tropical climates will spread north.

Debate how you would evaluate these claims. Explore the need for data, reliable models of the environment, methods for determining the accuracy of the model's forecasts, and how one would balance increases in farming productivity with increases in tropical diseases. In the process, you should recognize the need for the analysis of data subject to much uncertainty. Demonstrate the manner in which the scientific method is relevant to this analysis.

1.3 According to a *New York Times* (October 31, 1999) article:

> A ranking is easier to convey information to a large public, like a football ranking. . . . We can clearly say that Denmark is cleaner than Germany and Germany is cleaner than Botswana. But in between there may be some problems—saying that Kenya is cleaner than Tanzania, for example.

The article goes on to report that Bolivia's presidential election in 1997 was won on the basis of an anticorruption campaign that was bolstered by quoting rankings showing that Bolivia had a worse ranking on corruption than its neighbors.

Indicate the dangers of uncritical reliance on such figures. Debate an alternative strategy for evaluating the relative nature of corruption in two countries. What are some of the difficulties in collecting the appropriate data?

1.4 "Obesity Rate Rising Fastest in the South" was a headline in the *New York Times* (October 27, 1999) based on a telephone survey of 100,000 people in 1991 and 1998. The two samples used different people. Explore how you would evaluate the quality of the data that were used to make the claim that southerners' obesity rate jumped 67.2%.

1.5 In the *Economist* (August 5, 2000, p. 61), there is a quote from the American Consumer Satisfaction Index that a University of Michigan Business School indicator of consumer satisfaction shows that consumer satisfaction has fallen substantially in almost all areas since 1994 but mainly in the service industries. Discuss how you would devise a strategy to determine whether the decline represents more particular customers who are more willing to complain or a real decline in the services provided by firms.

1.6 "Scientist Differs with EPA on Malathion" is a headline in the the *New York Times* (August 18, 2000). The article indicates that Dr. Brian Dementi claims that the use of malathion to control mosquitos is a greater cancer risk than the EPA admitted. Explore the extent to which this debate rests, or should rest, on the accuracy and relevance of data; the degree of confidence in the theoretical science; and the procedures used to evaluate the data. Do you perceive how objective scientists might well differ on their recommendations whether or not to use malathion, even though they both have access to the same experimental and survey data?

1.7 In August 2000, Ford and Firestone had to recall millions of Firestone tires that had been declared potentially unsafe. Imagine that you are a manager at Firestone assigned the task of trying to assess the cost of this recall. Discuss the data requirements and what sort of modeling will be needed to come up with a "reasonable figure."

1.8 In the *Economist* (August 19, 2000), an article "Asbestos Claims Still Killing," points out that the claims against asbestos manufacturers are not only huge but growing rapidly. Indeed, the outstanding claims already are greater than the total net worth of the firms involved. Explain how you would use and assess the value of information in analyzing this situation.

The original research on the carcinogenic effects of asbestos were limited to specific types of asbestos and to workers in asbestos plants. Discuss the relevance of this evidence to situations in which asbestos of different types to those examined are installed and are not disturbed or "worked."

1.9 A quote from the *Economist* (August 5, 2000, p. 58) follows:

> Even in good times, some 40% of all new businesses fail within their first five years of operation, according to Census Bureau figures. In America as a whole,

more than 70,000 companies went bust during 1998, almost half as many as were started that year.

> By contrast, the drumbeat of Internet failures is still incredibly faint. There are at least 3,000 dot.com start-ups backed by American venture-capital firms, according to VentureOne, a consultancy. . . . Dotcomfailures.com lists a mere 20 [failures].

Imagine that you are analyzing investments in e-commerce companies. Explain how you would bring data and modeling to bear on this problem in trying to decide the near-term profitability of e-commerce firms.

1.10 The *Scientific American* (September 2000) included an article concerning the attempt to determine the relative importance of genes versus training for championship athletes. One finding is that sprinters and marathoners have very different proportions of slow versus fast myosin filament in the muscle fiber. Consider the role of data, modeling, and analysis in determining these results. How much credence do you suspect they have? Discuss the role of the scientific method in this process.

1.11 Airbus has committed itself to building the world's largest passenger airplane. Imagine that you are the engineer in charge of determining the potential cost to build and operate this plane. Alternatively, you might be on the marketing side and need to assess the financial viability of such a venture in the market. Discuss the strategy that you might follow to fulfill your task. Evaluate the data needs and how you would assess their accuracy and relevance.

1.12 "Worrying about Wireless. Researchers are still unsure whether cellular phones are safe" reads a headline in the *Scientific American* (September 2000). Explain how the resolution of this issue is one of relating data to theoretical concepts and being able to assess the accuracy and relevance of the data collected. Then discuss issues of how to collect the data.

CHAPTER
2

Types of Variables, Measurements, and Explanation

2.1　What You Will Learn in This Chapter

Statistics is in part about the measurement of variables. As we will learn in this chapter, there are different ways to measure variables. Each measurement provides opportunities for learning about observed experiments and sets limitations on how much we can learn. If we are to extract useful information from our observations, we need to know something about the strengths and limitations of our observations and our measurements. Some of the types of variables we will discuss are cardinal variables, discrete and continuous—for example, numbers of people, their incomes; ordinal variables, such as ranks in a race; and categories, such as eye color.

In this chapter, we will begin the long process of learning what is or is not a random variable and how to distinguish functional relationships you studied in high school from the more complex structural relationships that are the essence of everyday life. Functional relationships are illustrated by simple "if, then" situations. Structural relationships are more subtle in that specifying a set of conditions—for example, the "if" in the "if, then" of the functional relationship—gives rise not to a single predictable outcome—a "then"—but to a distribution of outcomes. Hooke's law for the extension of a spring to a weight is, up to measurement error, a functional relationship. The relationship between income and the consumption of butter is a structural relationship in that for any given income level for a group of individuals there will be a distribution of values for butter consumption, not a single amount.

Chapter 1 was abstract and provided the grand view. This chapter will be less abstract.

2.2　Introduction

We saw from the first chapter that the study of statistics deals with a concept called a *random*, or a *stochastic, variable*, but what this is precisely is still a mystery. In this chapter, we will begin the process of acquiring clear ideas about this elusive concept.

As we began to see in Chapter 1, the actual world of science is a blend of the familiar world of "cause and effect" with the less familiar world of "randomness." But to clarify the fundamental notions of statistics, we should concentrate in the beginning on purely random or purely deterministic phenomena. In Chapter 1, we described a **random variable** as one for which we can find no causal links, either to any other variable, or to its own past values; random variables are not predictable. **Deterministic variables,** in contrast, were those variables that had a causal explanation; that is, the theory specified a functional relationship between a deterministic variable and some other deterministic or controlled variable. Deterministic variables can be predicted. Variables are defined as random when we have run out of causal explanations. This is not a very precise definition, but it will do for a start.

We will try to do two things in this chapter. First, we will clarify the various concepts of a variable. Actually, the alternative concepts of a variable are really different ways of measurement. The reason this is important is that different ways of measuring "objects" determine what questions you can and cannot ask. The second task is to distinguish random variables from deterministic variables. Once we have settled on the type of objects we are discussing, the process of understanding the arguments in subsequent chapters will be easier.

2.3 Types of Variables

What is a *variable*, random or otherwise? This term has meaning only in the context of some theoretical interpretation of observed phenomena. For example, planetary orbits are an observed phenomenon; Newton's gravitational hypothesis is the theoretical interpretation of this observed phenomenon. The interpretation, or theory, is usually expressed mathematically, but this is not necessary. However, a mathematical formulation of a theory is useful in making statements precise and in aiding in the distinction between the "variables" and the "model coefficients," or "parameters," in a functional, or in a structural, relationship.

The same variables may have several hypothesized relationships between them, depending on the interest and background of the investigator. Consider data on the consumption of milk. An economist might be interested in the relationship between the quantity of milk consumed and the price of milk. A nutritionist might be more concerned about the effect milk consumption has on the probability of heart disease, whereas a sociologist might be interested in the relationship between milk consumption and social status. In each case, the researchers begin by postulating some relationship between those variables of interest to their field of research.

Before continuing, a brief note on notation will be helpful. Consider a typical textbook model for deterministic variables, such as Hooke's law, which relates the length of extension of a spring to the application of a force on it; we ignore for now problems of observation and experimental control. For modest weights, the mathematical representation might be:

$$y = a + bx$$

where y represents the length of the spring in millimeters and x represents the weight that is added to the spring, measured in grams; these are the **variables** of Hooke's law. The coefficients of the relationship, which describe the variation, are represented by the lowercase letters a and b. Theoretically, if y represents the *extension* of the spring caused by adding the weight, not its actual length, the value taken by the parameter a is zero; if you measure the length of the spring, the value taken by a will represent the length of the spring at zero weight. This equation is said to be a **functional relationship** between the variables y and x with **coefficients,** or **parameters** a and b.

In general throughout the book, variables will be represented by letters at the end of the alphabet, except where a particular choice will provide a useful mnemonic for remembering what the variable is; lowercase letters at the beginning of the alphabet will be used for representing the coefficients of the relationship. The coefficients specify the relationship. In our example using Hooke's law, we see that the relationship between weight and spring length is a linear one; the length of the spring with zero weight is given by the value assigned to a in the experiment, and the rate at which the spring extends in millimeters as the weight is increased in grams is given by the value assigned to b. The coefficient b has units of measurement associated with it; "units of y" per "unit of x." The units of measurement are "millimeters of extension" per "gram of weight." The parameter a also has units of measurement associated with it; in this case the units are "millimeters of extension."

Let us return to our example involving gravitational attraction. Recall that the attractive force (F) between two bodies is proportional to the product of their masses (m_1, m_2) and inversely proportional to the square of the distance (d^2) between them; mass and distance are the variables:

$$F = \frac{m_1 m_2 G}{d^2}$$

The constant of proportionality is in this case the gravitational constant (G), which is a parameter of the functional relationship between force, mass, and distance. The parameter indicates the "strength" of the relationship between the variables. Often, as in this case, parameter values are regarded as very important constants of a relationship.

Variables are the objects of interest in a postulated relationship; some variables may represent properties we are concerned about, some represent our ideas about how the former variables are influenced by other factors. In the previous examples, the economist regarded milk consumption as the variable of interest and the price was the factor (another variable) that affected the level of consumption. For the nutritionist, the variable of concern was heart disease and the factor (variable) explaining its incidence was the quantity of milk consumed. For the sociologist, the variable of interest was also the quantity of milk consumed, but the factor explaining milk consumption was one's social position. Of course, these hypotheses are not mutually exclusive.

When we suggest a mechanism, or a model, that relates carbon dioxide to atmospheric warming, we implicitly define at least two variables: some measure of carbon dioxide and some measure of atmospheric warming. Without specifying some mechanism relating the two objects, carbon dioxide and atmospheric temperature, we are merely indicating two characteristics of the atmosphere, the quantity of carbon dioxide in the atmosphere and some measure of the temperature of the atmosphere.

Now that we have some idea of what a variable represents, we should consider the various ways in which variables can be measured. We are going to discuss, mercifully only briefly, five types of measurement of variables.

Cardinal Measurement

Let us begin with the most familiar concept, **cardinal measurement.** Imagine comparing the lengths of three fishing poles. We compare the poles to some standard, say a meter. You might declare that the poles, labeled as Super Large, Large, and Not-so-Large have lengths of 2.35, 2.21, and 2.00 meters. The numbers 2.35, 2.21, and 2.00 are cardinal measurements of the lengths of the fishing poles. Not only can you decide which is the longest and which is the shortest but whether Super Large is larger than Large by more than Large is larger than Not-so-Large; it isn't. This idea of measurement is one with which you are already very familiar. Other phenomena that can be measured in terms of cardinal measurements include temperatures, weights, time, distance, and so on. The key concept is that not only can you use the measurement to order, or rank, comparable phenomena, but you can also interpret and compare the differences between measurements.

We can distinguish two subcategories of cardinal measurement. Those that have a meaningful zero, or origin, are said to have a **ratio scale.** Those that do not are said to have an **interval scale.** In the previous examples, weights and distance have easily interpretable zeros, or origins. Temperature—except when measured in degrees Kelvin—time, and IQ levels do not have meaningful origins.

For a **ratio scale variable,** such as weights or heights, where we have a clear origin, or zero, defined for the measurement system, we can declare, for example, that Tom at 6 feet is twice as tall as James at 3 feet, or that Betty, who weighs 200 pounds, is twice as heavy as Jane, who weighs 100 pounds. Ratios are meaningful for such variables.

For an **interval scale variable,** even though differences in measurements are meaningful and can be compared, we cannot interpret ratios. We cannot say, for example, that one measurement is twice that of another. If Jones has an IQ measurement of 100, Brown has one of 150, and Smith one of 200, we can compare intervals; that is, the difference between Jones and Brown is the same as the difference between Smith and Brown, which is no more than we have been saying. What we cannot do in this case is to say that Smith is twice as intelligent as Jones. The reason is that psychologists cannot agree on an interpretable origin for IQ levels. Intervals can be defined and compared but not ratios of the absolute levels. The same is true for measurements of time; the origin is essentially arbitrary. We can meaningfully talk about time differences, but we cannot take ratios of times and interpret them usefully.

There may be a little confusion here in that "time differences" and "temperature differences" are themselves ratio scale variables, because in both cases there is a natural definition for the origin, zero. We are most used to talking about time differences, not about absolute time measurements. This situation would change if we were able to specify the "big bang" as the origin for all time; then we could say that the time for one event was twice that for another.

These examples are all for continuous measurements, or by extension, **continuous variables.** The accuracy of the measurement can be as precise, in principle at least, as you wish. We could have measured our fishing rods to 30 places of decimals—that is, 30 digits to the right of the decimal point—given that we were masochistic enough to impose such a burden on ourselves and could have found a suitable measuring instrument. Continuous variables are represented by "real numbers" (if you remember your high school mathematics).

Cardinal variables also have another distinguishing characteristic that is too frequently forgotten, even in some textbooks. Such variables most often have units of measurement associated with them. The extension of the spring in Hooke's law might be measured in millimeters; weight in kilograms or pounds; current flow in amperes; national income in Canadian dollars or U.S. dollars, or in Finmarks; electrical capacitance in farads; astronomical distances in light years; gasoline in gallons or liters; electrical resistance in ohms; temperature in degrees Kelvin, and so on. The important aspect of these comments is that the units of measurement are an essential component in the description of the data. Kilograms and kilometers and kilograms squared or cubed are very different objects and cannot be directly compared to each other. If the units of measurement don't appear with the cited numbers, there is a temptation to forget this important constraint on our interpretation of measurements, and we are then liable to make some very foolish statements.

But not all variables can or should be so measured. Sometimes we merely need to count; for example, how many people consumed organic carrots on December 25, 1990, in Macon County? Or we might want to know the number of children in a family, the number of sales calls made in a day, or the number of accidents in a particular week at Houston and Mercer streets in New York. In each case, our measurement must be in discrete units; the integers must be precise. Variables that are measured in terms of integers are said to be **discrete variables.** Discrete variables can have negative values. If for example, you measure the number of net arrivals at a car wash, the number is negative if the number of departures of clean cars is greater than the number of arrivals of dirty cars. The key concept for cardinal measurement is still that differences are meaningful. If Fluffy Car Wash has 20 more cars in its lines than does Scruffy Car Wash and Eazy Wash has only 10 more than Lazy Wash, then the Fluffy–Scruffy difference is twice that of the Eazy–Lazy difference.

Ordinal Measurement

Suppose that you want to survey the bagel preferences of a group of New York University students, who are well known to have almost fanatical preferences about such important matters. If five varieties of bagels are being compared, then for each person you can rank, or order, their preferences from least to most preferred. The preference ranking can be expressed by assigning letters of someone's alphabet— Roman, Greek, or Hebrew—or to be confusing to students, by assigning "numbers."

These numbers are really rankings, or orderings, and the rankings of preferences could as easily be represented by letters; for example, A, B, C, D, where A is preferred to B, which is preferred to C, and so on. One is never tempted to claim that a preference for A over C is "twice as great as" a preference for C over D. Unfortunately, when we use numbers to represent rankings, there is a tendency to think that we can, in fact, interpret the differences between rankings, or orderings; we cannot. We also have to be careful in how we compare rankings. With our bagel rankings, for example, we can conclude that two individuals have the same rankings of bagels; that is, they agree on their rankings, but we cannot compare the intensity of their preferences.

Ordinal measurements represent rankings or orderings of the data. Consider another example: your rank in class. Suppose four students, A, B, C, and D, have the grades, 90, 89, 45, 43. Note that because zero is a natural origin for grades, and because the instructor has assigned the grades, they are deterministic, cardinal, ratio-scale variables. Now assign ranks to the four students; the ranks are in sequence 1, 2, 3, and 4. These ranks are ordinal measurements. The person in the third rank is one rank less than the person in the second, who is one rank less than the person in first place. From the ranks that is all that you can infer. However, if you had the grades, a cardinal measurement, you would realize that student B is only 1 grade unit behind A, but 44 units ahead of C. Further, C is only two units ahead of D, but 44 units behind B and has a grade that is one-half that of A.

All of this information is lost when you use an ordinal measurement. In one of the data files supplied for computer use with this text is a variable term *sales rank* for the sales of rock songs. You now recognize that the information that you can extract from such information is limited relative to the original cardinal, ratio-scale, actual sales figure.

Many observations can be recorded only in terms of ordinal measurements. Preferences for commodity bundles can only be given ranks; for example, you can rank your preferences for alternative soft drinks.

Categorical Variables

Yet another way to represent data is to "classify" them, or to put them into **categories**. Eye color, hair style, sex, race, and religious preference are examples of categories. Categories are recorded by counting the number of examples that belong to each classification. An alternative term to describe such variables is **nominal;** that is, these are variables that give names to objects, which facilitates the creation of categories.

Indices

Indices are the most prevalent type of variable you will ever encounter in economics; almost all economic data are in the form of indices. An **index** is a weighted sum of other variables. Now is not the time to go into the intricacies of creating indices, but an intuitive understanding of the basic idea will help.

Imagine that we would like to measure the output of a paper towel firm. The firm produces ten different types and quality levels of paper towel, but we need a single measure for the output of the firm. To do this, we create an index of the output of the firm. One naive way to do this is to define the index by adding up the output of each type of towel; 100,000 of Super-Soft plus 200,000 of Squishy-Soft plus . . . , plus 50,000 of Congealed Woodchips. But such an index might not be very useful if Super-Soft costs twice as much to produce as Congealed Woodchips.

Another way to create an index of output that will meet this objection is to define an index by weighting the output of each type of paper towel by its share of the total value of the product; that is, the weight to be associated with the first type of paper towel is the first's value of output relative to the total value of output, that for the second is the value of the second output to the total value, and so on. Suppose the revenues from Super-Soft were $100,000, from Squishy-Soft were $80,000, and so on for a total of $1,000,000. The weight for Super-Soft would be 0.1, for Squishy-Soft, 0.08, and so on. The weights obviously add to one, and the index value in any period is the sum of the individual outputs, each multiplied by its weight as described. The weight attached to each component in the index is a measure of the relative importance of that component in the index.

There are many other ways to create an index, but what they all have in common is a sum of components, each of which is multiplied by some weight. The individual components in an index can be indices themselves, and their components can be indices, and . . . ; you get the picture. Indices have to be treated with caution; one must be careful to understand what is in the index and how it was constructed. As we will see later in the book, different choices of indices can change the results of any analysis quite dramatically. Virtually all the actual economic or financial data that you will observe and that are cardinal variables will also be index numbers.

Time Series

Time series are sequences of data that are ordered in time; each observation has associated with it a particular point in time at which it was observed. The output by month of our paper towel firm is an example; the daily prices on the New York Stock Exchange are another. All macroeconomic variables, such as gross national product, national income, savings, investment, interest rate, and money supply, are time series of indices.

Time series may be indices, ordinal measurements, cardinal measurements, continuous, or discrete. The distinguishing characteristic is that the data are time ordered, and that time ordering can be very critical in the analysis of the data. A time series of categories is possible but usually would not be very interesting, unless the objects being categorized changed their categories over time; for example, hair color changes would change hair color categories over time and thereby create a different time series.

Data that are not time series are usually called **cross-sectional** to distinguish them. Cross-sectional data collected for a group of people or objects at a point in time are a "cross section" of that chosen group at that point in time. We could collect cross-sectional data at different points in time and so would then have a time series of cross-sectional data; such a collection is called **panel data.**

We could, for example, record for the year 1990 the income of each family for that one year; this would be a cross section of incomes. Alternatively, we could record an individual's income by year; this would be a time series. Or we could record the individual incomes of a selected group of people over time; this would be a panel data set.

2.4 Random and Deterministic Variables

Let us begin with the familiar, deterministic variables. We know already that we need some representation, or model, of the phenomena of interest that will relate the variables to each other. Consider Hooke's law once again; within bounds the extension of a spring is proportional to the weight that is attached. Here we have two variables, the weight and the extension of the spring. The postulated mechanism, or model, that represents the data is extremely simple; the degree of extension is proportional to the force applied in the form of weights attached to the spring. Let us for the moment ignore the fact that if we were actually to run this experiment, which you may well have done yourself, the results would vary from trial to trial. The results of the hypothetical (unrealistic) experiment might look like the graph shown in Figure 2.1. This is a linear relationship between weight in grams and the extension of a spring measured in millimeters; experimental and observational errors have been ignored.

This naive example illustrates a functional relationship between deterministic variables; for a given specified weight, there is a unique extension to the spring. This is a simple "if, then" type of relationship. The degree of extension is predictable, once we know the amount of weight that has been added and the conditions of the experiment. We control the weight variable, so we can regard it as deterministic in that we determine its values through our choices. The length of extension is deterministic in this simple version of the experiment, because we can find a causal mechanism—a function—relating a deterministic variable—weight that we physically control—to our variable of interest.

Now let us consider a random, or stochastic, situation. Suppose that we examine a roulette wheel and, to keep the discussion pure, let us ignore any problems caused by faulty wheels, square balls, or a crooked croupier. Under these pristine conditions, experience teaches us that no one that we are acquainted with, but most particularly ourselves, can predict where the roulette ball will land; the claim is that the slot in which the roulette ball lands is an example of a random variable.

Before we make any such rash conclusion, let us first consider some alternatives. One mechanism that someone might suggest as a model for this situation is that between the

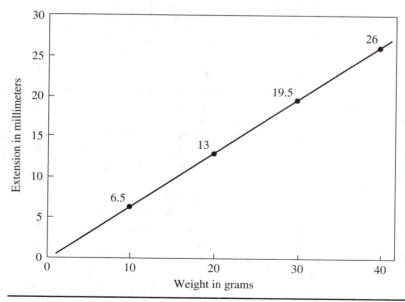

Figure 2.1   Illustration of an experiment on a hypothetical deterministic relationship between weight and length of extension of a spring.

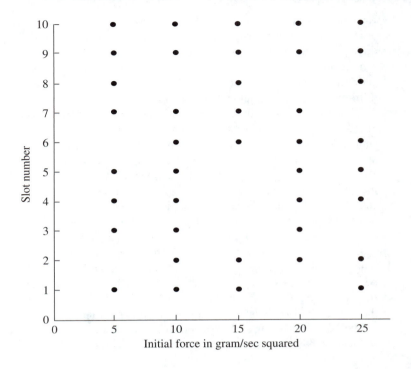

Figure 2.2   Illustration of an experiment on a random relationship between initial ball momentum and the value of the slot into which the ball lands. Ten trials are taken at each force level. Each • represents one or more hits.

relative momentum of the roulette ball when thrown and the value of the slot into which the ball comes to rest; that is, for a given speed of rotation of the roulette wheel, a more powerful throw will make the ball travel farther so that if the change in force of the throw is sufficiently precise, we may be able to "choose the slot in which to land." Because we will be controlling the momentum of the ball when thrown, it is best regarded as a deterministic variable. If we were to plot the values of the resting slots and the initial momentum of the ball entering the wheel, we might see something like the graph in Figure 2.2. This figure shows that if you perform the experiment many times any outcome is compatible with any level of initial momentum.

There are, of course, many other possible mechanisms that might influence where the ball will land that we could examine; but all would be similar to that shown in Figure 2.2. We could try, for example, to relate the value of the resting slot on a given trial to the values that occurred on previous trials. But as you suspect, this approach is not likely to work either.

We cannot predict the individual outcomes. Causal models, like that used for the spring extension, do not seem to exist in our roulette situation. We have here a different type of relationship, and we have a different type of variable to examine—a ran-

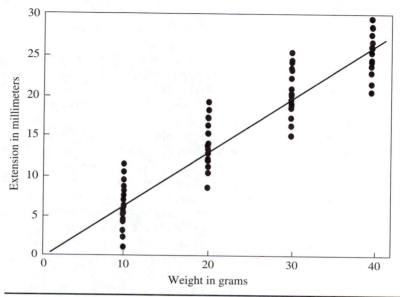

Figure 2.3   Illustration of an experiment on the relationship between weight and length of a spring. Each point on the graph represents an experimental outcome at each of the weights. The straight line represents a best linear fit to all the observed data.

dom, or stochastic, variable. These are variables for which we can find no causal relationship and for which we cannot predict the specific outcomes of any trial in an experiment.

Real experiments do not fall into either of these two extreme situations. The usual case is one in which there are deterministic elements and random elements. The real task of science is to separate the two and to discover how much one can say about such mixed situations. Recall, for example, the Hooke's law experiment. Actual experiments will produce different results each time, but we will observe for each weight that the extensions will cluster about some characteristic value and that characteristic value will increase linearly with the value of the weights (see Figure 2.3). Only occasionally has anyone managed to find the deterministic component in the roulette example, and then only when there were imperfections in the wheel or the ball.

We can pursue this idea of an "experiment" in the context of the social sciences—economics and politics, for example. In these situations, the incidence of experiments that combine deterministic and random elements is universal. But there is a subtlety in such data in defining the experiment that generates the data. Using economic data, economists formulate causal models linking prices, incomes, weather, and number of commodities sold. But once your study of economics takes you into the realm of examining actual data, you will immediately recognize that the "economic story" can only be part of the explanation because there will be a lot of variation left unexplained by the economist's models. Statistical theory and analytical techniques will be needed to separate the deterministic components from the random components.

You may still be puzzled by what is meant by an experiment in economics, or political science, when the data being examined are whatever occurred historically. Your income is whatever it is, you bought 5 pounds of potatoes and a pair of roller blades, and these are facts. There was no sense of anyone "experimenting" as in a laboratory. True, but we will discover that it will be useful for us to extend the notion of an experiment to include what we might label "nature's experiments." Your income can be regarded as an experiment when you recognize all the myriad circumstances and special events that led to your current situation. The level of GNP of any country is the outcome of millions of decisions, some very significant, some not so significant; further, from time to time, various matters that affect GNP occur with little or no warning and certainly with little control. For all these reasons, we say that the outcomes of the observed level of GNP, your income, or how many potatoes you bought last week are the outcomes of natural experiments.

Another way to illustrate nature's experiments is in terms of biology. A plausible model of how organisms adapt is through random genetic mutations. Those mutations that lead to improved adaptation to the organism's environment tend to survive, and those that do not improve adaptation do not survive. At any point in time we see only the survivors, not those that failed. We see the outcome of the experiment, not the running of it. Only if we pay close attention to the mechanism will we begin to recognize the extent of nature's biological experiments that are being carried out constantly. Merely to observe the current list of species misses the experimental process that underlies the observed outcomes.

As claimed, all these "real" experiments involve both aspects that are amenable to analysis by economists and other scientists and elements that are not so amenable. We will begin with the simplest situations first and treat, initially, all variables as if they were totally random; that is, there is no causal explanation. Even under these extreme assumptions we will discover that there is much for us to learn and more for us to say about the properties of economic variables treated as random variables. Later, particularly in Chapter 13 on regression, we will relax this stringent assumption and begin the process of showing the confounding interaction between random elements and deterministic ones.

There is an even more important reason for viewing the real outcomes of actual events as experiments, in that much of what the economist, or political scientist, does involves what-if speculations. What would the level of GNP have been if tax rates had been lowered as proposed? What would the outcome of an election have been if campaign financing reform had been implemented? In these situations, it is helpful to view the outcomes that we actually observe as being just one of very many potential outcomes that we could have observed. So from the perspective of observing merely one of very many potential outcomes in any given situation, we can label each observation as the outcome of an experiment run by nature.

Some of you may have spotted an anomaly in the characterization of random and deterministic variables. Is it possible that two random variables could be linked in a functional way? If we label one random variable X and the other Y, and

$Y = 10 + 2.5X$, do we have a problem with our definition of a random variable in that X and Y are related by a simple linear function? By labeling X and Y as random variables, we are saying that except for the functional relationship between X and Y, there are no causal links between X or Y and anything else that is itself deterministic. In this example, we can regard X and Y as the same random variable but expressed in different units. For example, X might have been temperature in degrees Fahrenheit and Y is in degrees Centigrade. The situation would have been different if Y were temperature, no matter how measured, and if X were a measure of heat input. In the latter situation, we have a potential causal relationship and a corresponding theory that links the relevant variables, heat and temperature.

Figure 2.3 illustrates the situation in which a distribution of a collection of values of a variable is dependent on another variable, either random or deterministic. In Figure 2.3, when the weight is 10 grams, we observe a distribution of values for the extension. Such relationships are called *structural*. A **structural relationship** is one between a variable and a statistical model, or distribution, for some random variable. For example, the distribution of income within an economy might depend on past levels of net investment; in this example, income is regarded as a random variable, at least in part, with a distribution of values that depends in part on the level of net investment, another variable. If the value of the variable income, rather than the distribution, had depended on the value taken by net investment, then we would have had a functional relationship between variables. If we regarded net investment as a deterministic variable, we would have defined income to be a deterministic variable also. We generally do regard both investment and income as random variables.

For those of you who have some prior computer experience, you may have wondered about the computer generation of random numbers. For a long time, numbers generated on the computer to simulate random numbers were called *pseudorandom numbers* to reflect the fact that they were not real random numbers. Often the mechanisms used to generate the pseudorandom numbers were surprisingly simple.

Although we have not yet developed the tools to do justice to this question, we can speculate about the existence of such numbers for our definition of a random variable. Many mechanisms have the following remarkable property: We can write down an equation linking a value of a variable to its previous value, for example, $x_{t+1} = 4.0x_t(1 - x_t)$, a simple quadratic. If we simulate the sequence starting at a pair of arbitrary initial points that are close together but still different, then as the two paths progress, they rapidly separate to produce two very different sequences. For such a sequence, a plot of x_{t+1} on x_t produces a smooth graph, whereas as we separate the pair of points that are plotted, say x_{t+10} on x_t, we get a plot that looks random; that is, we cannot predict x_{t+10} from x_t. The random number generators on most computers today are even more impressive in that simple iterated sequences of numbers are almost impossible to distinguish from the abstract idea of a random variable—that is, a variable whose values cannot be predicted—except by replicating the computer mechanism exactly. So here we have examples of seemingly obvious deterministic relationships that have the appearance of random phenomena.

Let us keep our naive definition; a random variable is one for which we cannot find a causal relationship—that is, a variable whose values we cannot predict.

2.5   Summary

Models of physical or social phenomena involve *variables, coefficients,* or *parameters.* Coefficients, or parameters, determine the specific properties of the behavior of the variables specified in the model. Variables are the main objects of interest in the model and represent the properties of the phenomena under examination.

In this chapter, we have made a series of distinctions between different types of variables, which represent different ways to measure. We have distinguished *cardinal* and *ordinal, categorical, indices,* and *time series variables.* Cardinal variables can be either *continuous* or *discrete* and *ratio scale* or *interval scale,* depending on whether a unique zero can be defined. Variables that are not time series are sometimes referred to as *cross-sectional.* Variables that are both cross-sectional and time series are called *panel data.*

A separate distinction is between random and deterministic variables, depending on the existence of causal explanations; *deterministic variables* have causal theoretical explanations and *random variables* do not. The theoretical explanation for random variables is given by the description of a distribution function, which describes the properties of large collections of data.

Deterministic variables are related by *functional relationships.* Random variables are related by *structural relationships;* that is, values of one variable, deterministic, or random, determine a distribution for the other variable, which will be a random variable. We also discussed the conundrum of the computer generation of random numbers (see page 31).

Random variables as well as deterministic variables can have any of the five different types of measurement; that is, we can have random time series, categories, ordinal measures, discrete, and of course, random continuous variables.

In the next several chapters, we will concentrate on figuring out how to understand random variables. The main task is to discover what we can say about such variables.

Case Study

Was There Age Discrimination in a Public Utility?

In Chapter 1, we introduced the age discrimination problem within a public utility that was undergoing reorganization. In this section, we examine the extent to which the lessons learned in this chapter apply to these data.

The major variables in the data that are stored in the Xfiles folder "Agedisc" are age of employee, wages earned by that employee before resigning, sex of employee, and a se-

ries of variables indicating "membership" in a specific class, such as over 40, under 40, internal applicant, external applicant, and so on. Our first major question from this chapter is how to characterize these variables.

Age is a cardinal ratio scale continuous variable that is only recorded in terms of discrete units of years. Similarly, wages are also measured in terms of a cardinal ratio scale continuous variable that has associated with it the units of measurement, U.S. dollars. The implications are that with these data we can engage the full roster of

continues on next page

(Continued)

analysis that is to follow in the chapters ahead. We know, for example, that we can compare salaries and ages and decide by how much one employee differs from another; if the income data were in terms of ranks we could not make such comparisons.

Whether either of these variables can be regarded as random variables depends on one's viewpoint and objective. If we regard the recorded numbers as the characteristics of a given specific set of named individuals at a particular point in time, they are most likely best treated as deterministic. But for our purposes, we are more interested in the data as representing the state of a group of employees with certain characteristics. At other times there will be different specific individuals making up the composition of the firm, so we are advised to regard the variables as observations on random variables in that the particular values associated with each individual are to some extent unpredictable. This distinction will become much clearer later in the text after we have developed probability theory and the concept of distributions of random variables.

The remaining variables are categorical. We could have defined ordinal variables from some of these data, if for example, we had replaced the income variable with income ranks, or the age variable with ranks. However, to have done so would have limited our analysis later in the text.

These data are all cross-sectional and are not time series.

Exercises

Before beginning the exercises, read the "Addendum to the Reader" at the end of Chapter 1 if you have not already done so.

Calculation Practice

2.1 In the following list of model statements, for each term identify whether they are variables, coefficients, or parameters.

a. $C_t = a + bYh_t$; C_t is aggregate consumption in year t, Yh_t is aggregate household income in year t.

b. $I_t = \alpha_0 + \alpha_1(Y_t - Y_{t-1}) - \delta K_{t-1} + \gamma r_t$; I_t is aggregate investment in year t, Y_t is net national product in year t, K_t is aggregate capital stock in year t, and r_t is the real interest rate.

c. $S_{it} = c_i + dA_{it}$; S_{it} is sales of firm i in year t, A_{it} is advertising expenditures in year t by firm i.

d. $M_t = e + fB_t - gB_t^2$; M_t is the infant mortality rate and B_t is the birth rate.

e. $E = Mc^2$; E is energy, M is mass, and c is the velocity of light.

2.2 *Worked. Objective: Illustrate determination of variable types.* In the following list of variables, specify how each should be measured; that is, identify what type of variable it is, or what type of measurement is applicable. There may be more than one alternative; if so, mention at least two. (We have omitted the arguments one would use to justify each choice; you can supply your own. The choices for some variables depend on your interpretation of the way in which the data are observed and measured; sometimes there is no single right answer.)

a. National income in year t. Answer: Random, time series, index, cardinal, ratio scale

b. Amount of fertilizer needed to enhance growth of lettuce. Answer: Deterministic, cardinal, continuous, ratio scale

c. Lettuce output. Answer: If measured by number of heads of lettuce: deterministic, cardinal, discrete

d. Dosage of aspirin in tablets. Answer: Deterministic, cardinal, discrete

e. Dosage of aspirin as a fluid. Answer: Deterministic, cardinal, continuous, ratio scale

f. Campaign contributions. Answer: Deterministic, cardinal, continuous, ratio scale

g. Political preferences as to "liberal," "moderate," and "conservative." Answer: Random, ordinal

h. Evaluating motor skills of a machinist in an equipment plant. Answer: Random, ordinal, cardinal

i. Classification of type of addiction. Answer: Categorical

2.3 In the following list of variables, specify how each should be measured, that is, identify what type of variable it is, or what type of measurement is applicable. There may be more than one alternative; if so, mention at least two.

a. Temperature by month at specified points on the Earth's surface

b. Number of earthquakes per year

c. Severity of earthquakes as indicated by the Richter scale

d. Scholastic aptitude test scores

e. Volume of a gas

f. Rate of arrival of patrons at a cinema

g. Hostility levels of student subjects

h. Reading speed and comprehension score

i. Train use by commuters (note several possibilities)

j. Preference for alternative mouthwashes

k. Cost of production of all automobiles in the United States by year

2.4 Examine the description of the data files on the computer in the folder Xfiles. (See Appendix B, Section B.4, "Data Files.") Select 15 variables; then decide which type of variable each one is. You will find examples of every type of variable mentioned in this chapter.

Exploring the Tools

2.5 For the following list of variables give your reasons why, or the extent to which, you think that each is a random or a deterministic variable. What criteria would you use to distinguish between the two categories of variables? What experiments would you perform to check your distinctions?

a. Extensions of a spring after adding weights

b. Picking cards from a shuffled deck (What role does "shuffling" play and why?)

c. Numbers in the lottery

d. Orbital periods of the same planets (that is, the times taken to complete one cycle)

e. Consumption of cigarettes by a specific individual

f. Purchase of cigarettes by a specific individual

g. Cost of production for a specific output by a particular firm

h. Service time at an auto repair facility

2.6 Resolve the paradox: Random numbers can be produced by a computer algorithm.

2.7 With respect to the distinction between deterministic and random variables and the idea of a structural relationship, compare and contrast the disciplines of astronomy and meteorology, or biology and economics, or psychology and political science.

2.8 If you write the equation:

$$y = a + bx$$

where x is a continuous deterministic variable and y is a discrete deterministic variable, what is immediately wrong with this formulation? Explain your answer.

2.9 *Worked. Objective: Illustrate random draws.* A random variable is one whose value cannot be predicted on any given trial. Let us illustrate this idea by generating values of a random variable by computer. [Computer directions: Start S-Plus. On the menu bar click on <u>Labs</u>, <u>Random Sampling</u>.] You will see ten columns of 10 boxes, labeled 1 to 100. We can run an experiment by generating random numbers; this is called *sampling*. The random numbers will be generated without replacement. [The 5 boxes selected are colored red. The yellow box is the mean of the sample selected. By clicking on the Sample button you will see a new random sample of 5 boxes and a new mean value. Change the number of random boxes selected on each trial by keying in a new value in the *n* box and clicking on Sample. Clicking on Reset will eliminate the previous means and calculate a new sample. Experiment with different values of *n*.] As you watch repeated generations of sample drawings from the 100 boxes, what conclusions can you draw? For example, try predicting one of the five outcomes, the occurrence of adjacent pairs, or the value of the maximum difference between numbers.

2.10 Worked. *Objective: Illustrate structural relationships as discussed in the text.* Create a graph of *horsepower* and *miles per gallon,* using data in the Cardata.xls file in the Misc subfolder.[Computer directions: Start S-Plus. To import the data file: On the menu bar click on <u>File</u>, <u>Import Data</u>, <u>From File</u>; select folder Xfiles, subfolder Misc. Click on file Cardata.xls; click Open. To select the two data columns you wish to graph: Click on the top of the mpg column, hold down the CTRL key, and click on the top of the hp column. (The first item checked will be on the graph's *x*-axis, the second on the *y*-axis.) On the menu bar click on <u>Graph</u>, <u>2D Plot</u>. Scroll to and click on <u>Fit-Linear Least Squares</u>. Click OK.] The straight line summarizes the effect of hp on mpg. The actual observed value of mpg depends on the sum of the effect of the level of horsepower and a random component. The deterministic part is represented by the line and the random component by the position of the dots relative to the line.

Repeat this exercise using the variables *midterm1* and *final* in file Grades.xls, subfolder Misc. If all

the dots lie exactly on the line, what would be implied about the relationship between midterm1 and final grades? What is your reaction to such a result?

2.11 Worked. *Objective: Illustrate structural equations and the effect of noise on the observed variable.*

a. Consider the equation

$$y_i = .5x_i + e_i$$
$$i = 1, 2, \ldots, 11$$

where $x = \{-5, -4, -3, -2, -1, 0, 1, 2, 3, 4, 5\}$, and we use the Uniform distribution with limits $[-1, 1]$ to generate 11 random variables for e_i. Calculate the values of y_i.

[**Computer directions:** Start S-Plus. (1) Create an empty data frame to hold the data: On the menu bar click on <u>Data</u>, <u>New Data Object</u>; select data.frame, and click OK. An empty data frame with a name (SDF#) in the upper left will appear on the screen.

(2) To generate 11 random numbers for the value of *e*: On the menu bar click on <u>Data</u>, <u>Random Numbers</u>. In the Random Number Generating dialog, key in $\boxed{11}$ in Sample Size. Distribution should be Uniform. Key in $\boxed{-1}$ for Minimum. In the Save As box, key in the name of the data frame just created in (1) (be sure the case of the data frame name is correct, e.g., SDF1). Uncheck the Print Results box. Click Apply. Next, change the name of the first column in the data frame. Double click on the word *sample* in the label position of column 1; key in $\boxed{e}$. Hit <Enter>.

(3) To create the *x*-variables, −5 to 5: Click on column 2 of the data frame. On the menu bar click on <u>Data</u>, <u>Transform</u>. In the Transform dialog in New Column Name key in $\boxed{x}$, and in Expression key in $\boxed{\text{seq}(-5,5,1)}$. Click Apply.

(4) To calculate the value of *y*: On the menu bar click on <u>Data</u>, <u>Transform</u>. In the Transform dialog in New Column Name key in $\boxed{y}$, and in Expression key in $\boxed{.5 * x + e}$. Click Apply.]

b. Plot y and x using the scatter plot with regression line, and print the graph.

[**Computer directions:** Select the two data columns you wish to graph, x and y. Click on the top of the x-column. Hold down the CTRL key, and click on the top of the y-column. On the menu bar, click on Graph, 2D Plot. Scroll to and click on Fit-Linear Least Squares. Click on OK. To put a label on the graph, highlight the graph. On the menu bar click Insert, Titles, Main. Key in the title in the box that appears on the graph. To print the graph, highlight the graph window you wish to print. On the menu bar, click File, Print Graph Sheet. Note: The straight line in the Fit-Linear Least Squares graph is the regression line discussed in the text.]

c. Generate a second set of 11 values for e as in (2); call the new variable $e2$. Recalculate y as in (4) using the new variable $e2$; call the new variable generated $y2$. Plot the scatter plot with regression line for $y2$ and x. (Note: You can copy and paste column x to the new data sheet.)

d. Repeat (c), substituting a new $e3$ and calculating a new $y3$.

e. Compare your graphs, and comment on the respective effects on y of the variables x and e.

Applications

2.12 Consider any one of the data files on the computer in folder Xfiles, subfolder Energy. (See Appendix B, Section B.4, "Data Files.") Consider a simple model of demand for energy that uses the variables that have been listed in that data file. Indicate whether the relationships are structural, and justify your answers. For each variable, specify what type of variable it is.

2.13 Consider the data files Age65.xls, Arms.xls, Cardata.xls, Chal.xls, and Coles.xls in the folder Xfiles, subfolder Misc. (See Appendix B, Section B.4, "Data Files.") For each of the variables listed, indicate whether it is deterministic or random, and further classify it as cardinal or ordinal, continuous or discrete, ratio or interval, and so on. Briefly justify your selections.

2.14 In terms of the definitions in the text, describe the variables listed in the data files in folder Xfiles, subdirectories Testscor and Wheatpr. (See Appendix B, Section B.4, "Data Files.") Justify your answers.

2.15 All relationships in economics must be postulated as structural. Debate this claim.

2.16 The difference between economic laws and physical laws is that the latter are deterministic and the former are structural. Comment.

2.17 If data are generated by an experiment, are the outcomes necessarily functional? If data are obtained by a survey, are they necessarily structural? Debate these issues.

PART TWO

Descriptive Statistics

CHAPTER

3

How to Describe and Summarize Random Data by Graphical Procedures

3.1 What You Will Learn in This Chapter

If we have data that we can neither predict nor relate functionally to other variables, we have to discover new methods for extracting information from them. We begin this process by concentrating on a few simple procedures that provide useful descriptions of our data sets and supplement these calculations with pictures. The median, the range, and the interquartile range are three such measures, and the corresponding picture is called a *box-and-whisker plot*. We will also discover the importance and use of histograms in portraying the statistical properties of data, in particular the all-important concept of a "relative frequency."

The most important lesson in this chapter is the idea of the "shape" of a histogram. The concept of shape involves the notions of location, spread, symmetry, and the degree of "peakedness" of a histogram.

Experiments in statistics are distinguished by the shapes of their histograms; different types of experiments produce different shapes of histograms. When there is a sufficiently large number of observations on the same experiment, the same experiment produces the same shape of histogram.

3.2 Introduction

Let us recall our preliminary, intuitive definition of a random variable: A random variable is a variable for which neither explanation nor predictions can be provided, either from the variable's own past or from observations on any other variable. Whereas variables that are predictable from the values of other variables can easily be summarized by stating the prediction rule, this is not possible with random variables. If you have only a few values to look at, then there is no problem; merely list the variable values. But if there are many values to consider, a simple listing will not be very useful.

Consider these examples. The list of values for a variable representing examination grades, midterms and a final, is shown in Table 3.1. As you can see, the entries in this

Table 3.1 **List of Midterm and Final Grades for 72 NYU Students**

Midterm I				Midterm II				Final			
88	60	60	88	96	84	96	80	82	66	62	86
60	84	88	84	64	88	88	76	74	78	80	74
84	72	74	100	56	88	68	88	60	74	80	74
56	60	52	80	56	76	76	88	42	68	60	86
64	92	88	52	84	96	80	36	86	80	60	52
92	68	72	60	96	88	88	80	92	70	58	70
48	48	84	76	36	40	76	84	48	46	60	70
76	44	76	64	74	52	68	92	66	48	66	76
88	52	60	80	76	52	68	92	78	56	68	76
48	36	60	74	84	68	68	88	66	46	52	66
84	68	68	56	92	72	76	84	72	60	58	66
72	92	64	56	88	72	88	80	62	32	62	58
64	80	68	60	64	80	68	76	74	70	78	68
84	76	92	92	80	80	88	84	66	68	64	90
60	80	84	88	84	52	84	68	64	56	70	64
90	76	72	84	96	60	76	64	78	66	70	78
72	64	72	76	72	56	56	72	60	60	60	58
92	84	72	72	92	84	84	84	74	78	76	82

table do not provide much understandable information or insight into the nature of student grades. Clearly, all the information that is available is contained in the entries in the table. But equally clearly that information is not in a form that enables you or me to learn very much from these data. Try this experiment. Close your eyes and then try to describe in your own words the data that you have just examined in Table 3.1. If you have a photographic memory, then you will be able to recall all the values, but that is not of much use; we still do not have any insight into the values taken by this

Table 3.2 **One Hundred Tosses of an Eight-sided Die**

3	2	2	4	5	8
1	4	8	2	7	3
5	8	4	1	7	6
7	8	5	6	5	4
3	5	8	4	7	7
1	6	5	4	8	8
1	8	3	2	5	5
5	4	2	2	6	8
8	6	3	1	2	7
7	1	5	3	8	3
1	7	1	2	8	
1	8	8	1	8	
6	1	3	7	8	
4	5	4	8	7	
7	7	6	8	1	
5	5	6	4	5	
3	1	1	7	5	
8	6	1	2	8	

random variable. As for the rest of us, we are in even worse shape because we cannot even recall more than a very few values from Table 3.1.

Consider another example. Table 3.2 lists the recorded numbers from tossing an eight-sided die. What do you learn from looking at these data? You may have noticed that the minimum and maximum values are 1 and 8, respectively. However, I doubt that you will learn much else by merely examining the raw numbers.

If the data are not predictable and cannot be related in any functional way to other variables, we will have to discover new ways to describe and summarize the data so that we have an opportunity to learn something. This is now our objective; find new ways to extract useful information from an otherwise unintelligible and indigestible mass of raw data.

Before we begin this important task, we should recall that there are different types of data to be described and that fact might make a difference to our choice of procedure. As we saw in Chapter 2, data can be continuous, discrete, categorical, cross-sectional, or time-dependent. In the beginning of this course and certainly for the next few chapters, let us restrict our attention to cross-sectional data of both the discrete and continuous types—some ratio scale, some interval—and to categorical data.

3.3 Describing Data by Box-and-Whisker Plots

If we want to learn something from a list of data as illustrated in Tables 3.1 and 3.2, we first have to decide what we want to learn. As an example, look at Tables 3.3 to 3.5, which show the revenue from movies produced by nine different studios over a period

Table 3.3 **Movie Revenues for B, C, and F Studios ($ millions)**

Studio B	Studio C		Studio F	
8.30	220.80	25.60	40.70	12.01
62.10	27.10	24.90	2.76	3.56
23.60	26.00	14.20	17.10	20.50
23.00	21.80	12.90	19.90	1.91
31.00	8.80	11.30	23.80	8.67
31.30	6.50	8.99	1.38	34.80
14.20	5.77	3.55	18.50	77.60
13.20	4.99	3.55	38.40	34.80
10.60	28.70	2.65	21.30	25.70
9.10	7.03	113.80	74.70	23.40
4.10	21.60	5.30	12.10	10.50
71.20	90.90	17.80	65.50	9.07
60.20	24.30	15.30	26.60	7.94
52.20	42.10	8.08	11.90	6.31
23.60	40.40	7.24	10.50	5.44
20.90	37.50	5.73	8.64	3.68
17.80	32.00	4.95	2.54	3.14
		4.21	75.90	2.27
		3.64		
		3.57		

Table 3.4   **Movie Revenues for M, O, and P Studios ($ millions)**

Studio M		Studio O		Studio P	
1.02	49.60	16.20	27.30	175.00	10.80
1.42	16.40	51.60	4.23	76.30	18.10
1.48	6.90	38.30	14.30	17.20	7.39
1.93	1.85	25.80	10.60	9.98	13.30
4.01	1.05	25.30	20.30	5.38	4.84
4.02	124.40	25.30	2.56	.46	10.50
4.09	8.89	4.86	38.00	79.90	176.60
6.13	4.29	8.61	89.40	18.30	109.30
6.73	18.50	10.50	20.50	5.83	69.70
7.51	1.61	11.70	7.61	30.30	36.40
8.59	7.04	38.50	131.70	10.50	24.20
13.00	1.70	8.62	7.72	33.00	12.50
17.50	1.31	4.20	28.40	3.68	4.32
27.50	38.80	17.10	5.61	23.30	169.90
35.90	13.80			65.80	40.20
38.80	37.20			4.79	18.90
41.10				6.56	79.50
29.80				7.66	6.59
					31.50

of 3 years. What would you like to learn from these data? Suppose that you are interested in investing in the movies. One obvious idea is to invest in the studio that makes the most money. But, as you look at Tables 3.3 to 3.5, you see that there is not just one value for film revenue for each studio but a large number of them. So our first problem is to get some idea of where each studio's movie list of revenues is "centered." (Where the data are centered is of interest with the examination grades too.)

Besides knowing the location of your data you might also like some idea of how the range of values of the nine lists of film revenues overlap, or how "spread out" the movie revenues are. (We are also interested in the spread of examination grades.)

The Median

One obvious idea for finding the center of a list of numbers would be to identify the value for which half of the remaining values are less than it and half are more. This measure of the center of a list is called the **median.** Let us see how to calculate it for our various lists of data.

First, let us make life easier by rearranging the observations from smallest to largest. If your collection of numbers is 7 2 9 4 6 3, the reordered collection is 2 3 4 6 7 9. Hereafter in this chapter, all our collections and lists of data will be reordered from smallest to largest as a first step in our analysis. (In the exercises and problems, you should reorder your data from smallest to largest as your first step in your analysis.) When we have reordered the data, we will call them a **sample distribution,** because it shows how the sampled, or observed, values of the variable are distributed by size; the data are no longer just a list of numbers. Now let us discover how to calculate the median.

Table 3.5   **Movie Revenues for T, U, and W Studios ($ millions)**

Studio T		Studio U		Studio W		
34.70	23.50	8.85	10.90	148.10	36.20	5.02
15.10	25.70	26.30	16.70	81.10	40.90	11.00
13.10	150.40	35.20	8.82	68.30	4.88	12.90
6.77	20.60	8.81	6.96	48.10	9.02	13.90
2.49	40.40	8.54	6.72	45.80	9.02	18.20
25.50	37.70	15.10	4.57	38.30	4.91	48.20
10.50	23.70	9.45	83.10	34.60	10.60	40.90
.86	12.20	8.07	200.10	28.00	41.40	26.10
47.90	48.60	27.40	2.24	26.10	49.30	48.60
5.41	32.10	7.34	5.79	21.50	55.30	42.60
14.20	54.90	4.77	12.20	20.10	59.50	42.70
3.09	12.30	5.59	12.80	1.46	61.30	
11.60	38.70	22.20	30.90	2.07	94.00	
12.90	33.90	11.10	47.10	4.74	10.00	
		20.40	47.10	17.50	8.67	
		45.40	12.70	12.40	9.81	
		42.40	44.90	7.82	11.70	
		38.10	10.90	6.65	11.90	
		36.00	14.90	5.32	13.40	

If there is an odd number of values in the distribution, then calculating the median is easy; pick the middle one. Suppose that your values are

(a) 1 2 3 4 5

The median is obviously the number 3 because 1 and 2 are less than 3, and 4 and 5 are greater than 3. What if your values are

(b) 9 10 11 12 13

The median this time is the number 11, because 9 and 10 are less than 11, and 12 and 13 are greater than 11.

Be careful to distinguish the *position* of the median from the *value* of the median. In our two examples, the position of the median was 3, because there were five numbers in each set. However, the value of the median was 3 in the first example and 11 in the second. The median is the value such that half the observations are below and half are above; so when we use the term *median* without qualification, we mean the value of the median.

Consider another example:

(c) 3 4 5 6 7 8 9

Here we have 7 numbers, so the position of the median will be in the fourth place regardless of the actual values of the numbers. The value of the median in this case is 6. If we were to add 10 to each of the numbers in (c), the position of the median would be unchanged, but the value of the median would now be 16.

What if there is an even number of values? Now there can be no actual number that is halfway between the rest. Think for a moment about your solution to this problem.

You might have guessed that a reasonable choice would be to pick a value that is halfway between the middle two numbers. Let us see how this would work. Consider:

(*d*) 1 2 3 4 5 6

We have six values, so the median must be between the third and the fourth values. Halfway between 3 and 4 is 3.5. But once again we must distinguish between the value and the position of the median. Try the following set of numbers:

(*e*) 2 4 6 8 10 12

Again we have six numbers, but we have different values. The position of the median is the same because there are still just six values. The value of the median, however, is 7, because 7 is halfway between the values of the middle two numbers, 6 and 8.

These operations can be summarized in the following rules: The position of the median is given by $(N + 1)/2$. The value of the median is the value of the observation at the position $(N + 1)/2$, if N is odd, and it is half the sum of the middle two observations if N is even. The letter N represents the number of observations or data points you have in your collection.

Let us see how these expressions work with our examples. In the first example (*a*), N took the value of 5; there were five numbers. The position of the median was $(5 + 1)/2$, which is 3. The position of the median in the second example (*b*) was also 3 because there were five numbers in that collection. The values of the medians in these two cases were 3 and 11, respectively. In the third example (*c*), there were 7 data points; the position of the median was $(7 + 1)/2$, which is 4. In the last two cases (*d* and *e*), there were six observations in each collection, so the median position was 3.5—that is, halfway between the third and the fourth positions. The number 3.5 is derived by $(6 + 1)/2$. In these last two cases, there is no actual observation in the collection that is the median, so we have to average the values of the middle two observations. We use as the value of the median half the sum of the two data points to either side of the median position; $(3 + 4)/2 = 3.5$ in (*d*) and $(6 + 8)/2 = 7$ in (*e*).

The Range

Now that we know where each of our collections of data are centered, our next task is to look at the range, or the "spread," of the distribution of numbers in our collection. The **range** is given by subtracting the smallest observation from the largest observation, or with our ordered data, by subtracting the first observation from the last observation. The range for each of our examples is

$$5 - 1 = 4 \quad (a)$$
$$13 - 9 = 4 \quad (b)$$
$$9 - 3 = 6 \quad (c)$$
$$6 - 1 = 5 \quad (d)$$
$$12 - 2 = 10 \quad (e)$$

The median and the range give us some useful information about our collections of data. The data on the movie revenues, for example, 304 observations, have a median of $15 million and a range of $220 million. But when we look at the individual firm's

Table 3.6

Median, Minimum, Maximum, and Range for Revenues ($ millions)

Firm	Median	Minimum	Maximum	Range	Observations
B	23.0	4.10	71.2	67.1	17
C	12.9	2.65	220.8	218.2	37
F	12.1	1.38	77.6	76.2	36
M	7.3	1.02	124.4	123.3	34
O	16.7	2.56	131.7	129.1	28
P	18.1	0.50	176.6	176.1	37
T	22.1	0.90	150.4	149.5	28
U	12.8	2.20	200.1	197.9	38
W	20.1	1.46	148.1	146.6	49
All	15.0	0.50	220.8	220.3	304

film revenues we find each firm has a different median and a different range (Table 3.6). For now, notice that a large median does not imply a large range nor the other way around. The median tells us about the "location" of our list of data. The range tells us about the spread of the values of the data.

Quartiles

However, our film revenue example indicates that the range does not quite give us enough additional information. Although there are a few really big revenue films with some studios, there are many more smaller ones, but still some are bigger than the median. Consequently, let us break up the range into quarters, called **quartiles** in the language of statistics. There is an easy way to do this. Recall that the median splits the range in half; so let us split each of these halves in half to get quarters of the whole spread of the data.

The first *quartile point* is the median of all the values to the left of the median position. The third quartile point is the median of all the values to the right of the median position. What is the second quartile point? It is the median.

There is an easy way to calculate the positions and the values of the quartile points; reuse the idea of the median. The first quartile point is halfway between the first (smallest) data point and the median; the third quartile point is halfway between the median and the last (largest) data point.

The following diagram will help you to see what is happening;

Suppose that we define the variables N_0, N_1, N_2, and N_3 by $N_0 = 4k$ observations, $N_1 = 4k + 1$, $N_2 = 4k + 2$, and $N_3 = 4k + 3$ observations, where k can be any number that you like. For example, if k is 1, $N_0 = 4$, $N_1 = 5$, $N_2 = 6$, and $N_3 = 7$; for $k = 2$, $N_0 = 8$, $N_1 = 9$, $N_2 = 10$, and $N_3 = 11$.

We let M denote the median and Q_1 and Q_3 denote the first and third quartiles, respectively.

In the diagram, an isolated ★ represents a single observation, and ★ ★ ★ ★ ★ represents a string of k points. There are $4k$ points in line N_0, $4k + 1$ points in line N_1, and so on. If an ↓ points to a blank space, then the corresponding quartile lies between the adjacent strings of k points. In the first line, all three quartiles lie between strings of points; in the last line, three points split up the whole set of points into four sets of k points each.

When a quartile lies between two strings of points, its value is calculated by averaging the two neighboring points; that is, its value is halfway between the two neighboring points. When a quartile is represented by an actual data point, then its value is the value of the represented point. When you calculate quartiles on your own, keep this diagram in mind and you will have no trouble.

Consider this example:

2, 4, 6, 8, 10, 12, 14, 16

which has eight data points. Eight divided by four is even with no remainder, so—as in line N_0—all three quartiles will be between actual data points. The median has a value of 9 and is halfway between data points 8 and 10. The first quartile point is 5, halfway between data points 4 and 6. (One-quarter of the number of data points is 2.) The third quartile point has a value of 13, halfway between 12 and 14. We see that the three quartile points, 5, 9, and 13, separate the eight data points into four quarters.

Box-and-Whisker Plots

Although calculating these numbers has been easy enough, a better way to examine the data is to create a diagram showing how the median, the range, and the quartiles are related. Such a diagram is called a **box-and-whisker plot.** A glance at Figure 3.1 and the box-and-whisker plots in Figure 3.2 will explain the name. The "box" part of the diagram shows the **interquartile range**, which is the difference between the third and first quartiles, as shown in Figure 3.1. The range is represented by the distance between the ends of the "whiskers." The median is represented by the horizontal line inside the box. The width of the box often indicates the relative sample sizes used to create the individual plots.

Another small modification you will often see is the display of the most extreme observations, called *outliers,* as isolated points (see Figures 3.2 and 3.3). These are lines beyond the whiskers. When there are outliers, the whiskers indicate the range of the *majority* of the data. Usually, the whiskers are picked to represent all the data that are within 1.5 times the length of the interquartile range (as in Figure 3.3); but the range is still represented by the difference between the most extreme observations. When the median line lies at one extreme of the box, this indicates that the data are highly concentrated in that region; so the median and one of the quartiles are close together.

Let us now see how we can put these ideas to work for us. Consider first the data on midterm and final grades for 72 NYU students in an economics examination; how did their performances differ across the three examinations? Table 3.7 summarizes the

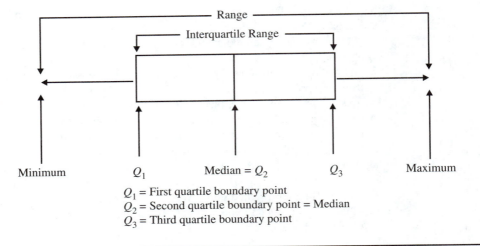

Q_1 = First quartile boundary point
Q_2 = Second quartile boundary point = Median
Q_3 = Third quartile boundary point

Figure 3.1   Explanation of a box-and-whisker plot

statistics we have been developing: the median, the range, the quartiles, and so on. The last column shows the results for the final grade, derived after dividing by two. This was done to enhance comparability because the possible total for the final was 200, whereas that for each midterm was 100. Figure 3.2 shows the same information in the form of box-and-whisker plots for the three examinations.

The three distributions of observations appear to be remarkably symmetric; the median is approximately in the middle of the interquartile range, and the range is approximately the same in all three cases. The two midterms are more alike than either is to the

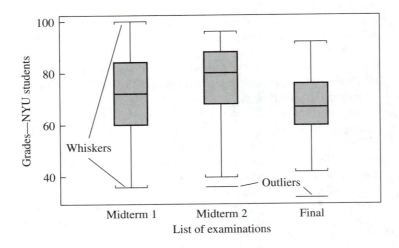

Figure 3.2   Box-and-whisker plots: NYU examination grades

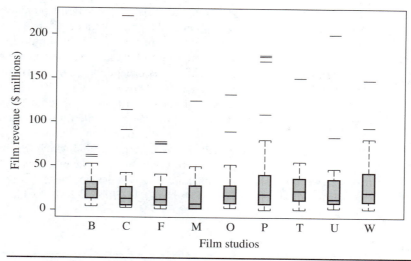

Figure 3.3   Box-and-whisker plots: Film revenues ($ millions)

final. The final is different in that both the median is lower and the size of the interquartile range is much smaller. We can conclude that the "average" grade is lower in the final (lower median), that the "B" and "C" students deviated less from the middle than was true in the midterms (smaller interquartile range), the "A" students did nearly as well as in the midterm (compare upper whiskers), and that with one exception the poorest students did not do as badly as in the midterms (bottom whiskers and outliers). Over the three examinations the middle-level students tended to concentrate more in the final about the median, as is reflected in the decline in the value of the interquartile range. Seemingly, this is an "average" class with about as many "below C" students as "above B" students—either that or the instructor grades according to a symmetric curve.

Now reconsider the film revenue example. Suppose that we wished to discover something about the differences in film revenues across different firms. The summarized data are shown in Table 3.6; the corresponding box-and-whisker plots for each film studio are plotted in Figure 3.3. As you can see, the box-and-whisker plots give a clear impression of the relative distribution of revenues across different film studios.

Table 3.7   **Statistics on Grades for 72 NYU Students**

Variable	Midterm1	Midterm2	Final
Sample size	72	72	72
Median	72	80	67
Minimum	36	36	32
Maximum	100	96	92
Range	64	60	60
Q_1	60	68	60
Q_3	84	88	76
Interquartile	24	20	16

They also show clearly the advantage of listing the extreme points separately. This procedure enhances our perception of the range of values by helping us to recognize the few very, very large values. We see that, except for the films of studios P and W, almost all film revenues are below $48 million, and even for these two exceptions over 75% are below that figure. With one exception, the medians are between $12 and 23 million, and the interquartile range is between $18 and 26 million, except for studios P and W again, which have an interquartile range of about $33 million. The nine studios differ most in the very large revenue films; the films for studios P and W have over a 25% chance of generating at least $36 million, although the film revenues for studios T and U are not far behind. We have not settled which firm we ought to invest in, but we do have a better idea of the variability of the revenues and of the comparisons between the various firms. Later, we will develop better procedures for answering this question. Meanwhile, if you had $2 million to invest, which firm would you choose and why?

3.4 Plotting Relative Frequencies

Although our box-and-whisker plots have been most helpful, there are other ways to examine large numbers of data. One of the difficulties we saw with the box-and-whisker plots is that there is no information about the distribution of the data within quartiles. Another difficulty is that when data are expressed in terms of categories, the drawing of a box-and-whisker plot does not make much sense.

Consider a sample of the eye colors of 50 students. For these data we merely have a string of letters, each letter representing an eye color. Clearly, box-and-whisker plots will not do in this situation. There is no concept of "degree of difference," merely different categories with different labels. However, there is something that we can do: count the number of occurrences of each eye color observed. This is called the **absolute frequency** of occurrence and is shown in the first column in Table 3.8.

There is a problem with merely counting the number of occurrences in each category—that is, recording the absolute frequency; the values that we obtain depend on the total number of people interviewed. Interview more people and there will be more entries in each category. This makes comparing categories difficult and comparing categories across different interview groups impossible. A simple solution to this problem is to look at relative frequencies instead.

A **relative frequency** for a category is the number of occurrences observed in that category divided by the total number of occurrences across all categories; that is, divide the number observed in each category by the total number of observations. The benefit of looking at relative frequencies instead of absolute frequencies can be illustrated by considering three groups of students that were observed in three different universities. Suppose that although the relative frequencies of eye color are the same for all three sets of students, the number of students that were surveyed in each university was 50, 300, and 1000, respectively. If we look only at absolute frequencies, we would not easily recognize that the relative frequencies were nearly about the same. To do that would require dividing each absolute frequency for each university by its corresponding university total. Consequently, it is best to give the relative frequencies to

Table 3.8   **Absolute and Relative Frequencies of Eye Color for 50 University Students**

Eye Color	Absolute Frequency	Relative Frequency	Cumulative Frequency	Cumulative Relative Frequency
Brown	21	.420	21	.420
Blue	10	.200	31	.620
Hazel	5	.100	36	.720
Green	8	.160	44	.880
Gray	6	.120	50	1.000

begin and supplement that information with the total count to obtain some idea of the size of the group that was surveyed.

In Table 3.8 there are four columns: absolute frequency, relative frequency, cumulative frequency, and cumulative relative frequency. These last two definitions of frequencies are discussed at some length in the next subsection. The cumulative frequencies, either absolute or relative, are simply accumulations, or additions, of the absolute or relative frequencies. In Table 3.8, we accumulate from the top down. Notice that the final value at the bottom of the column of cumulative relative frequencies is one. This result is, of course, always true and can provide a check on your arithmetic in calculating the frequency in each cell.

If we let N represent the total number of observations, F_1 denote the first absolute frequency and f_1 the first relative frequency, F_2 the second absolute frequency and f_2 the corresponding second relative frequency, and so on, then we see from Table 3.8 that

$$F_1 = 21 \qquad f_1 = \frac{F_1}{N} = .42$$

$$F_2 = 10 \qquad f_2 = \frac{F_2}{N} = .20$$

$$F_3 = 5 \qquad f_3 = \frac{F_3}{N} = .10$$

$$F_4 = 8 \qquad f_4 = \frac{F_4}{N} = .16$$

$$F_5 = 6 \qquad f_5 = \frac{F_5}{N} = .12$$

or, more generally:

$$F_1 + F_2 + F_3 + \ldots + F_k = N$$
$$\frac{(F_1 + F_2 + F_3 + \ldots + F_k)}{N} = \frac{N}{N} = 1$$

that is,

$$\left(\frac{F_1}{N} + \frac{F_2}{N} + \frac{F_3}{N} + \ldots + \frac{F_k}{N} \right) =$$
$$(f_1 + f_2 + f_3 + \ldots + f_k) = 1$$

In our eye color example, N, the total number of observations, is 50; k, the number of categories, is 5.

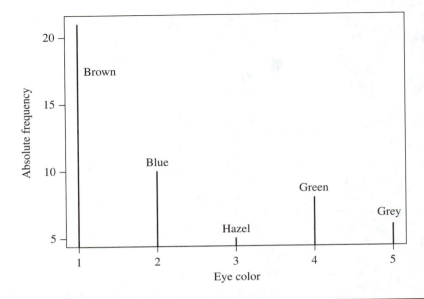

Figure 3.4   Line chart of absolute frequencies for eye color

Although this information is useful, it is not very visual; we need a picture. Figure 3.4 shows the same information as in Table 3.8 but in a more easily recognizable form. This figure is called a *line chart*. A **line chart** merely shows the plot of absolute or relative frequencies against each category. It is traditional to plot the categories on the horizontal axis and the absolute or relative frequencies on the vertical axis.

To appreciate the importance of relative frequencies as opposed to absolute frequencies, look at Table 3.2, which contains 100 data points on tossing an eight-sided die. Record the absolute and relative frequencies for the first 20 observations, the first 50 observations, and then all 100 observations. Plot the absolute frequencies and the relative frequencies for each choice, and compare the results. The problem is that the absolute frequencies confound two different pieces of information: the relative frequencies in each cell and the size of the observed group. When you compare frequencies across groups, it is useful to distinguish these two separate effects. This experiment should convince you that it is advisable to look only at relative frequencies when making comparisons across different groups of data.

Let us see what we can learn from these tables and diagrams. Consider the entries in Table 3.8 and Figure 3.4. Brown eyes are more than twice as frequent as any other eye color. Hazel is least frequent. This may not be earth-shattering news, but if you did not already know these facts, you have now learned something. What may be surprising and worth further investigation is why brown eyes are so much more prevalent than any other color—in fact, more prevalent than any other pair of colors.

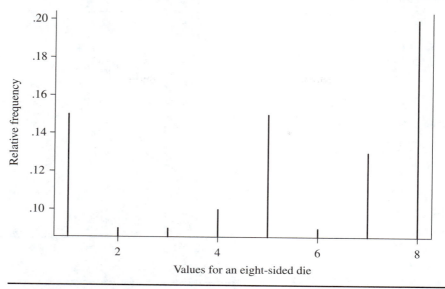

Figure 3.5   Line chart for an eight-sided die

Now look at the information in Table 3.2. These are discrete data; the only values that we can observe are integers, and in this case, only the integers from 1 to 8 representing the eight sides of the die. Just as with the categorical data (eye color) we can plot the relative frequency for each observed integer against that integer. This is shown in Figure 3.5 where we have plotted the relative frequencies for 1000 observations on an eight-sided die. You may have expected that the relative frequencies would all be the same; the line chart clearly indicates that the relative frequencies are not equal. Why? Are the die imperfect? Are the observed variations in the results plausible? If you had to bet with this die, would you regard it as fair; that is, would you expect that the relative frequencies would all be the same, or would you put your money on side 8?

A general word to represent the category for ordinal data, or the integer for discrete data, that can also be used for continuous data is **cell.** The categorical eye data have five cells, and the discrete, eight-sided-die data shown in Table 3.2 and Figure 3.5 have eight cells.

3.5   Cumulative Frequencies

With the eye color categories, the idea of cumulative frequencies was not very intuitive. However, with ordinal and cardinal data, cumulative frequencies are often very useful. The cumulative relative frequencies for the die-tossing experiment are plotted in Figure 3.6, and those for the recording of student grades are plotted in Figure 3.7. Suppose that we are interested in the percentage of observations that have less than two successes, or we are interested in the percentage of observations that are greater than four successes; or we are interested in the percentage of students with a grade

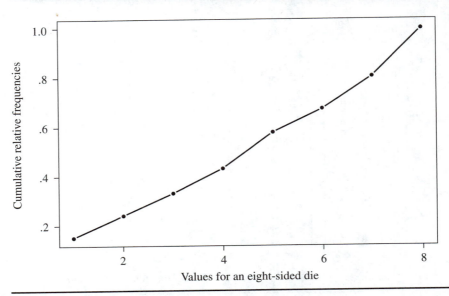

Figure 3.6   Cumulative relative frequency of an eight-sided die

of less than 75, or in the percentage of students with a grade greater than 80 percent. To see this type of information easily, it is useful to plot the **cumulative frequencies**—or the sum of the frequencies from the first, left-most cell to the last, right-most cell. If we label the relative frequencies in each cell f_1 for cell 1, f_2 for

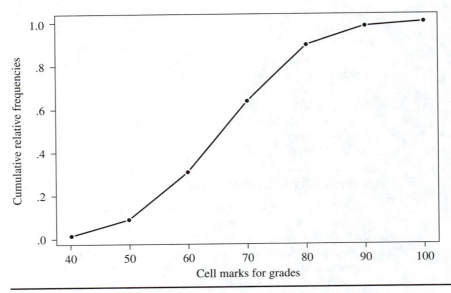

Figure 3.7   Cumulative frequency for grades

cell 2, and so on, and the cumulative frequencies $Cf_1, Cf_2, \ldots$, then the cumulative frequencies are

$$Cf_1 = f_1$$
$$Cf_2 = f_1 + f_2$$
$$Cf_3 = f_1 + f_2 + f_3$$
$$Cf_4 = f_1 + f_2 + f_3 + f_4$$
$$\ldots$$

The cumulative frequencies for the data in Table 3.2 are plotted in Figure 3.6, and the student grade data are shown in Figure 3.7.

We can use cumulative frequencies to represent such combinations as the relative frequency of cells 2, 3, and 4 or cells 5, 6, 7, 8, 9, and 10. For example, we might want to know the relative frequency of obtaining less than 8 but more than 4 in tossing an eight-sided die, or of obtaining less than 3 but more than 6. We can express these four relative frequencies as

$$Cf_5 - Cf_1$$
$$Cf_{11} - Cf_4$$
$$Cf_8 - Cf_4$$
$$Cf_2 + [1 - Cf_6]$$

This last calculation may require some explanation. Cf_2 represents the relative frequency of getting a value for the eight-sided die of less than 3—that is, of getting only a 1 or a 2. The expression $[1 - Cf_6]$ represents the relative frequency of getting more than a 6—that is, the relative frequency of getting a 7 or an 8. This expression is nothing more than one minus the relative frequency of getting something less than or equal to a 6. The sum of the two is $Cf_2 + [1 - Cf_6]$, the relative frequency of obtaining less than 3 but more than 6 in tossing an eight-sided die.

3.6   Histogram

So far we have plotted the relative frequency of both categorical and discrete data. But if we return to our data on film revenues or examination grades we will quickly see that we have a problem: these are continuous data. Reexamine Table 3.1, which contains the grades for NYU students. Some grades appear only once, whereas others appear several times; the same is true for the film revenues listed in Tables 3.3 through 3.5 if we look only at millions of dollars. But even for the values that appear several times we should recognize a problem. Grades and revenues can be measured to any degree of accuracy; so the reason there appears to be several observations in some cells, or intervals, is that the recorded data are only recorded to the nearest million dollars for the film data and to the nearest unit for the grade data. If we were to measure grades or revenues with sufficient accuracy, then, in principle at least, we could end up with one entry per measurement. This strategy produces the trivial result of a relative frequency that is either zero—no measurement observed—or the equally trivial result of $1/N$, where N represents the total number of observations in the collection. If we measure the film revenue data to sufficient accuracy we will have either 0, no entry, or 0.0033, which is 1/304.

This seems to be a simple problem, so it should have a simple solution. We should pick cells to facilitate our analysis. With continuous data the cells will have to be intervals. Of course, if we pick different cells, or different intervals, we are likely to get different results. But this is just a reflection of the idea that if you ask different questions, you will get different answers.

Let us look again at our revenue data to see if now we can get a more useful answer to our question about how film revenues seem to be distributed by size. We could also consider how the examination grades are distributed.

Our objective is to see how the relative frequency changes over different regions of revenues (or grades). In particular, we want to know the relative frequency of the highest revenue studios (and the brightest students). At this juncture our box-and-whisker plots will be very useful in giving us an idea of how to begin to determine our division of the data into cells. Reexamine Figures 3.2 and 3.3, the box-and-whisker plots of the examination grades and of the film revenues, respectively. These plots give us some idea of how to begin to set up our cells. If we just pick four cells we will not have improved matters over our box-and-whisker plots. However, what the box-and-whisker plot shows is that we have half the cells in the interquartile range and half outside it. Further, the box-and-whisker plot shows us the range that we have to cover.

As a practical matter, we need to have sufficient observations in each cell so that we gain some information, but we also want as many cells as we can. The extremes are to have so many cells that we only have one observation per cell, and the other is to have all our observations in one or two cells. In both cases we will not learn anything, so we need to seek a compromise between these two extremes. How many cells? Select as many as you can and still have at least five observations in the very smallest cells. The more data you have, the less you have to worry about how many observations are in each cell, and you can concentrate on getting a "smooth" shape. The ultimate with very large data sets is a smooth curve of relative frequencies, but with limited data you need enough observations in each cell to get a reasonably meaningful relative frequency. Why five? Five seems to be a reasonable lower bound, but the number 5 is purely arbitrary; you could choose 4 or 7 and get about the same results. Picking bigger numbers will be better if you can avoid having too many large cells—that is, cells with boundaries far apart. The more data you have, the easier all these decisions are.

Let us take a first cut at creating the cells by not being very elaborate; simply divide the range of the final examination data into eighths. Now that we have our cells, the next step is easy. Define the midpoint of each cell, as the **cell,** or **class, mark;** this enables us to identify each cell by its cell mark. Count all the observations that occur in each cell; this gives the absolute frequency in each cell.

When we count the numbers of observations lying in a cell we may run into the following problem. Suppose the following line and its divisions indicate the cell boundaries you created by dividing the range into eighths. We have eight cells, eight class marks (or midpoints of the cells), and nine boundaries.

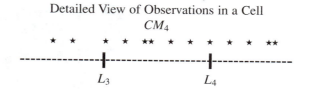

CM_i = cell mark in ith cell, or interval
L_{i-1} = lower boundary of ith cell
L_i = upper boundary of ith cell

Detailed View of Observations in a Cell
CM_4

★ ★   ★ ★ ★★ ★ ★ ★ ★ ★ ★★

L_3 L_4

Look at this blowup of the fourth cell where we have used ★ to represent observations in the cell. Suppose that by chance two data points land right on the cell boundaries L_3 and L_4. The question is into which cells do we assign these two data points? This is not a momentous decision, but we do have to be consistent. The data point at L_3 could go into cell 3 or cell 4, and that at L_4 could go into cell 4 or cell 5. A quick solution is to say that if a data point lies at the lower boundary of a cell include it and if on the upper boundary assign it to the next cell. You could do the opposite if you want. All that is important is to be consistent and inform the reader.

Often upper boundaries are open ended; for example, a list of incomes will usually have as a last cell "$100,000 or more." If so, your choice of using the lower boundary as the one to be included is a happy choice. With this decision, the data point at L_3 is counted in cell 4, and the one at L_4 is included in cell 5. This choice is often represented by the following device:

Cell boundaries for cell i: $[L_{i-1}, L_i)$

The bracket [indicates that data points at L_{i-1} are to be included in the ith cell, and the bracket) indicates that points at L_i are to be included in the next cell.

Having obtained the absolute frequencies, divide them by the total number of observations to get the relative frequencies. Finally, we can plot the relative frequencies against the cell marks.

We can do this in two ways: by a line as we did with the line charts, or we can fill in the whole area above the cells. The first way of doing things is shown in Figure 3.8 with the corresponding cumulative frequencies in Figure 3.7. The second way of doing things is shown in Figure 3.9. I think that you will agree that this last plot looks better and seems to provide more useful information. This plot is called a *histogram*.

A **histogram** plots relative frequencies as areas. Because, as we have already seen, relative frequencies add to one, it is also true that the total area under a histogram should be one. In the future, if we want to plot the relative frequencies of continuous data, we will use the histogram. But do remember that the total area under a histogram is always one.

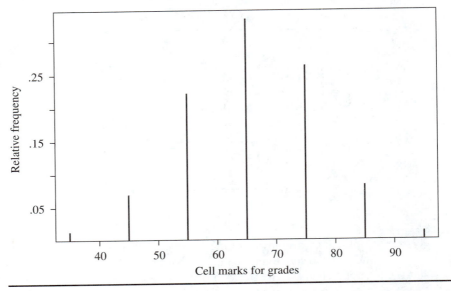

Figure 3.8   Line chart for final grades

When we plot histograms we should remember that what we are really plotting is the area of the bar, not the height of the bar above a given cell. Consequently, we must set relative frequency equal to the area of the bar and not to the height of the bar above the cell. When we plotted our final examination data in Figure 3.9, this problem did not arise because we made all our cells the same size; consequently, area was also proportional to the height on the vertical axis above each cell. But if we want to

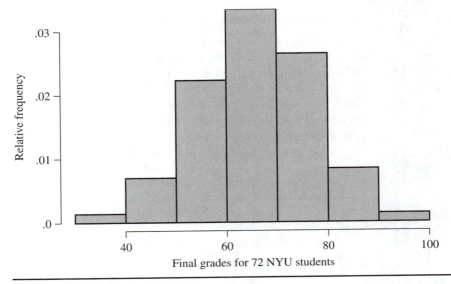

Figure 3.9   Histogram for final grades at NYU

use cells of different sizes—that is, of different lengths—then we will have to be careful to remember that relative frequency is to be made proportional to area of the bar.

We can improve our histograms by adjusting the size of the cells. The end cells can be made longer; the inner cells can be made shorter. This is often done to allow for wide variations in the relative density, or relative "sparseness" of your data; that is, some regions of the data have lots of observations and others have very few. Consequently, just one cell size does not fit all regions of the data equally well.

If we make relative frequency proportional to area, then the rule is very simple:

Area = Base times height

Area = Relative frequency

Relative frequency = Cell length times height

so that

$$\text{Height} = \frac{\text{Relative frequency}}{\text{Cell length}}$$

In short, we adjust the height of each cell so that the product of the cell's length and its height equals the recorded relative frequency for that cell. Cell length is simply $(L_i - L_{i-1})$ for the ith cell.

As an example of what happens when histograms fail to represent area, contrast Figures 3.10 and 3.11. Figure 3.10 shows the "histogram" of film revenues per film for all the major film studios. The last cell is open ended to the right because there is a small number of very large revenue producing films as we saw in the box-and-whisker plots. In Figure 3.10, the relative frequencies were made proportional to the height of the vertical axis, not to the area. In Figure 3.11, we show the histogram

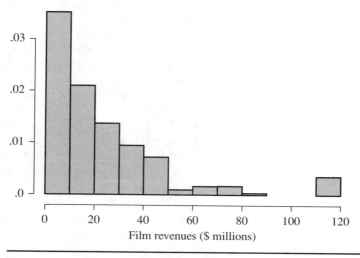

Figure 3.10   Histogram for film revenues: Incorrect version. All receipts greater than $90 million are recorded at $120 million.

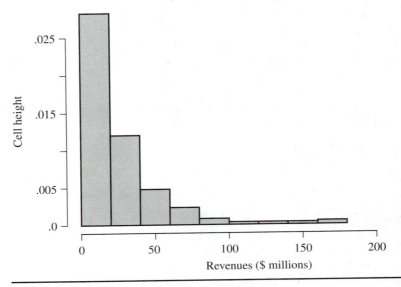

Figure 3.11   Histogram for film revenues: Correct version

drawn correctly—that is, with relative frequency drawn proportional to the area of the cell. (We had to cheat by using the largest value as an upper limit, as the last cell was really open ended; with an open-ended cell the idea of the "area" of the cell becomes problematical, although the relative frequency is still understandable.) From Figure 3.11, it is clear that the histogram of film revenues declines steeply from very small revenues to the very large and that the relative frequency of the very large revenue films is small. Figure 3.10 would mislead you into believing that the very large revenue films are much more frequent than they really are. A financial analyst was in fact so misled until she met a statistician.

Now that we have a handy tool to look at large collections of continuous data, let us explore its use. Quickly glance through the data sets shown in Figures 3.12 to 3.14. These sample histograms represent some basic shapes of histograms that one might observe, although by no means all of them.

First, a word of caution is needed. The graph routines for histograms in S-Plus plot the height (ht) of the cells on the y-axis, where ht = relative frequency/cell width. Consequently, for cells of fixed width, the height plotted on the y-axis is proportional to, but not equal to, the relative frequency. If the width is 1, the y-axis represents relative frequency directly; but if the cell width is $\frac{1}{2}$, the y-axis units represent twice the relative frequency. What is important is that the areas do add to 1 in every case, and even, more important, the shape of each histogram is correct.

Each histogram has been created by computer for the author's convenience, but each run represents a different type of "experiment," or survey, that could have been done. Recall from Chapter 2 that we are using the word *experiment* more broadly than restricting the idea to physical experiments in a laboratory. We are including here the concept of an experiment by nature. For example, we regard the level of investment in the economy on June 14, 1995, as an experimental outcome, even if it

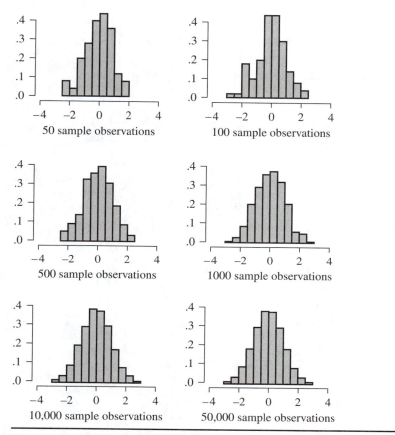

Figure 3.12   Histograms from Gaussian distributions at various sample sizes

may be difficult for us to describe fully the circumstances of the experiment. Similarly, we regard the recorded observations from a survey, for example on voter preferences, as recordings of an experiment by nature. What we actually observe is merely one outcome of a potentially vast array of feasible outcomes under the specified circumstances. An alternative way of viewing the matter is that in many cases we are contemplating hypothetical experiments and that the actual observations constitute one outcome from the hypothetical experiment that could have generated many other outcomes.

In the following paragraphs, we will discuss the relevance of each experiment in turn at some length. Most important, this collection of graphs of histograms provides a minilesson in the basics of statistics. We will spend the rest of the book filling in the details and refining the intuition that we will gain by carefully examining these graphs.

Having glanced through the large number of histograms plotted in Figures 3.12 to 3.14, you will notice a wide variety of shapes; some contain relatively small numbers

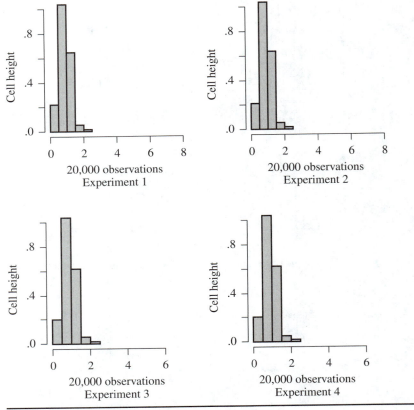

Figure 3.13   Four repetitions of the same Weibull experiment

of observations, some contain large numbers of observations. Some histograms are very tightly packed around a central value, others are spread out; some have sharp peaks, some are flat; some have long tails to the right, some to the left. Further, you might have noticed that the histograms with large numbers of data points were relatively more regular, or smooth, in their shapes, whereas the histograms with small numbers of data points were often quite irregular. Perhaps as a first step, we should explore this apparent dependence of the smoothness of the shape of a histogram on the number of available observations.

To this end, consider the histograms graphed in Figure 3.12. Notice that as the number of observations increases, the smoothness and regularity of the histogram improves. By about 1000 observations, at least in this instance, the graphs are beginning to look fairly smooth and regular. After this point there is improvement, but not at the same rate as that from 50 observations to 1000. The plots at 50 and 100 observations hardly look at all like the plots at 10,000 observations.

If we were to repeat this experiment of collecting data and plotting the histograms for ever larger numbers of observations for different situations, we would see that the

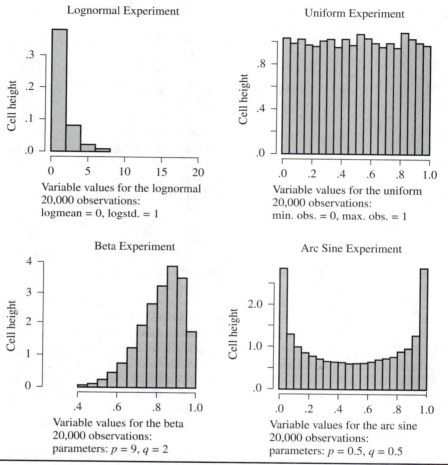

Figure 3.14   Histograms of four different experiments

result summarized in Figure 3.12 is universal. For any type of situation in which random variables are generated, and for which we can pick as many observations as we choose, we will recognize that as the number of observations increases, the smoothness and the regularity of the histograms increases.

Now consider Figure 3.13. This set of graphs shows the result of running a given type of experiment four times. We have picked a reasonably large number of observations to be portrayed given our experience in examining Figure 3.12. What do we see? The repetition of the same experiment seems to produce the same shape of histogram, if we are careful to look only at large numbers of observations. At 10,000 observations (not pictured) there are some noticeable differences, but the graphs clearly seem to be representing the same phenomenon. If we were to examine much larger collections of data, it seems reasonable that we would be able to obtain as close an agreement as we could wish between the histograms of data generated by repetitions of the same type of experiment.

The obverse side to this statement is that if we look at the histograms produced by other experiments we would see that different experiments produce different shapes of histograms. Compare the histograms in Figure 3.14 with one another and with those in Figures 3.12 and 3.13. All of the histograms plotted in Figure 3.14 are plotted at 20,000 observations, so that given the experience with the plots in Figures 3.12 and 3.13, we should be able to make meaningful comparisons. Some comparisons are very obvious to the eye, some are not. The key point still remains that different types of random variables have different shapes of histograms. Some histograms are sharply peaked, some are quite flat; some are skewed to the right—that is, have a long tail to the right—some are skewed to the left, some are symmetric. These shape characteristics we can easily see with our untrained eyes. We will discover more subtleties later.

Let us now reexamine the figures in light of a discussion about the experiments that might generate these results. Although the particular numbers that were used in the plots shown in Figures 3.12 to 3.14 were, as we said, generated by computer for the convenience of the author, they all have their origins in real experiments and real-world events. The computer was used to "simulate" real situations.

Notice that each histogram title refers to some "distribution"—for example, the Gaussian, the Weibull, the Uniform, and so on. These names refer to classes of experiments that have the same abstract features; that is, two experiments in two different fields of application may well be the same statistical experiment. For example, the statistical experiment might be the result of the outcome of trials that have only two outcome types, say {0,1}. The real experiment might be genetic, in which the outcome is a male, or a female; it might be the result of an industrial experiment on machine failure; or the result of an examination that is graded as "Pass/Fail." In the following few paragraphs, let us consider what the true experiments might have been.

The first example presented in Figure 3.12 could have been generated by the sum of many sources of error in the observation of the outcomes of an experiment. Indeed, this is how the Gaussian distribution was first discovered. Recall from Chapter 1 that *distributions* are the models that statistics uses to represent random data. The Gaussian distribution, or model, is also known as the *normal* distribution, but the latter name has unnecessary implications; there is nothing normal about the normal distribution. Some educators believe that student grades, or student abilities, are explained by the Gaussian distribution; we shall examine that claim in a subsequent chapter. The Gaussian distribution is a very important model as we shall see later in the book. Its importance arises from the fact that it is the model, or distribution, for "sums of random occurrences," even if this result holds only under certain circumstances.

In Figure 3.13, I have illustrated the Weibull distribution, which can represent the breaking strengths of materials and as such has found many applications in quality control work.

Figure 3.14 shows the histogram for an experiment governed by the beta distribution. This distribution arises in the context of random variables that are the products and ratios of squares of other random variables.

Figure 3.14 also shows an interesting *U*-shaped distribution. The arc sine distribution arises in experiments that involve sums of binary variables—variables that take on only two values, such as {0,1}. Imagine tossing a coin many times and recording whether you win, heads, or your opponent wins, tails. The distribution for the consecutive number of tosses for which you remain the winner, or reciprocally the number of tosses for which your opponent is the winner, is governed by the arc sine distribution. A surprising conclusion from this distribution is that in the coin-tossing game, it is more likely that one of you will be a winner for a long time than that the lead will change very frequently. Even before we get into this topic in detail in later chapters, you might want to try the experiment for yourself. Think about the implications of this idea for evaluating the performance of stock market analysts and money managers, if, as is sometimes claimed, the distribution of stock returns is a random phenomenon.

The "uniform" experiment illustrated in Figure 3.14 can be used to model the distribution of rounding errors. Recall that we considered measuring fishing rods in Chapter 2; note that given any measuring device we will inevitably "round off" the recorded measurement to the nearest mark. Such errors are modeled by the uniform distribution, although not necessarily on a scale of {0,1}! This model also arises in the processing of the distributions of other random variables.

The lognormal distribution shown in Figure 3.14 is a model for the *products* of random variables, whereas we said that the Gaussian distribution is a model for the *sum* of random variables. The lognormal distribution is the model for the size of many economic characteristics, such as incomes in a region at some point in time or the size of firms in terms of number of employees or the revenues generated. The lognormal distribution also models the distribution of critical doses for drugs and is useful in modeling many phenomena in agriculture, and in entomological research, and the sizes of earthquakes. As an aside, the plot of the lognormal histogram shown in Figure 3.14 does not include 58 observations between 20.2 and 58.3; these observations were deleted from the plot to get a better picture of the bulk of the distribution. If nothing else, this indicates that this distribution has a very large right-hand tail.

3.7   Summary

We began with lists of numbers. We produced *sample distributions* by reordering each list of numbers from smallest to largest as a first step in examining the distribution of the values of the variable.

Our first attempt to describe data was to define the *median,* that value of the observations such that half are less than it and half are greater. The value and the position of the median must be distinguished: the value refers to the quantitative characteristic of the number; the position refers to its location in the sample distribution.

The *range* of the sample distribution is determined by subtracting the value of the smallest from the value of the largest observation. The range tells us the spread of the sample distribution—how dispersed the observed values are about the median.

To determine the distribution of the values within the range, we defined the *quartiles:* the first quartile is the median of the observations to the left of the median of all the data; the third quartile is the median of the observations to the right of the median of all the data; the median itself is the second quartile. The quartiles split the data into approximately four quarters; the split is exact if the number of data points is exactly divisible by four. The illustration on page 44 is very helpful in figuring out the position of the quartiles. You should distinguish the values of the quartiles from the position of the quartiles.

The difference between the third and first quartiles is the *interquartile range;* this calculation tells us the spread of the middle half of the observations.

Box-and-whisker plots summarize in a graph all the preceding calculations. The box represents the interquartile range and its "cross-bar" the position of the median; the tails represent the spread of the first and fourth quartiles, respectively; and the whole plot represents the range. Box-and-whisker plots provide us with a lot of information about the sample distribution of a list of numbers; they are particularly useful in comparing different data sets.

If we have discrete, or categorical, data, then we can count the number of occurrences of each distinct value of the discrete variable, or count each occurrence of each category; these counts are called *absolute frequencies*. If we divide the absolute frequencies by the total number of observations, we get *relative frequencies*. The frequencies, absolute or relative, can be plotted against the values of the discrete variable, or against the category. These plots are called *line charts*.

Relative frequencies always sum to one.

Cumulative frequencies indicate the "running total," or the accumulation, of relative frequencies.

If we have continuous data, we cannot easily plot a line chart. For continuous data we plot instead a *histogram*. The range of the data is divided up into *cells,* or intervals, just as the quartiles divide the range into four "cells." The absolute frequency in each cell is just the count of the number of observations that lie in that cell. The midpoint of each cell is called the *class mark,* or the *cell mark;* its value represents the values taken by the observations in the cell. The length and the position of each cell are determined by the class, or cell, boundaries. Histograms plot the area of a cell equal to the relative frequency of that cell, so if the length of a particular cell is different from the length of another cell, then the heights above the cells must be adjusted to keep areas proportional to relative frequencies.

Histograms give rise to the notion of "shape." Histograms can be flat, peaked, symmetric, or asymmetric to the right or to the left.

The bigger the number of observations used to create the histogram, the "smoother" is the histogram. The same experiment leads to the same shape of histogram. Different experiments lead to different shapes of histograms.

These last three statements provide the key to the understanding of almost all of statistics. Briefly review all the histograms that we have plotted, and you will see very clearly that shape of the histogram is an important piece of information. The rest of this book will elaborate and refine the insights that we have gained in this chapter.

Case Study

Was There Age Discrimination in a Public Utility?

We can begin to understand these data if we use the procedures that we have developed in this chapter. Our first task is to gain some familiarity with the data to recognize how we might begin our analysis of the discrimination problem. Recall some of the questions that we posed in Chapter 1. Recall also that these are real data from an actual case, so we must be on the lookout for errors and inconsistencies. Part of the effort in this chapter is to examine the data with a view to noting, before we begin more formal analysis, if there are difficulties in the data that should be investigated first.

In this connection, if you examine the data in Discdata.xls carefully you will discover that there are obvious coding errors. For example, the variable "ext.appl" is coded "1" for an external applicant and "0" for former employees. However, if we look down the column when ext.appl = 1, we will see an entry for years of service that should refer only to the original employees. There are a few external applicant entries listing salaries; however, salaries were only collected for former employees. In the column headed "not.appl" a "1" indicates an internal applicant that did not apply. Strictly speaking all entries in this column for external applicants should be coded "NA" for not applicable and so be eliminated in analyzing the characteristics of internal applicants. Further, although a "1" in this field should correspond to only "9's" in the column headed "hire.stat," there are "0s" and "1s" as well.

Consequently, these data definitely do have coding errors. One of the first tasks in analyzing any data is to check for errors. If you are in the data collection stage, you can easily correct the mistakes. But if

you have long passed that stage, other strategies are needed. Sometimes, you can determine which component in an inconsistent set of entries is incorrect and therefore be able to correct it. Often, one cannot take that step. At the very least you should explore the extent to which your results depend on these errors. One of the benefits of the procedures discussed in this chapter is that it provides a mechanism for warning the analyst that there may be very large coding errors—for example, those caused by misplacing a decimal point or transposing digits in a number.

Our first steps are exploratory.

Let us start by creating a series of box-and-whisker plots of the age data for males and females. It will also be informative to examine the box-and-whisker plots for age separated by the categories "internal" and "external" candidates. In both cases, it is of interest whether the distributions of the data differ across these categories. We should also examine the distribution of wages in the same way. Another breakdown that is of interest in these data are the distributions by age and wages across the categories "rehired" and "not rehired."

Our first plot, Figure 3.15, shows the box-and-whisker plots for the age variable for the categories male = 0, female =1. We see that the median age for men is somewhat older than that for women and that the higher extremes are greater for men, but the minima are nearly the same. In the next plot, we see the breakdown for age by internal and external applicants (Figure 3.16). We see that although the minimum ages of both internal and external applicants were approximately the same, the maximum and median ages of external applicants were younger, especially for the extreme ages. But the difference in the medians was not very large.

continues on next page

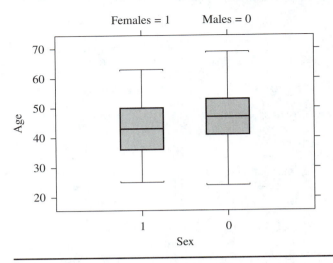

Figure 3.15   Discrimination case study: Age by sex

(Continued)

Next, we compare salaries across "hire status"; that is, how do salaries differ across those hired, those rejected, and those who did not even apply? We see the beginnings of an answer in Figure 3.17.

This result should be a surprise in that the distributions of salaries across all three groups are remarkably similar given the charge that was made by the union. Further, the difference between the

continues on next page

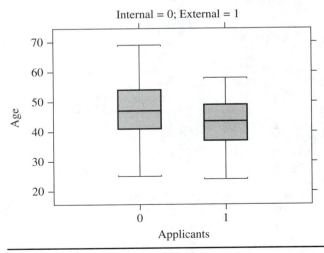

Figure 3.16 · Discrimination case study: Age by applicant status

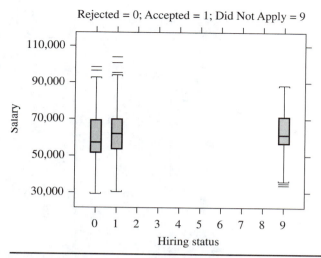

Figure 3.17   Discrimination case study: Salary by hiring status

(Continued)

hired and the rejected is very small indeed. To the extent that there are differences, the median salary of those rejected was slightly below that of those accepted.

Let us examine the distribution of ages across the same "hired/not hired" break-down (Figure 3.18). Again, rather surprisingly, the distributions of ages by hiring status are, except for the obvious exception

continues on next page

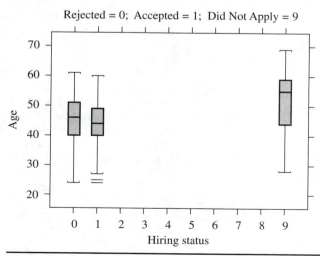

Figure 3.18   Discrimination case study: Age by hiring status

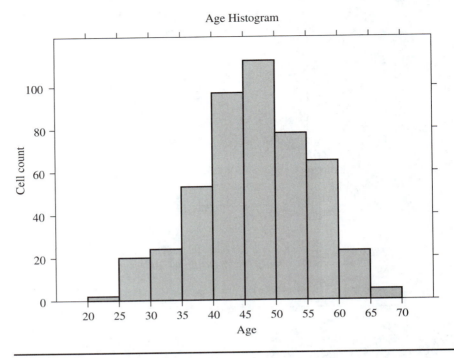

Figure 3.19   Discrimination case study: Age histogram

(Continued)

of the "Did not apply group" that contains mainly near retirees, remarkably similar. The median age of those hired is younger than for the rejected group, but the difference is very small given the variation around the median; the ranges of the two distributions are almost the same as are the interquartile ranges.

As our last effort in this chapter, let us examine the histogram of salaries and of ages to see how these data are similar to, or different from, the examples that we have seen so far. The histograms for age and salary are shown in Figures 3.19 and 3.20. These histograms look like some that we have seen before, the age histogram in particular. But there is a subtle difference. A popular choice for plotting histograms is to plot the actual counts—that is, the actual number of cell entries in each cell, not the relative frequency. The interpretation of the graph is slightly different, but the shape of the histogram is the same as that for the relative frequencies. Reexamine the histograms that we have looked at so carefully and see if you can spot the ones that are most similar. Note that these histograms were drawn using the absolute frequencies in each cell rather than the relative frequencies that we just used; the difference will have little effect on distinguishing shape. You may conclude that both distributions are similar to those we labeled "normal." But the histogram for salaries has a more irregular shape. Partly this is due to the small number of observations, but partly this is due, I suspect, to the wage and salary scales set by the firm; that is,

continues on next page

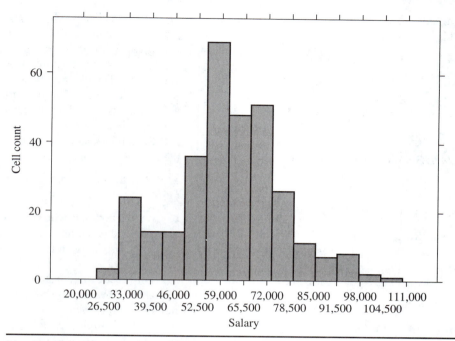

Figure 3.20   Discrimination case Study: Salary histogram

(Continued)
the firm uses various skill categories and levels, and each skill category has its own scale. Combining small numbers of employees into various skill categories may lead to a histogram that is irregular in shape.

The overall conclusions to be drawn from these graphs are that male wages are a little higher on average than those for women, and the maximum salaries are a little bigger. As between internal and external applicants, we note that external applicants have a simi-lar range of ages but on average are a little younger. As we examine the distributions of age and salary for internal applicants, we see little difference between those hired and those not hired; indeed those hired had on average slightly higher salaries. The major difference is that those who retired were on average much older, but of course, this is no surprise.

None of the box-and-whisker plots indi-cates any large outlying observations that might represent errors in coding.

Exercises

Recall the advice for tackling the Exercises that was presented in "Addendum for the Reader" at the end of Chapter 1.

Calculation Practice

3.1 Worked. *Objective: Practice calculation of the quartiles.* Find the minimum, maximum, range, interquartile range, and median for the following sets of data.

a. $-7, 0, 5, 6, -1, -2, 4$

Answer: Reorder data: $-7,-2,-1,0,4,5,6$;
Min $= -7$, Max $= 6$, Range $= 13$, $Q_1 = -2$,
$Q_3 = 5$, Interquartile range $= 7$, Median $= 0$

b. $1, 2, 8, 3, 6, 3$

Answer: Reorder data: $1, 2, 3, 3, 6, 8$; Min $= 1$,
Max $= 8$, Range $= 7$, $Q_1 = 2$, $Q_3 = 6$,
Interquartile range $= 4$, Median $= 3$

c. $0, 1, 100, 0, 90, 50, 2, 80, 100, 0, 10, 20$

Answer: Reorder data:
$0, 0, 0, 1, 2, 10, 20, 50, 80, 90, 100, 100$; Min $= 0$,
Max $= 100$, Range $= 100$, $Q_1 = 0.5$, $Q_3 = 85$,
Interquartile range $= 84.5$, Median $= 15$

d. $-10, 8, 3, -3, 13, 4, -7, 6, 5, 6, 1, 9, -2$

Answer: Reorder data:
$-10, -7, -3, -2, 1, 3, 4, 5, 6, 6, 8, 9, 13$;
Min $= -10$, Max $= 13$, Range $= 23$, $Q_1 = -2.5$,
$Q_3 = 7$, Interquartile range $= 9.5$, Median $= 4$

3.2 Find the minimum, maximum, range, interquartile range, and median for the following sets of data.

a. $25, -10, 13, -5, 9, 100, -1, 0, 15$

b. $76, 64, 50, 49, 47, 44, 45, 43, 55$

c. $65, 66, 65, 63, 62, 62, 62, 63, 57, 64$

d. $14, 22, 12, 25, 30, 35, 15, 8, 13, 17, 21, 32$

3.3 Construct box-and-whisker plots by hand for the four sets of data in Exercise 3.1.

a. Relate the details of the plot to your calculations.

b. Create a box-and-whisker plot on the computer. Compare the computer output with yours.

[*Computer directions:* In S-Plus, on the menu bar, click on Data, New Data Object, data.frame. Click OK. Key the numbers shown in Exercise 3.1(*a*) into the first column of the data frame just created. Highlight by clicking on the top of the column. On

the menu bar, click on Graph, 2D Plot. Scroll to Box Plot and highlight; click OK. To produce a title for your graph, click on Insert, Titles, Main, and enter a title for your graph. To print the graph: Highlight the graph, then click the Print button on the toolbar.] Repeat the computer directions for the remaining three data sets by adding columns to the data frame.

3.4 Construct box-and-whisker plots by hand for the four sets of data in Exercise 3.2.

a. Relate the details of the plot to your calculations.

b. Create a box-and-whisker plot on the computer. Compare the computer output to yours. Use the computer directions in Exercise 3.3.

3.5 For practice in constructing histograms, use the table below, which shows a frequency distribution (based on seven "classes") of the weekly wages of 65 employees at BagelBurger.

a. Show
(1) the lower limit of the sixth cell, or interval.
(2) the upper limit of the fourth cell, or interval.
(3) the class mark, or cell mark, of the third cell, or interval.
(4) the relative frequency of the third cell.
(5) the cell, or interval, having the largest frequency.
(6) the percentage of employees earning less than $80 per week.
(7) the percentage of employees earning less than $100 but at least $60 per week.

b. If a new employee were to be added to the staff of BagelBurger at the princely sum of $134.35 per week, what would you do to alter the histogram to include this observation?

Wages ($)	No. of Employees
50.00 – 59.99	8
60.00 – 69.99	10
70.00 – 79.99	16
80.00 – 89.99	14
90.00 – 99.99	10
100.00 – 109.99	5
110.00 – 119.99	2

3.6 Worked. *Objective: Examine the effect of the number of cells (bars or intervals) on the interpretation of histograms.* Consider the data on the film revenues for studio W; these are found in the folder Xfiles, subfolder Misc, file Film.xls.

a. Create a histogram for this studio's revenues.

[*Computer directions:* Start S-Plus. To import the data file: On the menu bar, click on File, Import Data, From File, folder Xfiles, subfolder Misc. Click on file Film.xls. Click Open. On the menu bar, click on Graph, 2D Plot. Scroll to and click on Histogram. Click OK. In the dialog that appears select "filmwrev" for x Column(s). Click on the Options tab; key in [8] in the Number of Bars box. Click OK. Print the Graph.]

b. Redo the histogram with half the number of cells (bars).

[*Computer directions:* Repeat the directions in (*a*). Key in [4] in the Number of Bars box. Click OK.]

c. Redo the histogram with 16 cells (bars).

d. Compare the results from (*a*), (*b*), and (*c*) with respect to the amount of information conveyed by each graph.

3.7 Repeat Exercise 3.6 using two other film studios. What general observations can you make about the choice of number of cells (bars)?

3.8 Repeat Exercise 3.7 using the data file Psatsat.xls in the subfolder Testscor on the variables psatmath and psatverb. As you vary the number of cells (bars), what information is lost or gained? What general conclusions can you draw about creating histograms?

Exploring the Tools

3.9 Consider film studio O discussed in this chapter. Suppose that you received the revenue data on this studio piece by piece, starting with the first 18 observations, which are summarized in the table below.

Fill in the table one line at a time. Examine the extent to which each of the measures that enter a box-and-whisker plot is altered by the addition of new data. Draw conclusions from this experience about the size of the sample of data that you might need to observe and not have the shape measures continue to change substantially.

Construct a box-and-whisker plot by hand for the first 18 observations only, and compare the results with the plot for all the data.

3.10 Consider the first three sets of random variables listed in Exercise 3.1. Suppose that data set (*a*) represented individuals' weight change in a month, data set (*b*) represented the number of weeks' vacation taken by workers in a firm, and data set (*c*) represented percentage changes in income. Does this statement create any problems in comparing the three sets? If so, identify. If not, why not? Suppose that data set (*a*) and (*b*) represented dollar changes in dollar income. Would it be easier to compare the variability of the two sets then? Why or why not?

3.11 If there are five cells (and therefore five relative frequencies), and if you know four of them, you must know the fifth. True? Explain.

For Exercise 3.9

Observations	Minimum	1st Quartile	Median	3rd Quartile	Maximum	IntQuartile Range	Range
First 18	4.2	9.09	15.25	25.68	51.6	16.59	47.4
20.30							
2.56							
38.00							
89.40							
20.50							

3.12 What relates the idea of a cell mark to the idea of a median? When does a cell mark give a great deal of information about the contents of a cell, and when does it tell us the least?

3.13 When discussing the construction of cells, the text states: "If we just pick four cells, we will not have improved matters over our box-and-whisker plot." Why not?

3.14 Imagine that you want to obtain precise information about the possible shifts in the public's opinions about five alternative candidates. You have a series of polls taken every 2 months that record the opinions of those polled. Explain in detail what you can do to present this information in an informative manner.

3.15 Using the cumulative distributions of heights for men and women aged 18 to 24 contained in file Htmw.xls in folder Xfiles, subfolder Misc. (see Appendix B, Section B.4, "Data Files"), by hand:

a. Construct a table showing the relative frequencies.

b. Construct a histogram from these data. What is your choice for the cell marks and the cell boundaries?

c. What differences do you observe between these two distributions?

d. What do the corresponding box-and-whisker plots look like? Comment on the advantages and disadvantages of the two presentations of the data.

3.16 At the campus cafeteria, there are two lines at lunchtime. Following is the time it takes, in minutes, for 15 different students to get an order placed and correctly served:

Line 1: 6 6 7 8 9 10 10 11 11 11 13 17 18 19 20
Line 2: 5 6 7 8 9 10 10 10 10 10 11 12 13 13 16
Line 3: 3 8 4 5 10 7 11 4 3 14 14 5 7 2 15

Which line would you choose, and why? Justify your choice of analytical tools; that is, explain why you chose the summaries of the data that you used.

3.17 If you know the fact listed in column A, what more (if anything) do you need to know to deduce the fact listed in column B? Explain how you would use the extra information to discover the fact in column B.

3.18 *Worked. Objective: To compare distributions.* In the text, we have seen examples of a

For Exercise 3.17

A	B
a. the minimum observation	the range of the observations
b. all absolute frequencies	all relative frequencies
c. nothing	the median's position in a set of ranked observations
d. the median	the second quartile
e. the third quartile	the interquartile range
f. all relative frequencies	all absolute frequencies
g. an even number of observations exist	the median's position in a ranked set of observations
h. the cell mark	the lower bound of the cell
i. the number of cells	the number of cell boundaries
j. nothing	the area of a histogram
k. the first quartile	the location of the "box" in a box-and-whisker plot
l. the location of the line inside the "box" of a box-and-whisker plot	the median
m. all but one relative frequency	all cumulative relative frequencies

large variety of distributions for different types of experiments. In this exercise, you will be able to explore a number of alternatives on your own. In the graphical output that you will create in this exercise you will see for each type of distribution both a histogram of 500 data points and overlaid on the peaks of the histogram a smooth curve. Later, we will learn what these smooth curves are, but for now regard them as representing the shape of the histogram you would see with a very large data set.

[*Computer directions:* Start S-Plus. On the menu bar, click on <u>Labs</u>, <u>How are Populations Distributed</u>? In the dialog that appears "Distribution Family" will be set to Normal. In Lab Option, click Simulated Data. Click Apply. Print the graph that appears by clicking on the Print button. To select another type of distribution, click on Chi-square in Distribution Family. Click Apply. Print the graph. Repeat these directions selecting Lognormal, Pareto, Uniform, and Beta in Distribution Family. You will have six graphs in all. Click on the Close button to exit.]

Review the histograms displayed in the text. You should recognize shape as key to relating distinct histogram shapes to unique experiments.

Applications

3.19 *Worked. Objective: To illustrate the use of box-and-whisker plots in understanding data.* In the folder Xfiles, subfolder Energy, there are six country files with the amount of energy used per capita by year. The country file names are Argnteng.xls, Auseng.xls, Koreng.xls, Noreng.xls, Phileng.xls, and Usaeng.xls; the relevant variable name is *energpc,* which represents the energy use per capita.

a. Create box-and-whisker plots to compare the distribution of energy use per capita across countries. To facilitate comparison the plots will be grouped on two graph sheets.

[*Computer directions:* Start S-Plus. To import the data file: On the menu bar, click on <u>File</u>, <u>Import Data</u>, <u>From File</u>. Select folder Xfiles, subfolder

Energy. Click on file Argnteng.xls; click Open. Repeat to import all the files in the Energy folder. Because the Philippines, Korea, and Argentina use energy per capita on a much smaller scale than the other countries, two sets of box plots need to be created.

(1) To create the box-and-whisker plots with three plots on one graph:
(a) Create a new data frame to group the data for the box plot. On the menu bar, click <u>Data</u>, <u>New Data Object</u>, <u>data.frame</u>. Click OK. Highlight the *energpc* column in Phileng. Click Copy. Highlight the first column in the new data frame; click Paste. Repeat these instructions for the Koreng and the Argnteng *energpc* columns.

(b) To label the columns that you have copied, double click on the name (e.g., V1), then key in the name you want (e.g., Phil).

(c) To produce the box plots, open the Commands window. At the Commands prompt (>), key in boxplot (SDF#). Enter. (Replace # with the actual number of the data frame you just created.) Print the graph.

(2) Repeat the instructions in (1), creating a new data frame for grouping Auseng, Noreng, and Usaeng (Australia, Norway, and USA) *energpc* data.]

b. What do you notice about the distribution of energy use across countries?

An analysis of the box-and-whisker plots of energy per capita use reveals some surprising results. Because we are comparing energy use, measured in the same units across countries per capita, we can easily compare the individual box-and-whisker plots. Considering first the comparison between Argentina, Korea, and the Philippines, we notice immediately that Korea's variation in energy use per capita over time is enormous relative to Argentina and the Philippines; this reflects Korea's enormous and very rapid industrial growth and its heavy reliance on heavy industry that is very energy intensive. By comparison, the variation in energy use for Argentina and the Philippines is minuscule. A further surprise may be that the median level of energy use in Argentina is greater than that for Korea; the fact that the Philippines is so low is not a surprise and reflects that country's continuing large reliance on agriculture.

The plots for Australia, Norway, and the USA are all very much bigger in energy use per capita than for any of the previous three countries. The range of variation in energy use for all three countries is remarkably similar; perhaps surprisingly, the range of variation for Norway is the biggest. You might also be surprised to note that the median energy use for Australia and Norway are similar. The USA, of course, is by far the largest user of energy per capita. But the USA is the country with one of the lowest average levels of energy costs and supplies the bulk of the world's products; that is, energy use per capita is high, but the energy use per dollar of output is much lower.

A quick glance at these three plots provides as you have now seen a wealth of information about the distribution of energy usage across a wide variety of countries.

Understanding data at an intuitive level requires practice and familiarity with your tools of analysis. You should now have a good appreciation of the information conveyed by box-and-whisker plots.

3.20 Following is the actual attendance and swimmer-and-surfer rescue information from the ten busiest beaches in Los Angeles County for June, July, and August 1988.

Beach	Attendance	Rescues
Dockweiler	3,246,350	90
Hermosa	1,658,000	92
Malibu	588,500	37
Manhattan	1,987,500	152
Redondo	1,511,700	58
Santa Monica	9,823,100	475
Torrance	712,000	18
Venice	3,700,500	385
Will Rogers	1,363,000	59
Zuma	2,713,000	400

a. Find the minimum, maximum, median, first quartile, third quartile, and range for beach attendance and for rescues.

b. Plot the box-and-whisker plots for both attendance and for rescues.

c. Calculate the fraction of rescues per 100,000 attendees. What implications for choosing a beach do you draw?

d. From this information, what do you learn about the distribution of attendance and rescues and the relationship between them, if any? Are the shapes of the distributions similar (other than the obvious differences in the medians and in the ranges)? How would this information affect your decision to attend these beaches?

3.21 You are an investment counselor trying to advise clients. On the computer in the folder Xfiles, subfolder Misc, use the file Ror.xls, which contains annualized rates of return for two fictitious firms. There are 40 observations on each stock. Note that the data are already ordered. Use S-Plus to create box-and-whisker plots and histograms for the returns of both stocks. Comment on the benefits and drawbacks of investing in each stock. Which would you recommend to

a. someone especially concerned with a safe, sure return?

b. someone who doesn't mind risk if there's a chance for a big return?

c. someone who has the alternative of a perfectly safe return of 3%?

d. someone who has the alternative of a perfectly safe return of 6%?

e. someone who has the alternative of a perfectly safe return of 9%?

[*Computer hint:* In S-Plus, import the Ror.xls file. Open the Commands window; key in boxplot (Ror). Enter. To create a histogram, highlight the column to graph. Click on Graph, 2D Plot, Histogram.]

3.22 The data in folder Xfiles, subfolder Misc, file Arms.xls shows arms transfers by the United States and the U.S.S.R. for the period 1981 to 1985, by recipient country, in millions of dollars. (The countries are organized alphabetically by continent and area. Not all countries are included.) By constructing a pair of box-and-whisker plots for the U.S. and U.S.S.R. shipments, examine the extent to which you can draw conclusions about the relative emphasis of the two countries in providing arms and the variation in those shipments across recipient countries. If there are outliers in the data try to explain them. The United States and the U.S.S.R. favored different countries for various political reasons, but can you detect any similarities or interesting differences in the respective distributions of arms shipments by the two countries?

3.23 The data in the folder Xfiles, subfolder Misc, file Age65.xls shows the percentage of the population aged 65 or over by state in 1980. Construct a box-and-whisker plot to summarize this information and use the results to comment on where your parents might wish to retire and the implications for health insurance costs. Cite possible reasons for the most sparsely populated and the most densely populated states. Is there anything interesting that you can say about the states that are near the median population density level?

3.24 In the folder Xfiles, subfolder Misc, file Geyser1.xls observations on the duration and the interval between eruptions of "Old Faithful" in Yellowstone National Park are recorded. By examining box-and-whisker plots of these data, what conclusions do you draw about the occurrence of eruptions?

[*Computer hint:* In S-Plus, import the Geyser1.xls file. Click on the top of the first column, date, in the data set. Click on the Remove Column button on the toolbar (or on the menu bar, click Data, Remove, Column). Open the Commands window, and key in boxplot(Geyser1). Enter.]

3.25 Open the folder Xfiles, subfolder Misc, file Rock.xls. In this file, which records sales information for rock tunes, the sales are recorded not in dollar amounts but as ranks. What limitations does this choice for recording sales present to you; that is, how much more information could you extract if you had the dollar amounts? If someone were to suggest that you calculate a box-and-whisker plot, explain and demonstrate why this would not be a useful suggestion.

3.26 In the folder Xfiles, subfolder Wheatpr, there are two files of wheat prices: one for Europe and one for France starting in the Middle Ages.

a. Do two separate box-and-whisker plots to compare these two distributions using the price variable (*priceind*) in the file Europe.xls and the price variable (*price*) in the file France.xls. What conclusions can you come to with respect to the differences between the distribution of wheat prices for Europe as a whole and those in France?

b. Create a histogram for each of the two prices and compare your conclusions with those obtained from the box-and-whisker plots.

3.27 In the folder Xfiles, subfolder Testscor is a file Psatsat.xls with the mathematics and verbal scores for both the PSAT and the SAT examinations. By computing both the box-and-whisker plots and the histograms for all four series, indicate what you can learn from these data about the relative mathematics and verbal performances. How similar are the two examinations? If you had a choice of which examination you could take, which would you choose and why?

[*Computer hint:* In S-Plus, import the Psatsat.xls file in the Testscor folder. Click on top of the third column and, holding down the CTRL key, click on the fourth column in the data set. Click on the Remove Column button on the toolbar. Open the Commands window, and key in boxplot(Psatsat). Enter. Print graph. Repeat the import of the file. This time remove columns 1 and 2. Open the Commands window, and key in boxplot(Psatsat). Enter.]

3.28 In the folder Xfiles a, subfolder GNP, use subfolder Intlgnp, which contains three data files Swegnp.xls, Ukgnp.xls, and Usgnp.xls with variables output (*output*) and price index (*priceind*). Using the tools of this chapter, compare the variation in output and price indices across the three countries.

[*Computer directions:* In S-Plus, import Swegnp.xls, Ukgnp.xls, and Usgnp.xls in the GNP subfolder.

a. Create a new data frame to group the data for the plot: on the menu bar click <u>Data</u>, <u>New Data Object</u>, <u>data.frame</u>. Click OK. Highlight column "output" in Swegnp. Click Copy. Highlight the first column in the new data frame; click Paste. Repeat for the UK and the US in columns 2 and 3.

b. To label the columns that you have copied, double click on the column name, (e.g., V1), then key in the name you want (e.g., Sweden). Enter.

c. To create the box-and-whisker plot: Open the Commands window. At the prompt >, Key in boxplot(SDF#) . Enter. (Replace # with the actual number of the data frame.) Print graph.

Note that the US price index (*priceind*) is much greater than the UK and Swedish indices. As a result, compare the UK and Swedish price indices separately from the US. Create a new data frame for the UK and Sweden *priceind* variable. In the Commands window, key in boxplot(SDF#) . Enter. Print graph.]

3.29 (You may want to do this exercise as a member of a team.) Pick three books, for example, a volume of Shakespeare's plays, a Faulkner novel, and an Agatha Christie mystery. Select a sequence of five pages at random in each book and produce a histogram of the sizes of words used. Compare your results across the different types of books. Comment. Do the distributions help to explain the relative popularity of the author?

3.30 Case Study: Was There Age Discrimination in a Public Utility?

The plaintiff's attorney suspects that hiring practices that have a disparate impact on a protected class of people (like those age 40 and over) can be detected by comparing the differences in the age composition of various groups of employees or potential employees. As a result, he has asked Econometrics Associates, your forensic economics consulting firm, to compare the representation of older individuals (age 40 and over) among (*a*) all individuals in the file Discdata.xls, (*b*) all former employees (internal), and (*c*) all external applicants.

a. You are asked to find for your supervisor the (*d*) minimum, (*e*) maximum, (*f*) range, (*g*) interquartile range, and (*h*) median age for
(1) all individuals 40 and over
(2) among all 40 and over, those who were hired
(3) all former employees (internal) 40 and over
(4) among former employees 40 and over, those who were hired
(5) all external applicants 40 and over
(6) among external applicants 40 and over, those who were hired

b. You are also asked to construct box-and-whisker plots for these six sets of data and to discuss your understanding of their information content for this case.

c. Prepare a comprehensive statistical analysis report for your supervisor. The data can be found in the Xfiles, folder Agedisc, file Discdata.xls.

[*Computer hint:* To create the six data sets for analysis: In S-Plus, on the menu bar, click on <u>Data</u>, <u>Subset</u>. To create a data frame for those age 40 and over, key in age>39 . Using the new "40 and over" data frame, click on <u>Data</u>, <u>Split</u> to create data frames with hired applicants (hire.stat). Use only the hire.stat =1 data frame. Repeat with splits of the "40 and over" data frame for former employees and external applicants (ext.appl), where 1 = external and 0 = former employees (internal). Split the internal and external data frames on hire.stat. See Computer Directions, Appendix B, Section F, "Subset" and "Split".]

CHAPTER
4

Moments and the Shape of Histograms

4.1 What You Will Learn in This Chapter

In Chapter 3, we discovered the essential role played by the shape of histograms in summarizing the properties of a statistical experiment. This chapter builds on that beginning. Pictures are well and good, but we need precise measurements of the characteristics of shape; this is the subject of this chapter. We will discover that almost all the information we might require can be captured by calculating just four numbers, called *moments*. **Moments** are merely the averages of powers of the variable values. In the process, we will refine the notions of the location, spread, symmetry, and peakedness of a histogram as measures of the characteristics of shape. We will recognize that once location and spread have been determined, it is more informative to look at standardized variables, or standardized moments, to measure the remaining shape characteristics.

4.2 Introduction

We saw in Chapter 3 that different types of experiments produce different shapes of histogram. Although the visual impression we have obtained from the histograms has been informative, transmitting this information to someone else is neither obvious nor easy to do. We need a procedure that will enable us to express shape in a precise way and not have to rely on visual impressions, useful as they have been. Our new objective is to develop expressions that will enable us to describe shape succinctly and to communicate our findings to others in an unambiguous manner.

A corollary benefit of this approach is that it will enable us to compress all the information contained in the data into a very small number of expressions. Indeed, in most cases we will be able to compress thousands of data points into only four numbers! If we succeed, then this will be a truly impressive result.

4.3 The Mean, a Measure of Location

In Chapter 3 we reduced shape to four characteristics: location, spread, peakedness, and skewness. Our easiest measure of shape is location, so let us begin with it. We already have a measure of location, the median. But the median is not very sensitive to changes in the values of data points. This can be an advantage, but for now we are more interested in reflecting changes in shape to changes in the data. Consider the following five numbers: 1 2 3 4 5.

The center of location as indicated by the median is clearly at 3. Now consider these five numbers: 1 2 3 4 8.

The median still insists that the center of location is at 3. But if we look at the data in a different light, the center of location should be more to the right. The data are plotted on a line as shown in Figure 4.1. While 3 is the observation in the middle, we are ignoring the size of the last digit. For example, what if the last digit instead of 8 were 30? The median would still insist that the center of location is 3! We need a new measure that will overcome the fact that the median does not reflect the magnitudes of individual observations, only the number that is greater or smaller than the median. We need a measure that in some sense "balances" the smaller and the larger observations; we need to allow for a very large observation to offset many small ones.

If we look at just two numbers, an obvious measure of the center of location is halfway between; that is, the center is given by $(a + b)/2$, where a and b are any two numbers. What if we had three numbers? Might not a useful definition be $(a + b + c)/3$? Try $a = 3$, $b = 6$, and $c = 9$. Is not 6 a reasonable choice for the center of location? Try plotting these three numbers. This approach to the definition of the center of location is called the **(arithmetic) mean,** or just the mean. For any given set of data, we calculate the mean by adding up all the values and dividing that sum by the number of data points added.

Let us consider some examples from our previous work. We listed the means and medians of some of the distributions from Chapter 3 in Table 4.1. Reexamine the corresponding histograms carefully and relate the difference between the median and the mean to the shape of the histogram. Note particularly whether the mean is bigger than

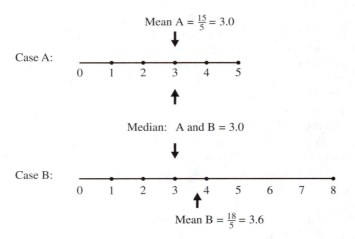

Figure 4.1   Illustrations of the difference between the median and the mean

Table 4.1   **List of Medians and Means for Chapter 3 Histograms**

Figure	Subject	Median	Mean
3.5	Tosses of an eight-sided die	5.00	4.80
3.9	Student final grades	67.00	67.30
3.11	Film revenues	15.00	26.50
3.12	Gaussian distributions	.05	.01
3.13	Weibull distributions	.95	.97
3.14	Beta (9,2) distribution	.90	.83
3.14	Arc sine distribution	.60	.49
3.14	Uniform distribution	.50	.52
3.14	Lognormal distribution	1.10	1.81

the median, or vice versa, when the histogram is asymmetric and how close they are when the histogram seems to be symmetric, as it is for the first two examples. When the distributions have long right-hand tails, for example, film revenues and the lognormal distribution, the mean is bigger than the median; the opposite is the case when there is a left-hand tail, as in the beta distribution.

An Aside on Notation

We need to be a little more formal in our statements. In the future, we will represent our observations by lowercase letters, especially from the end of the alphabet (e.g., x, y, w, v, z). Each lowercase letter will represent one variable, or the outcome from one experiment or one survey. To represent each observation on each variable, we will write a subscript to the variable. For example, if our data are from a variable called "wins," then its values

3, 1, 5, 8, 5, 1, 1, 0

could be represented by

$x_1, x_2, x_3, x_4, x_5, x_6, x_7, x_8$

or more succinctly by

$x_i, i = 1, \ldots, 8$

where $x_1 = 3$, $x_2 = 1$, $x_3 = 5$, and so on. Usually, the index refers to the order in which the data were recorded.

Another variable might be called y, with values indicated by y_i. The number of data points is traditionally labeled N. Sometimes we have different numbers of values for each variable, so we have to distinguish the number of variable values to add; we can do this by indexing N. N_1 or N_2 might represent 50 and 340 values of two different variables, respectively. A general statement for listing a variable's values is

$x_i, i = 1, \ldots, N_1$

or, for another variable

$z_j, j = 1, \ldots, N_2$

or, for yet another variable

$$y_k, k = 1, \ldots, N_3$$

These examples show the flexibility of the system of notation. In these examples, there are three variables, x, z, and y. They each have N_1, N_2, and N_3 observations. The indexing subscripts i, j, and k indicate the individual observations in each set of numbers.

One last notational convenience is the symbol $\sum$, which indicates that what follows is to be added. For example

$$3 + 5 + 7 + 9 + 14$$

can be represented by

$$\sum x_i$$

where $x_i, i = 1, \ldots, 5$ represents the numbers 3,5,7,9,14; so

$$\sum x_i = 38$$

the sum of the numbers 3,5,7,9,14.

Usually, the limits of the summation are clear, start at 1 and go to N. But where this is not so, the limits of summation will be indicated as follows:

$$\sum_{1}^{N} x_i$$

A more useful example is

$$\sum_{2}^{(N-1)} x_i$$

which indicates that only the numbers from 2 to $N - 1$ are to be added.

We can now use our new system of notation to reexpress the mean in a more succinct manner:

$$\bar{x} = \frac{\left(\sum x_i\right)}{N} \tag{4.1}$$
$$= N^{-1} \sum x_i$$

where $\bar{x}$ is a symbol that represents the mean and N^{-1} means divide by N. Equation 4.1 represents the operation of adding up N numbers and then dividing that sum by N.

Let us try another example to illustrate our new notation:

15 10 12 3 8 21

The mean of these six numbers is 11.5. N takes the value 6; the sum of these six numbers is 69, or $\sum x_i = 69$, where $x_1 = 15, x_2 = 10, \ldots, x_6 = 21$.

Without doing any formal calculations, quickly estimate the means the following:

1. {4, 8}
2. {3, 7, 5}

Table 4.2   **Blood Pressure Readings of Young Drug Users 17–24 Years Old**

Blood Pressure	Cell Mark	Absolute Frequency
85–90	87.5	1
90–95	92.5	0
95–100	97.5	1
100–105	102.5	6
105–110	107.5	9
110–115	112.5	12
115–120	117.5	16
120–125	122.5	14
125–130	127.5	14
130–135	132.5	12
135–140	137.5	6
140–145	142.5	4
145–150	147.5	2
150–155	152.5	1
Total		98

3. $\{1, 3, 20\}$
4. $\{-12, 2\}$

Draw a line on a scrap of paper and place the numbers that you are averaging and your estimate of the average on it to visualize the process. Add the median and the formal calculation of the mean, and compare the results.

Averaging Grouped Data

These calculations are easy enough, but what if the data we have are like those in Table 4.2? Here the data are in terms of absolute frequencies; we do not have a set of values to add up and divide by the number of entries. We have lost information because we do not have the original data that went into making the tables. But we would still like to discover the center of location. Consider for example the fourth cell in Table 4.2, the one that lies between the boundaries 100 and 105. Observe that there are 6 data points, and the class (cell) mark has the value 102.5. When we created cells for continuous data in Chapter 3, we chose the cell mark as the midpoint of the cell because that point was the best choice to represent the cell. With 6 data points in a cell, the value of the cell mark repeated 6 times represents the 6 unknown values in this cell. So it is with all the other cells. The cell mark represents each of the unknown entries in that cell; the number of representations is given by the absolute frequency in that cell.

Consequently, we may approximate the value of the actual mean that would be given by $N^{-1} \sum x_i$, if we had the actual entries, x_i, by the following approach:

1. In each cell, multiply the absolute frequency by the cell mark to get an approximation to the true sum in that cell.
2. Add up the values obtained over all cells.
3. Divide the final total by N, the total number of observations in the data set.

Table 4.3   **Cumulative Frequencies for the Data in Table 4.2**

C_j	F_j	$F_j \, C_j$
87.5	1	87.5
92.5	0	0.0
97.5	1	97.5
102.5	6	615.0
107.5	9	967.5
112.5	12	1350.0
117.5	16	1880.0
122.5	14	1715.0
127.5	14	1785.0
132.5	12	1590.0
137.5	6	825.0
142.5	4	570.0
147.5	2	295.0
152.5	1	152.5
Total	98	11,930.0

This somewhat lengthy expression is very simple as will become clear once we re-express it as follows:

$$\bar{x} \approx N^{-1} \sum_{1}^{k} F_j C_j$$

where "$\approx$" means that the left-hand side of the expression is only approximated by the expression on the right-hand side; k is the number of cells into which the data are placed; F_j is the absolute frequency in the jth cell, $j = 1, \ldots k$; and C_j is the cell mark for the jth cell. In Table 4.2, showing blood pressure for young drug users, there are 14 cells, $k = 14$; the total number of observations, N, is 98.

Let us list F_j, C_j, and the products $F_j C_j$, $j = 1, \ldots 14$ in Table 4.3:

$$N = \sum F_j = 98; \sum F_j C_j = 11,930$$

We conclude that the mean of the blood pressure data is approximately $11,930/98 = 121.7$; that is, for these data, using y to represent the blood pressure readings, we obtain:

$$\bar{y} \approx \frac{\left(\sum F_j C_j \right)}{N}$$

$$= 121.7$$

Recall that f_j, the relative frequency, is given by F_j/N; so the preceding expression can be rewritten as

$$\bar{y} \approx \sum_{j=1}^{k} f_j C_j = 121.7$$

Let's consider another example. Look at the data in Table 4.4, which shows household income in 1979. These data have 10 cells, so $k = 10$. Let w represent the variable "household income" and $\bar{w}$ its mean. The total number of observations

Table 4.4   **Household Income in 1979 for the United States**

Income in 1979	Cell Mark	Number of Households (millions)	Percent of Total
	C_i	F_i	$100 \cdot f_i$
Less Than $ 7,500	$ 3,750	17.1	21.2
$ 7,500–$ 14,999	$ 11,250	18.7	23.2
$ 15,000–$ 19,999	$ 17,500	11.4	14.2
$ 20,000–$ 24,999	$ 22,500	10.0	12.4
$ 25,000–$ 29,999	$ 27,500	7.4	9.2
$ 30,000–$ 34,999	$ 32,500	5.2	6.5
$ 35,000–$ 39,999	$ 37,500	3.4	4.2
$ 40,000–$ 49,999	$ 45,500	3.6	4.5
$ 50,000–$ 74,999	$ 62,500	2.6	3.2
$ 75,000–$149,999	$112,500	1.1	1.4

is 80.5 million households, so $N = 80.5$ million. The values of $f_j = F_j/N$ and C_j are listed in Table 4.5; $\bar{w} \approx \sum f_j C_j = \$20,520.0$.

It is important to remember that these last expressions for the mean in terms of the frequencies, relative or absolute, are only approximations to the true value of the mean that would be obtained by $N^{-1} \sum x_i$ if we had the orginal data used to make the frequencies. These original data are usually referred to as *raw,* as in "uncooked," data, and the data that are in cells are called *grouped* data.

Interpreting the Mean

We now have another possible answer to our question about which film studio we should invest in—that with the largest mean, see Table 4.6. Studio P has the largest mean with a value of $38.3 million, and the next largest is studio W with a revenue of $30 million. In contrast, the largest median was for studio B with a value of $23 million, and the next largest was for studio T with a value of $22.1 million. Reexamine the box-and-whisker plots in Figure 3.3 to put these results into perspective. The mean values are very sensitive to the large values in the "tails of the distributions." Based on

Table 4.5   **Household Income in the United States in 1979**

$f_1 =$ .212	$C_1 =$ $3,750	$f_1 \cdot C_1 =$ $795.0
$f_2 =$ .232	$C_2 =$ 11,250	$f_2 \cdot C_2 =$ 2,610.0
$f_3 =$ .142	$C_3 =$ 17,500	$f_3 \cdot C_3 =$ 2,485.0
$f_4 =$ .124	$C_4 =$ 22,500	$f_4 \cdot C_4 =$ 2,790.0
$f_5 =$ .092	$C_5 =$ 27,500	$f_5 \cdot C_5 =$ 2,530.0
$f_6 =$ .065	$C_6 =$ 32,500	$f_6 \cdot C_6 =$ 2,112.5
$f_7 =$ .042	$C_7 =$ 37,500	$f_7 \cdot C_7 =$ 1,575.0
$f_8 =$ .045	$C_8 =$ 45,500	$f_8 \cdot C_8 =$ 2,047.5
$f_9 =$ .032	$C_9 =$ 62,500	$f_9 \cdot C_9 =$ 2,000.0
$f_{10} =$ .014	$C_{10} =$ 112,500	$f_{10} \cdot C_{10} =$ 1,575.0
$\sum f_j = 1.000$		$\sum f_j C_j = \$20,520.0$

Table 4.6   **Mean and Median Revenues ($millions) for Film Studios**

Film Studio	Mean	Median
B	28.0	23.0
C	25.5	12.9
F	21.2	12.1
M	17.2	7.3
O	24.8	16.7
P	38.3	18.1
T	27.1	22.1
U	25.3	12.8
W	30.0	20.1
All	26.5	15.0

a comparison of the means, you might be tempted to choose studio P as your best choice.

But is this really the best choice? What if the two histograms looked like those shown in Figure 4.2, which shows two smoothed histograms—one with a larger mean and a larger spread. (For the moment, pay attention only to the shape of the histograms; the notations m_1 and m_2 will be explained in the next section.) With this larger spread, you can get larger revenues and a larger mean revenue, but you can also get smaller revenues. The choice is now not as clear as it seemed to be. Alternatively, we could think about a case in which one distribution has a larger mean but a smaller degree of spread than the other. Which is better in this case, and why?

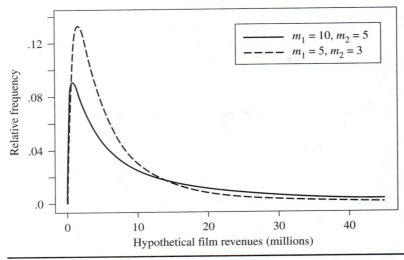

Figure 4.2   Comparison of two hypothetical smoothed histograms

However we choose to answer this question, we will need a measure of spread that is sensitive to the variations in the data about the mean. Neither the range nor the interquartile range is sensitive to variations in the data except for the extremes and for designating the percentage of terms that lie in the interquartile range.

4.4 The Second Moment as a Measure of Spread

As long as we do not change the value of the largest and the smallest observations, the value of the range stays the same. It is not very sensitive to changes in the data. For our purposes, however, it is important that we have information on values that are large, but still less than the largest. We will need more than one very large revenue producing film! So we need a measure of spread that will be sensitive to the value of each observation. Our examination of Figures 3.3 and 4.2 showed that it was the spread around the measure of location that seemed to be important, so it would appear to be sensible to measure spread about the mean.

Let us try the average difference between the data points and the mean, which we define by

$$m_1 = \frac{\sum (x_i - \bar{x})}{N} \tag{4.2}$$

In this expression we are adding up the differences between the x_i and their means and dividing by the number of additions. What would we get with actual data? Apply the expression to the film revenue data for studio B shown in Table 3.3. The mean for studio B is 28.02353. The 17 values for the differences between the observed revenues and the mean are

$-19.72, 34.08, -4.42, -5.02, 2.98, 3.28, -13.82, -14.82, -17.42, -18.92,$
$-23.92, 43.18, 32.18, 24.18, -4.42, -7.12, -10.22$

The sum of the differences is -0.00001, not exactly equal to zero because of rounding. Now try another data set, say studio C. The result is again approximately zero.

This does not seem to be a very useful measure for the spread of a histogram. But why? Rewrite Equation 4.2 as follows:

$$\begin{aligned} m_1 &= \frac{\sum (x_i - \bar{x})}{N} \\ &= \frac{\left[\left(\sum x_i \right) - \left(\sum \bar{x} \right) \right]}{N} \\ &= \frac{\left[\left(\sum x_i \right) - \left(\sum x_i \right) \right]}{N} \\ &= 0 \end{aligned} \tag{4.3}$$

Remember that in these expressions we are adding N terms, so that $\sum \bar{x}$ is merely N lots of $\bar{x}$, which in turn is simply:

$$N\bar{x} = N \frac{\sum x_i}{N} = \sum x_i$$

We see from this expression that m_1, the average sum of the differences, is identically zero; that is, it will be zero for any set of data.

Adding differences obviously does not work. The problem is that the positive differences above the mean offset the negative differences below the mean. This result is another way of saying that the mean is a "center of location." We could have defined the mean as that value such that the differences between the variable values and the mean add up to zero.

We need to consider an alternative approach. If we square the differences and then get the average squared difference, then we will not get zero identically—that is, zero for all possible variables. (There is one very special case for which the sum of squared "differences" is zero; all the values are the same.)

Let us write down the general expression:

$$m_2 = \frac{\sum (x_i - \bar{x})^2}{N} \tag{4.4}$$

where x_i represents the values of the variable, $\bar{x}$ represents the mean, and the whole expression means that we are "averaging" the squared differences between the x_i and $\bar{x}$ the mean.

Remember that we are using the word *averaging* to mean the simple operation of adding up all the terms and then dividing by the number of additions.

Let us try this operation on a few simple numbers. Consider:

$$\{1, 2, 3, 4\}$$

$$\bar{x} = 2.5$$

which you should verify for yourself. The individual differences are

$$\{(x_i - \bar{x})\} = \{(1 - 2.5), (2 - 2.5), (3 - 2.5), (4 - 2.5)\}$$
$$= \{-1.5, -0.5, 0.5, 1.5\}$$
$$\{(x_i - \bar{x})^2\} = \{2.25, 0.25, 0.25, 2.25\}$$
$$\sum (x_i - \bar{x})^2 = 5.0$$
$$\frac{\sum (x_i - \bar{x})^2}{N} = 1.25$$

because $N = 4$ in this example.

Let us carry out these calculations on a few examples from Chapter 3. The results are listed in Table 4.7 in the column under the heading "m_2." Our new measure of spread is called the **second moment**, and we give it the symbol "m_2." It is the average squared deviation of the variable's values from the mean; m_2 is obtained from a set of data using Equation 4.4.

We now have a measure of spread that is sensitive to the values taken by all the variables. Suppose that the second of the four previously listed values is 2.1 instead of 2.0; the mean is now 2.525 instead of 2.5. The squared measure of spread, the second moment, is now 1.227 not 1.25. A 5% change in one of the four variable values changes the total by only 1%, the mean by 1%, and the second moment by 1.8%.

Table 4.7   **Lists of Means and Second Moments for Chapter 3 Histograms**

Figure	Subject	Mean	m_2	$\sqrt{m_2}$
3.5	Tosses of eight-sided die	4.80	6.00	2.50
3.9	Student final grades	67.30	132.00	11.50
3.11	Film revenues	$26.50	$1050.50	$32.41
3.12	Gaussian	0.01	0.84	0.92
3.13	Weibull	0.97	0.02	0.14
3.14	Beta (9,2)	0.83	0.01	0.11
3.14	Arc sine	0.49	0.12	0.34
3.14	Uniform	0.52	0.09	0.30
3.14	Lognormal	1.81	6.66	2.60

There is one minor problem with using the second moment; the units are squared. For example, if we are observing film revenues in millions of dollars, the second moment will be in the units of millions of dollars squared. Or if we are observing household incomes in thousands of dollars, the second moment will be in thousands of dollars squared. If nothing else, these are large numbers. This is inconvenient, especially as we want to use the measure of spread to put the value of the mean into context. The way out is straightforward; take the square root of the second moment to get a measure of spread that has the correct units of measurement. The change in the square root of the second moment resulting from the 5% change in one of the data entries is now only 0.9%. The relationship of the square root of the second moment to the size of the mean is illustrated in Table 4.7. We need a name for the square root of the second moment, which is a mouthful for anyone. Let us define the **standard deviation**, albeit temporarily, as the square root of the second moment. We will have many occasions to use this term.

You may recall that when we only had frequencies we were able to approximate the mean by the expression:

$$\frac{\sum_1^k F_j C_j}{N} = \sum f_j C_j$$

where there are k cells of data with a total of N observations.

We can also approximate the second moment in a similar manner. With N observations on a variable x in k cells of data, we can approximate

$$m_2 = \frac{\sum (x_i - \bar{x})^2}{N}$$

by

$$m_2 \cong \frac{\left[\sum_1^k F_j (C_j - \bar{x})^2 \right]}{N}$$

$$= \sum_1^k f_j (C_j - \bar{x})^2$$

(4.5)

Table 4.8   **Entries from Table 4.2**

C_j	$(C_j - \bar{y})^2$	F_j	$F_j(C_j - \bar{y})^2$
87.5	$(-34.2)^2$	1	1169.64
92.5	$(-29.2)^2$	0	0.00
97.5	$(-24.2)^2$	1	585.64
102.5	$(-19.2)^2$	6	2211.84
107.5	$(-14.2)^2$	9	1814.76
112.5	$(-9.2)^2$	12	1015.68
117.5	$(-4.2)^2$	16	282.24
122.5	$(0.8)^2$	14	8.96
127.5	$(5.8)^2$	14	470.96
132.5	$(10.8)^2$	12	1399.68
137.5	$(15.8)^2$	6	1497.84
142.5	$(20.8)^2$	4	1730.56
147.5	$(25.8)^2$	2	1331.68
152.5	$(30.8)^2$	1	948.64
Total		98	12,969.88

where F_j is the absolute frequency in cell j, f_j is the relative frequency in cell j, f_j is F_j/N, and C_j is the class mark in cell j.

F_j represents the number of occurrences in cell j. C_j represents "the value taken" by the variable in cell j. Because we are looking at squared differences, we square the difference between C_j, the representative value, and $\bar{x}$, the mean.

An example of the second moment using the blood pressure data listed appears in Table 4.8. The values for C_j and F_j shown in Table 4.8 are the same as we used for calculating the approximation to the mean, which we calculated as $\bar{y} = 121.7$.

The sum of the weighted squares, $\sum F_j(C_j - \bar{y})^2$, is 12,969.88 and $\sum F_j$ is 98. So for these grouped data the approximate value for the second moment is 132.35; that is, $12,969.88/98 = 132.35$. The value for the square root of the second moment is 11.5.

4.5   General Definition of Moments

In working these examples you have noticed a similarity in the procedures for finding the **mean**, m'_1, and our measure of spread, m_2. In both cases we "averaged"; that is, we added something up and divided by the number of additions. This suggests an immediate generalization. If we can average the x_i and if we can average the squared differences, we can average any power of the data! This insight suggests a clever way of describing all these averages in a way that these similarities are stressed, so that we can take advantage of knowing one general procedure—"one expression fits all."

However, there is one difference between the mean and our measure of spread; for the mean we merely averaged, for the spread we averaged squared differences from the mean. With this in mind, let us define **moments**.

The **first moment about the origin** is the mean. The phrase "about the origin" merely means that we are looking at differences between the x_i and the origin, zero; that is, $x_i - 0$ is nothing more than x_i. We now generalize the idea:

$$m'_1 = \frac{\left(\sum x_i\right)}{N}$$

$$m'_2 = \frac{\left(\sum x_i^2\right)}{N}$$

$$m'_3 = \frac{\left(\sum x_i^3\right)}{N} \tag{4.6}$$

$$m'_4 = \frac{\left(\sum x_i^4\right)}{N}$$

and so on. The symbol m'_1 is called the first moment (about the origin) and is nothing more than our old friend the mean, $\bar{x}$; m'_2 is called the second moment about the origin; and m'_3 is the third moment about the origin.

Our measure of spread is also a moment, but this is a moment about the mean as we showed in Equation 4.4. We can generalize this idea too. Consider:

$$m_1 = \frac{\sum (x_i - \bar{x})}{N}$$

$$m_2 = \frac{\sum (x_i - \bar{x})^2}{N}$$

$$m_3 = \frac{\sum (x_i - \bar{x})^3}{N} \tag{4.7}$$

$$m_4 = \frac{\sum (x_i - \bar{x})^4}{N}$$

and so on. These moments are called **moments about the mean**. They are just the averaged values of the powers of the differences of the x_i from the mean. Compare the expressions for the two sets of moments carefully: m'_1 is the first moment about the origin and is simply the mean; m_1 is the first moment about the mean, and as we saw it is identically zero. We also saw that m_1 can be used as the definition of the mean. The symbol m_2, or its square root, $\sqrt{m_2}$, is our new measure of spread; we now see that m_2 is also called "the second moment about the mean." The symbol m_3 is the third moment about the mean, and so on.

So far we have seen a use for m'_1, the first moment about the origin, or the mean, and for m_2, or its square root, $\sqrt{m_2}$, the second moment about the mean. We will now see if the other moments will prove to be of any help. But do we use m'_r or m_r, $r = 1, 2, 3, \ldots$? Do we take moments about the origin, or about the mean?

One thought is that given that we have already discovered the location of the data, we are no longer interested in the first moment, so we can ignore it in our further examination of the data. In the hope that this will prove to be a good idea, let us proceed by looking only at m_r, the rth moment about the mean, where $m_r = N^{-1} \sum (x_i - \bar{x})^r$; that is, we look at averaged powers of differences of the raw data from the mean. We have in fact "subtracted out" the effect of the mean.

If you recall, we decided that there are four important indicators of the shape of a histogram: location, spread, skewness, and peakedness. Symmetry is the absence of skewness, and flatness is the absence of peakedness. We already have measures for the first two, location and spread; the measures are m'_1, the mean, and m_2, the second moment about the mean. Let us now have a look at the property of skewness.

Before we investigate the third and fourth moments in detail, let us consider a potential application of the higher moments. You may be aware, especially over the past decade, that there is considerable controversy in the United States about "income inequality." This discussion is definitely about the shape of the income distribution. Although there has also been some concern about the overall level of the income distribution, the main issue is whether the richest quintile has improved relative to the lowest quintile; a quintile is one-fifth of a distribution. The mean can tell us about the level of the overall distribution, and we can ask whether the mean of the income distribution did, or did not, increase over the past decade. We might also examine the second sample moment about the mean for a measure of the spread in income and ask whether it has changed over the last decade. But neither of these measures gets at the heart of the real question. It has been well known for a very long time that income distributions are highly skewed to the right, as is shown for example in the lognormal distribution (Figure 3.14). One important question is whether the distribution of income has become even more skewed to the right, or is it less skewed? A related question is whether the amount of the distribution in the tails of the distribution has changed, even if the measure of spread may not have changed very much. All these questions are about the *shape* of the distribution of income, not about its location or spread. To answer these questions we need new measures of shape, and to these topics we now turn.

The Third Moment as a Measure of Skewness

Reexamine Figures 3.12 to 3.14. Figure 3.12, at least for the large sample sizes, and the uniform and arc sine distributions in Figure 3.14 represent symmetric histograms. The beta distribution in Figure 3.14 represents a histogram skewed to the left; that is, it has a tail to the left. Figure 3.13 and the lognormal distribution in Figure 3.14 represent histograms that are skewed to the right; that is, they have tails to the right. Left-skewed distributions have observations that extend much farther to the left of the mean than the corresponding observations to the right of the mean. The opposite is the case for right-skewed distributions. With symmetric distributions the two sides balance.

We have discovered that the mean and the median are approximately equal when the distribution appears to be symmetric. We also saw that for distributions that are skewed to the right, the mean is bigger than the median and that for distributions skewed to the left the mean is less than the median. This observation does provide some idea of the sign of the skewness, positive or negative, right or left, but it is not a useful measure of the extent of the skewness. We need a measure that will be sensitive to all the observations.

Table 4.9   **The Third and Fourth Moments about the Mean for Chapter 3 Histograms**

Figure	Subject	m_3	m_4
3.5	Tosses of eight-sided die	−2.700	62.900
3.9	Student final grades	−555.100	57,366.000
3.11	Film revenues	101,008.000	15,404,336.000
3.12	Gaussian	0.070	1.800
3.13	Weibull	−0.002	0.001
3.14	Beta (9,2)	−0.001	0.001
3.14	Arc sine	0.002	0.022
3.14	Uniform	0.006	0.013
3.14	Lognormal	91.500	1787.000

We should also require of our measure of skewness that symmetric histograms have a measure of skewness that is zero, left-tailed histograms a negative measure, and right-tailed histograms a positive measure to reflect our observations about skewed histograms. These remarks lead to the following idea: Third powers of differences between x_i and $\bar{x}$ will certainly be negative for the x_i below the mean and positive for the x_i above the mean, and it is a good bet that the sum of third powers will be zero for symmetric histograms. This means that we should look at m_3.

The only way to find out is to try our new measure on some simple examples. Consider:

$$x_i = -2, -1, 0, 1, 2$$
$$y_i = 0, 1, 2, 3, 14$$
$$w_i = -12, -1, 0, 1, 2$$

The means of x, y, and w are, in turn: 0, 4, and –2. The second moments are, in turn: 2, 26, and 26. Now x, y, and w are respectively symmetric, skewed to the right, and skewed to the left. You can verify this by plotting each of the five points on a line. The cubed differences are

$$x_i:\ (-2-0)^3,\ (-1-0)^3,\ (0-0)^3,\ (1-0)^3,\ (2-0)^3$$
$$-8,\qquad -1,\qquad 0,\qquad 1,\qquad 8$$
$$y_i:\ (0-4)^3,\ (1-4)^3,\ (2-4)^3,\ (3-4)^3,\ (14-4)^3$$
$$-64,\qquad -27,\qquad -8,\qquad -1,\qquad 1000$$
$$i:\ (-12+2)^3,\ (-1+2)^3,\ (0+2)^3,\ (1+2)^3,\ (2+2)^3$$
$$w_i\quad -1000,\qquad 1,\qquad 8,\qquad 27,\qquad 64$$

The sum of the cubed differences are for x, y, and w: 0, 900, and −900, respectively. Dividing by five in each case gives us the third moment. We get for x, y, and w the values 0, 180, and −180, respectively. At least the third moment gets the signs correct; that is, the third moment is zero for symmetric distributions, negative for left-tailed distributions, and positive for right-tailed distributions.

Using our new tool, let us examine once again the data from some Chapter 3 figures. The results are presented in the column headed "m_3" in Table 4.9. The signs seem to be correct, except for the Weibull, which is a small puzzle. The values for Figures 3.11 to 3.14, except for the film revenues and the lognormal, seem to be essentially zero. But one obvious fact should impress you; the numbers go from very small to huge—this looks like a problem we will have to address.

We now have three useful measures of shape: m'_1 for location, m_2 for spread, and m_3 for skewness. If m_3 is negative, then the histogram has a left-hand tail; if positive, it has a right-hand tail; and if zero, it is symmetric about the mean. However, the units of measurement for the third moment, m_3, are in terms of the units for the original data cubed; this may present a problem.

The Fourth Moment as a Measure of Peakedness, or "Fat Tails"

Our last shape characteristic is peakedness. An alternative, but less elegant, description of what is measured by the fourth moment is "fat tails." A single-peaked histogram with a lot of distributional weight in the center and in the tails, but not in the shoulders is said to have "fat tails"; or it is "highly peaked." Recall that if one area of a histogram has more weight, somewhere else must have less, because the relative frequencies must sum to one.

Our approach using moments has been successful, so let us continue it. We will reexamine the same data by calculating this time m_4. Let us consider three simple examples:

$$x_i: \quad -2, -1, 0, 1, 2$$
$$y_i: \quad -2, 0, 0, 0, 2$$
$$w_i: \quad -2, -2, 0, 2, 2$$

Once again, plot these three sets of five numbers on a piece of paper to get some idea of the shape of these very simple distributions.

The means are zero in each case. The second moments are 2, 1.6, and 3.2. The fourth powers of the differences are

$$x_i: \quad -2^4, -1^4, 0^4, 1^4, 2^4$$
$$16, 1, 0, 1, 16$$
$$y_i: \quad -2^4, 0, 0, 0, 2^4$$
$$16, 0, 0, 0, 16$$
$$w_i: \quad -2^4, -2^4, 0, 2^4, 2^4$$
$$16, 16, 0, 16, 16$$

These differences raised to the fourth power and averaged for x, y, and w give 6.8, 6.4, and 12.8. But is 12.8 a large number? Is 6.8 a small number? At the moment we cannot tell.

Perhaps, if we examined more realistic examples of distributions we would be able to get a better idea. Let us list our figures from Chapter 3 in the rough order from flattest to most peaked. This gives us the order: arc sine, whose U-shape is actually "anti-peaked"; the uniform; Figures 3.9 and 3.12, the beta distribution; film revenues; the Weibull; and the lognormal. Looking carefully at these figures we see that the most peaked histograms also tend to have fat tails. This is because the total area under a histogram is one, so that if the middle of the histogram is characterized by a narrow peak (high frequency), the tails must be thin (low frequency) and spread out. A peaked histogram, relative to a flat histogram, has a lot of observations near the mean, and a few observations very far away from the mean. Note that a U-shaped distribution has very few observations near the mean, and most of them in the tails.

Table 4.10   **Comparison of Moments in Different Units of Measurement**

Moment	Height (in.)	Height (ft)
m'_1	65.37 in.	5.450 ft
m_2	11.24 in.^{2}	0.078 ft^2
m_3	−3.83 in.^{3}	−0.002 ft^3
m_4	283.20 in.^{4}	0.014 ft^4

If we raise the differences between the x_i and $\bar{x}$ to a high power, the "big" numbers will have a much bigger effect on the sum of the powers than the more numerous observations in the middle that produce small differences. When we calculate m_4, and if our intuition has been reliable, we should see the values of m_4 increase as we examine the distributions in the order we specified.

The results of these calculations are in Table 4.9. Unfortunately, the results do not match our expectations. The fourth moments of the distributions that we thought would be the smallest are not so, nor are the fourth moments we thought would be the largest so. We need to go back to the drawing board.

4.6   Standardized Moments

You may have noticed another problem with the third and fourth moments: what's large? It is not very helpful to say that m_4 is large for highly peaked distributions if we do not know what constitutes "large." Our cavalier attitude needs reassessment.

Even for m_3 we have a problem. If we want to compare two histograms that are both skewed to the left, for example, can we unambiguously say that one of them is more skewed than the other on the basis of the values that we obtained for m_3? Yet another problem is raised if we try the next experiment.

In Table 4.10, we recorded the first four moments on the heights of enrollees in a fitness class measured in inches. We converted these numbers into feet. We are essentially dealing with the same histogram of heights, so our conversion to feet was merely a re-scaling of the data; we should conclude that we have the same shape of histogram.

The mean is easy enough to understand; m'_1 in feet is just one-twelfth of m'_1 in inches. But the second moment is not so easy to interpret, and except for signs, m_3 and m_4 appear to be completely different between the two measurements. This is not desirable at all; our results should not depend on our choice of the units of measurement if we are to create a generally useful measure of shape.

Now suppose that we measure heights not from zero as we have done so far, but from 60 inches; the idea is that we are interested mainly in the deviations of actual heights from 5 feet. If we now recalculate all our moments, we get

$$m'_1 = \quad 5.37 \text{ in.}$$
$$m_2 = \quad 11.24 \text{ in.}^2$$
$$m_3 = \quad -3.83 \text{ in.}^3$$
$$m_4 = 283.20 \text{ in.}^4$$

Comparing the means we get what we might have expected: m'_1 for the data after subtracting 60 inches is just our original mean value of 65.37 inches less 60 inches. But what may be surprising is that m_2, m_3, m_4 are all exactly the same as the moments we obtained from the original data!

A moment's reflection may help you to see why this is so. Look at the definition of m_2, for example:

$$m_2 = \frac{\sum (x_i - \bar{x})^2}{N}$$

Define a new variable y_i by

$$y_i = x_i - 60$$

because we subtracted 60 from the height data in inches.

To emphasize the variable whose moment is being taken, let us change notation slightly to $m_r(y)$, $m_r(x)$, or $m_r(w)$ to represent the rth moment about the mean for the variables y, x, and w respectively.

Now calculate the mean for the new variable y:

$$\begin{aligned} m'_1(y) &= m'_1(x_i - 60) \\ &= m'_1(x_i) - m'_1(60) \\ &= 65.37 - 60 = 5.37 \end{aligned}$$

If you have any trouble following these steps, a quick look at Appendix A will soon solve your difficulty.

Now we calculate $m_2(y)$.

$$\begin{aligned} m_2(y) &= \frac{\sum (y_i - \bar{y})^2}{N} \\ &= \frac{\sum \left[(x_i - 60) - (m'_1(x) - 60) \right]^2}{N} \end{aligned}$$

where we have substituted

$$x_i - 60 \text{ for } y_i; \ \ m'_1(x) - 60 \text{ for } m'_1(y)$$

but,

$$\frac{\sum \left[(x_i - 60) - (m'_1(x) - 60) \right]^2}{N} = \frac{\sum (x_i - \bar{x})^2}{N}$$

because the two "60s" cancel in the previous line: $-60 - (-60) = -60 + 60 = 0$. We have shown that the second moments for the variables x and y, where y is given by $y = x - 60$, are the same.

This result will hold for all our moments about the mean. This property is called *invariance;* the moments $m_2, m_3, m_4 \ldots$ are all said to be **invariant** to changes in the origin. This means that you can add or subtract any value whatsoever from the variable and the calculated value of all the moments about the mean will be unchanged.

The qualification "about the mean" is crucial; this is not true for the moments about the origin.

We have solved one problem; we now know that, beyond the first moment, we need to look at moments that are about the mean and so invariant to changes in the origin. But the problem of interpreting the moments, detected with the heights, goes further than a change of origin. When we changed from inches to feet, we did not change the origin, it is still zero, but we did change the scale of the variable. But "scale" is like spread; a bigger scale will produce a larger spread and consequently a larger value for m_2, our measure of spread. Further, our measure of spread is squared. Reconsider the expression for m_2:

$$m_2(x) = \frac{\sum (x_i - \bar{x})^2}{N}$$

and consider changing from measuring x_i in inches to a variable y_i that is height measured in feet. We do this by dividing the x_i entries by 12:

$$\frac{\sum (y_i - \bar{y})^2}{N} = \frac{\sum \left(\frac{x_i}{12} - \frac{\bar{x}}{12}\right)^2}{N}$$

$$= \frac{\left[\dfrac{\sum (x_i - \bar{x})^2}{N}\right]}{144}$$

where $144 = 12^2$. Or more generally, if $y_i = b \times x_i$, for any constant b, then

$$m_2(y) = b^2 \times m_2(x)$$

Even more generally, if $y_i = a + (b \times x_i)$, for any constants a and b,

$$m_2(y) = b^2 \times m_2(x)$$

If we now apply this same approach to the higher moments, we will discover that, whenever

$$y_i = a + (b \times x_i)$$
$$m_2(y) = b^2 \times m_2(x)$$
$$m_3(y) = b^3 \times m_3(x)$$
$$m_4(y) = b^4 \times m_4(x)$$

and so on.

This business of changing variables by adding constants and multiplying by constants may still seem a little mysterious, but a familiar example will help. You know that temperature can be measured either in degrees Fahrenheit or in degrees Celsius. The temperature of your sick sister is the same whatever units of measurement you use; that is, how much fever your sister has is a given, but how you measure that temperature, or how you record it, does depend on your choice of measuring instrument.

To reexpress the idea, your choice of the units of measurement alters the measurement, but it clearly does not alter the degree of fever.

One choice is to measure in degrees Fahrenheit. Suppose that you observe a measure of 102 degrees Fahrenheit. That observation is equivalent to a measured temperature of 38.9 degrees Celsius. As you may remember from your high school physics, degrees Fahrenheit are related to degrees Celsius by

$$\text{deg.F} = 32 \text{ deg.F} + \left(\frac{9}{5}\right) \times \text{deg.C}$$

but this is just like

$$\text{deg.F} = a + b \times \text{deg.C}$$

where $a = 32$ deg.F and $b = \frac{9}{5}$.

The origin for degrees Fahrenheit, relative to degrees Celsius, is 32°F and the scale adjustment is to multiply by $\frac{9}{5}$. So, if you were interested in the shape of histograms of temperatures, you would not want your results to depend on how you measured the data [except, of course, for measures of location (that depend directly on origin and scale) and measures of scale or spread that should depend only on scale, not on the choice of origin.]

We can reexpress our results so far by saying that m'_1 indicates the chosen origin for the units of measurement and that $\sqrt{m_2}$ indicates the chosen scale of measurement; "$\sqrt{\ }$" is the traditional square root sign and means take the square root of its argument.

We now have the answer to our problem of trying to decide whether a third or a fourth moment is large or small. We also have our answer to the question of how to ensure that our measures of shape do not depend on the way in which we have measured the data. If we divide the third and fourth moments about the mean by the appropriate power of m_2, we will have a set of moments that will be invariant to changes in scale. This is equivalent to picking an arbitrary value for b in the equation $y_i = a + (b \times x_i)$.

We conclude that to discuss shape beyond location and scale in unambiguous terms, one has to measure shape in terms of expressions that are invariant to changes in origin or in scale. As we saw, any change in scale in the variable x is raised to the power 3 in the third moment and to the power 4 in the fourth moment. Thus an easy way to overcome the effects of scale is to divide m_3 by $(m_2)^{3/2}$ and m_4 by $(m_2)^2$.

Define $\hat{\alpha}_1$ and $\hat{\alpha}_2$, the **standardized** third and fourth **moments**, by

$$\hat{\alpha}_1 = \frac{m_3}{(m_2)^{3/2}}$$
$$\hat{\alpha}_2 = \frac{m_4}{(m_2)^2}$$

(4.8)

Our rationale for picking this "peculiar" notation, $\hat{\alpha}_1, \hat{\alpha}_2$, will be apparent in a few chapters. For the moment we need labels and $\hat{\alpha}_1, \hat{\alpha}_2$ are as good as any.

Consider any arbitrary change of origin and scale of any variable; that is, if x_i is the variable of interest, look at $y_i = a + (b \times x_i)$, for any values of a and b,

$$\hat{\alpha}_1(y) = \frac{m_3(y)}{(m_2(y))^{3/2}}$$

$$= \frac{b^3 m_3(x)}{(b^2 m_2(x))^{3/2}}$$

$$= \frac{m_3(x)}{(m_2(x))^{3/2}}$$

$$= \hat{\alpha}_1(x)$$

$$\hat{\alpha}_2(y) = \frac{m_4(y)}{(m_2(y))^2}$$

$$= \frac{b^4 m_4(x)}{(b^2 m_2(x))^2}$$

$$= \frac{m_4(x)}{(m_2(x))^2}$$

$$= \hat{\alpha}_2(x)$$

These two new measures, $\hat{\alpha}_1$ and $\hat{\alpha}_2$, are invariant to changes in both scale and origin and so may correctly be called measures of shape. Before looking at some practical uses of our new tools, consider the following set of simple examples that will illustrate the ideas involved.

A key concept involved in any discussion of the higher moments is that, because a measure of the center of location and of spread, or scale, have already been determined, their confounding effects should be removed from the calculation of the higher moments. For example, the value of the third moment about the origin will reflect the effects of the degree of asymmetry, the center of location, and the spread. However, until the latter two effects are allowed for, you cannot distinguish the effect of asymmetry on the third moment.

We define four simple variables to illustrate. The four variables are x_a, x_b, x_c and x_d:

$$x_a = 1, 2, 3$$
$$x_b = 1, 2, 9$$
$$x_c = -3, 1, 2$$
$$x_d = -1, 0(10 \text{ times}), 1$$

Before beginning, sketch the frequencies as a line chart on any scrap of paper. We now calculate the four moments for each variable as well as the standardized third and fourth moments:

$$m'_1(x_a) = 2 \qquad\qquad m_2(x_a) = \frac{2}{3}$$

$$m_3(x_a) = 0 \qquad\qquad m_4(x_a) = \frac{2}{3}$$

$$\hat{\alpha}_1(x_a) = 0 \qquad\qquad \hat{\alpha}_2(x_a) = \frac{3}{2} = 1.5$$

$$m_1'(x_b) = 4 \qquad m_2(x_b) = \frac{38}{3} = 12.66$$

$$m_3(x_b) = 30 \qquad m_4(x_b) = \frac{722}{3} = 240.66$$

$$\hat{\alpha}_1(x_b) = \frac{30}{45.1} = 0.67 \quad \hat{\alpha}_2(x_b) = \frac{240.66}{160.4} = 1.5$$

$$m_1'(x_c) = 0 \qquad m_2(x_c) = \frac{14}{3} = 4.66$$

$$m_3(x_c) = -6 \qquad m_4(x_c) = \frac{98}{3} = 32.66$$

$$\hat{\alpha}_1(x_c) = \frac{-6}{10.1} = -0.59 \quad \hat{\alpha}_2(x_c) = \frac{32.66}{21.78} = 1.5$$

$$m_1'(x_d) = 0 \qquad m_2(x_d) = \frac{2}{12} = 0.166$$

$$m_3(x_d) = 0 \qquad m_4(x_d) = \frac{2}{12} = 0.166$$

$$\hat{\alpha}_1(x_d) = 0 \qquad \hat{\alpha}_2(x_d) = \frac{12}{2} = 6$$

The variables x_a and x_d are symmetric, so the third moment is zero, and we do not have to worry about the scaling problem. But is x_b five times more asymmetric than x_c as the raw third moment values would indicate? The standardized third moments are 0.67 and -0.59, which seems to be much more reasonable in light of our drawings of the distributions. The unstandardized third moments are so different because the second moment of x_b is nearly three times greater than that of x_c'; that is, the unstandardized third moments have compounded the effects of the asymmetry with the differences in the values of the second moments, which indicate the degree of spread.

Looking at the fourth unstandardized moments, we would be misled into thinking that x_d has the smallest value for peakedness, that the value for peakedness for x_b is the largest by far, and that the value for x_c is much greater than that for x_a. All of these conclusions are wrong as we can see by examining our $\hat{\alpha}_2$ values, the values of the standardized fourth moments. Variable x_d has the largest value for peakedness as we might suspect if we look carefully at the relative frequency line chart. Interestingly, the values for peakedness for all the other variables are identical; again, we might suspect that fact from a glance at the frequency line charts.

Similarly, reconsider Figures 3.5 to 3.14 by examining the $\hat{\alpha}_1$ and $\hat{\alpha}_2$ values shown in Table 4.11 and the unstandardized moments in Table 4.9. Consider, for example, the $\hat{\alpha}_1$ values for Figure 3.11 and the lognormal in Figure 3.14; the latter is greater than the former, but for the unstandardized moments shown in Table 4.9 the opposite is true. This is due to the differences in the second moments. We noted previously that the lognormal distribution is a model for income distributions, and Figure 3.11 is the graph of the distribution for the film revenues. If these data are to be believed, we might wonder whether film revenues are less or more asymmetric than incomes.

Table 4.11 **List of Means, Second, and Standardized Third and Fourth Moments for Chapter 3 Histograms**

Figure	Subject	m_1	m_2	$\sqrt{m_2}$	$\hat{\alpha}_1$	$\hat{\alpha}_2$
3.5	Die toss	4.80	6.00	2.50	−0.18	1.70
3.9	Final grades	67.30	132.00	11.50	−0.37	3.30
3.11	Film revenues ($mm)	26.50	1050.50 ($mm)^2	32.41	3.00	14.00
3.12	Gaussian	0.01	0.84	0.92	0.09	2.60
3.13	Weibull	0.97	0.02	0.13	−0.80	4.10
3.14	Beta (9,2)	0.83	0.01	0.11	−1.10	4.10
3.14	Arc sine	0.49	0.12	0.34	0.04	1.60
3.14	Uniform	0.52	0.09	0.30	0.25	1.80
3.14	Lognormal	1.81	6.66	2.60	5.32	40.30

Using the data in Table 4.4, we can calculate that the second moment of household income is 3.1 times 10^8 dollars, and the unstandardized third moment is 13.1 times 10^{12} dollars. However, the standardized third moment for household income is 2.4 and the standardized third moment for the film revenue data is 3.0, which is only a little larger.

Recall that the household incomes data in Table 4.4 involve some considerable approximation, especially in that the very highest incomes, although of very low relative frequency, were not recorded in the table. We expect that the actual standardized third moment is greater than that calculated. In any event, we can conclude that film revenues are not substantially more skewed than incomes generally.

What of peakedness for these data? The fourth moment for the household income data is 114.2 times 10^{16} dollars, but the standardized fourth moment is 11.9. The corresponding values for the standardized fourth moments shown in Table 4.11 are 13.9 for the film revenue and 40.3 for the lognormal distribution. Recalling once again that the nature of our approximations for the household income data is likely to underestimate the fourth moment, we can put the film revenue results into some perspective; they are at least not substantially more peaked than the household income data.

Three distributions in Table 4.11 seem to have similar values for the standardized fourth moments. Figure 3.5 was for the die-tossing experiment, and we would expect intuitively that the distribution of outcomes would be flat and not peaked. The uniform distribution is the ultimate in flat distributions. The arc sine distribution is U-shaped; such a distribution might be thought of as anti-peaked, so it should have a very low value for the standardized fourth moment. The $\hat{\alpha}_2$ values are, respectively, 1.7, 1.8, and 1.6. The Weibull and beta distributions shown in Figures 3.13 and 3.14, respectively, have about the same standardized fourth moments as we would expect from looking at the figures; both have $\hat{\alpha}_2$ values of 4.1.

Some Practical Uses for Higher Moments

At last we are ready to compare our film revenue data to see which film studios we want to back. Before looking at the listing of all four moments for the nine different film studios shown in Table 4.12, it would be helpful for you to refresh your memory

Table 4.12 **The First Four Moments of Film Revenues ($ millions) for Nine Film Studios**

Film Studio	m'_1	m_2	$\sqrt{m_2}$	$\hat{\alpha}_1$	$\hat{\alpha}_2$
B	28.0	407.0	20.2	0.9	2.3
C	25.5	1578.8	39.7	3.6	16.7
F	21.2	457.7	21.4	1.5	4.3
M	17.2	549.4	23.4	2.9	13.2
O	24.8	748.7	27.4	2.5	9.6
P	38.3	2309.6	48.1	1.8	5.4
T	27.1	782.6	28.0	3.0	13.7
U	25.3	1120.1	33.5	3.8	19.9
W	30.0	775.5	27.8	1.9	7.8
All	26.5	1050.5	32.4	3.0	14.0

by reexamining Figure 3.3, which shows the box-and-whisker plots of the film revenue data.

Now let us see what we can learn from Table 4.12. With respect to the means, one procedure might be to look first at the studios that exceed the overall mean. With this criterion, we should look at B, P, T, and W, although C and U are very close. P has the biggest mean return by far, so one might be tempted to pick it. But might not this result be from the fact that P had a couple of very big wins? Remember the mean is sensitive to all the data values and P's median value is about the same as that of the others.

If we are to consider the variability of the returns, we will have to think of how to trade off large means against large second moments, on the presumption that a larger second moment is all things considered not a good idea. One way to do this is to plot the means and the square roots of the second moments so that both returns and spread, or "variability," are in the same units; see for example Figure 4.3. This figure plots the means against the square roots of the second moments of the film revenues.

If you now imagine that you have an innate sense of your willingness to trade off returns against variability, then you want to be on the lowest line that passes through at least two of the alternatives and leaves all the other points above and to the left of the line. Restricting yourself to such a line means that you can choose between the alternatives on the line using whatever other criteria you wish, but that you will not be able to find a larger mean without having to pay a bigger price in variability; or re-expressed, you cannot find a smaller variability without having to accept a smaller mean.

For our film revenues, the line joining studios B and P is just such a line. W is so close to that line that one should probably include it as an alternative as well. Studio W is an example of a studio with the biggest return for a given value for the second moment, or for a given measure of spread, relative to studios T and O. Studio B is an example of a studio with the minimum second moment for a given mean return. Studio P has the largest mean and the largest variation.

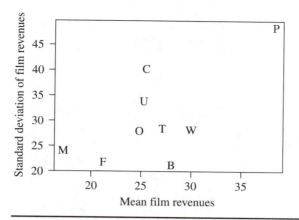

Figure 4.3   Means and standard deviations of film revenues ($millions)

Which studio you choose, or better still which combination of studios you choose, depends on your personal feelings about the trade-off between return and the variability of returns. You can get a specific combination of return and variability on the line joining B and P by putting part of your money into B and part into P.

The return–variability trade-off that we outlined in Figure 4.3 makes most sense when the distributions are nearly symmetric. But when the distributions are skewed to the right, this comparison loses a lot of its charm. One might want to consider the degree of asymmetry that is involved in the choices. For example, it happens that B, P, and W, which lie on our return–variability trade-off line, all have relatively small standardized third moments; those for C and U are the highest. If the measure of skewness is large, that implies that for a given mean and a given degree of variability, the value taken by the average return depends to a substantial extent on a relatively small number of very large returns; a small value for the standardized third moment implies the opposite. For a given variance, the distribution with the smaller standardized third moment is in a sense "less risky" in that your average return over a long period of time will depend less on the rare, but very large, return. In this particular example, you might well decide that the small size of the third moments for the three studios B, W, and P enhances your decision to look at these three.

This idea is more easily seen if we consider the comparison of two distributions of returns, one of which has a negative standardized third moment, the other a positive standardized third moment, with equal means and equal second moments. For the former return distribution, a large number of small positive returns is offset by an unusual, but very large negative return of, say, bankruptcy status. Merely to consider this choice is to recognize the importance of examining the third moment. The alternative distribution of returns is positively skewed so that the mean return is achieved by the averaging of a large number of very small—even negative—returns, with a few very large returns. As you contemplate these alternative distributions, you will recognize that your personal reaction to risk is affected by the presence of nonzero third moments.

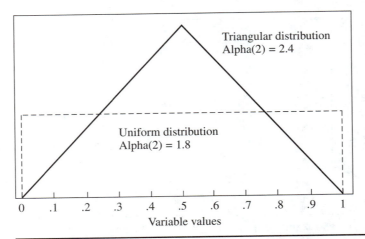

Figure 4.4   Comparison of two distributions with different alpha(2) values. The area under each curve represents probability.

We should now examine the usefulness of the standardized fourth moment in making our decision. As we have said, the fourth moment provides information about the peakedness of the distribution, or the existence of fat tails of the distribution—that is, the concentration of data about the mean as opposed to the tails of the distribution. The fourth moment is easiest to interpret when the distribution is symmetric; otherwise, one has to disentangle the effects of asymmetry from those due to the peakedness or fat tails problem. The standardized fourth moment was smallest when the distribution was flat, or anti-peaked as was the arc sine distribution. It is very large when the distribution has a narrow "spike" in the middle and large tails.

Figure 4.4 provides a comparison that is easier to visualize because the range of the data in both cases is restricted to the interval [0,1]. Two distributions are compared, the uniform that we have seen before in Tables 4.7 and 4.11 and in Figure 3.14, and a new one, the triangular distribution, for which the name is obvious. In interpreting Figure 4.4 remember that the areas under histograms add up to one, so that what is gained in relative frequency in one region has to be compensated for elsewhere. Remember also that you have to compare standardized fourth moments; that is, you have to allow for differences in the values of the second moments. The second moment for the triangular distribution is $(\frac{1}{3})(\frac{1}{2})^3$ and that for the uniform is $(\frac{1}{3})(\frac{1}{2})^2$; so the second moment for the triangular distribution is one-half that for the uniform. The triangular distribution's standardized fourth moment, $\hat{\alpha}_2 = 2.4$, is greater than that for the uniform, $\hat{\alpha}_2 = 1.8$, because the former distribution has fatter tails than the uniform, but only after allowing for the difference in the second moments.

We can get an even clearer picture of the role played by the standardized fourth moment if we examine Figure 4.5. In this figure I have listed the raw data on the extreme left and have plotted the standardized data in the middle of the figure; the

Unstandardized
Variable Values   Plot of Standardized Variable Values   Values of α_2

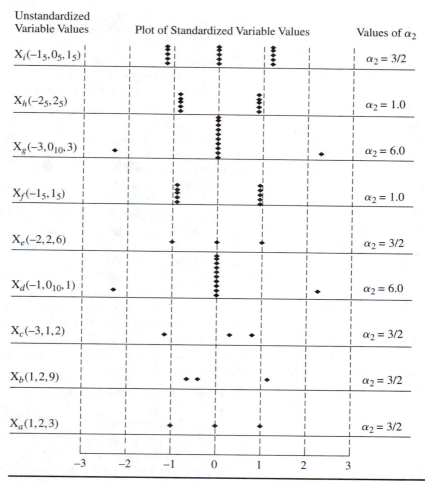

Figure 4.5   A comparison of alpha(2) values for standardized variables. Each diamond represents an observation.

values of $\hat{\alpha}_2$ are shown at the far right. The calculated values of $\hat{\alpha}_2$ vary from a low of 1.0 to a high of 6.0; uniformly distributed data have an $\hat{\alpha}_2$ value of $\frac{3}{2}$. Both x_f and x_h are U-shaped distributions and have $\hat{\alpha}_2$ values of only 1.0; x_d and x_g illustrate distributions that yield large values for $\hat{\alpha}_2$. It is worth some time comparing distributions and the corresponding values for the standardized fourth moment. Compare the distributions that have the same $\hat{\alpha}_2$ values, and compare x_f, x_i, and x_g with $\hat{\alpha}_2$ values ranging from 1 to 6.

We can illustrate these ideas with the film revenue data. Studios C, M, T, and U have the biggest values for $\hat{\alpha}_2$, whereas B, F, P, and W have the smallest. Of these, we have seen from Figure 4.3 that F is dominated by B in that B has a much larger mean revenue and a smaller second moment. P has a surprisingly low value for its standardized fourth moment given that it has the greatest range of all the alternatives. Somewhat surprisingly in this example, the examination of the standardized fourth moments also confirms that a choice between B, W, and P is best. In terms of determining the optimal combination of weights for choosing an optimal mix of the three studios, one might well place a higher weight on B because it has the smallest value for $\hat{\alpha}_2$. Other things equal, studio B is less risky than the other "mean variance" optimal alternatives, W and P.

You now have several ways to choose between the alternative studios. Clearly, choosing on the basis of the mean alone is not enough; some recognition of the variability of the data is important. The second moment measures the extent of that variability, but the third and the fourth moments help you to describe the nature of that variability. We have seen that the distribution of revenues can be quite different, even between distributions that have the same degree of variability as measured by the second moment. Just as we can consider our implicit and intuitive trade-off between return and variability, so we can consider our implicit and intuitive trade-off between distributions with different degrees of asymmetry and different degrees of peakedness. Normally, we might expect that people would prefer less asymmetry, given a level of return and degree of variability. Similarly, we might expect them to prefer less peakedness and hence thinner tails—that is, less reliance for a given average return on large, but low-frequency, occurrences. The choice now is up to the individual to evaluate the trade-offs in these various characteristics of the film revenue distributions.

4.7 Standardization of Variables

Before we began looking closely at our film revenue data, we recognized the importance of the effects of origin and scale in the measurement of our variables. As a consequence we had to define $\hat{\alpha}_1$ and $\hat{\alpha}_2$ to obtain scale and origin invariant measures of shape. This technique is very useful and provides a lot of simplification. It is easier to handle variables for which the mean is zero and for which the second moment is one. The process is known as *standardization of variables*. Standardization is a simple procedure: subtract the mean and divide by the square root of the second moment; the reason for the square root will be clear soon, if it is not already. Define the variable y_i by

$$y_i = \frac{(x_i - \bar{x})}{(\sqrt{m_2(x)})}$$

which is the general statement for "subtract the mean and divide by the square root of m_2."

The transformed variable, y_i, has a mean of zero and a second moment of one! Let's check this. Rewrite the equation expressing y_i as

$$y_i = \left[\frac{-\bar{x}}{(\sqrt{m_2(x)})}\right] + \left[(\sqrt{m_2(x)})^{-1}\right] \times x_i$$

but this is just

$$y_i = a + b \times x_i$$

where

$$a = \frac{-\bar{x}}{(\sqrt{m_2})} \text{ and } b = (\sqrt{m_2})^{-1}$$

If we now calculate the first two moments of y, we get

$$y = \frac{\left(\sum y_i\right)}{N}$$

$$= \left(\frac{-\bar{x}}{\sqrt{m_2(x)}}\right) + \frac{(\sqrt{m_2(x)})^{-1} \times \sum x_i}{N}$$

$$= \left[\frac{-\bar{x}}{(\sqrt{m_2(x)})}\right] + \frac{\bar{x}}{\sqrt{m_2(x)}}$$

$$= 0$$

$$\frac{\sum(y_i - \bar{y})^2}{N} = (\sqrt{m_2(x)})^{-2} \times \frac{\sum(x_i - \bar{x})^2}{N}$$

Because

$$y = a + b \times x = 0 \text{ and } (\sqrt{m_2(x)})^{-2} = (m_2(x))^{-1}$$

we get

$$\frac{m_2(x)}{m_2(x)} = 1$$

so, we conclude

$$\frac{\sum(y_i - \bar{y})^2}{N} = 1$$

Even more interesting is that we get yet another simplification:

$$\hat{\alpha}_1(y) = \frac{m_3(y)}{(m_2(y)^{3/2})} = m_3(y)$$

$$\hat{\alpha}_2(y) = \frac{m_4(y)}{(m_2(y)^2)} = m_4(y)$$

because $m_2(y) = 1$.

The variable y is called "x standardized." Standardized variables are very convenient in that their means are zero, their second moments are one, and their standardized third and fourth moments, $\hat{\alpha}_1$ and $\hat{\alpha}_2$, are easily calculated by the ordinary third and fourth moments of the standardized variables.

We get the same result for $\hat{\alpha}_1$ and $\hat{\alpha}_2$ whether we first standardize the variable and calculate the third and fourth moments or we calculate the third and fourth moments of the original variable and then divide by the second moment.

The Higher Moments about the Origin

All of this time we have ignored the higher moments about the origin, m_2', m_3', m_4'. This is because the moments about the mean are more useful for understanding the shapes of distributions. But the moments about the origin come into their own when we want an efficient way to calculate the actual values of moments about the mean. For example, for any variable x:

$$m_2(x) = \frac{\sum (x_i - \bar{x})^2}{N}$$

$$= \frac{\sum \left[(x_i^2 - 2 \times x_i \times \bar{x} + (\bar{x})^2 \right]}{N}$$

$$= \frac{\left[\sum x_i^2 - 2 \times \sum x_i \times \bar{x} + \sum (\bar{x})^2 \right]}{N}$$

$$= \frac{\sum x_i^2}{N} - (\bar{x})^2$$

where

$$\frac{\sum x_i \bar{x}}{N} = \bar{x}^2, \text{ and } \frac{\sum \bar{x}^2}{N} = \bar{x}^2$$

so

$$m_2(x) = m_2'(x) - (m_1'(x))^2 \tag{4.9}$$

This relationship between the second moments is very useful and we will use it a lot, so Equation 4.9 is a useful one to remember. Similar relationships hold for the rest of the moments, but we will not need them for awhile. However, examples are provided in the exercises to this chapter.

Higher Moments and Grouped Data

We can also calculate the grouped approximations to the third and higher moments. However, remembering that using the grouped data involves an approximation, we can easily see that raising the differences between the actual and the approximation to higher and higher powers will soon lead to huge differences between the true values of the moments and the approximations. The more the cell mark, C_j, differs from the actual values of the data within the cell, the greater the difference between the true moment values and the group approximations.

4.8 Summary

This chapter's objective has been to convert the visual ideas of shape discussed in Chapter 3 into a precise mathematical formulation. We implemented this idea by defining moments. *Moments* are simply averaged powers of the values of a variable. Four moments are all that are needed to characterize the shape of most histograms you will need to use. Moments can be defined in terms of *moments about the mean* or as *moments about the origin*. It is convenient to carry out all the discussion of the use of moments in terms of the moments about the mean for all moments after the first one. However, to calculate moments about the mean it is convenient to use moments about the origin.

The *mean* was defined in Equation 4.1, and its approximation using cell data was defined subsequently. The mean is a measure of location, and it is obtained by averaging the observed data. The mean is the first moment about the origin.

The general moments about the origin were defined in Equations 4.6 and moments about the mean in Equations 4.7. The *second moment about the mean* is particularly important as it is a measure of spread of the variable values. The second moment and its approximation using data in cells is presented in Equations 4.4 and 4.5. We temporarily defined the term *standard deviation* as the square root of the second moment; the standard deviation is important as it is the measure of spread that has the same units of measurement as the original data, whereas the second moments units are squared.

To capture the effects of skewness and peakedness, we discovered that we had to look at the standardized values of the third and fourth moments; these *standardized moments* are called $\hat{\alpha}_1$ and $\hat{\alpha}_2$, and their expressions are given in Equations 4.8.

Standardization is an important tool that simplifies much analysis. Standardization of any variable is achieved by subtracting the mean and dividing the result by the square root of the second moment. Standardized variables by their construction have zero means and second moments equal to one.

The second moment about the mean can usefully be reexpressed as the difference between the second moment about the origin and the square of the first moment as shown in Equation 4.9.

Case Study

Was There Age Discrimination in a Public Utility?

In Chapter 3, we examined some of the distributions of the data in this case to get a feel for what might be involved. In this chapter, we will use the tools that we have just developed to explore in more depth the issues previously raised. The first question to resolve concerns the shape of the distributions. We can use the menu command Moments in S-Plus to calculate the moments of the distributions and compare these calculations to the shapes of the observed histograms. Recall Figures 3.19 and 3.20.

However, before we begin calculating moments, recall the warnings given in Chapter 3 that these data contain coding errors. You have to decide how to handle this difficulty. One way is to recognize that although there are errors their effects on the calculations are minimal and so can be ignored, but note the problem for the reader of your work. An alternative is to run the analysis without the controversial data and tell the reader about your decision. In the following analysis, we will ignore the coding errors because they have little effect on our results at this stage.

We obtain using the menu command Moments on the <u>age</u> variable the following output for all individuals in the Discdata.xls file:

Age of all individuals in the file
First four moments about the mean
No. of observations = 479

continues on next page

(Continued)

First = 46.225
Second = 78.016
Standard deviation = 8.833
Third =−146.452
Fourth = 16664.98
Standardized moments beginning with
    the third = −0.213 2.738

We observe that the mean of the overall distribution of ages is 46 years with a standard deviation of about nine years. The distribution is nearly symmetric, but with a small left-hand tail, $\hat{\alpha}_1 = -0.21$. The amount of peakedness is modest at $\hat{\alpha}_2 = 2.7$. We know from Figure 3.15 that we would discover very little difference in these calculations if we were to separate men and women.

Of greater importance is to examine the difference in moments for the subgroups created by querying whether the person was a former employee(internal) or external.

Age of former employees
First four moments about the mean
No. of observations = 375
First = 47.259
Second = 75.637
Standard deviation = 8.697
Third = −132.341
Fourth = 15737.85
Standardized moments beginning with
    the third = −0.201 2.751

Age of external applicants
First four moments about the mean
No. of observations = 104
First = 42.5
Second = 68.865
Standard deviation = 8.299
Third = −225.288
Fourth = 10944.6
Standardized moments beginning with
    the third = −0.394 2.308

As we might guess from the box-and-whisker plots, the mean age and standard deviation of the former employees are greater than that for the external applicants, but the differences are not very large. Both distributions are skewed left, and there is a modest amount of peakedness.

Another comparison is between those hired, not hired, and those that did not apply as they transferred or were near retirement (see Figure 3.18). How do these distributions differ?

Age of former employees that were not
    hired
First four moments about the mean
No. of observations = 52
First = 49.058
Second = 31.093
Standard deviation = 5.576
Third = −1.862
Fourth = 2495.982
Standardized moments beginning with
    the third = −0.011 2.582

Age of former employees that were hired
First four moments about the mean
No. of observations = 204
First = 43.931
Second = 57.427
Standard deviation = 7.578
Third = −213.539
Fourth = 9958.013
Standardized moments beginning with
    the third = −0.491 3.020

Age of former employees that did not
    apply
First four moments about the mean
No. of observations = 119
First = 52.176
Second = 81.742
Standard deviation = 9.041
Third = −405.121
Fourth = 15071.32
Standardized moments beginning with
    the third = −0.548 2.256

Our first observation is that across these divisions, there seems to be little difference

continues on next page

(Continued)

between the three distributions with respect to shape as measured by the standardized third and fourth moments; all have very modest amounts of left skewness and moderate amounts of peakedness. The difference in ages between those hired and not hired does reflect the union's charges; those hired are on average younger than those not hired. However, the difference seems to be very small relative to the degree of dispersion in the age data. This conclusion is amply born out looking at the age distribution of those who did not apply; the mean and the degree of variation are far greater as one would expect.

Our overall conclusions on the age variable are that for all the subdistributions that we have examined, the shapes of the distributions are very similar. Indeed, the difference between our sample distributions and the normal distribution in Chapter 3 are very slight, but our distributions show some evidence of having a left-hand tail. With respect to the complaint, although we do observe that the ages of the internal applicants relative to the external applicants and the ages of those not hired relative to those hired are both older than the comparison group, the differences are very small, especially in light of the size of the second moments that we calculated. As an aside, we also observe that the second moments of those hired and those who did not apply were larger than those not hired, but the differences do not appear to be large.

In Chapter 3, we examined the breakdown of salaries by the same categories. Let us examine how the calculation of moments helps. The overall distribution of salaries (see Figure 3.20) has moments:

Salaries of all individuals on the
    Discdata.xls file
First four moments about the mean
No. of observations = 479
First = 61457.64

Second = 213976391
Standard deviation = 14627.93
Third = 256386072762
Fourth = 1.387142e+017
Standardized moments beginning with
    the third = 0.082 3.030

We immediately note striking differences with respect to our previous distributions. Here, the measures of shape indicate clearly that the distribution of salaries—although having moderate, but higher, levels of peakedness relative to the distribution of age—are in this case skewed to the right. We note that the mean for all internal employees is about \$61,500 with a standard deviation of about \$14,600. The salaries of most employees in this firm lie in a region from about \$32,300 to \$90,700. We now investigate how this overall distribution is altered by considering the various subcategories.

First, we ask what is the difference between the salaries of those who were hired from the former employees and those who were not?

Salaries of former employees that were
    not hired
First four moments about the mean
No. of observations = 52
First = 60026
Second = 238852724
Standard deviation = 15454.86
Third = 1546485329952
Fourth = 1.868219e+017
Standardized moments beginning with
    the third = 0.419 3.275

Salaries of former employees that were
    hired
First four moments about the mean
No. of observations = 219
First = 61803.43
Second = 222177292
Standard deviation = 14905.61
Third = 277031532737

continues on next page

(Continued)

Fourth = 1.459941e+017

Standardized moments beginning with the third = 0.084 2.958

From these figures we see that the average salaries of those hired were slightly greater than for those not hired. This result does not lend support to the union's contention that the firm was trying to save money by letting go the higher-priced employees.

Salaries of former employees that did not apply
First four moments about the mean
No. of observations = 121
First = 61758.62
Second = 166257253
Standard deviation = 12894.08
Third = –969433408053
Fourth = 8.044588e+016
Standardized moments beginning with the third = –0.452 2.910

The mean for those who did not apply is surprisingly very close to that for those hired, but the standard deviation is much less. Interestingly and somewhat surprisingly, this income distribution has a left-hand tail, whereas all the others have a right-hand tail. The reason presumably is that there are included in the group "did not apply" a number of very low-salaried people. Indeed, an examination of the corresponding box-and-whisker plots (see Figure 3.17) indicates that this is the case.

One cannot calculate the salary breakdown by the distinction between internal and external applicant as we have no information on the salaries of the external candidates.

Overall, the variations across the subgroups were with one exception very small. Indeed, the average salaries of those previous employees hired were greater by a small amount than the average salaries of those not hired. More surprisingly, the average income of those who retired was nearly equal to that of those hired. There are differences across the various groups in terms of the shape of the distributions, but they are all very small in extent.

Nevertheless, we have already learned a fair amount about the facts of this case. As we proceed, we shall learn more still.

Exercises

If you have not yet read the "Addendum to the Reader" at the end of Chapter 1, you will really need to do so for the exercises in this chapter.

Calculation Practice

Exercises 4.1 through 4.4 provide some basic practice on the use of summation notation and the elementary algebra that is needed for the rest of the book. See Appendix A, "Mathematics Appendix" for a more intensive review of these ideas.

For questions 4.1 to 4.4, use the following set of numbers:

$$\{x_i\} = \{1, 2, 3, 5, 7, 8, 9, 12\}, i = 1, 8$$

4.1 Use a hand calculator to calculate each of the following expressions. Indicate the relationships between your results.

a. $\sum x_i$

b. $\sum x_i^2$

c. $(\sum x_i)^2$

d. $3 \sum x_i$

e. $\sum 18 x_i$

f. $\sum x_i^3$

g. $(\sum x_i)^3$

4.2 Use a hand calculator to calculate each of the following expressions. Note that you can use the results from Exercise 4.1. Indicate which are moments, and define the moment.

a. $\sum x_i / N$

b. $\sum x_i^2 / N$

c. $(\sum x_i)^2 / N$

d. $\sum x_i^3 / N$

e. $(\sum x_i)^3 / N$

f. $\sum x_i^4 / N$

g. $(\sum x_i)^4 / N$

4.3 Use a hand calculator to calculate each of the following expressions. Indicate the relationships between these results.

a. $\sum (x_i - (\sum x_i / N))$

b. $\sum (x_i - \bar{x})$

c. $\sum (x_i - \bar{x}) / N$

4.4 Use a hand calculator to calculate each of the following expressions. Indicate the relationships between these results.

a. $\sum (x_i - \bar{x})^2$

b. $\sum (x_i - \bar{x})^2 / N$

c. $(\sum (x_i - \bar{x}))^2 / N$

d. $(\sum x_i^2 / N) - \bar{x}^2$

e. $(\sum x_i^2) / N - (\sum x_i)^2 / N$

4.5 *Worked. Objective: To link the preceding algebraic exercises to the use of the computer in "adding up."* Exercises 4.5 through 4.7 provide more practice on the use of summation notation

and elementary algebra. For these exercises, refer to the following set of numbers: $\{x_i\} = \{-4, 2, -1, 0, 5, 7, -2, 8\}$. Please calculate the following:

a. $\sum x_i$

b. $\sum x_i^2$

c. $(\sum x_i)^2$

d. $-2 \sum x_i$

e. $\sum 64 x_i$

f. $\sum x_i^3$

g. $(\sum x_i)^3$

4.6 Confirm by using a hand calculator that you get the same results as in the following computer method.

[*Computer directions:* To calculate the seven exercises in 4.5, the set of numbers x_i has been placed in a file Test.xls. Use the following directions:

Start S-Plus. On the menu bar, click on <u>File</u>, <u>Import Data</u>, <u>From File</u>, folder Xfiles, subfolder Misc. Click on file Test.xls. Click Open. On the menu bar, click on <u>Data</u>, <u>Transform</u>. In the Transform dialog in Expression:

a. Key in $\boxed{\text{sum}(x)}$. Click Apply. The answer will be in column V1 in the Test data frame (answer = 15).

b. Key in $\boxed{\text{sum}(x^2)}$. Click Apply. The answer will appear in column V2 (answer = 163).

c. Key in $\boxed{\text{sum}(x)^2}$. Click Apply (answer = 255).

d. Key in $\boxed{-2*\text{sum}(x)}$. Click Apply (answer = −30).

e. Key in $\boxed{\text{sum}(64*x)}$. Click Apply (answer = 960).

f. Key in $\boxed{\text{sum}(x^3)}$. Click Apply (answer = 915).

g. Key in $\boxed{\text{sum}(x)^3}$. Click Apply (answer = 3375).]

The answers from the computer should confirm your hand calculations.

Summarize your calculations by stating some general rules of summation that are illustrated by these questions.

4.7 Now try calculating the following expressions by hand using the set of numbers in Exercise 4.5.

a. $\sum x_i/N$

b. $\sum x_i^2/N$

c. $(\sum x_i)^2/N$

d. $\sum x_i^3/N$

e. $(\sum x_i)^3/N$

f. $\sum x_i^4/N$

g. $(\sum x_i)^4/N$

h. $\sum(x_i - (\sum x_i/N))$

i. $\sum(x_i - \bar{x})$

j. $\sum(x_i - \bar{x})/N$

k. Which of these are moments? Distinguish moments about the origin and moments about the mean.

l. Complete the exercise by confirming that the use of the computer gives the same results. If you get a different result, you should first check your use of parentheses to make sure that you are performing the same calculations by hand as by computer.

4.8 Using the set of numbers in Exercise 4.5 calculate:

a. $\sum(x_i - \bar{x})^2$

b. $\sum(x_i - \bar{x})^2/N$

c. $(\sum(x_i - \bar{x}))^2/N$

d. $(\sum x_i^2)/N - \bar{x}^2$

e. $(\sum x_i^2)/N - (\sum x_i)^2/N$

f. Summarize these calculations by stating some general rules that would apply to any data set.

g. Complete the exercise by confirming that use of the computer gives the same results.

Exploring the Tools

4.9 Moments about the mean can be reexpressed in terms of moments about the origin, and vice versa. For the first three moments derive the relationship between each moment about the mean and the moments about the origin. Similarly, derive the relationship between each moment about the origin and the moments about the mean, plus the mean itself. Can you detect a general principle?

4.10 As practice and as a reminder for the next few exercises, consider the following relationships. Try to follow the algebra for each statement, and verify the results when $a = 3$, $b = 2$. Then confirm the result when $a = 7$ and $b = 3$.

$$(a - b)^3 = (a - b)^2(a - b)$$
$$= (a^2 - 2ab + b^2)(a - b)$$
$$= a^3 - 3a^2b + 3ab^2 - b^3$$

$$(a - b)^4 = (a - b)^2(a - b)^2$$
$$= (a^2 - 2ab + b^2)(a^2 - 2ab + b^2)$$
$$= a^4 - 4a^3b + 6a^2b^2 - 4ab^3 + b^4$$

4.11 Using the numbers $\{x_i\} = \{-2, -1, 0, 1, 2, 6\}$, $i = 1, 6$, calculate with a hand calculator:

a. $\sum x_i/N$

b. $\sum(x_i - \bar{x})^2/N$

c. $\sum x_i^2/N - (\sum x_i)^2/N$

d. $\sum(x_i - \bar{x})^3/N$

e. $\sum x_i^3/N - 3(\sum x_i^2/N)\bar{x} + 3\bar{x}^3 - \bar{x}^3$

f. Using your results, algebraically express the second and third moments about the mean in terms of moments about the origin.

g. Complete the exercise by confirming that use of the computer gives the same results.

4.12 Using the same numbers listed in Exercise 4.11, calculate:

a. $\sum(x_i - \bar{x})^4/N$

b. $\sum x_i^4/N - 4(\sum x_i^3/N)\bar{x} +$
$6(\sum x_i^2/N)\bar{x}^2 - 4\bar{x}^4 + \bar{x}^4$

c. $\sum x_i^4/N - 4(\sum x_i^3/N)\bar{x} + 6(\sum x_i^2/N)\bar{x}^2 - 3\bar{x}^4$

d. Using your results, reexpress the fourth moment about the mean in terms of moments about the origin.

e. Complete the exercise by confirming that use of the computer gives the same results.

4.13 Under what circumstances is the second moment about the mean zero? When is the fourth moment about the mean zero? The first moment about the mean is identically zero. Explain and illustrate. How does this fact aid your understanding of the "mean"?

4.14 The second moment is an average squared deviation. This can be seen by noting that in the formula for a second moment, the sum of the deviations squared is divided by the number of observations. If there are N observations, there are N deviations from the mean. Let $N = 4$. Write out the formula for the second moment in longhand (do not use summation notation). For any N if possible, but for $N = 4$ if you must, prove that only $N - 1$ of the N deviations are independent (i.e., prove that if you know what $N - 1$ of the deviations are, you know what the Nth deviation is as well).

4.15 You observe your mother's temperature three times a day for many days while she is sick. Your thermometer is calibrated in degrees Fahrenheit. The attending nurse has also been taking your mother's temperature, except that her thermometer is calibrated in degrees Celsius. Explain how you would begin to check whether the distribution of the nurse's temperature readings is similar to yours. How would you specify "similar"?

4.16 Why does it make sense that skewness should be measured by a deviation raised to an odd power, as opposed to an even one?

a. Which observations in a data set do the most to increase the third moment?

b. Which observations in a data set do the most to increase the fourth moment?

c. If distribution A is shaped like a triangle and distribution B is shaped like a U, which distribution will have the larger value for the standardized fourth moment given the second moments are the same?

d. If distribution C is very flat and D has a single hump in the middle of the distribution, which has the larger standardized fourth moment given the second moments are the same?

e. What do the mean and the square root of the second moment have in common that the mean and the second moment itself do not?

f. A brand-new statistical software package freshly installed on your computer has calculated various statistics about the age and income distributions of a populous but less-developed country. You discover that the third moments of both variables are negative. Without hesitation, you call the software company and tell them you want your money back. Why?

g. Write out the expressions for $\hat{\alpha}_1$ and $\hat{\alpha}_2$. After examining these expressions specify the units in which they are measured.

h. Prove that the mean of a standardized variable is 0.

4.17 When do the average, $\bar{x}$, and median differ? If you were examining the following sets of data, which measure of location would you use and why? When might you use both? If you examine both, which do you think is larger and why?

a. income of households

b. length of fishing poles

c. number of family members

d. duration of unemployment

e. size of earthquakes

f. wind strength of hurricanes

g. number of felonies committed in a year

4.18 Worked. *Objective: To illustrate the use of the Moments menu command.* Recall the data on 72 NYU student grades, two midterms and a final, that we discussed in Chapter 3 (see folder Xfiles, subfolder Misc, file Grades.xls).

a. For the variable *midterm1*, calculate the first four moments using the following two computer procedures and compare your answers.

[**Computer directions:** Start S-Plus. On the menu bar, click on File, Data Import, From File, folder Xfiles, subfolder Misc. Double click on file Grades.xls.

Procedure 1: To calculate the moments step by step: on the menu bar, click on Data, Transform.

(1) To calculate the number of observations, n: In the New Column Name box key in $\boxed{n}$. In the expressions box, key in $\boxed{\text{length (midterm1)}}$. Click Apply. The answer will be in the n column (the answer will be repeated throughout the column) in the Grades data frame (answer = 72).

(2) To calculate $m1$, the mean, key in $\boxed{\text{mean}}$ for the New Column Name. In Expression, key in $\boxed{\text{sum(midterm1)}/n}$. Click Apply (answer = 72.31).

(3) To calculate $m2$, key in name $\boxed{m2}$ and $\boxed{\text{sum((midterm1-mean) }^2)/n}$. Click Apply (answer = 196.52).

(4) To calculate $m3$, key in name $\boxed{m3}$ and $\boxed{\text{sum((midterm1-mean) }^3)/n}$. Click Apply (answer = −824.28).

(5) To calculate $m4$, key in name $\boxed{m4}$ and $\boxed{\text{sum((midterm1-mean) }^4)/n}$. Click Apply (answer = 90505.14).

Procedure 2: To calculate all the moments: On the menu bar, click on Text Routines, Moments. In the dialog, select Data Frame, Grades. In Variable, select "midterm1." Click OK.] Compare the results from procedures 1 and 2. They will be the same. If not, you made a mistake; recheck your entries.

b. Repeat procedures 1 and 2 using the variable *final* in Grades.xls.

Now that you have had practice calculating moments step by step on the computer, you can use the Moments menu command as in procedure 2 whenever you need to calculate moments. Better still after this exercise, you will have no doubt about what it is that the computer is calculating on your behalf.

4.19 An absentminded professor has calculated the mean, second moment, and third and fourth moments for his economics class' final exam. The grades for his 24 students are as follows: 52 92 86 80 88 64 92 76 92 68 68 64 70 68 68 88 88 94 64 56 84 84 74 62

a. What are the results of the professor's calculations?

[**Computer hint:** In S-Plus, on the menu bar, click on Data, New Data Object, data.frame. Click OK. Key in the grades into the first column. On the menu bar, click on Text Routines, Moments. In the dialog, select Data Frame, SDF#. In Variable, select V1. Click OK. The plots in (*b*) can be created by clicking Graph, 2D-Plot on the menu bar and selecting the graph type desired.]

b. Create the box-and-whisker plot and a histogram for the professor's grades. Answer all the following questions *before* doing any calculations on the computer; use the computer merely to check your intuition.

(1) Having gone through all the work, the professor relaxes by drinking tea and petting his cat. Lifting the cat, he finds six ungraded and fur-covered exams. Suddenly he remembers that there are 30, not 24, students in his class. After grading the newfound exams, he finds that each of the six earned the mean score. Which of his previous calculations now need to be redone? Which can be left unchanged?

(2) Consider each of the moment calculations that must be changed. Without recalculating, in which direction will each result change? Remember that the number of grades included in the calculations has also changed.

(3) Add the six "mean" exams to the histogram. Does the histogram reflect what you said would happen in question (2)?

(4) Do you need to redraw the box-and-whisker plot?

4.20 More reflections on the absentminded professor. Do *not* use the computer for this exercise. Before he had found the last six exams and viewed the distribution of grades, he was thinking of changing his teaching, or at least his grading, methods. Why do you think he was considering this, and what do you think he should have changed? After considering the additional six exams, do you think it is still so imperative for him to change? Why or why not?

Late at night, just before falling asleep, the absentminded professor remembers that he has been grading so far on a scale of 50 to 100, not on a scale of 0 to 100. He wants to make the scores in 4.19a comparable to his other exams, and he wants the information on the moments to be comparable as well. What does he have to do to fix things? Be nice and do it for him; he's sleepy.

4.21 Worked. *Objective: To indicate the loss of information in using grouped data.* In the text it was explained that it is not very useful to use grouped or cell data to calculate the higher moments; even the second moment is not very accurate. This exercise will help illustrate this fact. The mathematics and verbal scores for both the PSAT and the SAT are recorded in the file Psatsat.xls.

a. For each score catagory calculate all four moments and the standardized third and fourth moments using the observed data.

[*Computer directions:* Start S-Plus. On the menu bar, click on File, Import Data, From File, folder Xfiles, subfolder Testscor. Click on file Psatsat.xls. Click Open. On the menu bar, click on Text Routines, Moments. In the dialog, select Data Frame, Psatsat. In Variable, select "psatmath." Click OK. Repeat the Moments command for each variable.]

b. Using the procedure developed in Chapter 3, the PSAT and the SAT data have been grouped into cells. A file, Psatcell.xls, has been created with the number of observations by cell (*pmobs, pvobs,* etc.) and the cell marks (*pmmark, pvmark,* etc.) for each of the variables in file Psatsat.xls. Use the following directions to calculate the moments from the cell data.

[*Computer directions:* On the menu bar, click on File, Import Data, From File. Select folder Xfiles, subfolder Testscor. Double click on the file Psatcell.xls. On the menu bar, click on Data, Transform.

(1) To calculate the number of observations, n: In New Column Name, key in n. In Expression, key in sum(pmobs). Click Apply. The answer will be in the Psatcell data frame in column n (answer = 520).

(2) To calculate $m1$, the mean: key in mean for the name. In Expression, key in sum(pmmark* pmobs)/n. Click Apply (answer = 45.75).

(3) To calculate $m2$, key in m2 for the name. In Expression, key in sum(pmobs*(pmmark-mean)^2)/n. Click Apply (answer = 135.78).

(4) To calculate $m3$, key in m3 for the name. In Expression, key in sum(pmobs*(pmmark-mean)^3)/n. Click Apply (answer = 149.83).

(5) To calculate $m4$, key in m4 for the name. In Expression, key in sum(pmobs*(pmmark-mean)^4)/n. Click Apply (answer = 48495.76).]

c. Calculate the moments for the other three variables from the cell data, and compare your answers with the moments calculated using the observed data in step (a).

4.22 Worked. *Objective: To illustrate the relationship between the shape of a distribution and its moments.* In Chapter 3, we mentioned a variety of different distributions that were generated by different types of experiments. In this chapter, we have shown that as the shape of the distribution changes, so do the moments. This exercise will illustrate this essential idea in terms of histograms from computer experiments and from idealized shapes of distributions (that is, in terms of histograms that are very smooth, such as might be generated by a very large set of data).

[*Computer directions:* Start S-Plus. Click on Labs, How Are Populations Distributed? In the dialog box in Lab Option, click Simulated Data. Click on each listed Distribution Family. Click Apply.]

Print your graphs so that you can examine them closely. Compare the shapes of the distributions to the values of the moments shown on the graph. Try to draw out general statements that you can make about the relationship between the values taken by the four moments and the observed distributions. Notice that the unstandardized third and fourth moments are not very informative, whereas the standardized third and fourth moments are very informative. Observe the extent to which the histograms you observe do, or do not, match the idealized distributions.

This is one of the most important exercises in this chapter. It is vital that you learn at an intuitive level the relationship between moments and the shapes of distributions.

4.23 *Worked. Objective: To relate moments to the shape of histograms.*

a. In Chapter 3, in Exercise 3.18, you generated a number of histograms from various distributions or experiments. In this exercise, we will calculate the moments from similar types of histograms. Compare your moment calculations, especially the standardized third and fourth moments, with the shapes of the histograms that you will generate in this exercise. First, generate six sets of 400 random numbers each based on a different distribution.

[*Computer directions:* Open S-Plus. On the menu bar, click on Data, Random Numbers.

(1) In the Random Number Generation dialog, in Sample Size, key in $\boxed{400}$. In Distribution scroll to

normal (it is the first entry in the list). In the Save As box, key in $\boxed{\text{Norm.den}}$ as a file name.* Uncheck Print Results. Click Apply.

(2) Follow the directions in (1). In the Distribution box scroll to LogNormal. Select a new file name.

(3) Follow the directions in (1). In the Distribution box scroll to Uniform. Select a new file name.

(4) Follow the directions in (1). In the Distribution box scroll to Chi-square. In the Deg. of Freedom 1 box, key in $\boxed{5}$. Select a new file name.

(5) Follow the directions in (1). In the Distribution box scroll to Weibull. In the Scale box, key in $\boxed{3}$. In the Shape 1 box, key in $\boxed{2}$. Select a new file name.

(6) Follow the direction in (1). In the Distribution box scroll to Beta. In the Shape 1 box, key in $\boxed{2}$. In the Shape 2 box, key in $\boxed{5}$. Select a new file name. (*Note: To open the files created, open the Object Browser and double click on the data frame names.)]

b. For each of these six data sets, generate the histograms, give them a descriptive title, and print out the results. Calculate the first four moments, including the standardized moments.

[*Computer directions:* Highlight the data column in the first dataset. On the menu bar, click on Graph, 2D-Plot, Histogram. Click on OK. To title the graph, on the menu bar, click Insert, Titles, Main. In the area that is highlighted on the graph, key in a title such as $\boxed{\text{Normal Density:}}$ $\boxed{\text{400 Obs}}$. Print the graph. Repeat for all six data sets.

To calculate the moments that correspond to the histograms: On the menu bar, click on Text Routines, Moments. In the dialog box, select Data Frame, Norm.den. In Variable, select "sample." Click OK. Repeat for each data set substituting the appropriate file name for Norm.den.]

Compare the variation in the moments, especially the standardized moments, with the variation in the shapes of the histograms.

c. Repeat the previous exercises with 200 observations.

d. Repeat the previous exercises with 600 observations.

e. As the number of observations increases what implications do you observe?

This exercise illustrates the point that each unique experiment has a corresponding distribution and that as the number of observations increases the smoothness and persistence of shape over repeated samplings is enhanced.

Applications

In all the following exercises, use the "Moments" function where appropriate.

4.24 In Exercise 3.23, we examined the distribution of the elderly across states; see folder Xfiles, subfolder Misc, file Age65.xls. Calculate the moments to provide more precise information about the distribution of the elderly. Are there any surprises in the results? The values that you are measuring are the percentages of the population in each state that are greater than 65 years old (*pct65*); so the mean, for example, is the mean percentage of those over 65. The mean is averaged over the percentages recorded in each state.

4.25 Using the data on weight and fat (see folder Xfiles, subfolder Misc, file Coles.xls), examine the differences that the weight loss program might have made to weight and fat content for the subjects involved. Was the program successful? How are you defining "successful"? The main question is, How different are the two distributions? Explain how you would characterize "different."

4.26 In Exercise 3.22, we examined the distributions of arms shipments by the United States and the U.S.S.R. (see folder Xfiles, subfolder Misc, file Arms.xls). Let us now consider calculating both sets of moments for the two distributions.

What conclusions can we draw about the differences between U.S. and U.S.S.R. policies from examining these moments? Pay particular attention to the higher moments about the mean, as the first moment in particular is, perhaps, intuitively obvious.

4.27 In the folder Xfiles, subfolder Gnp, subfolder Intlgnp, there are three files of GNP data: Swegnp.xls, Ukgnp.xls and Usgnp.xls for Sweden, the United Kingdom, and the United States, respectively. Clearly the means and variances of these very different countries will be different, even after conversion to a common monetary unit. However, it is not clear that the shapes of the distributions of GNP components will be different. Using both box-and-whisker plots and calculations of the first four standardized moments, explore the differences in the shapes of the distributions among the three countries with respect to the three variables "priceind," "consump," and "invest." What policy implications do you draw from your analysis?

4.28 In the folder Xfiles, subfolder Testscor, a file on scholastic aptitude tests, Psatsat.xls, contains four variables: PSAT scores and SAT scores for the mathematics and verbal tests.

a. Compare the shapes of the box-and-whisker plots of the math scores between the PSAT and SAT, recognizing that the two scores are measured on different scales.

b. Compare the shapes of the verbal scores between the PSAT and SAT, recognizing that the two scores are measured on different scales. Calculate the standardized moments.

c. Similarly, compare the verbal and math scores for the PSAT in the same way.

d. What conclusions about the performance of students on these two sets of tests do you draw?

4.29 In the folder Xfiles, subfolder Misc, file Geyser1.xls are recorded the durations of and the intervals between eruptions of Old Faithful in

Yellowstone National Park. By calculating the four moments of both variables, what conclusions can you draw about the eruptions of Old Faithful? What questions are you stimulated to ask from examining these data?

4.30 Recall the discussion in Chapter 2 on IQ and height. Using the variables on IQ and height in the folder Xfiles, subfolder Misc, file Psychol.xls, explore the relevance to the interpretation of the moments of each variable. Recall that IQ has no natural origin, but that height clearly does. If you were to shift your attention to IQ differences, relative to some benchmark individual, what would be the change in your interpretation of the moments?

4.31 Explain the difference between examining the moments of the variable sales rank (*slsrank*) in the file Rock.xls in the folder Xfiles, subfolder Misc and the corresponding moments that you would observe from the actual sales figures, if they were available. (*Hint:* Recall from Chapter 2 the difference between a measurement, such as "sales" which will have units of measurements attached, and the ranking of such a variable).

4.32 Obtain the data on stock prices in NASDAQ and NYSE from the folder Xfiles, subfolder Misc, file Nyseotc.xls. Calculate the first four moments, and indicate how they help you to answer the following questions:

a. Which market do you prefer if you are a broker?

b. Which market do you prefer if you are buying stocks for your retirement?

c. Which market do you prefer if you have recieved a small inheritance, and you are already well off?

4.33 Using the data in the file Cardata.xls from the folder Xfiles, subfolder Misc, calculate the first four moments of the variables *mpg, displace, horsepower, weight,* and *price.* Given the wide disparity in the definitions of these variables and the differences in the associated units of measurement, presumably comparing the means and the second moments will be of little interest, but what of the standardized sample third and fourth moments, $\hat{\alpha}_1$ and $\hat{\alpha}_2$? What general conclusions about the characteristics of cars can you draw from a comparison of $\hat{\alpha}_1$ and $\hat{\alpha}_2$ values across the variables that were recorded?

4.34 Case Study: Was There Age Discrimination in a Public Utility?

Along with the age discrimination charges, the plaintiff's attorney is interested in discovering evidence of differential treatment between male and female employees to enrich his case by adding gender discrimination charges. In response to this concern, you are asked to estimate the four moments of the salary for

a. all individuals in the Discdata.xls file under 40 years old by gender.

b. all individuals in the Discdata.xls file 40 years old and older by gender.

Write a short report for your supervisor explaining the practical importance of your findings for this case.

The data are stored in Xfiles in the folder Agedisc. **(See the Computer Hint for Exercise 3.30.)**

4.35 Case Study: Was There Age Discrimination in a Public Utility? The plaintiff's attorney suspects that hiring practices having a disparate impact on a protected class of people (like those of age 40 and over) can be detected by comparing the differences in the age distribution across various groups of employees or potential employees. He asked your Forensic Economics Consulting firm to compare the age distribution of older individuals (ages 40 and over) among (1) all individuals on Discdata.xls file, (2) all former employees(internal), and (3) all external applicants to the distribution for those employees that were hired within each one of these groups. You will make three sets of comparisons.

a. You are asked to estimate for your supervisor the four moments for the age variable for

(1) all individuals in the file 40 and over and among all individuals 40 and over, those who were hired

(2) all former employees (internal) 40 and over and among former employees 40 and over, those who were hired

(3) all external applicants 40 and over and among external applicants 40 and over, those who were hired.

b. You are also asked to discuss your understanding of the information provided by the data. Prepare a comprehensive statistical analysis report for your supervisor. The data are stored in Xfiles in the folder Agedisc.

[*Computer hint:* See Exercise 3.30. Use Data, Subset and Data, Split to create needed data frames.]

4.36 Case Study: Was There Age Discrimination in a Public Utility? The labor union asked your consulting firm to investigate the presence of a "wage mobility discrimination" problem within this age discrimination case. Mobility discrimination is said to exist if certain employees are prevented from advancing, even though everyone is paid equally for equivalent work.

a. You are asked to prepare for the investigation team the following estimates for their next meeting:

(1) the four moments for salary of all individuals on the Discdata.xls file

(2) the four moments for salary of all females

(3) the four moments for salary of all males

b. Write a short, summary report with your findings. In your report indicate the limitations of your analysis. The data are stored in Xfiles in the folder Agedisc.

CHAPTER
5

The Description of Bivariate Data

5.1   What You Will Learn in This Chapter

In this chapter, we extend the ideas about shape to the properties of pairs of random variables. The key insight here is that we can summarize the statistical relationship between two variables in terms of just one more number, the correlation coefficient, or the first cross product moment for the standardized variables. As such, the correlation coefficient is a simple generalization of the concept of moment that was introduced in Chapter 4. If the correlation coefficient is positive, the relationship between the variables is one in which on average larger values of one variable are associated with larger values of the other; if negative, larger values of one variable are associated with smaller values of the other; and if zero, there is no apparent association.

A corresponding picture, the "scatter plot," plots pairs of points. We also introduce in this context the idea of the slope of the straight line that approximates the scatter of point pairs and the associated notion of a linear structural relationship introduced in Chapter 2. Linear structural relationships will prove to be universally useful in decision making as we shall see in Chapters 13 and 14.

We generalize the concept of "correlation" by introducing a measure of association between the *ranks* of variables, instead of between the variable *values*. We further discover how the idea of "association" can be applied to categorical data.

5.2   Introduction

In Chapters 3 and 4, we discussed how to summarize observations on one variable at a time. But what if we have two or more variables? How will we summarize the relationship between them? Because we are still concerned with random variables, we know that we will not see a functional relationship between the variables but a "structural" or an "approximate" relationship (as we discussed in Chapter 2). We know that the individual values, or "realizations," of each random variable cannot be predicted exactly, but might there be something that we can discover about collections of pairs of random variables? For example, if we were to examine the midterm grades and final grades of students, students' heights and weights, or car mileage and car weight,

Table 5.1   **Summary Statistics of the Midterm and Final Grades of NYU Students**

Statistic	Moments	Midterm	Final
Sample size		72.00	72.00
Mean	m_1'	72.30	67.30
Spread	m_2	196.50	132.00
$\sqrt{\text{Spread}}$	$\sqrt{m_2}$	14.02	11.50
Skewness	$\hat{\alpha}_1$	−0.30	−0.37
Peakedness	$\hat{\alpha}_2$	2.34	3.30

we would not expect to see any simple deterministic relationship between the pairs of variables. Interest rates and changes in Gross Domestic Product indicate some form of association as do energy consumption and output. Wages and age are obviously not deterministically related, but they are not independent of each other either. Other relationships may be more problematic, such as whether tall men marry tall women or whether starting salaries are positively related to height of the employee. However, we do expect that there is something we can learn from observing the data; so let us try to see what we might discover.

As a first step, we could apply all the analysis that we used in Chapters 3 and 4 on each variable in turn. For example, Figure 3.2 shows the box-and-whisker plots for midterm and final grades. The same procedure could and should be performed on the pair of variables one by one. This preliminary analysis will help you to get a "feel for the data" and to spot at least the obvious coding errors—for example, where someone accidently multiplies a number by ten or drops a digit. The next preliminary step is to calculate the basic statistics we discussed in Chapter 4. Table 5.1 shows the corresponding first two moments and the standardized third and fourth moments for the midterm and final grades in an NYU economics course (calculated from data in the folder Xfiles, subfolder Misc, filename Grades.xls). But this still does not answer the question of whether there is anything we can say about the variables as a pair.

The main task that we face in this chapter is to discover how to express a "relationship" between two random variables. First, we need to define what we might mean by a "relationship between two random variables." We anticipated this discussion in Chapter 2, where we introduced the idea of a "structural relationship." This chapter will begin the elaboration of that concept. Let us begin.

5.3   Three-Dimensional Histograms

Histograms were very useful with observations on a single variable, so we might consider plotting histograms for pairs of points, or, as we shall refer to them from now on, **bivariate data**. *Bi* means "two," so bivariate data refers to pairs of data points. Although this can be done, the process requires some sophisticated graphing to be effective. An example is shown in Figure 5.1 for the heights and weights of British women in 1951.

The cells that we define are now two-dimensional cells as shown at the base of the three-dimensional plot in Figure 5.1. For an observation to be placed, for example, in

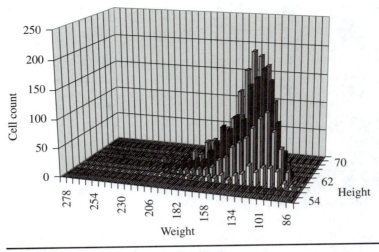

Figure 5.1   Three-dimensional histogram: Heights and weights

the cell bounded by weight between 158 and 162 and height between 60 and 62, a woman had to have been observed with height and weight that fell within those bounds. We are looking for the joint occurrence of a weight within a specified interval and a height within another specified interval. Similarly, the height of each of the blocks above the rectangular grid of midterm and final grades would represent the relative frequency of the pairs of grades that lie in the specified cell. From Figure 5.1 it would seem that the combination of heights and weights that a very large proportion of women have is about 110 to 140 in weight and about 54 to 64 for height; this is the group of cells with the largest relative frequencies. Few women had heights above 68 inches and weights above 206; even fewer had heights above 68 inches and weights below 110.

With **univariate data** (*uni = one,* or single variable), the area under the histogram was proportional to the relative frequency; with bivariate data it is the volume that is proportional to the relative frequency of the pairs of points. The height of the "third axis" on which the relative frequencies would be plotted above the axes for the cells for grades has to be chosen so that its height times the area of the two-dimensional cell would be proportional to the observed relative frequency.

These "three dimensional" diagrams are not very useful and are hard to draw. The only really effective way to present a three-dimensional histogram is to produce a physical model of the relative frequencies, but that is a little difficult to put into a book. It looks like we will have to try again.

5.4   Scatter Plots

A technique that professors often use to examine grades in a class is to plot the grades on a line to see how they are distributed; we did this when we were illustrating the properties of moments. But what if we had the grades from two examinations by the

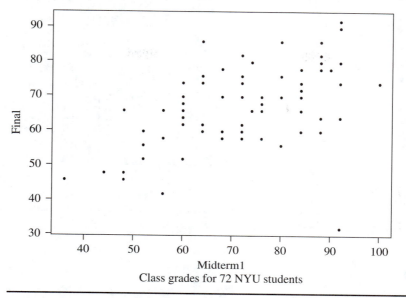

Figure 5.2   Scatter diagram: Midterm and final grades

same set of students, and we wanted to see if the better students in one examination were likely to do better in the other examination. If we want to compare midterm grades with final grades, how would we plot both of these grades to show this?

A direct solution to this problem is to set up two axes, or grids, one for each set of grades, and to plot on the pair of axes, the pair of grades received by each student. Figure 5.2 shows the grades plotted from the data that were summarized in Table 5.1, the first midterm against the final. Each pair of grades plotted refers to the first midterm and final grades earned by a single student. This figure is called a **scatter plot,** or **scatter diagram.**

Figure 5.2 does indicate some shape; the cloud of points seems to slope upward to the right. We also note that one student seems to have had a disastrous final grade, about 32, after a good performance in the midterm, about 92; such an observation is called an "outlier" because it lies well outside the range of the rest of the data. Another example showing a similar shape is presented in Figure 5.3, showing the heights and weights for a class of fitness students. The shape of this scatter plot is not as clear because there are a number of very heavy people who are also relatively short.

Now let us try another example. Figure 5.4 is a scatter plot of car weights and miles per gallon. Here we see that there is also some idea of shape, but that it is different from the previous examples. In this case the cloud of points slopes downward to the right.

Look at Figure 5.5. This is a scatter plot of heights and IQ levels; here we do not see much shape at all unless we call it "round." This figure also has an "outlier" in one individual who is not very tall but is most definitely smart.

What we have discovered looking at these figures is that there does seem to be an idea of "shape" when we look at scatter plots of pairs of variables. We now need

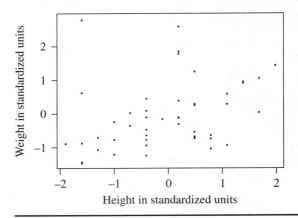

Figure 5.3   Scatter diagram: Height versus weight

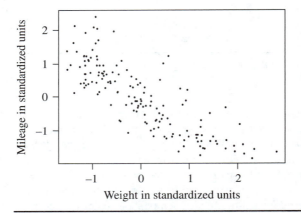

Figure 5.4   Scatter diagram: Mileage (mpg) versus weight

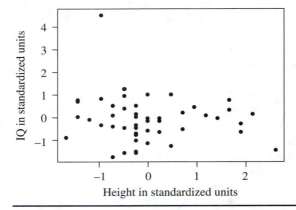

Figure 5.5   Scatter diagram: IQ versus height

some measure of shape that will capture the intuitive ideas that we have been discussing and make them precise.

5.5 Standardization for Pairs of Random Variables

Before we start to devise some notion of a measure of shape for pairs of variables, let us remind ourselves of some potential difficulties. Even with only one variable, we soon discovered the importance of allowing for "units of measurement" when we were trying to measure shape. We concluded that a wise tactic was to standardize our variables before trying to measure characteristics of shape beyond location and spread. Alternatively, we could standardize our measures of shape. This realization led to our definition of $\hat{\alpha}_1$ and $\hat{\alpha}_2$, the standardized third and fourth moments. We discovered that we could either standardize the variables and then calculate the higher moments, or we could standardize the higher moments themselves. In either case, standardization was important for the measurement of shape. We have a similar problem here.

Let us define

$$x_i^{st} = \frac{x_i - \bar{x}}{\sqrt{m_2(x)}}$$

$$y_i^{st} = \frac{y_i - \bar{y}}{\sqrt{m_2(y)}}$$

where the superscript st on the variables x and y reminds us that these variables have been standardized; that is, we have subtracted the mean and then divided by the square root of the second moment. Both x_i^{st} and y_i^{st} have means of zero and second moments of one. Further, and more important for our purposes at this time, is that the standardized variables are invariant to changes in origin and scale of the original variables. With standardized variables we can be sure that any measure of shape that we derive will represent the shape of the scatter plot and will not be an artifact of the choice of units of measurement.

Now let us use these standardized variables to examine the shape of distributions for pairs of random variables. First, compare Figures 5.2 and 5.6. The former figure is for the original data, and the second is for the standardized variables. In Figure 5.6 the mean values are zero for both variables, and the second moments are both one. These two graphs look very similar because the sophisticated graphing routine used to set up the axes here essentially allows for changes in both origin and scale. Careless graphing procedures might well lead to a misleading picture. Nevertheless, we will see a little later that even when we see little difference in the shape, the use of standardized variables is a great help. Beginning with Figure 5.3, the remaining figures were all plotted with the standardized variables. From these few figures we have a clear visual impression of at least one aspect of a "statistical relationship" between random variables: There seems to be a roughly positive association between the midterm and final grades (Figure 5.6), a roughly negative relationship between mpg and weights of cars (Figure 5.4), and apparently no relationship between IQ and height (Figure 5.5).

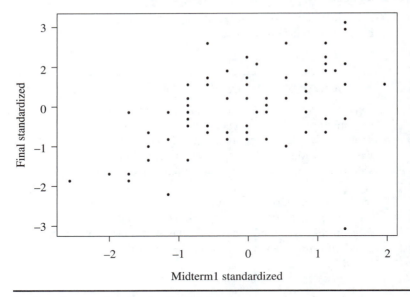

Figure 5.6   Scatter diagram for standardized data

In looking at Figures 5.2 and 5.6, one small, but important point may have been lost. We have not plotted any grade in one class with any grade in the other class, only those grades earned by the same person. Similarly with the other variables that we plotted, in each case the two variables were "related" by having the same individual in common for each pair of observations. This will always be true; that is, we will only plot pairs of observations that have a common "referent." The common referent may be the same individual, the same machine, or merely that the pairs of observations were observed at the same time. You can easily see that if we did not restrict our attention in this way that it would be unlikely that we would observe any shape for pairs of random variables.

Try this experiment. Consider the same midterm and final grades earned in the class, except that the order of the midterm grades is alphabetized by student names and the order of the final grades is that in which the students handed in their examination papers. The variables are plotted in Figure 5.7. Now we see no shape at all; in fact, this plot looks a little like that in Figure 5.5. This is because the "relationship" that existed between the two grades has been lost, and that relationship was created through the fact that each pair of grades represented a pair of characteristics for a single individual.

5.6   Covariation and m_{11}, the First Cross Product Moment

Like our box-and-whisker plots, our scatter plots are useful visually but not if you want to transmit that information to someone else. We still have to refine the idea of shape if we are to be able to measure it. Look back at Figures 5.3 to 5.6. In each of these figures, the plots are centered at zero; this is because the standardized variables

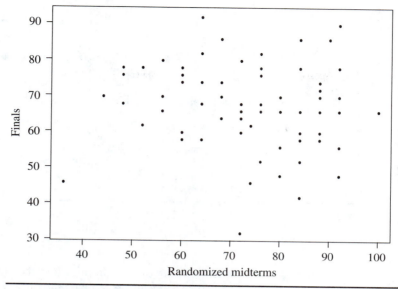

Figure 5.7   Scatter diagram: Final grades on randomized midterms

have zero means. In Figures 5.3 and 5.6, the points drift upward from lower left to upper right, whereas in Figure 5.4, the points drift downward from upper left to lower right, and in Figure 5.5, there is no drift at all.

Let us try to refine this notion of "drift." To simplify the discussion, label the variable on the horizontal axis in Figure 5.6, *x,* and the variable on the vertical axis, *y.* Now for an interval around each of several values of the variable *x*—say, $x_1, x_2, x_3, \ldots$—plot a box-and-whisker plot of the corresponding *y* values (see Figure 5.8).

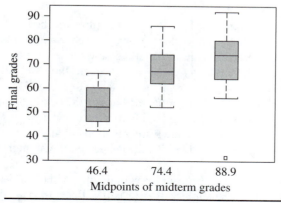

Figure 5.8   Box-and-whisker plots for NYU grades

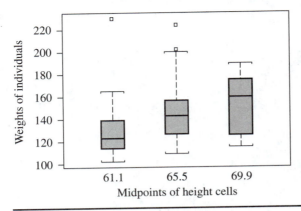

Figure 5.9   Box-and-whisker plots for weights given height

We are calculating box-and-whisker plots to discover how the distribution of y_i varies as we vary the value of x_i. The idea is to compare the final grades of students that all had approximately the same midterm grade with students that all had a different, but similar, midterm grade. In Figure 5.8 the midterm data were divided into three groups of low, medium, and high grades; the midpoints of these groups are 46.4, 74.4, and 88.9. The first box-and-whisker plot centered at $x_1 = 46.4$ is for all the final grades for students who had low midterms with a midpoint value of 46.4 in normal units. The last plot is for those students who had high midterm grades with a midpoint value of 88.9.

We see in Figure 5.8 that as we consider higher values for midterm grades, the distribution for the final grades moves up; the box-and-whisker plots are centered at higher median points. Although there is considerable overlap between the box-and-whisker plots, there is still a most noticeable increase in the "average position" of the plots. Another way to express this fact is to note that a reasonably straight line can be drawn through the medians, and that line through the medians has an upward slope.

In Figure 5.9, we plotted the box-and-whisker plots for the height and weight data. The line through the medians also slopes upward, even though there is considerable overlap between the plots. This result is telling us what we all know from long experience: there are short and tall heavy people and there are short and tall thin people, but on average the distribution of weight moves up the scale when we observe taller people.

If we were to draw a line through the medians of the box-and-whisker plots for the mpg and car weight data in Figure 5.10, it would be downward sloping. In this figure we observe something else that is interesting and potentially useful; the range and the second moments of the distributions of mileage decrease with higher values for the weight variable.

Last, if we were to repeat the exercise with the IQ and height data, we would observe that the line of medians in Figure 5.11 is flat. Except for the one outlier observation in the first box-and-whisker plot the ranges and spreads are similar.

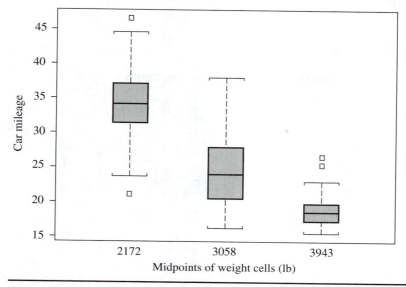

Figure 5.10   Box-and-whisker plots for car mileage (mpg) given car weight

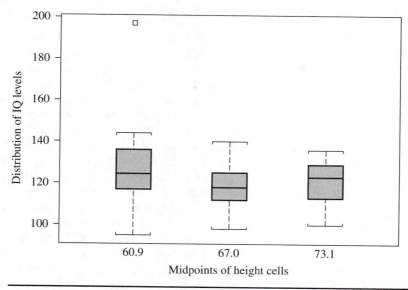

Figure 5.11   Box-and-whisker plots for IQ given height cells

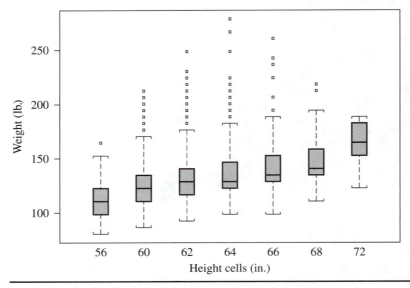

Figure 5.12   Box-and-whisker plots for weights given heights in cells

A more realistic example is provided by the data stored in the folder Xfiles, sub-folder Misc, file Htwtkst.xls, where the heights and weights of 4995 women were recorded in Britain in 1951. In Figure 5.12, we plotted the box-and-whisker plots for weights given seven classes of heights. Notice two aspects of the plots. First, the line of medians slopes upward in a nearly straight line; this we have seen before. In addition, the distribution of weights changes quite dramatically over the range of heights. The range of weights at the ends of the height range are much less, and the occurrence of large outliers is much greater for the intermediate heights than it is for either very small or very large heights. Similar plots could also have been carried out using weights as the "conditioning" variable and examining how the distribution of heights varied given weights.

In these examples, we plotted the box-and-whisker plots for the y variable given intervals of values for the x variable. We could have done the opposite; that is, we could have plotted the box-and-whisker plots for the x variable given intervals of values for the y variable. Except for exchanging the roles of x and y there would be no other effect, and the interpretation would be the same. There is in this discussion no idea of "causality"; we have merely related the distribution, or histogram, of one random variable to another and we can equally well carry out the relationship the other way around.

We now have an important indicator of shape for bivariate data, the slope of the approximating line through the medians. This line may be upward sloping, downward sloping, or flat. We could improve on our indicator by measuring the degree of slope of the approximating line.

However, you may remember that the median is not sensitive to variations in the data that do not change the number of data points either side of the median. For a measure of shape we want something that is sensitive to variations in the values of the data. Our previous solution was to average the values of the variable, but here we have two variables.

Consider Figure 5.6 again. Positive values of the standardized variable y tend to be associated with positive values of the standardized variable x; and negative values of y tend to be associated with negative values of x. In both cases, the product of x and y will be positive more often than not. If we were to average the products, we would expect to get a positive result. The opposite situation prevails with the data in Figure 5.4. In this figure positive values of the standardized x tend to be associated with negative values of the standardized y, and negative values of x tend to be associated with positive values of y. The result is that the products are usually negative. Consequently, if we were to average the products in this case, we would expect to get a negative value. Finally, in Figure 5.5, positive values of the standardized x are associated with both negative and positive values of the standardized y, and similarly for the negative values of x; so we would expect to get a small value for the average of the products of x and y, if not actually zero.

If this intuition proves to be reasonable, we can now attempt a definition of a measure of shape for bivariate data. Let us define m_{11}, the **first cross product moment** of the standardized variables x_i^{st} and y_i^{st} by

$$m_{11}(x^{st}, y^{st}) = N^{-1} \sum x_i^{st} y_i^{st} \tag{5.1}$$

By recalling how we defined x_i^{st} and y_i^{st}, we see that $m_{11}(x^{st}, y^{st})$ can be rewritten as

$$m_{11}(x^{st}, y^{st}) = N^{-1} \frac{\sum (x_i - \bar{x})(y_i - \bar{y})}{\sqrt{m_2(x)}\sqrt{m_2(y)}} \tag{5.2}$$

because $\bar{x}^{st}$ and $\bar{y}^{st}$ are both zero, and the definitions of x_i^{st} and y_i^{st} are

$$x_i^{st} = \frac{x_i - \bar{x}}{\sqrt{m_2(x)}}$$

$$y_i^{st} = \frac{y_i - \bar{y}}{\sqrt{m_2(y)}}$$

The name "first cross product moment" is a mouthful, but the idea underlying it should be intuitively clear. All we have done is to extend the idea that was used repeatedly in Chapter 4; we averaged. What is different in this case is that here we have averaged the products of two different, but related, random variables, instead of averaging the powers of a single random variable. Compare Equation 5.1 with the equation for the second moment, Equation 4.4. If y and x are the same variable, Equation 5.1 would give us the second moment, m_2, of the common variable, divided by m_2, to give 1 as a result.

We have postulated that the average of the products of the standardized variables for upward sloping median lines will be positive, negative for downward sloping lines, and approximately zero for flat lines. The "sign" of the first cross product moment should match the "sign" of the slope; and if we are lucky the magnitude of m_{11} will indicate the degree of slope that we observe.

Recall from Chapter 4 that we could calculate moments from standardized variables, or we could standardize the moments. The same situation applies here. In Equations 5.1 and 5.2 we have calculated m_{11} using the standardized variables, but we could as easily have calculated the first cross product moment using the original variables and then standardized the result. Let's see how this approach would work.

First, following our conventions about the symbols for moments, we note that m_{11} has no "prime," so that one would guess that this moment is being calculated about the means; that is so. (Recall the general definition of moments in Section 4.5; in particular, examine Equations 4.6 and 4.7.) If we write out the first cross product moment in terms of the original variables, we get

$$m_{11}(x, y) = N^{-1} \sum (x_i - \bar{x})(y_i - \bar{y}) \tag{5.3}$$

Equation 5.3 defines the **covariance** of the variables x and y; the covariance between two variables is nothing more than the **first cross product moment (about the means).** The covariance is the averaged product of the differences between each variable and its mean. Covariance is easier to say and does summarize the idea that we are looking at co-variation; but the first cross product moment term emphasizes that this measure of shape is an extension of all the work that we did in Chapter 4. Everything that we said about moments in that chapter applies to the first cross product moment.

We need to consider the effects of rescaling the variables in Equation 5.3. A little reflection will soon convince you that if you were to rescale either x or y, the result would be to rescale the value of m_{11} proportionately; to see this, merely substitute $b \times x$ or $a \times y$ into Equation 5.3 for any constants a or b. To eliminate this dependence on rescaling of the variables, we can follow our previous approach in standardizing random variables; divide by the square root of the second moment. However, in this case we have two second moments, $m_2(x)$ and $m_2(y)$, so we will have to divide by the square root of both of them. The standardized first cross product moment is

$$\frac{m_{11}(x, y)}{\sqrt{m_2(x)}\sqrt{m_2(y)}} = N^{-1} \frac{\sum (x - \bar{x})(y - \bar{y})}{\sqrt{m_2(x)}\sqrt{m_2(y)}} \tag{5.4}$$

$$= m_{11}(x^{st}, y^{st})$$

Equation 5.4 is nothing more than Equation 5.2 rewritten. Consequently, we conclude that m_{11} defined with respect to standardized variables is the same as the covariance between two variables that is standardized by dividing by the square root of the product of the two second moments. We conclude that $m_{11}(x, y)$ standardized is the same as m_{11} defined with respect to the standardized variables.

Consider the following four examples to see how to do the calculations. However, before examining the results, graph each pair of variables by hand; a simple sketch will do.

(a) $x = -1, 0, 1$

$y = 1.2, 1.8, 3.0$

$\bar{x} = 0; \bar{y} = 2$

$m_2(x) = \dfrac{2}{3} = 0.67; m_2(y) = \dfrac{1.68}{3} = 0.56$

$\sqrt{m_2(x)} = 0.819; \sqrt{m_2(y)} = 0.748$

$x_i^{st} = \dfrac{x_i - \bar{x}}{\sqrt{m_2(x)}}, y_i^{st} = \dfrac{y_i - \bar{y}}{\sqrt{m_2(y)}}$

$x_i^{st} = -1.22, 0, 1.22$

$y_i^{st} = -1.07, -0.27, 1.34$

$m_{11}(x^{st}, y^{st}) = N^{-1} \sum x_i^{st} y_i^{st}$

$= \dfrac{1}{3}((1.22 \times 1.07) + (0.0 \times -0.27) + (1.22 \times 1.34))$

$= \dfrac{1}{3}(1.31 + 0.0 + 1.63)$

$= \dfrac{2.94}{3}$

$= .98$

(b) $x = 2, 4, 9$

$y = 10, 5, 0$

$\bar{x} = 5; \bar{y} = 5$

$m_2(x) = \dfrac{26}{3} = 8.67; \sqrt{m_2(x)} = 2.94$

$m_2(y) = \dfrac{50}{3} = 16.67; \sqrt{m_2(y)} = 4.08$

$x_i^{st} = -1.02, -0.34, 1.36$

$y_i^{st} = 1.22, 0.0, -1.22$

$m_{11}(x^{st}, y^{st}) = N^{-1} \sum x_i^{st} y_i^{st}$

$= \dfrac{1}{3}((-1.02 \times 1.22) + (-0.34 \times 0.0) + (1.36 \times -1.22))$

$= \dfrac{1}{3}(-1.24 + 0.0 + -1.66)$

$= \dfrac{-2.9}{3}$

$= -.96$

(c) $x = -1, 0, 1$

$y = 3, 0, 3$

$\bar{x} = 0; \bar{y} = 2$

$m_2(x) = \dfrac{2}{3} = 0.67; \sqrt{m_2(x)} = 0.819$

$m_2(y) = \dfrac{6}{3} = 2.0; \sqrt{m_2(y)} = 1.414$

$x_i^{st} = -1.22, 0, 1.22$

$y_i^{st} = 0.71, -1.41, 0.71$

$m_{11}(x^{st}, y^{st}) = N^{-1} \sum x_i^{st} y_i^{st}$

$= \dfrac{1}{3}((-1.22 \times 0.71) + (0.0 \times -1.41) + (1.22 \times 0.71))$

$= \dfrac{1}{3}(-0.87 + 0.0 + 0.87)$

$= \dfrac{0}{3}$

$= 0$

(d) $x = -1, 0, 1$

$y = 1, 2, 3$

$\bar{x} = 0; \bar{y} = 2$

$m_2(x) = \dfrac{2}{3} = 0.67; \sqrt{m_2(x)} = 0.819$

$m_2(y) = \dfrac{2}{3} = 0.67; \sqrt{m_2(y)} = 0.819$

$x_i^{st} = -1.225, 0, 1.225$

$y_i^{st} = -1.225, 0, 1.225$

$m_{11}(x^{st}, y^{st}) = N^{-1} \sum x_i^{st} y_i^{st}$

$= \dfrac{1}{3}((-1.225 \times -1.225) + (0 \times 0) + (1.225 \times 1.225))$

$= \dfrac{1}{3}(1.50 + 0 + 1.50)$

$= \dfrac{3.00}{3}$

$= 1.0$

5.7   Linear Statistical Relationships and the Correlation Coefficient

We can now define the concept of a **linear statistical relationship.** Two random variables, x and y, are linearly related statistically if $m_{11}(x, y)$ is not zero. If m_{11} is greater than zero, the linear statistical relationship is positive; and if m_{11} is less than zero, the linear statistical relationship is negative. If m_{11} is zero, then there is no linear statistical relationship. In our four examples, the first showed a positive relationship, the second a negative relationship, the third, no relationship, and the fourth, a positive relationship of nearly one; m_{11} equal to one is a special result to be discussed in a moment.

The first cross product moment, m_{11} between standardized variables, is so useful and widely used that it has its own symbol, r, and its own special name, the **correlation coefficient.** Because we defined the correlation coefficient in terms of standardized variables, we know that it does not depend on the units of measurement of the original variables used to define it. If we start with any two variables, x and y, then the value taken by the correlation coefficient is the same no matter what the original units of measurement, or how we might remeasure them.

At this juncture it is useful to remind ourselves of the unifying idea that underlies all our moment calculations: We are averaging products, or powers, over the data values. In the first moment about the origin, $\bar{x}$, we average the values of the raw data; with the second moment, m_2, we average the squares of the differences from the mean; with the higher moments we average the higher powers of the differences from the mean; and finally with the first cross product moment, m_{11}, we are averaging the products of the data. Averaging for N terms, whatever those N terms might be, is quite simply: "add up and divide by N." The different measures of shape that we obtain are due to the different powers or products that are averaged.

Now that we have a useful measure of shape for bivariate data, let us see how r, the correlation coefficient, can be used to gain information about actual variables.

First, let us reconsider the data on student grades; what is the correlation between midterm and final grades? The value of r that we obtain is approximately .5:

$$m_{11}(\text{midterm1, final score}) = N^{-1} \sum (x_i - \bar{x})(y_i - \bar{y})$$

$$= 79.88$$

$$m_2(\text{midterm1}) = N^{-1} \sum (x_i - \bar{x})^2$$

$$= 196.50$$

$$\sqrt{m_2} = 14.02$$

$$m_2(\text{final score}) = N^{-1} \sum (y_i - \bar{y})^2$$

$$= 132.00$$

$$\sqrt{m_2} = 11.50$$

so that

$$r = \frac{m_{11}}{\sqrt{m_2(x)}\sqrt{m_2(y)}}$$

$$= \frac{79.88}{(14.02)(11.50)}$$

$$= .495$$

From this result, we see that although we cannot in any way predict final grades from midterm grades, it is true that the higher the midterm score, the higher the mean or median of the final score.

In contrast, consider the correlation for the height and weight data shown in Figures 5.3 and 5.9; the value for r is .26, a much lower figure, but still a positive statistical relationship. Another example is provided by the mpg and car weight data shown in Figures 5.4 and 5.10. Here, as expected, we get a negative value of $-.83$ for r. So, although mpg cannot be predicted by car weight, we can say that the location of the distribution of mpg is lowered as car weight increases and that the relationship is a strong one.

If we calculate the correlation coefficient for the height and IQ data, we do not get zero as we might have expected from our examination of the scatter plots but a negative value of $-.14$. Although r in this case is not zero, it is clearly not a very strong relationship; its value is much closer to zero than either of the other r values that we have examined.

However, these examples do raise a serious question that we will have to address sooner or later: how do we decide what is a small and what is a large value of r? The tools we have developed so far are no help in answering this question. At the moment, we have to rely on our own judgment, and each person's judgment as to what is large or small can differ substantially.

We are now beginning to see that we should develop a theory of histograms and their shapes to be able to provide more objective answers to such questions. Before we pursue that challenging task, let us explore the properties of our measure r, the correlation coefficient, a little more.

What we have observed so far seems to indicate that r may be bounded by -1 and 1; at least we have not yet seen any examples of r values outside that range, and we did see one example of $r = 1$. Let's explore that example, (d). Recall the values of the variables:

$$x = -1, 0, 1$$
$$y = 1, 2, 3$$

If you were to plot x and y, you would observe that

$$y_i = 2 + 1 \times x_i$$

or

$$y_i = a + b \times x_i$$

where $a = 2$ and $b = 1$.

Writing the relationship between x and y in this way suggests that there is a general statement that we can make. Recall that r can be expressed directly in terms of the values of x_i and of y_i as in Equation 5.4. Because $y_i = a + bx_i$, we can easily show that

$$\bar{y} = a + b\bar{x}$$
$$y_i - \bar{y} = b \times (x_i - \bar{x})$$
$$\bar{y} = \frac{\sum y_i}{N} = \frac{\sum(a + bx_i)}{N}$$
$$= \frac{(Na + b\sum x_i)}{N}$$
$$= a + b\bar{x}$$

so that

$$y_i - \bar{y} = a + bx_i - [a + b\bar{x}]$$
$$= b(x_i - \bar{x})$$

From these relations by substituting $b(x_i - \bar{x})$ for $(y_i - \bar{y})$ into the definitions of $m_2(y)$ and $m_{11}(x, y)$, we derive

$$m_2(y) = b^2 \times m_2(x)$$
$$N^{-1}\sum(x_i - \bar{x})(y_i - \bar{y}) = b \times N^{-1}\sum(x_i - \bar{x})^2$$
$$= bm_2(x)$$

By substituting these relationships into Equation 5.4, we obtain

$$r = \frac{m_{11}(x, y)}{\sqrt{m_2(x)}\sqrt{m_2(y)}}$$
$$= \frac{bm_2(x)}{\sqrt{m_2(x)}\sqrt{b^2 m_2(y)}} \tag{5.5}$$
$$= \frac{b}{\sqrt{b^2}}$$
$$= \pm 1$$

So if $y_i = a + b \times x_i$ and b is positive, $r = 1$; and if b is negative, then $r = -1$. The correlation coefficient, r, is therefore a measure of linear association; it takes the extreme values of $+1$ or -1 when y and x are functionally linearly related—that is, when $y_i = a + bx_i$. Otherwise the value of r is between -1 and 1.

Suppose that

$$y_i = bx_i + e_i \tag{5.6}$$

and that the e_i are errors about the values given by bx_i. Further, we might as well make life simple by assuming that $\bar{e}$ and $\bar{x}$ are both zero, which implies immediately that $\bar{y}$ is also zero. Let us also assume that our errors are not related to the x variable, so that $\sum x_i e_i \approx 0$; that is, $\sum x_i e_i$ is approximately zero. The idea of these specifications is that y is not quite a linear function of x. The smaller the variation in e_i, the closer y_i is to being a linear function of x_i. In the language of Chapter 2, the variables y and x are in a "structural relationship" to each other.

The question that we want to pursue is what can we say about the value of r? Further, if the degree of variation of the e_i is increased relative to the degree of variation of the x_i, what happens to the value of r? As we weaken the strength of the functional linear relationship, what happens to the value of r?

Recall Equation 5.3, which defines covariance:

$$m_{11}(x, y) = N^{-1} \sum (x - \bar{x})(y - \bar{y})$$

Substitute Equation 5.6 into Equation 5.3, and remember that $\bar{x}$ and $\bar{y}$ are both zero, to get

$$m_{11}(x, y) = \frac{b \sum x^2}{N} + \frac{\sum xe}{N}$$

$$= \frac{b \sum x^2}{N}$$

$$= bm_2(x)$$

where we rely on our assumption that $\sum x_i e_i \approx 0$.

We now derive the second moments for x and y. The second moment for x is the same as before, but that for y is now a little different:

$$m_2(y) = \frac{\left[b^2 \sum x^2 + \sum e^2 \right]}{N}$$

$$= \left[\frac{b^2 \sum x^2}{N} \right] \left[1 + \frac{\sum e^2}{\left(b^2 \sum x^2 \right)} \right] \tag{5.7}$$

$$= b^2 m_2(x) \left[\frac{1 + m_2(e)}{b^2 m_2(x)} \right]$$

where we have extracted the value $b^2 \sum x^2 / N = b^2 m_2(x)$ from inside the bracket. The second moment of e is $m_2(e)$; because e is zero, $m_2(e) = \sum e^2 / N$.

Our definition of r is:

$$r = \frac{m_{11}(x, y)}{\sqrt{m_2(x)} \sqrt{m_2(y)}}$$

$$= \frac{bm_2(x)}{\sqrt{b^2 m_2(x)} \sqrt{\left[1 + \frac{m_2(e)}{b^2 m_2(x)} \right]} \sqrt{m_2(x)}} \tag{5.8}$$

$$= \frac{(+/-)1}{\sqrt{\left[1 + \frac{m_2(e)}{b^2 m_2(x)} \right]}}$$

Forgetting the sign for the moment, this last expression is just 1 divided by the square root of a term that is bigger than 1, because $\sum e^2/(b^2 \sum x^2) = m_2(e)/b^2 m_2(x)$ is positive, except when all the e_i are zero. The square root of a term that is bigger than 1 is itself bigger than 1, so that r must lie between -1 and 1, depending on the sign of b. The bigger the size of $m_2(e)$ relative to that of $m_2(x)$ the less the value for the correlation coefficient, r, for any value of b. Conversely, if the size of $m_2(e)$ is very small, the relationship approaches that of a linear functional relationship, and the correlation coefficient approaches 1.

We now see that r, the correlation coefficient, is a measure of linear association in that its values lie between -1 and 1; it takes the extreme values of -1 and 1 only when there is an exact linear functional relationship between the two variables. When the relationship is a structural one, in that we can only relate the distribution of one of the variables to values given by the other variable, then the value of r is between -1 and 1. This sort of relationship we called "structural" in Chapter 2; one of the variables affects the distribution of the other. This aspect of the statistical relationship we saw very clearly in the box-and-whisker plots in Figures 5.8 to 5.12. The larger the degree of variation of the "errors" relative to the variation of the variable x, the smaller is the observed value of r and the less the distribution of either variable is dependent on the other.

The first limiting case is a functional relationship, so the variation of the errors is 0 and r is ± 1. The second limiting case is where the variation of the errors is much, much greater than that for the x_i, or equivalently, the coefficient b is 0, so that r is 0. We now see that we can interpret r as a standardized measure of the slope of a line between y_i and x_i after allowance for the presence of errors in the relationship—that is, after allowing for the fact that we may only have a structural relationship, not a functional one.

Look again at Figures 5.8 to 5.12, which show the box-and-whisker plots of values of one variable against given values of the other. Notice in Figure 5.10, which shows the plots for car mileage (mpg) and weight, that given the value of the x variable chosen, say $x_2 = 3058$ pounds, the plot of the y variable, mpg, is just like a box-and-whisker plot for any other random variable. So given that particular value of x we are still not able to predict a particular value of y, but we can say something about the histogram of y given that value of x. Thus, when $x_2 = 3058$ pounds, we know that the median of the distribution of mileage is 23, that the range of the standardized mileage is approximately 22, and so on. Further, if we look at different values of x in Figure 5.10, we see how the medians of the distributions of y change, how the range changes, and so on. These observations are even more striking for the plots in Figure 5.12 relating heights and weights. In short, what our linear statistical relationship tells us is how the histogram, or distribution of y, changes as we consider different values of x.

However, as we have already noted, we could as easily have plotted the values of car weights for given values of car mileage, or student heights for given weights. In short, whether we look at distributions for y for given values of x or we look at distributions for x for given values of y is immaterial to the analysis; the value of the correlation coefficient will be the same. This should be clear from the very definition of r, in which the roles of x and of y are completely interchangeable.

These comments should convince you that the structural relationship that we are discussing is not a causal one. If the correlation coefficient between x and y is r_0, then the correlation coefficient between y and x is also r_0. Given that we are discussing relationships between random variables, we do not expect to find causal relationships in any case.

5.8 The Correlation Coefficient and Slope

From our analysis of the case where y was a linear function of x, we saw that

$$m_{11}(x, y) = bm_2(x)$$

so we may solve for b to get

$$b = \frac{m_{11}(x, y)}{m_2(x)} \tag{5.9}$$

This b is the slope coefficient for the linear relationship between y and x and is in "units of y" per "units of x." This agrees with the fact that $m_{11}(x, y)$ is a product of x and y and therefore is in "units of x and y." We have already discovered $m_2(x)$ is in "units of x^2." Consequently, the ratio of m_{11} and m_2 is also in "units of y" per "unit of x."

The correlation coefficient was obtained by using the first cross product moment on the standardized variables. Presumably, there is a link between b, the slope coefficient between the original data, and the correlation coefficient, which is the slope between the standardized variables (as shown in Equation 5.8). Might it not be true that if we rescale the definition of b given in Equation 5.8 by multiplying by the appropriate ratio of $\sqrt{m_2(x)}/\sqrt{m_2(y)}$, we will discover that the standardized slope is in fact the correlation coefficient, r? It is, as we see in Equation 5.10:

$$b\left[\frac{\sqrt{m_2(x)}}{\sqrt{m_2(y)}}\right] = \left[\frac{m_{11}(x, y)}{m_2(x)}\right]\left[\frac{\sqrt{m_2(x)}}{\sqrt{m_2(y)}}\right]$$

$$= \frac{m_{11}(x, y)}{\sqrt{m_2(x)}\sqrt{m_2(y)}} \tag{5.10}$$

$$= r$$

If we can solve for b, the slope coefficient, exactly when there is a functional linear relationship, as in Equation 5.9, might we not use the same equation as an approximation when the relationship is structural? Indeed we can, and the analysis that we have already performed enables us to evaluate how good, or bad, that relationship is. Recall Equation 5.6, which defined y in terms of a structural relationship with the variable x. Substitute that definition for y into the expression for b given in Equation 5.9 to define

$$\hat{b} = \frac{m_{11}(x, y)}{m_2(x)} \tag{5.11}$$

We use the symbol $\hat{b}$ to indicate that we are defining an approximation to the parameter b as defined by Equation 5.9 when there is an exact functional relationship. As before to keep life simple, let $\bar{x} = \bar{e} = a = 0$, so that $y = bx_i + e_i$. We derive

$$\frac{m_{11}(x, y)}{m_2(x)} = \frac{\dfrac{\sum x_i y_i}{N}}{m_2(x)}$$

$$= \frac{\dfrac{\sum x_i(bx_i + e_i)}{N}}{m_2(x)}$$

(5.12)

$$= \frac{bm_2(x) + m_{11}(x, e)}{m_2(x)}$$

$$= b + \frac{m_{11}(x, e)}{m_2(x)}$$

In this last equation, $m_{11}(x, e)$ is the covariance between x and the error terms, e_i, which we originally assumed was approximately zero. To the extent that this assumption is true, the equation $b = m_{11}(x, y)/m_2(x)$ produces a good approximation to the value of b; and to the extent that this assumption is not true, the approximation to the value of b is not good. What constitutes a "small" or a "large" value for $m_{11}(x, e)$ depends on the size of $m_2(x)$. The assumption is really about the size of $m_{11}(x, e)$ relative to that of $m_2(x)$. Later, we will see that this approximation is the best that we can do.

We discussed the implication for $m_{11}(x, y)$ when the slope coefficient between x and y is not zero; so far the answer is that when b is nonzero, so is $m_{11}(x, y)$. This is not necessarily always true as the next example shows. Look at Figure 5.13, which shows 150 observations from the equation

$$x(t) = \begin{cases} 2x(t-1) & \text{if} \quad x(t) \leq 0.5 \\ 2 - 2x(t-1) & \text{if} \quad x(t) > 0.5 \end{cases}$$

(5.13)

Note that the slope between $x(t)$ and $x(t-1)$ for $x(t-1)$ less than 0.5 is 2 but that for $x(t-1)$ greater than 0.5 the slope is -2. Intuitively, you can see that the "average slope" over the whole range of the function, which will be generated by enough observations on the function, will be approximately zero. In the data set, in the folder Xfiles, subfolder Misc, filename Tent.xls, there are 598 observations on just such a function called a "Tent function." In the exercises to follow you will be asked to investigate this function and to calculate the correlation coefficient for the observed data.

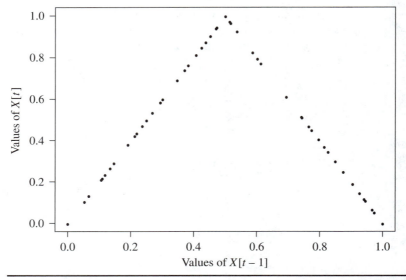

Figure 5.13   Time series plot of $X[t]$ on $X[t-1]$ for the Tent function. 150 observations generated.

5.9   Rank Correlation

So far, we have restricted our attention to cardinal variables—that is, variables for which we can compare differences and decide whether one difference is greater than another. This type of variable can be contrasted with variables that have only an ordinal measurement. As we recall from Chapter 2, with ordinal measurements we cannot compare differences as with cardinal measurements. One common way in which ordinal measurements are obtained is to replace the actual measurements by their ranks. The largest observation has a rank of 1, the next largest a rank of 2, and so on. One example is the data in the folder Xfiles, subfolder Misc, in the file Rock.xls, in which we recorded not the actual sales of rock songs but their rankings. Sometimes all we can measure are the ranks; for example, in stating preferences, one has only rankings: the most preferred item has a rank of 1, the next a rank of 2, and so on. Can we adapt our correlation results to those situations in which we have rankings, or ordinal, but not cardinal measurements? Such an extension would be most useful.

Before proceeding, we should recognize that if we actually have the cardinal measurements, we are best advised to use them rather than the associated rankings. This is because we clearly lose information in switching from cardinal to ordinal measurements. We will demonstrate the loss of information in some exercises.

Let us consider that we have two variables, say *car mpg* and *car weight,* as reported in the data folder Xfiles, subfolder Misc, file Cardata.xls; or we could consider the midterm and final grades of NYU students in the same folder. We have already considered the correlation between these two pairs of variables and have calculated their correlation coefficients. Let us consider what happens when we replace the actual figures with the corresponding ranks. We will examine as well the sales and the airtime for rock tunes that are recorded in Rock.xls in terms of ranks only.

Given that we have pairs of variables that are ordinal—that is, we have rankings only—can we measure the degree of association between them? The answer is, not surprisingly, yes; indeed the solution is almost obvious. In our formula for the correlation coefficient, why not try substituting for our cardinal measurements the ordinal rankings that we now have. Spearman did just that and thereby created what is called **Spearman's rank correlation coefficient.** Let the ranking of the mpg be denoted by s_i, $i = 1,2, \ldots , n$ and the ranking of weight by t_i, $i = 1,2, \ldots , n$. Similarly, we could define the ranking of the midterm grades by s_i, $i = 1,2, \ldots , n$ and the ranking of the final grades by t_i, $i = 1,2, \ldots , n$. Remember that the rankings for each variable must still refer to the same referent as was the case for the cardinal measurements. We define Spearman's rank correlation coefficient by

$$r_S = \frac{\sum s_i t_i - \left(\sum s_i \right) \left(\dfrac{\sum t_i}{N} \right)}{\sqrt{\sum s_i^2 - \dfrac{\left(\sum s_i \right)^2}{N}} \sqrt{\sum t_i^2 - \dfrac{\left(\sum t_i \right)^2}{N}}} \tag{5.14}$$

Look back to Equation 5.5 and recognize that the top line in 5.14 is nothing more than m_{11} for the rankings and the bottom line is the product of the square roots of m_2 for each ranking. In short, all that we have done is to substitute the rankings for the cardinal measurements that we used before. Because we are using rankings, there are some simplifications that we can use. Define d_i by $d_i = (s_i - t_i)$; that is, d_i is simply the difference in the rankings. Using d_i, we can rewrite r_S as

$$r_S = 1 - \frac{6 \sum d_i^2}{N(N^2 - 1)} \tag{5.15}$$

The "6" in this expression may be mysterious at first. But the answer lies in the fact that we have used the relationships

$$\sum s_i = \sum t_i = \frac{N(N + 1)}{2}$$

$$\sum s_i^2 = \sum t_i^2 = \frac{N(N + 1)(2N + 1)}{6}$$

After some tedious algebraic manipulation using these relationships and the definition of d_i, we can obtain Equation 5.15 from 5.14.

If we recall the data that we used as examples in the calculation of the correlation coefficients in Section 5.7, we can compare results using the ranks, instead of the actual values. First, we examined the midterm and final test scores of some NYU students and found a correlation of .495. Using our formula for Spearman's rank correlation coefficient as shown in Equation 5.14, we obtain .492, which is very close to the full correlation coefficient.

Using another example, we note that the value that we obtain for Spearman's rank correlation coefficient for the relationship between car mileage and weight is $-.83$, which is exactly what we obtained before. However, when we examine the Spearman's rank correlation coefficients for the relationship between student heights and weights and the correlation between IQ and heights, we get different results. In the former case, we obtain a value of .43, whereas the original number was .26, a substantial difference. In the latter case, we obtain $-.1035$, whereas before we obtained $-.138$, another noticeable difference. Nevertheless, between the two approaches all the results are similar, and some are remarkably close to each other. This would seem to lend some credence to our procedures.

Using an example for which we do not have the actual data, but only the ranks, consider the rank data on sales of rock songs in the folder Xfiles, subfolder Misc, in the file Rock.xls. The specific variables that we use to compare the relationship between sales and time on the air are *slsrank* and *airrank*. The value of Spearman's rank correlation coefficient is .29, which is much lower than expected.

5.10 Bivariate Categorical Data

In Chapter 3, we examined cases in which the data were in categories—for example, the number of students with different eye colors. We also recognized that sometimes we do not have the actual observations on a continuous, or a discrete, cardinal variable but merely recordings of the number of observations within a given interval, or cell. For example, the recording of blood pressure and age for the data in the folder Misc (in the file Bldpill.xls) is only in cells, or intervals, for each variable. In Chapter 3, we described such data by providing the frequency distribution of occurrence across the cells into which the data were divided.

In this section, we will explore ways to describe paired categorical data and look for the possibility of examining the data for some form of association between the variables. In the previous sections of this chapter, we have discussed at length the idea of "association" using pairs of cardinal variables and in the last section using pairs of ordinal data. We will now try to discover some form of association between pairs of categorical data.

Imagine that a survey has been taken and that each person has been asked whether they regard themselves as "conservative" or as "liberal." At the same interview, each person was also asked whether they favored Senator Bob Dole or then-President Bill Clinton as likely to win the next election. The sex of the interviewee was also recorded. Ignoring the sex of the interviewee for the moment, let us consider just the survey results. Each individual can be placed into one of four categories:

- Is conservative and favors Dole
- Is conservative and favors Clinton
- Is liberal and favors Dole
- Is liberal and favors Clinton

We can represent these data in a compact way by creating a two-by-two table, two rows for the conservative/liberal choice and two columns for the favor Dole or Clinton choice (see Table 5.2). Such a table is called a **contingency table.**

Table 5.2   **Contingency Table for Political Choices: The Data as Counts**

	Dole	Clinton
Conservative	24	8
Liberal	16	44

Table 5.3   **Political Choice Data: Row Comparisons and Entries in Relative Frequencies**

	Dole	Clinton	Row Totals
Conservative	.75	.25	32
Liberal	.27	.73	60

In Table 5.2, we see that 24 people declared themselves to be conservative and for Dole, whereas 44 people declared themselves to be liberal and for Clinton. What sort of information might we be able to extract from these data? We notice in the survey that more liberals were interviewed than were conservatives, 60 versus 32. Recall from our discussions in Chapter 3 that our examination of the data would be less confusing if we changed from absolute frequencies as are recorded in Table 5.2 to relative frequencies. But here we see that we have a choice. We can examine "row" relative frequencies, or we can examine "column" relative frequencies, or we can examine relative frequencies over the entire table—that is, over all four entries. What we choose to do depends on the questions that we ask.

Row Comparisons

Suppose we want to compare across the conservative/liberal distinction the support for Dole and Clinton using relative frequencies. We seek to answer such questions as whether a larger fraction of the conservative voters prefer Dole to Clinton as opposed to the liberal voters. So a natural way to pose this question is to divide each entry in Table 5.2 by its corresponding row total (see Table 5.3).

The entries in the body of Table 5.3 are relative frequencies in each *row*. The figure .75 in the cell "Conservative/Dole" is obtained by dividing the absolute frequency in that cell, 24, by the row total, 32. Similarly, the entry of .27 in the "Liberal/Dole" cell is obtained by dividing the absolute frequency, 16, by the row total of 60. Notice that each row's entries in Table 5.3 sum to 1; this is because each row is just like a table of relative frequencies (discussed in Chapter 3).

We observe immediately that each political group supports its own candidate by almost the same amount as is true for the other.

Sometimes authors prefer to present percentages instead of relative frequencies, so the entries in Table 5.3 would be as shown in Table 5.4.

However, one of the difficulties with presenting the data in percentages is that the row totals can provide useful information, but if only the percentages are given, this information is lost. For example in this case, the row totals in Table 5.3 tell us that

Table 5.4 **Political Choice Data: Row Comparisons and Entries in Percentages**

	Dole	Clinton	
Conservative	75	25	100
Liberal	27	73	100

Table 5.5 **Schematic Representation of Data in a Contingency Table**

	Category I.1	Category I.2
Category II.1	a	b
Category II.2	c	d

Table 5.6 **Schematic Representation of Row Comparisons: Entries in Relative Frequencies by Rows**

	Category I.1	Category I.2	Row Totals
Category II.1	$\frac{a}{a+b}$	$\frac{b}{a+b}$	$a+b$
Category II.2	$\frac{c}{c+d}$	$\frac{d}{c+d}$	$c+d$

nearly twice as many liberals as conservatives were interviewed. An immediate question here is whether there are twice as many liberals in the class of people selected for interview, or there was some sort of bias built into the survey procedure so that liberals were overrepresented. Presenting the totals provides another essential piece of information about how many people were involved in the survey. We already have some ideas from our experience from examining data in previous chapters that percentages based on a small number of observations are not likely to be as reliable as ones based on a large number of observations. Only with very large numbers of observations did the histograms in Chapter 3 begin to settle down to a consistent shape. Similarly, we suspect that the shape of our contingency table would require a lot of data to become consistent. By presenting the row and column totals we provide useful information, even if in the body of the table it is preferable for us to present the relative, rather than the absolute, frequencies.

What we have done can be clarified by presenting a schematic representation. Let the numbers of observations in each cell be represented by the letters a, b, c, and d, and assume that we have two categories. Table 5.5 presents the data in schematic form. In Table 5.5, there are a entries in the cell Category I.1/Category II.1 and d entries in the cell Category I.2/Category II.2, and so on. In Table 5.6, the data are reexpressed in terms of relative frequencies by rows. The row totals for the counts in each cell are presented in the last column. Obviously, rows in the body of the table add to 1, or 100, if one reexpresses the frequencies as percentages.

Table 5.7   **Political Choice Data: Column Comparisons and Entries in Relative Frequencies**

	Dole	Clinton
Conservative	$\frac{24}{40} = 0.60$	$\frac{8}{52} = 0.15$
Liberal	$\frac{16}{40} = 0.40$	$\frac{44}{52} = 0.85$
Column Total	40	52

Table 5.8   **Schematic Representation of Column Comparisons: Entries in Relative Frequencies**

	Dole	Clinton
Conservative	$\frac{a}{a+c}$	$\frac{b}{b+d}$
Liberal	$\frac{b}{a+c}$	$\frac{d}{b+d}$
Column Total	$a+c$	$b+d$

Column Comparisons

We have learned something about the differences and similarities of conservatives and liberals by comparing their choices for president. We could have as easily compared liberals and conservatives given their choice of president; that is, we could have examined the data by columns instead of by rows. The idea is similar; we are swapping rows for columns, and we proceed with exactly the same data. However, the question that we are asking is different. We are now asking: "For people, or objects, in Category I.1, what is the distribution of frequency across Category II, and how does that vary between Category I.1 and Category I.2?" Consider Table 5.7 for the political choice and political affiliation comparison in which the relative frequencies defined in terms of columns are presented.

From this latest table we see that by making column comparisons we learn some new facts about the survey respondents. Despite the imbalance between conservatives and liberals in the survey, there is not such an imbalance between those in the sample that are voting for Dole and those voting for Clinton. We note that of those voting for Dole, 60 percent are conservative; whereas among those voting for Clinton, 85 percent are liberals. Note that while we are using the same numbers we are doing so in a different way; actually we are asking different questions. In the first case with row comparisons, we implicitly asked: Given that you declare yourself to be conservative, or liberal, which candidate do you prefer? Now we are asking: Given that you prefer Dole, or Clinton, are you conservative, or liberal? In the first case, we are comparing conservatives and liberals; in the second case we are comparing Dole and Clinton supporters. We would get the same information from these two alternative ways of looking at the data if all conservatives are for Dole and all liberals are for Clinton; that is, in terms of our "algebraic notation," b and c are both zero.

Just as we created a schematic representation of the row comparisons, so we can make a schematic representation of the column comparisons as shown in Table 5.8.

Table 5.9   **Joint Comparisons: Entries in Relative Frequencies Based on Full Sample**

	Category I.1	Category I.2	Row Margins
Category II.1	$\frac{a}{n}$	$\frac{b}{n}$	$\frac{a+b}{n}$
Category II.2	$\frac{c}{n}$	$\frac{d}{n}$	$\frac{c+d}{n}$
Column Margins	$\frac{a+c}{n}$	$\frac{a+c}{n}$	$\frac{a+b+c+d}{n}=1$

Table 5.10   **Political Choice Data: Distribution of Joint Frequencies**

	Dole	Clinton	Row Margins
Conservative	$\frac{24}{92}=.26$	$\frac{8}{92}=.09$	$\frac{32}{92}=.35$
Liberal	$\frac{16}{92}=.17$	$\frac{44}{92}=.48$	$\frac{60}{92}=.65$
Column Margins	$\frac{40}{92}=.43$	$\frac{52}{92}=.57$	$\frac{92}{92}=1.00$

Joint Comparisons

We now consider the variation in cell counts relative to the total number of people surveyed. Let us begin with the schematic representation first, as that will immediately clarify what is being done.

Table 5.9 summarizes the most general situation. We define the total count in all cells as n; clearly $n = a + b + c + d$. We now have a third set of relative frequencies; these relative frequencies are relative to the total cell count in all cells. For example, in the cell Category II.2/Category I.1, the entry $\frac{c}{n}$ indicates that $100\frac{c}{n}\%$ of all the observations belong to this joint cell. Using this version of the problem we can compare each cell to the others. The results for our particular example are in Table 5.10.

We see immediately that 35 percent of this survey group label themselves conservative, but 43 percent favor Dole. There seems to be some sort of **association** between labeling oneself conservative and favoring Dole, or alternatively labeling oneself liberal and favoring Clinton. If there is no correlation between the categories liberal/conservative and favor Clinton/favor Dole, then knowing that someone is liberal (conservative) provides no information about the person's propensity to favor Clinton (Dole). Liberals are as likely to favor Dole as Clinton; the same is true of conservatives. Alternatively, if knowing that someone is a liberal (conservative) indicates a strong likelihood that he or she will favor Clinton (Dole), then there is a strong association between the two categories.

Maybe we could obtain some type of number that would represent the degree of association. In short, can we extend our ideas of association between variables that we developed in previous sections to the situation here? For example, one of the data sets that we have examined includes blood pressure groups and age groups. An immediate question is whether there is any "association" between the blood pressure cells and the age cells. In this case, because the cells can be ordered—that is, the cells for blood pressure can be ordered in terms of increasing blood pressure and the cells for age can also be ordered in terms of increasing age—we are close to having a situation similar to the bivariate ranks discussed in the previous section. Having a natural order to the cells provides more information than we had using the political choice data, because there was no meaningful way to order the preferences of conservative/liberal affiliation and which person is favored for president.

No matter how strong the association, that fact in itself provides no evidence for causality. I read somewhere that in Norway there is a strong association between the presence of storks and babies, that is, the relative frequency of the joint occurrence of babies and storks is very high. However, only the truly misinformed might interpret this fact as evidence of causality. An explanation that might reconcile the joint occurrence of storks and babies is that large numbers of babies implies large numbers of families with homes and therefore large numbers of chimneys in which storks nest.

Reconsider Table 5.8. If the two categories are not associated in any way, it would seem to be a reasonable idea that one way to express that notion is that column relative frequencies do not vary by row, or that row relative frequencies do not vary by column. What we are trying to do is to formalize the idea that if the proportion of people favoring Dole does not depend on whether one is conservative—or if the proportion of people that are conservative does not depend on whether one favors Dole—then the two classifications "conservative/liberal" and "favor Dole/favor Clinton" are not associated with each other. The two classifications are said to be **nonassociated, or independent.**

One way to express the independence of two classifications is

$$\frac{a}{a+b} = \frac{c}{c+d} \tag{5.16}$$

This is exactly equivalent to

$$\frac{b}{a+b} = \frac{d}{c+d}$$

because

$$\frac{b}{a+b} = 1 - \frac{a}{a+b}$$

and

$$\frac{d}{c+d} = 1 - \frac{c}{c+d}$$

The idea is that the proportion that a is of the first row should be the same proportion that c is of the second row. So to determine the relative frequency of Category I.1, it does not matter whether you also observe Category II.1, or Category II.2. In this sense, we can say that Category I and Category II are independent. We have defined independence by comparing relative frequencies in rows; we can derive the result that if Category I and Category II are independent by comparing rows, they are independent by comparing columns.

Equation 5.16 can be rewritten as

$$a(c + d) = c(a + b) \tag{5.17}$$

or

$$ad = cb$$

If we had begun with the idea of independence by examining columns we would have written

$$\frac{a}{a + c} = \frac{b}{b + d} \tag{5.18}$$

But this expression can also be rewritten as

$$a(b + d) = b(a + c) \tag{5.19}$$

or

$$ad = bc$$

and so we see that both criteria lead to the same equation; Equations 5.17 and 5.19 are the same. Note that the criterion says that the products of the two diagonals are equal for nonassociation to hold between any two categories.

If $ad \neq bc$, then we can agree that the categories are associated. This means that when two categories are associated—that is, we reject the idea of independence—we have the result that either $ad \geq bc$, or $ad \leq bc$. The difference is either positive or negative. If there is no order to the categories, then it is hard to interpret the sign; we decide merely whether the difference is very small, or not. For example, if our categories involve categories such as sex of respondent, hair color, did or did not vote, did or did not purchase an item, married, or unmarried, and so on, there is no useful meaning that we can attribute to the sign of the difference. We can always rearrange the categories to change the sign but leave the conclusion to be drawn intact.

However, if the categories are ordered, we want to interpret the sign. For example, using the blood pressure and age categories, we want to make sense of whether low blood pressure is associated with a young age and high blood pressure is associated with old age, or the reverse, low blood pressure is associated with old age and high blood pressure with a young age. In these circumstances the sign of the difference, $ad - bc$, can be used to choose between these two cases. The sign is important in this case because we cannot rearrange the order of either category without changing the interpretation of the categories; each has a unique agreed order of presentation.

If you recall the earlier discussion about the correlation coefficient, we realized that to investigate the shape of bivariate data we needed to allow for both location and scale; in short, we needed to standardize the data. When we defined the correlation coefficient we recognized the importance of a measure that did not depend on location and on scale of the units of measurement of the data. So here we have a similar problem; the size of the difference $ad - bc$ depends on the size of the survey that we have taken. Did we interview 90 people, or 900, or 9000? The size of $ad - bc$ depends on the answer, except in the unusual case where the difference is exactly zero. This discussion is, of course, just a repeat of the argument that we made when dis-

Table 5.11   **Joint Comparisons: Entries in Relative Frequencies Based on Full Sample**

	Category I.1	Category I.2	Row Margins
Category II.1	$\frac{a}{n}$	0	$\frac{a}{n}$
Category II.2	0	$\frac{d}{n}$	$\frac{d}{n}$
Column Margins	$\frac{a}{n}$	$\frac{d}{n}$	$\frac{a+d}{n} = 1$

Table 5.12   **Joint Comparisons: Entries in Relative Frequencies Based on Full Sample**

	Category I.1	Category I.2	Row Margins
Category II.1	0	$\frac{b}{n}$	$\frac{b}{n}$
Category II.2	$\frac{c}{n}$	0	$\frac{c}{n}$
Column Margins	$\frac{c}{n}$	$\frac{b}{n}$	$\frac{b+c}{n} = 1$

cussing the difference between absolute and relative frequencies in Chapter 3. Further, we want a measure that will be restricted to the interval $[-1, 1]$.

As it turns out, some careful, but inspired, manipulation of the terms involved reveals that if we define $\hat{\varphi}$, the **coefficient of association** for two-by-two contingency tables, as

$$\hat{\varphi} = \frac{ad - bc}{\sqrt{(a+b)(c+d)(a+c)(b+d)}} \tag{5.20}$$

we find that perfect association results in a value of $\hat{\varphi}$ that is ± 1, depending on the association between the two categories. We derived this result by noting that to get the bounds between ± 1 we need to rescale the observations by row and column totals. That we might need the square root as the numerator in Equation 5.20 involves the product of pairs and the product of all row and column totals requires a product of four terms. In the exercises, you will be asked to show that if we have the relationship shown in Table 5.11, the value for $\hat{\varphi}$ is 1, and that if we have the relationship shown in Table 5.12, the value of $\hat{\varphi}$ is -1. Of course, if $ad - bc$ is 0, then so is $\hat{\varphi}$. The symbol $\hat{\varphi}$ is the "correlation coefficient" for categorical data. You will be asked to demonstrate this relationship in the Exercises.

This entire discussion has been in terms of categories with only two subdivisions each. This was a matter of convenience to discuss the basic ideas. We can easily contemplate having two categories but where each has more than two subdivisions. Suppose that the question of party affiliation had been asked in Italy and each candidate for president had been listed; we would have two very large sets of divisions. Alternatively, suppose that one of the categories were levels of education, levels of income, a set of preferences for a group of products, or alternative colors, and so on. As you can see, the basic idea of association and its complement, independence, can be extended to these cases. The idea of independence is still the same: the categorical divisions by rows are independent of columns if the relative frequencies do not vary across columns; or, the alternative, categorical divisions by columns are independent of rows if the relative frequencies do not vary across rows. Some examples are explored in the Exercises.

Last, although we have restricted our attention to just two-by-two tables, we could have extended the ideas with another category. Recall our main political affiliation example where originally we said that the sex of the interviewee was recorded as well. In this case, we can visualize having two sets of two-by-two tables, one for each sex. This allows us to consider whether the relative frequencies over political affiliation and choice of candidate varies by the sex of the interviewee. In the Exercises, we will examine this issue a little further.

5.11   Summary

Bivariate data involve observations paired by having a single referent; that is, we have observations on two different characteristics of the same person, body, or object. By plotting the standardized variables, we were able to discover the shape of bivariate data very easily. We saw that the shape of bivariate data has either a general upward drift, a general downward drift, or no discernible drift at all. There is clearly no functional relationship between them, but the paired observations are not completely independent of each other.

The first question is what sort of "relationship" can we define for variables that are random; this chapter provides an answer. Essentially, our answer is to relate the distribution, or histogram, of one variable to the variable values of the other. This was shown by plotting a series of box-and-whisker plots for one variable at specified values for the other variable. The approximately straight line joining the medians of the box-and-whisker plots is either upward sloping, downward sloping, or no slope. In the first case, we would say that there is an approximately positive linear association between the two variables, in the second there is an approximately negative linear association, and in the last there is no linear association.

By combining our ideas about moments with these insights, we were able to define the *first cross product moment* of the standardized variables, $m_{11}(x^{st}, y^{st})$, as the average product of the standardized variables, x^{st} and y^{st} (see Equation 5.1). The first cross product moment of the unstandardized variables, $m_{11}(x, y)$, is called the *covariance* between the variables (see Equation 5.3).

The first cross product moment of the standardized variables has a special name; it is called the *correlation coefficient*, and it has a special symbol, r. The correlation coefficient is a measure of a "structural linear relationship" between any two random variables; this relationship is structural in that the correlation coefficient indicates the degree of the association between the two variables after allowance for the "errors" in the relationship. There is no implication of causality.

The relationship is also said to be *linear* because the approximate line joining the medians of the box-and-whisker plots of one random variable given values of the other random variable is a straight line. The range of possible values for r is $[-1, 1]$. A value of 1 or -1 indicates that the relationship between the random variables x and y is a linear function; that is, $y = a + bx$ for some values for the coefficients a and b in this linear equation. When this is the case, we really only have one random variable that is expressed in two sets of units of measurement—one relative to the x values and one relative to the y values (remember the temperature experiment). For values of r between these two extremes, the relationship between the random variables y and x is linear in the statistical sense as we defined it. Such a relationship is also said to be "structural" (as discussed in Chapter 2).

We were able to extend our results for cardinal measurements to ordinal measurements quite easily. All we had to do was to substitute into the definition for the correlation coefficient the rankings to derive what is known as *Spearman's rank correlation coefficient* (as shown in Equation 5.15).

Our next extension and relaxation of the idea of *association* was in the context of *contingency tables*, two-by-two tables that present the frequency of occurrence of pairs of events with two outcomes each. In this context, we defined the idea of *independence*, or *nonassociation*, the idea that the distribution of frequencies across rows does not change with the choice of column, or the distribution of frequencies across columns does not vary by choice of row. We provided a measure of association in terms of $\hat{\varphi}$, the *coefficient of association* for two-by-two contingency tables (see Equation 5.20). Two-by-two tables with only pairs of entries can be extended to two-by-two tables with more than two cases each. And we can extend examining pairs of tables to examining three sets of tables. This latest approach is best thought of as examining pairs of relationships, one pair for each division in the third category.

Case Study

Was There Age Discrimination in a Public Utility?

In previous chapters, we began to acquire some feel for the data involved in the union complaint about age and gender discrimination by a public utility. In this chapter, we can explore the extent to which the two main cardinal variables—that is, age and salary—are related. We begin by examining the scatter plots for the two variables.

Our first scatter plot is for all former employees (see Figure 5.14). The correlation coefficient as you might expect from examining the figure is positive, but small, with a value of .18. This result is for all employees that declared an age and a salary response. In line with our previous efforts, we might examine how the correlation might be modified by examining corre-

lations between age and salary when restricted to specific subgroups.

First, we examine the difference induced by separating the employees by sex. Figures 5.15 and 5.16 illustrate the difference. In both cases the correlations are very weak; but a little surprisingly, whereas the male correlation is positive with a value of .16, that for women is negative with a value of −.004. However, it is most likely given the very wide dispersion of the data that both correlations, but especially that for women, are 0. Indeed, a close examination of the scatter diagram indicates that there may be two distributions of income involved for women: one for incomes below $60,000 and another for incomes above that figure.

The effect of whether hired or not is examined in the next three figures, Figures 5.17 to 5.19. The first figure indicates the

continues on page 157

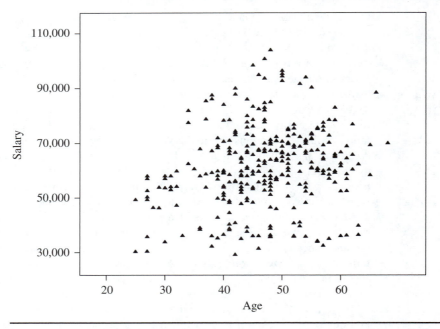

Figure 5.14   Discrimination case: Salary and age

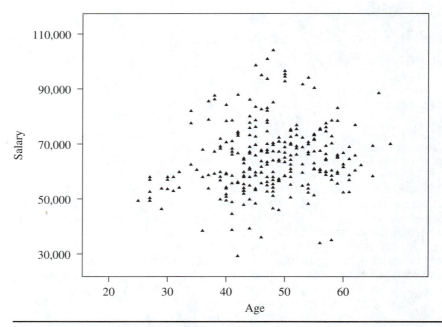

Figure 5.15   Discrimination case: Salary and age for males

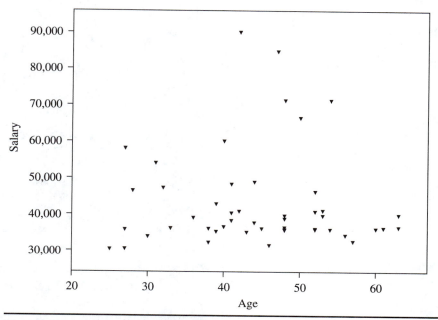

Figure 5.16   Discrimination case: Salary and age for females

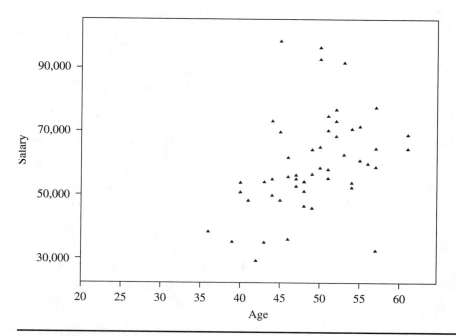

Figure 5.17   Discrimination case: Salary and age for rejected applicants

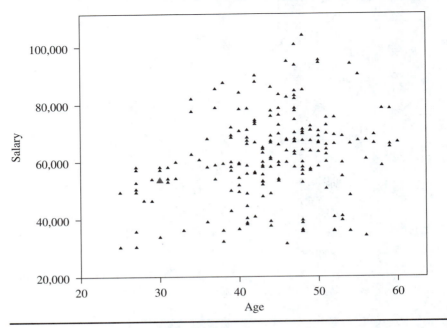

Figure 5.18   Discrimination case: Accepted applicants

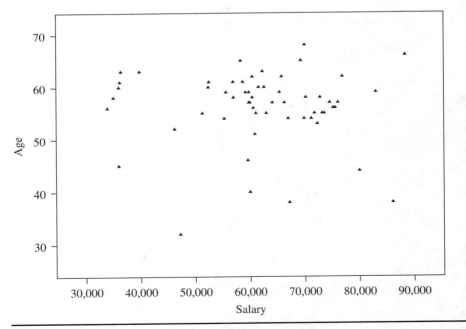

Figure 5.19   Discrimination case: Salary and age for those who did not apply

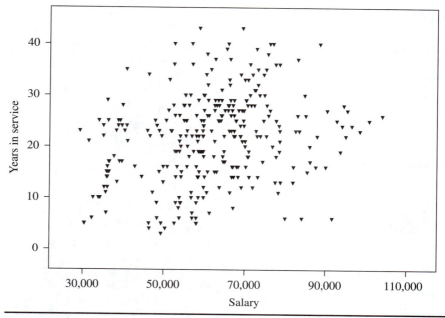

Figure 5.20   Discrimination case: Salary and years in service

(Continued)
relationship between age and salary for those former employees who applied but were not hired; the corresponding correlation is .39, the largest of this entire set. This evidence provides some weak evidence in favor of the union's hypothesis that the firm discriminated against older people in that the correlation between salary and age is positive; but do not rush to judgment, more analysis is to come.

Figure 5.18 reflects those hired, and the corresponding correlation is .26. So here as well we observe a small, but positive, relationship between age and salary. This result tends to undermine the union position in that if those hired from the pool had higher salaries, not much was being saved by eliminating the older employees. However, as we will investigate, the major issue is whether across the two groups, not hired and hired, the former had higher salaries and ages relative to the latter group. Next, examine the relationship for those who did not apply. The results are shown in Figure 5.19, and the corresponding correlation of −.04 is best regarded as essentially 0.

One criticism of these results is that what really counts is "years in service," not one's calendar age. To examine this claim, we have plotted the scatter plot for salary and "years in service" (see Figure 5.20). The corresponding correlation is .27, positive, but still quite small. Having obtained this disappointing conclusion, consider splitting the "years of service" variable into two subcomponents by sex. The scatter plots are shown for each in Figures 5.21 and 5.22. The corresponding correlations are .15 for

continues on page 159

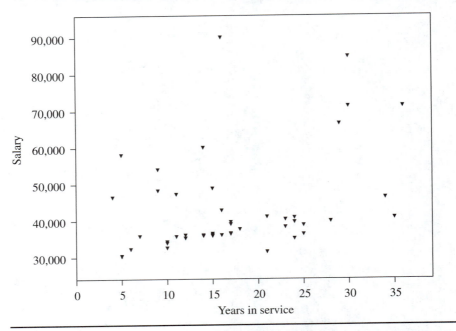

Figure 5.21   Discrimination case: Salary and years in service for males

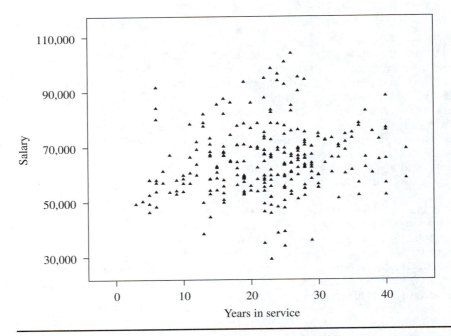

Figure 5.22   Discrimination case: Salary and years in service for females

(Continued)

men and .35 for women. One perhaps should not read too much into this difference, because the number of women in the sample is small and the graphs appear to indicate that a very small number of women with long experience and relatively high salaries dominate the results.

The overall conclusion is that for these data there is little relationship between age and salary. Further, breaking up the data into subgroups to reflect differences by gender, and whether hired or rehired, has not added very much to our understanding of the data. There is a positive correlation for those not hired but also for those hired.

What is missing in these figures is a breakdown by skill category. I suspect that a number of very different types of skills, and hence pay scales, have been amalgamated into the aggregate figures. Such a situation would indicate a reason for the lack of clear relationships between any of the variable pairs that we have examined in this chapter.

Nevertheless, the case for the union is not very convincing so far.

Exercises

Calculation Practice

5.1 Using the following numbers calculate by hand the first cross product moment for the variables, the covariance, the standardized variables, the correlation, and the individual second moments and their square roots:

$$\{x_i\} = \{-3, -2, -1, 0, 1, 2, 3\}$$
$$\{y_i\} = \{-8.9, -6.2, -2.7, 0.1, 2.8, 6.1, 8.8\}$$

Plot the data in a scatter plot. Confirm your visual impressions from the graph with your calculations.

5.2 Repeat the directions from Exercise 5.1 for the following data. Compare your results:

$$\{x_i\} = \{-3, -2, -1, 0, 1, 2, 3\}$$
$$\{y_i\} = \{9.1, 5.8, 3.3, 0.1, -3.2, -5.9, -9.2\}$$

5.3 Repeat the directions in Exercise 5.1 for the following data:

$$\{x_i\} = \{-3, -2, -1, 0, 1, 2, 3\}$$
$$\{y_i\} = \{7.2, 6.8, 7.3, 6.6, 7.1, 6.8, 7.0\}$$

Compare the calculations in the scatter diagrams and these three exercises.

5.4 Without performing any calculations, but after graphing, guess the value of the correlation coefficient between the following pairs of variables:

$$\{x_j\} = \{1, 2, 3, 4, 5\}$$
$$\{y_j\} = \{3, 1, -1, -3, -5\}$$

$$\{x_j\} = \{1, 2, 3, 4, 5\}$$
$$\{y_j\} = \{6, 9, 12, 15, 18\}$$

$$\{x_j\} = \{1, 2, 3, 4, 5\}$$
$$\{y_j\} = \{2, 4, 1, 3, 5\}$$

Confirm your guesses by calculating the correlation coefficient in each case.

5.5 *Worked.* *Objective: To confirm the computer algorithm for calculating correlation coefficients.* In Exercises 5.1 to 5.4 you calculated the correlation coefficients by hand. In this exercise, using the same data sets, recalculate the correlation coefficients using the computer algorithm. Compare the results with your hand computations.

[*Computer directions:* Open S-Plus. Click on Data, New Data Object, data.frame. Click OK. Enter the $\{x\}$ values into the first column, using the "down arrow" to move down the rows. Enter the $\{y\}$ values into the second column; the computer will automatically label the two columns "V1" and "V2." To calculate the correlation coefficient, on the menu bar, click on Statistics, Data Summaries, Correlations. Select All Variables. Click Apply. The answer will be in the Report window and should match what you have already obtained by hand. If not, check your entry of the data in the data frame and your original calculations.]

Warning: If you click on Covariance in the Correlation dialog, you will not get the same numerical result as in your calculation of the covariance. This is because the computer algorithm divides all second moments by $(n-1)$ instead of by n. Provided all second moments involved in the calculation of the correlation coefficient are calculated by dividing by the same number, n, or $(n-1)$, the calculated correlation will be the same. This mysterious difference will be explained later, but for now ignore it.

This exercise and the next are to help you understand precisely what the computer provides as output when the correlation routine is called. It is important that you avoid the easy use of "computer black boxes."

5.6 Worked. *Objective: To confirm the computer algorithm for calculating correlation coefficients.* In the folder Xfiles, subfolder Misc, in the file Cardata.xls, use the observations on *mpg, displacement, weight,* and *price.*

a. Plot the pairs: *mpg* and *weight*; *mpg* and *displacement*; *weight* and *price.*

[*Computer directions:* Start S-Plus. On the menu bar, click on File, Import Data, From File. Select folder Xfiles, subfolder Misc. Click on Cardata.xls. Click Open. Click on top of the mpg column. Hold down the CTRL key, and click on the weight column. On the menu bar, click on Graph, 2D Plot; select Scatter Plot. Click OK. Print the Graph. Repeat directions for other pairs of variables.]

Note: the first variable (column) selected will be on the X axis, and the second column selected with the CTRL key held down will be on the Y axis.

b. Calculate the corresponding correlation coefficients and comment. Follow the computer directions for calculating the moments and the standardized variables and use the results to calculate the correlation coefficient for mpg and weight.

[*Computer directions:*

(1) Procedure 1:

■ To calculate the moments for mpg (the first two moments will be used to create the standardized variable): On the menu bar, click on Text Routines, Moments. In the dialog, select Data Frame, Cardata. In Variable, select "mpg." Click OK. (Answer $m1 = 28.75$, $m2 = 53.91$; no. of observations $= 150$.)

■ To calculate the standardized variable for mpg: On the menu bar, click on Data, Transform. In New Column Name, key in mpgstd. In Expression, key in (mpg-28.75)/sqrt(53.91). Click Apply.

■ To calculate the moments for weight: On the menu bar, click on Text Routines, Moments. In the dialog, select Data Frame, Cardata. In Variable, select "weight." Click OK. (Answer $m1 = 2676.2$, $m2 = 364{,}148.6$.)

■ To calculate the standardized variable for weight: On the menu bar, click on Data, Transform. In New Column Name, key in wtstd. In Expression, key in (weight-2676.2)/sqrt(364148.6). Click Apply.

■ To calculate the correlation coefficient: In New Column Name, key in corr. In Expression, key in sum(mpgstd*wtstd)/150. Click Apply (answer $= -.82576$).

(2) Procedure 2:

■ To calculate the correlation coefficient: On the menu bar, click on Statistics, Data Summaries, Correlations. In the Correlations and Covariance dialog, in Data Frame, select Cardata. In Variable, select "mpg." Scroll to "Weight." Hold down the CTRL key and click on "Weight." Click Apply. The answer in the Report window should match that obtained in Procedure 1.]

c. Calculate the correlation coefficient for the other two pairs of variables. Verify that the two sets of calculations are the same in all these cases.

Now that you have had practice calculating the correlation coefficient step by step on the computer, you can use the correlation function in S-Plus, as in Procedure 2, for future calculations.

5.7 In the folder Xfiles, subfolder Misc, find file Coles.xls. Plot the variables *height* with *preweight* and *height* with *postweight*. Calculate the correlation coefficients for *height* and *preweight*, *height* and *postweight*, and *preweight* and *postweight*. Can you draw any conclusions about the effectiveness of the program from the difference in results?

5.8 Using data in the folder Xfiles, subfolder Misc, file Grades.xls, plot a Fit-Linear Least Squares graph and then calculate the correlation coefficient for the pairs of variables *midterm 1* and *midterm 2*, *midterm 1* and *final*, and *midterm 2* and *final*. Do you notice anything of interest in comparing these results?

Exploring the Tools

5.9 In Exercises 5.1 to 5.3, you calculated the value of *r*, the correlation coefficient. If you think that there is a linear functional relationship between the variables that is observed with error, then obtain the value of the slope coefficient directly from *r*. Explain what you are doing. Reexamine your results for Exercises 5.1 to 5.3.

5.10 Using the results in Exercise 5.6, examine the correlation coefficients for each relationship.

Comment on your results and relate them to the concept of "causality."

5.11 Suppose that a correlation coefficient has already been computed between *height* and *IQ*. On the basis of 48 observations, the correlation coefficient has been determined to be $-.14$. Let us label the height variable as H and the *IQ* variable as I.

a. Add John Kenneth Galbraith. He is over $6\frac{1}{2}$ feet tall, and he is very smart. What is the sign of the deviation of H_{49} (Galbraith's height) from the mean height? What is the sign of the deviation of I_{49} from the mean IQ? Will the correlation coefficient be increased or decreased by adding this observation?

b. Please add Milton Friedman. He is short but very, very smart. What is the sign of the deviation of H_{50} (Friedman's height) from the mean? What is the sign of the deviation of I_{50}? Will the correlation coefficient be increased or decreased?

c. Please add Joe Average. His height equals the current mean. His IQ equals the current mean. What is the sign of the deviation of H_{51} from the mean? What is the sign of the deviation of I_{51}? Will the correlation coefficient be increased or decreased?

5.12 What is the relationship between a scatter diagram and a histogram? What is the relationship between a scatter diagram and a correlation coefficient?

5.13 Consider the following sets of data:

$$\{x_i\} = \{-3, -2, -1, 0, 1, 2, 3\}$$
$$\{e_i\} = \{.2, -.3, .1, .2, -.1, -.2, .4\}$$

Let $y_i = 5 + x_i + e_i$, where the $\{e_i\}$ represent errors in observing the relationship. Calculate the correlation coefficient; label this case 1. Multiply $\{e_i\}$ by 2 and recalculate r; label this case 2. Multiply $\{e_i\}$ by 10 and recalculate r; label this case 3. Divide the original $\{e_i\}$ by 4, recalculate r; label this case 4. Divide the $\{e_i\}$ by 100 and recalculate r, label this case 5.

Comment on your results. If instead of changing the $\{e_i\}$ we had divided the slope coefficient in the first three cases and multiplied in the last case, would we have achieved the same qualitative result? Explain. In case 5 we divided the $\{e_i\}$ by 100 and in case 4 by 4; based on these two results what can you say would be the outcome if we divided by 1000, or even 100,000?

5.14 *Worked. Objective: To illustrate that correlation can be zero when the relationship is nonlinear.* Consider the data in folder Xfiles, subfolder Misc, file Tent.xls called the "Tent function" that was discussed at the very end of Section 5.8. Calculate the correlation coefficient between the variable in Tent.xls named *genvarbl* and itself lagged one period. We are examining the correlation between genvarbl at time period t and itself at time period $t - 1$; recall the graph of the tent function that plots this relationship.

[***Computer directions:*** Start S-Plus. Import Tent.xls.]

a. To create the lagged variable to use in the correlation calculation, copy and paste genvarbl -1. Click on the 2nd entry in genvarbl (.53). Use the fast scroll down button to scroll down to row 598. Hold down the Shift key, and click on the last entry in the first column. This will highlight the last 597 entries in genvarbl. Click on the Copy button. Highlight the top of column 2 in Tent and click the Paste button.

b. To calculate the correlation coefficient: On the menu bar, click on Statistics, Data Summaries, Correlations. In the dialog in Data Frame, highlight Tent. In Variables, select "all variables." In the Method to Handle Missing Values box, select "omit." Click Apply (answer: $r = -.0404$ is shown in the Report window).]

In light of the plot in Figure 5.13, comment on your calculations.

In the text it was pointed out that "linear correlation" is neither necessary nor sufficient for causality; this exercise illustrates the "necessity" part of that statement.

5.15 Imagine that two nurses are recording your temperature; one does so using a thermometer calibrated in degrees Fahrenheit and the other does so in degrees Celsius. Both also have measured your loss of fluids per hour in milliliters. Each has calculated a correlation coefficient between your temperature and your rate of fluid loss. Can you determine whether the two nurses are getting the same results? Explain.

5.16 *Worked. Objective: To compare bivariate distributions with different correlations.* In this experiment, you can observe samples of size 100 from a variety of bivariate distributions with correlation coefficients varying from $-.9$ to $.9$. Each time you execute the routine you will get a new set of data to observe.

[***Computer directions:*** Start S-Plus. On the menu bar, click Labs, Bivariate Descriptive Statistics, Scatterplots I. Click Apply. Click Apply several times.]

5.17 *Worked. Objective: To compare distributions with different correlations.* In this exercise, you can experiment by choosing the number of pairs of observations and the value of the correlation coefficient that applies.

[***Computer directions:*** Start S-Plus. On the menu bar, click Labs, Bivariate Descriptive Statistics, Scatterplots II. Vary the values of n and "rho" and click Apply.]

5.18 *Worked. Objective: To show the connection between slope, correlation, and degree of noise in structural relationships.* In this exercise, you can experiment with the relationship between the distribution of points in the scatter plot, the slope of the regression line, and the degree of fit as indicated by r^2. The square of the correlation coefficient, r^2, is listed in the dialog box in terms of a percentage between 10%—very low fit, large errors relative to the variation in the regressors—and 99%—very good fit, very small errors relative to the variation in the size of the regressors. For any value of r^2 that you choose, you can pick different values for the slope coefficient, b. You can also see what happens when you examine the regression lines plotted for a number of samples and for various sample sizes, n (the number of xy pairs in each regression). Note that each time you will have the same values for the regressors but different values for the error terms.

[*Computer directions:* Start S-Plus. On the menu bar, click <u>Labs</u>, <u>Bivariate Descriptive Statistics</u>, <u>Least Squares</u>. Click Apply. Vary the values of Sample Size, Number of Samples, Slope of True Line, and Desired R-square. Click Apply.]

5.19 *Worked.* *Objective: To investigate the relationship between correlation between pairs of variables and relationships involving multiple variables.* In the folder Xfiles, subfolder Misc, use the file Cardata.xls, which contains measurements on *acceleration* and *horsepower*, *horsepower* and *number of cylinders*, and *price of car per pound of car weight* and *mpg*. For each of these pairs, calculate the correlation coefficient, and comment on the fact that although we are examining pairs of variables clearly a larger number of variables are involved simultaneously. For example, mpg will depend on car weight, horsepower, number of cylinders, and acceleration. If there were only three main variables involved—say mpg, horsepower, and weight—speculate about what you would be seeing in the two-dimensional scatter plots of each pair in turn and the meaning of the pairwise correlation coefficients that you calculate.

One way to examine these issues visually is to plot a three-dimensional plot and then rotate the axes to view the three-dimensional plot from all viewpoints. The two-dimensional plots we use to calculate correlation coefficients are projections of the three-dimensional picture onto a two-dimensional plane. Consider a three-dimensional scatter plot, and imagine shining a light onto it parallel to one of the axes so that the shadows of the points are projected onto one of the planes; this is what you observe when you see a two-dimensional plot of a

relationship between three variables. These results can be illustrated in S-Plus.

[*Computer directions:* Import Cardata.xls. Select <u>Graph,</u> <u>Brush and Spin</u> in "columns," while holding down the CTRL key, select three of the related variables from Cardata. Click OK.]

You will see 3 two-dimensional plots, one for each pair of variables and a fourth panel that contains a three-dimensional axis. By clicking on the arrows in the top of the panel on the far right of the graph window, you can rotate the three-dimensional graph to any angle in three dimensions. Visually relate what you are seeing in the rotated three-dimensional graph to the 3 two-dimensional projections. Experiment on the data from Cardata and discover the limitations of the two-dimensional analysis we have been using so far. You might pick another data set and experiment further on your own.

In this chapter, we have restricted our analysis to the relationship between just two variables, but in many real situations more than two variables are involved. This exercise explores the effect of omitting a variable when it should be included in the analysis.

5.20 *Objective: To indicate the generalization of the coefficient of association.* This question is only for those who are familiar with the idea of determinants. When we calculated the coefficient of association for two-by-two contingency tables, we found that statistical independence was determined by the condition

$$ad - cb = 0$$

If we define the matrix A by

$$A = \begin{bmatrix} a & b \\ c & d \end{bmatrix}$$

then the condition for the statistical independence of the categories is that the determinant of A be zero; that is, $\det(A) = ad - bc = 0$. We can extend this notion to a matrix with three columns and three rows. If det (A), for A a three-by-three matrix of pairs of categories with three divisions each, is zero, we can declare the categories statistically independent. Let the matrix A be written:

$$A = \begin{bmatrix} a_{11} & a_{12} & a_{13} \\ a_{21} & a_{22} & a_{23} \\ a_{31} & a_{32} & a_{33} \end{bmatrix}$$

and let $a_{.1}$, $a_{.2}$, $a_{.3}$ be the column totals and $a_{1.}$, $a_{2.}$, $a_{3.}$ be the row totals.

Show that for such a matrix of category effects that statistical independence is determined by $\det(A) = 0$, and that if we define $\hat{\varphi}_3$ by

$$\hat{\varphi} = \frac{\text{Det}(A)}{\sqrt{a.1a.2a.3a1.a2.a3.}}$$

then $\hat{\varphi}$ will take the values ± 1 when there is a linear relationship between the rows of frequencies, or of course, between the columns of frequencies.

5.21 Worked: *Objective: To indicate the generalization of the coefficient of association.* This question is only for those who are familiar with the idea of determinants and who have done Exercise 5.20.

Recall the data folder Xfiles, subfolder Misc, and the data file Psychol.xls, in which the heights and IQ levels of some respondents are recorded.

a. Divide both height and IQ into two divisions each and calculate $\hat{\varphi}$, the coefficient of association. Our first step is to create a total of four cells, two by two, by dividing IQ into observations below and above 122 and by dividing height into two groups, those below and above 65 inches.

[**Computer directions:** Import file Psychol.xls. On the menu bar, click on Text Routines, Contingency Tables, Cell 2×2. In the dialog, select Data Frame, Psychol. In First Variable, select "iq." In Cut Point, key in $\boxed{122}$. In Second Variable, select "height." In Cut Point, key in $\boxed{65}$. Click OK. (Answer: $a = 13$, $b = 11$, $c = 15$, $d = 11$.)

Calculate the coefficient of association using Equation 5.20, and substitute the values obtained for a, b, c, d. (answer $= -.035$).]

b. Next, divide both height and IQ into three divisions each and calculate $\hat{\varphi}_3$. [**Computer directions:** IQ has been split into three cells: first cell: < 116; second cell: $>= 116$, but < 126; third cell: $>= 126$. The height has been split into three cells: first cell: < 64 inches; second cell: $>= 64$, but < 65 inches; third cell: $>= 65$ inches. On the menu bar, click on Text Routines, Contingency Tables, Cell 3×3. In the dialog, select Data Frame, Psychol. In First Variable, select "iq." In Cut Point 1, key in $\boxed{116}$. In Cut Point 2, key in $\boxed{126}$. In Second Variable, select "height." In Cut Point 1, key in $\boxed{64}$. In Cut Point 2, key in $\boxed{65}$. Click OK. (answer $a_{11} = 3$, $a_{12} = 5$, $a_{13} = 8$, $a_{21} = 7$, $a_{22} = 3$, $a_{23} = 7$, $a_{31} = 8$, $a_{32} = 2$, $a_{33} = 7$).] Refer to the equation for $\hat{\varphi}_3$ to calculate the coefficient of association.

c. Compare your results using $\hat{\varphi}$ and $\hat{\varphi}_3$. Comment. Also compare your results with those obtained using the correlation coefficient and Spearman's rank correlation coefficient, as discussed in the text.

5.22 Suppose that the relationship between two variables is given by the equation

$$y = a + bx + e$$

where e is the error in observing the relationship between y and x.

If you knew r, the correlation coefficient, how would you get an idea of b? If you had a calculation for b, how would you determine r? Explain the relationship between these two ideas.

Applications

5.23 The international GNP data files contain national income data, which have been converted into U.S. dollar equivalents. If, however, the data were in original units, so that, for example, output was measured in Swedish Kroner, in British pounds, and so on, could you make comparisons across countries for the correlations between consumption and output? If so, how?

5.24 Worked. *Objective: To illustrate the effect on correlation of transforming the data.* Use the data found in the folder Xfiles, subfolder Gnp, subfolder Domgnp, file Domgnp.xls.

a. Plot the variables industrial production (*indprod*) and real GNP (*rgnp*), and calculate the correlation between them.

b. Calculate the growth rates of real GNP and industrial production; the growth rate for a time series, $\{x_t\}$, is given by $gth = (x_t - x_{t-1})/x_{t-1}$. You will have to lose the "first" observation in each case. Calculate the correlation coefficient.

[*Computer directions:* Start S-Plus. Import file Domgnp.xls.

(1) To generate a variable for the growth rate of rgnp, highlight column rgnp. Click Copy. Highlight the second cell of a new column. Click Paste. Highlight the new column name. Key in $\boxed{\text{rngplag}}$. Enter. Repeat for column indprod, naming the new column "indprodlag." On the menu bar, click on Data, Transform. In the dialog in New Column Name, key in $\boxed{\text{rngpg}}$. In Expressions, key in $\boxed{\text{(rgnp-rgnplag)/rgnplag}}$. Click Apply. Repeat for indprod using "ipg." In Expressions, key in $\boxed{\text{(indprod-indprodlag)/indprodlag}}$. Click Apply.

(2) To calculate the correlation coefficient, on the menu bar, click on Statistics, Data Summaries, Correlations. In Variables, select "rgnpg" and "ipg." In Method to Handle Missing Values, select "omit." Click Apply. The answer will be in the Report window (answer = .8388).]

c. Plot the scatter diagram for the relationship between the growth rates for industrial production and real GNP. Are you surprised by the results? Compare carefully these results with those obtained in (*a*).

We have restricted our attention to "linear relationships." This exercise indicates that sometimes by suitable transformation of the variables involved one may be able to apply our techniques to a wider variety of cases.

5.25 Repeat the previous exercise using the international income and consumption data in the three files in the folder Xfiles, subfolder Gnp, subfolder Intlgnp. Comment on your results. Can you explain the differences between the results for levels and growth rates? Which set of results would you believe, and why?

5.26 Worked. *Objective: To illustrate the loss of information from using ranks.* In the text we discussed the correlations between mpg and weight (Cardata.xls) and between midterm grades and final grades (Grades.xls).

a. Generate the ranks for each variable, and plot the variable against the rank. What do you observe?

b. Calculate the Spearman rank correlation coefficient for the ranked data of each pair. Recall that the Spearman correlation is obtained by using the standard correlation function on the ranks.

[*Computer directions:* Start S-Plus. Import file Cardata.xls. On the menu bar, click on Data, Transform.

(1) To calculate the ranks: In New Column Name, key in $\boxed{\text{mpgr}}$. In Expression, key in $\boxed{\text{rank(mpg)}}$. Click Apply. Repeat for Column Name: key in $\boxed{\text{weightr}}$. In Expression, key in $\boxed{\text{rank(weight)}}$. Click Apply. The two columns mpgr and weightr will be added to the Cardata data frame.

(2) Plot a scatter diagram with a regression line of the ranked data and the unranked data. Highlight the two columns to be graphed: Click on column mpg. Hold down the CTRL key, and click on mpgr. On the menu bar, click on Graph, 2D Plot. Scroll to Fit-Linear Least Squares and highlight. Click OK.

(3) Calculate the correlation of the ranked data. On the menu bar, click on Statistics, Data Summaries, Correlation. In Variable, scroll to and highlight mpgr. Hold down the CTRL key, and click on weightr. Click Apply. The answer will be in the Report window (answer: rho = −.84235).]

Table 5.13 **Political Affiliation by Sex for Males**

	Dole	Clinton
Conservative	14	2
Liberal	8	17

Table 5.14 **Political Affiliation by Sex for Females**

	Dole	Clinton
Conservative	10	6
Liberal	8	27

c. Repeat this process for the other set of variables. Compare your results with the correlations obtained in the text. Explain the differences.

d. Ranks contain less information than the data from which they are often obtained. This exercise illustrates that loss of information. Use the original data, if you can obtain them; if not, note the limits on the implications that you can draw from just the ranks.

5.27 Consider the data sets in the folder Xfiles, subfolder Firmdata. For any two firms, examine the variables *sales*, *income*, and share price (*sharepr*). For each pair of these variables, for each firm:

a. Plot the scatter plots, and calculate the correlation coefficient.

b. Determine the ranks from the data.

[*Computer hint:* See step 1 of Exercise 5.26 to calculate the ranks to use for plotting.] Plot the corresponding scatter diagrams of the ranks, and calculate Spearman's rank correlation coefficient.

c. Examine your results and comment on the usefulness of Spearman's rank correlation coefficient and on the loss of information in using ranks instead of the actual data.

5.28 Identify situations with examples where using the ranks instead of the actual data will make no difference to the correlation value that you calculate. Clarify the circumstances under which using the ranks will reflect a loss of information.

5.29 Table 5.2, the contingency table on political affiliation, was created omitting the information about the sex of the interviewee. Suppose that the full data that includes information about the sex of the interviewee is as shown in Tables 5.13 and 5.14. Use this information to modify the results obtained in the text by recognizing the differences, if any, between the responses by the different sexes. Is there a "gender gap"?

5.30 In the folder Xfiles, subfolder Energy, and in each country's files—for example, Usaeng.xls— there are annual data on agricultural and industrial production, energy use per capita, gross domestic product, and population. Produce scatter diagrams and individual box-and-whisker plots for the following pairs of variables for each country.

a. In each case, calculate the correlation coefficient. Comment on energy use in each country as it might relate to aggregate industrial and agricultural economic activity.

(1) agricultural production (*agrprod*) and industrial production (*indprod*)

(2) energy per capita (*energpc*) and gross domestic product per capita (you will need to calculate the last variable)

[*Computer hint:* To calculate gross domestic product per capita: Import the Energy files. Click on Data, Transform. Enter gdppc in the New Column Name. For Expression, key in gdpmil/popmil.

Click Apply. The new variable will be in the last column of the Energy file. Use variables *gdppc* and *energpc* in the plots and correlation calculations. If missing values are encountered in the correlations, omit them.]

(3) agricultural production and energy per capita

(4) industrial production and energy per capita

b. Comment on your findings and compare the correlation coefficients across countries. Explain what property of correlation coefficients allows you to do this.

5.31 In the folder Xfiles, subfolder Testscor, file Psatsat.xls, four variables are recorded: the math and the verbal scores on each of the PSAT and SAT. Plot the scatter plots, and calculate the correlation coefficient between all pairs of the four variables. Comment on your results with respect to the PSAT as a "predictor" of performance on the SAT, the extent to which high math scores are at the expense of high verbal scores. Are there any surprises?

5.32 In the folder Xfiles, subfolder Misc, file Geyser1.xls, the duration of and interval between the eruptions of Old Faithful are recorded. Is there any relationship between duration and interval? Would looking at subsets of the data help? If so, what subsets?

5.33 In the folder Xfiles, subfolder Misc, file Coles.xls, the weights, pre- and postexercise program; fat measurement, both pre- and postprogram; and blood pressure, together with height and age are recorded. Using the tools of this chapter and the last, what can you determine about the effectiveness of the program in weight and fat reduction? Are there any differences due to height or age? How would you determine this? What role, if any, does blood pressure play?

5.34 In the folder Xfiles, subfolder Firmdata, there are seven files of data on firm performance by name of firm. For each firm, there are observa-

tions on a list of variables for the years 1975 to 1994. If you wanted to correlate share price with some other variable in the data sets, which one (or ones) would you choose and why?

5.35 In the folder Xfiles, subfolder Misc, use the file Food.xls. Plot and calculate the correlation coefficients for the pairs *qd* and *pd*, *qs* and *ps*, and *qd* and *year*. If you are an economics major, do you have some questions about the results given the definitions of the variables? If you are not an economics major, what are your reactions to your results?

5.36 In the folder Xfiles, subfolder Misc, use the file Housing.xls. Plot and calculate the correlation coefficient for the pairs of variables *hsestrts* and *gnp*, *hsestrts* and *intrate*, and *gnp* and *intrate*, where "hsestrts" are housing starts and "intrate" is an estimated real interest rate. What conclusions do you think you can draw from these results? Do the results meet your prior expectations?

5.37 In the folder Xfiles, subfolder Gnp, subfolder Intlgnp, there are three country files with variables that represent indices of output, consumption, investment, government expenditure, and the price level. For each country and for each of the following pairs of variables plot the relationships and calculate the correlation coefficients for output and government expenditure, output and investment, consumption and the price level. Compare the graphs and the calculations across the three countries. Can you draw any interesting inferences from these results?

5.38 Case Study: Was There Age Discrimination in a Public Utility? A senior associate of your Forensic Economics Consulting firm is interested in investigating the statistical relationship between age and salary among the hired and not hired former employees (internal applicants).

a. Prepare scatter plots and estimate the correlation coefficients for age and salary for those internal applicants who were hired and for those internal applicants who were not hired.

b. Prepare a statistical analysis report for the senior associate. In the Agedisc folder, use the Discdata.xls file.

[*Computer hint:* Use the Data, Split to create a data frame for former employees (internal applicants) "ext.appl" = 0.]

5.39 Case Study: Was There Age Discrimination in a Public Utility? The labor union asked your consulting firm to investigate the presence of any form of association between the age of applicants (hire.stat = 1 or 0) and the hiring decisions of the firm in this age discrimination case.

a. You are asked to prepare for the next meeting of the investigation team contingency tables of

(1) all applicants (hire.stat = 1 or 0) by age (40 and over, and below 40) and their hiring status (hired, not hired).

(2) all internal applicants by age (40 and over, and below 40) and their hiring status (hired, not hired).

(3) all external applicants by age (40 and over, and under 40) and their hiring status (hired, not hired).

b. Write a short, summary report of your findings. In the Agedisc folder, use the Discdata.xls file.

5.40 Case Study: Was There Age Discrimination in a Public Utility? The labor union is looking for statistical evidence that indicates substantial association between the age of an applicant and the firm's decision to hire the applicant or not. If such statistics reveal that the hiring decisions were associated with the applicant's age, then the union might be able to substantiate its claim of age discrimination during the firm's RIF (reduction in force) process.

a. You are asked to estimate the coefficient of association between age of applicants (those under 40 and those age 40 and over) and those applicants who were hired and not hired. In the Agedisc folder, use the Discdata.xls file.

b. Write a short explanation and interpretation of your estimate.

PART THREE

Probability and Distribution Theory

CHAPTER

6

The Theory of Statistics: An Introduction

6.1   What You Will Learn in This Chapter

So far all our analysis has been descriptive; we have provided parsimonious ways to describe and summarize data and thereby acquire useful information. In our examination of data and experiments, we discovered that there were many regularities that held for large collections of data. However, this led to new questions:

- If random variables are unpredictable, why is it that the same experiment produces the same shape of histogram?
- What explains the different shapes of histograms?
- Why do the shapes of histograms become smooth as the number of observations increases?
- How can we explain the idea of a structural relationship?

We now introduce the "theory" of statistics called *probability theory.* This theory will provide the answers to these and many other questions as yet unposed. In addition, at last we will formally define the idea of a random variable. The basic theory that we delineate in this chapter underlies *all* statistical reasoning. Probability theory and the theory of distributions that is to follow in the succeeding chapters are the foundation for making general statements about as yet unobserved events. Instead of having to restrict our statements to a description of a particular set of historically observed data points, probability theory provides the explanations for what it is that we observe. It enables us to recognize our actual data as merely a finite-sized "sample" of data drawn from a theoretical population of infinite extent. Our explanations move from statements of certainty to explanations expressed in terms of relative frequencies, or in terms of the odds in favor or against an event occurring.

You will discover in this chapter that besides "simple probability," there are concepts of joint and conditional probability as well as the notion of independence between random variables. The "independence" that we introduce in this chapter is "statistical independence." *Statistical independence* between two variables implies that we gain no information about the distribution of events of one of them from information on the values taken by the other.

This is a critical chapter because the theory that we will develop lies at the heart of all our work hereafter. All decision making depends one way or another on the concept of conditional probability, and the idea of independence is invoked at every turn.

6.2 Introduction

We began our study of statistics by giving an intuitive definition of a random variable as a variable that cannot be predicted by any other variable or by its own past. Given this definition we were in a quandary to start, because we had no way to describe, or summarize, large, or even small, amounts of data. We began our search for ways to describe random data by "counting"; that is, we counted the number of occurrences of each value of the variable and called it a frequency. We then saw the benefit of changing to relative frequencies and extended this idea to continuous random variables. With both frequency charts and histograms we saw that frequencies added to one by their definition and that the area under a histogram is also one. More important, we saw that different types of survey or experimental data took different shapes for their frequency charts or their histograms. Also, we saw that if we had enough data there seemed to be a consistency in the shapes of charts and histograms over different trials of the same type of experiment or survey.

We began with nothing to explain. We now have a lot to explain. What explains the various shapes of frequency charts and histograms? Why does the same shape occur if random variables are truly unpredictable? The stability of the shape seems to depend on the number of observations, but how? For some pairs of random variables, the distribution of one variable seems to depend on the value taken by the other variable. Why is this, and how does the relationship between the variables change? Why are some variables related in this statistical sense and others are not? Most important, can we predict the shape of distributions and the statistical relationships that we have discovered so far? Might we be able to discover even more interesting relationships?

The task of this chapter is to begin the process of providing the answers to these questions. What we require is a theory of relative frequencies. This self-imposed task is common to all sciences. Each science discovers some regularities in its data and then tries to explain those regularities. The same is true in statistics; we need to develop a theory to explain the regularities that we have observed. But if we spend the time to develop a theory of relative frequency, or a theory of statistics, as we shall now call it, what will we gain from our efforts?

First, we would expect to be able to answer the questions that we posed to ourselves in the previous paragraphs. But in addition, we would like to be able to generalize from specific events and specific observations to make statements that will hold in similar, but different, situations; this process is called *inference* and will eventually occupy a lot of our efforts. Another very important objective is to be able to deduce from our theory new types of concepts and new types of relationships between variables that can be used to further our understanding of random variables. Finally, the development of a theory of statistics will enable us to improve our ability to make decisions involving random variables or to deal with situations in which we have to make decisions without full information. The most practical aspect of the application of statistics and of statistical theory is its use in "decision making under uncertainty" and in determining "how to take risks." We will discuss both of these issues in later chapters.

If we are to do a creditable job of developing a theory of statistics, we should keep in mind a few important guidelines. First, as the theory is to explain relative frequency, it would be useful if we developed the theory from an abstraction and generalization of relative frequencies. We want to make the theory as broadly applicable, or as general as is feasible; that is, we want to be able to encompass as many different types of random variables and near random variables as is possible. Although we want the theory to generate as many new concepts and relationships as possible, it is advisable that we be as sparing as we can with our basic assumptions. The less we assume to begin, the less chance there is of our theory proving to be suitable only for special cases. Finally, we would like our theory's assumptions to be as simple and as noncontroversial as possible. If everyone agrees that our assumptions are plausible and useful in almost any potential application, then we will achieve substantial and broad agreement with our theoretical conclusions.

A side benefit to this approach is that we will be able to make our language more precise and that we will be able to build up our ideas step by step. This will facilitate our own understanding of the theory to be created. But, as with all theories, we will have to idealize our hypothesized experiments to concentrate on the most important aspects of each situation. By abstracting from practical details, we will gain insight. Let us begin.

This is a chapter on theory. Consequently, we are now dealing in abstractions and with theoretical concepts, not with actually observed data. However, we will illustrate the abstract ideas with many simple examples of experiments. Try not to confuse the discussion of the illustrative experiment with the abstract theory that is being developed. The notation will change to reflect the change in viewpoint; we will no longer use the lowercase Roman alphabet to represent variables or things like moments. Now we will use *uppercase* letters to represent *random* variables and Greek letters to represent theoretical values and objects like moments for theoretical distributions. This convention of lowercase Roman to represent observed variables and uppercase to represent random variables is restricted to variables; that is, we will need both upper and lowercase Roman letters to represent certain functions and distributions that will be defined in later chapters. The context should make it abundantly clear whether we are talking about variables or functions or distributions. However, much of the new notation will not come into play until the next chapter.

This chapter relies heavily on elementary set theory, which is reviewed in Appendix A, "Mathematical Appendix." The reader is advised at least to scan the material in the appendix to be sure that all the relevant concepts are familiar before proceeding with this chapter.

6.3 The Theory: First Steps

The Sample Space

Let us start with a very simple illustrative experiment that involves a 12-sided die. Each side is labeled by a number: 1,2,3, . . . ,10,11,12. Imagine the experiment of tossing this die; each toss is called a "trial" of the experiment. If you throw this die, it will land on one side and on only one side.

This situation is very common and is characterized by this statement:

Conjecture There is a set of events that contains a finite number of discrete alternatives that are mutually exclusive; the set of events is exhaustive for the outcomes of the experiment.

An **event** is an outcome or occurrence of a trial in an experiment. The set of outcomes (or events) of the experiment of tossing the 12-sided die is finite; that is, there are only 12 of them. The events are **mutually exclusive** because one and only one of the outcomes can occur at a time. The set of events is **exhaustive** because nothing else but 1 of the 12 listed events can occur. Events that are mutually exclusive and exhaustive are known as **elementary events;** they cannot be broken down into simpler mutually exclusive events.

The exhaustive set of mutually exclusive events is called the **sample space.** This is a somewhat misleading term because it (as well as all the other terms defined in this section) is an abstraction; it does not refer to actual observations. In our current experiment, a trial is the tossing of a 12-sided die; an event is what number shows up on the toss. The sample space is the set of 12 numbers: 1,2,3,4, . . . ,11,12; the events are mutually exclusive and exhaustive, because on each trial, or toss, only one of the numbers will be on top. Listing the 12 numbers as the outcomes of trials logically exhausts the possible outcomes from the experiment.

Look at Table 6.1, which shows the relative frequencies of 1000 tosses of a 12-sided die. The first few observed outcomes were

9,4,11,2,11,6,3,12,6,11, . . .

In the first ten trials of this experiment, there were three 11s and two 6s.

What would you have expected? Is this result strange, or is it unremarkable? One of the objectives of our theoretical analysis is to provide answers to this sort of question. These numbers are actual observed outcomes, but what we want to do is to abstract from this situation. We want to be able to speak about all possible tosses of 12-sided die, not just about this particular set of actual outcomes as we have done exclusively until now. This change in viewpoint is difficult for some at first, but if you keep thinking about the idea it will soon become a natural and easy one for you. Let us study another example.

Suppose that we have a coin with sides, heads and tails, and the edge is so thin that we do not have to worry about the coin landing on its edge. What we are really saying is that we want to study a situation in which there only two possibilities, "heads" and "tails," which are exhaustive and mutually exclusive. The sample space is $S = \{e_1, e_2\}$; in any trial, one and only one of e_1 or e_2 can occur, where e_1 represents "heads" and e_2 represents "tails."

Table 6.1   **Frequency Tabulation of a 12-Sided Die**

Die Value	Absolute Frequency	Relative Frequency	Cumulative Frequency	Cumulative Relative Frequency
1	74	.0740	74	.0740
2	91	.0910	165	.1650
3	81	.0810	246	.2460
4	91	.0910	337	.3370
5	88	.0880	425	.4250
6	91	.0910	516	.5160
7	86	.0860	602	.6020
8	81	.0810	683	.6830
9	82	.0820	765	.7650
10	76	.0760	841	.8410
11	66	.0660	907	.9070
12	93	.0930	1000	1.0000

Our language about "heads" and "tails" is colorful and helpful in trying to visualize the process, but the abstract language of sample spaces and events is more instructive and enables us to generalize our ideas immediately. Remember that throughout this and the next two chapters, the experiments that are described and the "observations that are generated by them" are merely illustrative examples. These examples are meant to give you insight into the development of the abstract theory that you are trying to learn.

Let us study a more challenging example. Suppose that we have two coins that we toss at the same time. At each toss we can get any combination of heads and tails from the two coins. To work out the appropriate sample space is a little more tricky in this example. Remember that we are looking for a set of mutually exclusive and exhaustive events. Here is a list of the potential outcomes for this experiment:

H, H
H, T
T, H
T, T

where the first letter refers to the first coin and the second letter to the second coin. As listed these four outcomes are mutually exclusive and exhaustive, because one and only one of these events can and will occur. But what if we had listed the outcomes as

$\{H, H\}; \{H, T \text{ or } T, H\}; \{T, T\}$

You might be tempted to list only three mutually exclusive and exhaustive events. This is not correct because *H* and *T* can occur together in two ways: *H, T* or *T, H*. The event {*H, T*} is not an *elementary event*, because it is composed of two subevents: *H, T* and *T, H*—that is, heads first, then tails, or the reverse order. But the notation {*H, T*} means that we are examining the pair *H, T* without worrying about order; {*H, T*} is the set of outcomes *H* or *T*. This example shows that our definition of a sample space must be refined:

A **sample space** is a set of *elementary events* that are *mutually exclusive* and *exhaustive*.

(An *elementary event* is an event that cannot be broken down into a subset of events.)

Table 6.2 **Frequency Tabulation for a Single-Coin Toss**

Elementary Event	Absolute Frequency	Relative Frequency	Cumulative Frequency	Cumulative Relative Frequency
0	50	.500	50	.500
1	50	.500	100	1.000

Table 6.3 **Frequency Tabulation for a Double-Coin Toss**

Elementary Event	Absolute Frequency	Relative Frequency	Cumulative Frequency	Cumulative Relative Frequency
1	21	.210	21	.210
2	30	.300	51	.510
3	23	.230	74	.740
4	26	.260	100	1.000

In a very real sense our elementary events are the "atoms" of the theory of statistics, or of *probability theory* as it is also called. So a sample space is a collection of elementary events, or a "collection of atoms." These are our basic building blocks. In the die example the sample space had 12 elementary events, the numbers from 1 to 12, or more abstractly, $\{e_1, e_2, \ldots, e_{12}\}$. In the single-coin toss experiment, the sample space had two elementary events, heads and tails, or more generally, e_1 and e_2; and in the last experiment involving the tossing of two coins, we had a sample space with four elementary events, e_1 to e_4.

Introducing Probabilities

Table 6.1 shows the relative frequency for an experiment with a 12-sided die, and Tables 6.2 and 6.3 show observed relative frequencies for 100 trials on each of two experiments—one with a single coin, one with two coins. We want to be able to explain these relative frequencies, so we need an abstract analog to relative frequency.

We define the **probability** of an elementary event as a number between zero and one such that the sum of the probabilities over the sample space is one; this last requirement reflects the fact that relative frequencies sum to one. To each elementary event, e_i, we assign a number between zero and one, call it p_i. We can write this as

$$S = \{e_1, \ e_2, \ \ldots \ldots, \ e_k\}$$
$$\downarrow \quad \downarrow \qquad \qquad \downarrow$$
$$p_1, \ p_2, \ \ldots \ldots, \ p_k\}$$

for a sample space having k elementary events; or, we can write this as

$$e_1 \to \text{pr}(e_1) = p_1$$
$$e_2 \to \text{pr}(e_2) = p_2$$
$$e_3 \to \text{pr}(e_3) = p_3$$
$$\ldots$$
$$e_k \to \text{pr}(e_k) = p_k$$

The expression pr(e_2) means "assign a specific number between zero and one to the elementary event that is designated in the argument," e_2 in this case; and the value given by that assignment is p_2. Our notation reinforces the idea that we are assigning a number to each elementary event.

But we are not at liberty to assign just any number between zero and one; there is one more constraint, namely $\Sigma p_i = 1$. If you look at the simplest example, where the sample space is $\{e_1, e_2\}$, "the tossing of one coin" experiment, you will see that this last constraint still leaves a lot of choice. If a probability of p_1 is assigned to e_1, $0 \leq p_1 \leq 1$, then our constraint merely says that pr(e_2) $= 1 - p_1 = p_2$ for any valid value of p_1. If we are to proceed with our examples we will have to resolve this issue.

There is one easy way out of our difficulty given our current ignorance about what values of probabilities we should assign to our elementary events; assume that they are all the same. Consequently, if there are k elementary events, the assumed probability is $1/k$ for each elementary event. This convenient assumption is called the **equally likely principle**, or following Laplace, the "principle of insufficient reason"; the former phrase is easier to comprehend. This principle is really an expression of our ignorance of the actual probabilities that would apply to this particular type of experiment. Until we begin to derive probability distributions, we will have to invoke this principle quite often; in any case, it does seem to be reasonable under the circumstances. Following this principle, we can assign a probability distribution to each of our three experiments:

- 12-sided die experiment: $S = \{1, 2, \ldots, 11, 12\}$; $p_i = \frac{1}{12} = .0833$, $i = 1, 2, \ldots, 12$
- Single-coin toss experiment: $S = \{e_1, e_2\}$; $p_i = \frac{1}{2} = .50$; $i = 1, 2$
- Double-coin toss experiment: $S = \{e_1, e_2, e_3, e_4\}$; $p_i = \frac{1}{4} = .25$, $i = 1, 2, 3, 4$

In each case, we have defined probability such that $0 \leq p_i \leq 1$, $i = 1, \ldots, k$, and $\Sigma p_i = 1$. This is called a probability distribution. A **probability distribution,** as its name implies, is a statement of how probabilities are distributed over the elementary events in the sample space.

An immediate question may occur to you. If probabilities are the theoretical analogues of relative frequency, then what can we say about the relationship, if any, between probability and relative frequency? Tables 6.1, 6.2, and 6.3 show the results of three actual experiments designed to illustrate the three sample spaces that we have been discussing. We get excellent agreement for experiment 2; the assigned probability is .50 and the relative frequency is .50. The results for experiment 1 are not so good; no relative frequency equals the assigned probability of .0833, but they do seem to be scattered about that value. With the last experiment, no relative frequency equals the assigned probability, but the relative frequencies do seem to be scattered about the assigned probability of .25. At first sight it would appear that we have not made much progress, but on reflection we recall that to get stable shapes we had to have a lot of data; so maybe that is our problem.

However, the question does raise an issue that we will have to face eventually; namely, when can we say that we have agreement between theory and what we observe? What are the criteria that we should use? We will meet this issue directly soon enough, but for now you should keep the problem in mind. We can conclude at this time only that the observed relative frequencies seem to be scattered about our assumed probabilities.

Probabilities of Unions and Joint Events

If this were all that we could do with probability, it would be a pretty poor theory. So far all that we have done is to assign probability to elementary events using the "equally likely principle." But what is the probability of getting on a single roll of the 12-sided die a 2, 4, or a 10? Another way of saying this is that we will declare the roll a "success" if on a single roll, we get one of the numbers 2, or 4, or 10. Given that each outcome from a single roll of a die is mutually exclusive, we will get only one of these three alternatives. If we obtain any other number, we will declare a "failure." The question is, What is the probability of success in any trial of this new experiment? Will our new theory help in this more complex, but more interesting, case?

Maybe we could just add up the individual probabilities to get the probability of the new event, $\{e_2, \text{ or } e_4, \text{ or } e_{10}\}$:

$$
\begin{aligned}
pr(e_2, \text{ or } e_4, \text{ or } e_{10}) &= p_2 + p_4 + p_{10} \\
&= .0833 + .0833 + .0833 \\
&= .25
\end{aligned}
$$

Because our development of the theory is meant to explain relative frequency, we might see how reasonable this guess is by looking at an experiment. A generous soul volunteered to toss a 12-sided die to get 2000 trials on the event $\{e_2, \text{ or } e_4, \text{ or } e_{10}\}$. The result was a relative frequency of .238, which at least seems to be close. The lesson so far seems to be that to obtain the probability of two or more elementary events all we need do is to add up the individual probabilities, but we should be careful and make sure that the current success is not a lucky break.

Let us try another experiment, and ask another question. What is the probability of the event of at least one head in the two-coin experiment? Our present theoretical answer is

$$
\begin{aligned}
pr(e_1, \text{ or } e_2, \text{ or } e_3) &= p_1 + p_2 + p_3 \\
&= .25 + .25 + .25 \\
&= .75
\end{aligned}
$$

Event e_1 is $\{H, H\}$, e_2 is $\{H, T\}$, and e_3 is $\{T, H\}$. But what is the value obtained by the experiment? Our generous soul reluctantly came to our rescue again to produce the result of .78.

Maybe we are onto something. So far for this first set of problems involving only elementary events, the probability of an event composed of two or more elementary events is just the sum of the probabilities of the individual elementary events; or, in our more abstract notation:

$$
pr(e_i, \text{ or } e_j, \text{ or } e_k, \ldots, \text{ or } e_m) = p_i + p_j + p_k + \cdots + p_m
$$

These new events are called **compound events,** because they are "compounds," or "unions," of the elementary events. In any trial, you declare that a compound event has occurred if any one of its members occurs. In our previous examples, the

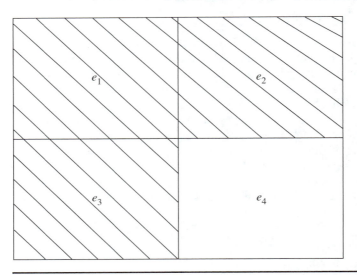

Figure 6.1   Table of elementary events for the two-coin toss experiment. Note: The lined region is the event "at least one head."

compound event was to get a 2, 4, or 10. So, if in any single trial in the 12-sided die example, you throw either a 2, 4, or 10, you have an occurrence of that compound event. In the two-coin toss experiment, the compound event was said to occur if you throw at least one "head" in a trial using two coins. Figure 6.1 illustrates this last case. "Success" is represented by the lined region, which is the "union" of the events $\{e_1, e_2, e_3\}$.

If we can discuss the probability of a compound event by relating it to the probabilities of the member elementary events, can we discuss the probability of two or more compound events? Think about this case; what is the probability of "at least one head *or* at least one tail" in the two-coin experiment?

To answer this question we need to know the relevant compound events. The compound event for "at least one head" is (e_1, or e_2, or e_3), call it a, and the compound event for "at least one tail" is (e_2, or e_3, or e_4), call it b. Let us call our event "at least one head or at least one tail," c. From our previous efforts, we have

$$\text{pr}(e_1, \text{ or } e_2, \text{ or } e_3) = p_1 + p_2 + p_3 = \text{pr}(a) = .75$$
$$\text{pr}(e_2, \text{ or } e_3, \text{ or } e_4) = p_2 + p_3 + p_4 = \text{pr}(b) = .75$$

So, is the probability of "at least one head or at least one tail" the sum of pr(a) and pr(b)? Try it:

$$\text{pr}(c) = \text{pr}(a) + \text{pr}(b)$$
$$= .75 + .75$$
$$= 1.5!$$

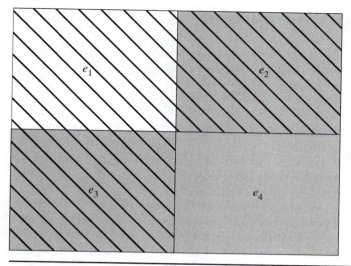

Figure 6.2   Table of elementary events for two-coin toss experiment. The lined region is the event "at least one head." The shaded region is the event "at least one tail."

Something is decidedly wrong! Probability cannot be greater than one. What worked so well for unions of elementary events does not seem to work for unions of compound events.

Let us look more closely at this problem. Study Figure 6.2, which reproduces Figure 6.1. Here we have put lines to represent the event a, which is "at least one head," and shaded the region corresponding to the event b, which is "at least one tail." Figure 6.2 gives us a clue to the solution to our problem, for we see that the elementary events e_2 and e_3 are represented twice, once in the event a and once in the event b. The event that is represented by the overlap between events a and b defines a new idea of a compound event. In this example, the overlap, or **intersection,** is the event defined by the occurrence of e_2 *and* e_3—that is, the occurrence of both a head and a tail on a single trial. In our first attempt at adding probabilities, the elementary events to be added were mutually exclusive, but the events a and b are not mutually exclusive. If $\{H, T\}$ occurs, this is consistent with declaring that event a has occurred, *and* it is also consistent with declaring that event b has occurred. Remember that a compound event occurs whenever any one member of its defining set of elementary events occurs on any trial. Events a and b are not mutually exclusive.

What is the way out of our difficulty? Well, we know how to add probability when the events are mutually exclusive, but what do we do when they are not? One solution is for us to convert our problem into one that only involves mutually exclusive events. To do this, we will have to develop some useful notation to ease our efforts.

A Mathematical Digression

Recall that we used the symbol S to represent the sample space. Compound events are collections of the elements, or members, of the set S. Suppose that A and B represent any two such compound events. From the events A and B, we create new events C and D:

■ Event C occurs if any elementary event in A *or* B occurs.

This is written as $C = A \cup B$.

■ Event D occurs if any elementary event in A *and* B occurs.

This is written as $D = A \cap B$.

The symbol "$\cup$" is called **union** and indicates that the event C is composed of the union of all the events in A or B (a **composite**) but without duplication. The symbol "$\cap$" is called "intersection" and indicates that the event D is composed of all elementary events that are in both compound events A and B. In our previous example with the two-coin toss, the event c was the union of the events a and b; that is, $c = a \cup b$. The elementary events that overlap between a and b form the intersection between the compound events a and b; that is, we define the event d by $d = a \cap b$, where d represents the compound event created by the intersection between a and b. The event d is composed of the elementary events $\{e_2, e_3\}$.

To make sure that we have a good understanding of our new tools, we should try another example. Consider the sample space for the 12-sided die experiment. To have something to work with, let us define the following compound events:

$$E_1 = \{1, 3, 5, 7, 9, 11\}$$
$$E_2 = \{2, 4, 6, 8, 10, 12\}$$
$$E_3 = \{5, 7, 9\}$$
$$E_4 = \{9, 10, 11, 12\}$$

Now we can practice our new definitions:

$$A = E_1 \cup E_2$$
$$= \{1, 2, 3, 4, 5, 6, 7, 8, 9, 10, 11, 12\} = S$$
$$B = E_1 \cap E_3$$
$$= \{5, 7, 9\} = E_3$$
$$C = E_3 \cup E_4$$
$$= \{5, 7, 9, 10, 11, 12\}$$
$$D = E_3 \cap E_4$$
$$= \{9\}$$
$$F = E_1 \cap E_2$$
$$= \emptyset$$

This last symbol $\emptyset$ means that F is an empty set; that is, F has no elements. Be careful to distinguish this from $\{0\}$, which is the set whose single element is zero. Events that have a null intersection are mutually exclusive, and vice versa.

One other useful notation is A^c, which means the **complement** of A. It contains all members of S that are not in A. For example, using our four events E_1, E_2, E_3, and E_4, we have

$$E_1^c = E_2$$
$$E_4^c = \{1, 2, 3, 4, 5, 6, 7, 8\}$$
$$\emptyset^c = S$$
$$S^c = \emptyset$$

Let us experiment some more with these relationships. By matching the lists of component elementary events, confirm the following relationships:

$$(E_1 \cap E_3) \cup (E_1^c \cap E_3) = E_3$$
$$(E_1 \cap E_2) \cup (E_1^c \cap E_2) = E_2$$
$$E_1 \cup E_1^c = S$$
$$E_1 \cap E_1^c = \emptyset$$

From these relationships we can build more. For example, what might we mean by the set operation:

$$A - B$$

We might guess that this expression means the set of all elements that are in A but are not in B. Let us formalize that notion by defining for any two sets A and B:

$$A - B = A \cap B^c$$

The right-hand side of the equation represents all those elements of the universal set S that are in A and in the complement of B—that is, in A but not in B.

We have defined numerous alternative compound events; one question that we have not yet asked is how many are there? This question can only be answered easily for the simple case in which we have a finite number of elementary events. Recall the single-coin toss example with only two elementary events, $\{e_1, e_2\}$. The total possible collection of events is

$$\{e_1\}, \{e_2\}, [\{S\} \text{ or } \{e_1, e_2\}], \emptyset$$

that is, four altogether. Now consider the total number of events for the two-coin toss experiment. We have

$$\{e_1\}, \{e_2\}, \{e_3\}, \{e_4\}, \{e_1, e_2\}, \{e_1, e_3\}, \{e_1, e_4\}$$
$$\{e_2, e_3\}, \{e_2, e_4\}, \{e_3, e_4\}, \{e_1, e_2, e_3\}, \{e_1, e_2, e_4\}$$
$$\{e_1, e_3, e_4\}, \{e_2, e_3, e_4\}, [S \text{ or } \{e_1, e_2, e_3, e_4\}], \emptyset$$

with a total of 16 events. The rule for determining the number of alternative events when there are K elementary events is given by 2^K. Each elementary event is included or not, there are just two choices. For each choice on each elementary event, we can choose all the others, so that our total number of choices is $2 \times 2 \times 2 \ldots 2$ (*k times*) $= 2^k$. In the first example there were only two elementary events, so the total number of events is 2^2, or 4. In the second example there were four elementary events, so there are 2^4, or 16, different events.

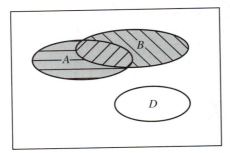

Figure 6.3   A Venn diagram illustrating compound events. The lined region \\\ is $A^c \cap B$. The lined region ≡≡≡ is $A \cap B^c$. The region is $A \cap B$. The shaded region is $A \cup B$. $A^c \cap D = B^c \cap D = D$. $A \cap D = B \cap D = \emptyset$.

Calculating the Probabilities of the Union of Events

With our new tools, we can easily resolve our problem of how to handle calculating the probabilities for compound events that are not mutually exclusive. Recollect that we know how to add probabilities for events that are mutually exclusive, but we do not yet know how to add probabilities for events that are not mutually exclusive. Consequently, our first attempt to solve our problem is to try to convert our "sum of compound events" into an equivalent "sum of mutually exclusive compound events." Look at Figure 6.3, which illustrates a sample space S and three arbitrary compound events A, B, and D. Notice that A and B overlap, so the intersection between A and B is not empty. But A and D do not overlap, so the intersection between A and D is empty, or $\emptyset$. The union of A and B is represented by the shading over the areas labeled A and B. This figure is known as a **Venn diagram;** it is very useful in helping to visualize problems involving the formation of compound events from other compound events.

While we work through the demonstration of how to add probabilities for compound events that are not mutually exclusive, focus on Figure 6.3. Suppose that we want to calculate the probability of the event E, given by the union of A and B; that is, $E = A \cup B$, which is composed of all the elementary events that are in either A or B. The idea is to reexpress the compound events A and B so that the new compound events are mutually exclusive. We can then express the probability of E as a simple sum of the probabilities of the component compound events that are mutually exclusive. From Figure 6.3, we see that there are three mutually exclusive compound events in the union of A and B: $\{A \cap B\}$, $\{A \cap B^c\}$, $\{A^c \cap B\}$.

Because both $A^c \cap A$ and $B^c \cap B$ are null (that is, $A^c \cap A = \emptyset$ and $B^c \cap B = \emptyset$), our three listed events are mutually exclusive. For example, none of the elementary events that are in $\{A \cap B\}$ can be in $\{A \cap B^c\}$ as well because $\{B \cap B^c\}$ is null; an elementary event cannot be in both B and B^c at the same time. Let us now reexpress the event $\{A \cup B\}$ in terms of its component events:

$$A \cup B = (A \cap B) \cup (A \cap B^c) \cup (A^c \cap B)$$

First, we should check that the equation is correct, which is illustrated in Figure 6.3, by making sure logically that no elementary event can be in more than one of the component events for $\{A \cup B\}$ and that any elementary event that is in $\{A \cup B\}$ is also in one of $(A \cap B)$, $(A \cap B^c)$, or $(A^c \cap B)$. All the elementary events that are in $\{A \cup B\}$ are in one, and only one, of $(A \cap B)$, $(A \cap B^c)$, or $(A^c \cap B)$.

Now that we have mutually exclusive compound events, we can use our old expression to get the probability of the compound event $\{A \cup B\}$:

$$\text{pr}(A \cup B) = \text{pr}(A \cap B) + \text{pr}(A \cap B^c) + \text{pr}(A^c \cap B)$$

Let us see if we can rearrange this expression to relate the left side to the probabilities for A and B. To do this, we use the following identities:

$$(A \cap B) \cup (A \cap B^c) = A$$
$$\text{pr}(A \cap B) \cup (A \cap B^c) = \text{pr}(A)$$
$$(B \cap A) \cup (B \cap A^c) = B$$
$$\text{pr}\left[(B \cap A) \cup (B \cap A^c)\right] = \text{pr}(B)$$

If we now add and subtract $\text{pr}(A \cap B) = \text{pr}(B \cap A)$ (why is this always true?) to the expression $\text{pr}(A \cup B)$, we will be able to rewrite the expression $\text{pr}(A \cup B)$ in terms of $\text{pr}(A)$ and $\text{pr}(B)$ to get

$$\text{pr}(A \cup B) =$$
$$\left[\text{pr}(A \cap B) + \text{pr}(A \cap B^c)\right] + \left[\text{pr}(A^c \cap B) + \text{pr}(A \cap B)\right] - \text{pr}(A \cap B) \qquad (6.1)$$
$$= \text{pr}(A) + \text{pr}(B) - \text{pr}(A \cap B)$$

This is our new general statement for evaluating the probability of compound events formed from the union of any two arbitrary compound events. If the compound events are mutually exclusive, as they are with elementary events, then the new statement reduces to the old because $\text{pr}(A \cap B)$ for A, B mutually exclusive, is 0.

The name given to the probability of the intersection of A and B is the **joint probability** of A and B; it is the probability that in any trial an elementary event will occur that is in both the compound events A and B.

Refer to our compound events E_1 to E_4 from the 12-sided die experiment:

$$E_1 = \{1, 3, 5, 7, 9, 11\}$$
$$E_2 = \{2, 4, 6, 8, 10, 12\}$$
$$E_3 = \{5, 7, 9\}$$
$$E_4 = \{9, 10, 11, 12\}$$

Let us calculate the probabilities of A to F, where

$$A = E_1 \cup E_2$$
$$= \{1, 2, 3, 4, 5, 6, 7, 8, 9, 10, 11, 12\} = S$$
$$B = E_1 \cap E_3$$
$$= \{5, 7, 9\} = E_3$$

$$C = E_3 \cup E_4$$
$$= \{5, 7, 9, 10, 11, 12\}$$
$$D = E_3 \cap E_4$$
$$= \{9\}$$
$$F = E_1 \cap E_2$$
$$= \emptyset$$

In each instance, we have two ways to calculate the required probability. We can reduce each compound event to a collection of elementary events and then merely add up the probabilities of the component elementary events; we can always do this. However, trying to calculate the probabilities by this procedure can easily get to be a tremendous chore. The alternative is to use our theory to find easier and simpler ways to perform the calculations.

Some results should be immediately obvious. For example, what are the probabilities for events A and F? The immediate answers are 1 and 0; do you see why? The probability of S, $\mathrm{pr}(S)$, is the probability that at least one of the logical outcomes will occur on any trial; because we have defined the set of elementary events to be exhaustive, we know that one of the outcomes must happen so the probability is 1. Correspondingly, the probability that none of the elementary events will occur is 0 by the same reasoning.

Now consider the probability of event $C = E_3 \cup E_4$. We have discovered that this probability is given by the sum of the probabilities of the individual component events less an allowance for the double counting that is caused by the intersection of the component events. The probability of C in this case is

$$\mathrm{pr}(C) = \mathrm{pr}(E_3) + \mathrm{pr}(E_4) - \mathrm{pr}(E_3 \cap E_4)$$
$$= \frac{3}{12} + \frac{4}{12} - \frac{1}{12}$$
$$= \frac{1}{2}$$

Recall that $E_3 \cap E_4 = \{5, 7, 9\} \cap \{9, 10, 11, 12\} = \{9\}$. $E_3 \cup E_4 = \{5, 7, 9, 10, 11, 12\}$. So, in both cases the probabilities are easily confirmed; $\mathrm{pr}(\{9\}) = \frac{1}{12}$ and $\mathrm{pr}(\{5, 7, 9, 10, 11, 12\}) = \frac{6}{12} = \frac{1}{2}$.

The Definition of Probability for Sample Spaces of Discrete Events

In the section "Introducing Probabilities," we defined the probability of an elementary event. That was fine as a beginning, but now we have broadened the notion of probability quite a bit. We now see that probability really is defined on *subsets* of the sample space rather than on the sample space itself. Indeed, we would like our definition of probability to be as general as we can make it. In this connection, for any sample space S we want to be able to define probabilities for any subset of S that is constructed by any combination of unions or intersections or complementarities. Logically, this means that we should be able to determine the probability of any set of events that are combined by the logical statements "and," "or," and "not." In short, given any subset of S formed in any way whatsoever using these procedures, we will be able to assess its probability.

Probability for a sample space of discrete events is a function defined on the class of all subsets of the sample space that satisfies the following conditions:

1. For any set A contained in S: $0 \le \text{pr}(\{A\}) \le 1$
2. For any disjoint sets A, B—that is $\{A \cap B\} = \emptyset$

$$\text{pr}(\{A \cup B\}) = \text{pr}(\{A\}) + \text{pr}(\{B\})$$

3. For any sets $\{A_i\}$ such that $\cup_i\{A_i\} = S$, that are mutually disjoint—that is, $\{A_i \cap A_j\} = \emptyset$ for all $i \ne j$

$$\text{pr}(\cup_i\{A_i\}) = 1$$

We are merely saying that for any set of events drawn from S, the probability is between 0 and 1, the definition of probability for the union of two events that are mutually exclusive is the sum of the constituent probabilities, and the sum of mutually exclusive and exhaustive events has a probability of 1. We are now ready to extend our notion of probability once again.

6.4   Conditional Probability

Often in life we face circumstances in which the outcome of some occurrence depends on the outcome of a prior occurrence. Even more important, the very alternatives that we face often depend on the outcome of previous choices and the chance outcomes from those choices. The probability distribution of your future income depends on your choice of profession and on many other events over which you may have no control. We can simulate such compound choices by contemplating tossing one die to determine the die to be tossed subsequently.

How do we use our probability theory in this situation? What is different from the previous case is that we now have to consider calculating probability conditional on some prior choice, and that choice itself may depend on a probability. Suppose that you are contemplating a choice of university to attend, and then given the university that you attend you face having to get a job on graduating. If you apply to ten universities, you can consider the chance that you will enter each, and given your attendance at each university, you can consider the chance that you will be employed within six months. The chance that you are employed within six months depends on the university from which you graduate. This situation can be more abstractly modeled by contemplating tossing a die to represent your first set of alternatives, which university you will attend. Given each university that you might attend, there is an associated chance that you will soon be employed; and this is represented by the toss of a second die, but which die that you get to toss depends on which university you actually attend. The various income outcomes from each university can be represented by tossing a die, and across universities the dice to be tossed will be different in that they will represent different probabilities.

The questions that we might want to ask include, What is the chance of getting a job whatever university you attend? or, For each university that you might attend,

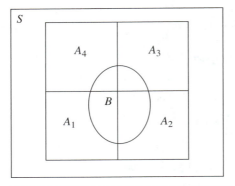

Figure 6.4   Illustration of the concept of conditional probability.

what are the chances that you will get a job? and How can you determine what those chances might be?

What we are really trying to do is to define a new set of probabilities from other probabilities that relate to a specific subset of choices or outcomes. A **conditional probability** is the probability an event will occur given that another has occurred. Look at the Venn diagram in Figure 6.4. What we are trying to do is illustrated in Figure 6.4 by the problem of defining a new set of probabilities relative to the event B. If we know that the event B has occurred, or we merely want to restrict our attention to the event B, then relative to the event B what are the probabilities for the events $\{A_i\}$, $i = 1, \ldots, 4$? You may think of the event B as attending university B instead of some other university. You can regard the events $\{A_i\}$ as the probabilities of getting different types of jobs.

If we are looking at the probability of the event A_i, $i = 1, 2, \ldots$, given the event B, then we are in part concerned with the joint probability of each of the events A_i, $i = 1, 2, \ldots$ and B—that is, with the probability of the events $(A_i \cap B)$, $i = 1, \ldots, 4$.

The event A_i given B is the set of elementary events such that we would declare that the event A_i has occurred and the event B has occurred; so far this is just the *joint event* of A_i and B. The change in focus from joint probability stems from the idea that now we would like to talk about the probability of A_i *relative* to the probability of B occurring. We are in effect changing our frame of reference from the whole sample space S that contains A_i and B to just that part of the sample space that is represented by the compound event B.

Figure 6.4 shows a sample space S containing four compound events, A_1, A_2, A_3, and A_4, together with an event, B, with respect to which we want to calculate the conditional probability of the A_i given B. As drawn, the A_i do not intersect, they are mutually exclusive; that is, the joint probability of $\{A_i \cap A_j\}$, for any i and j, is 0. This assumption is not necessary but is a great convenience while explaining the theory of conditional probabilities. Let the joint probability of each A_i with B be denoted p_i^b, that is, $\text{pr}(A_i \cap B) = p_i^b$, $i = 1, 2, 3, 4$. Since the $\text{pr}(S) = 1$ and the union of the compound events $A_i \cap B$, $i = 1, 2, 3, 4$ is certainly less than S (because B is not the whole of S), we know that $\text{pr}[\cup_i (A_i \cap B)]$, where

$$\text{pr}[\cup_i (A_i \cap B)] = \text{pr}[(A_1 \cap B) \cup (A_2 \cap B) \cup (A_3 \cap B) \cup (A_4 \cap B)]$$
$$= p_1^b + p_2^b + p_3^b + p_4^b$$

is not greater than 1; indeed, it is less than 1. But our intent was to try to concentrate on probability restricted to the event B. This suggests that we divide p_i^b by $\text{pr}(B)$ to obtain a set of probabilities that, relative to the event B, sum to 1.

We define the conditional probability of the event A given the event B by

$$\text{pr}(A|B) = \frac{\text{pr}(A \cap B)}{\text{pr}(B)} \tag{6.2}$$

The probability of an event A restricted to event B is the joint probability of A and B divided by the probability of the event B. It is clear that this procedure yields a new set of probabilities that also sum to one, but only over the compound event B.

A simple example is given by considering the two mutually exclusive events, A and A^c. The distribution of probability over A and A^c, where the event B intersects both is

$$\text{pr}(A|B) + \text{pr}(A^c|B) =$$

$$\frac{\text{pr}(A \cap B)}{\text{pr}(B)} + \frac{\text{pr}(A^c \cap B)}{\text{pr}(B)} = \frac{\text{pr}(B)}{\text{pr}(B)} \tag{6.3}$$

$$= 1$$

We can add the probabilities in this expression, because A and A^c are mutually exclusive. Further, it is always true that

$$(A \cap B) \cup (A^c \cap B) = B$$

for any events A and B. If you do not see this right away, draw a Venn diagram and work out the proof for yourself.

Many statisticians claim that conditional probabilities are the most important probabilities, because almost all events met in practice are conditional on something. Without going that far you will soon discover that conditional probabilities are very, very useful.

For now, let us try another simple example from the sample space where $S = \{1, 2, 3, \ldots, 11, 12\}$. Define the compound events a_i and b as follows:

$a_1 = \{1, 2, 3, 4, 5, 6\}$

$a_2 = \{7, 8\}$

$a_3 = \{9, 10, 11\}$

$b = \{6, 7, 8, 9\}$

So, the compound events formed by the intersection of a_i and b are

$a_1 \cap b = \{6\}$

$a_2 \cap b = \{7, 8\}$

$a_3 \cap b = \{9\}$

The corresponding joint probabilities are now easily calculated by adding the probabilities of the mutually exclusive (elementary) events in each set:

$$p_1^b = \mathrm{pr}(a_1 \cap b) = \frac{1}{12}$$

$$p_2^b = \mathrm{pr}(a_2 \cap b) = \frac{2}{12}$$

$$p_3^b = \mathrm{pr}(a_3 \cap b) = \frac{1}{12}$$

$$\mathrm{pr}(b) = \frac{4}{12}$$

The corresponding conditional probabilities are given by:

$$\mathrm{pr}(a_1|b) = \frac{p_1^b}{\mathrm{pr}(b)} = \frac{\frac{1}{12}}{\frac{1}{3}} = \frac{1}{4}$$

$$\mathrm{pr}(a_2|b) = \frac{p_2^b}{\mathrm{pr}(b)} = \frac{\frac{2}{12}}{\frac{1}{3}} = \frac{1}{2}$$

$$\mathrm{pr}(a_3|b) = \frac{p_3^b}{\mathrm{pr}(b)} = \frac{\frac{1}{12}}{\frac{1}{3}} = \frac{1}{4}$$

$$\sum_i \mathrm{pr}(a_i|b) = \frac{\sum_i p_i^b}{\mathrm{pr}(b)} = 1$$

Now that we understand the idea of conditional probability, it is not a great step to recognize that we can always and trivially reexpress ordinary, or "marginal," probabilities as conditional probabilities relative to the whole sample space. (**Marginal probabilities** are the probabilities associated with unconditional events.) Recognize for a sample space S and any set A that is a subset of S, that $A \cap S = A$ and that $\mathrm{pr}(S) = 1$. Therefore, we can formally state that the conditional probability of A given the sample space S is $\mathrm{pr}(A)$. More formally, we have

$$\mathrm{pr}(A|S) = \frac{\mathrm{pr}(A \cap S)}{\mathrm{pr}(S)}$$

$$= \mathrm{pr}(A)$$

Let us experiment with the concept of conditional probability in solving problems. We will use the popular game Dungeons & Dragons® to illustrate the idea of conditional probability. Imagine that you are facing four doors: behind one is a treasure, behind another is an amulet to gain protection from scrofula, and behind the other two are the dreaded Hydra and the fire dragon, respectively. With an octagonal (an eight-sided die), suppose that rolling a 1 or a 2 gives you entrance to

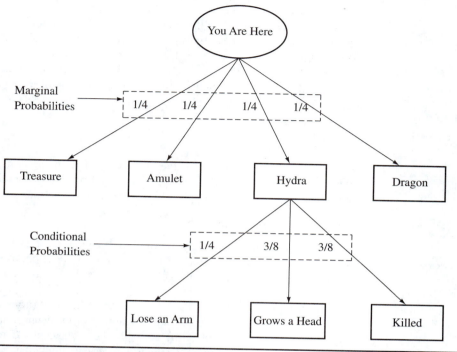

Figure 6.5   A probability tree for the Dungeons & Dragons® example.

the treasure, rolling a 4 or a 5 provides the amulet, and rolling a 6 or a 7 brings on the fire-breathing dragon. However, if you roll a 3 or an 8, you get the Hydra. The probability of this event using the "equally likely principle" is 2/8, or 1/4. These probabilities, labeled the "*marginal probabilities*," are illustrated in Figure 6.5.

If you rolled a 3 or an 8, you must now roll another octagonal die to discover the outcomes that await you through the Hydra door. If you then roll a 1 or a 2, you will lose an arm with probability 1/4; if 3, 4, or 5, the Hydra grows another head with probability of 3/8; and if 6 or more, the Hydra dies and you escape for another adventure with probability of 3/8. These probabilities are the conditional probabilities. What is the probability of your losing an arm given that you have already chosen the Hydra door? What is the probability of your losing an arm before you know which door you have to go through? The former probability is the conditional probability; it is the probability of losing an arm given that you have chosen the Hydra door, 1/4. The second probability is one we need to calculate. The conditional probabilities of the various alternatives before choosing the Hydra door are

- lose your arm; conditional probability $= \frac{2}{8} = \frac{1}{4}$
- Hydra grows a head; conditional probability $= \frac{3}{8}$
- Hydra killed; conditional probability $= \frac{3}{8}$

These three probabilities are of the form $\text{pr}(a_i \mid b)$, where a_i is one of the three alternatives facing you and b is the event "chose the Hydra door."

In this example, you have been given the conditional probability, but to work out the probability of losing an arm before you chose your door, you will have to know the probability of choosing the Hydra door. That probability, the marginal probability, as we calculated is $\frac{1}{4}$. Now how do we get the probability of losing an arm? Look back at the definition of conditional probability:

$$\text{pr}(A|B) = \frac{\text{pr}(A \cap B)}{\text{pr}(B)} \tag{6.4}$$

In our case $\text{pr}(A|B) = \frac{1}{4}$—that is, the probability of losing an arm given you drew the Hydra door—and $\text{pr}(B) = \frac{1}{4}$—that is, the probability of drawing the Hydra door—so, the probability of both drawing the Hydra door and losing your arm is

$$\text{pr}(A \cap B) = \text{pr}(A|B) \times \text{pr}(B) \tag{6.5}$$

We got this from Equation 6.4 by multiplying both sides of that equation by $\text{pr}(B)$. We conclude from Equation 6.5 that the joint probability of choosing the Hydra door and losing an arm has a probability of $(\frac{1}{4}) \times (\frac{1}{4}) = \frac{1}{16}$; because $\text{pr}(A|B) = \frac{1}{4}$ and $\text{pr}(B) = \frac{1}{4}$.

This last expression that we have used to obtain the joint probability of $\frac{1}{16}$ provides us with an interesting insight: the joint probability of the event A and B is the probability of A given B multiplied by the probability of the event B. This is a general result, not restricted to our current example. Further, we immediately recognize that we could as easily have written

$$\text{pr}(A \cap B) = \text{pr}(B|A) \times \text{pr}(A) \tag{6.6}$$

We could have defined joint probability in terms of this relationship; that is, the joint probability of two events A and B is given by the product of the probability of A given B times the probability of B. This is a type of "statistical chain rule." The probability of getting both A and B in a trial is equivalent to the probability of getting B first, followed by the probability of getting A, given B has already been drawn. We evaluate the events together, but for the purposes of calculation, we can think of them as events that occur consecutively.

Summing Up the Many Definitions of Probability

We started with one simple idea of probability, a theoretical analogue of relative frequency. We now have four concepts of probability:

- ■ (Marginal) probability: $\text{pr}(A)$, $\text{pr}(C)$
- ■ Joint probability: $\text{pr}(A \cap B)$, $\text{pr}(K \cap L)$
- ■ Composite (union) probability: $\text{pr}(A \cup B)$, $\text{pr}(K \cup L)$
- ■ Conditional probability: $\text{pr}(A|B)$, $\text{pr}(C|K)$

where A, B, C, K, and L each represent any event. We describe probabilities as "marginal" to stress that we are not talking about joint, composite, or conditional probability. So marginal probabilities are just our old probabilities dressed up with an added name. All of these concepts of probability are related to each other; we have discovered some of these relationships already.

A visual way of seeing some of these relationships is through a diagram called a **probability tree**, an example of which we present in Figure 6.5. In a probability tree, at each stage, except for the first, usually we have the conditional probabilities—that is, the probabilities of moving from the previous position to the next, given that one has managed to get to the previous position. At the very first stage, we have the marginal probabilities; for at that stage there are no conditioning events as yet. However, be careful, sometimes you are not given the conditional probabilities at a given stage but the joint probability of getting to the given point. In the Dungeons & Dragons® example, you could have been given not the conditional probability of killing the Hydra, given the choice of the Hydra door, but the joint probability of choosing the Hydra door and killing the dragon. That probability would be $(\frac{1}{4})(\frac{3}{8}) = \frac{3}{32}$. If you were given just the marginal probability of choosing the Hydra door and the joint probability of killing the Hydra, you could have then calculated the conditional probability of killing the dragon, given you had chosen the Hydra door; in this case the result would be simply $\frac{3}{32}$ divided by $\frac{1}{4}$, which is $\frac{3}{8}$. Conditional probability is given by the joint probability divided by the marginal probability.

Note that the probability of a union of events is the sum of the probabilities of the component events; the joint probability of two events we see as a restriction of probability. The probability of more and more elementary events gets bigger and bigger; the joint probability of more and more events gets smaller and smaller. Adding unions of events adds to the alternative states that constitute "success"; seeking the joint occurrence of more and more events increasingly restricts the region of sample space for which we seek the probability; fewer and fewer elementary events constitute "success." Probabilities are always positive and increasingly more restrictions can only reduce the probability to zero. The probability of unions involves "addition," and the probability of restriction involves "multiplication."

6.5 Random Variables: Intuition Made Formal

Until now we have dealt successfully with the probabilities of events; events have all had labels attached to them, such as a_i, b, heads, tails, or numbers as in the 12-sided die. But even in this last example, the numbers were still just labels used to identify the relevant event. Labels, however, are not going to be of much use when we try our newfound skills on continuous variables; we would need a lot of labels, indeed, an infinite number of them. Further, when dealing with events and their labels we are restricted to talking about the probability of occurrence only; for example, there is no way to obtain abstract generalizations of the "moments" that we discussed in the previous two chapters. We will have to reconsider our approach.

Our theoretical tools so far comprise the ideas of a sample space, elementary events, probabilities, compound events, and their probabilities. Compound events, as we saw, are collections, or subsets, of the elementary events in the sample space. We have seen that these collections, or subsets, of elementary events are the major building blocks of our theory so far; if the elementary events are the "atoms" of our theory, the compound events are the "molecules" of our theory.

Because numbers are easier to deal with than labels, what we would like to do is to convert our present notions into ones using numbers. The objective is to convert our discussion from statements involving "probabilities of events," where events are designated by "labels," into mathematical statements expressed in terms of functions with numbers as their arguments. The first step in this change in viewpoint is to redefine our "events" in terms of real numbers.

That is easily done. Let us define a **random variable** as a function (yes, a function), from subsets of the sample space to the real numbers. The easiest subsets to handle are the elementary events themselves. We have

$$S = \{e_1, e_2, e_3, \ldots \ldots, e_k\}$$
$$\downarrow \ \downarrow \ \downarrow \qquad\qquad \downarrow$$
$$r_1, r_2, r_3, \ldots \ldots, r_k$$

and we can associate the relevant probabilities with both the event labels and the corresponding random variable values. All that we have done so far is to assign a value, $r_i, i = 1, 2, \ldots, k$ to the ith event e_i. Using this relationship between events and the assigned variable values, we can now define the probability relationship:

$$\{e_1, e_2, e_3, \ldots, e_k\} \leftrightarrow \{r_1, \quad r_2, \quad r_3, \quad \ldots, \quad r_k\}$$
$$\downarrow \ \downarrow \ \downarrow \qquad \downarrow \qquad\quad \downarrow \quad \downarrow \quad \downarrow \qquad\qquad \downarrow$$
$$p_1, p_2, p_3, \ldots, p_k \leftrightarrow p(r_1), \ p(r_2), \ p(r_3), \ \ldots, \ p(r_k)$$

To get a better feel for this, let us reconsider our two-coin-tossing experiments. The sample spaces are

$$S_1 = \{H, T\}$$
$$S_2 = \{HH, HT, TH, TT\}$$

Some possible assignments of random variable values to the events include:

$$\{H, T\} \rightarrow \{0, 1\}$$
or $\{H, T\} \rightarrow \{4, 8\}$
or $\{H, T\} \rightarrow \{5.2, 6.9\}$
or ...

$$\{HH, HT, TH, TT\} \rightarrow \{1, 2, 3, 4\}$$
or $\{HH, HT, TH, TT\} \rightarrow \{3, 7, 1, 5\}$
or ...

From these examples we see that there are a lot of possibilities for defining random variables, even with the same sample space. The choice between the alternatives is usually one of simple convenience and ease of calculation. For example, with S_1, the simplest choice is $\{0, 1\}$, and for S_2, the simplest is $\{1, 2, 3, 4\}$.

The allocation of probability is as before. For the first sample space, we have

$$S: \quad \{H, \ T\} \ \leftrightarrow \{0, \ 1\}$$
$$\downarrow \ \downarrow \qquad \downarrow \ \downarrow$$
$$\text{pr} = \{.5, \ .5\} \ \leftrightarrow \{.5, \ .5\}$$

For the second sample space, we have

$$S_2: \quad \{HH, \ HT, \ TH, \ TT\} \ \leftrightarrow \{1, \ 2, \ 3, \ 4\}$$
$$\downarrow \quad \downarrow \quad \downarrow \quad \downarrow \qquad \downarrow \quad \downarrow \quad \downarrow \quad \downarrow$$
$$\text{pr} \ = \{.25 \quad .25 \quad .25 \quad .25\} \ \leftrightarrow \{.25 \ .25 \ .25 \ .25\}$$

Note that the definition for a random variable involved functions on *subsets* of the sample space, not the sample space itself and its component events. We can easily handle individual events as we did here because the probabilities are defined with respect to subsets consisting of single events. We should write for a single event that, for example:

$$\text{pr}(\{e_i\}) = p_i$$

and not

$$\text{pr}(e_i) = p_i$$

The {.} in the preceding statement stresses that we are seeking the probability of a subset, whereas the simple parentheses (.) would indicate trying to obtain the probability of an element of the sample space. All of this may sound like too much fuss over inconsequential differences, but the distinction will later become more important in its consequences. In any case, it is best to start by having the right idea. Remember, probabilities are defined on subsets of a sample space, not on the sample space elements themselves.

Incorporating the notion of a random variable into the assignment of probabilities, we now recognize that we can define a random variable on the sample space by choosing a function $Y = h(\{e_i\})$ to yield real numbers. We can define probability on the random variable by defining another function $f(Y)$:

$$\text{pr}(\{e_i\}) = f(Y) = f(h(\{e_i\})) \tag{6.7}$$

All we are saying here is that for each event $\{e_i\}$, we can, through the definitions of $h(.)$ and $f(.)$, assign the exact same probabilities. In short, the "random variable" is interposed between the events defined originally by subsets of the $\{e_i\}$ and the probabilities attached to them. The reason for this procedure is not yet fully clear, but its usefulness will be amply demonstrated in the next two chapters.

The function $f(.)$ defined on the random variable Y is called a **probability mass function.** As its name implies, it assigns some probability "mass," or "weight," to each discrete value of the random variable. The name is often shortened to the **probability function.** We will return to these definitions and the role of random variables in the next chapter.

An Example Using Two Random Variables

Many of our definitions and concepts can best be illustrated through a simple example, using a pair of random variables that have discrete values. Consider Table 6.4.

Here we have two random variables: X_1 takes on only two values, $\{0, 1\}$, and X_2 takes on three values, $\{-1, 0, 1\}$. X_1 might represent the sex of the individual and X_2 might represent whether someone passed or failed an examination. $X_2 = 1$ indicates

Table 6.4   **Joint Probabilities for the Random Variables X_1, X_2**

		X_2		
		−1	0	1
X_1	0	0	1/4	1/4
	1	1/4	1/4	0

the student passed the examination, $-1 =$ failed, and $0 =$ did not take the examination. Our sample space is given by:

$$S = (0, -1) \ (0, 0) \ (0, 1) \ (1, -1) \ (1, 0) \ (1, 1)$$
$$\text{Probability} = 0 \quad\quad 1/4 \quad 1/4 \quad 1/4 \quad\quad 1/4 \quad 0$$

The only difference between this table of probabilities and our previous ones is that the elementary events in this table are composed of pairs of numbers. Listing the values in a two-by-two table is merely a convenience. If we have defined a genuine set of probabilities, then the sum of the probabilities over the entire sample space will be one; it is, as you can easily check for yourself.

This is a table of joint probabilities; each entry in the table is the probability of a joint event—namely, the event specified by the values taken by the two defining variables. For example, the event $(0, 1)$, female and passed the examination, is the joint event: $\{X_1 = 0, X_2 = 1\}$. The event $(1, -1)$, male and failed the examination, is the joint event: $\{X_1 = 1, X_2 = -1\}$. The distribution of probabilities over the entries is called the **joint probability function.**

We can now use this table to demonstrate the relationships between the various concepts of probability. Because the entries in the table are joint probabilities, the first question is how we might recapture the marginal probability distributions from the joint probability distribution. The **marginal probability distribution** of the random variable X_1 is the probability distribution of X_1, regardless of the values taken by any other variable. The joint probability distribution is the probability distribution of the joint event defined by the pairs of values taken by both X_1 and X_2.

From Table 6.4, can we obtain the marginal probability distribution of X_1 by summing the joint probabilities over the values of X_2? Alternatively, can we obtain the marginal probability distribution of X_2 by summing the joint probability over the values of X_1? The rationale behind these suggestions is that the marginal probability is the union of the events involving the other variable and that the entries in the table of joint probabilities are mutually exclusive.

Table 6.5 sums the probabilities across each random variable added. For example, the event $\{X_1 = 0\}$, meaning the examination taker is female, is the union of the mutually exclusive events:

$$[\{X_1 = 0, X_2 = -1\}, \{X_1 = 0, X_2 = 0\}, \{X_1 = 0, X_2 = 1\}]$$

So, we can deduce from what we have learned that

$$\text{pr}(X_1 = 0) = \{\text{pr}(X_1 = 0, X_2 = -1) + \text{pr}(X_1 = 0, X_2 = 0) + \text{pr}(X_1 = 0, X_2 = 1)\}$$
$$\frac{1}{2} = 0 + \frac{1}{4} + \frac{1}{4}$$

Table 6.5   **Joint and Marginal Probabilities for the Variables in Table 6.4**

		X_2			Marginal Probability X_1
		−1	0	1	↓
X_1	0	0	1/4	1/4	1/2
	1	1/4	1/4	0	1/2
Marginal Probability X_2	→	1/4	1/2	1/4	1

Another example is the event $\{X_2 = 0\}$, meaning the individual did not take the examination, which is the union of the two mutually exclusive events:

$$[\{X_1 = 0, X_2 = 0\}, \{X_1 = 1, X_2 = 0\}]$$

So, we can also deduce that the marginal probability is

$$\text{pr}(X_2 = 0) = \{\text{pr}(X_1 = 0, X_2 = 0) + \text{pr}(X_1 = 1, X_2 = 0)\}$$
$$\frac{1}{2} = \frac{1}{4} + \frac{1}{4}$$

The formal statement of this operation is

$$\text{pr}(X_i) = \sum_j \text{pr}(X_i, Y_j)$$
$$\text{pr}(Y_j) = \sum_i \text{pr}(X_i, Y_j) \tag{6.8}$$

for any pair of random variables $\{X_i, Y_j\}$. To obtain the marginal probability distribution for one random variable from a table of joint probabilities for a pair of random variables, we sum the joint probabilities over the values of the other random variable.

Having shown how to obtain marginal probabilities from joint probabilities, let us relate conditional and joint probabilities. Recall the definition of conditional probability for pairs of events:

$$\text{pr}(A|B) = \frac{\text{pr}(A, B)}{\text{pr}(B)} \tag{6.9}$$

for any two events A, B.

With random variables, we have to define a conditional probability distribution. A **conditional probability distribution** is the probability distribution of one random variable given some specific value for the other random variable. Let us designate an arbitrary, but specific, value of the conditioning event by the notation y_j^0; that is, y_j^0 indicates specifying a particular value for the variable Y_j. Formally, we may state for a pair of random variables $\{X_i, Y_j\}_{i=1, \ldots}$:

$$\text{pr}(X_i|Y_j = y_j^0) = \frac{\text{pr}(X_i, y_j^0)}{\text{pr}(y_j^0)}$$

where $\text{pr}(X_i|y_j^0)$ is the conditional probability of the random variable X_i conditional upon, or evaluated at, the value y_j^0 for the variable Y_j; $\text{pr}(X_i, y_j^0)$ is the joint probability for the variable X_i and the specified value for Y_j, y_j^0; and $\text{pr}(y_j^0)$ is the marginal probability that Y_j will take the specified value y_j^0. The conditional probability distribution is obtained from the set of conditional probabilities for all X_i given the specified value for Y_j, y_j^0.

Let us use our joint distribution of X_1, X_2 shown in Table 6.4 to illustrate these ideas. Consider:

$$\text{pr}(X_1 = 0|X_2 = -1) = \frac{\text{pr}(X_1 = 0, X_2 = -1)}{\text{pr}(X_2 = -1)}$$

$$= \frac{0}{\frac{1}{4}}$$

$$= 0$$

$$\text{pr}(X_1 = 1|X_2 = -1) = \frac{\text{pr}(X_1 = 1, X_2 = -1)}{\text{pr}(X_2 = -1)}$$

$$= \frac{\frac{1}{4}}{\frac{1}{4}}$$

$$= 1$$

$$\text{pr}(X_1 = 0|X_2 = 0) = \frac{\text{pr}(X_1 = 0, X_2 = 0)}{\text{pr}(X_2 = 0)}$$

$$= \frac{\frac{1}{4}}{\frac{1}{2}}$$

$$= \frac{1}{2}$$

$$\text{pr}(X_1 = 1|X_2 = 0) = \frac{\text{pr}(X_1 = 1, X_2 = 0)}{\text{pr}(X_2 = 0)}$$

$$= \frac{\frac{1}{4}}{\frac{1}{2}}$$

$$= \frac{1}{2}$$

$$\text{pr}(X_2 = -1|X_1 = 0) = \frac{\text{pr}(X_1 = 0, X_2 = -1)}{\text{pr}(X_1 = 0)}$$

$$= \frac{0}{\frac{1}{2}}$$

$$= 0$$

$$\text{pr}(X_2 = 0 | X_1 = 0) = \frac{\text{pr}(X_1 = 0, X_2 = 0)}{\text{pr}(X_1 = 0)}$$

$$= \frac{\frac{1}{4}}{\frac{1}{2}}$$

$$= \frac{1}{2}$$

$$\text{pr}(X_2 = 1 | X_1 = 0) = \frac{\text{pr}(X_1 = 0, X_2 = 1)}{\text{pr}(X_1 = 0)}$$

$$= \frac{\frac{1}{4}}{\frac{1}{2}}$$

$$= \frac{1}{2}$$

If you were to calculate more conditional probability distributions from this table you would discover that usually the conditional probability distribution is not equal to the corresponding marginal probability distribution. Further, the conditional probability distribution of, say X_1 given X_2, is not the same as that of X_2 given X_1.

But in one case, we saw that the marginal probability distribution was equal to the conditional probability distribution—namely, the conditional probability distribution of X_1 given $X_2 = 0$. This raises an interesting question, Could we have the conditional probability distributions equal to the marginal distributions? And if we did, what would it mean? Let us weigh this idea with Table 6.5 in mind.

6.6 Statistical Independence

If the conditional probability distribution of X_2 given any value taken by the random variable X_1 is equal to the marginal probability distribution of X_2, then in effect we are saying that the probability distribution of X_2 is "independent" in some sense of the values taken by X_1. As we look at the conditional probability distribution of X_2 for various values of X_1 we would always get the same distribution, that of the marginal distribution of X_2. Intuitively, this seems like an interesting and potentially useful idea, so let us define a concept of statistical independence.

Statistical independence can be defined with respect to both the probabilities of events and the probability distributions of random variables.

Two events A, B are statistically independent if

$$\text{pr}(A|B) = \text{pr}(A) \tag{6.10}$$

And two random variables are statistically independent if

$$\text{pr}(X_i|Y_j) = \text{pr}(X_i) \tag{6.11}$$

for all values of Y_j.

The condition "for all" is important as we have already seen in Table 6.5. The conditional probability distribution of X_1 given $X_2 = 0$ is equal to the marginal probability distribution of X_1, but that is not true for $X_2 = -1$, or 1.

If the event A is statistically independent of the event B, is the event B statistically independent of the event A? Logically, that requirement would seem to make sense, but we should check that our definition meets it.

If A is statistically independent of B, then

$$\text{pr}(A|B) = \text{pr}(A)$$

but by the definition of conditional probability

$$\text{pr}(A|B) = \frac{\text{pr}(A, B)}{\text{pr}(B)}$$
$$= \text{pr}(A)$$

so, we have

$$\text{pr}(A, B) = \text{pr}(A) \times \text{pr}(B)$$

with the result that

$$\text{pr}(B|A) = \frac{\text{pr}(A, B)}{\text{pr}(A)}$$
$$= \frac{\text{pr}(A) \times \text{pr}(B)}{\text{pr}(A)}$$
$$= \text{pr}(B)$$

We conclude that "statistically independent" is symmetric; if A is statistically independent of B, then B is statistically independent of A. Similarly, we could show that if the probability distribution of the random variable X is statistically independent of the random variable Y, then the probability distribution of Y is statistically independent of the random variable X.

In both cases we have discovered an interesting result; if two events are statistically independent, or two random variables are statistically independent, then the joint probability, or the joint probability distribution, is obtained from the product of the marginal probabilities, or marginal probability distributions.

If events A and B are statistically independent:

$$\text{pr}(A, B) = \text{pr}(A) \times \text{pr}(B) \tag{6.12}$$

and if two random variables $\{X, Y\}$ are statistically independent:

$$\text{pmf}(X_i = x, Y_j = y) = \text{pmf}(X_i = x) \times \text{pmf}(Y_j = y) \tag{6.13}$$

where we use the notation $pmf(.)$ to denote a probability mass function. The $\text{pmf}(X_i = x)$ is to be read as the probability that the random variable X_i takes the value x, and the $\text{pmf}(X_i = x, Y_j = y)$ is to be read as the probability that the random variable X_i takes the value x *and* that the random variable Y_j takes the value y.

Returning to our example in Table 6.4, we see that X_1 and X_2 are not statistically independent because the conditional probability distribution of X_1 given $X_2 = -1$ is

Table 6.6   **Joint and Marginal Probabilities for the Variables $Y(1)$, $Y(2)$**

		Y_2			Marginal Probability Y_1
		−1	0	1	↓
Y_1	0	1/8	1/4	1/8	1/2
	1	1/8	1/4	1/8	1/2
Marginal Probability Y_2	→	1/4	1/2	1/4	1

not equal to the marginal probability distribution of X_1. We only need one case where the conditional probability distribution and marginal probability distribution differ to be able to declare that the two random variables are not statistically independent. But to verify that two random variables are statistically independent, we need to look at the conditional probability distribution for *all possible values* of the conditioning variable. You should verify for yourself that X_2 is not statistically independent of X_1.

Statistical independence is a very important concept in the theory and practice of statistics as we shall soon discover. One of its great advantages is that it simplifies many calculations because joint probabilities are the products of the marginals.

Try an experiment. Suppose that we have a pair of random variables $\{Y_1, Y_2\}$ that have the same marginal distributions as those of $\{X_1, X_2\}$ in Table 6.4 but are statistically independent. What does the joint probability distribution look like? Table 6.6 shows the answer. The probabilities entered in the body of the table were obtained by our new rule: joint probability equals marginal times marginal when the random variables are independent.

In Table 6.6, we see that both marginal probability distributions are the same as in Table 6.5, but that the joint probability distribution is different. You should confirm for yourself that the random variables Y_1 and Y_2 are statistically independent.

Application of the Results to Continuous Random Variables

So far, our illustrative mechanisms for generating random variables have used dice, coins, and other elementary events that produce discrete-valued variables. Now that we have defined random variables formally, we can extend our theory to continuous variables. Let us consider first a simple example.

Suppose that the sample space is now the "unit interval"—that is, the interval on the real line between 0 and 1. Let us assign probability to this unit interval by making the probability of an interval within the unit interval proportional to the length of the interval chosen. The assigned probability for the entire unit interval is, of course, 1. The probability of an interval of length .235 is .235 and of a collection of nonintersecting intervals of total length .56 is .56. This probability assignment is called a uniform probability distribution; we will meet it again in Chapter 8. In this new situation, as the sample space is based on an interval, not necessarily [0,1], our sets will be intervals, and we will want to be able to include in our collection of sets of intervals all intervals that can be obtained by the same operations of union, intersection, and complementation that we have used.

Unfortunately, there are some technical difficulties associated with this procedure that we will ignore in this text. Nevertheless, the same principles apply and the intuition is the same. For now, let us merely mention that we will need to extend our use of subsets of the sample space.

For example, in Chapter 8 we will discuss at length the properties of probability distributions based on continuous random variables and show the need to define the idea of a "density function," which specifies the "rate of change" of probability. Even in the discrete version of probability that we have developed so far, the most important elements of the theory were not the elementary events themselves but the compound events that we constructed from the elementary events by use of the operations of union, intersection, and complementarity. These operations will be even more important in the context of continuous random variables than they are for discrete random variables. That means, for our uniform probability distribution, for example, that we will want to be able to calculate the probability of any collection of intervals that can be obtained by the operations of union, intersection, and complementarity of other intervals.

Consequences of the Equally Likely Principle

There is a famous problem originally posed by Buffon in 1777, called the "Buffon Needle Problem." Let us consider a version of the basic problem that was originated by J. Bertrand in 1907 that generalizes the original problem in an informative manner. In the next few paragraphs, we will be dealing with geometrical objects, such as lines, points, and areas, not just the numbers that we have used so far.

Our objective in exploring this example is to indicate two main points:

- The "equally likely principle" is a statement about an empirical fact of an experiment.
- Different formulations of the equally likely principle can lead to quite different results, so the choice is important.

Let us begin by looking at Figure 6.6. Do not be put off by a seemingly complex graph; it is in fact quite simple but does require step-by-step discussion. The outer circle represents a circle with a radius of 1 (say inches). Inscribed in the circle is an equilateral triangle; that is, all sides are of equal length, and the length is $\sqrt{3}$ inches. The triangle provides us with a "benchmark," or a way to measure chords across the outer circle. A chord of a circle is any straight line that cuts the circle in two places; three examples are the lines c, d, and e in the figure.

What is the probability that a chord "chosen at random" has a length greater than $\sqrt{3}$, the length of a side of the triangle? For example, the lines c and e are less than $\sqrt{3}$ in length, but d is greater. Our real problem is what precisely do we mean by "chosen at random" in this context. We have three choices, and they give different answers! Consider each alternative in turn.

1. Any chord intersects a circle at two points by definition, say (C_x, C_y) for the line c. For our purposes, we might as well fix the first point, say C_x, anywhere and then we can assume that we can pick the second point, C_y, anywhere on the circumference of the circle using the equally likely principle.

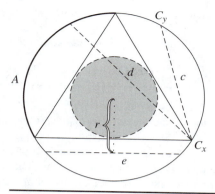

Figure 6.6   Some alternative formulations in geometric probability. Length of each side of the triangle is $\sqrt{3}$.

From the figure, we see that one third of the circumference is the only region within which C_y can lie and have chord length greater than $\sqrt{3}$. That region I have labeled A in the figure; chord d is an example. The probability of this event is one-third.

2. Our second way of formulating the problem is to recognize that a chord can be determined by its distance from the center of the circle, for example the chord e in the figure is a distance r from the center. The radius of the big circle is 1, so we can easily solve that the distance r has to be less than $\frac{1}{2}$ for the corresponding chord to be bigger than $\sqrt{3}$. If the random lengths of such distances are determined by the equally likely principle, the probability is $\frac{1}{2}$!

3. Our third solution is obtained by recognizing that the point of minimum distance from the chord to the center can occur anywhere in a circular area from the center and that if the chord is to have length greater than $\sqrt{3}$, then it must be contained in the shaded small circle with radius $\frac{1}{2}$. Now assume that the points of minimum distance are distributed over the large circle by the equally likely principle. The probability that we seek is given by the ratio of the area of the smaller circle, πr^2, where $r = \frac{1}{2}$, to that of the larger circle with area π. That probability is $\frac{1}{4}$!

We have here three different solutions for our problem starting from three different, but a priori, equally plausible assumptions using the equally likely principle. In an actual experiment, it is clear that at most one of these will apply. I say "at most" for it is not clear without experiment whether any of these geometrical objects are distributed in accordance with the equally likely principle.

There is a theoretical resolution of this problem in terms of abstract geometrical concepts; the solution is $\frac{1}{2}$; the empirical question, using actual circles and thin rods and mechanisms to drop them, requires experimentation to decide the issue.

Consider trying the experiment for yourself. Draw a large circle on a piece of cardboard, say 1 foot in radius, and create a corresponding equilateral triangle as a measuring device. Find a very thin rod at least 2 feet long to use as a chord. Experiment with how to drop the rod in a steady and systematic manner so that you get useful results. Measure the percentage of times out of your total number of trials that the rod cuts a chord that is greater than $\sqrt{3}$ feet. Can you decide which of the three alternatives applies in your experiment?

6.7 Summary

In this chapter, we began developing the theory of statistics, or probability theory, and prepared the way for discussing the theory of probability distributions that is to come in the next two chapters. This chapter marks an important shift in viewpoint from the first five chapters where the emphasis was on describing data. The development of the theory will enable us to interpret the results that we discussed in the first part of the course.

We began by defining the *sample space* that is given by a collection of *mutually exclusive* and *exhaustive elementary events*. When we defined sample space, we defined an experiment in statistical terms. On each trial, one and only one of the elementary events will occur. We defined and discussed *probabilities* and *probability distributions* by assigning probabilities to the elementary events assuming the *equally likely principle*. In the absence of evidence about the shape of the probability distribution that might apply, the equally likely principle is a useful way to begin.

Of even greater importance for the use of the theory is the development of *compound events*, which are defined by collections of elementary events. We saw that we could define "new" events from "old" by taking the *intersections* and the *unions* of events. Probabilities can be assigned to the new events from the old by summing probabilities for unions, or *composite* probabilities, and taking products of probabilities for intersections of events, or *joint events*. Probabilities can be added only if the constituent events are mutually exclusive. If a collection of events is not mutually exclusive, then to get the probability of the union, we must either transform the problem into one that involves only mutually exclusive events or allow for the effect of "double counting" due to the presence of non-null joint probabilities.

Our next step was to define *conditional probability* in Equation 6.3 and to show its connection to *joint probability*. The idea of a conditional probability is to define probabilities with respect to a subset of the sample space. Over the subspace, conditional probabilities also sum to one. We also saw that any joint probability can be defined as the product of a conditional probability and the corresponding *marginal probability*.

To facilitate the evaluation of long strings of dependent events, we defined a *probability tree*, or probability diagram. These diagrams enable us to lay out the interconnections between the various conditioning events in a simple visual way.

The next major contribution to our theoretical arsenal was to define a *random variable*. At first glance, the definition seems to be very artificial in that a random variable is a function defined on subsets of events of a sample space to the real line; that is, we assign real numbers to any possible subset of events that can be constructed from the given sample space. We did this because real numbers are much easier to use than "labels on events." For any given sample space, there are many alternative random variables. The choice between them is one of mathematical convenience. The benefit of shifting to this definition of random variables is that it allows us to handle a much wider variety of variables and sample spaces and paves the way for the more formal analysis to come. Having defined the concept of the random variable, we next had to define the function that assigned probabilities to the values of the random variable. That function is known as the *probability mass function*. Defining random variables also enabled us to extend our notions of probability to the *joint probability distribution*, which allocates the probability of occurrence of two random variables.

The last concept that we introduced was *statistical independence*, which can be defined for both discrete and continuous random variables. Two random variables are statistically independent if the *conditional probability distribution* of one of them does not depend on the values taken by the other (Equation 6.11). If two variables are statistically independent, then the joint probability distribution is given by the product of the *marginal distributions* (Equation 6.13). Statistical independence is one of the most important concepts in the whole of statistics and one of the least understood. We will meet this concept often.

Case Study

Was There Age Discrimination in a Public Utility?

In this chapter, we can continue our investigation of our public utility age discrimination complaint by examining some of the probabilities involved—more accurately, the observed relative frequencies. First, we need to inquire about the relative frequencies of those over 40 and compare them with those over 50 and under 35 to get some idea how these relative frequencies change with age.

We begin by asking, What are the marginal probabilities for the various age groups? What percentage of employees are in each category? About 80% were less than 55, so 20% were over 55. Correspondingly, the percentage less than 40 (the benchmark age chosen by the union) was 21% and the percentage less than 35 was only 10%; that is, 90% were older than 35. The percentage between the critical years of 40 and 55 was 58%.

Given that nearly two-thirds of all employees were between 40 and 55, let us use that age group as a benchmark for the breakdown over the hire status—that is, whether the individual was hired, hire.stat=1; not hired, hire.stat=0; or chose not to apply, hire.stat=9. The percentages in these three categories are hire.stat = 0, 33%; hire.stat = 1, 55%; hire.stat = 9, 12%. So in the critical age category over half of the employees were rehired and of those who chose to apply, the percentage was 62%. The question is whether the percentages that were hired among lower and older age groups are any different. Let us compare the percentages for the under 40 and the over 55 groups. For the under 40 group, hire.stat = 0, 31%; hire.stat = 1, 55%; and hire.stat = 9, 14%. These numbers are remarkably close to those for the 40 to 55 group. Now consider the over 55 group: for hire.stat = 0, 13%, hire.stat = 1, 14%, and for

continues on next page

Table 6.7   **Joint Probabilities across Sex and Hire Status**

Sex	Hire Status			Row Totals
	0	1	9	
Male = 0	120	183	101	404
	.251	.382	.211	.840
	(.240)	(.390)	(.210)	
Female = 1	19	36	20	75
	.040	.075	.042	.160
	(.046)	(.074)	(.040)	
Column Totals	139	219	121	479
	.29	.46	.25	1.00

(Continued)

hire.stat = 9, 73%. These numbers are very different from the previous two sets.

The ratio of the probabilities of those hired to those nonhired in the over age 55 category is $\frac{14}{13} = 1.08$, whereas in the reference group it is $\frac{55}{33} = 1.67$. In the over 55 category, the firm retained employees about one for one, whereas for the less than 55 group, the number retained was about 3 for every 2 not rehired. So here at last is some evidence that the union might be correct in its complaint. However, a critical question that we have not yet answered is what is the source of this difference; the observed difference may have nothing at all to do with the firm discriminating against those older than 55. For example, the over 55 category contains a much larger proportion of people very near retirement, so that of those that applied in this category, one would expect a greater proportion of the applicants would be indifferent between being hired and not, whereas that proportion would be much less among those less than 55 and certainly so for those less than 40.

We can examine another question. What difference does it make to break down the results by male and female? See Table 6.7. In this connection, we can look at a table of the actual joint probabilities across the categories of sex and hire status and compare these results with those that would obtain if sex and hire status were independent variables. We do this by looking at the joint probabilities obtained by multiplying the marginal probabilities. The probabilities if the categories are independent are in parentheses. Note that because of the presence of N/A's in the data, there are minor differences between the figures presented in Table 6.7 and those we quoted. The entries in Table 6.7 within each cell list the cell count, the joint probability for the cell, and the probability that would apply if the two categories were independent and had the <u>same</u> marginal probabilities. From the figures listed in the table we might well conclude that the categories of sex and hire status are independent.

Except for the over 55 category of employees, there is little difference in the probabilities of being hired or not. The difference for the over 55 category is most likely due to the fact that there are relatively few employees in this group and the proportion of those choosing retirement is relatively greater. The joint distribution across sex and hire status appears to be independent; that is, whether hired or not did not depend on the employee's sex.

Exercises

Calculation Practice

6.1 Using Venn diagrams to illustrate, define in words the meaning of the following operations on the sets $A, B, \ldots$, all contained within the universal set S. Remember $A, B, \ldots$ can be any sets whatsoever contained within S.

a. $A \cap B$

b. $A \cup B$

c. A^c

d. $A^c \cap A$

e. $A^c \cup A$

f. $(A \cup B)^c$

g. $(A \cap B)^c$

h. $A \cap (B \cup C)$

i. $A \cup (B \cap C)$

j. $(A \cap B) \cup (A^c \cap B)$

k. The result in (j) is known as a partition of the set B. Can you explain why?

6.2 Demonstrate and illustrate the following theorems that hold for any sets $A, B, \ldots$ within a universal set S.

a. $(A \cup B \cup C)^c = (A^c \cap B^c \cap C^c)$

b. $(A \cap B \cap C)^c = (A^c \cup B^c \cup C^c)$

6.3 If the following are compound events in S, the universal set, and their union equals S:

$E_1 = \{1, 3, 5, 7, 9\}$

$E_2 = \{2, 4, 6, 8\}$

$E_3 = \{1, 2, 3, 4\}$

$E_4 = \{5\}$

$E_5 = \{\emptyset\}$

a. Enumerate the elementary events in S.

b. How many different subsets can you construct from the set S?

6.4 Using the data in Exercise 6.3, list the elementary events that are defined by

a. $E_1 \cup E_2$

b. E_5^c

c. $E_2 \cap E_3$

d. $(E_1 \cup E_2)^c$

e. $E_3 \cap E_5$

f. $E_3 \cup E_5$

g. $(E_4 \cap E_3) \cup (E_4^c \cap E_3)$

h. $(E_4 \cup E_3) \cap (E_4^c \cup E_3)$

i. $E_3 \cup S$

j. $E_3 \cap S$

k. $E_4 \cap \emptyset$

l. $E_4 \cup \emptyset$

6.5 If A_i is the interval $(a - i/n, a + i/n)$ for any number a and $i = 1, 2, 3, \ldots, n$, what is $\cup_i \{A_i\}$, $\cap_i \{A_i\}$? Draw a figure to illustrate your answer.

6.6 For the following experiments define the sample space, and enumerate the elementary events. How do you decide whether you have enumerated all the elementary events and only the elementary events?

a. Tossing three coins.

b. Tossing two dice.

c. Lightbulbs are either working or have failed. If there are four lightbulbs in a room, what is the sample space?

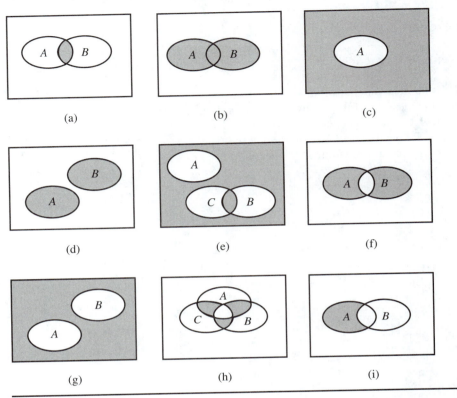

Figure 6.7   Venn Diagrams

d. The price of a stock either rises, falls, or stays the same. If you have four stocks, what is the sample space for changes in stock prices?

6.7 In the Venn diagrams shown in Figure 6.7, what events are being illustrated in the graphs (*a*) to (*i*)? Write down the theoretic statement that describes the set operation that is illustrated by the shaded portions of the graphs.

6.8 Refer to the compound events defined in Exercise 6.3. For the following sets, which are mutually exclusive, which exhaustive, and which neither?

a. E_1, E_2

b. E_2, E_3

c. E_1, E_4

d. E_5, E_3

e. $(E_1 \cup E_2), E_3$

f. E_5, E_5^c

g. $(E_1 \cap E_3), E_4$

h. E_3^c, E_2

6.9 Determine the sample space for the following situations:

a. two 6-sided dice and the sum is divisible by three

b. two 6-sided dice and the sum is odd

c. the odd red cards from a regular deck of cards

d. three 8-sided dice

6.10 Suppose that you have a sequence of sets that satisfy

$$E_0 = \{\emptyset\}$$

$$E_1 \subset E_2 \subset E_3 \subset E_4 \subset E_5 \ldots$$

Show that

a. $\cup E_i = \cup(E_i - E_{i-1})$

b. The sets $(E_i - E_{i-1})$ are disjoint in pairs; that is, $(E_i - E_{i-1}) \cap (E_j - E_{j-1}) = \emptyset$ for all $i \neq j$.

6.11 Determine, or describe, the sample spaces for the following situations:

a. committees of three to be drawn from a faculty of six

b. committees of three to be drawn from a faculty of six when the committee must have a female and there are only two females on the faculty

c. the market price of sowbellies at the St. Louis hog market

d. marital status of applicants for a job

6.12 With respect to Exercises 6.9 and 6.11, discuss the possible assignment of probabilities in the absence of factual knowledge about the relevant probability distributions.

Exploring the Tools

6.13 Show that $\text{pr}(A) = 1 - \text{pr}(A^c)$ for any set A in a universal set S. Illustrate your demonstration with a Venn diagram. This result is very useful to remember when $\text{pr}(A)$ is hard to calculate but $\text{pr}(A^c)$ is easy to calculate.

6.14 Many elementary textbooks define the probability of an event as a ratio of counts. They specify an event within a given context and ask what the corresponding probability is. They often term the elementary events in the specified event "successes." In this formulation, the probability of the event A is given as

$$\text{pr}(A) = \frac{\text{successes}}{\text{outcomes}} = \frac{\text{outcomes in event } A}{\text{total outcomes}}$$

In the context of determining the probability of the event A, obtaining a picture card out of a randomly shuffled deck of 52 cards, show that this formulation is an alternative way of expressing the probability of the event A that implicitly relies on the equally likely principle.

6.15 Show that the generalization of the general formula for "adding probabilities" when there are three events, A, B, and C is

$$\text{pr}(A \cup B \cup C) = \text{pr}(A) + \text{pr}(B) + \text{pr}(C) - [\text{pr}(A \cap B) + \text{pr}(A \cap C) + \text{pr}(B \cap C)] + \text{pr}(A \cap B \cap C)$$

Illustrate your argument with an appropriate Venn diagram. (*Hint*: Generalize the argument that we used leading up to Equation 6.1 for transforming the sets into a sequence of mutually exclusive sets.)

6.16 We have defined the set operation *union* $(A \cup B)$ as the set of elementary events that are in A or B; and implicitly we have included the condition "or in both." This is called the "inclusive or." There also is an alternative "or," called the "exclusive or." For the exclusive or, say "Xor," we have $(A \text{ Xor } B)$ contains all elements of S that are in A, or in B, but not in both. This verbal statement is still a bit confusing. In set terms, we have

$$(A \text{ Xor } B) = A \cup (B \cap A^c)$$

Demonstrate the following:

a. $\text{pr}(A \text{ Xor } B) = \text{pr}(A) + \text{pr}(B \cap A^c)$

b. $\text{pr}(A \text{ Xor } B) = \text{pr}(A \cup B)$

c. $\text{pr}(A \text{ Xor } B) = \text{pr}(A) + \text{pr}(B) - \text{pr}(A \cap B)$

6.17 In Exercises 6.6 and 6.9, you specified the sample space for a variety of situations. Determine suitable random variables that correspond to these sample spaces. Justify your choice.

6.18 "If the events A, B are mutually exclusive, they are not independent." By argument and using a Venn diagram to illustrate, show that this is a true statement.

6.19 If the discrete random variable Z_1 is independent of the discrete random variable Z_2, show that Z_2 is independent of Z_1.

6.20 *Worked. Objective: To compare observed relative frequencies and theoretical predictions.* In the text, we discussed the equally likely principle. In this lab, the equally likely principle is implemented in assigning the probabilities to the 100 boxes listed; that is, each box has a probability of 1/100 of being selected on any trial. As guided, draw five samples of size 20. For each of the five samples record the number of times the column 91–100 is hit (a box turns red).

[*Computer directions:* Start S-Plus. On the menu bar, click Labs, Random Sampling. In the dialog box Random Sampling, key in 20 into the *n* box. Click on the Sample button. The boxes selected will change to red. Count the number of red boxes in the column 91–100. Repeat four more times by clicking on the Sample button and count the red boxes.]

a. What is your calculation of the probability of getting a box labeled 91–100? (Answer = .1.) Can you explain why?

b. What is the observed relative frequency?

c. How do the observed relative frequencies vary as you sample repeatedly?

6.21 Repeat the previous experiment, but pick any row.

a. What is your calculation of the probability of getting a box in the row you chose?

b. What is the observed relative frequency?

6.22 Repeat the previous experiment, but pick any five boxes of your choice.

a. What is your calculation for the probability of observing one or more of your chosen boxes on any trial?

b. What is the observed relative frequency?

6.23 *Worked. Objective: To compare observed relative frequencies and theoretical predictions.*

[*Computer directions:* Start S-Plus. On the menu bar, click on Labs, Relative Frequency and Probability. On the screen, you will see a graph of 50 balls in 5 rows of 10. Six balls will be colored red and were selected randomly without replacement; that is, no ball can occur more than once when you activate the lab. In the dialog box, there is a Draw button; every time you click the button you get another draw of 6 red balls. Try it a few times. You will also notice a button Draw *n* Times and a box *n* set to 1. You can change *n* to any value and then click on the button Draw *n* Times; the computer will draw 6 balls at random, *n* times. On the graph are three numbers: "*n* draws," which keeps a running total of your draws; "*n* pairs," which records for all your draws the number of times a draw of 6 balls produced 2 next to each other horizontally—for example (26)(27); and "Relative Frequency," which is the relative frequency, over all your draws, of getting pairs. This is simply (*n* pairs)/(*n* draws).]

a. The probability of drawing at least one pair is .4874. To check that this calculation is correct try the following: [*Computer directions:* In the dialog box, set *n* to 100. Click on Draw *n* Times and record the relative frequency. Repeat a few times.]

b. What conclusions do you draw from your observations concerning the relevance of the theory that the probability of drawing at least one pair is .4874?

This exercise is to help you gain intuition for the relationship between theoretical statements and what is actually observed.

6.24 *Objective: To understand the probability of joint events and independence.* The probability of a "head" in a coin toss is .5. The probability of tossing two heads in a row is $(\frac{1}{2})(\frac{1}{2}) = .25$. You have just tossed a head and are about to toss again; your friend tells you that the probability of getting the next head is still .5. Explain.

Applications

6.25 Worked. *Objective: To explore the implications of conditional probability on the interpretation of test results, especially for rare events.*
Tests for diseases such as AIDS involve errors. There are false positives and false negatives. With *false positives,* the test indicates that an individual has AIDS when he or she does not, and the false negative indicates that a tested individual does not have AIDS when in fact he or she does. Let us consider the consequences of the first problem, false positives, when we contemplate testing a large class of people, or even the entire population. Suppose that 100 million people are tested. What information have we been given? $pr(test + |NoAIDS) = .05$, $pr(test-|AIDS) = .01$, and $pr(AIDS) = .005$. So, in a population of 100 million, we are looking for 500,000 people. The test is presumed to be quite accurate in that there is only a 5% error for false positives and a 1% error for false negatives.

What do we want to know? What is the probability of having AIDS, given that a person has tested positive? We will use our concepts of conditional probability extensively in answering this question. We want $pr(AIDS|test+)$. We derive

$$pr(AIDS|test+) = \frac{pr(AIDS, test+)}{pr(test+)}$$

And we can break up the $pr(test+)$ into its constituent states by

$$pr(test+) = pr(AIDS, test+) + pr(NoAIDS, test+)$$

where we recognize that the states AIDS and NoAIDS partition the state "test +." We can test positive if we have AIDS and if we do not have AIDS, and these two states are mutually exclusive. If we can work out these last two joint probabilities given our information, we will have the problem solved. We define

$$pr(AIDS, test+) = pr(test + |AIDS)pr(AIDS)$$
$$pr(NoAIDS, test+) =$$
$$pr(test + |NoAIDS)pr(No AIDS)$$

We have been given the information we need; $pr(AIDS)$ is .005, so that $pr(NoAIDS)$ is .995. We know that $pr(test + |AIDS)$ is .99, because $pr(test - |AIDS)$ is .01. It is also given that $pr(test + |NoAIDS)$ is .05. We can now calculate that

$$pr(AIDS, test+) = .99 \times .005 = .00495$$
$$pr(NoAIDS, test+) = .05 \times .995 = .04975$$

We can now solve our original problem:

$$pr(AIDS|test+) = \frac{.00495}{.00495 + .04975} = .0905$$

This result that the probability that one has AIDS given a positive reading is only about 10% may be surprising at first sight, but if you experiment with the calculations a bit you will begin to see the logic of the situation. The bigger the probability of AIDS in the first place, the bigger the probability given the test. So the surprising nature of the result is due to the relative low probability of AIDS in the whole population.

6.26 Given the facts stated in Exercise 6.25, determine the probability of not having AIDS, given that you have tested negatively. Rework both exercises if the probability of AIDS in the population is .2. Draw some policy conclusions about testing schemes from these calculations.

6.27 Frequently poll takers are required to ask sensitive questions. One strategy to overcome this problem is to make sure that the poll taker cannot know the respondents' answer. Imagine that you are requested to sample a group of students about their use of drugs; it is likely that most students will not want to give an honest answer. One solution is to prepare two questions; one is the sensitive question, the other is nonsensitive and such that you know the proportion of the population that will answer yes to the alternative question. For example, you ask, "Were you born in January?" and know that the proportion of the population born in January is .08.

Our strategy is to tell the respondent that he or she is to toss a coin without your seeing the outcome;

if heads, the respondent is to answer the sensitive question, if tails, the nonsensitive question. You are to see only the one answer, yes or no. Suppose that the proportion of "yes" answers is .06. Using similar procedures as in Exercise 6.26, determine the probability of your student sample using drugs.

6.28 This is a problem that was solved by Galileo, or so it is claimed. In the 17th century, Italian gamblers used to bet on the outcomes of throws of three 6-sided dice at a time. For a long time it was thought that getting a 9 or a 10 on throwing three dice was equally likely. Galileo showed that it was not. Try to determine which of these two events is the more probable and by how much. (*Hint*: Label the dice so that you can count the number of ways of getting 9 or 10. Recall that for three dice, there are a total of $6^3 = 216$ ways.)

6.29 "Roulette is a pleasant, relaxed, and highly comfortable way to lose your money." (Jimmy the Greek, *San Francisco Chronicle*, July 25, 1975.)

In the game of roulette, there are 36 numbers to bet on, from 1 to 36, and two colors, 18 red and 18 black. In addition, the roulette ball may land on a green 0, or 00—making 38 positions altogether.

In each of the following situations,

a. Determine the probability of winning, if you assume that the wheel is "fair"; that is, all numbers and the two colors red and black are equally likely events.

b. Determine the expected value for each game. For example, if you are betting on some single specific number, the house pays 35 to 1, or $35 for every $1 you bet. If the probability of winning is 1/38, what is the expected value of this game?

(1) Bet on a single number; it pays 35 to 1.

(2) Bet on red; it pays 1 to 1.

(3) Bet on even; it pays 1 to 1.

(4) Bet on two specified numbers adjacent to each other; this is called a "split." It pays 17 to 1. Compare this with the first answer.

(5) Bet on the numbers 2 to 12; this pays 2 to 1.

c. Recall that on any run of the wheel, the ball could land on green 0, or 00. If you have $1 million to bet, what is your expected return? Do you agree with Jimmy the Greek?

d. Which of these games is the least unfavorable?

6.30 Use the data set Age65.xls in the folder Misc, which contains the percentages of people over age 65 by state.

a. Is it plausible that the distributions of these percentages across states are equally likely?

b. Separate the list of states into "warm" and "cold" states. Is the average percentage higher in warm states?

c. What conclusions do you draw from these results about the distribution of elderly people?

6.31 Use the data file Arms.xls in the folder Misc, which contains the amounts of arms shipments to various countries from the United States and the the former U.S.S.R.

a. What is the probability of receiving arms from the United States?

b. What is the probability of receiving arms from the former U.S.S.R.?

c. What is the probability of receiving arms from the United States, given you are already receiving arms from the former U.S.S.R.?

d. What is the probability of receiving arms from the former U.S.S.R., given you are already receiving arms from the United States?

e. Should the previous two results be the same? If not, why not?

6.32 Use the data set Cardata.xls in folder Misc to answer the following:

Table 6.8   **Admissions Data for Graduate School UC Berkeley, 1973**

Major	Men Applicants	% Admitted	Women Applicants	% Admitted	Total
A	825	62	108	82	933
B	560	63	25	68	585
C	325	37	593	34	918
D	417	33	375	35	792
E	191	28	393	24	584
F	373	6	341	7	714
Total	2691		1835		4526

a. Is the distribution of the number of cylinders (*cyl*) equally likely over the range observed?

b. Is the distribution of the average value of mpg by country of origin (*origin*) distributed equally likely?

c. How about engine displacement (*displace*)?

d. Create a table with three columns, one each for low, medium, and high acceleration (*accel*) and with rows given by country of origin. In each cell, record the number of observations.

e. Do your entries represent a joint distribution?

f. If the country of origin is the United States, what is the probability the car has high acceleration?

g. If Japan?

6.33 Use the file Coles.xls in the folder Misc, which contains variable values collected for a fitness program.

a. Is there a difference in mean age by sex?

b. Separate the age variable into low and high cells. Is the average height in the younger age group taller than the older age group?

c. If *prewt* is less than its median, what is the probability *postwt* is less than its median?

d. If *prewt* is higher than its median, what is the probability that *postfat* is higher than its median?

6.34 Use the data set Cosize.xls in the folder Misc, which contains observations on characteristics of firms grouped by size of firm (*sizeco*).

a. If a firm is labeled small, what is the probability that sales per employee are less than the median?

b. If a firm is labeled large, what is the probability that sales per employee will be bigger than the median?

6.35 Examine the data file Food.xls in folder Misc. Break down the observations on food consumption (*qd*), production (*qs*), retail price (*pd*), price received by farmers (*ps*), and income (*y*) into the observations less than the median and those greater.

a. If retail price is below the median, what is the probability the price received by the farmers is below its median?

b. If the retail price is above the median and income is below the median, what is the probability that the quantity consumed is below its median?

c. If you ignore income, how does the probability change?

6.36 (Reference: Freedman, Pisani, and Purvis, *Statistics,* Norton & Co. 1978, p. 12). In the fall quarter of 1973, UC Berkeley had 8442 male applications, of which 44% were admitted, and 4321 female applications, of which 35% were admitted. At first sight, it would appear that UC Berkeley was discriminating against women by a substantial margin. But when individual department figures were examined the picture was quite different. For just six departments (identity unrevealed by UC Berkeley), the figures are shown in Table 6.8.

As you examine this table you will see that in only two cases was the male percentage larger than the female percentage. You will also see that there are wide disparities between the departments in terms of numbers of applications and in the numbers of those admitted. The figures of 44% and 35% were obtained by simply dividing the number of males, or females, admitted by the number that applied. But you can see that the problem here has something to do with the relationship between the distinction by sex and the differences in numbers applying by departments; men and women generally applied to different departments with different levels of acceptances. We can allow somewhat for this discrepancy by examining the weighted average of the percentages, weighted by the numbers of men and women applying. If we calculate the weighted sum of the two sets of percentages, where the weights are given by the proportion of each department's applicants to the total applicants (see the last column), the results are 39% for men and 43% for women. This is a reversal of the original inference!

a. What is the estimated probability of being admitted to department B, given that you are a female?

b. What is the estimated probability of being admitted to department D if you are a male?

c. What is the estimated probability of being admitted to UC Berkeley if you are a female? Note that there are several possible answers here but with different interpretations. Explain.

d. What are some of the policy implications of this analysis?

6.37 Case Study: Was There Age Discrimination in a Public Utility?

One of the team members that analyzes the public utility age discrimination case in your consulting firm made the following observation. "It appears to me that both younger and older applicants in this case had the same qualifications and were equally likely to be selected (hired) by the firm during its reduction in force process. If what I see is true, then the probability of being hired by the firm should be identical for both younger and older applicants. So, I propose to the team that we calculate those probabilities and compare them. If those probabilities are not equal, that should increase our suspicion that some kind of bias was introduced into the hiring process that requires further investigation."

a. The team assigns to you the task of calculating these probabilities. They expect you to start with a two-by-two contingency table showing the number of applicants hired and not hired by age group (age under 40 and age 40 and over). Then you should proceed with a second table replacing the number of applicants hired and not hired by age group with their joint probabilities (relative frequencies).

b. Calculate the marginal probabilities, and write a short report explaining your findings.

6.38 Case Study: Was There Age Discrimination in a Public Utility? You know, by now, that in age discrimination cases you are faced with the task of comparing the ages of those who were terminated with the ages of those who were similarly situated but not terminated. You compare the numbers of people over 40 years old in each group with those under 40 in each group.

Today, your Forensic Economics Consulting firm had a meeting with one of the attorneys of the law firm that handles this case. In this meeting, it was brought to the attention of your firm that this comparison may be open to debate. The complaint treats as fungible all terminated people 40 and older, although the rights of persons aged 50 and over should be protected from encroachment by persons of any other age, not just by persons under 40.

A senior associate of your firm indicated that one approach to deal with this problem is to vary the boundary age in your contingency tables.

a. Produce two-by-two probability contingency tables for this age discrimination case for the following age groups. In each case, you are looking for differences between those hired and those not hired:

(1) less than 45, and 45 and older

(2) less than 50, and 50 and older

(3) less than 55, and 55 and older

(4) less than 60, and 60 and older

b. Write a short, summary report of your findings.

6.39 Case Study: Was There Age Discrimination in a Public Utility? After reading Chapter 6, you decide to

a. Calculate the following conditional probabilities and present to your supervisor the importance of the information so obtained:

(1) the probability of being hired given that the applicant is younger than 40 years old

(2) the probability of being hired given that the applicant is 40 years old or older

(3) the probability of not being hired given that the applicant is younger than 40 years old

(4) the probability of not being hired given that the applicant is 40 years old or older

b. Write a short report explaining the relevance to the case of your findings.

CHAPTER 7

The Generation and Description of Discrete Probability Distributions

7.1 What You Will Learn in This Chapter

This chapter is about the theory of distributions, the theory that underlies the concept of histograms and enables us to interpret them. This chapter builds on the previous chapter on probability. Now we begin to examine how distributions are created and to specify the conditions under which different distributions will be generated. More precisely, we are concerned in this chapter with the specification of probability mass functions, or just "probability functions" (which we defined in Chapter 6). The term *probability mass function* stresses the functional relationship between the assignment of probabilities and the values taken by the random variable. The term *probability distribution* is broader; it stresses the idea of the distribution of probability and helps to maintain the link to the distributions of relative frequencies discussed in previous chapters. As examples of this process we derive two very important examples of discrete probability mass functions, the binomial and the Poisson. These two distributions provide the statistical explanation for an amazing array of different physical experiments as we shall see.

We will discover that probability distributions are characterized by their parameters and their theoretical moments. The theoretical moments are the theoretical analogues to the sample moments that we have discussed. The values of the theoretical moments determine the shape of the probability distribution, or probability mass function, just as the sample moments measured the shape of histograms. Further, we will discover a close connection between the values of the parameters of the distribution and the values of the moments and hence between the values of the parameters and the shape of the probability distribution.

In the process, we will introduce a technique called *expectation* that is the basis for the conclusions drawn from almost all pragmatic decision problems. Expectation is a generalization of the process involved in calculating theoretical moments. The derivation of the idea of expectation is deceptively simple, but this belies its very great importance.

7.2 Introduction

In Chapter 6, we learned how to manipulate probabilities and to obtain marginal probability distributions from joint probability distributions. But what we do not yet know is how to obtain a probability mass function, either joint or marginal, in the first place; that is the subject of this chapter and its extension to continuous variables in the next. All we have been able to do so far is to assign probabilities on the "equally likely principle." But as we recall, we do this because we don't know what the true probability function really is. Our next step is to discover how different experiments or different surveys lead to different types of probability mass function.

The major lesson to be learned in this chapter is that different hypothetical experiments generate different types of probability distribution. Once the nature of the hypothetical experiment has been determined, that specification of the experiment will also specify a particular corresponding type of probability distribution. Consequently, we now realize that probability distributions do not spring out of the thin air, or from the fervid imaginations of statistics professors, but arise naturally from the specification of an experiment.

Ultimately, our objective is to come back to real data and the outcomes of actual experiments or surveys. At that time, we will benefit from our recognition that there is a strong link between experiment and the form of a probability distribution. And our first task will be to discover what probability distribution applies to the situation in hand.

In this chapter, we will discuss only a few probability distribution functions but enough to show clearly the link between hypothetical experiment and corresponding probability function. We will also try to demonstrate how a probability function will change as we change the experiment. Indeed, this dependence of the specific form of the distribution on the precise formulation of the experiment will be emphasized. Before we can begin we will have to learn some new notation and some new mathematical tools. This is our next topic.

7.3 Combinations and Permutations

Suppose that we have n distinct objects, A_1, A_2, A_3, . . . , A_n. The objects might be different fruits, such as an apple, a pear, an orange, a banana, and so on. In how many distinct ways can we rearrange our n distinct objects, say our fruit, in a line? One arrangement is

Orange Banana Pear Apple

An alternative way of saying this is, "In how many distinct ways can we permute the order of our n distinct objects?" Suppose that we have only four fruits: an apple, a pear, an orange, and a banana. We also have four positions to fill:

———————   ———————   ———————   ———————

We have four choices for the first position. We might pick a banana, for example. But for each choice for the first position, we will have three choices for the second position. If our first choice was the banana, then for our second choice we have only the pear, orange, and an apple left. After that choice we have only two choices left for the next and third slot; and for the last slot, we have only one choice, in fact no choice at all.

We can generalize our discovery. If we have n distinct objects, then we have

n ways of picking the first in line
$(n - 1)$ ways of picking the second in line
$(n - 2)$ ways of picking the third in line
. . .
1 way of picking the last object

With each of the n ways of picking the first object, we have $(n - 1)$ ways of picking the second object, and with each of the $(n - 1)$ ways of picking the second object, we have $(n - 2)$ ways of picking the second object, and so on. Each possible choice for rearranging the distinct elements is called a **permutation**.

We conclude that the total number of permutations of n distinct objects is

$$n(n - 1)(n - 2)(n - 3) \ldots 1$$

The terms are multiplied because for each choice at every position, you can have any one of the remaining choices. This special product is called "n factorial" and is written "$n!$"; that is

$$n! = n(n - 1)(n - 2)(n - 3) \ldots 1$$

It is the simple product of all the numbers from 1 to n; for n distinct elements we have a total of $n!$ permutations.

In how many ways can we permute our four fruits? Because n takes the value "four," the answer is 4!, which equals 24.

Let's look at an even easier example but examine the alternative permutations specifically. Try the three letters A, B, and C. Their permutations are

$A\ B\ C$ $A\ C\ B$
$B\ A\ C$ $B\ C\ A$
$C\ A\ B$ $C\ B\ A$

With this example check that for each of the first three choices, you have two choices left; so that the number of permutations is 3 times 2. You might not relish permuting four different types of fruit, but if you relabel them as the letters A to D as we did here, you can permute them for yourself.

All this is easy enough, but we will also want to know how to figure out how many different ways we can select r objects taken from n distinct objects. This question would arise, for example, if we wanted to know how many ways we could select two fruits at a time from the set of four. What this is really saying is that, having selected our two objects, we do not care about the order of the remaining objects. How do we do this? We have two slots to fill, as shown, four choices for the first and three choices for the second slot.

   _____   _____

In general, if we have n objects and want to select r of them, then we have n choices for the first position, $(n - 1)$ choices for the second position, $(n - 2)$ choices for the third position, and so on:

$$n(n - 1)(n - 2)(n - 3) \cdots (n - r + 1)$$

Notice that as there are r terms, the index of the last term in the expansion is $(n - r + 1)$; this is because the first term in the expansion is $(n - 0)$.

Alternatively, if we do not care about the order of the remaining $(n - r)$ objects, even if we actually have them, then the number of distinct ways of selecting r objects out of n distinct objects is still

$$n(n - 1)(n - 2)(n - 3) \cdots (n - r + 1)$$

Returning to our four fruits, for example, if we want to select only two fruits, then $r = 2$, and $n = 4$; so the number of distinct choices is 4 times $3 = 12$.

It is instructive and useful to reexpress the problem in a slightly different way. If we are not interested in the order, or permutations, of the remaining $(n - r)$ objects, and given that we multiply our options at each position, then we should divide out those choices that we do not make. Our solution for the number of ways of selecting r objects out of n objects is by this reasoning:

$$n! = \text{total number of permutations of } n \text{ objects}$$

$$(n - r)! = \text{number of permutations of } (n - r) \text{ objects}$$

so the number of ways of selecting r objects and ignoring all permutations of the remaining $(n - r)$ objects not chosen is to divide out the unwanted permutations:

$$\text{No. of perms.} = \frac{1 \times 2 \times 3 \times \cdots \times (n - r) \times (n - r + 1) \times \cdots \times (n - 1) \times n}{1 \times 2 \times 3 \times \cdots \times (n - r)}$$

$$= (n - r + 1) \times (n - r + 2) \times \cdots \times (n - 1) \times n$$

$$\frac{n!}{(n - r)!} = \frac{1 \times 2 \times 3 \times \cdots \times (n - r) \times (n - r + 1) \times \cdots \times (n - 1) \times n}{1 \times 2 \times 3 \times \cdots \times (n - r)}$$

$$= n \times (n - 1) \times (n - 2) \times \cdots \times (n - r + 1)$$

Our answer is found by dividing out the unwanted permutations; the number to divide by is $(n - r)!$ for the $(n - r)!$ permutations of the $(n - r)$ remaining objects. The total number of objects is n so that the total number of permutations to be divided is $n!$. This is a good strategy to follow in general; figure out how many objects have permutations in which you are not interested and divide out by the appropriate factorial.

To make this idea work in full generality, we need a convention, an agreement, that

$$0! = 1$$

Let us return to our example of the four letters, A, B, C, and D. In how many ways can we choose two letters out of the four? Our expression yields

$$\frac{n!}{(n-r)!} = \frac{4!}{(4-2)!}$$

$$= \frac{4!}{(2)!}$$

$$= \frac{(1 \times 2 \times 3 \times 4)}{(1 \times 2)}$$

$$= 3 \times 4 = 12$$

by dividing out the common products, 1×2, in both the numerator and the denominator. To see this result clearly, let us write out the permutations:

AB CD AC AD BC BD

BA DC CA DA CB DB

This list shows the permutations in which we are interested. List the permutations in which we are not interested, the ones left out, and count them. You should have

$$(4! - 12) = 24 - 12 = 12$$

Yet another useful way of viewing this result is to answer the related question. How many distinct permutations are there for n objects of which $(n - r)$ are identical but the remaining r objects are distinct? Mathematically, this question is just like the previous question. You have n objects of which r are distinct and can be permuted, but the remaining $(n - r)$ objects are either the same or you are not interested in their permutations. In both cases, the total number of possible permutations with n objects is $n!$, but you want to divide out the $(n - r)!$ permutations that you cannot, or do not want to, distinguish. Let us consider a sample example of this alternative interpretation.

We have five objects, *A A A B C*, of which three are the same, so $n = 5$; $r = 2$; $(n - r) = 3$:

$$\frac{n!}{(n-r)!} = \frac{5!}{3!} = \frac{1 \times 2 \times 3 \times 4 \times 5}{1 \times 2 \times 3} = 4 \times 5 = 20$$

Here is the list:

A A A B C	*A A A C B*	*A A B C A*	*A A C B A*	*A B C A A*
A C B A A	*A A B A C*	*A A C A B*	*B C A A A*	*C B A A A*
B A A A C	*B A A C A*	*B A C A A*	*C A A A B*	*C A A B A*
C A B A A	*A B A A C*	*A B A C A*	*A C A A B*	*A C A B A*

Alternatively, if we have n objects, of which r are the same, then the number of distinct permutations is given by

$$\frac{n!}{r!}$$

But if we can calculate the number of permutations when either r or $(n - r)$ of them are the same, could we not calculate the number of distinct choices when there are both r and $(n - r)$ the same? We have n objects as before, but now we have r of them the same and $(n - r)$ of them the same but different from each other. Suppose that we have 4 As and 3 Bs. Here n is 7, r is 4, and $(n - r)$ is 3. Our expression tells us that out of a total of 7! permutations, we must divide out both the 4! and 3! permutations that we cannot distinguish. The expression is

$$\frac{n!}{r!(n - r)!} = \frac{7!}{3!4!}$$

$$= \frac{1 \times 2 \times 3 \times 4 \times 5 \times 6 \times 7}{(1 \times 2 \times 3) \times (1 \times 2 \times 3 \times 4)}$$

$$= 5 \times 7 = 35$$

The result of 35 you might find a little surprising with only two different letters to play with, but there are seven positions to fill!

This particular expression is used so often that it has a special name and a special symbol. The special name is **combination**. One asks how many combinations of n objects can be obtained if taken r at a time. Notice that with a combination we are not interested in the order of either the r items selected or the $(n - r)$ items not selected. If we know the total number of permutations for n objects, we can obtain the number of combinations by dividing out the unwanted permutations generated by the order within each selection and the order within each set not selected. The special symbol is shown in Equation 7.1:

$$\binom{n}{r} = \frac{n!}{(n - r)!r!} \tag{7.1}$$

Notice that the roles of r and $(n - r)$ can be interchanged with no effect on the value taken by the expression; that is

$$\binom{n}{n - r} = \frac{n!}{(n - r)!r!} = \binom{n}{r} \tag{7.2}$$

You might want to imagine that combinations can be obtained by placing the n objects into two boxes, one containing r objects, the other containing $(n - r)$ objects. The order of the objects within each box is unimportant.

The generic question with combinations is, "In how many ways can I separate n objects into two categories?" So we might consider how many committees of 5 can we select from 15 people; how many flower arrangements we can obtain from ten different flowers taken three at a time; how many ways there are to selecting three colors from six colors when producing maps; or how many car options there are if a consumer can select any 6 of them and there are 20 to choose from; and so on.

7.4 Generating Binomial Probabilities

The main objective of this chapter is to demonstrate how random variables are generated and to show how the shape of the probability distribution depends on the properties of the experiment. To accomplish this, we will discuss the determination of two particular probability mass functions, called the "binomial" and the "Poisson."

We will begin with the simplest possible example, the tossing of a coin. You might justifiably complain that such a subject might be of interest to statisticians but not to you. If we were only going to talk about coin-tossing itself, you would be right. "Coin-tossing," however, is merely a simple, but colorful way of talking about all experiments that have only two outcomes. Two-outcome experiments include many genetic experiments (but the probability is not usually one-half), decisions to buy or not to buy, guessing at true/false quizzes, and machine successes/failures. What really makes the coin toss example so useful is that a host of problems can be easily transformed into an equivalent coin toss experiment. Indeed, if you could learn about only one probability distribution, that one we are about to discover is it. It is called the *binomial probability distribution*, or the *binomial probability mass function*.

In Chapter 6, we defined a random variable as a function from subsets of a sample space to the real numbers. We argued that this very abstract, highly artificial, definition was a useful, even necessary, step for us to take. In this chapter, we will buttress those arguments substantially. The next two chapters could not have been written without the notion of a random variable.

Because we are dealing with the theory of statistics and random variables, the notation we use hereafter will reflect this change in viewpoint. Random variables will be represented by uppercase Roman letters and the parameters of the probability distributions we derive in the next two chapters will be represented by Greek letters. This is done to remind you that we are dealing with theoretical concepts. In the beginning of the text we used lowercase Roman letters because we were there dealing with actual observations and with functions of actual observations such as the sample moments, m_r. This convention is only for the variables; we will need both uppercase and lowercase Roman letters to represent distributions and functions.

Let us proceed with our first hypothetical, or prototypical, experiment. Imagine that we want to consider all experiments that have the coin toss characteristics: there are only two outcomes to any trial; exactly one of which must occur. On any trial, we have no way of knowing which outcome will occur. Further, as far as we can tell the outcome on any one trial does not depend on the outcomes in any previous trial. Finally, like a true coin-tossing experiment, the mechanism generating the outcomes seems to be stable over the whole experiment; that is, we do not expect our coin to wear unevenly or the firing mechanism to become faulty. Because we are in the world of theory, of hypothetical prototypes, we do not need to worry about these mundane details that would be very important in an actual experiment.

We could label the outcomes H, T (or "up," "down"; or anything that we choose), but we remember from Chapter 6 that it is useful to define instead a corresponding random variable. So let us define our random variable produced by any trial of this experiment by

$$X = \begin{cases} 1, & \text{if} \quad H \\ 0, & \text{if} \quad T \end{cases}$$

From our discussions in Chapter 6, we know that an assignment of probability to an elementary event is to pick some real number π, pronounced "pi," so that $0 \leq \pi \leq 1$ and the sum of all probabilities so assigned is 1. In our current case that is an easy task. We define

$$\text{pr}(X = 1) = \pi$$
$$\text{pr}(X = 0) = (1 - \pi)$$

This is fine, but if we are to make any real progress, we will need to express this assignment as a function of the random variable, X; that is, we need an expression to show how the various probabilities are related to the values taken by the random variable. A little introspection and some lucky guessing might lead you to try the following:

$$F(X) = \pi^X (1 - \pi)^{1-X} \tag{7.3}$$

If $X = 1$, then plugging this value into Equation 7.3 yields the number π. Plugging the value of $X = 0$ into the same expression yields the number $(1 - \pi)$. So truly the function $F(X)$, which is called a **probability mass function**, can be said to produce the value of the probability that is assigned to each value of the random variable:

$$F(X) = \begin{cases} \pi & \text{if} \quad X = 1 \\ (1 - \pi) & \text{if} \quad X = 0 \end{cases} \tag{7.4}$$

So far, except for being more formal than we were in Chapter 6, we have not yet added anything of substance, but that is just about to change. Suppose that we now contemplate running a series of n trials. Remember that we are still working under the hypothesis that there is no information about any one trial from any other, and that whatever value of π holds for a trial that same value will hold throughout our experiments.

Consider the following actual experiment to make these ideas less abstract. Recall the die-tossing experiment that we used in Chapter 3; Table 3.2 showed the outcomes of 100 tosses of an eight-sided die. Suppose that we declare that tossing a 1, 2, or 3 is a success, and that tossing any of the other values is a failure. The first major question is whether this experiment is one that meets our requirements. By defining the compound events as we have just done, we have produced a two-outcome experiment with probabilities of three-eighths and five-eighths, respectively. Presumably, the outcome on any one trial has no effect on the outcome on any other trial, and the mechanism generating the outcomes can reasonably be assumed to be stable; that is, the probability of three-eighths for the event 1, 2, or 3, can be expected to stay the same. So we can conclude that this proposed actual experiment is an example of the prototypical experiment that we are examining.

Our task is to discover how we can obtain the probability distribution of getting K successes in n trials of the type we have just proposed. In a coin-tossing experiment a success is throwing a 1; in our die experiment it is throwing a 1, 2, or 3. We now want to discover how to generate the probabilities that are associated with the outcomes of the experiment, using n trials on a simple coin toss type of experiment. But to be useful we want to do more than simply list the probabilities; such a list could be very long indeed. It would be better to have a function in which if we insert a value of the random variable, the function tells us what the corresponding probability is. This is precisely what we shall do.

Let our random variable be called K, and by its definition its possible values are

$0, 1, 2, 3, \ldots, n$

In any one experiment involving n trials of the simple coin toss we can have no success at all, so that the random variable K takes the value 0; we can have one success, so that $K = 1$; or we can have a success on every trial, so that $K = n$. We are trying to find a function that will enable us to write down the probability that is associated with each value of the random variable.

The Convolution Sum

Before we begin this task in earnest, you might have noticed that our random variable K was called the "sum" of n replications of our random variable X. However, the word "sum" is being used here to mean the union of the mutually exclusive outcomes. Suppose that n is 2. On the first trial X could be 0 or 1, and on the second trial X could be 0 or 1.

If we define a new random variable, Y, as the "sum" of two random variables, X_1 and X_2, we are really considering events in Y that are the union of events in X_1 and X_2. We determine each value of Y by adding each *potential* value for trial 1 to each *potential* value for trial 2; that is, to get all the possible values of K, we add the combinations of the values that the random variable X can take in each of the two trials. The values for $Y = X_1 + X_2$ are $\{0, 1, 2\}$. If both X_1 and X_2 are 0, we obtain $Y = 0$; if $X_1 = 1$ and $X_2 = 0$, or $X_2 = 1$ and $X_1 = 0$, we obtain $Y = 1$. If n were 3, the possible values for K would be $\{0, 1, 2, 3\}$; if n were 4, the possible values for the sum of the four random variables would be $\{0, 1, 2, 3, 4\}$.

As another example, recall the random variables X_1 and X_2 that were defined in Table 6.4, where $X_1 = \{0, 1\}$ and $X_2 = \{-1, 0, 1\}$. If we were to consider the domain of the random variable $Y = X_1 + X_2$, we would obtain $\{-1, 0, 1, 2\}$. For each value of X_1 we can have any value of X_2, or for any value of X_2 we can have any value of X_1.

This "sum" of random variables is called a **convolution sum** to reflect the manner in which one normally obtains the distribution of the sum from the distributions of the individual components, X_1 and X_2.

Deriving the Binomial Distribution

Let us consider a typical outcome of our hypothetical experiment. Suppose that n is 10; then a possible set of outcomes from 10 trials on the simple coin toss experiment might be

1 1 1 0 0 0 0 0 1 0

or,

1 0 1 1 1 0 0 1 0 0   (7.5)

or,

1 0 1 0 0 1 0 0 1 0

Before we begin deriving the probability distribution for the random variable K, let us look at something simpler, the probability of getting the first sequence—that is, four 1s and six 0s in the same order—1 1 1 0 0 0 0 0 1 0.

We already know from our work in Chapter 6 that to do this we need the joint probability distribution for the set of ten random variables $\{X_1, X_2, X_3, \ldots, X_{10}\}$, where each X_i represents the random variable associated with the ith trial. By the design of our experiment, we have built in statistical independence between all our ten random variables. We know from Chapter 6 that the joint probability distribution, F_j, is the product of the marginal probability distributions, $F(X_i)$, $i = 1, \ldots, 10$, or

$$F_j(X_1, X_2, X_3, \cdots, X_{10}) = F(X_1)F(X_2)F(X_3) \cdots F(X_{10}) \tag{7.6}$$

where

$$F(X_i) = \pi^{X_i}(1 - \pi)^{1-X_i}$$

To obtain the probability for the joint event

$$[X_1 = 1, X_2 = 1, X_3 = 1, X_4 = 0, X_5 = 0, X_6 = 0, X_7 = 0, X_8 = 0,$$
$$X_9 = 1, X_{10} = 0]$$

we need to insert these values for the ten random variables X_i, $i = 1, \ldots, 10$, into the joint probability distribution F_j. We get

$$F_j(1, 1, 1, 0, 0, 0, 0, 0, 1, 0)$$
$$= F(1)F(1)F(1)F(0)F(0)F(0)F(0)F(0)F(1)F(0) \tag{7.7}$$
$$= \pi \times \pi \times \pi \times (1 - \pi) \times (1 - \pi) \times (1 - \pi) \times (1 - \pi) \times (1 - \pi) \times \tag{7.8}$$
$$\pi \times (1 - \pi)$$
$$= \pi^4 \times (1 - \pi)^6$$

If our experiment was a simple coin toss, then we have just calculated the probability of our prescribed sequence of successes. If $\pi = .5$, then the probability of getting three heads, followed by five tails, a head, and a tail is

$$\left(\frac{1}{2}\right)^4 \times \left(\frac{1}{2}\right)^6 = \left(\frac{1}{2}\right)^{10} = 9.8 \times 10^{-4} = .00098$$

Similarly, we could have calculated the probabilities of the second or third sequences in (7.5). So that you can check that you are following the discussion, the probabilities, given that $\pi = .5$, for the second and third sequences in (7.5) are

- Sequence (2): $\left(\frac{1}{2}\right)^5 \times \left(\frac{1}{2}\right)^5 = \left(\frac{1}{2}\right)^{10} = 9.8 \times 10^{-4}$
- Sequence (3): $\left(\frac{1}{2}\right)^4 \times \left(\frac{1}{2}\right)^6 = \left(\frac{1}{2}\right)^{10} = 9.8 \times 10^{-4}$

You may have noticed that the first and third sequences have the same number of 1s and 0s, but in different sequences. Even if π did not equal .5, as in this example, the probabilities of the two sequences might be the same. This observation suggests that although we have been calculating the probabilities of specific sequences, the probability of each sequence might depend only on the number of 1s and 0s. We should explore this idea.

Although using $\pi = \frac{1}{2}$ is easy, it is so simple that it can confuse matters. Let us try another experiment. In our die example the assignment of π using the "equally likely principle" for the individual outcomes that we specified was $\frac{3}{8}$. Suppose that we had obtained exactly the same set of outcomes in (7.5). We shall redo our three calculations, but this time with $\pi = \frac{3}{8}$ instead of $\pi = \frac{1}{2}$. The probability of getting the first sequence is given by

$$\pi^4 \times (1-\pi)^6 = \left(\frac{3}{8}\right)^4 \times \left(\frac{5}{8}\right)^6 = .0198 \times .0596$$
$$= .00012, \quad \text{or} \quad 1.2 \times 10^{-4}$$

The previous probability for this sequence was 9.8×10^{-4}, using $\pi = \frac{1}{2}$.

If we try the next sequence we get

$$\pi^5 \times (1-\pi)^5 = \left(\frac{3}{8}\right)^5 \times \left(\frac{5}{8}\right)^5 = .0074 \times .0954 = 7.1 \times 10^{-4}$$

The previous probability for this sequence was also 9.8×10^{-4}.

The new values for the last sequence in statement 7.5 are

$$\pi^4 \times (1-\pi)^6 = \left(\frac{3}{8}\right)^4 \times \left(\frac{5}{8}\right)^6 = .0198 \times .0596$$
$$= .00012, \quad \text{or} \quad 1.2 \times 10^{-4}$$

The previous probability was 9.8×10^{-4}.

Now we see that when the number of successes (and failures) is the same, we get the same probability for the sequence for any given probability on a single trial. Further, we see that getting the very same probability for *all* sequences is a special result due to setting $\pi = \frac{1}{2}$—that is, when the probability for each of the two outcomes is the same.

It has taken us a while, but we now know how to calculate the probabilities for a given sequence. We determine the joint probability distribution as the product of the marginals and substitute the values of the variables into the joint probability function.

With this result in hand, we can now discover how to obtain the probability distribution for the random variable K. With respect to our three examples, where n is 10, consider the case where $K = 4$. If $K = 4$, then we are considering four successes and by implication six failures! Laboriously, we have calculated the probabilities for a particular given sequence containing four successes and six failures; those probabilities are 1.2×10^{-4} for $\pi = \frac{3}{8}$ and 9.8×10^{-4} for $\pi = \frac{1}{2}$. However, if we are to get the probability for $K = 4$, we will want to consider the probability of all sequences that contain four successes and six failures. We have the probabilities for each sequence, so all that is left to do is to figure out how to combine them.

A moment's reflection might reveal that each sequence is a mutually exclusive event; that is, whatever sequence occurs, that is the only sequence that occurs. From

Chapter 6, we know how to calculate probabilities for the union of events that are mutually exclusive; we add them. Thus, the probability for all sequences that have four successes and six failures in them is merely the sum of all the probabilities corresponding to sequences that have four successes and six failures. But the real question is how many such sequences do we have?

Look at the first sequence that we discussed in (7.5)

1 1 1 0 0 0 0 0 1 0

We have here ten objects of which four are of one type, 1s, and six are of another, 0s. The question is, How many sequences are there with four 1s and six 0s? or How many permutations can we get from ten objects, of which four cannot be distinguished and six cannot be distinguished? or, How many combinations can we get from ten objects, four of one kind and six of another? From our discussion of permutations, we know the answer:

$$\binom{10}{4} = \frac{10!}{4!6!} = 3 \times 7 \times 10 = 210$$

after cancellation of terms between the numerator and the denominator. From this expression, we can conclude that the probability of getting any sequence with exactly four 1s and six 0s, when the probability of a single success is $\frac{1}{2}$, is the probability that $K = 4$, and that probability we now know is given by

$$210 \times 9.8 \times 10^{-4} = .21$$

where 210 is the number of mutually exclusive sequences involved, and 9.8×10^{-4} is the probability of any one sequence with four 1s in it when the probability of a single success is $\frac{1}{2}$.

From this result, we can calculate the probability of any value of the random variable K. Let's try another example. What is the probability of getting eight successes out of ten when the probability of a single success is $\frac{1}{2}$ and when it is $\frac{3}{8}$?

For a probability of $\frac{1}{2}$ (.5) we obtain

$$\binom{10}{8} \times \pi^8 \times (1 - \pi)^{10-8}$$

$$= \binom{10}{8} \times \left(\frac{1}{2}\right)^8 \times \left(\frac{1}{2}\right)^{10-8}$$

$$= 45 \times .000977 = .04$$

and for a probability of $\frac{3}{8}$ (.375) we obtain

$$\binom{10}{8} \times \pi^8 \times (1 - \pi)^{10-8}$$

$$= \binom{10}{8} \times \left(\frac{3}{8}\right)^8 \times \left(\frac{5}{8}\right)^{10-8}$$

$$= 45 \times .00039 \times .39$$

$$= 45 \times .00015 = .0068$$

Table 7.1   **Binomial Probability Distribution**

Parameters: $n = 3$, $\pi = 1/2$

K	0	1	2	3
Probability	$\frac{1}{8}$	$\frac{3}{8}$	$\frac{3}{8}$	$\frac{1}{8}$

All we have left to do is to write down the general expression for this operation, and we will then have the probability function that we have been trying to derive. Let us define the *binomial probability mass function* in Equation 7.9:

$$B_\pi^n(K) = \binom{n}{K} \pi^K (1 - \pi)^{n-K}$$

$$\binom{n}{K} = \frac{n!}{K!(n - K!)} \qquad (7.9)$$

$$K = \{0, 1, 2, \ldots, n\}$$

The expression $B_\pi^n(K)$, which describes the probability function, depends on two values that we call parameters. **Parameters** are the "constants" of a function; they determine the precise way in which the value of the function varies in response to changes in the values of the variable, or the function's argument. In this case, the two parameters are n, the number of trials used, and π, the probability of a single success, and as we shall soon see, parameters depend on the nature of the experiment and, in turn, determine the shape of the probability function. Any function contains a variable value and the values of parameters. K is the argument of the function, or the variable in the function. The values of K are the values of the random variable, and the corresponding probabilities are given by the output of the function. $B_\pi^n(K)$ is called the *binomial probability distribution* with parameters n and π. The **binomial probability distribution** is the distribution of the probabilities of all possible binomial outcomes in a given number of trials, n. The expression $\binom{n}{K}$ is called a **combinatorial expression**, and sequences of terms $\binom{n}{K}$ for various values of K are known as **combinatorial coefficients**.

To illustrate this discussion, let us look at a simpler example. Suppose that $n = 3$ and $\pi = \frac{1}{2}$. The complete probability function is listed in Table 7.1.

Each term in Table 7.1 is obtained from the expression

$$B_{1/2}^3(K) = \binom{3}{K} \left(\frac{1}{2}\right)^K \left(\frac{1}{2}\right)^{3-K}$$

where $n = 3$, $\pi = \frac{1}{2}$, and $K = \{0, 1, 2, 3\}$. For each value of the argument, K (that is, for each value of the random variable), the function $B_\pi^n(K)$, given the specified values of n and π, produces the required probability.

An important question is whether we really have defined a genuine probability distribution; do the probabilities add to one as they should? We should check that this condition is indeed true. Pascal's triangle (which is defined in Appendix A,

"Mathematics Appendix," Section A.3) is one way to determine the coefficients in the expansion of $(a + b)^n$. Suppose that n is 4, and let us write down the appropriate row of Pascal's triangle, the fifth:

1 4 6 4 1

Now consider the sequence of binomial coefficients given by the combinatorial expression $\binom{4}{K}$, $K = 0, 1, 2, 3, 4$:

$$\binom{4}{0} = 1; \qquad \binom{4}{1} = 4; \qquad \binom{4}{2} = 6;$$

$$\binom{4}{3} = 4; \qquad \binom{4}{4} = 1$$

We see that they are the same. And if you were to repeat the experiment with different values of n, you would see that each time the Pascal's triangle expression and the sequence of combinatorial coefficients, $\binom{n}{K}$, give the same result.

Because $(\pi + (1 - \pi)) = 1$, $(\pi + (1 - \pi))^n = 1$. By using our new connection between Pascal's triangle and the binomial coefficients we can demonstrate that

$$(\pi + (1 - \pi))^n = \sum_0^n \binom{n}{K} \pi^K (1 - \pi)^{n-K} = 1$$

Let us now explore the use of this probability function in solving some simple problems in probability and in exploring the relationship between the values of the parameters and the shape of the distribution.

Imagine that you are facing a true/false quiz in a course that you detest so you are completely unprepared. Fortunately, you have studied your statistics so you can evaluate your chances of getting any specific grade, given that you answer all questions by tossing a coin. On each question you are either right or wrong, so let us score a 1 if right and a 0 if wrong. There are 20 questions, and we will assume that you are equally likely to be right or wrong. Here we have a situation that seems to be relevant to our first probability function.

First, what are your chances of getting the ultimate disgrace of 0 on the whole test? We have 20 trials, the probability on each trial is .5, and we have independence across trials. All this we know because that is how we set up our experiment. Using

$$B_\pi^n(K) = \binom{n}{K} \pi^K (1 - \pi)^{n-K}$$

where in our case $n = 20$, $\pi = .5$, and $K = 0$, the answer is

$$B_{\pi=.5}^{20}(0) = \binom{20}{0} \pi^0 (1 - \pi)^n$$

or 9.5×10^{-7}, or less than one chance in a million. Well, that's a relief! But what about your chances of getting 100% on the test? That probability is also 9.5×10^{-7}; if you do not see why this is so, remember that $\binom{n}{n}$ and $\binom{n}{0}$ have the same value, 1.

Much more realistically, let us find out what your chances are of getting an A, if to get an A you need to score at least 17 out of 20. The probability is given by

$$\sum_{K=17}^{20} B_{\pi}^{n}(K) = \binom{20}{17} \pi^{17}(1-\pi)^{20-17}$$
$$+ \binom{20}{18} \pi^{18}(1-\pi)^{20-18} + \binom{20}{19} \pi^{19}(1-\pi)^{20-19}$$
$$+ \binom{20}{20} \pi^{20}(1-\pi)^{20-20}$$

or numerically,

$$\sum_{K=17}^{20} B_{\pi}^{n}(K) = .0011$$
$$+ .00018 + .000019$$
$$+ .00000095$$
$$= .00130$$

So it would seem that your chances of getting an A by random trial are not very likely. How about settling for a C or better? If a C or better is to get a score of at least 7, we can calculate that probability too. But before you rush off to do that, wait a moment to think. Adding up all the probabilities from 7 to 20 is a pain; so instead why not add up the probabilities from 0 to 6 and subtract from 1? The answer is

$$1 - .0577 = .94$$

So by "guessing" you have a 94% chance of getting a C or better! You have only a 6% chance of failing the course. Now you know why professional testers, such as the Educational Testing Service in Princeton, deduct penalties for wrong answers—to penalize guessing.

Parameters and the Shape of the Probability Distribution

Now that we have seen how to use our probability function to answer some simple probability questions, let us explore the distribution itself and discover for ourselves what role the parameters play. Figures 7.1 and 7.2 show the plots of the probabilities for various values of n and π against the value of the random variable. The figures illustrate the binomial probability function that we presented in Equation 7.9.

Let us look at the plots of the theoretical probabilities. In Figure 7.1, $\pi = .7$, and the probability distribution is left tailed. Notice in Figure 7.2 that when $\pi = .5$, the probability distribution is symmetric, but as the value of π falls to $\pi = .05$ the symmetry decreases. The probability distribution for values of π less than .5 is right tailed. Notice that as the value of n increases the degree of asymmetry decreases. Further, you may notice that as the value of n increases the peakedness of the probability distribution decreases. We will need some more tools to explore the reasons for these observations; we will provide those tools in the next section.

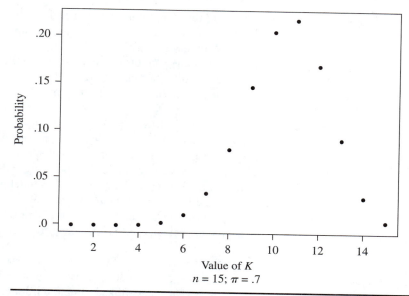

Figure 7.1   Plot of a binomial probability distribution

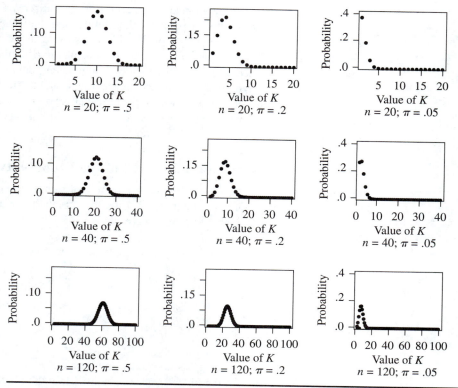

Figure 7.2   Comparison of binomial probability distributions with different parameters

We developed this theory to throw light on the empirical results that we obtained in previous chapters, but if we were to examine some experiments using the binomial probability distribution would we confirm our theoretical findings? Table 7.2 summarizes the results from running each of nine experiments a thousand times. The nine experiments were defined by setting the probability of a single success, π, to the values .5, .2, and .05 and by setting the number of trials, n, to the values 20, 40, and 120.

Imagine that in the first experiment with $\pi = .5$ and $n = 20$ we ran the experiment and got some number between 0 and 20 as an outcome. We then repeated that experiment 1000 times; on each run we would get an outcome that is a number between 0 and 20, which is the range for the random variable. For each setting for π and n we get 1000 numbers that are obtained experimentally from a binomial probability distribution that has parameters π and n. Using these data we can calculate the various sample moments that we examined in Chapter 4. We use the phrase "sample moments" advisedly to stress that the calculations are obtained from observing the outcomes of actual experiments.

Examining the summary statistics shown in Table 7.2, we see that the sample mean increases with the value of π and with the value of n. The sample second moment seems to behave in the same way. The standardized sample third moment, $\hat{\alpha}_1$, is near zero for $\pi = .5$. It increases as π gets smaller but declines as n increases. The sample fourth moment, $\hat{\alpha}_2$, stays near the number 3.0, except for $\pi = .05$ at $n = 20$.

From the calculated sample moments, we appear to have discovered that as the parameters are varied, both the shape of the distribution and the values taken by the sample moments change in seemingly predictable ways. But can we claim that we have confirmed our theory; that is, are the observed results in agreement with the theoretical claims? They seem to be approximately in agreement, but we do not yet know how to measure the extent of the difference, nor how to evaluate the difference, when measured. We still have to discover how to decide what is and is not an example of disagreement between theory and observation. That task will take us the remainder of the text. For now, we need new tools to proceed.

Theoretical Moments and the Shape of the Probability Distribution

In previous chapters, we discussed shape and the role of sample moments in the context of histograms. Given that probability distributions are the theoretical analogues of histograms, we should be able to extend the basic idea of a "moment" to probability distributions.

Let us recall the simplest moment, the mean, both in terms of raw data and in terms of data in cells:

$$m'_1 = \frac{\left(\sum_1^n x_i \right)}{n} \cong \sum_1^k f_j c_j \tag{7.10}$$

where "$\cong$" indicates that the right side is only approximately equal to the left side, f_j is the relative frequency in the jth cell, c_j is the cell mark in the jth cell, and the n ob-

Table 7.2 **Sample Moments from a Series of Binomial Distributions**

n	π	m'_1	m_2	$\hat{\alpha}_1$	$\hat{\alpha}_2$
20	.50	10.05	4.39	−0.023	2.69
40	.50	20.21	9.56	−0.028	2.95
120	.50	59.96	27.80	−0.084	2.93
20	.20	4.07	3.53	0.450	3.22
40	.20	8.10	6.63	0.045	3.03
120	.20	24.18	19.02	0.013	3.15
20	.05	1.02	0.88	1.040	5.87
40	.05	2.00	2.01	0.690	3.32
120	.05	5.93	5.80	0.340	2.96

servations are in k cells. The first definition using raw data can also be interpreted in terms of relative frequencies if we regard $1/n$ as the relative frequency of a single observation in a set of size n. We can abstract from this idea by noting that the sample moments we defined previously are weighted sums of the values of the variable, where the weights are given by the relative frequencies. Because probabilities are the theoretical analogues of relative frequencies, we have an immediate suggestion for a theoretical extension of the notion of "moment."

Let us define **theoretical moments** as the weighted sums of the values of the random variable, where the weights are given by the probability distribution. More formally, we write

$$\mu'_1 = \sum_1^n X_i \mathrm{pr}(X_i)$$ (7.11)

to express the first theoretical moment about the origin for a discrete random variable with n elements in the sample space and probabilities given by $\mathrm{pr}(X_i)$.

The use of the Greek letter μ is to remind us that this definition is theoretical and therefore to be distinguished from sample moments, which are defined with respect to actual data. We have already discussed this important issue of notation, but it bears repeating. In the chapters to come, you will frequently have to distinguish between observations, represented by lowercase Roman letters especially at the end of the alphabet; random variables that have distributions attached, represented by uppercase Roman letters, and parameters and properties of probability distributions, represented by Greek letters.

For example, if you see m'_1 you know that it represents adding up n observed numbers and dividing by n, the number of data points observed; m'_1 is a quantity. That means it is a number with units of measurement attached and is, through the observed data, observed itself. In contrast, when you see μ'_1, you know that this is a theoretical concept and is therefore an abstraction.

Random variables and probability distribution functions and theoretical moments are concepts enabling us to think about what we are observing. What we actually observe and the operations we perform on those observations are different. We use our theoretical ideas to interpret what we see. Force, momentum, velocity, and mass are all theoretical ideas in physics used to explain, or interpret, what we see and feel. But, a tennis ball hitting you smack in the face is reality; interpreting the event in terms of force, mass, and velocity is the abstraction. The symbol μ'_1 is a theoretical concept used to interpret the reality of the quantity m'_1.

Let us return to developing our concepts of theoretical moments. We define the rth theoretical moment about the origin as

$$\mu'_r = \sum_1^n X_i^r \operatorname{pr}(X_i) \tag{7.12}$$

$$r = 1, 2, 3, \ldots, n$$

where μ'_r is nothing more than the weighted sum of the values of a random variable raised to the rth power; the weights are given by the corresponding probabilities.

When we dealt with moments of actual data, we found that the moments about the mean were the most useful. Similarly in this case, we will discover that our most useful theoretical moments are moments about the "mean"; but what "mean"? A good guess is to use μ'_1; and indeed μ'_1 is (as is m'_1) called the mean. By now you are getting the picture that the word "mean" has a lot of meanings!

We define theoretical moments about the mean by

$$\mu_r = \sum_1^n (X_i - \mu'_1)^r \operatorname{pr}(X_i) \tag{7.13}$$

$$r = 1, 2, 3, \ldots, n$$

where μ_r is the weighted sum of differences between the values of the random variables and the theoretical mean raised to the rth power; the weights are the corresponding probabilities.

We have introduced the idea of theoretical moments to help us measure the various characteristics of the shape of probability distribution functions. We have done this in analogy with our use of sample moments to measure the characteristics of histograms. Let us now explore these new ideas using our first experimentally motivated probability function, the binomial probability function. Remember that our objective is to explain the change in shape of the binomial probability distribution in response to the changes in the values of the parameters.

If we use the binomial probability distribution in the definition of μ'_1, let us see what we get:

$$\mu'_1 = \sum X_i \operatorname{pr}(X_i)$$

$$= \sum_{K=0}^n K \binom{n}{K} \pi^K \pi^{n-K} \tag{7.14}$$

where $K = 0, 1, \ldots, n$ are the values of the random variable represented in the defining equation for μ'_1 by X_i, $i = 0, 1, 2, \ldots, n$. The first term in this expression drops out because $K = 0$:

$$\sum_{K=1}^{n} K \binom{n}{K} \pi^K (1-\pi)^{n-K}$$

$$= \sum_{K=1}^{n} K \frac{n!}{K!(n-K)!} \pi^K (1-\pi)^{n-K} \tag{7.15}$$

We can divide K into the $K!$ to get

$$\sum_{K=1}^{n} \frac{n!}{(K-1)!(n-K)!} \pi^K (1-\pi)^{n-K}$$

What we want to do now is to try to rewrite the last expression in terms of a binomial expansion from zero to its upper limit as we did when we proved that the binomial probability distribution was a genuine probability distribution. But why? Because that expansion gives us a value of 1, so that whatever is left over is what we want. If we can reexpress the last expression in this way, we have solved our problem. Consider what happens in the last expression if we extract the product $n\pi$ from the summation:

$$\sum_{K=1}^{n} \frac{n!}{(K-1)!(n-K)!} \pi^K (1-\pi)^{n-K}$$

$$= n\pi \sum_{K=1}^{n-1} \frac{(n-1)!}{(K-1)!(n-1-(K-1))!} \pi^{K-1} (1-\pi)^{n-1-(K-1)} \tag{7.16}$$

Equation 7.16 is now easily reexpressed as a sum of binomial probabilities, which we know is one. In anticipation we have already reexpressed $(n-K)$ as $(n-1-(K-1))$. We can sum $K^* = (K-1)$ from 0 to $(n-1)$, instead of summing K from 1 to n. We can do this because $(K-1)$, when $K=1$, is 0 and is $(n-1)$ when $K=n$.

Consequently, we have a sum over K^* of binomial probabilities from 0 to $(n-1)$, where the numerator in the combinatorial coefficient, $\binom{n-1}{K^*}$, is $(n-1)$. As we now know this sum is one. We conclude that the mean, or the first theoretical moment about the origin, for the binomial probability distribution is $n\pi$. As we suspected from the empirical results contained in Table 7.2 the mean is an increasing function of both n and π.

In a similar manner, we can derive the higher theoretical moments of the binomial probability distribution (you are shown how to do this in the Exercises for this chapter) as follows:

$$\mu_2(X) = n\pi(1-\pi) = n\pi q \tag{7.17}$$

where $q = (1-\pi)$;

$$\mu_3(X) = n\pi q(1-2\pi) \tag{7.18}$$

and

$$\mu_4(X) = 3 \times (n\pi q)^2 + n\pi q(1-6\pi q) \tag{7.19}$$

Before we start to use these theoretical moments to represent the shape of the probability distribution, we recognize from our experience in Chapter 6 that it is probably important to standardize the theoretical moments beyond the second to allow for both origin and scale effects, just as we had to do for the higher sample moments.

Following the precedent set in previous chapters, we define

$$\alpha_1 = \frac{\mu_3}{\mu_2^{3/2}}$$
$$\alpha_2 = \frac{\mu_4}{\mu_2^2}$$

(7.20)

where α_1 and α_2 are the standardized theoretical moments in the sense that any change in the origin for measuring the random variable or in the chosen scale for measuring the random variable will leave the value of the standardized third and fourth theoretical moments invariant. For example, if the random variable represents temperature readings, then the values of α_1 and α_2 are the same no matter whether the temperature readings are recorded in degrees Fahrenheit or degrees Celsius.

Notice that the "little hats" are gone from α_1 and α_2. This is because we are now dealing with the theoretical entities and not their sample analogues. If we were to use our usual practice, we would have written a_1 and a_2 for the sample standardized moments in agreement with using m_r for μ_r, but as you now see that would have been an unfortunate choice given our use of a for so many other terms. This trick of using little hats to indicate that we are talking about the sample analogues, not the theoretical quantities, will be used quite extensively in the next few chapters.

Let us write down our first two theoretical moments, followed by our standardized third and fourth theoretical moments for the binomial probability distribution:

$$\mu_1' = n\pi; \quad \mu_2 = n\pi q$$

where $q = (1 - \pi)$;

$$\alpha_1 = \frac{\mu_3}{\mu_2^{3/2}}$$
$$= \frac{n\pi q(1 - 2\pi)}{(n\pi q)^{3/2}}$$
$$= \frac{(1 - 2\pi)}{\sqrt{n\pi q}}$$

(7.21)

$$\alpha_2 = \frac{\mu_4}{\mu_2^2}$$
$$= \frac{3(n\pi q)^2 + n\pi q(1 - 6\pi q)}{(n\pi q)^2}$$
$$= \frac{3 + (1 - 6\pi q)}{n\pi q}$$

(7.22)

We can now explore the relationship between theoretical moments, parameters, and the shape of the probability function. Let us review the summary calculations

Table 7.3 **Theoretical Moments for the Binomial Distribution for Various Parameters**

Parameter Values		Theoretical Moments			
n	π	μ_1'	μ_2	α_1	α_2
20	.50	10	5.00	0.00	3.15
20	.20	4	3.20	0.33	3.26
20	.05	1	0.95	0.92	4.00
40	.50	20	10.00	0.00	3.08
40	.20	8	6.40	0.24	3.13
40	.05	2	1.90	0.65	3.50
120	.50	60	30.00	0.00	3.03
120	.20	24	19.20	0.13	3.04
120	.05	6	5.70	0.35	3.17

shown in Table 7.3 and the plots of the theoretical probabilities shown in Figure 7.2 to see the extent to which our theoretical results are useful. For the nine alternative combinations of n and π that we have examined, we should compare the theoretical moments with the values obtained for the sample moments using the experimental data summarized in Table 7.2.

On comparing the theoretical values with the values obtained from the experiments, we observe a close, but by no means exact relationship, between the two sets of numbers. Thinking about these numbers and their comparisons, we may realize that a major problem that faces us is how to decide what is and is not close. How do we decide when an empirical result "confirms" the theoretical statement, given that we know that it is most unlikely that we will ever get perfect agreement between theory and observation? This is an important task that will have to be delayed until Chapter 9.

The values for the theoretical moments listed in Table 7.3 and the expressions that we derived for the theoretical moments enable us to confirm the conjectures that we formulated on first viewing the summary statistics in Table 7.2. We see even more clearly from the algebraic expressions that μ_1' increases in n and π; that μ_2 increases in n and π up to .5; that the standardized third and fourth theoretical moments decrease in n to minimum values that are 0.00 and 3.03, respectively. As π approaches 0 or 1 both α_1 and α_2 get bigger for any given value of n; alternatively expressed, the minimum for both $|\alpha_1|$ and α_2 is for $\pi = .5$.

The effect that n has on the shape of the distribution is quite remarkable. No matter how asymmetric the distribution is to begin with, a sufficiently large increase in n will produce a distribution that is very symmetric; the symmetry is measured by the value of α_1. The limit as $n \to \infty$ for α_1 is 0, and the limit for α_2 is 3. We will soon see that these two values for α_1 and α_2 keep occurring as the limits for the values of α_1 and α_2 as a parameter n gets bigger and bigger. We might suspect that these particular values for the theoretical moments represent a special probability distribution, as indeed they do.

Consider a simple example. Suppose that the distribution of births by sex within a specified region over a short interval of time is given by the binomial distribution with parameters n, being the total number of births in the region, and π, the probability of a male birth. Usually, the value of π is a little greater than .5, say .52. If $n = 100$, the mean of the distribution, $\mu_1' = n\pi = 52$. What this means is that the value about which actual numbers of male births varies is 52; for any given time period it might be less, or it might be more, but over a long period we expect the variations to average approximately 52.

The square root of the variance of the distribution is given by $\sqrt{n\pi(1-\pi)}$, which in this case is 5. We can expect very approximately that about 90% of the time the number of male births will lie between 42 and 62. Certainly, we would be very surprised if the number of male births fell below 37 or exceeded 67.

Given that the standardized third moment is negative, but very small, this distribution is approximately symmetric about 52; it is equally likely to have fewer than 52 male births as it is to have more. The standardized fourth moment is not too much less than 3, so that we can conclude that our distribution has neither thin tails nor fat ones. Very large and very small numbers of male births are neither very frequent nor very rare.

We can summarize this section by pointing out that what we have discovered is that

- the conditions of an experiment determine the shape of the relevant probability function.
- the effects of the experimental conditions are reflected in the values taken by the parameters of the distribution.
- the shape of the distribution is measured in terms of the theoretical moments of the probability function.
- the theoretical moments are themselves functions of the parameters.

7.5 Expectation

This section is not what you might expect; it is about a very useful operation in statistics called taking the expected value of a random variable, or **expectation**. You have in fact already done it—that is, taken an expectation of a random variable—but you did not know it at the time. The operation that we used to determine the theoretical moments was an example of the procedure known as expectation. Once again, we will be able to obtain both insight into and ease of manipulation of random variables and their properties by generalizing a specific concept and thereby extending our theory.

Taking expected values is nothing more than getting the weighted sums of functions of random variables, where the weights are provided by the probability function. Let us define the concept of expectation formally as follows:

The expected value of any function of a random variable, X, say $g(X)$, is given by

$$E\{g(X)\} = \sum_{1}^{n} g(X)\mathrm{pr}(X) \tag{7.23}$$

We have already performed this operation several times while calculating the theoretical moments. For μ_1', the function $g(X)$ was just X; for μ_2 the function $g(X)$ was $(X - \mu_1')^2$; and so on. The function $g(X)$ can be any function you like. Whatever choice you make, the expectation of $g(X)$, however defined, is given by Equation 7.23.

Consider the simple coin toss experiment with probability function discussed in Chapter 6. The distribution function was

$$F(X) = \pi^X (1 - \pi)^{1-X}$$
$$X = \{0, 1\}$$

The expectation of X,

$$E\{X\} = \sum_X X \pi^X (1 - \pi)^{1-X}$$

$$= \pi$$

takes the value $\frac{1}{2}$ in the case of a true coin toss. Note that I used the notation Σ_X to indicate "summation over the values of X."

What does this simple result mean? Clearly, it does not mean that in a coin toss one observes "$\frac{1}{2}$" on average. All one observes is a string of 0s and 1s, not a single $\frac{1}{2}$ in sight. What the "average," or "mean," of the variable given by the expectation operation implies is that it is the value for which the average deviation is zero. Recall from Chapter 3 that we define the sample mean as that value such that the average deviations from it are zero; that is

$$\sum (x_i - \bar{x}) \equiv 0$$

Similarly, we note that μ'_1 satisfies

$$\sum (X_i - \mu'_1) \text{pr}(X_i) \equiv 0$$

where

$$\mu'_1 = E\{X\}$$

Recalling our definition of a random variable (which is a function on all subsets of a sample space to the real numbers), we recognize that $g(X)$ is also a random variable. This is because it is a function of a random variable that is, in turn, a function of subsets of some sample space, so that $g(X)$, through X, is itself a random variable. As such $g(X)$ will have associated with it a corresponding probability function, say $h(Y)$, where $Y = g(X)$. For the student comfortable in calculus this approach is explored in the Exercises in terms of the concept termed "transformation of variables."

But we have also seen that any probability function has associated with it a set of theoretical moments. The first of these is the mean, or μ'_1. From the definition of μ'_1,

$$\mu'_1 = \sum Y_i h(Y_i) \tag{7.24}$$

where $Y_i = g(X_i)$ and $h(Y_i)$ is the probability function for the random variable Y_i.

Let's make sure that we understand what is going on here. We began with a random variable $X_i, i = 1, 2, \ldots, n$, with corresponding probability function $f(X_i)$. We then decided to create a new random variable Y, with values Y_i, by defining $Y_i = g(X_i)$, for example, $Y_i = (X_i - \mu'_1)^2$. We have claimed that there is some probability function, say $h(Y_i)$, that provides the distribution of probabilities for the random variable Y. At the moment we do not know how to find the probability function $h(Y_i)$, but because we know that Y is a random variable, we do know that there exists some probability function for the random variable Y; we are just giving it a name.

So if we knew the probability function $h(Y_i)$, we could obtain the mean of the random variable Y. But that is often a problem; it is sometimes not easy to get the probability function $h(Y_i)$ from information on X_i, $g(X_i)$, and $f(X_i)$. Here is where the operation of expectation comes to the rescue. Using the expression for expectation, we have

$$E\{g(X)\} = \sum_{i=1}^{n} g(X_i)\text{pr}(X_i) \tag{7.25}$$

where $\text{pr}(X_i)$ is the probability function for the random variable X. From this expression, we see that we can get the mean of the random variable $Y = g(X)$ without having to find out what the probability function $h(Y)$ is. We have in fact the result

$$E\{Y\} = \sum_{i} Y_i h(Y_i) = \sum_{i} g(X_i)\text{pr}(X_i)$$

All the theoretical moments are examples of expectations; μ_1' is the expectation of the random variable X; $\mu_2(X)$ is the expectation of the random variable $(X - \mu_1')^2$; and so on. As we know, all of these theoretical moments are merely weighted sums of the values of the appropriate function of the random variable X. The weights are given by the probabilities associated with each value of X or with each value of some function of X.

You might get a better feel for the idea of expectation if we consider a case where the number of variable values is two:

$$E\{g(X)\} = \pi g(X_1) + (1 - \pi)g(X_2) \tag{7.26}$$

and π is the probability that $X = X_1$ and $(1 - \pi)$ is the probability that $X = X_2$.

Suppose that $X_1 = 1$, $X_2 = 2$, and that we let π have various values. As an example, you might be contemplating an investment opportunity in which there are two possible outcomes: \$1,000 in one case and \$2,000 in the other; the probability of the first case occurring is represented by π.

Let us try $\pi = 1, \frac{3}{4}, \frac{1}{2}, \frac{1}{4}$, and 0. For each of these values of π, recall that $(1 - \pi)$ will have values $0, \frac{1}{4}, \frac{1}{2}, \frac{3}{4}$, and 1. We can write down for each choice of π the corresponding value of the expectation

$$\pi = 1 : E\{X\} = 1 \times 1 + 0 \times 2 = 1$$

$$\pi = \frac{3}{4} : E\{X\} = \frac{3}{4} \times 1 + \frac{1}{4} \times 2 = \frac{5}{4}$$

$$\pi = \frac{1}{2} : E\{X\} = \frac{1}{2} \times 1 + \frac{1}{2} \times 2 = \frac{6}{4}$$

$$\pi = \frac{1}{4} : E\{X\} = \frac{1}{4} \times 1 + \frac{3}{4} \times 2 = \frac{7}{4}$$

$$\pi = 0 : E\{X\} = 0 \times 1 + 1 \times 2 = 2$$

Table 7.4 **Expectations of Various Functions for Binomial Probability Functions**

Function	Expectations for				
	$\pi = 1$	$\pi = \frac{3}{4}$	$\pi = \frac{1}{2}$	$\pi = \frac{1}{4}$	$\pi = 0$
$g: x^2$	1	$\frac{7}{4}$	$\frac{5}{2}$	$\frac{13}{4}$	4
$f: x + 5$	6	$\frac{25}{4}$	$\frac{13}{2}$	$\frac{27}{4}$	7
$h: 2 + 3x$	5	$\frac{23}{4}$	$\frac{13}{2}$	$\frac{29}{4}$	8
$k: (x-1)^2$	0	$\frac{1}{4}$	$\frac{1}{2}$	$\frac{3}{4}$	1

We see that as we shift the weight of the probability from being all on the value "1" to being all on the value "2," the expectation shifts from the value 1 to the value 2 correspondingly. The value of the expectation is always between 1 and 2 in these examples. If you try doing this for probabilities with three values for the random variable and then for random variables with four values, you will soon see that as we allow the probability to vary over its whole possible range that the value for the expectation for any probability function must lie between the minimum and the maximum observations; that is, if $X_{(1)}$ and $X_{(n)}$ are the minimum and the maximum, respectively, of a random variable and pr(X) is the probability function, then,

$$X_{(1)} \le E\{X\} \le X_{(n)} \tag{7.27}$$

The smallest $E\{X\}$ can be is $X_{(1)}$, when the probability of $X_{(1)}$ is one and, of course, the probabilities of all other values are 0. The largest that $E\{X\}$ can be is $X_{(n)}$, when the probability of $X_{(n)}$ is one and the probabilities of all the other values are 0.

Similar statements can be made about the expectation of any function of a random variable X. With the five alternative probability distribution functions used in the example where $X_1 = 1$ and $X_2 = 2$, try obtaining for yourself the expectations of

- $g(X) = X^2$
- $f(X) = X + 5$
- $h(X) = 2 + 3 \times X$
- $k(X) = (X - 1)^2$

You should get the results shown in Table 7.4.

Notice that there are some simple relationships between the various expectations and the functions $g(.), f(.), h(.),$ and $k(.)$. It would be convenient to formalize this observation. Consequently, consider the following claim: If a random variable Y is related to a random variable X by

$$Y = a + bX$$

for a and b, which can be any constants, then

$$E\{Y\} = a + bE\{X\} \tag{7.28}$$

You can easily demonstrate this for yourself by substituting the definition of Y into the definition for expectation:

$$Y = g(X) = a + bx$$

$$E\{Y\} = E\{g(X)\}$$

$$= \sum g(X_i)\mathrm{pr}(X_i)$$

$$= a\sum \mathrm{pr}(X_i) + b\sum X_i\mathrm{pr}(X_i)$$

$$= a + bE\{X\}$$

What if we define Y by

$$Y = a_1X_1 + a_2X_2 + a_3X_3 + \cdots + a_nX_n \tag{7.29}$$

where the $\{X_i\}$ are a set of n random variables. Suppose that the expectations of the X_i, $i = 1, 2, \ldots, n$ are $\epsilon_1, \epsilon_2, \ldots, \epsilon_n$ respectively; that is, $E\{X_i\} = \epsilon_i$. What is the expectation of Y in terms of the $E\{X_i\}$?

By a slight extension of the preceding argument we see that

$$E\{Y\} = \sum [a_1X_1 + a_2X_2 + a_3X_3 + \cdots + a_nX_n]\mathrm{pr}(X_1)\mathrm{pr}(X_2) \cdots \mathrm{pr}(X_n) \tag{7.30}$$

where $\mathrm{pr}(X_1)\mathrm{pr}(X_2) \cdots \mathrm{pr}(X_n)$ is the joint probability function for the n random variables $\{X_i\}$, $i = 1, 2, \ldots, n$, assuming that the $\{X_i\}$ are statistically independent.

Applying the elementary probability concepts that we learned in Chapter 6, we see that

$$E\{Y\} = \sum_i [a_i \sum_j X_{ij}\mathrm{pr}(X_{ij})]$$

where X_{ij} represents the jth value of the ith random variable. So

$$E\{Y\} = \sum_i a_i\epsilon_i \tag{7.31}$$

In the chapters to come we will use these concepts and results repeatedly, so make sure that you thoroughly understand these ideas.

Let us try a simple example using the random variables X_1 and X_2, where $E\{X_1\} = 3$, $E\{X_1^2\} = 9$, and $E\{X_2\} = 4$. Let us assume that we know nothing further about the distributions of X_1 and X_2. To find the expectation of

$$Y = 2X_1 + 5X_2$$

and of

$$W = (X_1 - 2)^2 = X_1^2 + 4 - 4X_1$$

we obtain by substitution

$$E\{Y\} = 2 \times 3 + 5 \times 4$$

$$= 26$$

$$E\{W\} = E\{X_1^2\} + 4 - E\{4X_1\}$$

$$= 9 + 4 - (4 \times 3) = 1$$

In Equation 7.30, we defined the expectation of a "sum of variables" with respect to random variables that were independently distributed. Let us now extend that definition to variables that are not independently distributed. Let $F(X_1, X_2)$ be the joint distribution of X_1, X_2 where $F(X_1, X_2)$ cannot be factored into the product of the marginals. Consider:

$$E\{a_1 X_1 + a_2 X_2\} = \sum_{X_1, X_2} \{a_1 X_1 + a_2 X_2\} F(X_1, X_2)$$

$$= \left\{ a_1 \sum_{X_1, X_2} X_1 F(X_1, X_2) + a_2 \sum_{X_1, X_2} X_2 F(X_1, X_2) \right\}$$

$$= \left\{ a_1 \sum_{X_1} X_1 F_1(X_1) + a_2 \sum_{X_2} X_2 F_2(X_2) \right\}$$

$$= a_1 E\{X_1\} + a_2 E\{X_2\}$$

In this development, we used the result that the marginal distribution is obtained from the joint distribution by adding up the probabilities over the "other variable" (as was discussed in Chapter 6); $\sum_{X_2} F(X_1, X_2) = F_1(X_1)$. The notation $\sum_{X_1, X_2}$ implies that one sums over the values of both X_1 and X_2. In the previous expression, we used the idea that

$$\sum_{X_1, X_2} X_1 F(X_1, X_2) = \sum_{X_1} X_1 \sum_{X_2} F(X_1, X_2)$$

$$= \sum_{X_1} X_1 F_1(X_1)$$

where $F_1(X_1)$ is the marginal distribution of X_1.

We can easily extend this idea to weighted sums of functions of the variables, one at a time. For example,

$$E\{a_1 g(X_1) + a_2 h(X_2)\} = \sum_{X_1, X_2} \{a_1 g(X_1) + a_2 h(X_2)\} F(X_1, X_2)$$

$$= \left\{ a_1 \sum_{X_1} g(X_1) F_1(X_1) + a_2 \sum_{X_2} h(X_2) F_2(X_2) \right\}$$

$$= a_1 E\{g(X_1)\} + a_2 E\{h(X_2)\}$$

So far, it would seem that there is no difference between the independent and the nonindependent cases. That is because we have not looked at any functions involving the products of X_1 and X_2. Consider, using the same distribution:

$$E\{X_1 \times X_2\} = \sum_{X_1, X_2} \{X_1 \times X_2\} F(X_1, X_2)$$

No further simplification is possible. However, if the variables X_1 and X_2 are independent, the situation is different:

$$E\{X_1 \times X_2\} = \sum_{X_1, X_2} \{X_1 \times X_2\} F(X_1, X_2)$$

$$= \sum_{X_1, X_2} \{X_1 \times X_2\} F_1\{X_1\} F_2\{X_2\}$$

$$= \sum_{X_1, X_2} \{X_1 F_1\{X_1\} F_2\{X_2\} \times X_2 F_1\{X_1\} F_2\{X_2\}\}$$

$$= \sum_{X_1} \{X_1 F_1\{X_1\}\} \times \sum_{X_2} \{X_2 F_2\{X_2\}\}$$

$$= E\{X_1\} E\{X_2\}$$

Let us explore this result using the simple bivariate distribution defined in Chapter 6. Table 6.4 gave the joint distribution of $X_1 = \{0, 1\}$ and $X_2 = \{-1, 0, 1\}$. We obtain

$$E\{X_1 \times X_2\} = \sum_{X_1, X_2} \{X_1 \times X_2\} F(X_1, X_2)$$

$$= (\{X_1 = 1\} \times \{X_2 = -1\}) \times \frac{1}{4}$$

$$= -\frac{1}{4}$$

where all other terms have dropped out because zeros are involved in the multiplication. In contrast, consider the expectation of the product of the independent random variables $\{Y_1, Y_2\}$ that were defined in Table 6.6 and have the same marginal distributions as those of $\{X_1, X_2\}$.

$$E\{Y_1 \times Y_2\} = \sum_{Y_1, Y_2} \{Y_1 \times Y_2\} F(Y_1, Y_2)$$

$$= (\{Y_1 = 1\} \times \{Y_2 = -1\}) \frac{1}{8} + (\{Y_1 = 1\} \times \{Y_2 = 1\}) \frac{1}{8}$$

$$= -\frac{1}{8} + \frac{1}{8} = 0$$

after having dropped all terms involving multiplication by zero. So even for two distributions where the values taken by the random variables are the same and the marginal probabilities are the same, there is a considerable difference in the expectation of a product between variables that are independent and nonindependent.

Moment-Generating Functions for Discrete Variables

This section is for the student who is comfortable with integral calculus and higher-order derivatives. The remainder of the book can be read with full comprehension even if you do not follow the material in this section. However, if you can follow the material, the depth and richness of your understanding of the theory underlying statistical analysis will be enhanced.

We have defined the general idea of expectation of any function of a random variable. There is a very special function that provides useful insight into the relationship between the shapes of probability functions and moments. Recall the exponential function, $e^{s \times X}$, for some random variable X. Formally, we can write the expectation of this function for a discrete random variable X with probability distribution function $F(X)$ as

$$E\{e^{s \times X}\} = \sum_X e^{s \times X} F(X)$$

$$= M_X(s)$$

for some function $M_X(s)$ that depends on the function $F(X)$. So far, there is nothing remarkable about this calculation. However, once we recall one way to define the function $e^{s \times X}$—namely,

$$e^{s \times X} = 1 + s \times X + \frac{(s \times X)^2}{2!} + \frac{(s \times X)^3}{3!} + \frac{(s \times X)^4}{4!} + \cdots \qquad (7.33)$$

and take expectations on both sides we obtain in the case of the discrete random variable

$$M_X(s) = 1 + s \times \mu_1' + \frac{s^2}{2!}\mu_2' + \frac{s^3}{3!}\mu_3' + \frac{s^4}{4!}\mu_4' + \cdots \qquad (7.34)$$

In short, we see that the function $M_X(s)$ is a weighted sum of the moments about the origin of the random variable involved. Further, if we now take the derivative of $M_X(s)$ once we will obtain

$$M_X(s)^{(1)} = \mu_1' + \frac{2s}{2!}\mu_2' + \frac{3s^2}{3!}\mu_3' + \frac{4s^3}{4!}\mu_4' + \cdots \qquad (7.35)$$

Setting $s = 0$, we get

$$M_X(0)^{(1)} = \mu_1'$$

Let us now take the second derivative. We obtain

$$M_X(s)^{(2)} = \frac{2!}{2!}\mu_2' + \frac{3 \times 2s}{3!}\mu_3' + \frac{4 \times 3s^2}{4!}\mu_4' + \cdots \qquad (7.36)$$

or

$$M_X(0)^{(2)} = \mu_2'$$

And, let us do so once again, to obtain

$$M_X(s)^{(3)} = \mu_3' + \frac{4 \times 3 \times 2s}{4!}\mu_4' + \cdots \qquad (7.37)$$

or

$$M_X(0)^{(3)} = \mu_3'$$

We now see that by taking higher and higher derivatives of the function $M_X(s)$ and setting the variable s to zero, we can derive the moments about the origin for the random variable X. The notation $M_X(s)$ stresses that we have a **moment-generating function**; that is, it is the function that generates the moments for a random variable X, and it is a function of the variable s. The label s is in fact a "dummy" variable; we could have called it anything; s serves a role similar to that of an index.

In summary, we have

$$M_X(0)^{(r)} = \mu'_r \tag{7.38}$$

which holds for any r for discrete random variables.

Let us use a simple example (there are more in the Exercises). Suppose that we are considering a random variable, Y, that can take only the two values $\{1, 0\}$ with probabilities π and $(1 - \pi)$; that is, we are considering a binomial distribution with $n = 1$. We can easily evaluate the corresponding moment-generating function:

$$
\begin{aligned}
M_Y(s) = E\{e^{s \times Y}\} &= e^s \pi + e^0 \times (1 - \pi) \\
&= e^s \pi + (1 - \pi) \\
&= \pi \times \left(1 + s + \frac{s^2}{2!} + \frac{s^3}{3!} + \cdots\right) + (1 - \pi) \\
&= 1 + \pi s + \pi \frac{s^2}{2!} + \pi \frac{s^3}{3!} + \cdots
\end{aligned}
\tag{7.39}
$$

From this we see that by taking the rth derivative of the function and evaluating the derivative at $s = 0$, we obtain, in each case, the value π for all values of $r \geq 1$.

This result is useful for obtaining the moments when we can easily derive the moment-generating function itself. But the moment-generating function has some other useful properties. Consider, for any constant a:

$$
\begin{aligned}
M_{X+a}(s) = E\{e^{s(X+a)}\} &= E\{e^{s \times a} e^{s \times X}\} \\
&= e^{s \times a} M_X(s)
\end{aligned}
$$

At the moment this result seems unremarkable, but if we let $a = -\mu'_1$, we obtain

$$M_{X-\mu'_1}(s) = e^{-s \times \mu'_1} M_X(s) \tag{7.40}$$

In short, we can easily obtain from this expression the moments about the mean from the moments about the origin by merely multiplying the moment-generating function for the moments about the origin by the expression $e^{-s \times \mu'_1}$. We derive:

$$
\begin{aligned}
&1 + \frac{s^2}{2!}\mu_2 + \frac{s^3}{3!}\mu_3 + \frac{s^4}{4!}\mu_4 + \cdots \\
&= \left(1 - s \times \mu'_1 + \frac{s^2}{2!}(\mu'_1)^2 - \frac{s^3}{3!}(\mu'_1)^3 + \cdots\right) \times \\
&\quad \left(1 + s \times \mu'_1 + \frac{s^2}{2!}\mu'_2 + \frac{s^3}{3!}\mu'_3 + \cdots\right)
\end{aligned}
$$

By multiplying together the last two brackets and equating coefficients, we can easily derive the moments about the origin. We can apply this result to our example to obtain (letting $\eta = \mu_1'$):

$$1 + \frac{s^2}{2!}\mu_2 + \frac{s^3}{3!}\mu_3 + \cdots$$

$$= 1 + \frac{s^2}{2!}[\mu_2' - 2\eta^2 + \eta^2] + \frac{s^3}{3!}[\mu_3' - 3\eta\mu_2' + 3\eta^3 - \eta^3] + \cdots$$

$$= 1 + \frac{s^2}{2!}[\mu_2' - \eta^2] + \frac{s^3}{3!}[\mu_3' - 3\eta\mu_2' + 2\eta^3] + \cdots$$

$$= 1 + \frac{s^2}{2!}[\pi(1 - \pi)] + \frac{s^3}{3!}[\pi - 3\pi^2 + 2\pi^3] + \cdots$$

Moment-generating functions have another useful property; namely, that for any constant c,

$$M_{c \times Y}(s) = E\{e^{c \times s \times Y}\} = M_Y(c \times s) \tag{7.41}$$

This property becomes even more useful when we add the next property for the sum of independent and identically distributed random variables. Let

$$Z = \sum_{i=1}^{k} Y_i$$

so that for the moment-generating function we have

$$M_Z(s) = E\left\{e^{s \times Z}\right\} = E\left\{e^{s \times \sum_{i=1}^{k} Y_i}\right\}$$

$$= \prod_{i=1}^{k} E\{e^{s \times Y_i}\} \tag{7.42}$$

$$= \prod_{i=1}^{k} M_{Y_i}(s) = (M_{Y_i}(s))^k$$

For example, if we reconsider our example and ask what is the moment-generating function for the sum of n independent random variables with individual moment-generating functions given by Equation 7.39, we have

$$(M_Y(s))^n = [e^s \times \pi + (1 - \pi)]^n \tag{7.43}$$

This is the moment-generating function for the binomial distribution with parameters n and π. A sequence of derivatives of this function evaluated at $s = 0$ will produce the moments about the origin for the binomial distribution. Further, if we examine the moment-generating function

$$e^{-n \times \pi \times s}(M_Y(s))^n = e^{-n \times \pi \times s}[e^s \times \pi + (1 - \pi)]^n$$

we will obtain the moment-generating function for the binomial in terms of moments about the mean, $n \times \pi$.

7.6 The Cumulative Distribution Function

We have derived our first probability function. This function tells us what the probability associated with any specified value of the random variable is; the probability given, of course, is the probability of that particular value of the random variable occurring. However, when we were using histograms and relative frequencies, we found it convenient to consider the accumulating sum of relative frequencies, the cumulative relative frequency. Similarly here, it is often convenient for us to consider the accumulating sums of probabilities; these sums are called cumulative probabilities and the function that prescribes their values is called the **cumulative distribution function** (CDF). The cumulative distribution function is given by

$$\text{CDF}(x_0) = \sum_{X \le x_0} \text{pr}(X) \qquad (7.44)$$

where $\text{pr}(X)$ is the relevant probability mass function. Look back at Table 7.1, which showed the binomial probability distribution for parameter values $n = 3, \pi = \frac{1}{2}$. The corresponding cumulative probabilities are

X	0	1	2	3
$\text{pr}(X)$	$\frac{1}{8}$	$\frac{3}{8}$	$\frac{3}{8}$	$\frac{1}{8}$
$\text{CDF}(x_0)$	$\frac{1}{8}$	$\frac{4}{8}$	$\frac{7}{8}$	$\frac{8}{8}$
x_0	0	1	2	3

Why did we use the lowercase x_0 in the definition of the cumulative distribution function? In this case, x_0 is being used as a limit of the operation of adding up probabilities from the minimum possible value to the assigned upper bound; as such the upper bound is then not a random variable, it is a specified limit on the collection of values that can be taken by the random variable itself. The cumulative distribution function is a sum of probabilities over all possible values of the random variable that are less than the fixed, and hence deterministic, upper bound. For example, if x_0 has the value 2, then in $\text{CDF}(x_0)$, we are adding up the probabilities from $X = 0$ to $X = 2$—that is, for $X \le x_0$.

7.7 The Poisson Probability Distribution

In the first part of this chapter, we saw how the binomial probability distribution could be generated from the conditions of an experiment. We will now see how to generate the characteristics of a different, but related, distribution by altering the conditions of the hypothetical experiment.

Consider the following problem. In writing this text, every once in a while I made a typographical error. If we imagine the text as a very large line, then every so often in the line, I would have an error. If we are willing to believe that the occurrence of these errors cannot be predicted by any means, then we can seek to discover the relevant probability distribution. An example is the number of telephone connections to a wrong number. A different example is to consider the number of particles emitted by a radioactive source in a given interval of time. Another version is the probability of an occurrence within a given volume, or area, the size of which is indexed by the radius; an example of this was the distribution of V2 bombs on the city of London during World War II. Yet another is the distribution of bacteria colonies on a petri dish.

Using these examples, can we abstract from their particularities to get a new general prototypical experiment that will generate a probability distribution? Imagine that we are considering the following type of hypothetical physical process. Events are occurring over time, or over "space" such as a length, or over the number of typed characters, but in an unpredictable way; that is, given any past history of the phenomenon, we still cannot determine what the next outcome will be, nor when it will occur. This is just like our emission or typographical error examples. However, let us suppose that we can determine that the following conditions prevail in the statistical experiment.

If we pick any interval of time, or length of interval, then the probability of occurrence of an event in that interval seems to be independent of the occurrence of events in past periods or prior lengths; that is, we cannot predict future outcomes given knowledge of the past history.

If we make the length of the interval small enough, then it is reasonable to assume that the probability of occurrence is proportional to the length of the interval; that is, the probability of occurrence of an event in a small interval is given by $(b\Delta t)$, where Δt represents the length of a small interval and b is some constant whose precise value depends on the conditions of the experiment. Suppose that it is also true that the probability of occurrence in any interval of given size does not change with the point in time or space that is considered; that is, if we calculate the probability for an interval of length Δt at some time t_0 and at some other point in time $t_0 + \delta$, the two calculations should be the same. Finally, we imagine that if we pick an interval small enough, then the probability of getting two or more events occurring in the same interval is essentially zero.

These assumptions seem to characterize fairly closely the type of process we had in mind when we looked at the emissions and typographical error models, except that in the typographical error model "time" was replaced by "number of characters typed." Many other actual physical processes meet these conditions; for example, defective items on an assembly line, cars entering a freeway (at least under certain conditions), phone calls into an exchange, the number of lightbulbs that fail in a given interval within a large office, the number of people that contract a noncontagious disease, the number of Prussian soldiers that were killed by mule kicks (yes, this is an actual and very early example of the use of this distribution), and so on for more pragmatic, but less colorful, examples.

Before we accept the claim that these real situations actually do approximate the theoretically specified conditions, we should question these claims further. At least, we should see whether there are circumstances when the conditions are not met. For example, whereas calls to an exchange might under normal circumstances meet the conditions stated, it is very clear that if a flying saucer were to be spotted, then you would be foolish to expect that the probability is constant over time for equal length intervals, or that the probability of a call one minute after the first flying saucer call is independent of that first flying saucer call. Entry onto a freeway may often be usefully regarded as an example of this mechanism—but not just after the football game has ended. The number of people in line at the supermarket checkout is a bad example, because people choose their checkout line with the objective of trying to minimize their time in line. Consequently, the probability of an arrival at a particular line is not independent of the existing length of the line. Each proposed situation must be carefully evaluated to determine as best one can that the specified conditions are at least approximately met.

Now what we would like to know is how does this specification of the conditions of the experimental situation determine a probability function, and what probability distribution is it? This is the question to which we now turn.

Let us imagine time along a straight line as illustrated. We imagine that a given segment of the line is divided up into a string of small intervals, or cells. Suppose that there are n intervals.

$$Arrivals: \quad \star \qquad \star \quad \star \qquad \qquad \star$$
$$Intervals: \quad - \quad - \quad - \quad - \quad - \quad - \quad - \quad - \quad - \quad -$$

Each interval, or cell, has an arrival that occurs in it, or it does not (arrivals are indicated by the "stars"). But given that we are proposing that an arrival in any cell is independent of arrivals in any other cell, that the probability of two or more arrivals in a single cell is virtually zero, and that the probability of arrival is constant all along the line, it is a reasonable conclusion that the distribution of the number of cells filled is given by the binomial probability distribution. There are n cells, so the range of the random variable is from 0 to n; the probability of arrival in any one cell is π_n. We do not know what the value of π_n is, but we do know that it is proportional to $1/n$. This is because the probability of arrival in a cell of length $1/n$ is proportional to $1/n$ by the specifications we listed. The probability that there are K cells filled is then

$$\binom{n}{K} \pi_n^K (1 - \pi_n)^{n-K} \tag{7.45}$$

So far all that we have done is to derive the binomial probability distribution in a different context. Indeed, if we were to stop here, then that is exactly what we would have, a binomial probability distribution. However, we are now about to change that situation. You may have noticed that the probabilities of occurrence, π, all had subscripts n; that was to remind ourselves that the probability in each cell depends on the size of the cell and therefore on the value of n that determines the number of cells into which a given length of time or interval has been divided.

What we are going to do is to see what happens when we let the length of each interval become arbitrarily small—that is, as the size of n becomes arbitrarily large. Although it is true that for each value of n we have a binomial probability distribution, the limiting result as n becomes arbitrarily large, so that the length of a cell becomes arbitrarily small, may be different.

Essentially, we are examining what happens to a binomial probability distribution when the probability of a single success, π_n in this case, becomes very, very small. You might also recognize that the distribution that we are about to obtain is an approximation for the binomial probability distribution when the parameter π is very small; this is where the Prussian soldiers dying of mule kicks came in; there were a lot of mules, even if the probability of getting kicked to death was rare.

What we have to do is to take limits of the binomial probability function as n, the number of cells, gets big, and correspondingly as π_n, the probability of an arrival, gets small. But, because π_n is proportional to the length of an interval, or cell, and the length is itself proportional to $1/n$, we soon realize that $n \times \pi_n$ is a constant! Let us call this constant, whatever value it has, λ.

More formally, we have, after setting g as the length of the whole interval to be divided into n equal subintervals, each of length $\Delta\gamma$, and letting b be the factor of proportionality relating probability to the length of an interval:

$$\pi_n = b\Delta\gamma$$

$$\Delta\gamma = \frac{g}{n}$$

where both b and g are constants; b is the unknown constant of proportionality for π_n, and g is the arbitrary original length that we are dividing into n cells. By substituting $\Delta\gamma = g/n$ into $\pi_n = b\Delta\gamma$, we get

$$\pi_n = b\Delta\gamma = b \times \frac{g}{n}$$

so that

$$n \times \pi_n = b \times g$$

and we have agreed to call the constant $b \times g$, λ.

We want to take limits of the expression in Equation 7.45 as $n \to \infty$; the symbol "$\to \infty$" means let n get arbitrarily large. The simplest probability to examine in this fashion is the probability of no arrivals in any cell—that is, the probability for $K = 0$. This probability is shown in Equation 7.46.

$$\binom{n}{0} \pi_n^0 (1 - \pi_n)^n = (1 - \pi_n)^n$$

$$\pi_n = \frac{(n\pi_n)}{n} = \frac{\lambda}{n} \tag{7.46}$$

We obtain as a limit as $n \to \infty$ the expression:

$$\lim_{n\to\infty} \left(1 - \frac{\lambda}{n}\right)^n = e^{-\lambda} \tag{7.47}$$

The symbol e stands for the exponential constant with a value of 2.71828 (and is fully discussed in Appendix A, "Mathematical Appendix" for those who are unfamiliar with this expression). If you do not yet know this useful concept you should learn about it, because it plays an important role in the continuous compounding of interest.

We now have the limiting probability for $K = 0$. Next, we shall find the limits for $K \neq 0$:

$$\lim_{n\to\infty} \binom{n}{K} \pi_n^K (1 - \pi_n)^{n-K} \tag{7.48}$$

Substituting λ/n for π_n in the previous expression, we obtain

$$\lim_{n\to\infty} \frac{n!}{K!(n-K)!} \left(\frac{\lambda}{n}\right)^K \left(1-\frac{\lambda}{n}\right)^{n-K}$$

We now extract all terms not involving n from the limit process:

$$\frac{\lambda^K}{K!} \lim_{n\to\infty} \frac{n!}{(n-K)!} \left(\frac{1}{n}\right)^K \frac{(1-\lambda/n)^n}{(1-\lambda/n)^K}$$

$$\lim_{n\to\infty} \left(1-\frac{\lambda}{n}\right)^n \to e^{-\lambda}$$

$$\lim_{n\to\infty} \left(1-\frac{\lambda}{n}\right)^K \to 1^K \to 1 \qquad (7.49)$$

$$\frac{n!}{(n-K)!} \left(\frac{1}{n}\right)^K = \frac{(n-K+1)(n-K+2)\cdots n}{n^K}$$

$$\lim_{n\to\infty} \frac{(n-K+1)(n-K+2)\cdots n}{n^K} \to 1$$

We can conclude that as $n \to \infty$

$$\lim_{n\to\infty} \binom{n}{K} \pi_n^K (1-\pi_n)^{n-K} \to e^{-\lambda}\frac{\lambda^K}{K!} \qquad (7.50)$$

The distribution that we have just derived is called the **Poisson probability distribution**, or the **Poisson probability mass function**; it expresses the probabilities for the number of arrivals in any given time period. If a random variable X has a Poisson probability distribution, its range of values is $\{0, 1, 2, 3, \ldots\}$; recall that we let n go to infinity. We can define a symbol to represent the Poisson probability function:

$$Po_\lambda(K) = e^{-\lambda}\frac{\lambda^K}{K!} \qquad (7.51)$$
$$K = 0, 1, 2, 3, \ldots$$

This distribution has only one parameter, λ, which is called the "mean rate of occurrence"; an obvious name given our derivation.

Our first question is whether the sum of the probabilities adds up to one as it should. We can in fact demonstrate that fact quite easily:

$$\sum \frac{\lambda^K}{K!} = 1 + \frac{\lambda}{1!} + \frac{\lambda^2}{2!} + \frac{\lambda^3}{3!} + \cdots$$
$$= e^\lambda$$

by the definition of the exponential function. Consequently, by putting both these components together we have

$$\sum e^{-\lambda}\frac{\lambda^K}{K!} = e^{-\lambda}e^\lambda = 1$$

One way of characterizing the Poisson probability distribution is that it is the limiting form of a binomial probability distribution when π, the probability of a success in a single trial, is small and the number of trials is very large. This was the rational for the "Prussian soldiers' deaths from mule kicks"; the probability of being killed was very small, the number of trials was large because the number of soldiers was large, and the assumption of independence between events was reasonable. In short, the Poisson probability distribution is the relevant distribution for "rare events" as well as for the occurrence of independent arrivals over time.

As we did for the binomial probability distribution, we should now consider the theoretical moments of this distribution. We will derive the mean but will leave the derivation of the remaining moments to the Exercises. By definition of μ_1', we have

$$\mu_1' = \sum_K K \frac{e^{-\lambda}\lambda^K}{K!}$$

$$K = 0, 1, 2, 3, \ldots$$

(7.52)

and by dividing K into the $K!$, letting $Y = K - 1$, and then pulling out a common λ, this last expression can be rewritten as

$$\lambda \sum_{Y=0} \frac{e^{-\lambda}\lambda^Y}{Y!}$$

But this summation is nothing more than the sum of the definition of the Poisson probability distribution itself multiplied by λ. Consequently,

$$\lambda \sum_{Y=0} \frac{e^{-\lambda}\lambda^Y}{Y!} = \lambda$$

Using similar arguments, we can show that the remaining theoretical moments are

$$\mu_2(X) = \lambda$$

$$\mu_3(X) = \lambda$$

$$\alpha_1 = \frac{\lambda}{\lambda^{3/2}} = \lambda^{-1/2}$$

$$\mu_4(X) = \lambda + 3\lambda^2$$

$$\alpha_2 = \frac{(\lambda + 3\lambda^2)}{\lambda^2} = 3 + \lambda^{-1}$$

(7.53)

From these expressions, we see that the shape of the Poisson probability distribution is always positively skewed, $\alpha_1 = \lambda^{-1/2} > 0$, and that its degree of kurtosis, or peakedness, is greater than 3; recall that by definition λ is positive. Three is the same value that we found as a limit for the binomial probability distribution when n gets arbitrarily large, but the probability of a single success, π, is constant at π. In any event because the Poisson has a value for α_2 that is greater than 3 the distribution has a greater probability for large observations to occur than is true for the binomial distribution.

It is interesting that we have discovered two different limits for the binomial probability distribution as n, the number of trials, increases without limit. In the first case, the

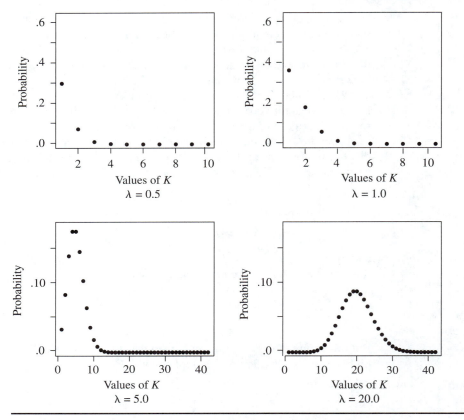

Figure 7.3   Poisson probability distributions with different parameter values

limiting theoretical moments were 0 and 3; this was the case where $n \to \infty$, but π remained fixed. In the other limiting result, where $n \to \infty$, $\pi_n \to 0$, but $n \times \pi_n = \lambda$, a constant for all n, the limiting theoretical moments for α_1 and α_2 are $\lambda^{-1/2}$ and $3 + \lambda^{-1}$. When α_1 is positive the corresponding distribution is positively skewed; that is, it has a right-hand tail. And when α_2 is greater than 3, the distribution is more peaked than the binomial distribution; equivalently the distribution is said to have "fatter tails"; that is, the probability of very large values for K is greater than it is for the binomial.

If we consider Poisson probability distributions for which λ gets very big, then we see that for the Poisson probability distribution, as well as for the binomial probability distribution, the limiting theoretical moments are, respectively, 0 and 3. The four figures in Figure 7.3 illustrate these comments clearly. You can easily see that as the value of λ increases, the symmetry of the probability function increases and you can guess that the standardized fourth moment is decreasing to 3.

Now let us put our new distribution to work. Suppose that you are considering hiring a new typist for the office; two applicants each submit a typing test of 200 pages that was corrected by computer. Let us suppose that we are told that the statistical model that is relevant here is the Poisson probability distribution for each typist, but

Table 7.5 **A Poisson Comparison of Two Typists**

Theoretical Moments	Distribution 1 $\lambda = 0.500$	Distribution 2 $\lambda = 1.0$
μ_1'	0.500	1.0
$\sqrt{\mu_2}$	0.707	1.0
α_1	1.414	1.0
α_2	5.000	4.0

that the parameter λ that applies is different between the two; typist A has a parameter λ with a value of 0.5 and typist B has a parameter value of 1.0. The question is, of course, which of the two typists should you hire? The relevant theoretical moments are summarized in Table 7.5. The typist with the smaller mean number of mistakes is A, and A also has the smaller variation about the mean. But typist A also has a larger value for α_1 and a larger value for α_2. How you choose between them depends on your own requirements. It might seem clear at first sight that the typist to hire is the one with the smaller average number of errors per page and the smaller variance. But that typist has the larger values for α_1 and for α_2, as we noted. If you are much more concerned about the occasional occurrence of a large number of errors, then you might lean to typist B.

7.8 Summary

This chapter dealt with three themes: the development of two probability distributions, the binomial and the poisson; the definition of theoretical moments; and the definition of expectation.

As a mathematical preliminary, we developed the ideas of *permutations, combinations* (Equation 7.1), and *combinatorial coefficients*. Permutations are the number of ways distinct elements can be rearranged in a line when order of occurrence is important. Combinations are permutations after allowing for permutations that cannot be distinguished—that is, where order of occurrence is not important. Combinatorial coefficients are elements in the expansion of the expression $(\pi + (1 - \pi))^n$.

Probability distributions are functions that indicate how probabilities are distributed over the values of the random variable. We derived two specific probability distributions, the *binomial* (Equation 7.9) and the *Poisson* (Equation 7.51). We also defined the *cumulative distribution function*, CDF, as the cumulative sum of the probabilities associated with the random variable by increasing the value of the random variable. We recognized the need for a "special definition" of the "sum" of random variables, the *convolution sum*. The convolution sum of two random variables, X_1 and X_2, represents for each value of their sum the union of the values for the variables X_1 and X_2 that make up that sum.

We have seen how the shape of the theoretical probability distribution depends on the choice of the *parameters* of the distribution, and how in turn the *theoretical moments* reflect the shape of the distribution. The theoretical moments are the weighted sums of the values of powers of the variable weighted by the associated probability.

In addition, we have seen how the values of the theoretical moments themselves depend on the values taken by the parameters of the distribution.

We defined *expectation* as an operation that generalizes the concept of calculating moments. The expectation of a function of a random variable is simply the weighted sum of the values of the function, where the weights are the probabilities that are associated with the values of the variable or of the function.

Case Study

Was There Age Discrimination in a Public Utility?

In this section, we will consider which discrete distributions are relevant to our case. It should be immediately clear that the distribution of sex, male or female, is binomial. The parameter π may have the approximate value .84, which is the calculated value of the relative frequency of males to females in the firm.

A number of other characteristics have multiple, more than two, responses and so are likely to be distributed as multinomial. This is an important distribution in practice even though we have not introduced it in this chapter. The multinomial is a generalization of the binomial. The probability distribution for three distinct outcomes, x_1, x_2, x_3, with n trials has the form

$$pr(x_1, x_2, x_3) = \frac{n!(\pi_1)^{x_1}(\pi_2)^{x_2}(\pi_3)^{x_3}}{x_1!x_2!x_3!}$$

$$x_1 + x_2 + x_3 = n$$

$$\pi_1 + \pi_2 + \pi_3 = 1$$

There are several examples in our case: the variable <u>hire status</u>; "eeo" the coding for race and gender; and the description of successful applicants.

There are no recorded examples of the relevance of the Poisson distribution, but if we had observed the distribution of annual resignations it would likely be Poisson. Other examples might be the number fired in a year and the number of sick days per employee per year.

Exercises

Calculation Practice

7.1 A construction firm builds tract homes for moderate income families. Its homes have three basic floor plans. Also, each home can be built with a single or double garage or carport. Each can be outfitted with one of three different types of kitchen cabinets, each can have one of four different fireplaces, and each can have one of seven different carpets laid. How many variations of this firm's tract homes can be built?

7.2 If a restaurant serves 3 salads, 5 entrees, 4 vegetables, 6 drinks, and 7 desserts, in how many different ways can one get 2 entrees, 2 vegetables, and 2 desserts? If a complete dinner includes two of everything, how many different dinner combinations are being offered?

7.3 There is a group of seven males and three females. In how many different ways can a committee of five be formed if

a. it must consist of three males and two females?

b. it must consist of at least four males and one female?

7.4 If each participant in a ten-player tournament must play every other participant, how many plays must be made?

7.5 If you have a random variable X_1 distributed as a Poisson with parameter λ_1, and X_2 is distributed independently of X_1 as Poisson with parameter λ_2, what is the domain of definition for the random variable $Y = X_1 + X_2$; that is, what is the range of possible values that Y can take? What is the mean of Y?

7.6 If X_1 is distributed as Poisson with parameter λ_1, and X_2 is distributed independently of X_1 as binomial with parameters n and π and $Y = X_1 + X_2$, what is the domain of definition of Y? What is the mean of Y?

7.7 If X_1 and X_2 are as defined in Table 6.4, what is the domain of definition of the random variable $Y = X_1 + X_2$? (*Hint:* Be careful. What is the mean of Y?)

7.8 If Y_1 and Y_2 are as defined in Table 6.6, what is the domain of definition of the random variable $Z = Y_1 + Y_2$? What is the mean of Z? Compare these answers with those in the previous question.

7.9 A certain portfolio consists of ten stocks. The investor feels that the probability of any one stock going down in price is .45 and that price movements of stocks are independent.

a. What is the probability that exactly five stocks will decline?

b. What is the probability that five or more stocks will decline?

c. Does the assumption of independence seem logical here? If not, is the binomial distribution the appropriate probability distribution for this problem?

7.10 Sales representative Ann Dolittle plans to try to sell an innovative product that her company has developed to ten plant managers. She estimated that her chance of landing a sale with any one manager is .6. Assuming statistical independence, what is the probability:

a. that she will make no sales?

b. that she will make ten sales?

c. that she will make less than two sales?

d. that she will make at least five sales?

7.11 A professor of a class of 20 students assumes that the probability of any one student passing a national aptitude test is .95. If all students take the test, what is the probability (assuming statistical independence) that

a. all the students will pass the test?

b. at least 90% of the students will pass the test?

c. at least 15 students will pass the test?

7.12 The probability that a venture capitalist can persuade an entrepreneur to sell his or her company is .4. The venture capitalist makes a presentation to five entrepreneurs. Assuming statistical independence, what is the probability that

a. all five entrepreneurs will sell their companies?

b. none of the entrepreneurs will sell?

c. exactly one entrepreneur will sell?

7.13 The random variables X and Y have the joint distributions shown in Table 7.6.

a. Find the marginal distributions of X and Y.

b. Show that X and Y are dependent variables but uncorrelated.

c. Find $E(X)$ and $E(Y)$.

d. Calculate the expectation of $Z = 2X + 3Y + 5$.

e. Calculate $E(-2X + 2)$.

f. Show how you can create two new variables X_1 and Y_1 that have the same values as X and Y and

Table 7.6 **Table of Joint Probabilities**

		X		
		-1	0	1
	-1	$\frac{1}{8}$	0	$\frac{1}{8}$
Y	0	0	$\frac{1}{2}$	0
	1	$\frac{1}{8}$	0	$\frac{1}{8}$

the same marginal distributions but are independently distributed.

7.14 The number of patients visiting Dr. Surecure's clinic between 9:00 A.M. and 10:00 A.M. on Monday is distributed according to the Poisson distribution, with a mean of 8. What is the probability that

a. no patients will visit Dr. Surecure's clinic on a given Monday?

b. one or two patients will visit Dr. Surecure's clinic on a given Monday?

c. exactly two patients will visit Dr. Surecure's clinic on a given Monday?

7.15 The number of defective articles in any batch of products produced by a manufacturing process is distributed according to the Poisson distribution, with a mean of 4.

a. What is the probability that no more than three defectives will occur in a given batch of articles?

b. What is the probability that more than four defectives will occur?

7.16 A family has five children.

a. What is the probability that all are girls?

b. What is the probability that two are girls and three are boys?

c. What assumptions did you make to answer (a) and (b)?

d. Evaluate the probabilities if the probability of a girl is .53.

e. Evaluate the probabilities if the probability of a girl is .47. Compare this with your previous answer and comment.

7.17 In the 1972 presidential election approximately one-third of the voters chose George McGovern and two-thirds chose Richard Nixon. Suppose five people are selected at random from those who voted.

a. What is the probability that no one in the sample voted for McGovern?

b. What is the probability that everyone in the sample voted for McGovern?

c. What is the probability that a majority in the sample voted for McGovern?

d. Suppose the five people chosen for the sample were picked not randomly but out of the same office. How might that interfere with your being able to use the idea of a binomial variable in these problems?

e. In (a) through (c), what event did you categorize to be a "success," and which event did you categorize as a "failure"?

f. Surely some other reader who completed (a) through (c) did it the other way around—chose your "success" variable as the "failure" and your "failure" as the "success." Show that this other reader would have gotten the same answers.

7.18 Proverb: "If at first you don't succeed, try, try again." OK, suppose the probability of success in one try is .40.

a. What is the probability of success the first time?

b. What is the probability of success on the second try, given that you failed the first time?

c. Before you try at all, what is the probability that you will succeed only on the second try?

d. What is the probability that you will succeed at least once in two tries?

e. What is the probability that you will succeed in two tries, given that you quit as soon as you succeed?

f. What is the probability that you will succeed at least once in four tries?

g. What is the probability that you will succeed in four tries, given that your quit as soon as you succeed?

7.19 Calculate:

a. $\binom{5}{1}$

b. $\binom{5}{2}$

c. $\binom{5}{3}$

d. $\binom{5}{4}$

e. $\binom{5}{5}$

7.20 Back in the dark ages of computers, a programmer would write a program on keypunch cards. The program would be represented by the placement of punched holes; the computer would read the punched cards in order and follow the directions on them.

Careful programmers would take up some of the blank space and number the cards so that if they got out of order they could be put back together easily. Some programmers were not so careful. One, in particular, tripped on his way into the computer room. His nine keypunch cards went flying in all directions and ended up scattered all over the floor. None fell together; they landed randomly. The programmer hurriedly picked them up. He picked them up randomly, only making sure they all faced the right direction.

a. How many different ways could the cards be picked up?

b. How likely is it that the randomly picked-up cards would be picked up in their original order?

c. Out of all the ways the cards could be reassembled, one would cause the computer to "crash" and do $500,000 worth of damage in wages paid to the people who "bring the system back up" to working order. What is the probability that the cards would be reassembled in such a way?

d. Out of all the ways these cards could be reassembled, five would create a program that (although it probably wouldn't work as the original was intended) the computer would actually be able to do. What is the probability that the cards would be picked up in one of these ways?

7.21 The Department of Economics at Savant University offers 30 different classes in any of the 30 separate time slots.

a. How many different five-class schedules can students take if they want to take nothing but economics?

b. There are 15 economics professors at Savant University, and each is qualified to teach any of the 30 classes (these are very knowledgeable people). How many different ways can instructors be assigned so that each teaches two classes?

c. You sign up for "Economics of the Environment." What is the probability of getting your favorite instructor?

7.22 Trams University gives classes at five different times during the day. At each time, 36 classes are available. How many different course schedules are there?

7.23 Five airplanes are circling above Mega Airport waiting to land. In how many different ways can they land?

7.24 Wisdom U.'s Book Center sells all the books for the university's 300 classes. Each class assigns two books; no two classes assign the same book. Each student takes three classes. Any class schedule is possible (there are no time conflicts). Each student buys six books. How many different six-book bundles can the Book Center sell?

7.25 Before Halloween, 13 different costumes were ordered by 13 different individuals. The company mailed out the 13 masks, 13 pieces of clothing, and 13 hats separately to its 13 customers. The company, however, mailed out the masks, clothing, and hats randomly to those customers. Consider a mask, a piece of clothing, and a hat to be a costume, even if the three don't go together.

a. How many possible costumes could have been constructed this way?

b. What is the probability that one individual will get a costume for which all of the pieces match?

7.26 An odd custom has arisen in Isoland, which no one ever leaves and to which no one ever immigrates. Two individuals who want to get married must have been born in the same year. This year 30 children were born: 15 boys and 15 girls.

a. How many different married couples can there possibly be out of this batch?

b. How many different married couples could there have been if 20 boys and 10 girls had been born?

7.27 A "ztlaw" is a musical composition that has 43 different notes, playable one at a time, sequentially, and on a piano. Pianos can play 88 different notes.

a. How many different ztlaws can there be?

b. How many different ztlaws could there be if the ztlaw law was that you could not ever use the same note twice?

7.28 Yolanda Yuppie is a stockbroker. She is trying to put together a portfolio of ten stocks for her client. A stock could be a good stock, or it could be a disaster. Let the probability of picking a good stock be $\frac{4}{5}$ and the probability of picking a disaster be $\frac{1}{5}$.

a. What is the probability Yolanda will pick ten good stocks?

b. What is the probability Yolanda will pick five good stocks and five disasters?

c. What is the probability Yolanda will pick nine good stocks and one disaster?

d. What is the probability Yolanda will pick at least five good stocks?

e. What is the probability Yolanda will pick at least nine good stocks?

Exploring the Tools

7.29 *Worked. Objective: To illustrate the dependence of the shape of binomial probability distribution on its parameters.* We begin by exploring how the binomial distribution depends on its two parameters n and pi.

[*Computer directions.* Start S-Plus. On the menu bar, click <u>Labs</u>, <u>Statistical Tables</u>, <u>Binomial</u>. In the dialog box, set "No. of trials" to 10. Set "Prob. of success" to .5. Set "No. of successes" to 8. Click Apply. The results are in the Report window.]

a. Vary the No. of successes between 0 and 10 to explore the variation in probabilities. Do you really have to calculate every outcome?

b. Vary the No. of trials, n, keeping Prob. of success, pi = .5, and the No. of successes = 8.

c. Vary the Prob. of success, pi, and examine the effect on probabilities of getting 8 successes.

d. Try to summarize what you have learned from these experiments.

We have repeatedly stressed the relationship between "shape" and the moments. In this exercise, we extend that relationship to the parameters of a distribution. We have three related characteristics of a distribution: shape, moments, and parameters.

7.30 Consider the example in the text in which a coin flip is denumerated "Heads = 1; Tails = 0."

Write out $F(x)$, $F(1)$, and $F(0)$, where $F(X)$ is the probability function.

a. What difference would it make if the coin flip were denumerated "Heads = 3; Tails = 0"?

b. What difference would it make if the coin flip were denumerated "Heads = 4; Tails = 2"?

7.31 Worked. *Objective: To explore the shape of the Poisson distribution as a function of its parameters.* In this experiment, we will examine the Poisson distribution.

[**Computer directions:** Start S-Plus. On the menu bar, click on <u>Labs</u>, <u>Statistical Tables</u>, <u>Poisson</u>. In the dialog box, set "lambda" to 5. Set "count" to 2. Click on Apply. Repeat, varying "count," in turn, to 3, 5, 8, 10. The results will be in the Report window.]

a. Set lambda to 3, and repeat the experiment.

b. Set lambda to 7, and repeat the experiment.

c. Set lambda to 1, and repeat the experiment.

d. Set lambda to 10, and repeat the experiment.

e. Work up a table that has as entries the probability of getting a given count for a given lambda. Create a column for each lambda and a row for each count value; you will have a table with five rows and five columns. Comment on the properties of the Poisson probability distribution.

We have repeatedly stressed the relationship between "shape" and the moments. In this exercise, we extend that relationship to the parameters of a distribution. We have three related characteristics of a distribution: shape, moments, and parameters.

7.32 Worked. *Objective: To illustrate the Poisson distribution as an approximation of the binomial.*

[**Computer directions:** Start S-Plus. On the menu bar, click on <u>Labs</u>, <u>Sampling From 0-1 Population</u>, <u>Approximating Binomial Probabilities</u>, <u>Poisson Approximation</u>. In the dialog box, set n to 100. Set "pi" to .01. Click Apply. The graph has the Poisson distribution in red and the binomial in blue. Print the graph.]

a. With pi = .01, in turn, vary n to 50 and 20. Print the graphs.

b. Set pi = .25, in turn, vary n to 100 and 20. Print the graphs.

c. Set pi = .5, in turn, vary n to 100 and 20. Print the graphs.

d. Examine your graphs carefully and comment on the nature of the approximation between the Poisson distribution and the binomial as a function of n and pi.

This exercise indicates that besides our three-way relationship between shape, moments, and parameters, we have the example of one distribution providing an approximation to another. Later, we will discover more examples of distributions approximating other distributions.

7.33 Suppose that you have n objects, of which r_1, r_2, and r_3 are the same and $r_1 + r_2 + r_3 = n$. The number of combinations that one can obtain in these circumstances is

$$\frac{n!}{r_1!r_2!r_3!}$$

Suppose that you consider permutations of

$$AA, BB, CC$$

in which $n = 6$, $r_i = 2$, $i = 1, 2, 3$. How many permutations are there? List the first six permutations in this case.

7.34 If the list of objects to be permuted is

$$AAA, BB, CCC$$

How many permutations are there? List five of them.

7.35 If the list of objects were

$$AAAA, B, CCC$$

How many permutations are there? List five of them.

7.36 Suppose that you have n objects for which there are six groups with $r_1, r_2, \ldots, r_6$ in number in each group, and one does not care about permutations within a group. $\Sigma_i r_i = n$. How many permutations are there?

7.37 Without calculating, but knowing that you have a binomial distribution with parameters n and π, guess the answer to the following questions. When you are finished check your answers by calculation.

a. Is α_1 positive or negative for $\pi = .2$?

b. Is α_1 positive or negative for $\pi = .7$?

c. Is α_2 larger or smaller for $\pi = .2$ versus $\pi = .5$?

d. Is α_2 larger or smaller for $\pi = .7$ versus $\pi = .5$?

7.38 For what values of π in the binomial distribution is the variance maximum? the standardized third moment maximum? the fourth standardized moment maximum? What are the maximum values?

7.39 For what values of π in the binomial distribution is the variance minimum? the standardized third moment minimum? the fourth standardized moment minimum? What are the minimum values?

7.40 The Poisson distribution is an approximation to the binomial distribution when $n \to \infty$, $\pi_n \to 0$, but $n\pi_n$ is a constant. If $n = 10$ and π_n takes the values $\{.2, .1, .01, .001\}$, and you are calculating the probabilities $\text{pr}(K \leq 1)$, $\text{pr}(K \geq 9)$, and $\text{pr}(4 \leq K \leq 5)$:

a. What are the differences in calculating the probabilities by the two distributions?

b. What difference does being in the tails of the distribution make?

7.41 If in Exercise 7.40, n were only 5 and you were considering the probabilities $\text{pr}(K \leq 1)$, $\text{pr}(K \geq 4)$, and $\text{pr}(2 \leq K \leq 3)$, what difference in probabilities could you detect between the two distributions?

7.42 For any distribution of a random variable, X, show that:

$$E\left\{(X - \mu_1')^2\right\} = E\{X^2\} - \mu_1'^2$$

7.43 Use the result in Exercise 7.42 to show that for the $B_\pi^n(K)$:

$$\mu_2(X) = n\pi(1 - \pi)$$

7.44 An interesting correspondence took place in 1693 between Samuel Pepys (author of the famous diary) and Isaac Newton, in which Pepys posed a probability problem to the eminent mathematician. The question originally stated by Pepys was

A has 6 dice in a box, with which he is to throw a 6.

B has 12 dice in another box, with which he is to throw two 6s.

C has in another box 18 dice, with which he is to throw three 6s.

Newton replied and said essentially, "Sam, I do not understand your question." Newton asked if A, B, and C were to throw independently and if the questions pertained to obtaining exactly one, two, or three 6s or at least one, two, or three 6s.

After an exchange of letters, in which Pepys supplied little help in answering these queries, Newton decided to frame the question himself. In modern language, Newton's wording would appear as follows:

If A, B, and C toss dice independently, what are the probabilities that

a. A will obtain at least one 6 in a roll of 6 dice?

b. B will obtain at least two 6s in a roll of 12 dice?

c. C will obtain at least three 6s in a roll of 18 dice?

Answer (*a*) through (*c*).

7.45 For each of the following statements, determine whether the situation can be summarized by a binomial probability. If not, briefly give the reason.

a. It could rain, sleet, or snow.

b. People in the class are of different ages.

c. Weather can be good or bad.

d. Some rolls of a pair of dice are "doubles."

7.46 Consider your performance next semester as an application of a binomial probability distribution. Suppose you take five courses and care whether you pass or fail but don't care about the grade beyond that.

a. What is the relevant distribution function?

b. What assumptions do you have to make about class performance to use this function?

c. Use the probability function to express the probability that next semester you will fail one (and only one) course.

d. Use the probability function to express the probability that next semester you will pass one (and only one) course.

e. Use the probability function to express the probability that next semester you will pass at least one course.

7.47 The third and fourth moments about the mean can be reexpressed in terms of the first three and four moments about the origin, respectively. Derive this relationship using Pascal's triangle or the binomial coefficients.

7.48 (For the student with calculus.) *Objective: To illustrate the concept of the moment-generating function.* The following equation is called the "moment-generating function" for the binomial distribution, $B_\pi^n(K)$.

$$[(1 - \pi) + \pi e^s]^n$$

The moment-generating function was derived in Section 7.5. The rth derivative of this function evaluated at $s = 0$ yields the rth moment about the origin. Check the function by rediscovering the first two moments. Using this function and the expansion showing the relationship between moments about the mean and moments about the origin, prove that the third and fourth moments about the mean are

$$\mu_3(X) = n\pi(1 - \pi)(1 - 2\pi)$$

$$\mu_4(X) = 3(n\pi(1 - \pi))^2$$
$$+ n\pi(1 - \pi)(1 - 6\pi(1 - \pi))$$

7.49 In the text, the first moment of the Poisson distribution with parameter λ was derived. Use the same procedure again to show that $E\{K^2\} = \lambda^2 + \lambda$, so that $E\{(K - \lambda)^2\} = \lambda$; that is, the variance equals the mean!

7.50 (For the student with calculus.) **Worked.** *Objective: To introduce the concept of the moment-generating function.* The moment-generating function that made getting the moments of the binomial distribution so easy has a simple rationale. The moment-generating function, $M(s)$, for a probability distribution, $pr(x)$ is given by

$$E\{e^{sX}\} = E\left\{1 + sX + \frac{(sX)^2}{2!} + \frac{(sX)^3}{3!} + \cdots\right\}$$

$$E\{e^{sX}\} = \sum_x e^{sX} pr(X)$$

From expanding the expression e^{sX} and its derivatives with respect to s and by taking expectations, we quickly see the logic of this process. For example, the first derivative of $E\{e^{sX}\}$ is:

$$\frac{D}{ds}(E\{e^{sX}\}) = E\left\{\frac{D}{ds}(e^{sX})\right\}$$

$$= E\left\{X + sX^2 + \frac{s^2X^3}{2!} + \cdots\right\}$$

and by setting $s = 0$, we see that all the terms beyond the first go to zero to give us the first moment. Taking the derivative with respect to s once again and setting the value of s to zero, we see that the expectation of that operation yields the second moment about the origin. We can proceed in this way indefinitely.

Table 7.7 **Joint Probability Distribution of X_1 and X_2; Dependent**

		X_2		
		−1	0	1
X_1	0	$\frac{1}{4}$	$\frac{1}{4}$	0
	1	0	$\frac{1}{4}$	$\frac{1}{4}$

Table 7.8 **Joint Probability Distribution of X_1 and X_2; Independent**

		X_2		
		−1	0	1
X_1	0	$\frac{1}{8}$	$\frac{1}{4}$	$\frac{1}{8}$
	1	$\frac{1}{8}$	$\frac{1}{4}$	$\frac{1}{8}$

The derivation of the moment-generating function for the Poisson is very simple. Here it is

$$E\{e^{sK}\} = \sum_K e^{sK} \frac{e^{-\lambda}\lambda^K}{K!}$$

$$= \sum_K \frac{(e^s\lambda)^K}{K!} e^{-\lambda}$$

$$= \sum_K \frac{(e^s\lambda)^K e^{-(e^s\lambda)}}{K!} e^{\lambda(e^s - 1)}$$

$$= e^{\lambda(e^s - 1)}$$

where we have used once again the trick of rewriting the expression so that the summation goes to 1 exactly.

7.51 (For the student with calculus.) For a Poisson probability distribution demonstrate that the third moment about the mean is λ and the fourth moment about the mean is $\lambda + 3\lambda^2$. The relatively easy way to accomplish this is to use the moment-generating function for the Poisson:

$$\exp[\lambda(e^s - 1)]$$

Taking the rth derivative of this function and evaluating the result at $s = 0$ yields the rth moment about the origin. Confirm that the first two moments agree before proceeding.

7.52 For each of the following functions, show that the stated relationships hold for the expectation of the function. Draw diagrams to illustrate your proof.

If $pr(X)$ is any probability distribution, prove and illustrate the following:

a. $g(X) = a + bX : E\{a + bX\} = a + bE\{X\} :$
$\min(a + bX) \leq E\{a + bX\} \leq \max(a + bX)$

b. $g(X) = X^2 : \min(g(X)) \leq E\{g(X)\}$
$\leq \max(g(X))$

c. For $0 \leq X \leq 1$ and
$g(X) = X^2; E\{g(X)\} \geq g(E(X))$

d. If $E\{g(X)\} = g(E\{X\})$, what can you say about $g(X)$?

7.53 Consider the two joint distributions that we discussed in Chapter 6 (reproduced in Tables 7.7 and 7.8). In Table 7.7, X_1, X_2 are dependent, but they are independent in Table 7.8. Evaluate the following equations with respect to the entries in Table 7.7 and Table 7.8. Comment on what you have learned.

a. $E\{X_i\}$, $E\{(X_i - E\{X_i\})^2\}$

b. $E\{Y = X_1 + X_2\}$

c. $E\{W = X_1 - X_2\}$

d. $E\{(Y - E\{Y\})^2\}$

e. $E\{(W - E\{W\})^2\}$

7.54 Calculate the expectation of the random variable $W = X_1 X_2$ in two cases and compare the results. The two cases are given by considering the two distributions listed in Exercise 7.53. In the first part, calculate the expectation when the variables are independent. In the second case, calculate the expectation when the two variables are not independent. Derive the result using the conditional distribution of X_2 given X_1 and then using the distribution of X_1 given X_2. By these means show that the two approaches yield the same result when the variables are not independent.

7.55 Note that for any two variables X and Y, in general,

$$E\left\{\frac{X}{Y}\right\} \neq \frac{E\{X\}}{E\{Y\}}$$

This exercise will illustrate this important point. In the folder Firmdata, you will find financial data for seven different firms. Try the following experiment.

a. Calculate the variable sales per long-term debt—that is, $salesltd = sales/ltdebt$—and obtain the mean and standard deviation of the sales per long-term debt for each of the seven firms.

b. Calculate mean sales and mean ltdebt for each firm. Calculate for each firm the ratio of mean sales to mean ltdebt. Compare your results.

c. Comment on the difference between the ratio of standard deviations and the standard deviation of the ratio.

7.56 In Exercise 7.55, you explained the statistical difference between the mean of a ratio and the ratio of means. If you are interested in the amount of sales supported by long-term debt, which ratio

is more useful to you? Discuss this question, keeping in mind your objectives.

7.57 Reassess your discussion in Exercises 7.55 and 7.56 with respect to a measure of sales per employee.

7.58 *Worked:* For the student with calculus. In Section 7.5, "Expectation," we discussed the notion that we could evaluate the expectation of a function $g(X)$ either with respect to the probability mass function for X, or by taking the expectation of a variable Y defined by $Y = g(X)$, which has a probability mass function $h(Y)$ that can be obtained from that of the random variable X. In this exercise, we provide an example of that process.

Let the discrete random variable K be distributed as binomial with parameters n and π. Suppose that we want to know the distribution of the associated random variable Y that takes the values $\{0, 1, 4, 9, \cdots, n^2\}$; that is, Y is defined by $Y = K^2$. Our question is, What is the probability mass function for the variable Y? Clearly, the distribution of Y depends on that for K. The procedure that follows will show you how to derive the probability function for Y from that of K:

$$p(K) = \binom{n}{K} \pi^K (1 - \pi)^{n-K}$$
$$K = 0, 1, \ldots, n$$

The basic rule in all these derivations is to recognize that because the new random variable is a function of the old random variable, the probabilities match. Indeed, this must be so because the same underlying sample space is involved; we are merely redefining the values taken by the random variable, which is in turn a function of subsets of the sample space. We have therefore:

$$\text{pr}(Y = y_0) = (K^2 = y_0)$$
$$= \text{pr}(K = \sqrt{y_0})$$
$$= \binom{n}{\sqrt{y_0}} \pi^{\sqrt{y_0}} (1 - \pi)^{n-\sqrt{y_0}}$$

is true for all values y_0 in the set $\{0, 1, 4, \ldots, n^2\}$. We conclude that the probability mass function for the random variable Y that takes the values $\{0, 1, 4, \ldots, n^2\}$ is $h(Y)$ defined by

$$h(Y) = \binom{n}{\sqrt{Y}} \pi^{\sqrt{Y}} (1 - \pi)^{n - \sqrt{Y}}$$

Applications

7.59 An insurance company offers a 45-year-old man a $1000 one-year term insurance policy for an annual premium of $12. Assume that the number of deaths per 1000 is 5 for persons in this age group. What is the expected gain for the insurance company on a policy of this type?

7.60 In the folder Misc, use the file Rock.xls, which contains various measures of the probability distributions for sales characteristics of rock music.

a. What do you think is the relevant distribution for the number of weeks on the sales top 100 list (*wksslstop*)?

b. To what extent does the distribution for the number of weeks on the airplay top 100 list (*wkairtop*) differ from the previous distribution? Can you speculate why?

7.61 There is a discrete distribution known as the discrete uniform distribution. If there are N values, the probability associated with any one of the N values is $1/N$, that is, the outcomes are equally likely.

Using the data set Grades.xls in the folder Misc, answer the following questions:

a. Using final grades, which distribution, uniform, Poisson, or binomial, do you think is the most relevant? Present your arguments.

b. If you examine the midterm grades do you come to the same conclusion?

c. If you examine the square root, the log, or the square of final grades, to what extent do you change your mind?

d. If you were able to choose whether you wanted grades to be listed as grades, the square root of grades, the log of grades, or the square of grades, which would you pick?

e. If only ranks were recorded, what difference would that make?

7.62 Consider the Old Faithful geyser data in the folder Misc; there are two files, Geyser1.xls and Geyser2.xls.

a. Is the binomial or the Poisson distribution more relevant to the duration data?

b. Is the binomial or the Poisson distribution more relevant to the interval data?

c. What characteristics of the binomial and Poisson distribution did you use to make your comparisons?

d. Is the mean duration time in Geyser1 data the same as that in Geyser2? Comment on the observed difference.

e. Is the mean interval time in Geyser1 the same as in Geyser2?

f. Plot the histograms for the Geyser2 duration data, the square root of duration data, and the log of duration data. Calculate the first four moments and the standardized moments for the square roots and the logs. Comment on your results in light of the discussion in the text on the expectation of functions of random variables.

g. By using Geyser1 data, do you confirm the previous results?

7.63 (I am indebted to my colleague Professor Richard Borowsky for this example.) Daddy long-legs normally have eight legs, but encounters with spiders' webs and other dangers mean that they sometimes lose one or more legs. As an experiment, a team of 6-year-olds collected a group of 59 daddy longlegs and counted the number of extant legs on each insect. The results were

Leg Count	Specimens
8	18
7	19
6	13
5	8
4, or fewer	1

Is this distribution well represented by the Poisson distribution? Are the mean and the variance approximately the same? You can justify the Poisson distribution on the grounds that in each random encounter the daddy longlegs loses only one leg and that they do not learn from their experiences. But if they were to learn, one should see a truncation of the distribution after the first loss. Discuss the assumptions needed to carry out this analysis, and try to assess their plausibility. Can you explain the results by means other than that postulated (single-event random losses by animals that do not learn)?

7.64 Ventures Limited, Inc., is considering a proposal to develop a new calculator. The initial cash outlay would be $1 million and development time would be one year. If successful, the firm anticipates that revenues over the five-year life cycle of the product will be $1.5 million. If moderately successful, revenues will reach $1.2 million. If unsuccessful, the firm anticipates zero cash inflows. The firm assigns the following probabilities to the five-year prospects for this product: successful, .60; moderately successful, .30; and unsuccessful, .10. What is the expected net profit?

7.65 In the folder Misc, use the file Htmw.xls, which contains the heights of men and women. One might guess that the average height of men is greater than that of women.

a. Is this so with these data?

b. Besides mean height, what other similarities or differences across gender do you detect in the distribution of heights? Be specific.

7.66 Examine the file Housing.xls, in the folder Misc.

a. Plot the histograms for the number of housing starts (*hsestrts*) for the entire data set, and by quarters. In what way do the distributions of housing starts vary by quarter? Be as specific in your answer as you can.

b. Repeat the exercise for low-interest rate periods and high-interest rate periods. What conclusions do you draw?

c. In interpreting your previous answer, what is the effect if low-interest rates are more associated with certain quarters than with others?

7.67 An early version of the New York lottery distributed prizes according to the following schedule:

■ No prize: 999,000

■ $50: 900

■ $500: 90

■ $5000: 9

■ $50,000: 1

for a total of 1,000,000 tickets.

a. What is the expected value of a ticket?

b. If the price of a ticket was $.50, was the lottery a "fair game"? Why might you guess that the lottery was not a fair game?

c. What is the expected value of a prize, given that you have won some prize?

d. Some people buy multiple tickets. Suppose that you bought 100 tickets. What is the expected value of your investment?

e. What is the variance of your return from buying 100 tickets? Would you recommend buying 1000 tickets?

7.68 A very large number of people engage in bungee jumping.

a. Suppose that the probability of dying during a jump is 2×10^{-7}? What is likely to be the appropriate probability distribution? What are the mean and variance of this distribution?

b. If an outfit claimed that in a million jumps, only two people died, would you regard this outfit as relatively safe? What is your argument?

7.69 Case Study: Was There Age Discrimination in a Public Utility? Suppose that you know that the probability distribution of the firm's employees by gender (male, female) is binomial. You are asked by your supervisor to calculate the mean (first theoretical moment about the origin) for the probability distribution of

a. all employees by gender.

b. all employees age 40 and older by gender.

c. all employees age 50 and older by gender.

d. all employees younger than 40 by gender.

7.70 Case Study: Was There Age Discrimination in a Public Utility? You suspect that the probability distribution of the firm's decision about the employment status of all employees who applied for reemployment (hired, not hired) is binomial. You want to discuss this issue with your peers. Prepare arguments supporting your suspicion.

CHAPTER

8

The Generation of Some Continuous Probability Distributions

8.1   What You Will Learn in This Chapter

In this chapter, we move from discrete probability distributions to distributions involving continuous random variables. Key to this is the concept of a density and its relationship to probability; the **density** is the "rate of change in probability." With continuous random variables we can no longer talk about the probability of observing a particular value of the variable—that probability is zero—but only about the probability of observing the variable within some stated range.

Density functions are characterized by their parameters just as the probability distributions were characterized by theirs. Further, the shape of the density function is measured by the values taken by the theoretical moments of the distribution as was the case for the probability distributions (discussed in Chapter 7). It is also true that there is a very close connection between the parameters of the density function and its theoretical moments—and, hence, with the shape of the density function.

We provide two universally important distributions: the normal and the uniform. The uniform distribution is the distribution of measurement errors and similar types of events. The normal is so famous that you are probably already familiar with the term. However, we will soon discover that we need to be careful to distinguish the actual properties of the normal from the myths that tend to surround it.

In the process of deriving the normal distribution, we will discover another famous theorem, the "central limit theorem." This theorem can rightly be said to be the kingpin of all statistical analysis. The central limit theorem tells us that the distribution for the average of independent events approaches the normal distribution as the number of terms grows without bound.

Last, we discuss a famous bound on the calculation of probabilities that applies to almost all distributions, the Chebyshev inequality.

8.2   Introduction

Chapter 7 showed us how to obtain probability distributions from the analysis of the conditions of an experiment. But the analysis in that chapter was restricted to random variables that were discrete; that is, even though the number of variable values might be infinite, the values were all integers (for example, the Poisson distribution). However, many of the examples that we have seen involve continuous random variables—variables such as heights, incomes, prices, gasoline consumption, speed and distance, and interest rates. Consequently, to be able to apply the basic ideas of probability that we examined in Chapter 6, we need to develop some new procedures.

Recall our examination of histograms in Chapter 3. One conclusion that we reached was that as n, the number of observations, increased, the smoothness of the histogram increased. This was due to two factors. With more observations, we were able to decrease the width of those cells in regions that had a high relative frequency. The other reason was that as n increased, the observed relative frequency in any given fixed interval seemed to settle down to a fixed proportion. Intuitively, therefore, we can see that if we increase n substantially, then we can decrease the maximum size of an interval, or a cell, and still have an ever-increasing number of observations in each cell. As we do this, we will see a smoother shape for our histograms evolving from the ever-larger data sets. An example of this is shown in the graphs in Figure 8.1. As n goes from 1000 observations to 100,000 observations, we see that the width of the cells decreases and that the shape of the histogram begins to settle down.

The remainder of this chapter requires a number of basic concepts from calculus, such as limit and continuity, differentiability, and "areas under curves." The reader is advised to review the material in the Mathematical Appendix before proceeding. You need to have some intuitive understanding of the concepts involved; algebraic details will not be stressed.

8.3 How to Express Probability in Terms of Continuous Random Variables

We began our discussion of how to generate discrete probability distributions by assigning probabilities under the assumption of the "equally likely principle." Later, we showed how to generate the probability distributions for more complicated collections of events. We generalized the approach by defining random variables and the probability mass function that assigned a probability to each value of the discrete random variable. Let us begin our analysis of continuous random variables in the same way.

Our objective is to discover how to define probability concepts in terms of variables like income, prices, weight, height, gasoline consumption, or distances. All these measurements are continuous variables, and in principle we can refine our measurement to be as exact as we wish. Is our fishing pole 2, 2.1, 2.08, 2.084, or 2.08365 meters long? Given that we can refine our measurement indefinitely, one immediately sees that there will be difficulty in assigning a probability to a *particular value* for a continuous random variable. To this difficulty we now turn.

Imagine a line that represents the possible outcomes that could occur from an experiment. Let us say, to be explicit, that $[a,b]$ is the interval over which the continuous random variable is defined. Two examples of this type of random variable were mentioned in Chapter 3; both the uniform and the arc sine distributions were defined over the unit interval—that is, the interval $[0,1]$. The histogram for the uniform distribution was flat and that for the arc sine distribution was U-shaped.

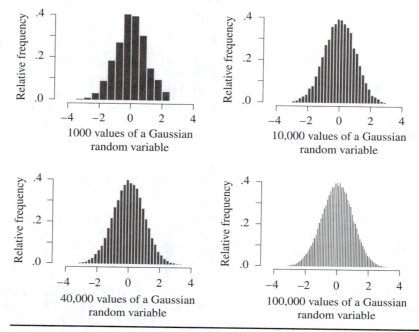

Figure 8.1 A sequence of histograms for a Gaussian random variable

Let us divide the interval $[a,b]$ into n cells of equal lengths. As we did with the Poisson probability distribution, let us also assign a probability pr_i to the ith interval; Δx is the width of the ith interval. We have assumed that this width is the same for all intervals, an assumption that is not essential but is convenient. There are n intervals and therefore n probabilities assigned, pr_i. The ith interval contains the following values of the variable X:

$$[X_0 + (i-1)\Delta X, X_0 + i\Delta X]$$
$$\min(X) = X_0 = a; \max(X) = X_0 + n\Delta X = b$$
$$\text{range}(X) = b - a = n\Delta X; \Delta X = \frac{(b-a)}{n}$$

What we are imagining is that there is some mechanism underlying the generation of probabilities that we are assigning to these intervals. At the moment we are not concerned about how the probabilities are generated, but we are interested in discovering how any distribution of probabilities will be affected by examining increasingly smaller intervals. In particular, we are not assuming that the probabilities are equally likely over the interval. The uniform distribution is an example where the equally likely principle seems to hold and the arc sine distribution is one where it does not.

We can draw one conclusion immediately. If pr_i is the probability in the ith interval, then as ΔX, the width of the ith interval approaches zero; $pr_i \to 0$. We can show this by using a similar argument that we applied with histograms and relative frequencies. As you

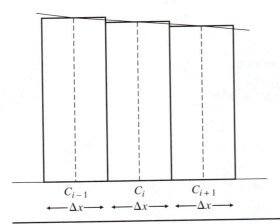

Figure 8.2   Expanded view of three approximating cells

may recall from Chapter 3, the relative frequency of a single point is $\frac{1}{n}$ and therefore approaches zero as the number of observations increases. We may conclude that the probability of a single point is zero. Intuitively, as we look at increasingly finer divisions of any given interval with a given probability attached, the probability in that interval is spread over more and more subintervals, so that the probability of each subinterval approaches zero. Another way of seeing this is to note that the limiting area under a section of histogram as the base of a given cell goes to zero is zero; it becomes a "line." But to continue the analogy, even though each component interval goes to zero and each histogram "bar" goes to zero as well, the total area under the histogram remains equal to one. Figure 8.2, which shows a blowup of a small section about the ith cell of a histogram, illustrates the idea. The three cells shown in the figure approximate the area under the curve—that is, the probability that the variable lies within the interval indicated in the figure. The little triangular sections between the curve and the approximating rectangles indicate the degree of approximation of the sum of the rectangles to the actual area under the curve.

As we examine the plot in Figure 8.2, we discover that while the area of each rectangle goes to zero as the base goes to zero, the height of the histogram remains approximately constant at the point $X_0 + (i-1)\Delta X + \frac{\Delta X}{2} = c_i$, which is the middle of the ith cell. For example, the random variable X might represent household income and the ith cell might be that between the income levels \$25,000 and \$27,000. If we let $f(X_i)$ denote the height of the histogram at the point $X_i = X_0 + (i-1)\Delta X + \frac{\Delta X}{2}$, then the value of the probability at the point X_i with interval size ΔX is

$$\mathrm{pr}_i \approx f(X_i) \times \Delta X$$

The symbol "$\cong$" means that pr_i is only approximated by the expression "$f(X_i) \times \Delta X$." Actually, if we allow ourselves the privilege of being able to pick a specific value of X within each cell, we can always achieve equality; that is,

$$\mathrm{pr}_i = f(X_i^*) \times \Delta X$$

where X_i^* is chosen so that equality holds. It is true that pr_i goes to zero as $\Delta X \to 0$, but our histogram analogy suggests that

$$f(X_i) \approx \frac{\text{pr}_i}{\Delta X}$$

is not going to zero. Indeed, we can define the function $f(X_i)$ by

$$f(X_i) \equiv \lim_{\Delta X \to 0} \frac{\text{pr}_i}{\Delta X} \tag{8.1}$$

In most cases of interest to us the derived function $f(.)$ can be shown to be a continuous function of the variable X; that is, there are no "gaps," or "breaks," in the function $f(X)$, it is smooth everywhere. The function $f(.)$ is known as a **density function**. The density function indicates the "rate of change" in the probability distribution. We can see this more clearly when we recognize that the probability of being in the ith cell is the probability that X is contained in the interval: $[X_0 + (i - 1)\Delta X, X_0 + i\Delta X]$. If $Y(X_0)$ represents the probability of X being less than X_0, then our initial probability, pr_i, is nothing more than ΔY evaluated over the ith interval. Consequently, because the limit of $\frac{\Delta Y}{\Delta X}$ as $\Delta X \to 0$ is the "rate of change in probability," we have obtained a derivative.

We also know by the manner in which we have derived this function, that the area under the function, $f(X)$, or the sum of the relative frequencies, is one. Indeed, this realization enables us to see how to relate our function, $f(X)$, to the probabilities that we started with. Suppose that we reconsider the n intervals dividing up the range of the variable X; the range was assumed to be $[a, b]$. And now suppose that we would like to calculate the probability of X being in the ith interval—that is, in the interval $[X_0 + (i - 1)\Delta X, X_0 + i\Delta X]$. We could go back to our original assignment of probabilities; the probability assigned to the ith interval was pr_i. But we now have a different way to do this; the probability in the ith cell is represented by:

$$\text{pr}_i \approx f(X) \times \Delta X \tag{8.2}$$

for any X in the ith interval. Remember that the symbol "$\approx$" means that the statement on the left side is approximated by the expression on the right side. Look back at our blowup of the histogram in the region of the ith interval in Figure 8.2; $f(X)$ is approximately the same for all X in the small interval of size ΔX. And if it were not, then we would only have to refine our mesh covering $[a,b]$ by dividing $[a,b]$ into more intervals.

Evaluating probabilities has now become the equivalent of adding up areas under the density function $f(X)$. For example, how do we discover the probability that the random variable X lies in the interval $[X', X'']$ as shown in Figure 8.3? Consider as an illustration that X represents individual incomes and that the interval $[X', X'']$ is the income range \$5,000 to \$25,000. We seek the probability that any individual has an income that lies within these bounds. The answer is given by

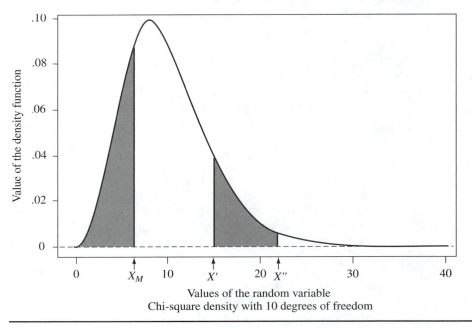

Figure 8.3 Probabilities as areas under a density curve

adding up all the areas under the curve from X' to X''. More formally, the answer is given by

$$\text{pr}[X' \leq X \leq X''] = \sum_{j=k}^{m} \text{pr}_j$$

$$\approx \sum_{j=k}^{m} f(X_j)\Delta X \tag{8.3}$$

where X_j is some value of X in the jth interval and the symbol "$\text{pr}[X' \leq X \leq X'']$" represents the probability that X belongs to the interval $[X', X'']$. The interval $[X', X'']$ is assumed to be subdivided into the set of subintervals labeled $\{k, (k+1), \ldots m\}$. Each point in the interval $[X', X'']$ is in one of the subintervals labeled $\{k, (k+1), \ldots m\}$, and each point that is in some subinterval is in $[X', X'']$.

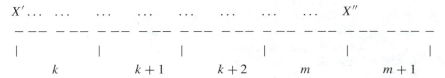

Also shown in Figure 8.3 is the probability that the random variable X is less than the value X_m. Formally, this probability is given by

$$\text{pr}[a \leq X \leq X_m] = \sum_{a \leq X_j \leq X_m} \text{pr}_j$$

$$\approx \sum_{a \leq X_j \leq X_m} f(X_j)\Delta X \tag{8.4}$$

where we recall that $\text{pr}[a \leq X \leq X_m]$ represents the probability that X belongs to the interval $[a, X_m]$. In Figure 8.3, a takes the value "0," but in many problems the a will represent "$-\infty$."

If you remember our experience when we first defined the probability of a union of events, you will wonder how we can add probabilities across the cells as we have been doing in these last few examples. The difficulty you will recall is that we can only add probabilities if the associated events are mutually exclusive. That is exactly the situation in this case; each cell defines a compound event mutually exclusive from the others. If a point lies in one cell, it does not lie in any other cell. Consequently, we can add the probabilities of individual nonoverlapping cells to get the probability for any interval, or union of intervals. We can always improve our approximation of

$$\text{pr}[a \leq X \leq X_m] = \sum_{a \leq X_j \leq X_m} \text{pr}_j$$

by letting ΔX get smaller. There is a limit to the ratio $\frac{\text{pr}_j}{\Delta X}$ as $\Delta X \to 0$—namely, $f(X)$. Consequently, we can state

$$\text{pr}[a \leq X \leq X_m] = \lim_{\Delta X \to 0} \sum_{a \leq X_j \leq X_m} f(X_i)\Delta X \tag{8.5}$$

The phrase "adding up the probabilities," or "adding the areas under the curve $f(X)$ between the limits X_0 and X_1," is a little tedious; we need a more succinct way of writing this. The notation we are going to use is

$$\int_{X_0}^{X_1} f(X)dx \equiv \lim_{\Delta X \to 0} \sum_{j=1}^{n} f(X_j^*)\Delta X$$

$$\approx \sum_{j=1}^{n} f(X_j^*)\Delta X \tag{8.6}$$

where the interval $[X_0, X_1]$ has been divided into n subintervals and X_j^* is some value of the variable within the jth interval. The symbol "$\equiv$" implies that this is a definition; that is, the left side is defined by the expression on the right. Equation 8.6 also reminds us that the sum of n discrete values of $f(X_j^*)\Delta X$ provides us with an approximation to the limit process shown in the previous line of the equation. We have added another approximation in that X_j^* is any value of X that is contained in the jth interval. As long as the interval width ΔX is small enough, the choice of the X value to represent the jth interval will make no essential difference to the result.

The left side of Equation 8.6 is a shorthand way of talking about the limit on the right side as ΔX gets small. For a not very small ΔX, the right side is only a rough approximation of the limit expressed on the left. The dX in the left expression is to remind us that we have obtained our result by taking limits as the size of an interval, ΔX, goes to zero. You can accurately express what this symbol means by defining it as "the area under the curve $f(X)$ from X_0 to X_1." We also know that this same symbol means "the probability that the random variable X lies in the interval $[X_0, X_1]$."

The symbol $\int$ is called the *integral sign*; the process of "adding up the areas" is called *integration*; the function whose area is being added is called the *integrand*; the result is called the *integral*: we integrate the integrand to obtain the integral. In going to the limit as $\Delta X \rightarrow 0$, we pass from Σ_j, "adding up discretely," to $\int$, "adding up continuously."

If the random variable's entire range is between the limits a and b, then from the fact that a histogram's area is one, we deduce that the area under the density function, $f(X)$, from a to b is also one. Symbolically,

$$\int_a^b f(X)dX = 1 \tag{8.7}$$

Often a random variable has no obvious boundaries within which it takes its values, or it has only one obvious boundary. We express this idea by the symbol "∞." For example, the notation

$$\int_0^\infty f(X)dX \tag{8.8}$$

and the notation

$$\int_{-\infty}^\infty f(X)dX \tag{8.9}$$

mean, respectively, "add up the area under the curve $f(X)$ from 0 to as far as you want to approximate the probability," and "add up the area under the curve $f(X)$ from as small a value of X as is practical to a value as big as is practical."

The integral symbol $\int_{-\infty}^\infty f(X)dX$ is both easier to write and to understand once the idea of integration has become familiar. There are many clever tricks and stratagems to figure out algebraically how to evaluate an integral, but the root idea is still the same. We are adding up areas as the change in the value of X gets smaller and smaller, so that the function $f(X)$ becomes smooth and the area between ΔX and $f(X)$ is well approximated by $f(X) \times \Delta X$. Look again at Figure 8.2 and imagine the size of the intervals becoming ever smaller. With this picture in mind it is now easier to understand why the probability of intervals that get increasingly smaller is zero, so that in particular the probability of a point is zero; but that the density function, which is the limit of the ratio of probability of an interval to the length of the interval is not zero. Remember that the density function that we have just derived is in fact nothing more than the "rate of change of probability"; that is, at the point X_0, $f(X_0)$ measures the rate of change in the probability as expressed in terms of the cumulative distribution function, $\text{CDF}(X_0) = \int_{-\infty}^{X_0} f(X)dX$, or $f(X_0) = \frac{d(\text{CDF}(X))}{dX}$ evaluated at the point X_0. Recall from the Mathematics Appendix that we can call the "integral" an "antiderivative"; this stresses the intimate relationship between integration and taking the derivative. Taking the derivative to get the rate of change is the opposite operation to integrating ("adding up") the rates of change to obtain the probability. And taking the derivative of the probability to get its rate of change yields the density function.

There is a convention to represent nearly all density functions with a range of $(-\infty, \infty)$. This is easily done by defining a new function that is the same as the original function everywhere that it is defined and zero everywhere else. For example, if $g(X)$ is our density function and it is defined over the interval $[a,b]$, then we can define a new density function $f(X)$ by

$$f(X) = \begin{cases} g(X) & \text{if } a \leq X \leq b \\ 0 & \text{otherwise} \end{cases} \tag{8.10}$$

We can define the corresponding probability function for which the density $f(X)$ is the rate of change of probability by

$$F(X) = \int_{-\infty}^{X} f(u)du \tag{8.11}$$

Correspondingly, we have

$$f(X) = F'(X) \tag{8.12}$$

where $F'(X)$ is the first derivative of $F(X)$. We call $F(X)$ the **probability function**. It is the probability of observing on any one trial a value of the random variable less than or equal to the limit X.

We may relate our new concept of a density function to our old idea of probability by the cumulative distribution function, first introduced in Chapter 6. As you will recall, the cumulative distribution function for discrete random variables is

$$\text{CDF}(X_0) = \sum_{X \leq X_0} \text{pr}(X) \tag{8.13}$$

The cumulative distribution function for a continuous random variable is defined analogously by

$$\text{CDF}(X_0) = \int_{-\infty}^{X_0} f(X)dX \tag{8.14}$$

The cumulative distribution function is in this case the same as the probability function evaluated at some specified point X_0. In both the discrete and continuous cases the idea of the cumulative distribution function is the same; it is the probability that the random variable X takes a value less than the specified limit, say X_0. Figure 8.4 illustrates the idea of the cumulative distribution function and its relationship to the density function. From our past discussion, we surmise that $\text{CDF}(X_0)$ is the area under the density function, $f(X)$, up to the value X_0, and that $\text{CDF}(X_1)$ is the area under the density function up to the value X_1. The CDF evaluated at X_0 and X_1 indicates the area under the curve, $f(X)$, up to the indicated limits, X_0 and X_1 (see the right axis of Figure 8.4).

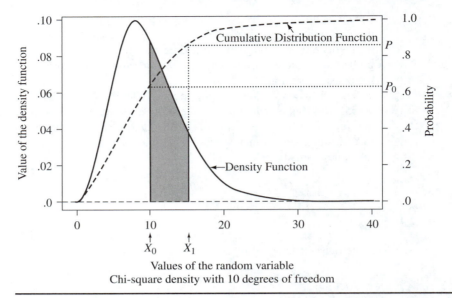

Figure 8.4   Relationship between the density and the cumulative distribution functions

Indeed, we can use the idea of the cumulative distribution function to reexpress the probability that a random variable X lies in the interval $[X_0, X_1]$:

$$\text{pr}[X_0 \le X \le X_1] = \text{CDF}[X_1] - \text{CDF}[X_0] \tag{8.15}$$

Here we see that the probability can be expressed as a difference in areas (see the shaded region) under the density function, $f(X)$. This is a useful way of expressing the probability of the random variable lying in the interval $[X_0, X_1]$. Given our definitions, we can conclude that

$$\text{CDF}[X_1] - \text{CDF}[X_0] = \int_{-\infty}^{X_1} f(X)dX - \int_{-\infty}^{X_0} f(X)dX \tag{8.16}$$

$$= \int_{X_0}^{X_1} f(X)dX \tag{8.17}$$

$$= \text{pr}[X_0 \le X \le X_1]$$

The probability of having an income between $X_1 = \$25,000$ and $X_0 = \$5,000$ is given by the difference in the probability of having an income up to $25,000 and the probability of having an income below $5,000.

If we define $Y_0 = \text{CDF}[X_0]$, $Y_1 = \text{CDF}[X_1]$, then the difference is $\Delta Y = Y_1 - Y_0$. The limit of the ratio $\frac{\Delta Y}{\Delta X}$ as $\Delta X \to 0$ is as we already know the density function, $f(X)$. But this confirms that the density function is the rate of change of the cumulative distribution function, and the cumulative distribution function is the integral, or antiderivative, of the density function. In the analysis to follow we will have occasion to look at both functions, so be sure that you have grasped the link between these two ways of expressing probability relationships.

8.4 Theoretical Moments and Density Functions

So far we have relied heavily on the concept of theoretical moments for characterizing our probability distributions, but how do we define theoretical moments when we have density functions instead of probability distributions? What we need to be able to do is to determine the location and the spread of the density function, and to characterize its shape. We should be able to talk about the mean of the income distribution as well as the spread of the errors in measuring distances of lengths or heights. We require theoretical moments for density functions as much and for the same reasons as we did for the discrete distributions.

Let us recall how we defined theoretical moments in the context of probability distributions:

$$\mu_r = E\{(X - \mu_1')^r\} = \sum_i (X_i - \mu_1')^r \operatorname{pr}(X_i) \tag{8.18}$$

The rth theoretical moment about the mean is the weighted sum of the values of the rth power of the difference between X_i and μ_1', where the weights are the probabilities. But our density function gives us a method to approximate the required probabilities. Let us substitute for $\operatorname{pr}(X_i)$ in Equation 8.18 its approximation in terms of the density function:

$$\mu_r = E\{(X - \mu_1')^r\} = \sum_i (X_i - \mu_1')^r \operatorname{pr}(X_i)$$
$$\approx \sum_i (X_i - \mu_1')^r f(X_i)\Delta X \tag{8.19}$$

The limit as $\Delta X \to 0$ is expressed by

$$\mu_r = E\{(X - \mu_1')^r\} = \int_{-\infty}^{\infty} (X - \mu_1')^r f(X)dX \tag{8.20}$$

$$\int_{-\infty}^{\infty} (X - \mu_1')^r f(X)dX = \lim_{\Delta X \to 0} \sum_i (X_i - \mu_1')^r f(X_i)\Delta X \tag{8.21}$$

In the former expression for the theoretical moment μ_r, the summation was over all values of the random variable X as indexed by the subscript i. In the second expression, the "adding up of area" is over all possible values of X as is indicated by the range on the symbol $\int$, which is $(-\infty, \infty)$. This is the general expression; in particular situations, the interval can be $(-\infty, b)$, (a, ∞), or $[a,b]$. We can always extend the definition of any function defined on an interval like $[a,b]$ to one defined on $(-\infty, \infty)$ by defining a new function that is the same as the old one over the interval $[a,b]$ and is zero everywhere else. This is a convenience, because we now have one expression that fits the integral of all functions.

In Equation 8.20, we defined the moments about the mean. As in Chapter 6, we can also define the moments about the origin:

$$\mu_r' = E\{X^r\} = \int_{-\infty}^{\infty} X^r f(X)dX \tag{8.22}$$

We will not actually solve, or evaluate, such expressions explicitly in this text, but it is important for our understanding to be able to tie the concept of theoretical moments to our development of random variables that includes continuous random variables and their corresponding density functions.

Now that we have defined the general notion of a density function for continuous random variables and related that concept to probability, we are ready to discover how to generate a probability function or a density function from a specific type of experiment. As before, we want to explore the relationship between the conditions of the experiment and the shape of the probability function or the shape of the density function.

8.5 The Uniform Distribution

Given our definition of a density function, our next task is to show how we can generate an example of a density function from a prototypical experiment. As we did with the probability distributions in Chapter 7, we will also show how the conditions of the experiment affect the shape of the density function and thereby the values taken by the theoretical moments. The change in the experimental conditions is also reflected in the values taken by the parameters of the density function, just as was the case with the probability distributions. Consequently, we can relate the values taken by the parameters to the values taken by the theoretical moments of the density function.

Let us begin with a very simple example of deriving a density and a probability distribution for a continuous random variable. Consider the process of "rounding down" any measurement to the nearest subunit; for example, suppose that we are measuring the lengths of a boat that we are building and our tape measure has no units less than 0.1 inch and that, for our purposes, the nearest tenth of an inch is acceptable. However, it is clear that all our measurements, if we were to measure to a much finer scale, say to the nearest ten-thousandth of an inch, would differ from the measurement to the nearest tenth. We can use the equally likely principle to claim that any measurement difference between zero and 0.1 inch is equally likely. Actually, this is not very precise as this statement merely says that the probability of any given measurement is zero. True, but what we really want to say is that any *interval* of say 0.001 inch is equally likely to contain our "actual measurement." In this example, the bounds on the variation of our random variable are 0 and 0.1 inch.

We can generalize this statement by assuming that we are dealing with a finite interval $[a,b]$ and assume that by the equally likely principle that obtaining an observation in any interval of length r that is less than $(b - a)$ has the same probability of occurrence as an observation in any other interval of the same length. Further, let us assume that the probability of an observation within a given interval is strictly proportional to the length of the interval. These assumptions on our hypothetical experiment are very similar to those we made in Chapter 7; the difference here is that we are dealing with a continuous random variable, and so we have to talk about the occurrence of observations within intervals, rather than the occurrence of the observations themselves. One way to think about this "experimental design" is that a particular round-off, say 0.007 inch, designates an interval of length, say 0.001, that is centered at 0.007.

Following the analysis in the previous section, the probability of an observational round-off in the interval $[c,d]$, where $a \leq c \leq d \leq b$, is

$$\text{pr}[c \leq Y \leq d] = \sum_{i=1}^{n} \text{pr}_i$$

$$= \lim_{\Delta Y \to 0} \sum_{i} f(Y_i) \Delta Y$$

where the interval $[c,d]$ has been divided into n subintervals and in taking the limit we consider dividing $[c,d]$ into more and more intervals of length ΔY.

In this first example of deriving a density function, the function $f(Y)$ is easily obtained. Remember $f(Y)$ is the limit as $\Delta Y \to 0$ of $\frac{\text{pr}_i}{\Delta Y}$. But pr_i is assumed proportional to the length of the interval (and the same for all intervals of the same length); that is,

$$\lim_{\Delta Y \to 0} \frac{\text{pr}_i}{\Delta Y} = k, \text{ for any } i$$

where k is some constant. The constant k is easily obtained by the constraint that $\text{pr}[a \leq Y \leq b]$ must be 1, and therefore the constant k is simply $\frac{1}{b-a}$. Recall that

$$k \int_{a}^{b} dy = k(b-a)$$

so that if $k = \frac{1}{b-a}$, we have

$$\text{pr}(a \leq Y \leq b) = \int_{a}^{b} \frac{dy}{b-a} = 1$$

Remember that the integral

$$\int_{a}^{b} dy$$

can be represented by the area under the curve, $f(y) = 1$ between the endpoints $\{a,b\}$. A more detailed explanation of this concept and of the derivation of the moments that is to follow is provided in the Mathematical Appendix and as the first three exercises in the "Exploring the Tools" section of this chapter; those readers not yet comfortable with the ideas of integration and differentiation should review the Mathematical Appendix and do these exercises.

The cumulative probability distribution function can be defined from the density function by

$$\text{pr}[a \leq Y \leq Y_0] = \int_{a}^{Y_0} \frac{1}{b-a} dY$$

$$= \lim_{\Delta Y \to 0} \sum_{i} \frac{1}{b-a} \Delta Y$$

(8.23)

where the density function in this very simple example is

$$f(Y) = \frac{1}{b-a} dY \tag{8.24}$$

This density function is known as the **uniform distribution function.**

The formal expression for the cumulative probability distribution function for the uniform distribution is

$$CDF[Y_0] = \frac{Y_0 - a}{b - a} \tag{8.25}$$
$$a \leq Y_0 \leq b$$

We can derive the first four moments quite easily; further details are provided in the Exercises. Let us examine a very simple version of the uniform distribution in which the interval over which the distribution is defined is the unit interval $[0,1]$. The reader should verify that

$$\int_0^1 dY = 1$$

Further, if you recall that the algebraic formulation of the integral of y^n is $\frac{y^{n+1}}{n+1}$, which is easily checked by taking the derivative of the latter expression, then one can verify that

$$\mu_1' = \int_0^1 Y \, dY = \frac{Y^2}{2} \Big|_{Y=0}^{Y=1} \tag{8.26}$$

$$= \frac{1^2}{2} - \frac{0^2}{2} = \frac{1}{2} \tag{8.27}$$

$$\mu_2 = \int_0^1 \left(Y - \frac{1}{2}\right)^2 dY = \frac{1}{12}$$

$$\mu_3 = \int_0^1 \left(Y - \frac{1}{2}\right)^3 dY = 0$$

$$\mu_4 = \int_0^1 \left(Y - \frac{1}{2}\right)^4 dY = \frac{1}{80}$$

And the corresponding values for α_1 and α_2 are

$$\alpha_1 = 0$$

$$\alpha_2 = \frac{1/80}{(1/12)^2} = \frac{9}{5} \tag{8.28}$$

From these results, we see that the uniform distribution is symmetric and that its degree of peakedness is apparently quite small; this is consistent with the shape of the distribution's histogram.

The uniform distribution is widely used and one of the oldest. Besides providing the probability distribution for "round off" errors, it has some very important theoretical properties, partly because it is a very simple distribution to use!

8.6   The Normal, or Gaussian, Density Function and the Central Limit Theorem

Our second example of a continuous random variable is as universally applicable and has as long a history as the uniform; it is called the **normal**, or **Gaussian**, distribution. With this distribution, it will be instructive to relate the values of the parameters of the distribution to the properties of the distribution and the corresponding theoretical moments.

However, first we need to dispel the notion that the normal density function is in any way "normal"; that is, the name "normal" does not mean that the distribution is "standard" or "regular" or that it sets a "norm." The distribution is, however, quite common in practice. The confusion with the name would not have occurred if we had used the European names for this distribution, "Gauss" or "Laplace," after the two famous mathematicians that did so much to develop our knowledge about this distribution. To this end, I will use the names "normal" and "Gaussian" interchangeably to emphasize that "normal" is just a name.

The original discovery of the normal, or Gaussian, density function was by a French mathematician by the name of De Moivre, who derived it by taking limits of the binomial probability distribution as n, the number of trials in a binomial experiment, increases to ever-larger values of n. We have already done this. Recall from the last chapter that we examined the limit of the standardized third and fourth moments as n, the number of trials increased without limit. The derived standardized moments were 0 and 3, respectively. As we will see, these are the same third and fourth moments of the distribution to be derived in this section. We could repeat the examination of the binomial probability distribution, but it will be more instructive if we think about a prototypical experiment that will demonstrate the potentially wide applicability of the Gaussian distribution.

We want to consider a situation in which the variable that we observe is the sum of a large number of components, each one of which is a random variable. Further, we would like the individual components to be distributed independently of each other. This is precisely the situation that we observed with the derivation of the binomial probability distribution; the number of successes in n binomial trials is the sum of n independent component trials. We seek to generalize that result.

Another example of this type of mechanism is the generation of errors of measurement; indeed, this was one of the early uses of the normal density function. The idea is simple. Any observed error is the result of adding up a large number of very small effects, each of which is independently distributed from the others. Enough talk; let's begin.

We have n independent trials on *any* random variable. The random variable could be a discrete random variable, or it could be continuous. Using our existing theory we know that the joint probability distribution for the n trials is given by

$$F_j(X_1, X_2, \ldots X_n) = G(X_1)G(X_2)G(X_3)\ldots G(X_n)$$

where $F_j(\cdot)$ represents the joint probability distribution and $G(\cdot)$ represents the probability distribution for the "original" random variable; that is, $F_j(\cdot)$ is the joint probability distribution for n-fold independent replications of the random variable X with distribution function $G(\cdot)$. Note the usefulness of this notation in that it does not matter at this stage of the analysis whether the variables, X_i, are discrete or continuous.

In the subsequent discussion we do not need to know any more about the distributions $G(\cdot)$ or $F_j(\cdot)$. It is important to recognize how little we have assumed; basically our only assumptions are that we have independence and that we are dealing with replications of the same experiment.

Our main interest is in deriving the shape of the probability distribution of the sum, or better, of a standardized version of the mean of the X_i, $i = 1, \ldots n$. As we have learned before, we can do this by calculating the theoretical moments of the random variable of interest. From the values of the first four theoretical moments, we can deduce the shape of the corresponding probability distribution. If we are to concentrate on the shape of this distribution, then our previous experience also teaches us that we should immediately standardize our variables. Let us assume that in our prototypical experiment, the first four theoretical moments of the distribution $G(\cdot)$ are given by

$$\mu'_1 = \gamma_1, \qquad \mu_2 = \gamma_2, \qquad \mu_3 = \gamma_3, \qquad \mu_4 = \gamma_4 \tag{8.29}$$

What the actual values of these theoretical moments are we do not know, nor for our purposes, do we care, other than that they should have finite values. Our first task is to derive the theoretical moments of the sum of these X_i, or of some closely related function of the sum. Let W^* be defined by

$$W^* = \sum_i X_i$$

then the mean and second moment of W^* are

$$\mu'_1(W^*) = n \times \gamma_1$$
$$\mu_2(W^*) = n \times \gamma_2$$

If you have any difficulty with this operation, reexamine Section 7.5, "Expectation."

Before continuing, we should standardize our random variable W^*. Remember that our main concern is about the shape; neither the location nor the spread of the distribution is of interest.

So let us define a new random variable W by

$$W = \frac{(W^* - n\gamma_1)}{\sqrt{n\gamma_2}} \tag{8.30}$$

and we now have a random variable that for all values of n has a mean of 0 and a second moment of 1. Let us reexpress W as a sum of n individual random variables, each with a mean of 0 and a second moment of 1. This is easily done by defining a random variable Y_i by

$$Y_i = \frac{(X_i - \gamma_1)}{\sqrt{\gamma_2}} \tag{8.31}$$

By design the mean and variance of Y_i are 0 and 1, respectively, and the third and fourth moments of Y_i are

$$\mu_3(Y_i) = \frac{\gamma_3}{\gamma_2^{3/2}}$$

$$\mu_4(Y_i) = \frac{\gamma_4}{\gamma_2^2}$$

and W is

$$W = \left(\frac{1}{\sqrt{n}}\right) \sum Y_i \tag{8.32}$$

You should verify that W does have the stated reexpression in terms of Y_i. Also note that the $\{Y_i\}$ that we have defined are independently distributed because the $\{X_i\}$ are, and that $W = \sqrt{n}\bar{Y}$.

Now comes the tricky part, what are the third and fourth moments of the random variable W? (You have already done this type of calculation in the Chapter 7 Exercises; you might also like to review in the Mathematics Appendix Section A.3, "Sigma Notation," which reviews the expansions to follow in detail.) This time we will work out the calculations together. By definition $\mu_3(W)$ is

$$\mu_3(W) = E\{W^3\} = E\left\{\left[\left(\frac{1}{\sqrt{n}}\right)\sum Y_i\right]^3\right\}$$

$$= \left(\frac{1}{\sqrt{n}}\right)^3 E\left\{\left[\sum Y_i\right]^3\right\} \tag{8.33}$$

If we can determine the value of $E\{[\sum Y_i]^3\}$, we can easily obtain the value for $\mu_3(W)$. To do that we have to expand the expression for $(\sum Y_i)^3$:

$$E\left\{\left[\sum Y_i\right]^3\right\} = E\left\{\sum Y_i^3 + \sum_{i \neq j} Y_i^2 Y_j + \sum_{i \neq j \neq k} Y_i Y_j Y_k\right\}$$

$$= \frac{n\gamma_3}{\gamma_2^{3/2}} + 0 + 0 \tag{8.34}$$

because the $\{Y_i\}$ are independent and $E\{Y_i\} = 0$:

$$E\left\{\sum_{i \neq j} Y_i^2 Y_i\right\} = \sum_{i \neq j} E\{Y_i^2\}E\{Y_j\}$$

$$= 0$$

$$E\left\{\sum_{i \neq j \neq k} Y_i Y_j Y_k\right\} = \sum_{i \neq j \neq k} E\{Y_i\}E\{Y_j\}E\{Y_k\}$$

$$= 0$$

We can conclude

$$E\{W^3\} = \left(\frac{1}{\sqrt{n}}\right)^3 \frac{n\gamma_3}{\gamma_2^{3/2}}$$

$$= \left(\frac{1}{\sqrt{n}}\right) \frac{\gamma_3}{\gamma_2^{3/2}} \tag{8.35}$$

Let us make sure that we understand this result. The first term in Equation 8.34 should be easy enough if we recall that the Y_i are all independent of each other and that they all have the same third moment, $\gamma_3/\gamma_2^{3/2}$ (see Equation 8.31 and keep in mind that γ_3, γ_2 are the third and second moments, respectively, of the X_i). But now the remaining terms should also be clear, because by independence the expectation of any term involving a single power of Y_i is 0.

With this result in hand, we can confidently and easily proceed to the fourth moment:

$$E\{W^4\} = E\left\{\left[\left(\frac{1}{\sqrt{n}}\right)\sum Y_i\right]^4\right\}$$
$$= \left(\frac{1}{\sqrt{n}}\right)^4 E\left\{\left[\sum Y_i\right]^4\right\}$$

(8.36)

We expand the term $[\sum Y_i]^4$:

$$E\left\{\left[\sum Y_i\right]^4\right\} = E\left\{\sum Y_i^4 + \sum_{i\neq j} Y_i^2 Y_j^2 + \sum_{i\neq j} Y_i^3 Y_j\right.$$
$$\left. + \sum_{i\neq j\neq k} Y_i^2 Y_j Y_k + \sum_{i\neq j\neq k\neq l} Y_i Y_j Y_k Y_l\right\}$$

By exploiting the independence of the Y_i, that the distribution for each Y_i is the same as for any other Y_j, and that the fourth moment of Y_i is $\frac{\gamma_4}{\gamma_2^2}$—the γ_i being the unknown moments for the original variable $\{X_i\}$—the first term in the expansion is just $\frac{n\gamma_4}{\gamma_2^2}$. Still exploiting the independence and the fact that $E\{Y_i\} = 0, i = 1, 2, \ldots, n$, we see that all the remaining terms, but the second, are 0.

The expectation of the second term is by independence $3n(n-1)$, but the term needs some explanation; it's not obvious! First, remember that $E\{Y_i^2\} = 1$ (Equation 8.31). Further, in both Equations 8.34 and 8.36, expressions of the type "$\sum_{i\neq j} Y_i^3 Y_j$" mean that one sums over $i \neq j$, for all choices of indices $\{i, j\}$. Thus, to get squared terms out of the product of four terms, Y_i, Y_j, Y_k, Y_l, we need to select two groups the same out of four different terms, this is simply $4!/(2!2!) = 6$. But, if we recognize that $E\{Y_i^2\} = E\{Y_j^2\} = 1$, so that the order in which we get the squares is irrelevant, then we see that we have in fact only $\frac{1}{2}$ as many terms. Finally, we now have to sum over $n(n-1)$ terms where $i \neq j$; that is, we can sum over i first, n terms, and then over $j \neq i$, $(n-1)$ terms. Pulling the two arguments together, we obtain a total of $6n(n-1)/2 = 3n(n-1)$ terms involving a product of squares.

We are now ready to express the fourth moment of W:

$$E\{W^4\} = \left(\frac{1}{\sqrt{n}}\right)^4 \left[\frac{n\gamma_4}{\gamma_2^2} + 3n(n-1)\right]$$
$$= \left(\frac{1}{n^2}\right) \left[\frac{n\gamma_4}{\gamma_2^2} + 3n(n-1)\right]$$
$$= \frac{\gamma_4/\gamma_2^2}{n} + 3\left[\frac{(n-1)}{n}\right]$$

(8.37)

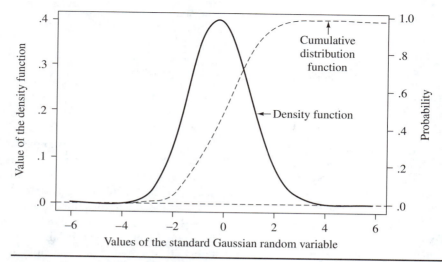

Figure 8.5   Density and cumulative distribution functions for the standard Gaussian

Let us recall what we have done. The theoretical moments of the random variable W for any n are

$$\mu_1'(W) = 0; \; \mu_2(W) = 1;$$

$$\mu_3(W) = \frac{\gamma_3/\gamma_2^{3/2}}{\sqrt{n}}; \; \mu_4(W) = \frac{\gamma_4/\gamma_2^2}{n} + 3\left[\frac{(n-1)}{n}\right] \qquad (8.38)$$

We can now answer the question concerning the limiting distribution of the random variable W as n, the number of terms in the sum, increases without limit. The answer is immediate. As $n \to \infty$,

$$\mu_3(W) \to 0; \; \mu_4(W) \to 3,$$
$$\alpha_1(W) \to 0; \; \alpha_2(W) \to 3 \qquad (8.39)$$

We define the density function that has theoretical moments with values

$$\mu_1' = 0; \; \mu_2 = 1; \; \mu_3 = 0; \; \mu_4 = 3 \qquad (8.40)$$

as the *standard normal density function,* or as it is often termed the *standard Gaussian density function.* The Gaussian, or normal density function, is that distribution associated with the standardized sums of independent random variables as the number of terms gets to be very large.

Figure 8.5 shows the shape of the density function that we have just derived and its corresponding cumulative distribution function. The area under the density function shown in Figure 8.5 sums to one as required and the "summing of the area" is represented by the height of the curve labeled cumulative distribution function.

The formal expression for the standard normal density is

$$\phi(X) = (2\pi)^{-1/2}\exp\left[-\frac{1}{2}(X)^2\right] \tag{8.41}$$

and the CDF is

$$\Phi(X_0) = \int_{-\infty}^{X_0} \phi(X)dX \tag{8.42}$$

which means that $\Phi(X_0)$ is obtained by "adding up the area under $\phi(X)$ from as far left as is practicable to X_0." In Figure 8.5, the density curve $\phi(X)$ is represented by the solid symmetrical graph; values of the density can be read from the left axis. The integral of the density up to each point on the ordinate is given by the CDF, $\Phi(X_0)$, expressed in Equation 8.42. The corresponding probabilities can be read on the right scale. The maximum density is at $X = 0$ with a value of .3989. The corresponding point for the CDF is an inflection point; that is, the probability is increasing at an increasing rate before $X = 0$ but only at a decreasing rate thereafter.

When writing the Gaussian density, e, EXP, and "exp" all refer to the same constant, 2.718 . . . (see the Mathematical Appendix).

Now we see the importance of the phrase "as far left as is practicable"; in this case it is where the function $\phi(X)$ is so close to the x-axis that for all intents and purposes there is no area under the curve. There is "high contact between the function and the axis." For the curve plotted in Figure 8.5 the points of "high contact" begin at about 4.5 units to either side of zero, which is the mean of the random variable X. The density function given by $\phi(X)$, evaluated at these extreme points, yields

$$\phi(-4.5) = \phi(4.5) = .399 \times \exp(-10.125)$$

and $\phi(6)$ is a minuscule $(2\pi)^{-1/2} \times \exp(-18)$. Notice that the CDF for this density function is practically 0 for all points to the left of -4.5 units from 0, $\Phi(-4.5) = .000003$, and is virtually 1 for all points to the right of 4.5 units past 0, $\Phi(4.5) = .999997$.

Standard Deviation and the Nonstandard Gaussian

It is useful at this juncture to recall the term *standard deviation,* which is the square root of the second moment. We assign a special symbol to it, "σ," because we will make a lot of use of this concept hereafter. By taking the square root of the second moment, we obtain a measure of spread in the same units as the original random variable X. The second moment of our current random variable is one by construction so that the standard deviation, σ, is also one, but now the units of measurement are in "natural" units, not squared units. The units used to construct the graph in Figure 8.5 were "units of standard deviation." In Figure 8.5, the numbers on the x-axis are numbers of standard deviations above and below the mean of zero, so that -2 is "2.0 standard deviations below the mean."

Table 8.1 shows some values of the density and the cumulative distribution functions to provide a better idea of the Gaussian density function and how to use it. The numbers in the first column are the units of standard deviation that we have just defined; the second column, CDF, contains the probabilities that X is less than the stated

Table 8.1 **List of Densities and Probabilities for the Standard Normal Distribution**

Standard Deviations	CDF	Density
-3	.001	.004
-2	.023	.054
-1	.159	.242
0	.500	.399
1	.841	.242
2	.977	.054
3	.999	.004

amount in the first column; and the third column, Density, contains the values of $\phi(X)$ evaluated at units of standard deviations above or below the mean. Notice the symmetry of the density values and that the maximum at $X = 0$ is .399, which is the solution to $(2\pi)^{-1/2}$. Also notice that the CDF begins by increasing slowly, then much more rapidly between -2 standard deviations and 0, then it begins to increase much less rapidly after that point.

When we derived the Gaussian density function, we did so with respect to a random variable that was standardized; that is, it has a mean of 0 and a second moment, or as we now know, a standard deviation of 1. But what we would like is to be able to consider any Gaussian density function with arbitrary mean and standard deviation; that is, we would have the same shape, but the location would be different from 0 and the spread would be different from 1. By recalling how we standardized random variables in the first place, we can see how to "de-standardize." If we call our current variable X, then the de-standardized variable, call it Y, is given by

$$Y = \mu + \sigma X \tag{8.43}$$

because with such a definition X is given back to us by

$$X = \frac{(Y - \mu)}{\sigma} \tag{8.44}$$

We say that the distribution of the random variable Y is a Gaussian density function with mean μ and standard deviation σ. The actual density function is expressed by

$$\phi(X; \mu, \sigma) = N\left(\mu, \sigma^2\right)$$
$$= \left(2\pi\sigma^2\right)^{-1/2} \exp\left[-\frac{1}{2}\frac{(Y - \mu)^2}{\sigma^2}\right] \tag{8.45}$$

The notation $N(\mu, \sigma^2)$ is easier to remember and to use, but both will appear in your readings. The main point of writing down in full the density function for the Gaussian is to let you see that this is a two-parameter distribution: μ and σ, or σ^2. Recall, however, that μ and σ also represent the mean and standard deviation. This is not a coincidence; μ and σ^2 are, respectively, the mean and the second moment of this distribution, so that in this *unique* case the two parameters of the distribution

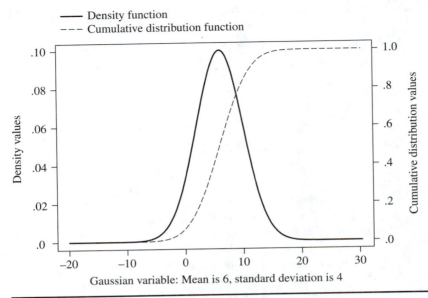

Figure 8.6 Density and cumulative distribution functions for an $N(6,4)$ Random Variable

represent the first two moments as well. Figure 8.6 shows the shape of the Gaussian, or normal, density function for different parameter values; as indicated by Equation 8.45, $\mu'_1 = 6$ and $\sigma = 4$, or $\sigma^2 = 16$. Note that although the mean and the variance are different, the shape is the same as in Figure 8.5. In comparing Figures 8.5 and 8.6, note that the location of the distribution in Figure 8.6 is shifted six units to the right of that in Figure 8.5. Because the density shown in Figure 8.6 has a standard deviation of 4, the density is significantly nonzero over a range that is four times as long as that shown in Figure 8.5.

The derivation of the normal distribution that we summarized in Equations 8.39 and 8.40 is a version of the proof of the famous **central limit theorem.** It says that if $\{Y_i\}$ is a sequence of independently and identically distributed standardized random variables (these are the same assumptions we used), then the limiting distribution of the random variable $\sqrt{n}\bar{Y}$, or $\Sigma_i \frac{Y_i}{\sqrt{n}}$, as $n \to \infty$ is the standard Gaussian distribution. Interpret carefully what this theorem says; the limit is for the *standardized variables*. However, having obtained the limit we can say that as an *approximation* for *finite* values of n, the random variables $\bar{X}$, or ΣX_i, are approximately distributed as Gaussian, but with means of γ_1 and $n\gamma_1$, and variances $\frac{\gamma_2}{n}$ and $n\gamma_2$, respectively.

The Gaussian, or Normal, Distribution as an Approximation to the Binomial Distribution

The Gaussian density function was derived as a limiting density function as the number of component terms increased indefinitely, provided that the individual terms are distributed independently. Let us explore this idea by some examples. First, let us

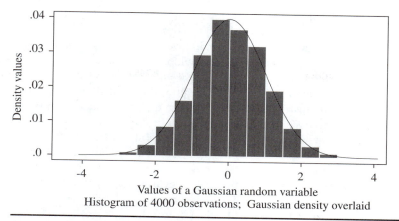

Values of a Gaussian random variable
Histogram of 4000 observations; Gaussian density overlaid

Figure 8.7   A comparison between a Gaussian density and histogram

look at an example of such a distribution. In Figure 8.7, 4000 observations on a simulated experiment involving the sum of a very large number of independent sources of "error" are shown in terms of a histogram; overlaid on that histogram is a normal density function. Notice the good fit.

Now consider Figure 8.8. Here we have repeated a binomial probability distribution experiment 4000 times, where the parameters of the binomial probability distribution are π, with a value of 0.2 and n, which represents the number of independent trials, is 100. Each of the 4000 trials represents a drawing from a binomial distribution with parameters $n = 100$ and $\pi = .2$. If we plot the histogram of the binomial experiment and overlay it with the graph of a Gaussian density function with the same

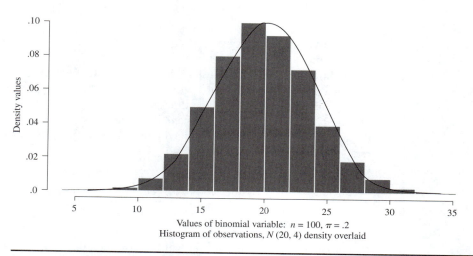

Values of binomial variable: $n = 100$, $\pi = .2$
Histogram of observations, $N(20, 4)$ density overlaid

Figure 8.8   A comparison between a normal density and a binomial histogram

theoretical moments as the binomial probability distribution—that is, $\mu'_1 = 20$ and $\sigma^2 = 16$—we get a remarkably good fit.

Recall that in Chapter 7 we discovered that the limiting theoretical moments, α_1, α_2, for the binomial probability distribution were 0 and 3, respectively; and these are the same theoretical moments of what we now call the Gaussian, or normal density function. So in effect, we have already proved that the limiting distribution for the binomial probability distribution is the Gaussian density function. Consequently, it would seem that the Gaussian density function can be used, at least under the circumstances indicated, as an approximating distribution for the binomial probability distribution.

Before proceeding, let us make sure that we know what we mean by "a limiting distribution." In a very real sense, the binomial probability distribution used in this example is the binomial probability distribution regardless of the value of n. The idea of the Gaussian density function as a limiting distribution is that it can be regarded as an approximation to the binomial probability distribution, and that approximation improves as n, the number of trials, increases. In short, you can use the Gaussian density function to calculate probabilities of binomial events with negligible error. The reason you would want to do this is because the task of calculating the actual probabilities from the binomial probability distribution directly is often a daunting prospect, especially when n is very large. However, although with powerful personal computers the actual time saved is now not so great, the need to understand the principles of the statistics that are involved is still as great as ever.

Let us examine in more detail the use of the Gaussian density function instead of the true, actual, binomial probability distribution. Imagine that we are contemplating an experiment in which the probability on any trial is .5, there are to be 100 independent trials, and we want to know the probability of getting between 40 and 60 successes in 100 trials. The straightforward approach is merely to "plug the numbers" into the binomial probability distribution:

$$\text{pr}(40 \leq X \leq 60) = \sum_{40}^{60} \binom{100}{K} \pi^K (1-\pi)^{100-K}$$

Now that you have the expression, consider working out the first few terms. Even with a computer, this is not a trivial task.

But how do we use the Gaussian density function? We believe that the shape of the binomial probability distribution with a large value for n is approximately a Gaussian density function, but we need to settle on the relevant mean and standard deviation. Obviously the mean, μ'_1, and the standard deviation, σ, that we want is the mean and the standard deviation for the assumed binomial probability distribution; in our current situation they are

$$\mu'_1 = n\pi = 100 \times \frac{1}{2} = 50$$

$$\sigma = \sqrt{\mu_2} = \sqrt{n\pi(1-\pi)} = \sqrt{100 \times \frac{1}{2} \times \frac{1}{2}} = 5$$

Our problem is to calculate the probability that, for a Gaussian density function with a mean of 50 and a standard deviation of 5, the corresponding normal random variable lies in the interval (40, 60); that is, we want the area under the Gaussian (normal) density function between the limits 40 and 60. Using our notation, we want the probability of a random variable distributed as $N(\mu_1' = 50, \sigma^2 = 25)$ to lie in the interval [40, 60].

An Aside on Calculating the Normal Probability Distribution   But how do we calculate the area under the Gaussian density function between the limits 40 and 60? Have we not traded one difficult problem for another? The answer is no, but only because some helpful souls have already done almost all the hard work for us. Back in the days before computers, calculating any probability was always a time-consuming, if not difficult, task, so ways were devised to economize on effort. One obvious way to do this was to create a series of tables of calculations that were designed to be used by a wide variety of users. One of the most famous of these books of tables is the *Biometrika Tables for Statisticians* (edited by E. S. Pearson and H. O. Hartley), first published in 1954; it is a revision of the tables that was first compiled under the auspices of *Biometrika* in 1914. It is difficult for a reader today, who is accustomed to the ubiquitous presence of powerful personal computers, to appreciate the difficulty in carrying out statistical calculations and the incredible boon from having tables of entries readily available. The Pearson and Hartley *Biometrika Tables* are still in use and are the source of almost all the tables quoted in statistics textbooks.

In an earlier version of this text, this section was called "An Aside on the Use of the Normal Probability Tables," and I spent many paragraphs discussing how to use the tables of the normal probability distribution. However, we will eschew the tables in favor of calculating the probabilities directly by computer. Because each of you has access to a computer and the programs that came attached with this text, we can easily solve all our problems by calculating the probabilities directly. The section of S-Plus where the normal probabilities are calculated is in the menu item Statistical Tables under Labs.

One matter that is consistent with the use of the standard tables in textbooks is the need to standardize the normal distribution. The computer will calculate the normal probabilities for a "standard normal" random variable and will give you as output three items: $\mathrm{pr}(Z \leq z_0)$, $\mathrm{pr}(Z \geq z_0)$, and $\mathrm{pr}(|Z| \geq z_0)$ for any assigned value z_0. The reason is that the computer algorithms are set up to calculate probabilities for a particularly simple normal distribution because the probability for any other normal distribution can be obtained by easy transformations of the variables involved. In short, we calculate the probabilities for one benchmark function that will represent all possible normal variables.

Any other normal random variable—that is, any other normal random variable with a different mean and a different standard deviation—can always be "included in your calculations" by the simple expedient of "standardization," a task that is by now very familiar. Once we have a probability for the $N(0,1)$, we can always obtain the probability for any other normal density function, say X, that is distributed as $N(\mu, \sigma^2)$, where μ is the mean and σ^2 is the standard deviation by the transformation:

$$Z = \frac{(X - \mu)}{\sigma}$$

To understand what is happening here, look at Figure 8.5. Consider first an arbitrary value for the standard normal density, say z_0. We want to calculate either the probability that $Z \leq z_0$, or the probability that $Z \geq z_0$. Enter S-Plus and click on Labs, Statistical Tables, Normal. In the dialog that appears enter your chosen value of z_0, say 1.5, and click "Apply." As output in the S-Plus Report window, you will see three probabilities listed: $\text{pr}(Z \leq 1.5)$, $\text{pr}(Z \geq 1.5)$, and $\text{pr}(|Z| \geq 1.5)$. The first probability is represented by the area under the standard normal density function from "$-\infty$" to 1.5 (look carefully at Figure 8.5), the second probability is represented by the area under the density function from 1.5 to "∞," and the last probability is represented by the area under the density over the two regions $(-\infty, -1.5)$ and $(1.5, \infty)$. If you want the probability that Z is contained between two arbitrary bounds, it is easy to subtract probabilities. For example, what is the probability that Z lies in the interval -1.8 to 2.1? We want to calculate $\text{pr}(-1.8 \leq Z \leq 2.1)$. By examining Figure 8.5, you will see that we obtain this probability by

$$\text{pr}(-1.8 \leq Z \leq 2.1) = \text{pr}(Z \geq 2.1) - \text{pr}(Z \leq -1.8)$$
$$= .9821 - .0359 = .9462$$

Figure 8.9 illustrates these calculations schematically by representing the probability integrals as areas under the normal density function.

Sometimes we want to discover the value of z_0 that will produce a particular probability; that is, we have a probability in mind and want to discover what bound on Z will yield that probability. This also has been programmed for you. Consider an example. Suppose that we want to know the value of z_0 such that $\text{pr}(Z \leq z_0) = .9821$. We do this in S-Plus by going to the "Inverse Statistical Tables." By clicking on Labs, Inverse Statistical Tables, Normal and entering .9821 in the box that appears, we obtain as output in the S-Plus Report window 2.0992, which is reasonably close to 2.1 for our purposes.

This discussion has demonstrated how to use the computer to carry out the probability integrals that we have been discussing for the standard normal distribution, but to be completely general we need to be able to handle any normal variable with arbitrary mean and variance. Suppose that we have a normal random variable X with mean value $\mu = 2.4$ and variance $\sigma^2 = 3.5$ and that we want to discover the probability that $X \leq 4.8$. We solve this problem by transforming it into one that we have solved already; we transform the problem into an equivalent problem in terms of the standard normal distribution. We do this by recognizing that

$$\text{pr}(X \leq 4.8) = \text{pr}\left(\frac{X - \mu}{\sigma} \leq \frac{4.8 - \mu}{\sigma}\right)$$
$$= \text{pr}(Z \leq 1.283)$$
$$= .9003$$

The last calculation was obtained from S-Plus's "Statistical Tables." The calculation works because the probabilities remain the same if we perform the same transformation on both X and its limit 4.8; we subtract the mean value 2.4 from both, and we then divide both by $\sqrt{3.5} = 1.8708$.

Back to the Normal as an Approximation to the Binomial Distribution After this long discussion on the use of probability calculations we return to our problem of

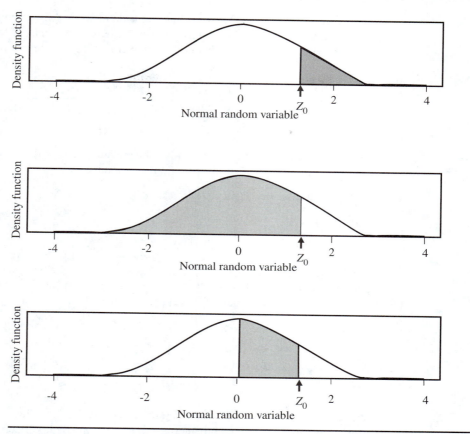

Figure 8.9   Three alternative ways of expressing $N(0,1)$ probabilities

how to approximate the binomial probability distribution. Recall the problem; we have a binomial probability distribution with parameters $\pi = .5$ and $n = 100$, so that the mean is 50 and the standard deviation is 5. This binomial probability distribution is to be approximated by a Gaussian, or normal, density function with a mean of 50 and a standard deviation of 5.

We want

$$\text{pr}(40 \leq X \leq 60)$$

where X is distributed as $N(50, 25)$; but the S-Plus's "Statistical Tables" are for a random variable Z that is distributed as $N(0,1)$. Let us transform our problem from one in terms of the random variable X to one in terms of the random variable Z. To convert X to Z, we use

$$Z = \frac{(X - 50)}{5}$$

But, to maintain the equivalent inequality inside the probability statement, we need to change the boundaries in exactly the same way that we changed the variable X into the variable Z; that is, subtract the mean and divide by the standard deviation. We have

$$\text{pr}[40 \leq X \leq 60] = \text{pr}\left[\frac{(40-50)}{5} \leq \frac{(X-50)}{5} \leq \frac{(60-50)}{5}\right]$$
$$= \text{pr}[-2 \leq Z \leq 2]$$

Be sure you understand why we can use the equality signs in this expression. The compound event $40 \leq X \leq 60$ is the same compound event as

$$\frac{(40-50)}{5} \leq \frac{(X-50)}{5} \leq \frac{(60-50)}{5}$$

so the probability of each is the same.

The probability that $-2 \leq Z \leq 2$ is given by the area under a $N(0,1)$ density function between the limits $-2, 2$. To use S-Plus's "Statistical Tables," we rewrite the probability statement so as to convert all the probability statements into those that can be calculated directly. Reexpress the probability statement as

$$\text{pr}(-2 \leq Z \leq 2) = \text{pr}(Z \leq 2) - \text{pr}(Z \leq -2)$$
$$= [1 - \text{pr}(Z \geq 2)] - \text{pr}(Z \leq -2)$$
$$= [1 - \text{pr}(Z \geq 2)] - \text{pr}(Z \geq 2)$$
$$= 1 - 2\text{pr}(Z \geq 2)$$

We can calculate $\text{pr}(Z \geq 2)$ using Figure 8.9 as a guide. In S-Plus, clicking on <u>Labs</u>, <u>Statistical Tables</u>, <u>Normal</u>, and entering "2," we obtain .023. We derive the required probability that an $N(0,1)$ random variable is in the interval $(-2, 2)$ from the last line in the previous equation:

$$1.0 - (2 \times .023) = 1.0 - .046 = .954$$

We conclude that the probability of getting a random variable X that is distributed as binomial with parameters $\pi = .5$ and $n = 100$ to lie in the interval $(40, 60)$ is approximately .95.

How accurate is this approximation? Well, if you were to calculate the actual probability you would get an error of only about .001, so for our purposes we need not worry about the degree of approximation. We might need to worry, if the value of π were close to 0 or 1 or if the value of n were very small; these issues are explored in the Exercises.

You may have noticed that by chance the tails of the distribution that were excluded were symmetric, $[0, 40]$ is symmetric with $[60, 100]$, so that given the symmetry of the distribution the shaded regions in Figure 8.10 that correspond to the probability of $X \leq 40$ and of $X \geq 60$ are also symmetric. You might find it interesting that the same probability could have been obtained from only one side, as with the lined right region in Figure 8.10 that begins at 1.68 standard deviations from the mean zero; 1.68 in stan-

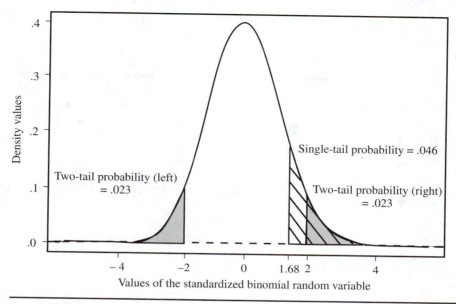

Figure 8.10 Calculating binomial probabilities using a normal approximation

dardized units corresponds to 58.4 in the original units described by the binomial distribution. We obtain "58.4" from

$$1.68 = Z = \frac{(X - 50)}{5}$$
$$X = (5 \times 1.68) + 50 = 58.4$$

What we have here is the idea that the probability of the union of events ($[-\infty \leq Z \leq -2]$ and $[2 \leq Z \leq \infty]$) is equal to the probability of the event $[-\infty \leq Z \leq -1.68]$, or equivalently to the probability of the event $[1.68 \leq Z \leq \infty]$. This result anticipates some calculations that we will be doing in the next two chapters, in which we will be concerned with the trade-off between the probability of lying in one tail and the probability of lying in either tail.

An example of a situation in which the probability of the underlying binomial distribution is very small is illustrated in Figure 8.11. The figure shows the probability distributions for both the binomial and the Poisson distributions; also plotted in the same figure is a normal approximation in terms of probabilities and the continuous approximation given by the density function.

The binomial probability distribution is for a distribution with $\pi = .001$ and $n = 1000$. Recall from Chapter 7 that when π is very small and n is large, the Poisson probability distribution is the appropriate approximating distribution with parameter λ taking the value $n\pi$, which in this case is 1.0. The approximation by the Poisson is so good that it is difficult to distinguish the two plots in Figure 8.11.

If we plot the differences between Gaussian cumulative distribution functions to get Gaussian approximations of the binomial probabilities, we see from the figure

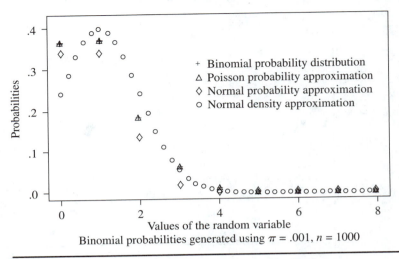

Figure 8.11   Comparison of binomial, Poisson, and normal approximations

that the approximation is not very good. In this example, as the change in probability is very small between adjacent random variable values, each difference is only .001, we can examine the Gaussian density function with the same mean and standard deviation as that for the binomial—that is, $\mu = 1$ and the standard deviation = 0.9999. The density approximation interpolates between the probability differences that we just calculated. In any event, the approximations are not very good.

We conclude that, while the Gaussian provides a useful approximation to the distributions of a wide array of random variables, the use of the Gaussian is by no means a universal phenomenon. The key is to examine closely the conditions of the experiment to discover the type of probability distribution that might be appropriate.

Moment-Generating Functions for Continuous Variables

This section is for the student who is comfortable with integral calculus and higher-order derivatives. The remainder of the book can be read with full comprehension even if you do not follow the material in this section. However, if you can follow the material, the depth and richness of your understanding of the theory underlying statistical analysis will be enhanced.

In Chapter 7, we introduced the concept of the moment-generating function. In this section, we extend that notion to continuous random variables. Recall Equation 7.32, which defined the moment-generating function as

$$E\{e^{s \times X}\} = \sum_X e^{s \times X} F(X)$$

$$= M_X(s)$$

The corresponding function for a continuous random variable is

$$E\{e^{s \times X}\} = \int_X e^{s \times X} f(X) dX$$
$$= M_X(s)$$

(8.46)

where $f(X)$ is the density function for the continuous random variable X.

The same rules and properties apply. By taking derivatives of the function $M_X(s)$ and evaluating them at $s = 0$, we can obtain all the moments of the density function $f(X)$. As before, we have the relationships

$$M_X(0)^{(r)} = \mu'_r$$

(8.47)

$$M_{X+a}(s) = E\left\{e^{s(X+a)}\right\} = E\left\{e^{s \times a} e^{s \times X}\right\}$$
$$= e^{s \times a} M_X(s)$$

(8.48)

$$M_{c \times X}(s) = E\left\{e^{c \times s \times X}\right\} = M_X(c \times s)$$

(8.49)

$$M_Z(s) = E\left\{e^{s \times Z}\right\} = E\left\{e^{s \times \Sigma_{i=1}^k Y_i}\right\}$$
$$= \prod_{i=1}^k M_{Y_i}(s) = (M_{Y_i}(s))^k$$

(8.50)

for Z defined by

$$Z = \sum_{i=1}^k Y_i$$

Consider an example. The Laplace distribution was discovered, by Laplace, as a distribution for the absolute values of errors of observation in measurements. As such, it is sometimes known as the first law of Laplace; the second law of Laplace generated the Gaussian distribution. The form of the distribution is given by its density function:

$$g(X) = \frac{1}{2} e^{-|X|}$$
$$-\infty < X < \infty$$

(8.51)

We obtain the moment-generating function by

$$M_X(s) = \int_X e^{s \times X} g(X) dX$$
$$= \int_X e^{s \times X} \frac{1}{2} e^{-|X|} dX$$
$$= \frac{1}{2} \left[\int_{-\infty}^0 e^{s \times X} e^{-|X|} dX + \int_0^\infty e^{s \times X} e^{-|X|} dX \right]$$

(8.52)

We solve each integral in the square brackets as follows:

$$\int_{-\infty}^{0} e^{s \times X} e^{-|X|} dX = -\int_{0}^{\infty} e^{-(1+s)X} dX$$

$$= -\frac{1}{1+s} \left\{ e^{-(1+s)X} \right\}_{0}^{\infty}$$

$$= -\frac{1}{1+s} \{0 - 1\}$$

$$= \frac{1}{1+s}$$

And for the other integral, we have

$$\int_{0}^{\infty} e^{s \times X} e^{-|X|} dX = \int_{0}^{\infty} e^{-(1-s)X} dX$$

$$= -\frac{1}{1-s} \left\{ e^{-(1-s)X} \right\}_{0}^{\infty}$$

$$= -\frac{1}{1-s} \{0 - 1\}$$

$$= \frac{1}{1-s}$$

We complete the derivation by adding the two terms together:

$$M_X(s) = \frac{1}{2} \left[\frac{1}{1+s} + \frac{1}{1-s} \right]$$

$$= \frac{1}{2} \left[\frac{1-s+1+s}{1-s^2} \right] \tag{8.53}$$

$$= \frac{1}{1-s^2}$$

The moments are easily generated from this function by taking the derivatives of $M_X(s)$ and setting $s = 0$. Clearly, because the distribution is symmetric about zero all the odd moments are zero. The even moments are given by

$$\mu_r(X) = r!$$

So far we have proceeded as if all moments of all orders existed for every distribution. Unfortunately, nothing could be further from the truth. The existence of moments we now see depends very much on the convergence of the sums, or integrals defining the moment-generating function. When we are dealing with discrete random variables with a finite set of values, there is no difficulty. However, such is not the case when we are examining distributions for continuous random variables. We will meet this problem directly in Chapter 10, but for now you can see that there may well be density functions $g(X)$ such that, for any nonzero value of s, the integral defined in Equation 8.46 does not converge.

This discussion raises a more difficult issue, the so-called problem of moments. The main issue is whether a given set of moments determines a distribution uniquely or not. In the case of discrete random variables with a finite set of values taken by the random variable, there is no difficulty. The problems arise with continuous distributions and then only when the range is infinite. Fortunately, these difficulties are best labeled "pathological," and the problem is not one that the average statistician need really be concerned about. It is useful to be aware of this problem, but it is not one that will occupy your thoughts very much until graduate school. We now know to modify our earlier cavalier treatment of moments to represent distributions by noting that for some distributions some or all of the moments may not be defined and that with continuous distributions that the moments may not uniquely determine the density function.

The Chebyshev Inequality

This short subsection introduces a useful inequality called the *Chebyshev inequality*, but its explanation requires a little more familiarity with calculus than we have allowed ourselves to use so far. We have introduced in this chapter two examples of density functions for continuous random variables. In later chapters we will introduce more, for example the Student's *T*, the chi-square, and the *F* density functions. Each distribution has its own set of moments, shapes, and properties. Consequently, it is rather remarkable that one can find inequalities on probabilities that will hold for *any* distribution; the **Chebyshev inequality** allows us to do this. One of the most difficult and important tasks before the statistician is to discover the probability distribution that may be involved in any problem. Thus, if one is unsure what the underlying distribution is, it is comforting to know that there are some universal inequalities that can give us some useful information; at the very least the Chebyshev inequality allows us to bound how far away from the mean the random variable could be.

Suppose that $F(X)$ represents a probability distribution for a random variable X with density function $dF(X)$. Suppose further that the mean is given by μ_1' and that the second moment is μ_2. We want to derive some bound on how far X can be from μ_1' in terms of μ_2. The following clever idea derives such a condition and is usually attributed to Chebyshev, who published the result in 1867, although Bienaymé discovered the inequality first in 1853 (in those days there were no Internet linkages and computerized literature searches).

Consider the following expectation after we redefine the variable to remove the mean μ_1'. This will simplify the calculations and will not detract from the generality of the result. In terms of the variable $x = X - \mu_1'$ and for an arbitrary variable t, we have

$$E\left\{1 - \frac{x^2}{t^2}\right\} = \int_{-\infty}^{\infty}\left(1 - \frac{x^2}{t^2}\right)dF(x)$$

$$= 1 - \frac{\mu_2}{t^2}$$

(8.54)

We now come to the clever bit. Break up the integral into three intervals: $(-\infty, -t)$, $(-t, t)$, (t, ∞). Recognize that for a large enough t the integrals over the first and last intervals can be made very small. Let us rewrite Equation 8.54:

$$\int_{-\infty}^{\infty} \left(1 - \frac{x^2}{t^2}\right) dF(x) = \int_{-\infty}^{-t} \left(1 - \frac{x^2}{t^2}\right) dF(x) + \int_{t}^{\infty} \left(1 - \frac{x^2}{t^2}\right) dF(x)$$
$$+ \int_{-t}^{t} \left(1 - \frac{x^2}{t^2}\right) dF(x) \tag{8.55}$$

In this last equation note that the arguments to the first two-tail integrals are negative, as over these intervals x^2 is larger than t^2. This enables us to conclude that

$$1 - \frac{\mu_2}{t^2} \leq \int_{-t}^{t} \left(1 - \frac{x^2}{t^2}\right) dF(x) \leq \int_{-t}^{t} dF(x) = F(t) - F(-t) \tag{8.56}$$

or

$$F(t) - F(-t) \geq 1 - \frac{\mu_2}{t^2}$$

If we express t^2 in terms of units of the second moment, μ_2—that is, set $t = \lambda\sqrt{\mu_2}$, or to use our alternate notation for the second moment, $t = \lambda\sigma$—we can reexpress the result as

$$\text{pr}\{|x| \leq \lambda\sigma\} \geq 1 - \tfrac{1}{\lambda^2} \tag{8.57}$$

or

$$\text{pr}\{|x| \geq \lambda\sigma\} \leq \tfrac{1}{\lambda^2}$$

or

$$\text{pr}\left\{\left|X - \mu_1'\right| \geq \lambda\sigma\right\} \leq \tfrac{1}{\lambda^2}$$

where we recall that X was the original variable with mean value μ_1'.

Let us consider what Equation 8.57 tells us. By just knowing the mean and the value of the standard deviation, σ, we can set bounds on the probabilities for any distribution. But we should expect that if we have such generality, we may not have very tight bounds. Before we explore that difficulty, let us see how we might use the information in Chebyshev's inequality. Suppose that you are only told the values of the mean and standard deviation of random radioactive emissions from an at-risk nuclear station. Even without knowing or having to take the time to discover the appropriate distribution for this situation, what is the maximum probability of observing a radiation level greater than three standard deviations above mean radiation levels? Chebyshev's inequality enables you to find the answer. Recently, scientists have recognized the risk Earth faces from very large meteors. Some effort has been made to determine the mean size of meteors and the variation in size. However, the number of meteors recorded is still sufficiently small that it is difficult to determine the appropriate distribution. What is the probability of being hit by a meteor greater in size than five times the standard deviation above the mean?

Table 8.2 **Comparison of the Chebyshev Inequality Bounds to Some Actual Bounds**

λ Value	Chebyshev Bounds	Gaussian	Chi-Square(9 d.f.)	Student's T (4)
2	.25	.04600	.0416	.0480
3	.11	.00160	.0098	.0132
4	.06	.00006	.0021	.0048

Once again, Chebyshev's inequality comes to the rescue in providing at least an approximate answer.

But how tight is this broadly applicable inequality? We can calculate the Chebyshev inequality and contrast that value with the exact calculation obtained from knowing the probability function as indicated in Equation 8.58:

$$\text{pr}\{|x| \geq \lambda\sigma\} = \int_{-\infty}^{-\lambda\sigma} dF(x) + \int_{\lambda\sigma}^{\infty} dF(x) \tag{8.58}$$

The results of a quick review are summarized in Table 8.2, using Equation 8.58. The Chebyshev inequalities are listed in the second column, and the actual probabilities for the Gaussian distribution are listed in the third column. For comparison, we list similar calculations for two other distributions (that we will discuss at length later in the text). For now, merely view the next two entries as alternative examples of distributions for which we have calculated the probabilities exactly; one is the chi-square distribution with 9 degrees of freedom and the other is called the Student's T distribution with 4 degrees of freedom. As we suspected, the Chebyshev bounds are very wide; they give very conservative results relative to the distributions that we have examined. So if you do know the distribution, then you should use it; otherwise you will lose information and your probability bounds will be unnecessarily large.

Terminology

We can conclude this chapter with a quick summary of some potentially confusing terminology. We have used the terms *distribution, probability function, distribution function,* and so on, frequently throughout the past three chapters. Although there are some general conventions, there is some widespread ambiguity in the use of the terms that you will soon discover in looking at other texts.

Distribution is used in this text as a generic term to refer to all the probability functions and density functions that we have discussed so far (and more that we will discuss in later chapters). Distribution reminds the reader that he or she is concerned with the allocation of probability across values of the random variable and that this discussion of probabilities arose out of our examination of the distribution of relative frequencies. When we began our theoretical development of probability in Chapter 6, we defined *probability distributions* in terms of allocating probabilities across the subsets of a sample space.

When we moved to the theoretical development involving random variables, we refined our ideas to talk of *probability functions*—that is, functions that generate probabilities. We saw that if the random variable was discrete, we defined the probability mass function; and if the random variable was continuous, we defined the (probability) density function, where the density function is the rate of change in the probability function. The probability function in the context of continuous random variables yields the probability of obtaining on a single draw any value that is less than the argument of the function. The *cumulative distribution function* in the context of a continuous random variable is a function that generalizes the idea of accumulating probabilities that we first defined in Chapter 7. In the continuous case we have the integral of the density function up to some specified upper limit.

8.7 Summary

We began by deriving in general terms the concept of a *probability density function* (see Equation 8.1), and later we related the concept of probability to density functions (Equation 8.6). We also defined the probability function for continuous variables. The next step was to redefine the concept of a cumulative distribution function in terms of the integrals of density functions (Equation 8.14).

These definitions enabled us to extend the idea of theoretical moments to continuous random variables. In Equations 8.20 and 8.22, the moments for continuous random variables were defined.

In all this discussion the main change from the analysis in Chapter 7 is that summations have been replaced by integrals, integration being a form of "continuous summation." In addition, we recognize that with continuous random variables there is no useful meaning to "the probability of a specific value of the random variable"; we have to restrict our discussion of probabilities to probabilities of "intervals." We have to talk not of the probability of X occurring but of the probability of X being in some designated interval.

With these theoretical preliminaries completed, we were able to derive our first continuous density function, the *uniform distribution*. The density was presented in Equation 8.24 and the corresponding cumulative distribution function was given in Equation 8.25. The theoretical moments were derived from the density function in Equations 8.26 and 8.28. This is the distribution of "round off" and is one of the first continuous distributions discovered; it is also very important theoretically.

The second distribution was the *normal*, or *Gaussian*, distribution. The density was presented in Equation 8.41 and the corresponding cumulative distribution function in Equation 8.42. The normal distribution is the distribution of the sum of independent and identically distributed errors. Deriving the normal distribution in the limit as n, the number of independent events, grows without bound is a variant of a famous theorem called the *central limit theorem*. The normal distribution, because of the central limit theorem, is one of the most important distributions in statistics. However, the reader is warned not to confuse the importance of the normal distribution with any idea about its "normality" or being "standard." For this reason, it is often referred to as the Gaussian distribution. An alternative way of referring to the distribution is $N(\mu, \sigma^2)$ (see Equation 8.45).

We gave an example of the normal distribution as an approximation of the binomial distribution. In contrast, we also examined a comparison in which the Poisson distribution provided a far better approximation. At the least, this example indicates that the Gaussian distribution is not the appropriate limit for all situations.

We concluded by discussing the *Chebyshev inequality* as a very approximate, but universally applicable, upper bound on probabilities for a wide variety of distributions (Equation 8.57).

Case Study

Was There Age Discrimination in a Public Utility?

There are only two continuous random variables involved in this case, age and salary. Let us consider salary first. We recall from Chapter 4 that for the salaries of all individuals in the age discrimination data set the standardized third and fourth moments were 0.08 and 3.03. These values are not exactly 0 and 3, respectively, but they are very close; so at the least we might well claim that the distribution of salaries is approximately normal (see Figure 3.20).

The distribution of age might also for similar reasons be regarded as approximately normally distributed. In Chapter 4,

we observed that the standardized third and fourth moments for the ages were −0.21 and 2.74, not as close as for the salaries but still reasonable. An alternative is looking at whether the age data are uniformly distributed between say 20 and 65—20 being the youngest age at which the firm can hire and 65 being the mandatory retirement age. The standardized third and fourth theoretical moments for this distribution are 0 and 1.8, respectively. In addition, the theoretical mean is 42.5 and the variance is 176.25 in contrast to the observed mean and variance of 46.2 and 78.0. From these results, we can be excused for concluding that the distribution of ages is more likely Gaussian than uniform over the interval 20 to 65.

Exercises

Calculation Practice

8.1 Use the standard normal probability integral routines in S-Plus to calculate the indicated probabilities for each of the following situations.

[*Computer directions:* Start S-Plus. On the menu bar, click on Labs, Statistical Tables, Normal. Click on Single Value. Enter the Z value; click Apply. The probability is in the Report window.]

a. $\text{pr}(Z \geq 2.35)$ $\text{pr}(-1.6 \leq Z \leq 1.3)$

b. $\text{pr}(Z \geq -2.35)$ $\text{pr}(Z \leq -1.2, \text{ or } Z \geq 1.3)$

c. $\text{pr}(Z \leq -2.78, \text{ or } -1.2 \leq Z \leq 0.7, \text{ or } Z \geq 2.6)$

In each case, draw a sketch of the probability required.

8.2 Use the standard normal probability integral routines in S-Plus to obtain the following probabilities. (*Hint:* The tables refer to Z values; the question refers to X values.)

[*Computer Directions:* Start S-Plus. Click on Labs, Statistical Tables, Normal. Click on Single Value. Enter the Z value; click Apply. The probability will be in the Report window.]

a. For X distributed as $N(25, 4)$, obtain the probabilities for the regions indicated.

(1) $X \geq 27.2$

(2) $X \leq 23.1$

(3) $24 \leq X \leq 25$

(4) $X \leq 22.8$, or $X \geq 27.1$

b. For X distributed as $N(5, 3)$, obtain the probabilities of

(1) $-1 \leq X \leq 11$

(2) $X \leq -4$, or $X \geq 14$

(3) $0 \leq X \leq 2$

(4) $X \geq 5$

8.3 *Objective: To illustrate the use of the standard Gaussian and the Gaussian distributions.* Use the standard normal probability integral routines in S-Plus to obtain the following probabilities.

[*Computer directions:* Procedure 1 (To generate probabilities for ordinate values): Start S-Plus. Click on Labs, Statistical Tables, Normal. Click on Single Value. Enter the Z value; click Apply. The probability will be in the Report window.

Procedure 2 (To generate ordinate values for probabilities): Start S-Plus. Click on Labs, Inverse Statistical Tables, Normal. Click on Single Value. Enter the probability; click Apply. The Z value will be in the Report window.]

a. Let X be distributed as $N(0, 1)$. Calculate the following probabilities. For each answer provide a diagram showing the area computed.

(1) $X > 3$

(2) $-3 < X < 3$

(3) $-2 < X < 2$

(4) $-4 < X < 4$

(5) Compare all of your answers with the probabilities that the Chebyshev inequality yields for intervals of 2, 3, and 4 standard deviations away from the mean.

(6) Provide an interval centered around the mean (0) of probability .90.

(7) Provide an interval centered around the mean of probability .95.

(8) Provide an interval centered around the mean of probability .99.

(9) What is the value of z_1 if $\mathrm{pr}(X > z_1) = .9$?

(10) What is the value of z_2 if $\mathrm{pr}(X > z_2) = .95$?

(11) What is the value of z_3 if $\mathrm{pr}(X > z_3) = .99$?

(12) What is the value of z_4 if $\mathrm{pr}(-1.4395 < X < z_4) = .9$?

(13) What is the value of z_5 if $\mathrm{pr}(z_5 < X < 2.17) = .95$?

b. Let X be distributed as $N(20, 25)$. Calculate the following probabilities. For each answer, provide a diagram showing the area computed.

(1) $X > 35$

(2) $5 < X < 35$

(3) $10 < X < 30$

(4) $0 < X < 40$

(5) Compare all of your answers in the following section with the z_1 to z_5 values calculated in (a). What common pattern can you see in the probabilities you have computed?

(6) What is the value of x_1 if $\mathrm{pr}(X > x_1) = .9$?

(7) What is the value of x_2 if $\mathrm{pr}(X > x_2) = .95$?

(8) What is the value of x_3 if $\mathrm{pr}(X > x_3) = .99$?

(9) What is the value of x_4 if $\mathrm{pr}(12.8025 < X < x_4) = .9$?

(10) What is the value of x_5 if
$pr(x_5 < X < 30.85) = .95$?

(11) How are x_1, x_2, x_3, x_4, and x_5 related to
z_1, z_2, z_3, z_4, and z_5, respectively?

8.4 Illustrate use of the uniform integral.

a. Calculate the following probabilities by hand
for the uniform distribution defined over the interval [0,1].

(1) $X \leq .3$

(2) $X \geq .6$

(3) $X > .15$

(4) $.2 < X \leq .7$

(5) $X < .3$, or $X \geq .78$

b. Check your hand calculations in (*a*) by using
the computer.

c. For the uniform distribution defined over the interval $[-1, 1]$, obtain the following probabilities.

[*Computer directions:* Start S-Plus, Click on <u>Labs</u>,
<u>Statistical Tables</u>, <u>Uniform</u>. As an example for (1),
set "Uniform minimum" to -1 and "Uniform max-
imum" to 1 for the interval. To calculate the probability for $.2 < X < .3$, in "*x* minimum" key in $\boxed{.2}$
and in "*x* maximum," key in $\boxed{.3}$. Click Apply. The
probability, .05, will be in the Report window.]

(1) $.2 < X < .3$

(2) X is positive

(3) $X < -.3$

(4) $X \geq .72$

(5) $.2 \leq X < .4$

8.5 Calculate the following probabilities by hand
for the uniform distribution defined over the interval
$[a,b]$. Let c and d be two positive numbers such that
$0 < a < c < d < b$. Complement each answer with
a diagram that shows the area under the probability
distribution function that you are computing.

a. $c \leq X \leq d$

b. $a \leq X < \frac{a+b}{2}$

c. $\frac{a+b}{2} < X \leq b$

d. $a < X < \frac{a}{4} + \frac{3}{4}b$

e. $\frac{3}{4}a + \frac{b}{4} < X \leq b$

f. What are the values of the first and third quartiles of this distribution? What is the value of the
first quintile?

8.6 A car dealer sells used 1996 Ford Tauruses.
The value of this model could range between a
minimum of $10,000 (the "lemon") and a maxi-
mum of $15,000 (the "peach"). The car dealer will
never reveal the car's past (who drove it, how
many accidents it had, and so on) so any value is
equally likely. Without any prior knowledge of the
car's quality:

a. What is the expected value of a 1996 Ford
Taurus bought from this dealer?

b. Would you buy one of these cars from this
dealer at $13,000? Justify your answer.

c. Would you buy one of these cars at $11,000?
Why?

d. Provide an interval centered in the total range of
dollar values in which you would expect to find
half of the cars sold at this venue.

e. Provide an interval centered in the total range of
dollar values in which you would expect 75% of
the cars sold at this venue. (*Hint:* This is the interquartile range.)

f. For this distribution, give the interval for which
the Chebyshev inequality would imply that at least
75% of the cars are contained in it. Compare it
with the result of the previous question. (*Hint:*
This interval is the one given by two standard deviations from the left and the right of the mean.)

Exploring the Tools

8.7 It is easy to calculate, using calculus, the theoretical moments for the uniform distribution.
Before doing this exercise, review Appendix A.5,

"Elements of Calculus." Consider the particular case where $0 \leq X \leq 1$ and the density function is

$$f(X)dx = dx$$

so that

$$E\{X\} = \int_0^1 X dx = \frac{1}{2}X^2 \Big|_0^1 = \frac{1}{2}$$

Find $\mu_2(X)$, $\mu_3(X)$, and $\mu_4(X)$. (*Hint:* Expand the powers first and evaluate each integral in turn and then simplify.) Calculate α_1 and α_2 for this distribution.

8.8 (For the student with calculus) Using the uniform distribution for $-1 \leq X \leq 1$, the density function is

$$f(X)dx = \frac{dx}{1 - (-1)} = \frac{dx}{2}$$

Note that

$$E\{X\} = \frac{1}{2} \int_{-1}^1 X dx = \frac{1}{4}X^2 \Big|_{-1}^1 = 0$$

Find the probability, using calculus, where necessary, that

a. $X \leq 0$

b. $X = -1$

c. $X \leq .5$

8.9 Using the same uniform distribution as in Exercise 8.8—namely, for $-1 \leq X \leq 1$, $f(x)$ is uniform—obtain the first four moments and α_1 and α_2. Compare your results with those obtained for the uniform distribution defined over $[0, 1]$. In both cases, sketch the distribution. Comment.

8.10 Recall that for the standard normal distribution, the probability $Z \leq -4$ and the probability $Z \geq 4$ are both nearly zero. Compute the probabilities for X, distributed as uniform over the interval $[-4, 4]$ for the intervals: $[-4, -3]$, $[-3, -2]$, $[-2, -1]$, $[-1, 1]$, $[1, 2]$, $[2, 3]$, and $[3, 4]$.

Compare the probabilities obtained with those obtained for the standard normal distribution. Sketch the two density functions, and interpret your results.

8.11 In the text, we used the normal distribution to approximate the binomial distribution for $\pi = .5$ and $n = 100$. The standard deviation for the binomial distribution is given by $\sqrt{\pi(1 - \pi)n}$ and the mean is $n\pi$. Calculate the binomial and approximate normal probabilities for K, the binomial random variable, for $\pi = .2, .5, .7$ and $n = 30, 60$ for the following values of K:

a. $K \leq \text{mean} - 2.5$ standard deviations

b. $K \leq \text{mean} - 1.75$ standard deviations

c. $K \leq \text{mean} - .75$ standard deviations

d. $K \geq \text{mean} + 2.5$ standard deviations

e. $K \geq \text{mean} + 1.75$ standard deviations

f. $K \geq \text{mean} + .75$ standard deviations

Comment on your results in detail with respect to the degree of accuracy of the approximation of the normal for the binomial. Remember that you are comparing the binomial probabilities with those calculated for the normal density function with the same mean and standard deviation.

8.12 Why is $\text{pr}(Z \geq 2.35) = \text{pr}(Z > 2.35)$ for any continuous random variable Z, where " $>$ " implies "greater than, but not equal to"?

8.13 *Worked. Objective: To explore the continuous uniform distribution as a function of its endpoints.*

[*Computer directions:* Start S-Plus. On the menu bar, click on <u>Labs, How are Populations Distributed?</u>. In the dialog box, set Distribution Family to Uniform and Lab Option to Curves. Click Apply. You will see four alternative uniform distributions defined by different endpoints. Print the Graph. In the dialog box, set Lab Option to Simulated Data. Click Apply. The 500 simulated data observations are displayed in a histogram. Note the values of the sample moments that are printed on the graph.]

Repeat this experiment several times with simulated data to get a feel for the variation in the observed histograms over repeated trials. Each trial will use a different set of randomly generated simulated data.

We have repeatedly stressed the relationship between shape and the moments; in this exercise we extend that relationship to the parameters of a distribution. We have three related characteristics of a distribution: shape, moments, and parameters.

8.14 *Worked. Objective: To explore the dependence of the normal distribution on its parameters.*

[*Computer directions:* Start S-Plus. On the menu bar, click on Labs, How are Populations Distributed?. In the dialog box, set Distribution Family to Normal and Lab Option to Curves. Click Apply. Notice that although the mean and spread may change as indicated in the graphs, the shape of the distribution is always the same. Set Lab Option to Simulated data, and click Apply to see a histogram of 500 observations.]

Repeat the experiment with simulated data several times by repeatedly clicking Apply. You will get a feel for the variation in the observed histograms over repeated trials with new sets of data.

We have repeatedly stressed the relationship between shape and the moments; in this exercise we extend that relationship to the parameters of a distribution. We have three related characteristics of a distribution: shape, moments, and parameters.

8.15 *Worked. Objective: To illustrate the central limit theorem.*

[*Computer directions:* Start S-Plus. On the menu bar, click on Labs, Central Limit Theorem.

a. In the dialog box, set Choice to Parent-Curves. (The other boxes are not active when Parent-Curves is selected). Click Apply. The resulting plot

shows the four distributions from which the samples will be drawn.

b. Return to the dialog box, set Choice to "500 samples," set Sample from to "Uniform," set Sample Size to "10," and click Apply.] The resulting graph shows a histogram of sample means of size 10 from the uniform distribution; 500 sample means have been generated for the histogram. The normal curve with the same mean and second moment as would be calculated from the properties of the uniform distribution is superimposed in red on the graph. Repeated clicking on Apply will generate new histograms of 500 observations of sample means of size 10 for the uniform distribution.

c. Experiment with various values for Sample Size.

The central limit theorem is one of the most important concepts in all of statistics, but it takes a long familiarity with the concept to really understand it. This exercise prepares you for obtaining that understanding.

8.16 Repeat Exercise 8.15 using the Exponential distribution. [In the "Sample from" box, click on Exponential(1).]

8.17 Repeat Exercise 8.16 using the "0-1 distribution," known as the "Point Nomial," which is the same as the binomial with $n = 1$ and $\pi = .5$. [In the "Sample from" box, click on "0-1".]

8.18 *Worked. Objective: To compare the dependence of convergence to normal across different types of distributions.* If you have completed the previous exercises, you will have gained considerable insight into the effect of the central limit theorem. For each of the distributions listed, the distribution of the mean converges to the normal, but the rate will differ, depending on the nature of the parent distribution.

[*Computer directions:* Start S-Plus. On the menu bar, click on Labs, Central Limit Theorem. Choose a low value for Sample Size to begin, say 5, and set Choice to "500 samples." Set "Sample from" one by one to the uniform, Exponential, and 0-1 distributions. Print each graph in turn. Examine the histograms produced for the different distributions. Increment the sample size used to calculate the mean from each distribution and repeat. Print each graph in turn.]

In light of these results, comment on the dependence of the central limit theorem on the sample size and form of the parent distributions.

This exercise explores the different rates at which normality is approached, depending on the shape of the parent distribution.

8.19   Worked. *Objective: To illustrate the normal approximation to the binomial probability distribution.*

[**Computer directions:** Start S-Plus. On the menu bar, click on Labs, Sampling From 0-1 Populations, Approximating Binomial Probabilities, Normal Approximation. In the dialog box, set $n = 10$ and pi = .5. Click Apply. Print the graph.]

a. Repeat the directions, setting: $n = 40$ and pi = .5, $n = 40$ and pi = .25, $n = 10$ and pi = .25, $n = 5$ and pi = .25, $n = 10$ and pi = .01, $n = 40$ and pi = .01.

b. Examine your graphs, and comment on the normal approximation to the binomial as a function of n and pi.

This exercise illustrates one of the more important examples of the approximation of one distribution by another.

8.20   Worked: For the student who is comfortable with calculus. In Chapter 7, in Section 7.5, we introduced the idea of expectation. And in Exercise 7.57, we explored in the context of discrete random variables the notion of "transformation of variables." In this exercise, we reconsider that idea in the context of continuous random variables. Recognize that the same basic principles apply here as well; the key is to equate probabili-

ties. Review Exercise 7.57 at this time. We begin with a general statement of the problem.

Consider that we have a continuous random variable X and another continuous random variable Y that is related to X by the function $Y = h(X)$. Let the density function for X be denoted by $f(X)$ and that for Y by $g(Y)$; our task is to discover what $g(.)$ is.

Consider a small interval in the domain for X, call it I_X, $I_X = [x', x' + \Delta x]$, so that the probability for X to lie in the interval I_X is given by the area under the density function $f(X)$ over the interval I_X—that is, between the bounds $[x', x' + \Delta x]$. The length of this interval is Δx. We can also consider a corresponding interval for the variable Y; $I_Y = [h(x'), h(x' + \Delta x)]$ and the probability of observing Y in this interval is given by the area under the density function over this interval. The length of this interval is Δy. The two probabilities are the same as they represent the same subset of the sample space but expressed in different "units." We have, using the symbol "$\in$" to indicate "belonging to":

$$\text{pr}\{X \in I_X\}\} = \text{pr}(Y \in I_Y) \tag{8.59}$$

We have

$$\text{pr}\{X \in I_X\}\} \simeq f(x')\Delta x$$

and

$$\text{pr}(Y \in I_Y) \simeq g(y')\Delta y$$
$$= g(h(x'))[h(x' + \Delta x) - h(x')]$$

For small Δx, we have:

$$f(x')\Delta x \simeq g(h(x'))\Delta y \tag{8.60}$$

or

$$f(x') \simeq g(h(x'))\frac{\Delta y}{\Delta x}$$

And we now have

$$\lim_{\Delta x \to 0} \frac{\Delta y}{\Delta x} =$$

$$\lim_{\Delta x \to 0} \frac{[h(x' + \Delta x) - h(x')]}{\Delta x} = h'(x') \tag{8.61}$$

We have assumed for simplicity that $h(x' + \Delta x) > h(x')$ and that the required limits exist. If $h(x' + \Delta x) < h(x')$, the limit becomes $-h'(x')$. However, all we need is to obtain the ratio of scales between the intervals I_X and I_Y, so that we only need the absolute value of the rate of change between Y and X. Substituting this last result into the equations yields:

$$f(x') = g(h(x')) \times |h'(x')| \tag{8.62}$$

An easy way to remember this result is that to convert $f(X)dX$ to $g(Y)dY$, where $Y = g(X)$, we need to consider the rate of change between Y and X, dY/dX, so that

$$f(X)dX = g(h(X))\frac{dY}{dX}dX$$
$$= g(Y)dY \tag{8.63}$$

An example will help. This first example is in fact very important in the theory of statistics. In the preceding general discussion, consider the function $h(X)$ to be the integral of $f(X)$ itself; that is, we define

$$Y = h(X) = \int_{-\infty}^{X} f(u)du \tag{8.64}$$

so that

$$\frac{dY}{dX} = f(X) \tag{8.65}$$

and the domain for the variable Y is $[0,1]$. We do not have to consider the absolute value in this case because the function $h(X)$ in this case is one that never decreases; the derivative is always positive. Substituting Equation 8.65 into Equation 8.63, we derive

$$dY = g(Y)dY$$

or

$$g(Y) \equiv 1$$

We have shown that the density function for Y as we have defined it is the uniform distribution for continuous random variables over the interval $[0,1]$.

Note that this result is true for any density function $f(X)$ for which the transformation is defined.

Here is a slightly more complex example. Let X be a standard normal distribution. We have

$$\phi(X) = \frac{e^{-\frac{X^2}{2}}}{\sqrt{2\pi}}$$

Let our transformation be defined by $W = X^2$. The inverse transformation is $X = \pm\sqrt{W}$, and here we have a difficulty in that the transformation is not "one to one"; that is, for each value of W there correspond two values for X, one positive and one negative. Because the normal distribution is symmetric, we can easily solve this problem in that over each of the intervals $(-\infty, 0)$ and $(0, \infty)$ the transformation is one to one. So, we can assign half the probability to one interval and half to the other. We have first the result:

$$\left|\frac{dX}{dW}\right| = \left|\frac{d(-\sqrt{W})}{dW}\right| = \left|\frac{d\sqrt{W}}{dW}\right| = \frac{1}{2\sqrt{W}}$$

so that the density function for W is

$$g(W) = \frac{1}{2\sqrt{W}}\left\{\frac{e^{-\frac{W}{2}}}{\sqrt{2\pi}} + \frac{e^{-\frac{W}{2}}}{\sqrt{2\pi}}\right\} \tag{8.66}$$
$$= \frac{1}{\sqrt{2\pi}}W^{-\frac{1}{2}}e^{-\frac{W}{2}}$$

This result is a special case of a distribution that we will meet more generally in Chapter 10; it is the chi-square distribution, defined in this case with what is called "1 degree of freedom."

Applications

8.21 Consider the data in folder Wheatpr, file French.xls, and in particular the variable *price* for the French wheat price data.

a. After calculating the first four moments, the third and fourth standardized, and plotting the histogram, do you think that the Gaussian distribution is a better fit than the uniform distribution?

b. How does your assessment change if you look at the log of prices?

[*Computer hint:* In S-Plus, to create the log of *price*, with file French.xls open, click on Data, Transform. Enter a column name, and in Expression, key in log(price) . Click Apply.]

c. Reevaluate your conclusions after examining the distribution and moments of the *priceind* variable and its log for the European data in the Europe.xls file in the same folder.

8.22 *Worked. Objective: To illustrate the central limit theorem.* In the previous exercise, you calculated the first four moments for the price of French wheat and for a European index. The central limit theorem tells us that averages of these prices will be distributed a lot closer to Gaussian than the raw data. In this exercise, we will evaluate this idea.

The Central Limit Theorem in Text Routines performs the following steps when applied to the French wheat data. Random selections at various sample sizes are made from the 370 French wheat price data. The selection is repeated 100 times, drawing each time a random sample of size 5, 10, 20, 40, and 60. The means of these 100 sample observations are then calculated.

$$\bar{X}_5 = \frac{1}{5}\sum_{1}^{5} X_i, \ \bar{X}_{10} = \frac{1}{10}\sum_{1}^{10} X_i, \ldots$$

Histograms of the means for each sample size are plotted. The standardized moments are calculated.

[*Computer directions:* On the menu bar, click on Text Routines, Central Limit Theorem. In the dialog, select Data Frame French. In Variable, select "price." Click OK. Five histograms will be generated. The Report window contains one row for each specified sample size. The six entries in each row are the first four moments; the last two entries are the standardized third and fourth moments.]

Examine the sequence of histograms carefully and draw your conclusions.

Here, you get to observe the effect of the central limit theorem with real data relevant to economic analysis.

8.23 Repeat the previous exercise using the six-month bill rate (*bill6mo*) and the five-year note (*note5yr*) in the Monyld.xls file in the Intrate folder. Comment on your results.

8.24 In the file Monyld.xls in the Intrate folder, are the interest rate variables, or their logarithms, distributed more nearly to the Gaussian or to the uniform distribution? How can you tell?

8.25 In the folder Gnp, use the subfolder Domgnp, file Domgnp.xls. In this file are the variables Gross National Product (*gnp*), Gross National Product per capita (*gnppc*), unemployment (*unemp*), consumer price index(*cpi*), and the real wage(*rwage*). All these variables are indices of time series and clearly are continuous random variables. In trying to decide on the appropriate distribution, examine the related question whether some transformations of the raw data are more nearly distributed as Gaussian or as uniform than the original data.

a. For each of the variables, plot and print the histograms and calculate the first four moments, especially the standardized moments. Comment on the extent to which the Gaussian distribution or the uniform distribution seems to be a reasonable choice.

b. Next, convert each variable into a growth rate; that is for each variable x_t, calculate $xgth_t = (x_t - x_t - 1)/x_t - 1$. Using the growth rates, generate the histograms and calculate the first four moments and the standardized moments. Compare your results very carefully with those obtained using the raw data.

[*Computer directions:* To generate a variable for the growth rate of *gnp*, highlight column "gnp." Click on Copy. Highlight the second cell of a new column. Click Paste. Double click on the new column name, and key in gnplag . Enter. On the menu bar, click on Data, Transform. In the dialog in New Column Name, key in gnpg . In Expression, key in (gnp-gnplag)/gnplag . Click Apply. The new column, gnpg, will be in the Domgnp data frame. Repeat for each variable using appropriate names, and in Expression substitute the correct variable names. The histograms can be plotted by highlighting the growth rate column to be graphed and clicking on Graph, 2D Plot, Histogram. Click OK.]

c. Take a natural logarithm of each variable and using the log, generate the histograms and calculate the first four moments and the standardized moments.

[*Computer directions:* To generate a variable for the log of *gnp*, on the menu bar, click on Data, Transform. In New Column Name, key in gnpl. In Expression, key in log(gnp). Click Apply. Repeat for each variable. The histograms can be plotted by highlighting the log column to be graphed and clicking on Graph, 2D Plot, Histogram. Click OK.]

Compare your results with those obtained using the raw data.

d. Finally, examine in the same manner the first differences in the logs and repeat the exercise.

[*Computer directions* to calculate the first differences in the logs: Use the logs calculated in (*c*). Highlight column "gnpl." Click on Copy. Highlight the second cell of a new column. Click Paste. Highlight the name of the new column, and key in gnpllag. Enter. On the menu bar, click on Data, Transform. In the dialog in New Column name, key in gnpld. In Expression, key in (gnpl-gnpllag)/gnpllag. Click Apply. Repeat for all four variables in this exercise, replacing with appropriate new variable names. Create histograms of the first differences in the logs. Print the graphs.]

What do you conclude about the Gaussian or uniform distribution as useful approximations of these various transformations of the data?

e. Mathematically, what is the relationship between the variables defined in (b) and (d)?

8.26 Consider the data in the Testscor folder. Use the four variables *psatmath*, *psatverb*, *satmath*, and *satverb* in the Psatsat.xls file. Examine only the SAT variables. Are they best described by the uniform or the Gaussian distribution? What evidence do you bring to bear on this problem?

8.27 Repeat the central limit theorem experiment outlined in Exercise 8.22 using the *satmath* and the *satverb* scores in the Psatsat.xls file.

8.28 Summarize the similarities and differences in the distributions of *satmath* and *satverb* scores. What do you conclude from this evidence? How best can you summarize the similarities and differences in the distributions for the SAT scores and the PSAT scores?

8.29 In the folder Gnp, use the folder Domgnp, file Domgnp.xls. For each of the variables real gnp (*rgnp*), industrial production (*indprod*), employment level (*emp*), money supply (*money*), and velocity (*vel*) examine the extent to which the variables, the growth rates, the logs of the variables, and the first differences in the logs are distributed as Gaussian. (See Exercise 8.25 for computer directions.)

Given these empirical results, what conclusions do you draw about the relevance of the Gaussian distribution to these GNP data?

8.30 Case Study: Was There Age Discrimination in a Public Utility?

Much of the discussion in the discrimination case involves the distribution of salaries and ages. Underlying any statistical analysis using these variables will be assumptions about the types of distribution that are involved. Examine both the age and salary variables for all individuals in the Discdata.xls data set in the Agedisc folder, and provide arguments for and against that these two variables are distributed as Gaussian. Produce both theoretical and empirical arguments in support of your conclusions.

P A R T   F O U R

Basic Principles of Inference

CHAPTER 9

Elementary Sampling Theory

9.1   What You Will Learn in This Chapter

This chapter introduces the third part of our development of statistics and statistical theory. In the first five chapters we showed how to describe data in a parsimonious manner. In Chapters 6 through 8, we developed the underlying theory in terms of probability theory and the related theory of distributions and density functions. In this chapter, we begin the process of linking these two branches together. This chapter introduces the notion of *inference,* even though we will not formally define it until Chapter 10.

We achieve this task by defining the concept of a "sample." We now recognize that all the data that we examined in the first five chapters represented samples, or "drawings" from some theoretical distribution. **Inference** is the task of trying to infer from actual observations—that is, from a sample—the precise relevant theoretical distribution; this in turn is achieved by inferring the values of the parameters of the distribution. Sampling is the physical process by which one achieves that result, and statistical theory provides the necessary framework. The study of sampling indicates the circumstances under which we can validly relate what we observe to our theoretical statements and assess the probability of our errors.

We begin the analysis by considering very large samples, so we can ignore variations due to the sampling process. We then move to cases where we have only modest-sized samples and examine the statistical properties of our observations. We conclude by indicating alternative sampling procedures designed to reduce the variance of errors of inference in special circumstances.

9.2   Introduction

Because we are about to embark on a new phase of our development of statistical theory, we should briefly review our progress to date. As you recall, our first task was to discover how to summarize actual data. That task led to the discovery that histograms had definite shapes and that those shapes seemed to be related to the type of experiment, or survey, that was under consideration. Further, we saw that the moments that we calculated were able to characterize the shape of histograms quite well; specific shapes of histograms led to specific values for the moments.

Our next task was to generate a "theory of the shape of histograms"—that is, probability theory. This exploration led to the generation of probability distribution functions and density functions. With respect to these theoretical constructs, we derived an analogue to moments—namely, theoretical moments. We saw that the theoretical moments, like the moments of histograms, characterize the shape of probability distribution functions and density functions. Further, and more important, we saw that probability distribution functions and density functions each depended on a small number of parameters that summarized the effects of the specification of the underlying prototypical experiment. Thus, we now see that by defining the conditions of a hypothetical experiment, we implicitly specify the values of the parameters of the probability distribution function as well as specifying the function itself. Consequently, we also see that this specification leads to a particular set of values for the theoretical moments and that the values of the theoretical moments depend on the values of the parameters in the probability distribution function.

So far, to illustrate the theoretical ideas that we have been discussing, we have casually and informally compared the shape of the theoretical probability distribution function or density function to the shape of a histogram of data generated by an actual experiment. Until now we have had no real justification for doing this, but the practice seemed to be a natural extension of our intention to use theoretical ideas to explain what we observe. Nevertheless, the practice was rewarding because we discovered a seemingly close fit between the theoretical probability distribution function and the actual observed histogram.

This experience suggests our next step: to figure out how to relate our theoretical ideas to what we observe and to discover how to interpret, or "explain," what it is that we see in real situations. In short, we want to work out how to link theory and practice. Numbers are numbers; what counts is how we interpret them. Theory is needed to interpret what we see. Theory is also needed to enable us to extrapolate from what we actually observe to be able to make statements about events that we have not observed; that is, we wish to draw "inferences from the data."

We now wish to address the following types of problems: If we observe a sequence of numbers, how do we know what probability distribution function applies; that is, what prototypical experiment might have generated the data actually observed? If we think that we know the relevant probability distribution function, how do we check that we are right? Even if we know the probability distribution function that applies, how do we discover the specific values of the parameters that are usually left unspecified by the experimenter? If we have a small number of observations, how do we use them to facilitate making decisions that involve knowledge about the future occurrence of the same type of event? Lastly, what specific procedures do we use to link theoretical constructs to the outcomes of particular experiments? We will try to answer the last question first, simply because its solution provides the basis for everything else that we will do in the text. The questions involving the type of distribution that is relevant are much more difficult to answer and require analytical tools that can only be obtained in a more advanced course.

The process of acquiring observations in accordance with a particular probability distribution function is called **sampling,** and the theory of that process is called **sampling theory.** The theory of sampling specifies (1) those conditions under which we can relate probability theory to the outcomes of particular experiments and (2) procedures to implement the link between theory and observation.

Some of the questions that we raised here are answered in the theory of inference that is to follow. Those answers will rely heavily on the answers that we will produce in this chapter. For example, the theory of inference uses the results of the theory of sampling to show how to make statements about the specific values taken by the parameters of a probability distribution function based on the observation of experimental outcomes.

9.3   An Illustrative Example

Suppose that you are trying to choose a publisher for your hot new novel that involves a number of tricky puns and subtle clues as to the true identity of the murderer. Consequently, you are most anxious to be sure that the publisher will produce as few typographical mistakes as possible. Being a realist, or at least having taken the first part of this course, you recognize that finding a publisher with no errors is impossible, or should we say, "finding an error-free publisher is an event with nearly zero probability." You also know that the incidence of errors is most likely to be random, in that you cannot predict the errors and that you cannot even predict how many errors that any given publisher will produce. Besides, the number of errors is likely to vary from book to book in an unpredictable fashion, at least for the type of books that we are now discussing; although a book on statistics is likely to have far more errors than a book without all those queer symbols!

Let us also suppose that by dint of careful and diligent research, or simply by asking the black sheep of your family, who happens to be a statistician, you learn that the relevant probability distribution function is the Poisson probability distribution. But you do not know the value of the parameter, λ. Let us be sure what it is that we do know. When we say that we know that the relevant probability distribution function is the Poisson probability distribution, we are really saying that an examination of the mechanism generating errors in a publishing house seems to be very similar to the prototypical experiment that we used to generate the theoretical distribution called the Poisson probability distribution. Clearly, whether or not the Poisson probability distribution does apply to your situation is a matter of fact, not of theory. For now we will skip this difficult issue and assume that we have convinced ourselves that the Poisson probability distribution does indeed apply to our specific case.

We now come to the key issue. How can we use our theory when we do not know the value of the parameter, λ? What can we do? Seemingly, the only avenue open to us is to see if we can use actual data from a particular publisher to discover something about the value of λ. This comment raises a tricky question: What data and how is it collected? In our situation, an observation is the number of errors in a

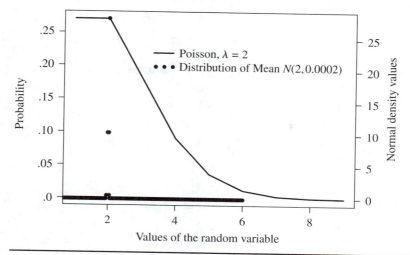

Figure 9.1   Comparison of a Poisson distribution, $\lambda = 2$, with the normal approximation to the mean using 10,000 observations

block of pages, say 100; that is, we will observe in a given block of pages 0, or 1, or 2, or 3, or more errors. We record the number of errors in that block, and that is our first observation. We will need to repeat this experiment n times with different blocks of pages to obtain a set of n observations on our error process.

Now if we had a huge amount of data, we could plot the histogram and then see which theoretical probability distribution function had the most similar shape; but that does not seem to be a very practical method. To apply it we really do need a lot of data. If we had a single observation, what could we learn from that? We know that the probability distribution function of errors is a Poisson probability distribution so that we can call our first observation our first "drawing" from our Poisson probability distribution with unknown λ. Say that we get an observation of "3." What does that mean? Not much, for we could have obtained any value at all. If you look at Figure 9.1 you see that with a λ value of 2, you can easily get on a drawing any number between 0 and about 8. But maybe what we should look for is a most likely value—that is, that value with the highest probability. When we plotted the probability distribution functions for the Poisson for various values of λ, we saw that the most likely value was certainly below the value of the mean of the distribution, which is λ. So maybe we could interpret our drawing as a lower bound on the value of λ. But as we say this, it is beginning to be clear that this procedure is not very satisfactory either.

We need to rethink the situation. You may remember that in deriving the normal distribution, we had to rescale the variance as a function of n, the number of terms in the sum. Let us recall from Chapter 8 our calculation of the variance of the random variable, $\bar{X}$, defined by $\bar{X} = (\Sigma X_i)/n$, where the X_i were n independently and identically distributed random variables. If you recollect, $\mu_2(\bar{X})$ was σ^2/n, where σ^2 is the second moment of the X_i. Now as $n \to \infty$, $\mu_2(\bar{X})$ gets to be very small; indeed, we

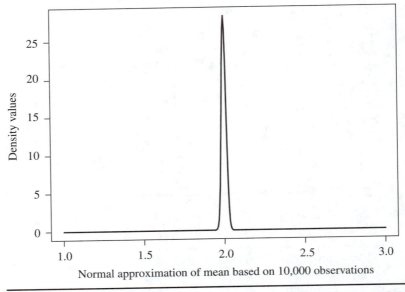

Density values

Normal approximation of mean based on 10,000 observations

Figure 9.2   Zoom view of the normal approximation to the mean shown in Figure 9.1

could get the variance to go to zero, at least approximately. If the variance of $\bar{X}$ is nearly zero, then whatever the value of the random variable $\bar{X}$ that we might observe, it cannot be very far from its mean. We already know that the mean of $\bar{X}$ is λ, when the mean of the individual X_i is λ. Now this looks like a promising line of attack, so let us pursue it.

The basic idea is simplicity itself. If we collect a very large number of observations on the process and calculate a mean of those observations, then we know from our theory that the theoretical distribution that is associated with that definition of a random variable has a mean of λ and a variance of λ/n, because the second moment of a Poisson random variable is also λ. If that is the case and we select, say, 10,000 observations from our publisher and calculate their mean, then whatever value we obtain, we will know that the probability is high that our mean value is not far from the unknown value of λ. For example, suppose that the unknown value of λ is 2. The variance of a random variable that is created by adding up 10,000 independent random variables, each having a Poisson probability distribution with parameter λ, is by our previous work, $\lambda/10,000$. In this case, the variance is $2/10,000 = .0002$; so the standard deviation is about .0141. Now look again at Figure 9.1, which shows two graphs overlaid. The first graph is the theoretical probability distribution for a Poisson with parameter $\lambda = 2$. The other graph in Figure 9.1 is the graph of the theoretical probability distribution function for the random variable defined by $\Sigma X_i/n$, where each X_i has a Poisson probability distribution with parameter $\lambda = 2$ and $n = 10,000$. As you can see very easily, a drawing from this distribution, indeed any drawing at all, no matter how improbable, will yield a value that is very close to the unknown parameter value for λ. Figure 9.2 shows the approximate normal distribution for the

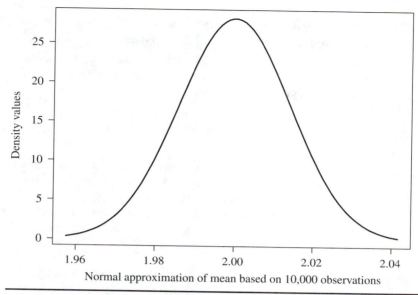

Figure 9.3   Zoom view of the normal approximation to the mean shown in Figures 9.1 and 9.2

mean but at an enlarged scale. The scale in Figure 9.1 is from 0 to 9 and in Figure 9.2 from 1 to 3. Figure 9.2 clearly demonstrates the small degree of variation about the value "2." Figure 9.3 shows yet a further enlargement; the range here is from 1.96 to 2.04, and now the normality of the approximating distribution is clear.

This simple idea is at the root of all the discussion of sampling theory that is to come. If you understand this example, then you will have no problem with everything that is to follow.

Let us return to the beginning of our example to discover any pitfalls that we might face. Our insight into how we can discover an unknown value of some parameter requires some careful handling. For a start we need to be sure when collecting our data that the relevant distribution is the same throughout the collection process. We also require that the random variables be independent. But before we even begin the process of trying to confront our theories with actual data, we should be sure that our theory is in fact relevant. For example, do we really believe that there is only one distribution involved? Surely, the error rate for technical books is higher than it is for novels. Is it not plausible that the error rate is higher at night than during the day? What if the firm hires an incompetent typesetter; would not the error rate rise? If the typesetter tends to exchange "*i*" and "*e*" in his work, then we will not have independence between the occurrence of events. All of this is to demonstrate that as soon as you begin to try to relate your theory to actual data and real experiments, then problems arise that require careful attention. The theory of sampling is in large part a prescription to avoid the worst of some of these problems. It is also an attempt to clarify the procedures required to be able to perform the trick we successfully used here to "infer" the value of the unknown parameter.

9.4 An Introduction to the Theory of Simple Random Sampling

What is our task? Actually, there are two related tasks that we face. The first is to identify the circumstances under which we can be fairly sure that a single probability distribution applies. The second task is to be sure that we obtain our observations in such a way that

- We do not change the relevant probability distribution
- The sequence of observations is represented by a set of independent random variables.

These requirements arise out of our successful attempt with the publisher example. The current discussion is needed to see how to abstract from the details of the example to provide a general strategy that will be of wide use. The key to our prior success is that one, and only one, distribution was involved in the process and that independence was maintained over the repetitions of the "experiment"—that is, our survey of the publishing house. To proceed, it will be useful to clarify the discussion with some new concepts.

We should define the words *sampling* and *sample*. A **sample** is a "drawing of observations" from some probability distribution function; that is, when we run an experiment, or observe some experiment "run by nature," or if we survey people or objects, the observations are meant to be realizations, or outcomes, of an actual experiment that is very close in design to one of our prototype experiments. The idea in all cases is that there is some experiment that is assumed to be generating the observations (although to be accurate this idea is seldom explicitly stated). We say that some theoretical probability distribution function is postulated to "describe, or predict," the properties of the outcomes. The observations are often said to be "realizations" of the theoretical probability distribution function. We have a language for the theory, but we do not yet have a language for the process of acquiring data in accordance with our theory; the vocabulary of sampling provides that language. It is important to recognize that we are acquiring data in a particular way. Again, the acquiring of data in accordance with our theory is called *sampling*. So when we sample, we are trying to obtain observations on, or from, a given specific probability distribution function. The observations so obtained are called collectively, the sample.

When we take a sample, we obtain a set of observations on which we will perform numerous calculations, just as we did in our example. Each of these is called a **statistic;** a statistic is a function of the sample values. The simplest statistic is a single observation. From our theory and assuming that the theory is applicable, we know that if we take many samples, they will all probably be different; the probability of there being two samples the same is small. Why is this? We are dealing with random variables, so we do not expect to be able to predict the actual values that we obtain in any specific sample, or set of "realizations" of the probability distribution function. This idea applies, even when we are obtaining observations by taking a survey, or collecting information on, or about, a specific group of objects, or people.

In each case, our strategy is to postulate the existence of a probability distribution function so that we can characterize the observations as "realizations" of that probability distribution function. Suppose that we are observing the eye color of a group of people. Our strategy is to regard our observations of eye color as realizations of a discrete probability distribution function. When we begin we may not know what the probability distribution function is, but we proceed on the presumption that there is an underlying probability distribution function to be discovered. Further, we proceed on the presumption that the observations on eye color will provide us with the information needed to discover the probability distribution function and the value of its parameters, provided, of course, that we have enough data.

Often, this process of discovering the relevant probability distribution function is not easy. For example, consider the situation where we have a pond containing fish; we wish to know something about the distribution of different types of fish in the pond. If we are only interested in this particular pond and are not concerned about extending our information to any other pond, then one view is that whatever fish are in this pond, they are the fish in the pond. What you see is what you have.

We could say that in this case we have a "finite population" of fish in the pond. One can take this viewpoint, but such a viewpoint is limiting in terms of the inferences that one can make. If one regards the specific fish in the pond at some particular instant in time as a "population," then one cannot make any inferences about the fish in the pond at any other time. After all, even if the distribution of fish by type remains the same the actual fish in the pond will change over time. It is, therefore, far better to assume that the actual fish in the pond at a particular point in time is itself a sample from an underlying hypothetical distribution of fish.

If we take the naive viewpoint that what is in the pond is what is in the pond—that is, we have a *particular* finite population—we lose the benefits of most of the theory that we have been developing. We cut ourselves off from many interpretations and insights that we can obtain from our theory. In addition, we should recognize that with a particular finite population, the very process of sampling may alter the population itself. Consider, for example, our pond and see that as we take fish out of the pond, we are changing the composition of the fish population. Of course, if we throw all the fish back no great damage is done, and we might then claim that we have a sample of a given finite population of fish in a particular pond at a specific date.

But, such an approach is very limiting. We are restricted to a very specific population, and we would then be very limited in what it is we could say more generally. The way out is to recognize the fish in the given pond at a particular point in time as a sample itself from a hypothetical population of fish. We do this by postulating a hypothetical probability distribution of fish from which the actual fish in the pond are to be regarded as drawings from that distribution.

A probability distribution function provides far more information than does a histogram. For example, we can usefully pose such questions as what would be the distribution of fish if the size of the pond were to be halved. This question might be very important because the other half of the pond is needed for construction and the pond supposedly contains some rare subspecies of fish. This problem is amenable to analysis by use of our probability theory, but if we take the naive view, we are stuck with descriptive statements of the existing pond as it is. We are not justified in making any statements about the fish composition if there is any alteration at all to the pond. In fact, logically we cannot make any statements about the fish composition of this particular pond at any other time, like next month. We avoid all such barriers to extrapolating our knowledge, by taking the logical route of postulating an appropriate underlying probability distribution function, whose properties we seek to discover as best we can from observations on the current fish population in the pond. Besides, even from a practical viewpoint, the pond is not a fixed entity. It is instead composed of actual fish that breed and die constantly, so that in a sense, we are forced into taking the probability route. Only in this way can we pose in a meaningful way the idea of a constant composition of types but a continually changing population of actual identifiable fish.

We have defined a statistic as a function of the sample values. If you think back to the beginning of this text, you will remember that we spent a lot of time calculating things that we called "moments"; we now recognize, provided that there is an underlying probability distribution function, that those moments were, in fact, statistics! We began the course by calculating statistics but without calling them that at the time. To help distinguish them from the theoretical moments, we will also know them as **sample moments.** If you are beginning to think that we are merely adding new words without distinction, the following examples of statistics will clarify the idea that statistics is a general term of which sample moments are a particular instance:

$$\log \left(\sum x_i \right)$$

$$e^{ax}$$

$$\cos(x^2)$$

are all examples of functions of the data and so are statistics, but they are not sample moments.

Let us return to our main task of determining the conditions under which we can learn from our data guided by our probability theory. Our first task is to ensure that a single well-defined probability distribution function is applicable to our situation. For example, in our publishing illustration, we have already speculated on the problems involved in trying to specify the conditions of our survey, so that we could be reasonably sure that a single Poisson distribution held. Although this part of the sampling process is sometimes not discussed in textbooks, it is in fact the most important part of the process of acquiring, or generating, observations on random variables.

Let us now assume that we have indeed managed to define our problem so that we are sure that a single, known, probability distribution function applies. However, what we do not know are the values of the parameters contained in that distribution. Our next task is to specify how to obtain a set of observations on the random process—that is, obtain a sample, such that we can use it to learn about the unknown parameter values.

There are three basic criteria that we should apply to the sampling process. The first is to be sure that a single probability distribution function continues to be relevant while the experiment, or survey, is being carried out. By extension of this idea, the results of our analysis of the sample may be used in the future, or in different circumstances, so that if our results are to be relevant, we need some assurance that the same probability distribution function will still apply. For example, if we were to observe typographers in training at a given publishing house, then we would expect to see the error rate change over time; that is, the relevant probability distribution function would change while we gathered the data. The Poisson may still be the relevant type of distribution, but the parameter value would be changing. As the typographers learn, the mean error rate will fall; alternatively expressed, λ decreases. A more subtle example is provided by the situation in which you collect information on, say, highly technical books, and then try to use the results for books written in simple English; it is likely that a different value of λ applies.

The next important criterion to be met by our sampling procedure is to ensure that our process of observation, or of collecting the data, does not itself alter the relevant probability distribution function. We can alter the probability distribution in at least two ways. Easiest to see is where the physical process of sampling—that is, the physical process of collecting the data—alters the probability distribution function directly. For example, in our pond illustration, if we sample fish from the pond without throwing them back in and the pond is not very large, then as we sample we are changing the relevant probability distribution; indeed this type of example is so important that a special distribution has been derived for the case where there are just two types; it is called the *hypergeometric distribution*. We can alter the relevant probability distribution when observing an experiment. Consider the situation where we closely observe our typographers as they work; either they will be very, very cautious, or they will get nervous. In either case, the probability distribution function will not be the same.

The second way in which we can alter the relevant probability distribution by our choice of sampling procedure is when we collect information by a survey. A very famous example is provided by a poll taken just before the presidential election in 1936 between Alfred M. Landon, Republican candidate, and Franklin D. Roosevelt, Democratic candidate. The *Literary Digest* magazine mailed a questionnaire to about 10 million people; now that's a sample! The *Literary Digest* predicted that Landon would win comfortably against Roosevelt; but what happened was that Roosevelt won by a margin never seen before in U.S. history. The key to the error is that the lists that the *Literary Digest* used for its mailing, such as its own subscription lists, telephone directories, and automobile registrations represented Republican voters in a far higher proportion to Democrats than was true of the total population of voters. The probability distribution relevant to the *Literary Digest* poll recipients was not the same as that relevant to the group of voters that actually went to the polls in that election. In our language, the sampling procedure used by the *Literary Digest* "altered" the relevant distribution; or rather, in this case the poll had one distribution and voters had another. Another aspect of this example that illustrates a further type of error is called "response bias." Response bias is introduced when those responding to a questionnaire have different characteristics than the group of people selected for the sample. For example, if you send out a questionnaire that asks, "Do you advocate the violent overthrow of the U.S. government?" you are most likely to get responses only from those who will answer yes; almost everyone else will not take the questionnaire seriously.

An even more common case is to ask sensitive questions. The characteristics of those respondents who actually answer will often differ markedly from the population being sampled. "Are you a thief?" "Do you have AIDS?" "Do you believe in God?" are all questions that illustrate vividly the potential for misleading answers.

How you pose a question frequently affects the outcome. Compare the questions "Do you favor murdering unborn children?" to "Should a woman have free choice?" Obviously, the answers to these questions definitely depend on the way in which they are phrased. Even the context can alter the responses. Consider the question "Are you a virgin?" asked by

- a medical sex researcher at a respected research institute
- your friends
- your mother
- your date
- guys in a sports locker room

The answer to this question depends more on the context in which it is asked than on the actual truth.

A recent article in the *New York Times* (February 8, 1999) by Greg Schneiders and Jo Ellen Livingston, "Can You Trust the Polls? Well, Sometimes" illustrates the difficulties. The authors were responding to a survey conducted by the *National Law Journal* that indicated that three-quarters of "potential jurors" would ignore a judge's instructions. The authors point out that if this result were truly the norm, our justice system would be in serious trouble.

The statement actually posed was, "Whatever the judge says the law is, jurors should do what they think is the right thing." There are a number of aspects of this "question" that make any inference from survey results generated by it suspect. As the authors point out, given vaguely worded statements with unclear import it has been found that survey respondents have a strong tendency to respond to a reasonable sounding statement—in this case, "jurors should do what they think is the right thing." Second, when respondents are given a complex statement, they tend strongly to focus on the last clause. Third, it has been found that the word *whatever* is a signal that the "correct" response is to ignore the whatever clause and agree with the second half of the statement.

Schneiders and Livingston demonstrated that by changing the question to "Regardless of how they personally view the case they are hearing, jurors should always follow the instructions of the judge concerning the law in the case," they could reverse the result; 74 percent of their respondents agreed with their statement, almost an exact reversal of the original poll results. Their question is not without criticism either, but their objective was merely to demonstrate the sensitivity of poll answers to how questions are phrased.

All of this discussion can be summarized very neatly in our new language of probability. Let us define the joint probability distribution function of the proposed sample by

$$F_j(X_1, X_2, \ldots, X_n | \text{C.E.})$$

The symbol "|C.E." is to emphasize that we are evaluating the distribution conditional on the conditions of the experiment. A first objective of sampling is to ensure that the joint probability distribution function $F_j(\cdot)$ can be expressed as

$$F_j(X_1, X_2, \ldots, X_n | \text{C.E.}) = F(X_1)F(X_2) \ldots F(X_n); \tag{9.1}$$

where $F(\cdot)$ is the relevant probability distribution function for performing a single trial of the experiment. When we come to actually draw the sample, we will observe a set of n numbers, x_i, that we will interpret as a drawing from the distribution $F_j(X_1, X_2, \ldots, X_n)$. This type of sampling is called **simple random sampling,** in that the objective is that specified in Equation 9.1. This terminology is used to distinguish it from other types of sampling with different objectives in mind. We want to discover the values of the parameters of the distribution $F(\cdot)$. With this information in hand we can now usefully reevaluate the publisher's errors example.

In our case, the required distribution is a Poisson probability distribution with unknown parameter λ; that is, $F(\cdot)$ in Equation 9.1 is the Poisson. If we are careful to sample appropriately, so that the joint probability distribution function is just the product of the marginals, then using tools we have already developed, we can easily draw inferences about the value of the unknown value of λ. What do we know from our theory? The random variable, call it $\bar{X}$, is the number of errors that occur in a block of ten pages. If we knew λ, then we would know that the mean and variance of X are both λ. But if we consider the statistic $\bar{x}$ defined by

$$\bar{x} = \frac{\sum x_i}{n} \tag{9.2}$$

we can regard this as a drawing, or an observation from, the distribution of the random variable $\bar{X} = \sum X_i / n$. From Equation 9.1, we can derive

$$E\{\bar{X}\} = \lambda$$
$$E\{(\bar{X} - \mu'_1(\bar{X}))^2\} = n^{-2}(n\lambda)$$
$$= \frac{\lambda}{n} \tag{9.3}$$

The statistic $\bar{x}$ that will be drawn as a sample is regarded as a realization of the probability distribution function of the random variable $\bar{X}$. Now let n, the sample size, take the value 10,000. The mean of $\bar{X}$ is λ and the variance is $\lambda/10,000$, presumably a very small number. Look back at Figure 9.1. As we saw then, if we make but a single drawing from the distribution of $\bar{X}$—or alternatively expressed, from the distribution $F_j(X_1, X_2, \ldots, X_n)$—then no matter what happens, we cannot be very far from the true, but unknown, value of the parameter λ. Figures 9.2 and 9.3 show close-up plots of the normal approximation in Figure 9.1. Examining these we see that the normal distribution does indeed apply but over a very tiny scale of variation. If we are prepared to be indifferent to an error of no more than 0.04, then Figure 9.3 shows that with a sample of 10,000, given our problem, we are guaranteed to achieve this accuracy.

This approach is a solution to our initial problem, but it is not very practical in that we have to obtain huge samples. We need to go back to the drawing board to figure out how we can get information on parameters without having to obtain such large samples. What we will have to do is to compromise on the exactness of our answer. But in exchange we will be able, through our theory, to assess the accuracy of our estimates of parameter values in terms of probabilities.

9.5 Stratified Random Sampling

In the last section, we discussed simple random sampling. In this section, we will discuss a different type of sampling, *proportionate stratified random sampling,* to give you a better idea of what is involved in simple random sampling and to shed more light on the process of sampling in general. We can use any sampling technique that we like as long as we can still identify the parameters of the distributions that are involved. For example, if we were to sample from a distribution of fish in a large pond

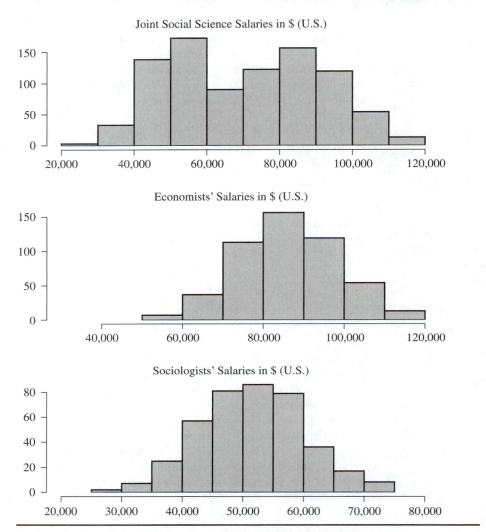

Figure 9.4   An examination of the effects of combining two distributions into one

by accepting only those fish with hooks in their mouths, we would not have any idea of the distribution involved with what parameters, even if we did know the distribution involved for sampling fish at random. Of course, if someone were to give us information on the distribution of fish with hooks in their mouths, then we might be able to identify the parameters of the new distribution.

Suppose that we are interested in the mean salary of social scientists in the United States, because we want to compare their salaries with those of physicists. However, we are aware that in the social sciences we have economists, sociologists, and anthropologists. Let us restrict our analysis to just the first two groups to simplify the algebra. Examine Figure 9.4, which illustrates the density functions for social scientists as a group, for economists, and for sociologists. We notice immediately that the variation about the mean for the group of social scientists is very much bigger than it is for either group on its own. This is because the means in the two groups are widely separated; the mean for economists is \$85,545 and for sociologists \$51,738, and the respective standard deviations are \$12,348 and \$8,952. If we use simple random sampling from the density function for social scientists we will be sampling from a density function with a very large standard deviation, \$20,274. But if we sample from each distribution separately, we will be sampling from density functions with much smaller variances. If we can combine the two means of the subgroups in some way, we may be able to reduce the variance of the observations in our sample for any given sample size relative to simple random sampling.

Let us therefore consider creating two *strata*. A **stratum** (strata is the plural) is a subpopulation; the entire target population is partitioned into a set of strata. This is to ensure that each member of the target population is in one and only one stratum. Let us note that there are N_1 economists and N_2 sociologists.

Our first task is to define what we might imply by the mean income for social scientists. Thus, if μ_1 is the mean for economists and μ_2 is the mean for sociologists, what do we understand by the phrase "the mean for social scientists"? One answer is $\mu_1 + \mu_2$, but that does not seem correct if the sizes of the two populations are very different. Suppose that N_1 is three times the size of N_2; merely adding the two mean values does not seem to be representative of the group. An alternative is to define the group mean for social scientists, as

$$\mu_J = \frac{N_1}{N_1 + N_2}\mu_1 + \frac{N_2}{N_1 + N_2}\mu_2 \tag{9.4}$$

The corresponding variance for the group "social scientists" is somewhat trickier to derive. This is because we want to examine the variation of individual social scientists about the mean value, μ_J, not each about their respective means, μ_1 and μ_2. Let $N = N_1 + N_2$. The terms $\frac{N_1}{N}$, $\frac{N_2}{N}$, which add to one, can be regarded as weights on the respective populations. One way to view the matter is that one picks the first population with a probability of $\frac{N_1}{N}$ and the second with a probability of $\frac{N_2}{N}$. We define the group variance as σ_g^2:

$$
\begin{aligned}
\sigma_g^2 &= E\{(X - \mu_J)^2\} \\
&= \frac{N_1}{N}E_1\left\{(X_1 - \mu_J)^2\right\} + \frac{N_2}{N}E_2\{(X_2 - \mu_J)^2\} \\
&= \frac{N_1}{N}E_1\{[(X_1 - \mu_1) + (\mu_1 - \mu_J)]^2\} \\
&\quad + \frac{N_2}{N}E_2\{[(X_2 - \mu_2) + (\mu_2 - \mu_J)]^2\} \\
&= \frac{N_1}{N}\left[\sigma_1^2 + (\mu_1 - \mu_J)^2\right] + \frac{N_2}{N}[\sigma_2^2 + (\mu_2 - \mu_J)^2]
\end{aligned}
\tag{9.5}
$$

where we have implicitly assumed that the two subpopulations are independent of each other. In Equation 9.5 the subscripts "1" and "2" indicate the two subpopulations. The overall variance reflects the sum of the variances of the subpopulations and the squared differences between the subpopulation means and the overall mean, μ_J. The weights $\frac{N_1}{N}$ and $\frac{N_2}{N}$ reflect the relative probability of picking each subpopulation. This is the population from which we will consider taking a sample of size n.

Our first simple way to do this is merely to treat the two subpopulations as one whole population and sample by simple random sampling; that is, we will sample exactly as we have done, and each social scientist has the same probability of being included in the sample. We will ignore the fact in this situation that we are sampling from a finite-sized population; we do this to keep the analysis as uncomplicated as we can. Our sample mean will be

$$\bar{x}_g = \frac{1}{n} \sum x_i = \$70,741$$

and its expected value is

$$\begin{aligned}
E\{\bar{x}_g\} &= \frac{1}{n} \sum E\{x_i\} \\
&= \frac{N_1}{N}\mu_1 + \frac{N_2}{N}\mu_2 \\
&= \mu_J
\end{aligned} \tag{9.6}$$

So far, so good. The variance of this statistic is

$$\begin{aligned}
\text{var}\{\bar{x}_g\} &= E\{(\bar{x}_g - \mu_J)^2\} \\
&= \frac{1}{n}\sigma_g^2
\end{aligned} \tag{9.7}$$

where we have used the same procedures, and σ_g^2 is the variance for the random variable defined by joining the two subpopulations. Our estimate of this joint variance for $\bar{x}_g$ is \$456,693 squared, or a standard deviation for this mean of \$676.

Now let us compare this result with that obtained by using the two strata, and we will sample the two strata *proportionately* to their respective sizes. We have two strata in that we sample from each stratum separately; one each for economists and sociologists. The strata are sampled proportionately in that the ratio of sample sizes equals the ratio of people in the two subpopulations. This is known as **proportionate stratified random sampling.** We chose to sample n_1 observations from the first population and n_2 observations from the second population, so that

$$n_1 = \frac{N_1}{N}n$$

$$n_2 = \frac{N_2}{N}n$$

so that

$$\frac{n_1}{n_2} = \frac{N_1}{N_2}$$

Our proportionately sampled statistic is

$$\bar{x}_p = \frac{N_1}{N}\bar{x}_1 + \frac{N_2}{N}\bar{x}_2 = \$70,741$$

and x_1 and x_2 are the means of each subpopulation. The expected value of this estimator is

$$E\{\bar{x}_p\} = \frac{N_1}{N}\mu_1 + \frac{N_2}{N}\mu_2$$

$$= \mu_J \tag{9.8}$$

And now we will see the real advantage of this way of sampling. As we will show in Chapter 10, the variance of $\bar{x}_p$ can be written as a weighted sum of the constituent variances. The variance of this statistic is

$$\text{var}\{\bar{x}_p\} = \text{var}\left\{\frac{N_1}{N}\bar{x}_1 + \frac{N_2}{N}\bar{x}_2\right\} \tag{9.9}$$

$$= \left(\frac{N_1}{N}\right)^2\text{var}\{x_1\} + \left(\frac{N_2}{N}\right)^2\text{var}\{x_2\}$$

$$= \left(\frac{N_1}{N}\right)^2\frac{\sigma_1^2}{n_1} + \left(\frac{N_2}{N}\right)^2\frac{\sigma_2^2}{n_2}$$

$$= \left(\frac{N_1}{N}\right)^2\frac{\sigma_1^2}{n}\frac{N}{N_1} + \left(\frac{N_2}{N}\right)^2\frac{\sigma_2^2}{n}\frac{N}{N_2}$$

$$= \frac{1}{n}\left[\left(\frac{N_1}{N}\right)\sigma_1^2 + \left(\frac{N_2}{N}\right)\sigma_2^2\right]$$

$$= \$130,281 \tag{9.9}$$

The corresponding standard deviation is $361.

Let us compare the two variances as shown in Equations 9.5, 9.7, and 9.9. The standard deviation for the group variance obtained from simple random sampling is $676, whereas the standard deviation for the stratified sample is only $361—not quite half, but still a substantial reduction. The variance for the simple random sampling is larger to the extent that the two subpopulation means differ. The bigger the squared difference between μ_1 and μ_J and between μ_2 and μ_J, the bigger the variance for simple random sampling relative to that for proportionate stratified sampling. The importance, of course, is that for any chosen level of precision—that is, for any chosen size of variance for our statistic—using proportionate stratified sampling will enable us to use a smaller sample size. Given that sampling is a costly exercise, this is an important gain.

9.6   Summary

This short chapter marks the beginning of a fundamental change in viewpoint. The first part of the text concerned issues of how to describe data. The second part developed the theory of probability and of distribution functions. To this point the two parts are seemingly separate; the former involves analyzing actual data and the latter presents the theory. What is missing is how to link the two. This chapter begins the process of linking theory and observation.

We began with an illustrative example where we assumed that we could always obtain as large a sample as needed. The idea was to illustrate *sampling*, the process of drawing observations in accordance with a particular probability distribution.

We saw that the observations and all the functions that we might calculate using these observations were called *statistics*. We recognized that all the sample moments that we calculated in Chapters 3 to 5 were in fact statistics.

When dealing with seemingly finite populations, such as the number of fish of various types within a pond, we saw that it made sense to recognize the "existing population of fish" as in fact a *sample* from a hypothetical distribution of fish of various types.

In any event, the importance of *sampling theory* is to specify the conditions under which we can use observations on actual data to make inferences about the values of unknown parameters. A particularly simple sampling strategy is to sample in such a way that we have an independently and identically distributed sample obtained from a single distribution; this is known as *simple random sampling*. Our sampling procedure does not alter the relevant probability distribution, and we can identify the unknown parameters involved in the distribution of the statistic.

We concluded by defining *proportionate stratified sampling* and demonstrating that by sampling in such a manner using the information about the relative sizes of two subpopulations, we could reduce the sample size needed to achieve any desired level of accuracy.

Case Study

Was There Age Discrimination in a Public Utility?

In this chapter, we learned the importance of examining carefully how our data are sampled. As we will soon learn in the chapters to follow, the validity of all our procedures depends critically on the nature of the sampling process.

In this case study, we have a fairly typical situation; a problem has to be resolved with respect to a particular set of named individuals. This is especially true in this situation as it involves a court case that will, or will not, award damages from a named firm to a set of named individuals. Consequently, we could regard the data collected as observations on a particular set of individuals at a particular point in time at a specific firm. Using an old terminology, we would have in our approximately five hundred individuals a "population," the population of these specific individuals at this particular firm at a precise moment in time. In this view there is no sampling. We can calculate all sorts of statistics, but the interpretations that we have begun to make in this chapter and that will be elaborated in later chapters will <u>not</u> be applicable. There is

continues on next page

(Continued)

no thought about distributions, nor really about random variables, except that we do not expect to find any deterministic relationships. There will be no room for "inference," the process of inferring general ideas from the observation of specific events. Whatever we observe is what we have and no general conclusions can be drawn.

However, this strict interpretation of our data is probably too limited even for the courts. Even the courts will want to know if "events occurred by chance, or if the outcome was of some design." The whole notion of discrimination suits rests on the effect of deliberate actions in addition to the random perturbations that are normal in everyday life. The courts want to know if discriminatory activity is detectable, not in an environment where everyone is exactly the same in the same circumstances, but where everyone is different and one is striving to find a "common average effect." Clearly, the courts require an approach that allows for random variations. Thus, our only alternative is to regard our observations as a sample from some, to be specified, distribution. To this notion we now turn.

If we are to regard the data that we have been examining as a sample, we now know that we need to inquire how the sample was taken and what "experiment" was performed by nature that generated these data. Clearly, we have observed at a particular point in time the incomes, ages, demographic characteristics, and so on of a group of individuals working for a given firm. These observations are similar to, but quite distinct from, a survey, or our example of the fish in a pond. In a survey, we can justify the idea of sampling more easily because we may have taken a random sample of all individuals within a specified group, or in the fish pond example, we

sampled the fish. But in this case we have looked at all employees; in what way then is this a sample?

The key to this question lies in the notion that distributions from which our samples are drawn are hypothetical. In this situation, the hypothetical joint distributions are specified by postulating that our observations form one particular realization of a joint distribution of public utility firm employee characteristics. So to observe this firm at some other time, or to observe employees at a similar firm (having specified what we mean by "similar") also represents random drawings from the hypothetical distribution. Roughly paraphrased, our hypothetical joint distribution might be the "distribution of public utility employee characteristics in the '90s." We can postulate that the individual outcomes that we observe—A's income, B's age, C's sex, D's race, E's skill level—are all random drawings from this joint distribution, because each actual realization is the outcome of the effects of a myriad of small random factors that impinge on who works where, when, and how. Our sample was not taken by a formal sampling procedure, but unless we have reason to believe otherwise, except for the common characteristic that all the people in the sample have worked at or applied to the same firm, we may proceed as if we have a random sample.

Actually, we have a conditional sample—a sample of employee characteristics conditional on being in the same firm at the same time. In the chapters to follow, we will rely heavily on this concept that what we have observed in these data is a drawing from the conditional joint distribution of employee characteristics, conditional on being in the same firm at the same time. Much of our analysis will hinge on the implications of this common conditioning.

Exercises

Exploring the Tools

9.1 Pick some object that you can measure with a ruler to fractions of an inch and have a group of students measure the length of the object. Plot box-and-whisker plots of all the measurements. How would you describe the distribution of measurements about the mean? Comment.

9.2 (Reference: *Judgement under Uncertainty: Heuristics and Biases*, Cambridge, 1998.) Consider the situation of tossing a fair coin ten times. First, ask five friends, who have not taken a statistics class, to write down what they believe to be a representative sample size of ten from a fair coin. Second, using S-Plus generate ten samples from a binomial distribution with parameters $\pi = .5$ and $n = 1$; the possible values of each trial are $\{0, 1\}$. Compare the two sets of outputs. What can you say about the "randomness" generated by your friends as compared with the actual randomness generated by the computer? Repeat the computer portion of the experiment. What conclusions do you draw from your observations?

[*Computer directions:* Start S-Plus. On the menu bar, click on <u>Data</u>, <u>Random Numbers</u>. Set Sample Size to "10," set Distribution to "binomial." For the parameters, key in $\boxed{.5}$ for Probability, and $\boxed{1}$ for Sample Size. Check the Print Results box. Click Apply. The results will be in the Report window.]

9.3 (This exercise should be done as a team.) Artists have noted certain regular proportions for the human body. For example, the distance from eye to chin is equal to the distance from eye to ear, that the eyes are halfway between chin and top of the skull, or that the length of the body is naturally divisible into eight equal sections. Explore the accuracy of these and other suggested regularities by measuring student volunteers. Given your measurements, what conclusions can you draw concerning these assumptions by artists?

9.4 For each of the following sequences of "heads and tails," state whether you believe that the sequence is random. Calculate the probability of each sequence occurring if the probability of a "head" is .5, and review your assessment of randomness.

a. *H H H H H T T T T T*

b. *H T H T H T H T H T*

c. *H H T T H H T T H H*

d. *H H H H H H H H H H*

e. *H H H T H H H H T H H*

9.5 Conduct a survey of student hours of studying, political affiliation, and drinking when under age and whether the respondent has ever stolen anything. Conduct the survey in a straightforward manner. All questions are to have simple "Yes or No" answers. Record and describe your observations.

9.6 Repeat the experiment with a different group of students, except that the sampling strategy is to be altered as follows. Obtain the actual distribution of students in your college by month of birth. For each question of interest, proceed in the following manner:

a. The interviewee is to toss a coin. If heads, the student answers the survey question, if tails he or she answers the question, Were you born in July, August, or September? The survey questioner must *not* see the outcome of the coin toss.

b. Using the procedures on conditional and joint probabilities learned in Chapter 6, and having observed the average outcome of the survey, calculate the estimated average outcome for the survey question. Compare results across the different survey questions. Is this a sensible way to survey for sensitive questions? Comment on your findings.

9.7 Pick three locations on your campus, such as the entrance to the mathematics department, the entrance to the men's locker room in the gym, the library, the student union. At each location, survey student's heights, or weights, or both. Calculate the means and the variances of your surveys, and comment on the results. To what extent are your survey locations liable to produce biased—that is, nonrandom—sampling?

9.8 Worked. *Objective: To illustrate two alternative sampling mechanisms from a finite population.* In the text, we discussed alternative ways of viewing sampling and stressed that usually the relevant parent distribution was a hypothetical population, not one composed of the actual existing members; our example was of fish in a pond. Sometimes, we want to consider the actual fish in a given pond, and we regard that group of fish as a population, not as a sample at a specific point in time from the hypothetical distribution. It now matters to our results very much indeed how we sample. We label this situation "sampling from finite populations."

a. We have two choices, sampling with or without replacement. In this experiment, we will compare the two procedures.

[**Computer directions:** Start S-Plus. On the menu bar, click on Labs, Sampling from 0-1 Populations, Sampling With and Without Replacement. In thee dialog box that appears, the box labeled N is the size of the population, the box labeled n is the size of the sample, the box labeled *pi* is the proportion in the population of one type and $(1 - pi)$ is the proportion of the second type; there are only two types in the population. Set N to "1000," set n to "10," set *pi* to ".5." Click Apply. Print Graph.] The graph shows the probability of getting k counts (or successes), $k = \{1, \ldots, 10\}$, of type 1 when sampling with replacement, these are the blue lines; and the results obtained without replacement are the red lines. At our current settings, $N = 1000$, $n = 10$, $pi = .5$, there is no discernable difference.

b. Repeat the experiment with $N = 50$, $n = 10$, pi = .02, and notice the substantial difference of the results of sampling with and without replacement.

c. Repeat the experiment with various combinations of N, n, pi. What general conclusions do you draw?

This exercise illustrates the importance of how we interpret our data in light of the objectives of our analysis. It also illustrates the importance of how one samples.

9.9 Worked. *Objective: In this exercise you will use the lab to experiment with the shape of the Poisson distribution for various values of n, sample size, and π (pi), the probability of an event occurring in a single trial.* Recall λ, the parameter in the Poisson distribution, is given by $\lambda = n\pi$. Choose various values for n and for π (pi), especially very small ones to observe the differences in the probability distribution.

a. Try values of n and π, such that $n\pi = 1$. Comment on the results.

b. For a fixed value of π, consider what happens as you increase n. Comment on the results.

c. Fix n at 200. Step through the values of π. Comment on the results.

[**Computer directions:** Start S-Plus. On the menu bar, click on Labs, Sampling From 0-1 Population, Approximating Binomial Probabilities, Poisson Approximation. In the dialog box, set n and *pi* to desired values. Click Apply. The graph has the Poisson distribution in red, and the binomial distribution in blue. Print the graphs.]

9.10 *Objective: To demonstrate that sampling of rare populations by related characteristics can be more effective than a simple random sample.*

Although still relatively rare, the occurrence of multiple human births (triplets, quadruplets, and so on) has been on the rise in recent years. For example, in late December of 1998 a woman in Texas gave birth to octuplets; the year before, septuplets were born. Assuming that the rate of multiple births is low (1 in 100,000 as announced by the U.S. Department of Vital Records), how would you go about taking a sample to confirm that the published number of multiple births was correct? How would your sampling procedure change if you knew that women who were taking fertility drugs had a greater occurrence of multiple births than women not taking fertility drugs?

9.11 Using the data provided on interest rates in the file Monyld.xls in folder Intrate, generate the yield curve (computed as the difference between the interest rate on the ten-year Treasury note (*note10yr*) and that on the three-month Treasury bill (*bill3mo*)). Given this sample, what can you say about the probability of the yield curve being negative; that is, what is the probability that the short-term interest rate will exceed the long-term interest rate? From what distribution does the yield curve sample seem to have been drawn? Describe this sample distribution as precisely as you can.

9.12 *Objective: To demonstrate that polling results can be affected by survey question phrasing and the characteristics of pollers.* (This exercise should be done as a team.)

The issue of welfare versus workfare is currently under debate. The task at hand is to determine whether the polling results on the welfare/workfare debate are influenced by the phrasing of the question or the characteristics of the poller. Select three members of the team to be pollers 1, 2, and 3. Each poller asks the following corresponding question:

(1) Do you favor welfare or workfare?

(2) Should a woman be forced to participate in a workfare program and place her child in daycare, instead of being allowed to stay home, receive benefits, and care for her children herself?

(3) Do you support or oppose an individual having to earn her own living by working for her income?

a. Take a sample of 30 students, 10 students per question, and record their responses.

b. Do your polling results differ across questions?

Now repeat the procedure with six pollers—three men and three women. (*Note:* Your sample size will increase to 60—six groups of 10.) Do your results differ across questions? across the gender of pollers? Can you explain any differences in the results?

9.13 *Objective: To illustrate that as sample size increases, the variance decreases.*

You are provided with data for miles per gallon for various makes and models of cars in the file Cardata.xls in folder Misc. The complete data set contains 150 observations. Using only the first 20 observations, calculate the first and second moments (about the mean). Repeat this calculation six times, each time bringing in 20 more observations. (*Note:* Your final calculation will involve 140 observations—the last 10 will be excluded.)

a. What can you conclude about the relationship between sample size and the size of the second moment?

b. What important implicit assumption have you made? Can you intuitively explain this result?

Applications

9.14 *Objective: To explore the implications of generalizing the findings obtained from one population and extending them to other populations.*

On August 9, 1992, the *Wall Street Journal* published an article entitled "Late Childbearing Is Found to Raise Risks." The article presented conflicting evidence on the dangers to the fetus of women giving birth in their thirties and beyond. One group of researchers reviewed the records of 174,000 Swedish women having their first child from 1983 through 1987. The study found that women over thirty faced a 40% greater risk of the fetus dying after 28 weeks of gestation. Additionally, very low birth weights, very premature delivery, and small full-term babies increased with maternal age by a range of 20% to twofold [100%]. These results contradict other studies showing that older mothers are no more likely than younger mothers to have a poor pregnancy outcome, although they are likely to have more difficult pregnancies. The Swedish researchers argue that the sample sizes of previous studies were not large enough to disclose the higher risk, or were not representative of the population. Should women in the United States be discouraged from giving birth in their thirties and beyond based on this Swedish study? Can you think of any characteristic differences between Swedish and American women? Do these differences reduce the applicability of the Swedish study results to the women of the United States?

9.15 *Objective: To illustrate how anonymity of respondents affects sampling results.*

On November 13, 1992, the *New York Times* ran an article entitled "Study Finds Many Heterosexuals Are Ignoring Serious Risk of AIDS." Joseph Catania conducted a survey regarding condom use and multiple sex partners. For the survey, more than 10,000 Americans were questioned by telephone about their sexual practices. Respondents were selected by a random digit-dialing system and represented people from the ages of 18 to 75, married and single, living in major cities and in rural areas. How do you think the results of the survey would have changed if, rather than speaking anonymously with respondents over the telephone, pollers had met with respondents in person to ask about the respondents' usage of condoms, number of sex partners, and so on? What would you hypothesize about the direction of bias in the mean and variance for condom usage? for the number of sex partners?

9.16 *Objective: To demonstrate that polling results are affected by survey question phrasing and the characteristics of pollers.*

On Tuesday, September 7, 1993, the *New York Times* printed an article entitled "Pollsters Enlist

Psychologists in Quest for Unbiased Results." The article cites the following two questions related to campaign financing:

■ Should laws be passed to eliminate all possibilities of special interests giving huge sums of money to candidates?

■ Do groups have a right to contribute to the candidate they support?

The first question is from a survey Ross Perot conducted in March of 1992, whereas the second is from a similar survey conducted by an independent polling concern. Not surprisingly, when asked the "Perot" question, 99% of respondents indicated "yes," whereas only 40% of respondents favored limitations on contributions when asked the second question. The author of the article concludes that the second question is a more "neutral" question. Would you agree with this statement? How might you rephrase the second question to make it even more neutral? What other differences (aside from the question asked) can you think of that could help to explain the difference in results?

9.17 "Can you tell the difference?" Marketers in general, wine and tea growers in particular, are very interested in blind taste testing. They want to know if people can taste the difference, or sometimes if they cannot taste the difference; for example, a manufacturer of margarine would want to know if people can tell the difference between its product and actual butter.

One way to do this is to give "taste testers" four samples, say of wine, two of one kind and two of another; that is, there are pairs of identical products. Suppose that no one can tell the difference between the two products, so that they are forced to choose randomly.

What is the probability of picking the correct pairs at random, and what is the relevant distribution? What is the variance of this distribution? If out of 100 independent trials the correct pairs were chosen 5 times, would this result indicate people can tell the difference?

9.18 There is a debate about the use of sampling procedures in taking the census. Although there are many political issues involved, the key statistical issues concern cost and accuracy. A sample involves less cost because fewer people are interviewed, but there is sampling error. A count involves far greater cost, everyone in principle is "counted," but an attempt to count everyone introduces its own errors and the larger the group to be counted, the greater the potential errors.

Use the insights gained in this chapter to assess the relative benefits and costs of sampling and a full count. How would you advise the government?

9.19 If you were asked by a credit card company to determine the distribution of the "timeliness" of repayments, how would you design a sample to estimate the mean arrival time of payment past the billing date?

What difference would it make to your answer if you recognized the different distributions of bill-paying practices between large corporations, small firms, and individual households?

9.20 Case Study: Was There Age Discrimination in a Public Utility?

The data in this case were obtained by interviewing each employee in the employ of the firm at the time of the transfer. In light of the discussion in the text, assess the relevance of sampling procedures to the analysis of salary and age distributions.

If plaintiffs were to claim that we have a given fixed finite population so that standard sampling theory does not hold in this case, how would you defend or rebut that claim? In your answer, state clearly the implications for the outcome of the case of either interpretation of the situation.

Estimation of Theoretical Moments and the Parameters of Probability Distributions

10.1   What You Will Learn in This Chapter

At last, in this chapter we formally introduce *inference*. We will use inference to estimate distributional parameters or theoretical moments. Our world is one in which we know the form of the relevant distribution, but we do not know the values of the relevant parameters of the distribution. Our task is to use observed data to infer the values of the unknown parameters or theoretical moments. We achieve this by defining "estimators" that are in fact functions of the underlying random variables and that are chosen to provide information about the unknown parameters. *Estimators* are themselves random variables and have their own distributions. When we take a sample of observations and perform the same calculations on the observed values as we specified for the definition of the estimator, we obtain an "estimate." Our statistical theory enables us to interpret the value of the estimate so obtained as providing information about an unknown parameter value.

We develop the theory of estimation in the context of several examples. At each stage, we consider either a different distribution for the underlying experiment, assume less information, or pose a different statistical problem to be solved. In particular, we consider obtaining estimates for the means of binomial, Poisson, and normal distributions and for the variance of a normal distribution.

In the process, we define the concepts of "bias" and "consistency," two very important properties of estimators. They are functions of the random variables used to make inferences about the parameters of the distributions.

10.2 Introduction

We now recognize the important role played by distributions, whether it be the binomial, the Poisson, the Gaussian, the uniform, or one of many others to follow. But what we have not settled is how to identify a particular distribution; that is, if we have a situation involving a binomial distribution we will usually not know the value of π. Alternatively, we may be facing a situation involving the Gaussian distribution, but we will not know the values of the parameters μ and σ. Referring to some of the data sets that we have examined, we will want to know the value of the mean for the examination grades; whether the midterm grade was equal on average to the final grade; the probability of AIDS occurring in a random selection of individuals and how accurate that number is; the mean effect of weight on gasoline mileage; the variance of interest rates about their mean value, a result that is important for evaluating portfolio risk; how often Old Faithful erupts and how much variation about that mean there is; whether the mean value of U.S. arms shipments exceeds those of Russia; and the mean horsepower for U.S. and foreign cars and how much variation there is about these means. All of these practical issues are examples of one general problem: How can we obtain information about the parameters of distributions from observing data, and how can we assess the accuracy of that information?

The main lesson from Chapter 9 is that actual data can be regarded as realizations of an experiment. Further, we presume that there is some prototypical experiment that generates the theoretical probability distribution function. In short, we have begun the process of using our theory to interpret actual data and to guide our decisions. The link between data and statistical theory is two-way; theory is used to interpret, or explain, data, and data are used to select the appropriate specific distribution by assigning values to the distribution's parameters. The general notion is called inference. **Inference** is the process of "inferring"—that is, drawing conclusions about the specific properties of probability distribution functions and of density functions. A major, but by no means exclusive, aspect of this process is the "drawing of conclusions" about the values of parameters in probability distribution functions. Another and related task is to infer, or draw conclusions about, the values of the theoretical moments associated with a given probability distribution function. A more difficult form of inference is to attempt to infer the form of the probability distribution function itself, not just the values of the parameters. We will begin with the easier forms of inference.

The idea behind the notion of inference is that by only observing the values of a few statistics, we can, in conjunction with our theory, learn some general facts about the process being observed and about all other processes that have the same underlying prototypical distribution. This underlying distribution is known as the **parent distribution.**

Inference should be distinguished from deduction. In Chapters 6 to 8, we made many deductions about probability and about distribution functions. For example, having derived the binomial probability distribution we deduced that the first two theoretical moments were expressible in terms of the parameters as $n\pi$ and $n\pi(1-\pi)$, respectively. In Chapter 7, which deals with probability, we deduced from first principles that when two random events are mutually exclusive the probability of the sum is just the sum of the probabilities, but that when the random events are not mutually exclusive, we must allow for the probability of the simultaneous occurrence of both. With deduction we know that our conclusions are correct whenever the premises on which they are based are correct, provided, of course, our proof of the relationship has been correctly carried out.

But with inference the matter is not so simple. When we try to establish a link between theory and fact, which is what inference is all about, we can never know whether the world that we observe will continue to be represented by our chosen prototypical experiment. The problem is that the decision as to whether the theory is, or is not, relevant is purely an empirical issue; it is a question of fact about real events, not of fact about some theory. Because there is no way to deduce that the postulated distribution applies, we are left with our surmise that our chosen distribution is relevant at any given time. Consequently, there is no way that we can *know* that a given distribution applies; we can only proceed on the *presumption* that it does, carefully check the implications of that assumption against other real facts, and then act accordingly. If our presumption is constantly reinforced by implications that agree with the observed facts, then we will have great confidence in our use of the presumed distribution. But if we begin to get disagreement, then we had better reconsider the situation.

Our first venture into inference is **estimation.** This is the process of trying to infer the values of the parameters and of the theoretical moments of some specified probability distribution from the observed values of actual data—that is, from a sample. The remainder of this chapter is about estimation. We will begin with the estimation of theoretical moments and then proceed to the estimation of parameters. Our basic strategy is to start from where we left matters in the last chapter and then proceed to develop more sophisticated tools of analysis. As we go, we will be able to handle increasingly more difficult situations.

10.3   Estimating Theoretical Moments: Large Sample Results

We begin with the estimation of theoretical moments. We start by imagining that we have an almost unlimited supply of data; that is why the title of this section includes "large sample" results.

Let us begin with the mean. Suppose that we have settled our sampling problems, so that we are sure that a single probability distribution function applies to our situation and that our sampling procedure is such that the joint probability distribution function is the product of the marginals. At this stage of the analysis, we can even ignore the actual form of the distribution; we merely need to know that there exists an unknown first and an unknown second theoretical moment. We seek to discover the values of the unknown theoretical moments from information contained in the data. How do we do this?

The clue lies in the results of the last chapter. Let us repeat that process. Consider the random variable defined by $\bar{X} = \Sigma X_i / n$ and its first two theoretical moments. If the first two moments of the unknown, parent distribution (the distribution of the random variable X), are labeled as μ_1' and μ_2, then the first two theoretical moments of the random variable $\bar{X}$ are given by

$$E\{\bar{X}\} = \mu_1'$$

$$E\left\{(\bar{X} - \mu_1')^2\right\} = \frac{\mu_2}{n} \tag{10.1}$$

Consider the sequence $\{x_i\}_{i=1,\dots,n}$, which is a *sample* of size n from the parent distribution. If we interpret $\bar{x}$, defined by $\bar{x} = \Sigma x_i / n$, as a drawing from the probability distribution of the random variable $\bar{X}$, the mean and variance of which we listed in Equation 10.1, we can interpret the meaning of our statistic $\bar{x}$.

Let us be quite careful about what we are saying here. We are using roman capitals to denote random variables and lowercase roman letters to indicate the corresponding drawings, or sample, from the probability distribution function. Our discussion about X_i and $\bar{X}$, their theoretical moments, and their probability distribution functions are all discussions about random variables. Random variables have probability distributions associated with them; they are not observed directly as they are theoretical constructs. The x_i and the $\bar{x}$, however, are actual numbers that we obtain from a physical process of either generating observations ourselves, or we take a survey; x_i and $\bar{x}$ are statistics. Our theory enables us to interpret these statistics as a sample of observations from a given distribution with specified properties. What you see is reality. But how you interpret and what you infer are theory; that is an abstraction. Only the numbers are real.

Returning to our theoretical interpretations of a sample, we know from our theory that the random variable $\bar{X}$ has associated with it a probability distribution function that we have not yet derived, except for specifying the first two theoretical moments. We are now going to see that if the sample size, n, is large enough, we do not have to worry about what the form of the associated probability distribution function for X_i actually is. Nor do we have to worry about the form of the probability distribution function for the random variable $\bar{X}$.

Indeed, if n is truly huge, then the distribution of the random variable $\bar{X}$ is a constant! This is true at least as far as any reasonable approximation is concerned. Such a distribution is said to be **degenerate**, meaning that the probability distribution function has collapsed onto a single point with a variance of zero. Any drawing from such a distribution will always yield the same number. However, this result is not as exciting as it first appears because the result requires a very, very large sample size. Obviously, the larger the variance of the underlying distribution, the bigger n must be for any reasonable approximation of a degenerate distribution to be obtained. In Chapter 9, we saw an example with the Poisson probability distribution where the variance was 2, and we looked at a sample size of 10,000, which gave a variance for $\bar{X}$ of .0002.

We have reached a stage at which we will have to improve our language; we need some new terms. A *statistic* is a function of the sample observations, but this is a general term. When we are discussing estimation, we will require some more specific terms.

An **estimator** is a function of a set of random variables that provides information about some property of a probability distribution function, such as the theoretical moments or the parameters of a distribution. An estimator is a random variable with its own probability distribution function. The reason for defining an estimator is that the properties of its probability distribution yield more information on the unknown theoretical moment or parameter than that of the original, or parent, probability distribution. Different estimators have different distributions, even with the same parent distribution.

An **estimate** is an observation on the estimator; it is a statistic, a function of the observed sample. Thus, *estimator* is to *estimate* as *random variable* is to *statistic*. In the example discussed in Equation 10.1, $\bar{X}$ is the estimator with a probability distribution function that has the theoretical moments described in that equation. The corresponding estimate is $\bar{x}$, a statistic calculated from the observation of actual data. $\bar{X}$ is a random variable; $\bar{x}$ is a number; $\bar{X}$ is a concept in theory, $\bar{x}$ is reality. All the moments that we calculated in Chapters 4 and 5 were sample statistics, drawings from the probability distribution functions of the corresponding estimators that we are about to define.

The property in which the variance of $\bar{X}$ goes to zero as $n \to \infty$, so that the distribution collapses onto a single point in the limit (Equation 10.1) is called **consistency**. The estimator $\bar{X}$ is consistent in that the distribution of $\bar{X}$ collapses onto the parameter μ that it is estimating. This involves two limits. First, the mean of the distribution of the estimator, $\bar{X}$ in this case, must converge onto the parameter; in our case that is trivially true. Further, the *variance* of the estimator must converge to zero; that is, as n gets to be very large, the variation of the estimator about the parameter value lessens.

Consider a random variable Y, with parent distribution $g(Y; \theta)$ that depends on some parameter θ. Consider the joint distribution obtained from n independent repetitions of $g(Y; \theta)$—that is, the joint distribution of the sequence of random variables $\{Y_i\}$. An estimator $\hat{\theta}$, which is a function of the random variables $\{Y_i\}$, is said to be consistent for the parameter θ if the probability limit of $\hat{\theta}$ is θ. We write

$$p \lim(\hat{\theta}) = \theta$$

The **probability limit** of an estimator, $p \lim(\hat{\theta})$, is defined by

$$p \lim(\hat{\theta}) = \tilde{\theta} \tag{10.2}$$

if and only if

$$\lim_{n \to \infty} P(|\hat{\theta} - \tilde{\theta}| < \varepsilon) = 1$$

for any $\varepsilon > 0$. The idea is that as $n \to \infty$ the probability distribution, or the density function, collapses onto the constant $\tilde{\theta}$. All the mass of the distribution is concentrated about the point $\hat{\theta}$. The probability of any observed value of $\hat{\theta}$ differing from $\tilde{\theta}$ by more than ε approaches zero.

Although the probability is approaching zero, that condition does not imply that all values of $\tilde{\theta}$ are infinitely close to $\tilde{\theta}$.

An example provided by Phoebus Dhrymes illustrates the difference. Suppose that the probability distribution for an estimator $\hat{\theta}$ is given by $f(\hat{\theta})$:

$\hat{\theta}$	$f(\hat{\theta})$
θ	$1 - \dfrac{1}{n}$
n	$\dfrac{1}{n}$

As $n \to \infty$, $P(|\hat{\theta} - \theta| < \varepsilon) \to 1$; that is, $p \lim(\hat{\theta}) = \theta$, while the probability that $\hat{\theta} = n$ approaches zero.

A sufficient, but not necessary, condition is that $\hat{\theta}$ be consistent for θ; that is, a sufficient, but not necessary condition, that $p \lim(\hat{\theta}) = \theta$, is

$$\lim_{n \to \infty} E\{(\hat{\theta} - \theta)^2\} = 0 \tag{10.3}$$

This is the same condition that we had in the preceding example with $\bar{X}$. What is this definition telling us? Note that we could well have indexed each of our estimators by the number of the jointly independent random variables involved, for example:

$$\hat{\theta}_n = \bar{X}_n = \sum_{i=1}^{n} \frac{X_i}{n}$$

The expectation of $\hat{\theta}_n$ is a function of n in general as is also the expectation of its second moment. These sequences of expectations yield a sequence in n, and Equation 10.3 says that we take the limit of this sequence. In the case of $\bar{X}$, the sequence of second moment expectations and the limit as $n \to \infty$ is

$$E\{(\bar{X} - \mu_1')^2\} = \frac{\mu_2}{n}$$

$$\lim_{n\to\infty} \frac{\mu_2}{n} = 0$$

One of the most useful properties of consistency is that for any continuous function $g(\cdot)$, it is true that if $\hat{\theta}$ is consistent for θ, then $g(\hat{\theta})$ is consistent for $g(\theta)$. Although a formal proof of this is beyond our scope at the moment, the result makes intuitive sense. If $\hat{\theta}$ is consistent for θ, then as $n \to \infty$, the variation of $\hat{\theta}$ about θ decreases to zero as measured by the second moment of $\hat{\theta}$. In turn, this implies that the variation of $g(\hat{\theta})$ about $g(\theta)$ must also go to zero, provided however we can still evaluate the expectation.

Now let us consider another example. Under the same circumstances as for Equation 10.1, define the estimator

$$M_2(X) = \sum \frac{(X_i - \bar{X})^2}{n} \tag{10.4}$$

where the use of the capital italicized letters reminds us that we are dealing with a random variable with a specific probability distribution function. For now, let us merely examine the first theoretical moment of the distribution for this estimator. The corresponding statistic would be written as

$$\sum \frac{(x_i - \bar{x})^2}{n}$$

where the x_i are n observations on the experiment. Let us derive the expectation of the estimator defined in Equation 10.4. The expectation is given by

$$E\left\{\sum \frac{(X_i - \bar{X})^2}{n}\right\} = \frac{1}{n} E\left\{\sum_i X_i^2 - n\bar{X}^2\right\} \tag{10.5}$$

Taking the expectation of the first term on the right:

$$E\left\{\sum X_i^2\right\} = \sum E\{X_i^2\} = \sum (\mu_2 + (\mu_1')^2)$$
$$= n(\mu_2 + (\mu_1')^2)$$

Taking the expectation of the second term on the right:

$$nE\{\bar{X}^2\} = nE\left\{\left(\frac{1}{n}\right)^2\left(\sum X_i\right)^2\right\}$$

$$= \left(\frac{1}{n}\right)E\left\{\sum X_i^2 + \sum_i\sum_{i\neq j}X_iX_j\right\}$$

$$= \left(\frac{1}{n}\right)[n(\mu_2 + (\mu_1')^2) + n(n-1)(\mu_1')^2]$$

$$= \mu_2 + (\mu_1')^2 + (n-1)(\mu_1')^2$$

$$= \mu_2 + n(\mu_1')^2$$

so, we finally see that

$$E\left\{\sum\frac{(X_i - \bar{X})^2}{n}\right\} = \left(\frac{1}{n}\right)E\left\{\sum X_i^2\right\} - nE\left\{\bar{X}^2\right\}$$

$$= \left(\frac{1}{n}\right)[n(\mu_2 + (\mu_1')^2) - (\mu_2 + n(\mu_1')^2)]$$

$$= \left(\frac{(n-1)}{n}\right)\mu_2 \neq \mu_2$$

And here we have a surprise! The expected value of the estimator $\sum(X_i - \bar{X})^2/n$ is not μ_2 but $((n-1)/n)\mu_2$. This result is called **bias**. An estimator is said to be biased when its expectation is not equal to the value of the parameter that it is estimating. The $\bar{X}$ that we examined in Equation 10.1 is unbiased, because

$$E\{\bar{X}\} = \mu_1'$$

However, although $\sum(X_i - \bar{X})^2/n$ is biased, there is obviously an easy fix; we can multiply our estimator by $n/(n-1)$ to get

$$\frac{n}{(n-1)}\sum\frac{(X_i - \bar{X})^2}{n} = \left(\frac{1}{(n-1)}\right)\sum(X_i - \bar{X})^2$$

$$E\left\{\frac{1}{(n-1)}\sum(X_i - \bar{X})^2\right\} = \sigma^2$$

This unbiased estimator is used so frequently in statistics that it has a special symbol, S^2. It is called the **sample variance** and its square root, S, is called the **sample standard deviation**.

$$S^2 = \frac{1}{(n-1)}\sum(X_i - \bar{X})^2 \tag{10.6}$$

S^2 is unbiased for σ^2. But, we can show that S is still biased for σ .

How important is this result for S^2? For very large n, as is now the case under discussion, there is virtually no difference between the two estimators. For small n, there may well be a reasonable difference between the two, so one is advised to use S^2, instead of our usual estimator for the second moment. For $n = 100$, the use of $n = 99$ is a difference of about 1%, which is not usually worth worrying about. But for $n = 25$, the use of 24 implies a difference of about 4% and now one may begin to be concerned. The bias is given by $\mu^2 - (n - 1)/n\mu^2 = (1/n)\,\mu^2$, so that it is declining in n.

We can also show that both S^2 and $M_2(X)$ are consistent. But there is a subtle difference between the two cases. Remember that S^2 is unbiased, whereas $M_2(X)$ is biased, although we note that the bias of $M_2(X)$ is going to zero in n. The condition for consistency in Equation 10.3 involves the expectation of the square of the deviations of the estimator from the *parameter*, not the deviations from the *expectation of the estimator*. Of course, when the estimator is unbiased, there is no difference. But when the estimator is biased there is a difference. Formally, this is seen by expanding Equation 10.3 as follows:

$$\lim_{n\to\infty} E\{\hat{\theta} - \theta\}^2 = \lim_{n\to\infty} [E\{(\hat{\theta} - E\{\hat{\theta}\})^2 + (E\{\hat{\theta}\} - \theta)^2\}] \tag{10.7}$$

where we have added and subtracted the term $E\{\hat{\theta}\}$ on the left side and recognized on the right side that

$$E\{(\hat{\theta} - E\{\hat{\theta}\})(E\{\hat{\theta}\} - \theta)\} = 0$$

In Equation 10.7, the expression on the left side is the limit of the mean squared error; and we see from that equation that the mean squared error is the sum of the variance, $E\{(\hat{\theta} - E\{\hat{\theta}\})^2\}$, and the bias squared, $(E\{\hat{\theta}\} - \theta)^2 y$. Later, we will examine some alternative estimators that consider the possible trade-off between bias squared and variance.

We now see that consistency requires two conditions in one. If $\lim_{n\to\infty} E\{\hat{\theta} - \theta\}^2$ is to go to zero, then we require that

$$\lim_{n\to\infty} E\{(\hat{\theta} - E\{\theta\})^2\} = 0$$

$$\lim_{n\to\infty} (E\{\hat{\theta}\} - \theta)^2 = 0$$

In short, we require both that the estimator be unbiased in the limit—that is, $\lim_{n\to\infty} (E\{\hat{\theta}\} - \theta)^2 = 0$—and that the variance of the estimator—that is, $\lim_{n\to\infty} E\{(\hat{\theta} - E\{\hat{\theta}\})^2\}$—approach zero. The former expression is the bias squared. In the Exercises, you will be led through a proof that $\lim_{n\to\infty} E\{(S^2 - \mu_2)^2\} = 0$. We will not go through a demonstration that the higher-order sample moments are consistent; the proofs are left to an exercise, but the proofs are the same as those used for the first two moments.

The Dhrymes example that we presented illustrates these comments very well. Using that example, we have

$$\lim_{n\to\infty} E\{(\hat{\theta} - \theta)^2\} = \lim_{n\to\infty} \left[(\theta - \theta)^2 \left(1 - \frac{1}{n} \right) + (n - \theta)^2 \frac{1}{n} \right]$$

$$= \lim_{n\to\infty} \frac{n^2 + \theta^2 - 2n\theta}{n} = \infty$$

The expression

$$\lim_{n\to\infty} E\{(\hat{\theta} - \theta)^2\}$$

is known as the limit of the **mean squared error** as $n \to \infty$. We have seen that an estimator can be consistent in that the probability limit of the estimator is equal to the parameter being estimated, even though the mean squared error is infinite. In the example, the asymptotic bias is 1 and the variance goes to infinity.

We can conclude that, if we have an enormous amount of data, the estimators corresponding to the sample moments are all consistent estimators for the corresponding theoretical moments. These estimates are said to be **point estimates**; they produce a single point as an estimate.

So far, we have demonstrated that we can link theory and reality through sampling. We can infer the values of unknown moments from observations on the corresponding sample moments. We have established the principle that a specific probability distribution function can be discovered through observations on an actual experiment if certain conditions are met. When you recall that we began this text with the observation that the subject matter of statistics comprises data for which there is no causal explanation, you will see that we have come a long way from that initial state of complete ignorance.

Let us consider an example. Suppose that we have a sample size of 2400, which is not very big for getting the variances of our estimates to converge to zero, but is large enough to demonstrate what we are doing. With this sample, suppose that we have calculated the following statistics:

$$\bar{x} = \sum \frac{x_i}{n}$$

$$s^2 = \sum \frac{(x_i - \bar{x})^2}{(n-1)}$$

$$m_3 = \sum \frac{(x_i - \bar{x})^3}{n}$$

$$m_4 = \sum \frac{(x_i - \bar{x})^4}{n}$$

$$\hat{\alpha}_1 = \frac{m_3}{(s^2)^{3/2}}$$

$$\hat{\alpha}_2 = \frac{m_4}{(s^2)^2}$$

(10.8)

Note the slight change in the estimate of the standardized third and fourth moments; we used s^2 instead of m_2. Our empirical findings are

$$\bar{x} = 5.94$$
$$s^2 = 11.2$$
$$m_3 = 43.23$$
$$m_4 = 592.1$$
$$\hat{\alpha}_1 = 1.04$$
$$\hat{\alpha}_2 = 4.72$$

We see that this distribution is skewed to the right and that it has more peakedness than a normal distribution. But how accurate are our results? As it happens, our sample

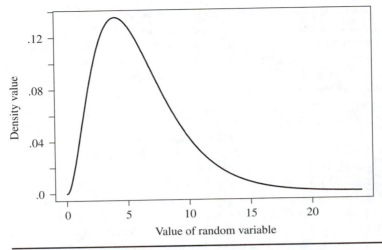

Figure 10.1   Parent density: Chi-square distribution with 6 degrees of freedom

was generated by computer according to a type of distribution that is known as the chi-square density function, a distribution with a single parameter. We set the value of the parameter to 6. With this information, we can figure out the values of the theoretical moments. The distribution is illustrated in Figure 10.1. The values of the theoretical moments are

$\mu'_1 = 6$; % estimation error $= 1\%$

$\mu_2 = 12$; % estimation error $= 7\%$

$\mu_3 = 48$; % estimation error $= 14\%$

$\mu_4 = 720$; % estimation error $= 18\%$

$\alpha_1 = 1.16$; % estimation error $= 7\%$

$\alpha_2 = 5.0$; % estimation error $= 6\%$

Looking at these results, we see that the percentage of estimation error increases with the order of the moment. The low-order moments have quite reasonable levels of accuracy, but the higher-order moments are quite large. A further benefit from looking only at standardized variables is clear from these results; the percentage of estimation errors for α_1 and α_2 are similar to that for the variance; those for the unstandardized moments are not.

So far the only course of action open to us is to increase sample size if we are to improve the accuracy of our estimates. But this may well be very expensive in terms of the costs of running an experiment, or the costs of taking a larger sample. Once again we have to go back to the drawing board to try to discover a better method.

What are our options? We could consider estimating the parameters of the distribution directly. But because the theoretical moments are just simple functions of the parameters, it is not likely that we will gain much from taking this approach. However, what we can try to do is to determine if we can use our theory to increase our knowledge about the accuracy that we can achieve with modest sample sizes. Our results using the concept of consistency have not relied on the form of the underlying probability distribution function. Consequently, our approach has not yet stressed the fact that estimators are random variables and have their own theoretical moments; the work to come will have to rely heavily on that idea. This extra information we will put to good use to improve our knowledge about our estimates. Now we begin the real task of inference.

10.4 Estimating Moments and Parameters: Confidence Intervals and Small Sample Results

Let us begin with a very simple example. Suppose that our prior research has demonstrated that the outcomes from a given experiment can be described by the normal density function. Examples from our data sets and case studies include the wages of the public utility workers, energy consumption per capita or per dollar of output, the cost of housing, interest rates, and so on. We already know that the Gaussian density function has two parameters, μ and σ^2, representing the mean and variance, respectively. Our first task is to estimate the mean of this distribution. Let us pretend that we already know the value of σ^2. You are quite right to argue that if we do not know the mean, it is even more likely that we do not know the variance. That is very true, but our task at the moment is to begin to learn how to obtain estimators, not to be as realistic as we can; that will come later.

If we are prepared to assume that we know the value of σ^2, then we might go the whole way and assume that the value of σ^2 is 1; for if not we could easily redefine the random variable so that the variance is 1. We are dealing with a normal density function with an unknown mean, but a variance of 1; this is the parent distribution. Further, we will assume that our sampling procedures are such that the sample's joint probability distribution function is the product of n independent random variables, each having the normal density function with mean μ and variance 1.

Our first example is doubly simple because the unknown parameter is μ, which is also the first theoretical moment, μ'_1; estimating μ is like getting two estimates in one! With this hint, we can easily guess what to do next; examine the distribution of the estimator $\bar{X}$. Part of this task has already been accomplished. In Equation 10.1, we showed that the first two theoretical moments of the estimator $\bar{X}$, are

$$E\{\bar{X}\} = \mu'_1 = \mu$$

$$E\{(\bar{X} - \mu)^2\} = \frac{\mu_2}{n} = \frac{\sigma^2}{n} = \frac{1}{n}$$

Now what else do we know? Well, if n is very large, then the distribution of $\bar{X}$ is approximately a normal density function with mean μ and a variance of $1/n$. The result follows because we have here a case in which we have a sum of a large number of independently and identically distributed random variables, each with mean and variance given by μ and 1. This result would be true for any probability distribution function as we saw when we derived the normal density function; this was the result of the central limit theorem (Chapter 8). Our big question is, What is the distribution for the random variable $\bar{X}$ for *any* value of n, when the underlying, or parent, distribution is itself a normal density function?

One way to derive the appropriate probability distribution function is to calculate the theoretical moments for a random variable defined by the sum of two random variables. It will be instructive to do this for a pair of normal density functions, because if we can show that the distribution of the sum of any two normal random variables is again normal, then we have shown that any sum of normal random variables has a normal distribution. This follows because any sum of n variables can be made up of the sums of pairs of the same random variables, and then each of these can be summed in pairs, and so on.

Suppose that X_1 and X_2 are two random variables, each of which is distributed as $N(\mu_i, \sigma_i^2)$, $i = 1, 2$ (Chapter 8). What is the distribution of the random variable Y, where Y is defined by $Y = X_1 + X_2$?

$$E\{Y\} = E\{X_1\} + E\{X_2\}$$
$$= \mu_1 + \mu_2 = \mu(Y)$$

$$E\{(Y - \mu)^2\} = E\{Y^2\} - \mu^2$$
$$= E\{(X_1 + X_2)^2\} - \mu^2$$
$$= E\{X_1^2 + X_2^2 + 2X_1X_2\} - \mu^2$$
$$= \sum_i (\mu_i^2 + \sigma_i^2) + 2\mu_1\mu_2 - \mu^2$$
$$= \sigma_1^2 + \sigma_2^2 = \sigma^2(Y)$$

using the fact that $\mu^2 = \mu_1^2 + \mu_2^2 + 2\mu_1\mu_2$.

We conclude that the sum of two independent normal random variables has a mean that is the sum of the means and that the variance is the sum of the variances of the two random variables. In the Exercises you will be led through the steps needed to continue this process for the third and fourth theoretical moments. The result is that the standardized third moment is zero and the standardized fourth is 3. But these are the third and fourth moments of the normal distribution.

Consequently, the sum of any two independent normal random variables $N(\mu_i, \sigma_i^2)$, $i = 1, 2$ is $N(\mu, \sigma^2)$, where $\mu = \mu_1 + \mu_2$ and $\sigma^2 = \sigma_1^2 + \sigma_2^2$. If you think about our result you will soon realize that we have in fact shown that the sum of any number of independently distributed normal random variables has a normal density function. This more general result follows from the observation that the sum of any number of random variables can be obtained from the sum of them two at a time. We now know the distribution of our estimator, $Y = \Sigma X_i$; it is a normal density function with a mean that is the sum of the means of the random variables X_i, $i = 1, 2, \ldots, n$, and a variance that is the sum of the variances of the random variables X_i. We can determine the distribution of the estimator, $\bar{X} = \Sigma X_i / n$, by merely rescaling that of Y to allow for division by n. Further, we can also allow for all the means and variances to be the same. The result is that the distribution of the estimator, $\bar{X}$, when the sample is independently and identically distributed as normal with common mean μ and

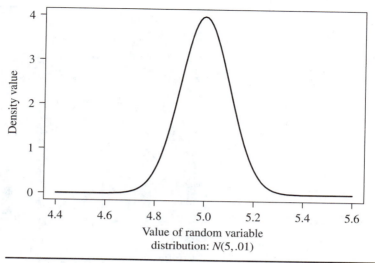

Value of random variable
distribution: $N(5, .01)$

Figure 10.2   Density function for the mean drawn from a parent distribution $N(5, 1)$

common variance σ^2, is normal with mean μ and variance σ^2/n; and in our special case $\sigma^2 = 1$, so the variance of $\bar{X}$ is $1/n$.

Now we have to figure out how to use this information. Remember that we wish to discover how to use a specific sample outcome, a statistic, to draw inferences about the unknown value of the mean μ of the parent distribution. Suppose that the parent distribution for the random variable X is $N(5,1)$; that is, X has a mean of 5 and a variance of 1. If we consider an interval of length ± 5 standard deviations, we know almost certainly that μ is in the interval $[0, 10]$. Now consider the distribution of $\bar{X}$ and the intervals for μ derived from it.

Figure 10.2 shows the theoretical distribution for $\bar{X}$, the estimator for μ, when $n = 100$. This distribution is a normal density function with mean $\mu = 5$ and a variance of $\frac{1}{100}$, or a standard deviation of $\frac{1}{10}$. If we consider a drawing from this distribution, we could easily get any value from 4.5 to 5.5—that is, any value between -5 and 5 standard deviations away from the mean of 5. By our reasoning, we are virtually certain to be within the interval $[4.5, 5.5]$, which is a lot more precise than the interval obtained using the parent distribution.

We can get any value between 4.5 to 5.5, but the probability for any interval of given size in the extreme tails of the distribution is much less than it is for intervals of the same size near the mean; glance again at Figure 10.2 and reconsider Table 8.1. The varying probabilities of alternative intervals may provide a clue to our puzzle. Although with limited data we cannot state precisely what the value of μ is, we could seek to assign probabilities to intervals. So instead of saying "the mean μ is 4.8," we could say something like "the probability that the mean μ is in the interval $[4.8, 5.3]$ is about .9." Such a statement is not as comforting as the former, but it is probably the best that we can do under the circumstances. The trick is to figure out how to find our interval and how to relate that interval to the unknown value of μ.

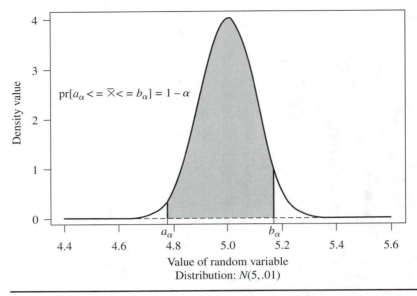

$\text{pr}[a_\alpha <= \bar{X} <= b_\alpha] = 1 - \alpha$

Value of random variable
Distribution: $N(5, .01)$

Figure 10.3   Illustration of a confidence interval with arbitrary bounds

Reexamine Figure 10.2, which shows the density function for the distribution of our estimator, $\bar{X}$. If we *knew* μ, then we certainly could define an interval about μ to express the probability of a draw on $\bar{X}$ being in the specified interval. Let us choose an interval such that the probability of a draw in that interval is $(1 - \alpha)$ and the probability of not being in the interval is α. We usually choose α small. Our reason for doing this is that we want to achieve a reasonably high probability of being in the prescribed interval. When we have taken the draw, then we will have an observation on the random variable $\bar{X}$, say $\bar{x}$; keep in mind that $\bar{x}$ is a number. On any given draw, either $\bar{x}$ is in the interval, or it is not. But the probability of being in the interval, before the draw is made, is $(1 - \alpha)$ and the probability of not being in the interval is α.

This is all very well, but it has not solved our problem yet. So far we have an interval that relates an observable $\bar{x}$ and the unknown μ. Let us see if we can "invert" the statement about the interval by using a "thought experiment." Suppose that we assign the interval, say $[a_\alpha, b_\alpha]$, about μ in such a way that the probability of a draw of the random variable $\bar{X}$ in the interval is $(1 - \alpha)$. (See Figure 10.3.) We have

$$
\begin{aligned}
(1 - \alpha) &= \text{pr}[a_\alpha \le \bar{X} \le b_\alpha] \\
&= \text{pr}[a_\alpha - \mu \le \bar{X} - \mu \le b_\alpha - \mu]
\end{aligned}
$$

(10.9)

Clearly, the probability statements in the two lines are the same, because all we have done in moving from line 1 to line 2 is to subtract μ from each term in the expression. Let us complete the standardization of the random variable $\bar{X}$ by dividing $\bar{X} - \mu$ by the standard deviation of $\bar{X}$, which in this case is 0.1. If we do the same

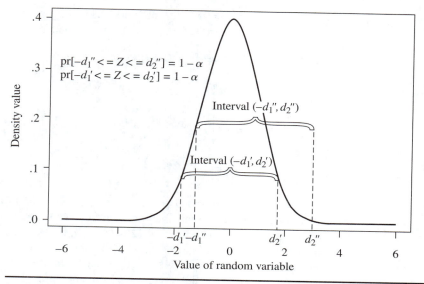

Figure 10.4　An example of different confidence intervals with the same confidence level

to each part of the expression inside the probability statement, we will still have the same inequality, but reexpressed for our purposes. Consequently,

$$\text{pr}[a_\alpha \leq \bar{X} \leq b_\alpha] = \text{pr}[(a_\alpha - \mu) \times \sqrt{n} \leq (\bar{X} - \mu) \times \sqrt{n} \leq (b_\alpha - \mu) \times \sqrt{n}]$$

$$= \text{pr}[(a_\alpha - \mu) \times 10 \leq (\bar{X} - \mu) \times 10 \leq (b_\alpha - \mu) \times 10] \quad (10.10)$$

where we have used the fact that the standard deviation of $\bar{X}$ is in our case $1/\sqrt{n}$, $n = 100$, and dividing by $1/\sqrt{n}$ is the same as multiplying by $\sqrt{n}$. Let us take stock of where we are. The bounds on the inequality involve the unknown μ, but everything else is known. The random variable $(\bar{X} - \mu)\sqrt{n}$, let's call it Z, has a normal density function with parameters 0 and 1; that is, the mean of Z is zero and the variance is 1, so that the *distribution of Z involves no unknown parameters.*

The problem is, Can we use this reformulation of the question to find our answer? We begin by choosing a confidence level of $(1 - \alpha)$ and defining a corresponding interval from an $N(0, 1)$ distribution. Let's rewrite Equation 10.10 to get an inequality statement about μ in terms of Z (see Figure 10.4):

$$(1 - \alpha) = \text{pr}[-d_1 \leq Z \leq d_2] \quad (10.11)$$

where we choose d_1 and d_2 such that the required probability is $(1 - \alpha)$. Because the random variable Z has a distribution with all known parameters, we can easily determine the bounds needed to obtain a probability of $(1 - \alpha)$ as is shown in Figure 10.4.

Suppose that d_1', d_2' are the *chosen* values for the bounds on the interval; that is, the probability that Z with an $N(0,1)$ distribution will yield a drawing in the interval

$[-d'_1, d'_2]$ is $(1 - \alpha)$. We now rewrite Equation 10.11 using d'_i, $i = 1, 2$, and substitute for Z its definition in terms of $\bar{X}$, μ, and $\sqrt{n}$. We obtain

$$\mathrm{pr}\left[-d'_1 \leq Z \leq d'_2\right] = \mathrm{pr}\left[-d'_1 \leq (\bar{X} - \mu)\sqrt{n} \leq d'_2\right]$$

$$= \mathrm{pr}\left[\frac{-d'_1}{\sqrt{n}} \leq (\bar{X} - \mu) \leq \frac{d'_2}{\sqrt{n}}\right]$$

$$= \mathrm{pr}\left[\left(-\bar{X} - \frac{d'_1}{\sqrt{n}}\right) \leq -\mu \leq \left(-\bar{X} + \frac{d'_2}{\sqrt{n}}\right)\right] \qquad (10.12)$$

$$= \mathrm{pr}\left[\left(\bar{X} - \frac{d'_2}{\sqrt{n}}\right) \leq \mu \leq \left(\bar{X} + \frac{d'_1}{\sqrt{n}}\right)\right]$$

where in the last step we multiplied by -1 and reversed the order of the inequality signs. This last statement looks like the one we have been trying to derive. By our derivation the probability in Equation 10.12 is $(1 - \alpha)$, the bounds are functions only of components that we know d'_i, and $\sqrt{n}$, or will know from a sample realization on $\bar{X}$. The bounded term is just μ. This is exactly what we have been looking for, a probability statement involving the unknown value of the parameter μ.

Notice carefully what the statement says. The interval centered at $\bar{X}$ of width $[-d'_2/\sqrt{n}, d'_1/\sqrt{n}]$ has a probability of covering the unknown μ equal to $(1 - \alpha)$. We have in fact created a new concept, a "random interval." This particular interval is random only with respect to its center of location, which is given by the random variable $\bar{X}$. Now we know how to use a sample to estimate the mean of a normal density function.

The estimate that we have provided is not a point estimate but an interval estimate. The interval is called a **confidence interval** and the probability assigned to it is called the **confidence level.** In our example, having taken a sample we have

$$\left[\frac{\bar{x} - d'_2}{\sqrt{n}}, \frac{\bar{x} + d'_1}{\sqrt{n}}\right] \qquad (10.13)$$

Equation 10.13 shows the observed confidence interval, and $(1 - \alpha)$ is the corresponding confidence level. Before sampling, there is a probability of $(1 - \alpha)$ that the interval will cover μ. After sampling, the observed interval either does, or does not, cover μ. Nevertheless, the corresponding confidence level indicates our degree of confidence that our observed interval covers μ.

The actual procedure to get numbers is simplicity itself. Collect a sample of size n in accordance with our sampling theory (Chapter 9). Calculate the statistic $\bar{x} = \Sigma x_i/n$ from the observed data. This is your point estimate that corresponds to a drawing from the random variable defined by $\bar{X} = \Sigma X_i/n$, where each random variable X_i is distributed as $N(\mu, 1)$. Our theory allows us to interpret this single number, $\bar{x}$, as a drawing from the distribution $N(\mu, 1/n)$. Finally, our theory allows us to assign a probability of $(1 - \alpha)$ to the coverage of the unknown μ by an interval of the chosen length, the interval $[\bar{x} - d'_2/\sqrt{n}, \bar{x} + d'_1/\sqrt{n}]$ is centered at $\bar{x}$.

If you look closely at Figure 10.4, you will see that there are two sets of interval bounds marked, d'_i and d''_i, $i = 1, 2$. Both intervals have a probability of $(1 - \alpha)$!

Now that you have seen the result, it will be easy to realize that there is an infinite number of such intervals; all you have to do is to ensure that the associated probability is $(1 - \alpha)$ and the d_i' can be adjusted in pairs to achieve this result. If you experiment with a pencil, paper, and the normal probability calculations in S-Plus [Labs, Statistical Tables, Normal], you will soon discover that the size of the interval is different for different choices of bounds, even though you can maintain the same probability level. Alternatively, you could use [Labs, Inverse Statistical Tables, Normal] to make the same discovery. You should compare the areas under the curve given up to the areas gained on the other side; that is, compare the probability given up on one side to the probability gained on the other.

Here is the clue to the solution of the choice of interval and whether we can find a unique one. Let us agree to choose the interval with the smallest length; such a choice will minimize the size of the interval containing the unknown mean, or equivalently will maximize the probability of coverage for a given size of interval. Look at Figure 10.4. Because the normal density function is symmetric about the mean, then it should be clear, especially after some experimentation with Figure 10.4, that the minimum size of interval is obtained when the interval boundaries are symmetric about the mean. Try the experiment of setting a symmetric boundary in Figure 10.4 of any size, determine its probability, and then try to increase the associated probability by moving the interval of fixed size about the graph. A minute will convince you that the symmetric interval has the highest probability for any interval of its size.

We could have discovered this result more logically. If you recall that the density function represents the rate of change in probability, then the maximum probability for a given interval length, or equivalently, the minimum interval length for a given probability, will be achieved when the two density values are equal. For example, suppose that you pick an interval and that the density values at the chosen bounds are equal. Now consider moving one bound slightly inward toward the middle; one has to move the other boundary outward to maintain the probability. But the loss in probability of coverage from moving the left boundary inward will be much greater than the gain in probability in moving the right boundary outward an equal amount. The interval is the shortest length for a given probability when the bounds are set so that the density values are equal.

We conclude this discussion about the choice of bounds for a symmetric distribution, the Gaussian in particular, by restating Equation 10.13 given we recognize that $d_1 = d_2 = d$ for the optimal interval for symmetric distributions:

$$\left[\bar{x} - \frac{d}{\sqrt{n}}, \bar{x} + \frac{d}{\sqrt{n}} \right] \tag{10.14}$$

To be sure you have the idea, consider Figure 10.5, which shows a nonsymmetric distribution. Repeat the experiment that you just performed on this density. You will soon discover that the maximum probability for an interval of given length is obtained when the value of the density is the same at the boundary points. So the rule to maximize the probability of an interval of given length, or to minimize the length for a given probability, is to equate the values of the density at the two boundary points. In Figure 10.5, the optimal bounds are d_1', d_2' and the nonoptimal bounds are d_1'', d_2''.

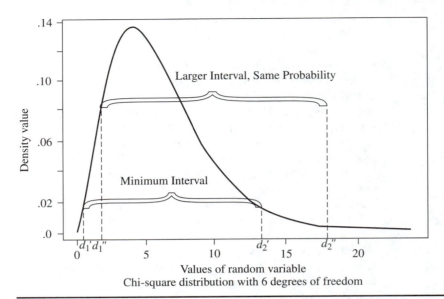

Figure 10.5   Illustration that the minimum interval length requires equal density values at the boundaries

If you read another textbook, the exposition of this topic may not match ours. It is common to ignore obtaining the minimum interval length by simply setting the tail probabilities equal. However, you now know that this casual practice is inaccurate.

We have one last generalization to make. In our discussion, we assumed that the variance of the parent distribution was 1. But this is seldom true; the usual case is that the variance of the parent distribution is $\sigma^2 \neq 1$. If you recall that in Equation 10.14 the term $1/\sqrt{n}$ is the standard deviation for the *mean* given that the parent distribution's variance is 1, the solution is clear. If the variance of the parent distribution is σ^2, the variance of the mean is σ^2/n, so that we can rewrite Equation 10.14 as

$$\left[\bar{x} - \frac{d\sigma}{\sqrt{n}}, \bar{x} + \frac{d\sigma}{\sqrt{n}} \right] \tag{10.15}$$

It is easy to remember the effect of the various components in this expression. Clearly, for larger variances for the parent population, the confidence intervals will be bigger at the same confidence level. A higher confidence level implies a longer confidence interval, giving less precision to offset the greater confidence; and finally a larger sample size implies a smaller variance for the mean, so that at the same confidence level the interval will be smaller.

Where did the value of α, and its complement $1 - \alpha$, come from? We could have as easily chosen interval bounds $[d_1', d_2']$, or, equivalently, we could have chosen an interval length. However, we cannot choose both α and an interval or an interval length. We can either choose α and then deduce, as we have done, the interval bounds; or, we can choose interval bounds and then deduce the corresponding value of α. In the Exercises you will be given practice in doing this. However, whichever choice we take, we are still left with the decision about the value of α or the length of the interval. What decision you make depends on your requirements for the confidence interval. Others, especially those who created the *Biometrika Tables* (Chapter 8), chose intervals with large probabilities associated with them. But with a personal computer you do not have to be bound by this convention. You can choose your own values of α or your own interval bounds. For example, suppose that you are producing bearings that must meet very precise tolerances on bearing diameter. In this situation you are better off determining an interval length and achieving a required probability $(1 - \alpha)$ by picking a large enough sample size. In this example, we have added another element: the ability to control both the α level and the interval length by picking a suitable sample size. Clearly, one could not even begin to think along these lines without the theory that we have been developing.

Let us summarize the mechanics of what we have been doing with an example. In the data file, the folder Testscor contains a file Psatsat.xls with four variables that represent the PSAT and SAT test scores of about 1800 students who took the examinations in 1981; the file contains a random selection from the total data set with 520 observations. Let us consider estimating confidence intervals for the mean PSAT verbal and mathematics scores. Of course, we do not know the variance, but for now let us assume that the variance is given by its sample estimate. Thus, the sample variance for the verbal score is 115.41 and that for the mathematics score is 124.96; these numbers were obtained from the sample by calculating S^2 for each set of scores. We calculate the means, $\bar{x}_j = \frac{1}{n_j}\Sigma x_{ij}$ with n_j observations for each set of scores, $j = 1,2$. The mean for the verbal score is 42.59. We now want to construct a 90% confidence interval on the assumption that we know the variance of the parent distribution; in our case the variance is 115.41. We also assume that we *know* that the parent distribution is Gaussian.

Recall Equation 10.15. For a chosen value for $(1 - \alpha)$, which in this case is .90, so that $\alpha = .1$, or $\alpha/2 = .05$, we can determine the values for the bounds on a Gaussian random variable Z. We know that $d_1 = d_2 = d$. The size of the excluded intervals on either side of the included interval are the same and have the same probability attached, $\alpha/2$ in our case.

We obtain the common value of d from the <u>Labs</u>, <u>Inverse Statistical Tables</u> in S-Plus for the standard normal (Gaussian) distribution. The z_0 value is 1.645; this is our d value for a probability of $\alpha/2 = .05$ in each tail. We have

$$(1 - \alpha) = .90 = \mathrm{pr}[-1.645 \leq Z \leq 1.645] \tag{10.16}$$

But Z is defined by $Z = (\bar{x} - \mu)/\sigma_{\bar{x}}$, where in our case $\sigma = 115.41$ and $\bar{x}$ has been observed to be 42.59; $\sigma_{\bar{x}}$ is given by $\sigma/\sqrt{n}$. If the variance of the parent distribution is 115.41, then the variance of the mean based on 520 observations is 115.41/520, so that the square root is $\sqrt{115.41}/\sqrt{520} = 10.74/22.80$. We substitute the definition of

Z into Equation 10.16 and rearrange the expression as we did in Equation 10.15 to obtain the 90% confidence interval for the PSAT verbal mean score:

$$\left[42.59 - 1.645\frac{10.74}{22.80}, 42.59 + 1.645\frac{10.74}{22.80}\right]$$
$$= [42.59 - 1.645 \times 0.47, 42.59 + 1.645 \times 0.47]$$
$$= [42.59 - 0.77, 42.59 + 0.77]$$
$$= [41.8, 43.4]$$

We have a confidence interval for the mean verbal score. How does the corresponding mathematics score compare? The observed mean mathematics score is 46.25 and the assumed value for the variance is 124.96. We continue to assume that the scores are distributed as Gaussian. If we are calculating another 90% confidence interval, then the d value will be the same, 1.645, and the only changes from the previous calculation are that the observed mean is different and that the assumed variance is different. Following exactly the same procedure, we substitute the definition of Z, $Z = (\bar{x} - \mu)/\sigma_x$, where now $\bar{x} = 46.25$, $\sigma^2 = 124.96$, $\sigma = \sqrt{124.96} = 11.18$, but n, the number of observations is the same, 520. The 90% confidence interval is given by

$$\left[46.25 - 1.645\frac{11.18}{22.80}, 46.25 + 1.645\frac{11.18}{22.80}\right]$$
$$= [46.25 - 1.645 \times 0.49, 46.25 + 1.645 \times 0.49]$$
$$= [46.25 - 0.81, 46.25 + 0.81]$$
$$= [45.4, 47.1]$$

In comparing the two results we see that the length of the confidence interval is nearly the same for the two scores, but that the confidence interval for the mathematics score lies to the right of the interval for the verbal score; it is likely that the mathematics score is greater by about 3 points than the verbal score.

Estimating a Binomial Probability

Now that we have mastered the estimation of the mean of a normal density function, let us try something a little more tricky. Consider the binomial probability distribution with parameters n and π. Examples from our data sets include the number of retained workers in the public utilities case, number of damaged O-rings in the *Challenger* disaster, number of students with a BA in a given city, number of males participating in an exercise program, the outcome on an experiment investigating the effect of rocking on crying babies, number of fatal car accidents, and so on. Usually we know the value of n, but we do not know the value of π. Let's go with custom and assume that we know that we are dealing with the binomial probability distribution and that we know the value of n. Our task is to find an estimator for π. Recall what π represents; it is the probability of a success on a single trial. But if we observe n trials, independent of course, we will obtain k successes, for some value of k; and k/n would be the observed relative frequency of successes. Might k/n indicate a useful estimator? There's only one way to find out, try it.

Accordingly, let us define the random variable $\hat{\pi} = K/n$, where K is a random variable distributed as a binomial with parameters n, known, and π, unknown. Our first task is to discover the first two moments of our potential estimator. We derive

$$E\{\hat{\pi}\} = \frac{E\{K\}}{n} = \frac{n\pi}{n} = \pi$$

$$E\{(\hat{\pi} - \pi)^2\} = E\{\hat{\pi}^2\} - \pi^2$$

$$E\{\hat{\pi}^2\} = n^{-2}E\{K^2\} = n^{-2}(n\pi(1-\pi) + (n\pi)^2)$$

therefore

$$E\{(\hat{\pi} - \pi)^2\} = \frac{\pi(1 - \pi)}{n} \tag{10.17}$$

Recall from Chapter 7 that the second moment about the origin of the binomial distribution with parameters n and π is $n\pi(1 - \pi) + (n\pi)^2$. We can conclude that the estimator $\hat{\pi} = K/n$ is unbiased because $E\{\hat{\pi}\} = \pi$ and that the variance declines in n, so that the estimator is also consistent. However, the distribution of the random variable $\hat{\pi}$ is not a binomial probability distribution, even though K is. An easy way to recognize this is that the binomial distribution is a distribution on the integers from 0 to n, whereas the distribution of $\hat{\pi}$ involves nonintegers over the interval zero to one.

But that is not the full problem that we face. Look at the definition of the variance of the estimator; it involves the parameter π! In short, the variance of our estimator depends on the very parameter that we are trying to estimate. We are back in a quandary; how do we determine a confidence interval if the variance that we need to determine it depends directly on the very parameter that we are trying to estimate?

In this particular case, we are lucky because someone else has taken the time to solve this problem for us. The task that the early researchers faced was how to allow for the uncertainty in the variance calculation. A simple way out, that can be justified when n is large, is to substitute $\hat{\pi}$, an estimator for π, in the calculation of the variance. Otherwise, the exact mathematical solution is complicated, so that tables and charts were provided to enable a researcher to determine, at least approximately, the length of a confidence interval with any given associated probability level, or confidence level. In our case, the solution is even easier in that we can use the actual mathematical algorithm used to produce those tables on our own computer. This is done in S-Plus, by choosing [Labs, Calculating Confidence Intervals, select "pi (exact)"] as we shall see.

We collect a sample of size n of independently and identically distributed random variables, each of which is distributed as $F(X)$, where $F(X) = \pi^X(1 - \pi)^{1-X}$. As our estimator is defined by $\hat{\pi} = K/n$, where K is the number of successes in n trials, our estimate is given by k/n, where k is the observed value of the random variable K in a single drawing from the binomial probability distribution.

For example, suppose that in an experiment the observed sample size, n, was 24, and that the observed relative frequency, k/n is 0.3. We can obtain the exact confidence interval having solved our mathematical problem by using [Labs, <u>Calculating Confidence Intervals</u>, choosing "pi (exact)" and setting $n = 24$, $p = 0.3$, where p represents the estimator $\hat{\pi}$, and alpha to 0.05]. The answer is read in the S-Plus Results window. For this example, the 95% confidence interval for π is [0.126, 0.511]. If we had chosen an alpha level of 0.1 instead, we would have obtained a confidence interval of [0.146, 0.479]. Notice that as we reduce the confidence level, we are able to decrease the length of the interval; that is, by increasing our probability that we will not cover the true value of π we can correspondingly decrease the length of the interval.

Let us consider another example. In the data file, the folder Misc and file Die8.xls contain a sample of independent tossings of an eight-sided die. Suppose that we wish to estimate the probability of getting no more than a "6" from these data. We reinterpret the data by agreeing that we will record a "success" whenever any side numbered from 1 to 6 appears and record a "failure" whenever any other side occurs. The recorded number of successes in 100 trials is 67, so that $\hat{\pi} = K/n = 0.67$. The 95% confidence interval with 100 observations is [0.569, 0.761].

There is a better method if n is greater than about 40. Recall from Chapters 7 and 8 that for large n the binomial probability distribution is well approximated by the normal density function. Consequently, if K is approximately distributed as $N(n\pi, n\pi(1-\pi))$, then $\hat{\pi} = K/n$ is approximately distributed as $N(\pi, \pi(1-\pi)/n)$. However, we still have our difficulty that the same parameter we are trying to estimate is in the expression for the variance. This is where the benefit of a large n comes to the rescue. From Equation 10.17, we see that $\hat{\pi}$ is consistent for π and hence $\hat{\pi}(1-\hat{\pi})$ is *consistent* for $\pi(1-\pi)$. Thus, we can substitute our consistent estimate for the variance into our procedure for calculating a confidence interval. Let us see how this works in practice.

Our estimator is $\hat{\pi}$ and is approximately distributed for large n as $N(\pi, \pi(1-\pi)/n)$. Our estimate will be $p = k/n$ and is to be regarded as a drawing from the distribution $N(\pi, \pi(1-\pi)/n)$. In Equation 10.12 we showed the procedure for determining the confidence interval for the mean of a normal density function. We repeat that procedure here setting $\sigma_\pi^2 = \pi(1-\pi)/n$:

$$\mathrm{pr}\left[-d \leq \frac{(p - \pi)}{\sigma_\pi} \leq d\right] = \mathrm{pr}\left[-d\sigma_\pi \leq (p - \pi) \leq d\sigma_\pi\right]$$

$$= \mathrm{pr}[(p - d\sigma_\pi) \leq \pi \leq (p + d\sigma_\pi)] \tag{10.18}$$

The difficulty is apparent. The bounds on π are themselves functions of π. However, we agreed that our "solution" is to rely on the consistency of $\hat{\pi}$ for π in the expression for the variance and to substitute for σ_π the consistent estimate, $\sqrt{p(1-p)/n}$. This fix to the difficulty is to be regarded as a "big n" ploy, not something that should be done when n is of only modest size. The official term for this is that it is "a large sample size" result.

Let us try an experiment. Consider that we have a sample from a binomial probability distribution with parameter $\pi = .4$ and $n = 100$. We will use both the exact confidence interval using S-Plus's algorithm and the normal approximation incorporating the "consistency argument" to evaluate the confidence interval for π. The parameter value in our experiment is $\pi = .4$, so $\pi(1 - \pi) = .24$, $n = 100$, and $\pi(1 - \pi)/n = .0024$. The sample results are

$$p = .39$$

$$\frac{p(1 - p)}{n} = .00238$$

$$\sqrt{\frac{p(1 - p)}{n}} = .0488$$

In this lucky situation the sampled value of $\hat{\pi}$ is so close to the correct theoretical value that our consistent estimate of the variance is nearly identical to the true value. Nevertheless, let us compare the confidence intervals obtained by both the normal approximation and from the direct calculation. We choose a confidence level of .95, or 95%, and use the normal approximation. For

$$d = 1.96$$

$$\text{pr}[-1.96 \leq Z \leq 1.96] = .95$$

Because $\hat{\sigma}_\pi^2 = p(1 - p)/n$ we can derive

$$\text{pr}[(p - d\hat{\sigma}_\pi) \leq \pi \leq (p + d\hat{\sigma}_\pi)]$$
$$= \text{pr}[.29 \leq \pi \leq .49] = .95 \tag{10.19}$$

where $p - d\hat{\sigma}_\pi = .29$, and $p + d\hat{\sigma}_\pi = .49$.

The result from the use of "pi (exact)" in [Labs, Calculating Confidence Intervals] is [.29, .49]. In our sample we were very lucky in that the sample estimate of σ_π was nearly equal to the theoretical value. The normal approximation is very good at n equal to 100.

Let us review our example using the eight-sided die. Previously, we calculated the exact 95% confidence interval and obtained the result [.57, .76]. What if we use the normal approximation? With $\hat{\pi} = .67$, the square root of the variance is $\sqrt{\hat{\pi}(1 - \hat{\pi})/100}$ $= \sqrt{.67 \times (1 - .67)/100} = 4.7021 \times 10^{-2}$. Using the same 95% confidence level, we have the same bounds, $d = 1.96$, so that substituting our calculations into the expression shown in Equation 10.19, we obtain

$$\text{pr}[(p - d\sigma_\pi) \leq \pi \leq (p + d\sigma_\pi)]$$
$$= \text{pr}[(.67 - 1.96 \times \sigma_\pi) \leq \pi \leq (.67 + 1.96 \times \sigma_\pi)]$$
$$= \text{pr}[(.67 - 1.96 \times .047) \leq \pi \leq (.67 + 1.96 \times .047)]$$
$$= \text{pr}[(.67 - .09) \leq \pi \leq (.67 + .09)]$$
$$= [.58, .76]$$

These bounds are also very close to those obtained from the exact calculation, [.57, .76.] In passing, we might note that a perfectly symmetrical eight-sided die would have a probability of .75 of getting no more than a 6. While the confidence interval covers the theoretical value, it only just does so; we might be a little suspicious of the experiment or of the symmetry of the die. Certainly, further experimentation is needed.

Estimating the Poisson Parameter

We have already noted that an important alternative distribution to the binomial is the Poisson. The Poisson is most likely the distribution of choice when the events have very low probability of occurring but the population is very large. Examples include the analysis of diseases; the occurrence of AIDS, heart attacks, car accidents, volcanic eruptions, and earthquakes; detection of concealed weapons at an airport or the presence of a bomb on an airplane; the analysis of rate of eruptions of Old Faithful; the identification of numbers of people that are illiterate; and so on.

Let us now look at estimating the parameter, λ, for the Poisson probability distribution. Here we run into two difficulties. First, as we recall, the Poisson probability distribution has a variance of λ, so we have the same problem. Worse, the Poisson probability distribution has a value for α_1, the standardized third moment, of $\lambda / \sqrt{n}$; the distribution is not symmetric. After all the discussion that we have had, you may well have forgotten that the choice of confidence interval depends on the shape of the density function. When the density is symmetric, as it has been so far, then the "optimal" confidence interval is also symmetric about the point estimate. But when the distribution is not symmetric, then the required interval should not be symmetric about the point estimate (recall our discussion about Figure 10.5). Choosing a symmetric interval around the mean of the Poisson is inappropriate as we have argued, but many algorithms ignore the effect and simply substitute tail intervals with equal probabilities. This "habit" stems, I believe, from the days before the universal availability of computers when people had to rely on tables in books for these probability calculations.

Let us try an example. Suppose that we have observed 15 occurrences of an event that we have verified is generated by a Poisson probability distribution; for example, 15 errors within a block of 100 pages of text selected at random. This single statistic, or estimate, is regarded as a drawing from a Poisson probability distribution with unknown parameter, λ. Before continuing, you might note a peculiarity of the Poisson—namely, that the value of λ is proportional to the size of the interval, or block. This result follows from the prime assumptions underlying the distribution that the occurrence of events is independent across nonoverlapping intervals, or blocks, and that the probability of occurrence within any interval, or block, is proportional to the size of the interval, or block. So in specifying a value of λ, we need to associate it with a specified interval, or block size.

In S-Plus, click on Labs, Calculating Confidence Intervals. In the dialog, click on Pois.lambda. In "xbar," key in 15. In Level of Confidence, "alpha," select ".05." Click OK. In the Report window you will see the 95% confidence interval [8.4, 24.7]. These bounds are the 95% confidence bounds for the observed estimate of λ of 15. What then would be the 95% bounds on the expected errors for a book with 1000 pages? These bounds were for a block of 100 pages, so the 95% confidence interval for 1000 pages is ten times greater, or [84, 247]; whichever block size we pick, this is not a very efficient publisher! However, if the same statistic had been obtained in a block of 10,000 pages—that is, you had observed 15 errors in a sample of 10,000 pages—then your 95% confidence interval would still be [8.4, 24.7] from the probability calculation. However, this is now an estimate per 10,000 pages, not per 1000 pages. The corresponding bounds for your 1000-page book are now [.84, 2.47], and that is a much better publisher.

Some researchers do not bother trying to achieve the minimum size of confidence interval for a given confidence level but merely set the tail probabilities to equal values. The interval chosen in the preceding calculation follows this convention. The differences are not great if the distribution is not too asymmetric; that is, in this example, the value of λ is not very small.

Consider two interesting examples that are quoted from William Feller's *An Introduction to Probability Theory and Its Applications* (1967, Vol. 1, p. 160). The first example involves data from an experiment on radioactive decay by Rutherford and colleagues in 1920. They recorded within 2608 consecutive time periods of 7.5 seconds each a total of 10,094 particle emissions. The total exposure time is $7.5 \times 2608 = 19,560$ seconds. In this example, we have 2608 drawings from a Poisson distribution; each drawing is the number of particle emissions within a time period of 7.5 seconds. One of the special characteristics of the Poisson distribution is that the sum of n independent drawings from a Poisson distribution with parameter λ is itself Poisson with parameter $n\lambda$. This enables us to simplify the calculations of the confidence intervals.

The mean number of emissions per second is 10,094/19,560, where 19,560 is the product of 7.5 seconds and 2608 observations. This ratio, call it $\hat{\lambda}$, is .516 and is an estimate of λ in terms of the number of emissions per second. The value of $n\hat{\lambda}$ is $2608 \times .516 = 1345.7$. To obtain the confidence interval for the estimate .516: in S-Plus, click on <u>Labs</u>, <u>Calculating</u> <u>Confidence</u> <u>Intervals</u>. In the dialog, click on Pois.lambda. In "xbar," key in 1345.7. In Level of Confidence, "alpha," select ".05." Click OK. In the Report window, you will see the confidence intervals for $n\hat{\lambda}$. Divide by 2608, the number of observations, to get the confidence bound for $\hat{\lambda} = .516$. The result is [.489, .544].

The second instructive example from Feller involves the incidence of flying bomb hits on London during World War II. An area of south London was divided into 576 one-quarter square kilometer areas, and in each the number of hits by flying bombs over a fixed period of time was recorded. The total number of hits was 537 over all areas, so that the average number of hits per quarter square kilometer section was $537/576 = .93$. If we assume that the incidence of flying bomb hits is distributed as Poisson, then our point estimate for λ is .93. So, the number of observations, n, is 576, and an estimate of λ is .93. From the Labs in S-Plus, we obtain the bounds for the total number of hits (537 at the 95% confidence level) and divide those bounds by 575 to get the bounds per square area. The result is [0.865, 1.01].

Both of these examples from Feller were checked for the agreement between the distribution of emissions or hits and the number that would be predicted by the Poisson distribution with the same mean. The fits were remarkably close, so that we can be fairly confident that we are indeed dealing with observations from a Poisson probability distribution. If the distributions involved were Poisson, then the estimated variances should be very close to the estimated mean values. In the radioactive decay example the estimated mean number of emissions per 7.5-second period is 3.87 and the estimated variance is

3.63, a close fit. In the flying bomb example, the estimated variance is .93 and the estimated mean is .93, an even better fit!

As another example consider the file Geyser2.xls in the data folder Misc, which recorded the durations and intervals between the eruptions of "Old Faithful." Let us concentrate on the interval times. We can easily convert these data into the number of eruptions within a 200-minute period. Doing so produces 110 observations. Given our development of the Poisson distribution in Chapter 7, one might suspect that the distribution of the eruptions would be distributed as Poisson. If so, we can use our procedures to estimate the unknown value of λ. The mean number of occurrences over a period of 200 minutes is 2.71 and the variance is .37; the range of values is from 0 to 4. Following a now well-established procedure, in "xbar," key in 298.1, where $298.1 = 2.71 \times 110$, for the estimated total number of eruptions and choose an α value of .05. Divide the bounds in the Report window by 110 to get the interval for the average number of hits to obtain the interval [2.41, 3.04].

Given that we have a sample size of 110, perhaps we can use the Gaussian approximation as indicated by the central limit theorem. Given that we have 110 independent observations on the random variable $\hat{\lambda}$, we can use the central limit theorem to claim that the distribution of the mean of these $\hat{\lambda}$ values will itself be distributed, at least approximately, as Gaussian with mean λ and variance λ/n, where n is the sample size, 110 in our case. If we further rely on the consistency of the estimator for the variance, we can use the normal distribution to write down a 90% confidence interval. From Equation 10.15, setting $(1 - \alpha) = .90$, $d = 1.64$, and noting that the variance of the parent distribution is thought to be equal to $\hat{\lambda}/n = 2.71/110 = 2.46 \times 10^{-2}$, with a standard deviation of $\sqrt{2.71/110} = .16$, we substitute these values into Equation 10.15. We obtain the following 90% confidence interval:

$$[\bar{x} - \frac{d\sigma}{\sqrt{n}}, \bar{x} + \frac{d\sigma}{\sqrt{n}}]$$
$$= [2.71 - 1.64 \times .16, 2.71 + 1.64 \times .16]$$
$$= [2.71 - .26, 2.71 + .26]$$
$$= [2.45, 2.97]$$

This result is quite close to the result that we obtained using the Poisson distribution directly.

We just mentioned that the variance of a Poisson distribution is λ when the mean is λ, but our estimated variance is .37, which is well outside the 90% confidence interval for the mean. Thus, it is likely that the conditions underlying the Poisson distribution do not hold in this case; in short, the eruptions of Old Faithful are not distributed as Poisson. This example is useful in helping you to see the vast importance of the theory in determining the appropriate procedures and the interpretation of the results. In this example, we interpreted the results and determined our procedures on the basis of assuming that the Poisson distribution was relevant.

What if we had merely assumed that we had an independent sample from some distribution but not Poisson? Our calculation of the variance and its use in our calculation of the confidence interval would have been different. We would have regarded the sample variance, .37 in this instance, as an estimate of the variance of the parent distribution. Our procedure then would either have followed those used in this section, assuming that we *know* the variance, or we could have used Student's T distribution (to be discussed next). The confidence intervals would have been quite different as would the interpretation of the results.

The Student's T Distribution

We have been moving from difficulty to difficulty. The next step is important, because it removes an unrealistic assumption that we have had to make until now. Let us return to our normal distribution example, but this time we will not assume that the variance is known. We are faced with two problems: how to obtain confidence intervals about the mean and how to obtain confidence intervals about the variance. Let us take them one at time. If the variance is unknown, then the variance must be estimated from the data. We have already tackled this issue when n is large with the "large sample theory result." That result depended on the consistency of the estimator. The task now is to find a confidence interval when n is small.

First, let us recall what we know. We know that we have a random sample from a normal distribution with fixed, but unknown, mean μ, and a fixed, but unknown, variance σ^2. The sample size is n, and n is not large. Previously, our estimator for the mean was $\bar{X} = \Sigma X_i / n$, and our estimator for the variance was $S^2 = \Sigma (X_i - \bar{X})^2 / (n-1)$. In the large sample case, we used S^2 as a point estimator for σ^2 in the standardization of $\bar{X}$. Further, an important aspect of our standardization was that the distribution of $Z = (\bar{X} - \mu)/\sigma$ did not depend on any unknown parameters, except for μ. Consequently, we were able to reexpress the interval for $\bar{X}$ in terms of μ as a probability interval for μ, without introducing any unknown values. We now face the problem of the distribution of our estimator, $\bar{X}$, depending on the unknown value of σ.

Thus, if we are able to derive another expression involving $\bar{X}$ that would be completely specified *except* for μ, then we would have our problem solved. We already know that the variance of $\bar{X}$ depends on the unknown σ^2; but it is also true that the mean value of S^2 is σ^2. Consequently, it would seem plausible that a ratio of $\bar{X}$ to S might not depend on the unknown value of σ. More precisely, we know that $\frac{(\bar{X}-\mu)}{\sigma}\sqrt{n}$ is distributed as $N(0,1)$, where $\bar{X}$ is the mean for n independently and identically distributed normal random variables. If S^2 is the sample variance for a variable distributed as $N(\mu, \sigma^2)$, then S^2/σ^2 is the sample variance for $N(\mu, 1)$. Consequently, it is plausible to consider the ratio

$$\frac{(\bar{X} - \mu)}{\sigma} \frac{\sqrt{n}}{\sqrt{\frac{S^2}{\sigma^2}}} = \frac{(\bar{X} - \mu)}{S} \sqrt{n}$$

In this ratio, we see that the unknown σ is canceled. W. S. Gosset, writing under the pen name of "Student," discovered that the distribution of the random variable T, defined by

$$T = \frac{(\bar{X} - \mu)}{S} \sqrt{n}$$

(10.20)

does not depend on any parameters that are unknown. More precisely, the distribution of the random variable T does not depend on the unknown value of σ. Unfortunately, some sophisticated calculus concepts involving the transformations of variables are needed to derive this result formally.

The corresponding density function for this new random variable is

$$g(T) = (K(v)\sqrt{v})^{-1}\left[1 + \frac{T^2}{v}\right]^{-.5(v+1)} \tag{10.21}$$

where $K(v)$ is a constant that ensures that the area under the curve

$$\left[1 + \frac{T^2}{v}\right]^{-.5(v+1)}$$

adds up to one as it should if the curve is to represent a density function. The one parameter, v, takes the known value of $(n-1)$. Consequently, this distribution does indeed depend only on known parameters. As we shall soon see, this result enables us to define a confidence interval for μ.

It is customary to refer to the Student's T distribution as Student's t, lowercase. I have departed from tradition to maintain our rule that *uppercase* italicized letters refer to *random variables* and *lowercase* to *observations* on random variables. I mention this only because you will see the lowercase used, even when the random variable is being referenced. In this text at least there will be no confusion as to which is which; the random variable is Student's T, the corresponding statistic is Student's t, where

$$t = \left(\frac{\bar{x} - \mu}{s}\right)\sqrt{n}$$

A Digression on Degrees of Freedom The one parameter in this distribution, v, is called the *degrees of freedom*. Degrees of freedom is not a hard concept to understand but tends to be treated somewhat mysteriously at times. Imagine that you have some joint probability distribution function of n random variables, X_i, that cannot be reexpressed in terms of fewer than n random variables without losing information about one or more of them. With n independent variables we have n independent bits of information. A joint probability distribution for n independent variables is said to have n degrees of freedom. Now imagine that, for example, you define new random variables, Y_i by $Y_i = X_i - \bar{X}$. There are clearly n random variables, but there are only $(n-1)$ degrees of freedom, because we have imposed a constraint on the behavior of the n variables. That constraint is that the Y_i have to add up to zero:

$$\sum Y_i = \sum X_i - n\bar{X} = \sum X_i - \sum X_i = 0$$

So we lose degrees of freedom when we impose constraints on the variation of the random variables. Suppose that n is merely 2. Then it is easily seen that Y_1 and Y_2 are jointly determined; if Y_1 occurs, then Y_2 must have occurred, because Y_2 satisfies the condition that it is equal to $-Y_1$. Starting with 2 random variables and imposing a con-

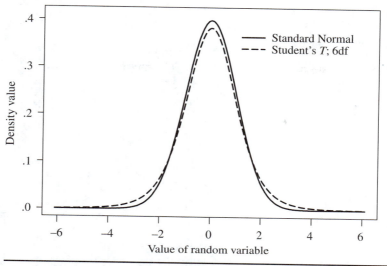

Figure 10.6   A Comparison of the normal and Student's *T* distributions

straint yields just one random variable that is not perfectly determined by the other. If we began with 3 random variables and imposed a constraint, then we would end up with just 2 random variables that are not perfectly determined by the others. The third is not truly a random variable because its value is determined exactly by the values taken by the other two. Remember that the very idea of a random variable was that we could not predict its value, either from its own past or from the values of any other variables. Including these "constrained variables" in our definition of random variables without modification, would cause us some considerable trouble in interpretation.

Thus, the term **degrees of freedom** represents the idea of independent bits of information. In general, when we sample *n* terms from some distribution, we obtain *n* independent bits of information, or *n* degrees of freedom. But as we have seen, if we impose constraints on the values taken by the observations we lose degrees of freedom. So degrees of freedom are measured by the number of independently sampled observations less the number of independent constraints that we impose on the data. In this text, we will restrict ourselves to very simple constraints, such as that imposed by subtracting the mean from a sample of observations.

Back to the Student's T Distribution   We now return to the Student's *T* distribution and its properties. First, notice that the distribution is symmetric about zero (see Figure 10.6). In your next course in statistics you will be able to show that the first four theoretical moments of the Student's *T* distribution are

$$\mu_1' = 0, \ \mu_2 = \frac{\nu}{(\nu - 2)}, \nu > 2$$

$$\alpha_1 = 0, \ \alpha_2 = 3 + \frac{6}{(\nu - 4)}, \nu > 4$$

(10.22)

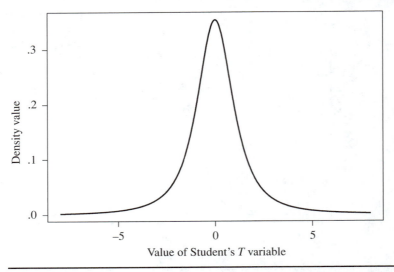

Figure 10.7 Example of a distribution with no second moment: Student's *T* distribution with 2 degrees of freedom

and from these four theoretical moments, in a manner that is by now beginning to be very familiar, you will easily recognize that as $n \to \infty$, consequently as $\nu \to \infty$, $\alpha_2 \to 3$ and α_1 is already 0.

So as the degrees of freedom increase without limit the Student's *T* distribution approaches the normal! We have

$$\mu'_1 = 0, \alpha_1 = 0$$
$$\lim_{\nu \to \infty} \mu_2 = 1, \lim_{\nu \to \infty} \alpha_2 = 3$$

For *n* relatively small, the variance of the Student's *T* distribution is larger than that for the standard normal. For example, if ν is 10, then the variance for the Student's *T* distribution is $\frac{10}{8} = 1.25$, which is a 25% increase over the variance for the $N(0,1)$. Figure 10.6 illustrates the comparison between a Student's *T* distribution with 6 degrees of freedom and an $N(0,1)$ distribution.

Before we leave our discussion of the properties of the Student's *T* distribution, we should consider one very curious fact. The variance of the random variable *T* was said to be $\nu/(\nu - 2)$, but if ν were 2 we would be in trouble! The variance for a Student's *T* distribution does not exist for degrees of freedom below 3. We have just been dealt a serious blow. So far we have confidently proceeded on the presumption that all distributions had moments of all orders, and here we suddenly discover that a variance does not exist. Even worse, perhaps, is that the fourth theoretical moment does not exist until the degrees of freedom have reached the value of 5! Figure 10.7 has plotted the Student's *T* distribution for $\nu = 2$ to give some idea of what a distribution with "infinite variance" looks like. At first glance there seems to be little to see, but on closer inspection what we observe is that the tails of the distribution are fatter than those for the standard normal distribution.

Is all lost? As it turns out, the answer is no, although its solution will require more work and mathematical preparation than we have time for at present. But we now know to be careful about our statements concerning the existence of theoretical moments. Henceforth, we will cautiously restrict our statements about theoretical moments to those distributions that actually have them. For now we will avoid small values of v.

Before leaving this topic, we can get some idea of the problem. What seems to be happening is that the rate of decay of the density function to zero is more than offset by the increase in squared terms in the definition of μ_2. If this is so, then we would expect that the moments of higher order than the variance would also not exist, because the limiting expression we derived for theoretical moments with continuous random variables does not exist. Recall the definition:

$$\mu_r = \lim_{\substack{n \to \infty \\ \Delta X \to 0}} \sum (X_i - \mu_1')^r \operatorname{pr}(X_i) \tag{10.23}$$

where $\Delta X \to 0$ as $n \to \infty$ in such a way that

$$\lim_{n \to \infty} \frac{\operatorname{pr}(X_i)}{\Delta X} = f(X)$$

for some X in the ith interval, so that in the limit as $\Delta X \to 0$ and $n \to \infty$:

$$\mu_r = \int (X - \mu_1')^r f(X) dX \tag{10.24}$$

is *finite*. Otherwise, if the limits do not exist, neither does the integral. If the product $(X_i - \mu_1')^r \operatorname{pr}(X_i)$ does not decline to zero fast enough as the absolute value of X_i gets big, the ever-increasing number of terms keeps adding sufficiently large additional terms that the sum no longer has a finite limit. Under these circumstances we say that the "integral does not exist." We now see clearly that if the second moment does not exist in the sense defined in Equations 10.23 or 10.24, then all moments above the second do not exist in the same sense.

Examine the graphs in Figure 10.8 after a quick review of Figures 10.6 and 10.7. In Figures 10.6 and 10.7 we saw that the Student's T distribution has "fatter tails" than the normal distribution, but nevertheless even the Student's T distribution seems to have high contact with the axis after eight units above and below the mean. Recall that the second moment is defined as a limit of a sum of the products of the variable squared and the value of the density function over the range of the variable. The limit as $\Delta X \to 0$ is the integral of the curve given by

- $Z^2 \times \phi(Z)$; in the normal case, $\phi(Z)$ is the normal density
- $T^2 \times g(T)$; in the Student's T case, $g(T)$ is the Student's T density

and we need to add up the areas under these curves to evaluate the second moments. Figure 10.8 shows the result of this operation for the normal and Student's T densities; the area is clearly finite under the curve $Z^2 \times \phi(Z)$. Now look at the

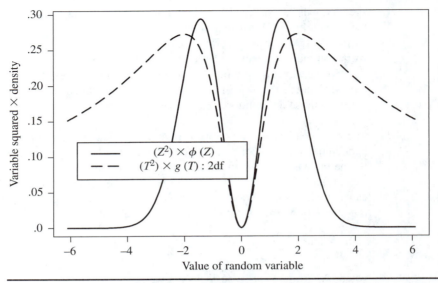

Figure 10.8   Illustration of the curves defining the second moments: Normal and Student's *T* with 2 degrees of freedom

curve $T^2 \times g(T)$. Here we see a completely different picture. It is intuitively plausible that the area under the curve $T^2 \times g(T)$ is not finite. This illustrates pictorially the difference between the normal density function and the Student's *T* distribution with 2 degrees of freedom; for the former the variance exists, for the latter the variance does not exist.

A Return to Student's T Confidence Intervals   We now focus our efforts on obtaining a confidence interval for the mean of a normal distribution with unknown mean and unknown variance. The random variable *T* with a Student's *T* distribution can be used to generate a confidence interval. The Student's *T* distribution is symmetric, so we know immediately that the confidence interval should be symmetric about the mean for the estimator, $\bar{X}$, and about the origin for the variable *T*. From the routines in S-Plus we can, for any given value for the sole parameter, ν, in the Student's *T* distribution, determine the probability of any specified interval. For example, in S-Plus [click on <u>Labs</u>, <u>Statistical Tables</u>, <u>Student's *t*</u>, select a value for the observed statistic, t_0, and choose a value for ν, that is referred to as "degrees of freedom"]. Experiment with some calculations of Student's *T* probabilities for various choices of the degrees of freedom parameter. Note that you can always calculate the probability of any interval, even when the *T* distribution does not have any moments defined; the density function always integrates to 1!

Recognizing that the Student's *T* distribution is symmetric, we can calculate a confidence interval by

$$\text{pr}[-d \leq T \leq d] = (1 - \alpha)$$

for some assigned value of $(1 - \alpha)$:

$$T = \frac{\bar{X} - \mu}{S} \sqrt{n},$$

$$S^2 = \sum \frac{(X_i - \bar{X})^2}{(n - 1)} \tag{10.25}$$

We choose a value for α so that we can calculate the value for d, say d_α. We use d_α and $(1 - \alpha)$ to determine the confidence interval:

$$\text{pr}[-d_\alpha \leq T \leq d_\alpha] = \text{pr}[-d_\alpha \leq \frac{\bar{X} - \mu}{S} \sqrt{n} \leq d_\alpha] \tag{10.26}$$

$$\text{pr}\left[\frac{-d_\alpha S}{\sqrt{n}} \leq (\bar{X} - \mu) \leq \frac{d_\alpha S}{\sqrt{n}}\right] \tag{10.27}$$

$$= \text{pr}\left[\bar{X} - \frac{d_\alpha S}{\sqrt{n}} \leq \mu \leq \bar{X} + \frac{d_\alpha S}{\sqrt{n}}\right]$$

The actual determination of a confidence interval is completed by substituting the sample statistics $\bar{x}$ and s^2, as well as the value of n in the expressions in Equation 10.27.

Notice something quite important in the formulation of this confidence interval. Relative to the case where the variance is known, we have less information. The interval in this case is "doubly random." The interval is random as before because the location of the interval depends on the value taken by $\bar{X}$, a random variable. *This interval also has random length.* The length of the interval in the unknown σ^2 case depends on S, where S^2 is also a random variable. This "double" randomness of our T confidence interval is illustrated in Figure 10.9. Our lack of information is also reflected in the value of d_α that is obtained from a Student's T distribution. For a given confidence level the value of d_α for the Student's T distribution is larger than the corresponding value for d_α using the normal distribution. This result reflects the "bigger tails" of the Student's T distribution relative to the normal distribution. The bigger tails of the Student's T distribution reflect our ignorance about the value of σ^2. Nevertheless, the probability that this random interval will cover the unknown mean is still given by $(1 - \alpha)$.

Now that we have developed the Student's T distribution to handle those cases in which we do not know the variance, which is just about all the time, let us compare the confidence intervals that we can calculate with the Student's T distribution versus the results that we obtained by assuming that our sample estimate of the variance was equal to the value of the unknown variance. Recall that we examined the confidence intervals for the means of the verbal and mathematical scores. We obtained the 90% confidence intervals: [41.8, 43.4] for the verbal score, and [45.4, 47.1] for the mathematical score. Let us obtain the confidence intervals using the Student's T distribution. Recall that the sample size was 520 in both cases; the sample means are 42.59, 46.25, respectively; and the sample variances were 115.41 for the verbal and 124.96

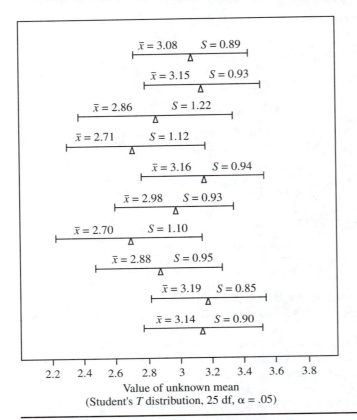

Figure 10.9   Comparison of ten sampled confidence intervals

for the mathematics scores. The values of S are 10.74 in the former case and 11.18 in the latter.

Using Equation 10.26 and the same confidence level of 90%, we can write for the verbal score:

$$\text{pr}\left[\bar{X} - \frac{d_\alpha S}{\sqrt{n}} \le \mu_1' \le \bar{X} + \frac{d_\alpha S}{\sqrt{n}}\right]$$

or

$$\text{pr}\left[42.59 - 1.645 \times \frac{10.74}{\sqrt{520}} \le \mu_1' \le 42.59 + 1.645 \times \frac{10.74}{\sqrt{520}}\right]$$
$$= \text{pr}[42.59 - 0.775 \le \mu_1' \le 42.59 + 0.775]$$
$$= \text{pr}[41.82 \le \mu_1' \le 43.37]$$
$$= 0.9$$

The corresponding values for the mathematical scores are

$$\text{pr}\left[\frac{\bar{X} - d_\alpha S}{\sqrt{n}} \le \mu_1' \le \bar{X} + \frac{d_\alpha S}{\sqrt{n}}\right]$$

or

$$\text{pr}\left[46.25 - 1.645 \times \frac{11.17}{\sqrt{520}} \le \mu_1' \le 46.25 + 1.645 \times \frac{11.17}{\sqrt{520}}\right]$$

$$= \text{pr}[46.25 - 0.806 \le \mu_1' \le 46.25 + 0.806]$$

$$= \text{pr}[45.44 \le \mu_1' \le 47.06]$$

The "d_α" values were obtained from the use of the Inverse Statistical Tables under S-Plus, Labs. Notice that the d_α value obtained is identical to that obtained using the normal distribution. At 520 degrees of freedom, the Student's T and the Gaussian distributions are virtually identical. This is because to all intents and purposes, 520 degrees of freedom are effectively infinite so that in both cases the d_α values are the same. However, there is still a major difference between the two cases. In the Student's T interval, the interval *width* is a *random variable* that depends on the sample values obtained for S. This is not the case in the Gaussian intervals where the interval width is fixed because the variance is assumed to be known and constant across repeated samplings.

A more enlightening example is provided by the data in the file Chal.xls in the data folder Misc. These are data on the occurrence of damaged O-rings in space shuttle flights. It is a stretch of the imagination to believe that the number of damaged O-rings is distributed as Gaussian, because they are integers and only a very few are recorded. Nevertheless, it is instructive to compare the difference in result using the Gaussian confidence interval assuming the variance is known and the Student's T–based confidence interval when the number of degrees of freedom are relatively small, in this case, 22. The estimated mean value for the number of damaged O-rings per flight is 0.39 and the estimated standard deviation, the square root of the sample variance is 0.66. If we use the Gaussian distribution assuming that this estimated standard deviation is actually the standard deviation of the parent distribution, we have from Equation 10.15:

$$\left[\bar{x} - \frac{d\sigma}{\sqrt{n}}, \bar{x} + \frac{d\sigma}{\sqrt{n}}\right]$$

$$= \left[0.39 - 1.96 \times \frac{0.66}{\sqrt{22}}, 0.39 + 1.96 \times \frac{0.66}{\sqrt{22}}\right]$$

$$= [0.39 - 0.28, 0.39 + 0.28]$$

$$= [0.11, 0.67]$$

using a 95% confidence interval.

Now consider the interval that we would obtain with the Student's T distribution at the same confidence level of 95%. From Equation 10.26, using the

<u>Confidence Intervals</u> under <u>Labs</u> in S-Plus, and specifying 22 degrees of freedom, we have

$$\text{pr}[\bar{X} - \frac{d_\alpha S}{\sqrt{n}} \leq \mu_1' \leq \bar{X} + \frac{d_\alpha S}{\sqrt{n}}$$

or

$$\text{pr}\left[0.39 - 2.07 \times \frac{0.66}{\sqrt{22}}, 0.39 + 2.07 \times \frac{0.66}{\sqrt{22}}\right]$$
$$= \text{pr}[0.39 - 0.29, 0.39 + 0.29]$$
$$= \text{pr}[0.10, 0.68] = 1 - \alpha = 0.95$$

Even in this case the difference between the two intervals is not striking; the Student's T interval is slightly bigger because the Student's T distribution has fatter tails than the normal, and so the value of d_α will be larger, 2.07 versus 1.96, for the normal distribution. However, there is still one very important difference in the interpretation of the results. With the Student's T interval the width of the interval is recognized as being a random variable itself, so that in repeated samplings from the parent distribution one would expect variation in the length of the confidence interval in addition to the variation from sample to sample for the center of the interval as indicated by the sampled value of the mean. In any event, the practical benefit of using the Student's T distribution is apparent only at very small sample sizes.

The Chi-square Distribution and Confidence Intervals for the Variance

We now come to our last example of finding estimators in this chapter. One unfinished piece of business is to produce, if we can, a confidence interval for the variance. Our need for information about the variance should be clear. Every time we need information about a mean, we also recognize that we require information about the variance as well to evaluate the accuracy of our mean estimate. In addition, the variance is often of great interest. For example, when evaluating a portfolio, a key aspect is the degree of risk involved and that involves measuring the variance. When we were comparing the revenues of alternative studios, we recognized that a key component in the comparison involved allowing for the very large differences in the variances of film studio revenues. An important aspect to evaluating the risk of an earthquake in California, or tornadoes in the Midwest, is to be able to evaluate the variances involved.

We already have an estimator for the variance, S^2. We know that it is a consistent unbiased estimator, but the question now is whether or not we can find a confidence interval. As we saw in the last example the answer to that question depends on whether or not we can find a probability distribution function that does not involve any unknown parameters besides σ. If so, then we should have no difficulty in defining a confidence interval.

Some very clever experimentation with the estimator S^2 discovered the following remarkable result. Suppose that Z_i, $i = 1, 2, \ldots, n$, is a set of independently and identically distributed random variables, each distributed as $N(0, 1)$. Then the distribution of $V = \Sigma Z_i^2$ is called chi-square with n degrees of freedom. Figure 10.1 is an example of a chi-square distribution with 6 degrees of freedom. This distribution was obtained from an $N(0,1)$ by deriving the distribution of the random variable V from the joint distribution of the Z_i. The mathematical tools used are beyond the level required for this text. The density function has the form

$$\chi_\nu^2(V) = K(\nu) V^{\frac{\nu}{2}-1} \exp\left[\frac{-V}{2}\right]$$
$$V \geq 0$$

(10.28)

where $K(\nu)$ is a constant chosen such that

$$K(\nu) \int_0^\infty V^{\frac{\nu}{2}-1} \exp\left[\frac{-V}{2}\right] dV = 1$$

The single parameter, ν, is called the degrees of freedom parameter, just as in the Student's T distribution. The first four theoretical moments for this distribution, including the standardized third and fourth, are

$$\mu_1' = \nu$$
$$\mu_2 = 2\nu$$
$$\mu_3 = 8\nu$$
$$\mu_4 = 48\nu + 12\nu^2$$
$$\alpha_1 = 4/\sqrt{2\nu}$$
$$\alpha_2 = 12/\nu + 3$$

(10.29)

The key point is that this distribution has a single parameter that is known. Consequently, if we can transform our problem into a random variable that has the chi-square density function, we can obtain a confidence interval for σ^2. But this is actually quite easy if we start with random variables that have a normal distribution.

Let us return to a sample of size n from the normal density function that is independently and identically distributed with mean μ and variance 1. The random variable defined by

$$W^* = \sum(X_i - \bar{X})^2$$

(10.30)

is itself distributed as a chi-square density function with parameter $(n - 1)$, which is the number of degrees of freedom for the distribution. We are nearly home free; all we now have to do is to recognize that if the parent distribution is $N(\mu, \sigma^2)$, then the random variable defined by $W = W^*/\sigma^2$ where W^* is defined by Equation 10.30, is distributed as a chi-square density function with parameter $\nu = (n - 1)$. When the X_i are from $N(\mu, \sigma^2)$, W^* is not itself distributed as a chi-square density function, although W is; the only difficulty is that we have to allow for scaling by σ^2. We can now produce a confidence interval for the variance when the parent distribution is $N(\mu, \sigma^2)$.

Suppose that we have a sample of n independently and identically distributed random variables, where each is distributed as $N(\mu, \sigma^2)$; we define W and W^* as in Equation 10.30. Because $W = W^*/\sigma^2$ is distributed as a chi-square density function, we can choose a probability level, say $(1 - \alpha)$, and then calculate d_1 and d_2:

$$\text{pr}[d_1 \leq W \leq d_2] = (1 - \alpha)$$

so that by replacing W by W^*/σ^2, we obtain

$$\text{pr}\left[\frac{d_1}{W^*} \leq \frac{1}{\sigma^2} \leq \frac{d_2}{W^*}\right] = (1 - \alpha)$$

or

$$\text{pr}\left[\frac{W^*}{d_2} \leq \sigma^2 \leq \frac{W^*}{d_1}\right] = (1 - \alpha) \tag{10.31}$$

And we now have a confidence interval for the parameter, σ^2. Once again with an asymmetric distribution we have the problem of choosing the smallest interval by appropriate choice of the critical bounds. But in this case we have a difficulty in that the interval is originally expressed in terms of $W = W^*/\sigma^2$, which naturally produces an interval for $1/\sigma^2$, not σ^2 itself. The consequence is that if we pick the smallest interval for $1/\sigma^2$, we pick the biggest for σ^2 itself. To get the smallest interval for σ^2 we will have a complicated problem to solve. In what follows, we, as have many others, take the easy route and choose intervals for W such that the probabilities are equal both above and below the confidence interval. This is the choice in the Labs that you will use later to calculate confidence intervals. However, to demonstrate to you the effect on the length of a confidence interval in the case of asymmetric distributions a special Lab routine, "Asymmetric Confidence Intervals," has been provided.

The actual use of this result is much easier than its derivation. Define the statistic:

$$s^2 = \sum \frac{(x_i - \bar{x})^2}{\nu}$$
$$\nu = n - 1$$

Choose an appropriate value for $(1 - \alpha)$ and consequently for α as well. For example, suppose that we have an independently and identically distributed sample of size 20 on a parent distribution that is $N(\mu, \sigma^2)$ and suppose that the sample value obtained for the statistic s^2 is 282.24. What is a 95% confidence interval for σ^2, when the degrees of freedom are 19? We can easily calculate this result using S-Plus, [click on Labs, Calculating Confidence Intervals, select case 4, enter the number of observations in menu n, and the value of s^2 in its menu]. The results are shown in the S-Plus Results window; the interval is [163.2, 602.1], which is not a very small interval. As with the Student's T distribution the length of this interval is random as it depends on the random variable S.

Let us apply our interval estimates to the problems that we examined in the previous sections with a view to examining the potential effect on the confidence intervals we used when we recognize our knowledge of the variance depends on an estimator and that we need to calculate confidence intervals for the variance as well. In each case, we will restrict our attention to a 95% confidence interval. Our first example is from the data on PSAT scores. We discovered that the sample variances for the verbal and mathematical scores based on 520 observations were 115.41 and 124.96, respectively. We calculated confidence intervals based on these results in two ways; in one we assumed that the estimated variance was equal to the unknown true variance, and in the other we recognized the sampling variability of our variance estimate and used the Student's T distribution to determine a confidence interval. Because we had such a large sample there was virtually no difference in the recorded size of the intervals, but there was a difference in interpretation. In both cases the recorded sample variances of 115.41 and 124.96 were used to determine the lengths of the intervals. Using our technique, we can provide a 95% confidence interval for both of the variances. We will use a subsample of only 200 observations to estimate the variance; we obtain the values 116.3 and 128.2. Once again, using [Labs, Calculating Confidence Intervals, and selecting Sigma^2], we obtain intervals for the variances of [96.4, 143.0] and [106.3, 157.6], respectively. Our choice of estimates, 115.41 and 124.96 as the actual variances may well be far from the truth given these results. It is a useful exercise to get a feel for the effect of the variation in the estimates of the variance of the parent distribution to calculate the confidence intervals for the mean using the upper and lower bounds of the confidence interval of the variance.

As a last example, consider the estimate of the mean number of damaged O-rings in the space shuttle. We had 23 observations, the mean number was 0.39 and the estimated sample variance was 0.4356. We questioned the relevance of the Gaussian distribution in this situation, but it is still instructive to consider a confidence interval for the standard deviation when the degrees of freedom are only 22. Substituting for s^2 and n at a confidence level of 95%, we obtain the interval [0.261, 0.873].

10.5 Maximum Likelihood Estimators

This section is for the student comfortable with calculus. Other students can skip this chapter without concern that doing so will impede their understanding of material presented subsequently in the text.

So far we have derived our estimators in a fairly simple and intuitive manner. We began by recognizing that, if we wanted to estimate the theoretical moments of a distribution, a reasonable first choice was to calculate the corresponding sample moment and then to examine its distributional properties. This approach, known as the **method of moments,** has its limitations. When we are primarily interested in the theoretical moments of the distribution, the procedure is simple and effective, but when we are more interested in the parameters of a distribution, or in nonlinear functions of the moments, the procedure loses its appeal. What we need is some principle, some general rule, that will allow us in a wide variety of circumstances to derive estimators. This is what the *maximum likelihood principle* does for us.

Recall the daddy longlegs example (Chapter 7). There we had reason to believe that the loss of legs could be modeled by the Poisson distribution. We estimated the value of the parameter λ, which is also the mean of the distribution, by the sample mean. Let us reconsider this example in the context of the estimation procedure that we are about to develop. First, let us review the statement of the probability distribution for the Poisson:

$$Po(K) = \frac{e^{-\lambda_0}\lambda_0^K}{K!} \tag{10.32}$$

Note that in this equation we are indicating that the parameter λ takes a specific value, λ_0, and that the random variable is K taking values $\{1, 2, \ldots\}$. For any choice of K, given the known parameter value λ_0, we can evaluate the probability associated with K; this is what we did in Chapter 7. Now suppose that we know that the data are generated by a Poisson probability distribution, we have observed a value, k_0, but we do not know the value of λ. We may redefine Equation 10.32 to summarize our information:

$$L(\lambda|k_0) = \frac{e^{-\lambda}\lambda^{k_0}}{K_0!} \tag{10.33}$$

$L(\lambda|k_0)$ is called the **likelihood.** It is the probability distribution rewritten with the parameters regarded as unknowns and the random variable replaced by the observed realization. For example, suppose that we had observed the value $k_0 = 3$; we would have

$$L(\lambda|3) = \frac{e^{-\lambda}\lambda^3}{3!} \tag{10.34}$$

This is a function of the unknown value for λ. We will use the **maximum likelihood principle,** which says, choose that value of the parameter that maximizes the likelihood function, to find a suitable value for λ, say $\hat{\lambda}$. The result of this calculation is known as the *maximum likelihood estimate*. Often abbreviated as MLE, the **maximum likelihood estimate** is the estimate that maximizes the observed likelihood function. More formally, we define the estimate in general by

$$L(\hat{\theta}|x_0) \geq L(\theta|x_0) \tag{10.35}$$

What this equation says is that after writing down the likelihood function given the observed realizations, x_0, we choose $\hat{\theta}$ such that the likelihood function is maximal over all other possible values of θ. When the likelihood function is differentiable, as in our Poisson case, we can find the maximum likelihood estimate, or MLE, by taking the derivative and setting it to zero. In the Poisson example we obtain $\hat{\lambda} = 3$. The derivative of Equation 10.34 for given k_0 is

$$\frac{D\left(\frac{e^{-\lambda}\lambda^{k_0}}{k_0!}\right)}{d\lambda} = \frac{e^{-\lambda}\lambda^{k_0}}{k_0!}\left[-1 + \frac{k_0}{\lambda}\right] \tag{10.36}$$

or

$$\left[-1 + \frac{k_0}{\lambda}\right] = 0$$

The solution is simply, $\lambda = k_0$.

However, differentiability of the likelihood function is not needed; all we require is to be able to determine a value for the parameter, say $\hat{\theta}$, that yields a maximum over all possible values for the parameter given the observed realizations of the sampling process. One way to do this is to graph the likelihood function to find a near approximation to the solution; the final solution can then be obtained by implementing a grid search. Thus, we calculate the likelihood function for a range of values in the neighborhood of the graphically determined value and search for the maximum.

We have defined the maximum likelihood estimate in terms of the observed data. However, what we really need to do is to define the **maximum likelihood estimator,** that function of the random variables that maximizes the likelihood function expressed in terms of the underlying random variables. We can do this very simply because we seek that value of $\hat{\theta}$ that maximizes the likelihood function for *any realization;* viewed theoretically, $\hat{\theta}$ is a function of the random variables $\{X_i\}$ and so is itself a random variable with its own probability distribution that can be derived from that of the $\{X_i\}$. The corresponding definition of the maximum likelihood estimator is to choose $\hat{\theta}$ such that

$$L(\hat{\theta}|X) \geq L(\theta|X) \tag{10.37}$$

So far we have illustrated the situation with a single observation. What if we have more than one observation? We can still apply the maximum likelihood principle, but we modify the likelihood function. If $F(X|\theta)$ represents the distribution function for a random variable X, and we have a sample of n independent drawings producing the observations $\{x_1, x_2, \ldots, x_n\}$, the realized likelihood function is

$$
\begin{aligned}
L(\hat{\theta}|\{x_1, x_2, \ldots, x_n\}) &= \prod_i L(\hat{\theta}|x_i) \\
&= \prod_i F(x_i|\hat{\theta})
\end{aligned}
\tag{10.38}
$$

The maximum likelihood estimate is that value of $\hat{\theta}$ that maximizes Equation 10.38. Equation 10.38 also indicates that the likelihood function for multiple observations obtained from independent sampling is simply the product of the likelihoods for each observation and that the likelihood is the distribution reexpressed in terms of known observed values and unknown parameter values. We can simplify the calculations by looking at the log likelihood function so that products are converted into sums:

$$
\begin{aligned}
\mathcal{L}(\hat{\theta}|\{x_1, x_2, \ldots, x_n\}) &= \log\left[L\left(\hat{\theta}|\{x_1, x_2, \ldots, x_n\}\right)\right] \\
&= \sum_i \log\left[L\left(\hat{\theta}|x_i\right)\right]
\end{aligned}
\tag{10.39}
$$

We discover the MLE from Equation 10.39 by choosing that value of $\hat{\theta}$ that maximizes the expression; one way to do that is to take the derivative and solve the resulting equation as was demonstrated for the Poisson example. However, if you follow this procedure, you need to be sure that you have indeed isolated the maximum, not a minimum. Fortunately, in most examples it is clear that a maximum has been obtained; graphing the likelihood is always advisable. The corresponding maximum likelihood estimator is obtained by substituting for the observed $\{x_i\}$ the random variables $\{X_i\}$. Thus, the maximum likelihood estimator is given by maximizing with respect to $\hat{\theta}$, the expression

$$
\begin{aligned}
\mathcal{L}(\hat{\theta}|\{X_1, X_2, \ldots, X_n\}) &= \log\left[L\left(\hat{\theta}|\{X_1, X_2, \ldots, X_n\}\right)\right] \\
&= \sum_i \log\left[L\left(\hat{\theta}|X_i\right)\right]
\end{aligned}
\tag{10.40}
$$

Let us return to our Poisson example for the daddy longlegs case. Rewriting Equation 10.40 in terms of the Poisson distribution for n observations, we have

$$
\begin{aligned}
\sum_i \log\left[L\left(\hat{\theta}|K_i\right)\right] &= \sum_i \log\left[\frac{e^{-\lambda}\lambda^{k_i}}{k_i!}\right] \\
&= \sum_i [-\lambda + k_i \log\lambda - \log(k_i!)] \\
&= -n\lambda + \sum_i k_i \log\lambda - \sum_i \log(k_i!)
\end{aligned}
\tag{10.41}
$$

Taking the derivative of the function defined in Equation 10.41 with respect to λ, summing, and setting the result to zero yields

$$
\frac{D\mathcal{L}}{d\lambda} = -n + \frac{\sum k_i}{\lambda} = 0
\tag{10.42}
$$

The solution is simply

$$
\hat{\lambda} = \frac{\sum k_i}{n} = \bar{k}
\tag{10.43}
$$

The result is the same estimator that we originally proposed informally in Chapter 7, the mean of the observations; the value obtained for $\hat{\lambda}$ is 1.49.

We initiated this discussion by looking at a simple example of a discrete random variable. We can as easily apply the principle to continuous random variables; the only difference is that the likelihood is now defined with respect to the density function. Instead of writing the density function as a function of a random variable given known values for the parameters, the likelihood is the same function rewritten in terms of unknown values for the parameters given known values for the observed realizations. In deriving the corresponding estimator, we express the likelihood function in terms of the random variables $\{X_i\}$.

One important aspect implicit in this discussion is that for continuous random variables the MLE is by design best regarded as a "modal" estimator; that is, the estimator's value is determined by the location of the mode of the density function. This is because the region in the vicinity of the mode is where the maximum mass of the density function will occur. When we contemplate a density function, we expect that the most likely range of observations on the random variable will occur in the vicinity of the mode. Correspondingly, when we fit a parameter to the likelihood function given a set of data, we will in fact reproduce that notion by picking a parameter value that will place the observed data as close to the mode as possible.

Recall that the mode is the ordinate at which the density function is maximal. The standard normal distribution has a single mode at zero; the chi-squared density function has a single mode at the point of maximum density given by $\nu - 2$, where ν denotes the degrees of freedom; the continuous uniform distribution has no unique mode; and there exist bimodal distributions.

A moment's reflection indicates that when the mode is close to the mean value for the distribution, the MLE will provide a useful solution to finding an estimator for the mean. But where the mode and the mean differ substantially, or there is no unique mode, then the MLE will not be very useful. For example, the chi-squared distribution is skewed to the right and the mode is less than the mean; $[\nu - 2] < \nu$, so that the MLE will be biased downward. Similarly, if the mode is larger than the mean because the distribution is skewed to the left, the MLE will be biased upward.

Nevertheless, maximum likelihood estimators are very important and provide useful solutions to the problem of generating estimators in a wide variety of circumstances. Partly, this is because the maximum likelihood principle provides a mechanical way for generating estimators; partly, it is because MLEs often have very useful distributional properties. Under easily specified conditions of the estimation problem, MLEs are distributed asymptotically as Gaussian; are asymptotically unbiased and consistent; and often can be shown to have a "minimum variance property" (that is, they achieve a theoretically derived minimum variance bound for any estimator obtained from "well-behaved" density functions). However, pursuing these topics is beyond our scope at this stage.

Elaborations on these introductory notes and a number of exercises on the derivation of MLEs are contained in the Exercises.

10.6 Summary

This chapter introduced the concept of *inference,* the process of drawing general conclusions from observing specific events. Inference should be distinguished from deduction. Deduction derives universally correct results by logical argument from a given set of premises. Inference involves the process of relating observed events to theoretical statements. Because of this relationship to the real world one can never be sure that the theoretical statements involved are relevant to the phenomena under analysis.

The main concern in this chapter is *estimation,* a special case of inference. We began by defining the *parent distribution,* and by applying the sampling theory from Chapter 9 we demonstrated the principles that define an estimator. Our initial effort was to assume very, very large sample sizes, so that the distribution of the estimator was *degenerate.* In the process we recognized the need to distinguish the *estimator* from the *estimate,* the former defines a random variable and, therefore, has associated with it a probability distribution. The latter is an observation on, or a drawing from, the distribution for the estimator. Estimates are real and are observed; estimators are theoretical entities. The estimation procedure used in the first section is based on large sample theory and involved *point estimates.*

To make useful progress, we needed to extend our ideas to samples of only modest size. To this end we defined two important properties of estimators, *consistency*

(Equation 10.3) and *bias*. Consistency involves the convergence to zero of the second moment of the estimator as $n \to \infty$. It is a very useful property in that if $\hat{\pi}$ is consistent for π, then $g(\hat{\pi})$ is consistent for $g(\pi)$. Bias implies that the expectation of the estimator is not equal to the parameter being estimated. In this connection we discovered that $M_2(X)$ is biased, but S^2 (Equation 10.6) is unbiased. For modest-sized samples, point estimates are not very useful, so we need *confidence intervals*. We explored this technique with several different examples that illustrated increasingly complex situations.

The first was to derive a confidence interval for the mean of a random normal variable when the variance is known. In this situation, we were able to prove that the distribution of a mean of normal random variables is itself normal. The second step was to define a confidence interval for the mean when the variance is unknown; this procedure involved defining the *Student's T distribution* (Equations 10.21 and 10.22) for the moments. In the process, we defined the notion of *degrees of freedom*. The Student's T distribution made us realize that seemingly well-behaved density functions might well not have moments of all orders. Implicitly, up to this time, we have assumed that the first four moments always exist. Now we have to be much more careful.

When we examined confidence intervals for both the binomial and Poisson distributional parameters, we recognized that special procedures were needed because the width of the confidence interval depended on the very parameter that we were trying to estimate. We did not solve this problem ourselves, but we relied on the solution of others who provided the algorithms that we needed to calculate the appropriate confidence interval when we cannot rely on the asymptotic convergence of the variance estimator to the true variance. Our last example was a confidence interval for σ^2; this involved defining the *chi-square distribution*, Equation 10.28, and Equation 10.29 for its moments. The confidence interval for σ is shown in Equation 10.31.

We concluded the development of estimators in this chapter with a brief discussion of the *maximum likelihood principle* and *maximum likelihood estimators*; this analysis was for those students comfortable with calculus. The maximum likelihood principle provides an algorithm for finding estimators in a wide variety of circumstances. Further, the MLEs so derived often have desirable distributional properties; in particular, they can usually be shown to be distributed asymptotically as Gaussian and are asymptotically unbiased and consistent. However, the reader should remember that MLEs are essentially "modal" estimators. The MLEs have the most desirable properties when the mode and the mean coincide; they have less desirable properties when the mode and the mean differ substantially.

Case Study

Was There Age Discrimination in a Public Utility?

The application of the tools developed in this chapter is immediate. We begin with the simplest procedures: What are the confidence intervals for the means of age and salary of former employees? Given that we are investigating a real problem, it is clear that we do not know the variance, so we should use the Student's T distribution, even though the degrees of freedom are

continues on next page

(Continued)

large. We already concluded in Chapter 8 that the assumption of normality for these data is reasonable. Further, as we discovered in this chapter, there will be little if any difference in the actual numbers if we use the Student's T distribution instead of the Gaussian, but there is a difference in the interpretation. By using the Student's T statistic we clearly recognize the variability of the variance estimator in the calculation of the confidence interval. We know that, unlike the normal case, the width as well as the position of the interval will change from sample to sample.

If you feel that we are being a bit pedantic on this matter, you are right, but to start, it is better to err on the side of caution and strict adherence to the correct procedures. This way you will not be surprised if in looking at a similar, but different sample, the confidence interval is observed to be much smaller or much larger.

Let us choose a confidence level $(1 - \alpha)$ of .80 to trade tightness of the interval for probability of coverage. For the mean of salary, the point estimate is $61,510, the degrees of freedom are 312, the estimated variance is 215565875.0 in dollars squared, and the 80% confidence interval is [60,442, 62,577]. The corresponding mean value for the age variable is 47 years for the point estimate, the variance estimate is 76, and the 80% confidence interval is [46.4, 47.7] based on 375 degrees of freedom. We might

also consider in passing the results for years in service; the mean is 22 and the 80% confidence interval is [21.4, 22.6] using 375 degrees of freedom. This is a rather remarkable result; with a lower bound estimate of mean years of service greater than twenty years, it would seem that this firm had very dedicated employees.

Given that we are dealing with real data, it is clear that we do not know the value of the variance. Let us produce an 80% confidence interval for each of the variances on the continuing assumption that the distributions involved are approximately normal. The point estimate for the variance of salaries is 2.155×10^8 and the 80% confidence bound is [1.95×10^8, 2.40×10^8]. Similarly, the point estimate for the variance of age is 76, and the 80% confidence bound is [69.0, 84.0].

The number of people who are male, or female, is the outcome of a binomial distribution. Our estimate of the probability of being female is .16 and the corresponding 80% confidence interval based on 375 degrees of freedom is [.14, .19]. To get an estimate of the proportion of people hired to those not hired, or who did not apply, we can rearrange the hire.stat variable to have just two cases, hired and not hired for whatever reason. We now have an outcome from a binomial distribution. The point estimate for the probability of being hired is .54, and an 80% confidence interval based on 375 degrees of freedom is [.51, .58]

Exercises

Calculation Practice

10.1 *Objective: To evaluate the degree of approximation involved in using the "large sample normal" approximation instead of the exact calculation.* Use S-Plus to calculate the exact and approximate confidence intervals for given values of $\hat{\pi}$ and n.

a. Calculate the exact 95% confidence intervals varying the values of $\hat{\pi}$ and n as shown in Table 10.1.

[*Computer directions:* Start S-Plus. On the menu bar, click on Labs, Calculating Confidence Intervals. In Parameter for Confidence Interval, click on "pi(exact)." In Level of Confidence, set

Table 10.1 **Binomial Estimates**

$\hat{\pi}$	n
0.8	16
0.3	16
0.1	16
0.3	40
0.2	40
0.3	200
0.05	200

"alpha" to ".05." In One Sample Cases, set n to "16," set "p" to ".8." Click Apply. The confidence interval will be in the Report window. Repeat for other Table 10.1 entries].

b. Calculate the approximate 95% confidence intervals for the values of $\hat{\pi}$ and n shown in Table 10.1. [Vary the computer directions by clicking on the "pi(approx)" parameter.] Compare the confidence intervals from the exact calculation to those obtained using $\hat{\pi}(1 - \hat{\pi})/n$ as an estimator for the variance of $\hat{\pi}$ and the normal distribution as an approximation to the actual distribution.

10.2 Repeat Exercise 10.1 for a confidence level of 99% and an assumed normal critical bound of 2.6.

10.3 If you are sampling from a Gaussian distribution with unknown mean and a known variance, $\sigma_0^2 = 25$, and the sample size $n = 100$, answer the following questions:

a. If you choose a confidence level of 95%, what is the length of the confidence interval? at a level of 90%? at a level of 99%?

b. If you choose to fix an interval length of 1, what is the corresponding confidence level? for a length of .9? for a length of .5?

c. Determine the sample sizes needed to achieve

(1) an interval length of 10 at a confidence level of 99%.

(2) an interval length of 5 at a confidence level of 90%.

(3) an interval length of 5 at a confidence level of 99%.

(4) an interval length of 1 at a confidence level of 99%.

10.4 *Objective: To illustrate the use of the* χ^2 *distribution.* Use the chi-square probability integral routines in S-Plus to obtain the following probabilities.

[*Computer directions:* Procedure 1: Start S-Plus. Click on Labs, Statistical Tables, Chi-Square. Click on Single Value. Enter the degrees of freedom and the chi-square statistic; click Apply. The probability will be in the Report window.

Procedure 2: Start S-Plus. Click on Labs, Inverse Statistical Tables, Chi-Square. Click on Single Value. Enter the degrees of freedom and the probability; click Apply. The chi-square statistic will be in the Report window.]

a. Let X be distributed as χ^2 with 6 degrees of freedom. Calculate the following probabilities. For each answer provide a diagram showing the area computed.

(1) $X < 12.592$

(2) $1.237 < X < 14.449$

(3) $0.676 < X < 9.236$

(4) $4.35 < X < 18.548$

(5) Provide a centered interval of probability .90.

(6) Provide a centered interval of probability .95.

(7) Provide a centered interval of probability .99.

(8) What is the value of x_1 if $pr(X > x_1) = .9$?

(9) What is the value of x_2 if $pr(X > x_2) = .95$?

(10) What is the value of x_3 if $pr(X > x_3) = .99$?

(11) What is the value of x_4 if $pr(1.942 < X < x_4) = .9$?

(12) What is the value of x_5 if $pr(x_5 < X < 15.7774) = .95$?

10.5 *Objective: To illustrate the use of the Student's T distribution.* Use the Student's T probability integral routines in S-Plus to obtain the following probabilities.

[*Computer directions.* Procedure 1: Start S-Plus. Click <u>Labs, Statistical Tables, Students</u> t. Click on Single Value. Enter the degrees of freedom and the t statistic; click Apply. The probability will be in the Report window.

Procedure 2: Start S-Plus. Click on <u>Labs, Inverse Statistical Tables, Students</u> t. Click on Single Value. Enter the degrees of freedom and the probability; click Apply. The t statistic will be in the Report window.]

a. Let T be distributed as Student's T, with 5 degrees of freedom. Calculate the following probabilities. For each answer provide a diagram showing the area computed.

(1) $T > 3$

(2) $-3 < T < 3$

(3) $-2 < T < 2$

(4) $-4 < T < 4$

(5) Provide an interval centered around the mean (0) of probability .90.

(6) Provide an interval centered around the mean of probability .95.

(7) Provide an interval centered around the mean of probability .99.

(8) What is the value of x_1 if $pr(X > x_1) = .9$?

(9) What is the value of x_2 if $pr(X > x_2) = .95$?

(10) What is the value of x_3 if $pr(X > x_3) = .99$?

(11) What is the value of x_4 if $pr(-1.6994 < X < x_4) = .9$?

(12) What is the value of x_5 if $pr(x_5 < X < 3.003) = .95$?

(13) Compare your answers with the probabilities obtained from the standard normal distribution for the same values.

b. Let T be distributed as Student's T, with 30 degrees of freedom. Calculate the following probabilities. For each answer provide a diagram showing the area computed.

(1) $T > 3$

(2) $-3 < T < 3$

(3) $-2 < T < 2$

(4) $-4 < T < 4$

(5) Provide an interval centered around the mean (0) of probability .90.

(6) Provide an interval centered around the mean of probability .95.

(7) Provide an interval centered around the mean of probability .99.

(8) What is the value of z_1 if $pr(X > z_1) = .9$?

(9) What is the value of z_2 if $pr(X > z_2) = .95$?

(10) What is the value of z_3 if $pr(X > z_3) = .99$?

(11) What is the value of x_4 if $pr(-1.4774 < X < x_4) = .9$?

(12) What is the value of x_5 if $pr(x_5 < X < 2.2783) = .95$?

(13) Compare your answers with the probabilities obtained from the standard normal distribution for the same values.

c. Based on your answers to (*a*) and (*b*), what can you say about the relationship between the standard normal distribution and the Student's T as the degrees of freedom increase?

10.6 **Worked.** *Objective: To explore the sampling properties of confidence intervals in a variety of situations for various parent distributions.*

[**Computer directions:** Start S-Plus. On the menu bar, click on Labs, Interpreting Confidence Intervals. Accept the default values in the dialog; click Apply. Examine the output in the Report window and the graph carefully. Repeat the exercise by setting n1, alpha, Parent Distribution, and Parameter for Confidence Interval to the various allowed options.]

This lab helps you to gain an intuitive feel for the concept of a confidence interval in a variety of situations. The most important lesson is to recognize the random character of the intervals and the relationship between the choice of α and the observed relative frequency of coverage.

10.7 You have a parent distribution $N(\mu, \sigma^2)$, and you know neither μ nor σ^2, but you do have a sample of observations of size 100, $\bar{X} = 3.6$, $s^2 = 12.3$. Construct confidence intervals for the unknown mean based on this information for the alternative confidence levels of 90%, 95%, and 99%.

10.8 If you have a parent distribution $N(\mu, \sigma^2)$, where neither parameter is known, the sample size is 100, and the observed value of s^2 is 36.4, obtain 95% and 99% confidence intervals for σ^2.

a. If the sample size is only 60, what are your intervals?

b. If the sample size is only 30, what are your intervals?

c. If the sample size is only 15, what are your intervals?

d. If the sample size is only 6, what are your intervals?

Comment on your results and illustrate your answer with diagrams comparing the confidence intervals.

10.9 You have observed 13 occurrences of an event within a given fixed block of time of 100

minutes. You know that the relevant parent distribution is the Poisson. Using the routine in S-Plus for calculating a confidence interval for the Poisson parameter, provide 90%, 95%, and 99% confidence intervals for the unknown value of λ.

Repeat the exercise when you observe 5, 21, and 35 occurrences.

By comparing your results what do you conclude about the relationship between confidence level, observed number of occurrences, and confidence interval length?

10.10 A random sample of 100 firms was drawn from a large number of clothing manufacturers. The average cost of capital was $10.1 million for the sample with a standard deviation of $2.5 million.

a. Construct a 99% confidence interval for the mean.

b. What is the meaning of a 99% confidence interval?

c. What would be the effect, if any, on the length of the interval in (*a*) if a lower level of confidence were used?

d. If a sample of 20 firms rather than 100 firms were selected, assuming the same level of confidence and the same standard deviation, what would be the confidence interval for the mean?

10.11 Out of 400 randomly selected managers in a nationwide sample of firms, 350 stated that they have an MBA degree. Construct a 95% confidence interval for the proportion of all managers who have MBA degrees.

10.12 In a sample of 579 randomly selected imprisoned convicted killers in penitentiaries nationwide, 16 were sentenced to death. Construct a 95% confidence interval for the proportion of all killers on death row.

10.13 In a sample of 200 randomly selected New York City residents, 12 had been victims of robbery in the streets at least once within the last year. Provide a 99% confidence interval for the proportion of New York City residents mugged at least once last year.

10.14 The average number of damaged O-rings in the fuel tanks of the *Challenger* space shuttle in its 23 flights was 0.391 with a standard deviation of 0.656. Provide a 99% confidence interval for the true average number of damaged O-rings and a 95% confidence interval for the true variance.

Exploring the Tools

10.15 Reconsider your answers to Exercise 10.3 when $\sigma_0^2 = 4$. By comparing your answers across these two questions and comparing results within each question draw out general conclusions on the relationship between the size of the parent distribution's variance, sample size, confidence interval length, and confidence level.

10.16 In Exercises 10.3 and 10.15, the size of the unknown mean was never stated. By comparing alternative sizes of the unknown means, say $\mu_1' = 0.1, 1.0, 5, -5, 20, 50$, comment on the usefulness of the confidence interval concept.

10.17 In Exercise 10.6, regard the estimate $s^2 = 12.3$ as being almost exactly equal to the true, but unknown, variance. Using the normal distribution, calculate the 90%, 95%, and 99% confidence intervals based on $\bar{x} = 3.6$ at a sample size of 100. Compare your intervals with those obtained in Exercise 10.6, and comment.

10.18 Evaluate the relevance of the claim that s^2 is consistent for σ^2 and s is consistent for σ. How quickly does it appear that s^2 converges to σ^2 in these situations? How quickly does s converge to σ?

10.19 *Worked.* Objective: To illustrate the algebraic derivation of the third and fourth moments

for the sum of two independent Gaussian variables. In the text, I promised to derive the third and fourth moments for the sum of two Gaussian variables. Let $Y = X_1 + X_2$, where both X_i are distributed as Gaussian with zero mean and unit variance and are independent. We can assume zero means and unit variances without loss of generality because in the text we have already derived the mean and variance for Y when the means and variances of the X_i are arbitrary.

The third moment of Y is therefore

$$E\{Y^3\} = E\{X_1^3 + X_2^3 + 3X_1^2 X_2^1 + 3X_1^1 X_2^2\}$$
$$= 0$$

so that

$$\alpha_1(Y) = 0$$

because the third moment of X_i is zero as is the mean, and X_1, X_2 are independent. Now examine the fourth moment:

$$E\{Y^4\} = E\{X_1^4 + X_2^4 + 4X_1^3 X_2^1 + 6X_1^2 X_2^2 + 4X_1^1 X_2^3\}$$

$$E\{Y^4\} = 3 + 3 + 6 = 12$$

because

$$E\{X_i^4\} = 3, \ E\{X_i^2\} = 1, \ E\{X_i\} = 0$$

so that $\alpha_2(Y)$ is

$$\frac{12}{\mu_2(Y)^2} = \frac{12}{2^2} = 3$$

We conclude that the sum of independent Gaussian variables is itself Gaussian.

10.20 In the text, we defined the concepts of bias and consistency. Having explained to your sister these ideas, she suggests that you should consider dividing by $2n$ instead of n—that is, consider $\tilde{X} = 1/2n \sum_i^n X_i$ as an estimate of the mean μ. She also suggests that maybe what you should consider is the size of the variance plus the bias squared; this is called the mean squared error (MSE). If $\hat{\theta}$ is an estimator of θ, the MSE($\hat{\theta}$) is given by

$$E\{(\hat{\theta} - \theta)^2\}$$
$$= E\{(\hat{\theta} - E\{\hat{\theta}\} + E\{\hat{\theta}\} - \theta)^2\}$$
$$= E\{(\hat{\theta} - E\{\hat{\theta}\})^2\} + E\{(E\{\hat{\theta}\} - \theta)^2\}$$
$$= E\{(\hat{\theta} - E\{\hat{\theta}\})^2\} + (E\{\hat{\theta}\} - \theta)^2$$
$$= \text{var} + \text{bias}^2$$

The cross-product term $E\{(\hat{\theta} - E\{\hat{\theta}\})(E\{\hat{\theta} - \theta)\}$ is zero because $(E\{\hat{\theta}\} - \theta)$ is a constant, or zero if the bias is zero, and $E\{\hat{\theta}\} - E\{\hat{\theta}\}$ is zero by definition.

Suppose you are considering an independently and identically distributed sample from a Gaussian distribution with a mean of μ and a variance of 1. Explain to your sister the full implications of her suggestion and comment on the implications for the idea of mean squared error.

10.21 On getting the results in Exercise 10.20, your sister now suggests using $\bar{X}_a = 1/(n + k)\Sigma_i^n X_i$ for some k, $0 \le k \le n$, $\lim_{n \to \infty} \frac{k}{n} = 0$. Explain to her the implications of this suggestion and for the concept of mean squared error. For various values of k illustrate the trade-off between bias squared and the variance.

10.22 The manager of a pipe manufacturing plant would like to estimate the average length of the pipe she produces. The manager randomly samples 16 pipes and finds a sample mean of 54 feet and sample standard deviation of 5 feet. Moreover, she constructs a confidence interval of [51.336, 56.664]. What is the confidence level associated with the manager's interval estimate?

10.23 (Reference: *Judgement under Uncertainty: Heuristics and Biases*, Cambridge University Press, 1998.)

Answer the following question, and justify your answer using the principles of inference that you have learned so far.

"A certain town is served by two hospitals. In the larger hospital about 45 babies are born each day,

and in the smaller hospital about 15 babies are born each day. About 50% of all babies are boys; however, the exact percentage varies from day to day. Sometimes it may be higher than 50 percent, sometimes lower.

For a period of 1 year, each hospital recorded the days on which more than 60% of babies born were boys.

Which hospital do you think recorded more such days?

a. the larger hospital

b. the smaller hospital

c. about the same

10.24 When you calculate a confidence interval for estimating the mean of a distribution and interpret your results, you will use some factual information, you will require some background knowledge of the distribution involved, and you will need some statistical theory. Write down an explanation of confidence intervals being very careful to identify which elements are known facts and which facts we assumed. Elucidate the elements of the theory. Identify what is random and what is not.

10.25 We have emphasized that the estimators that we have derived in this chapter are themselves random variables. This exercise and others to follow will help you confirm that idea. In each repetition of the experiment you will observe the theoretical distribution of $Z = (\bar{X} - \mu)\sqrt{n}/\sigma$ and a histogram produced by sampling $\bar{X}$ 500 times. We also have 500 samples of Z because we know μ, σ and n in this experiment.

[*Computer directions:* Start S-Plus. On the menu bar, click on Labs, Sampling Distributions. In the dialog box, set Statistic to "Z," "Sample from" to "Normal (0,1)," and "n1" to "5." Click Apply. Print the graph.]

Repeat several times with larger values for n1. Each time print the graph. Compare the graphs and comment.

10.26 Repeat Exercise 10.25, but this time set "Sample from" in the dialog box to (a) Uniform and (b) Exponential, varying $n1$ in each case. Print the graphs, and comment on the results. Compare with your results from Exercise 10.25. In particular, note the effect of increasing sample size, $n1$, on the usefulness of the Gaussian approximation as the appropriate distribution for the statistic $Z = (\bar{X} - \mu)\sqrt{n}/\sigma$.

10.27 This question supplements Exercise 10.25. Now assume that we do not know the variance. In each repetition of the experiment you will observe the theoretical distribution of $T = (\bar{X} - \mu)\sqrt{n}/S$ and a histogram produced by sampling 500 times the statistic t, $t = (\bar{x} - \mu)\sqrt{n}/s$. Note that in fact we get 500 samples of $\bar{x}$ and of s, and calculate t as shown.

[*Computer directions:* Start S-Plus. On the menu bar, click on Labs, Sampling Distributions. In the dialog box, set Statistic to "One sample t," "Sample from" to "Normal (0,1)," and "$n1$" to "5." Click Apply. Print the graph.]

Repeat the experiment several times with larger values for $n1$. Print the graphs and compare results.

10.28 Repeat Exercise 10.27, but this time set "Sample from" in the dialog box to (a) Uniform and (b) Exponential, varying $n1$ in each case. Print the graphs, and comment on the results. Compare with your results from Exercise 10.27. In particular, note the effect of increasing sample size, $n1$, on the usefulness of the Student's T distribution as the appropriate distribution for the estimator $T = (\bar{X} - \mu)\sqrt{n}/S$.

10.29 When we compare two distributions, say $N(\mu_1, \sigma^2)$ and $N(\mu_2, \sigma^2)$—that is, we are assuming that we have Gaussian distributions with possibly different means but the same variances—we can formulate the so-called Two-sample t statistic for estimating the difference in the means:

$$t = \frac{(\bar{x}_1 - \bar{x}_2) - (\mu_1 - \mu_2)}{\sqrt{s_p^2(\frac{1}{n_1} + \frac{1}{n_2})}}$$

where $\bar{x}_i$ are the means calculated from each sample, s_i^2 are the sample variances from each sample with sample sizes n_i, and s_p^2 is the pooled estimate of the variance:

$$s_p^2 = \frac{(n_1 - 1)s_1^2 + (n_2 - 1)s_2^2}{n_1 + n_2 - 2}$$

We further assume that the two distributions are independent of each other. (Note: We lose 2 degrees of freedom in calculating s_p^2, using $n_1 + n_2 - 2$, because we have used the data to estimate the two means, $\bar{x}_1$ and $\bar{x}_2$.)

The following exercise compares the theoretical distribution of the estimator T to the histograms produced by sampling $\bar{x}_1$, $\bar{x}_2$, s_1^2, and s_2^2 500 times and calculating t in each case. The estimator

$$T = \frac{(\bar{X}_1 - \bar{X}_2) - (\mu_1 - \mu_2)}{\sqrt{S_p^2(\frac{1}{n_1} + \frac{1}{n_2})}}$$

is distributed as Student's T with $(n_1 + n_2 - 2)$ degrees of freedom.

[*Computer directions:* Start S-Plus. On the menu bar, click on Labs, Sampling Distributions. In the dialog box, set Statistic to "Two sample t," "Sample from" to "Normal (0,1)," "$n1$" to "5," and "$n2$" to "5." Click Apply. Print the graph.]

Repeat the experiment with varying values of $n1$ and $n2$; pay particular attention to cases where $n1$ = $n2$ and where they differ substantially.

10.30 Repeat the experiment performed in 10.29, setting "Sample from" to (a) Uniform and (b) Exponential. Compare your results with those in Exercise 10.29. Comment.

10.31 Similar to Exercises 10.28 and 10.29, this exercise examines the extent to which the theoretical distribution for the variance estimator approximates closely the sample histograms. The estimator that we are examining is $W = (n - 1)S^2/\sigma^2$, and for this experiment we know σ^2; the corresponding sample statistic is $w = (n - 1)s^2/\sigma^2$.

[*Computer directions:* Start S-Plus. On the menu bar, click on Labs, Sampling Distributions. In the dialog box, set Statistic to "Chi-square," "Sample from" to "Normal (0,1)," and "n1" to "5." Click Apply. Print the graph.]

Repeat for increasing values of *n*. Repeat with "Sample from" set to (*a*) Uniform and (*b*) Exponential. Print your graphs and compare results. In particular examine the effect of increasing sample size *n1* on the results using "Sample from" set to Uniform and Exponential.

10.32 The chi-square distribution was introduced as the distribution of the sum of squares of a random variable distributed as Gaussian with zero mean and unit variance. This experiment enables you to examine how the shape of the distribution changes with the degrees of freedom parameter, df. As the degrees of freedom (df) increase what do you think is happening to the third and fourth standardized moments, α_1, α_2?

[*Computer directions:* Start S-Plus. On the menu bar, click on Labs, Z, t, Chi-square, F, Chi-square Curves. In the dialog box, vary the values of "df" by clicking on the df+ and df− buttons.]

10.33 In the text, we discovered the connections between the assigned alpha level; the number of observations, *n*, or equivalently the number of degrees of freedom, *n* − 1; and the critical value d_α. In the exercises that follow we will explore this relationship for the distribution Z, $Z = (\bar{X} - \mu)\sqrt{n}/\sigma$.

[*Computer directions:* Start S-Plus. On the menu bar, click on Labs, Z, t, Chi-square, F, Critical Values. In the dialog box, set Distribution to "Z," "alpha" to ".05," and Test Type to "Two-sided." Click Apply.]

Repeat the experiment, but set alpha to different values and observe the corresponding confidence interval lengths.

10.34 In this exercise, we continue examining the relationship between confidence levels, confidence interval lengths, and the corresponding critical bounds, but this time we examine the Student's *T* statistic.

[*Computer directions:* Start S-Plus. On the menu bar, click on Labs, Z, t, Chi-square, F, Critical Values. In the dialog box, set Distribution to "t," "df1" to "5," "alpha" to ".05," and Test Type to "Two-sided." Click Apply.]

Experiment with various combinations of df1 and alpha. Choose the same alpha levels used in the previous exercise, so that you can compare the effect of the approximation of the Student's *T* distribution with the Gaussian.

10.35 In this exercise, we examine the confidence intervals for the chi-square statistic.

[*Computer directions:* Start S-Plus. On the menu bar, click on Labs, Z, t, Chi-square, F, Critical Values. In the dialog box, set Distribution to "Chi-square," "df1" to "5," "alpha" to ".05", and Test Type to "Two-sided." Click Apply.]

Experiment with the various combinations of df1 and alpha. Note that the confidence intervals in this lab are created by assigning equal probabilities to the lower and upper regions; see the next exercise for the choice of bounds equating the density values. Print your graphs and after examining them carefully draw some conclusions about confidence intervals for variances.

10.36 In the text, we discussed the problem of how to assign the critical bounds for any assigned α level and noted that when the distribution is asymmetric, choosing bounds such that the densities at those bounds are equal produces the smallest interval length. This lab illustrates that idea.

[*Computer directions:* Start S-Plus. On the menu bar, click on Labs, Asymmetric Confidence Intervals. Set "alpha" to the desired level and choose *n* for the degrees of freedom.]

Examine the output in the Report window and the graphs that are produced. Experiment with the choice of alpha and *n*.

10.37 In Figure 10.9, we illustrated the sampling distribution for confidence intervals based on the Student's T distribution. This exercise enables you to experiment with creating your own sample of confidence intervals and to be able to explore their sampling variations.

[*Computer directions:* Start S-Plus. On the menu bar, click on Labs, Interpreting Confidence Intervals. In the dialog box, set "$n1$" to "20," Number of Intervals to "100," "Sample from" to "Normal (0,1)," "alpha" to ".05," and Parameter to "mu." Click Apply.]

a. Repeat the experiment observing each time what happens to the distribution of confidence intervals. Note that the interval length changes. Count the number of intervals that do not overlap the theoretical mean value, 0 in this case. Does the number match your alpha level?

b. Repeat the experiment, but set "Sample from" to (i) Uniform and (ii) Exponential.

c. Repeat the experiment, but vary $n1$ and compare interval lengths. Is the variation less for larger values of n? Compare the results and comment.

d. Vary the alpha level and count the number of noncovering intervals. How accurate is the theory?

10.38 *Worked. Objective: To illustrate the application of the maximum likelihood principle to estimation in the context of continuous random variables.* For the student comfortable with calculus.

To estimate μ in the Gaussian distribution using n independent samples the log likelihood function is

$$\log(L(\mu|\sigma_0^2, \{x_i\})) = (\log(2\pi)^{-\frac{n}{2}}) + \log(\sigma_0)^{-n} +$$

$$\sum_i \left\{ -\frac{1}{2} \left(\frac{x_i - \mu}{\sigma_0} \right)^2 \right\}$$

Expand the quadratic in the previous equation and simplify terms to show that the first derivative of the likelihood is

$$\frac{\partial \log(L(\mu|\sigma_0^2, \{x_i\}))}{\partial \mu} = \frac{n}{\sigma_0^2}(\bar{x} - \mu)$$

By setting this derivative to zero we derive the solution that the MLE is $\bar{x}$; we can easily demonstrate that this solution provides a maximum. For example, plot the likelihood in the neighborhood of $\bar{x}$.

10.39 For the student comfortable with calculus. Consider the likelihood for the binomial distribution:

$$L(r|\pi) = \binom{n}{r} \pi^r (1-\pi)^{n-r}$$

$$r = 0, 1, 2, \ldots, n$$

Show that the first derivative of the likelihood is

$$\frac{\partial L(r|\pi)}{\partial \pi} = L\frac{n}{\pi(1-\pi)} \left(\frac{r}{n} - \pi \right)$$

or

$$\frac{\partial L}{\partial \pi} \propto \frac{n}{\pi(1-\pi)} \left(\frac{r}{n} - \pi \right)$$

so that the MLE is the mean of the data.

10.40 For the student comfortable with calculus. Consider the Gaussian distribution where the mean is known to be zero but the standard deviation, σ, has to be estimated. For a sample of size n of independent drawings, derive the log likelihood function and discover the maximum likelihood estimate. Is the estimator biased for σ? Can you explain this result?

10.41 For the student comfortable with calculus. If the distribution is uniform over the interval $[0, \theta]$; that is, the density function is given by

$$dF(X) = \frac{dX}{\theta}, 0 \le X \le \theta$$

find the maximum likelihood estimator for θ.

Applications

Now that you have gained experience calculating confidence intervals, you can use the computer routines contained in S-Plus to calculate confidence intervals in the following exercises. In each case, what is important is your interpretation of the results and your statement about what you have learned from the calculations.

10.42 *Worked. Objective: To give you experience in using the routines in S-Plus for calculating confidence intervals by inputting the requisite information.* This exercise uses the data set Birds.xls in folder Misc.

a. Estimate confidence intervals for the mean and variance of the basal rate for various classes of birds in the data set. Choose your alpha level, but justify your choice.

[*Computer directions:* Start S-Plus. Import file Birds.xls in folder Misc. On the menu bar, click on Statistics, Data Summaries, Summary Statistics. In the dialog, set Variables to basalrat. In Statistics select Mean, Number of Rows, and Variance. Click Apply. In the Report window: Mean = 640.1, Total N = 32, Variance = 440232.0. Next, on the menu bar, click on Labs, Calculating Confidence Intervals. In the dialog box that appears, set Case to "mu, var unknown," set "alpha" to ".05"; set "n" to "32"; set "xbar" to the Mean value above; set s^2 to the Variance above. Click Apply. In the Report window the lower limit = 400.9 and the upper limit = 879.3.]

b. Estimate the confidence intervals for the mean and variance for basal rate per unit body mass.

[*Computer directions:* Create a new variable *ratemass* by clicking on the menu bar. Click on Data, Transform. In New Column Name, key in ratemass. In Expression, key in basalrat/bodymass. Click Apply. Use ratemass instead of basalrat in the computer directions.]

The main results are that Mean = 0.737, Variance = 0.0576, and the 5% Confidence interval is [0.65, 0.82]. Comment on the results from (*a*) and (*b*).

c. Plot the box-and-whisker plots for both variables *basalrat* and *ratemass*.

[*Computer directions:* Highlight the basalrat column in the Data window. On the menu bar, click

on Graph, 2D Plot. Select Box Plot. Click Apply. Repeat for ratemass.]

Note the implications for your conclusions that are drawn from the mean and sample variance. Using the menu command Text Functions, Moments, obtain the standardized third and fourth moments for both variables.

[*Computer directions:* On the menu bar, click on Text Routines, Moments. In the dialog, select Data Frame Birds. In Variable, select "basalrat." Click Apply. Repeat for "ratemass."]

Comment on your results. Note the difference between the variance calculated and the second moment from the moments routine! Do you recall why?

Commentary:

The 95% confidence interval for "basalrat" is [400.9, 879.3]; under the assumptions of the problem the probability that a random interval of the type calculated covers the true, but unknown, theoretical mean is .95. Similar comments apply for the confidence interval for the variable "ratemass," the estimated interval for which is [0.65, 0.82]. We recognize that in these calculations not only will the location of the interval change from random sample to sample but also the width as well. The estimation of ratemass, which shows the basal rate per unit of body mass, is probably the more informative measure in that it allows for variations in body mass. The rate gives information on the "efficiency" of various birds and may well vary between whether flighted or not.

The standardized third and fourth moments indicate to us clearly that basalrat is a distribution that is highly skewed to the right and has "fat tails." In contrast, the ratemass variable is nearly normal in shape and certainly much less skewed; as such it is the easier variable to analyze using conventional tools. Use the latter variable, unless there are overriding reasons otherwise.

The difference between the results obtained for the variances and standard deviations from the two sets of calculations stems from the difference in the degrees of freedom used, $(n-1)$ for the "Summary Statistics" and n for the "moments" menu command.

This exercise gives you practice in developing your understanding of confidence intervals and in using the computer to do the routine calculations. Also, you will gain experience in checking the validity of your assumptions and the effect that mistakes in your assumptions may have on your output and its interpretation. In this regard, pay particular attention to the values of the standardized third and fourth moments in the two cases.

10.43 Repeat Exercise 10.42 (*a*), but create two subgroups of basalrat data, one flighted and one flightless. What conclusions do you draw from a comparison of your calculations on the two groups? As you vary the alpha level, what implications does your choice have on your comparison between flighted and flightless birds?

[*Computer hint:* Click on Statistics, Data Summaries, Summary Statistics. In the dialog box, set Variables to "basalrat" and Grouping Variables to "flight." Click Apply. The mean, variance, and confidence interval will appear in the Report window. Repeat the procedure for "ratemass."]

10.44 Obtain confidence intervals for the mean and variance of the number of bombs ("bombs") discovered on airline flights as noted in data set Airbomb.xls in the folder Misc. Repeat the exercise for the number of bombs per passenger screened.

[*Computer directions:* Create the new variable *bombpass* by clicking on Data, Transform. In New Column Name, key in bombpass. In Expression, key in bombs/screened. Click Apply.]

Do you feel relieved by the second set of calculations?

10.45 Obtain confidence intervals for the percentage of people holding BA degrees and graduate degrees that are cited in the data set Cities2.xls in the folder Misc. What conclusions can you draw about the relative percentages of people with BA degrees and graduate degrees? What provisos ought to be mentioned in making this comparison?

10.46 In the folder Misc, data set Geyser2.xls, the interval times in minutes between eruptions of Old Faithful are recorded. The inverse of the interval times records the number of eruptions per minute, and if you multiply the inverse by 60 you will obtain the number of eruptions per hour.

[*Computer directions:* Start S-Plus. Import Geyser2.xls. On the menu bar, click on Data, Transform. In the dialog in New Column Name, key in numperhr. In Expression, key in (1/interval)*60. Click Apply.]

If the number of eruptions per hour were distributed as Poisson, an estimate of the mean would estimate the mean number of eruptions per hour. Provide a set of confidence intervals for the mean number of eruptions per hour at different alpha levels, and comment. How might you check the assumption that the distribution is Poisson?

10.47 In the folder Misc, data set Enerstus.xls, the energy consumption per capita in millions of BTUs in 1991 across states, is recorded. At the 90% confidence level, estimate the mean and variance of energy use per capita. Obtain the box-and-whisker plots, and comment.

10.48 In the folder Misc, data set Highway3.xls, are two variables: number of fatalities per 1000 population and number of fatalities per 1000 licensed drivers. At a 95% confidence level, obtain the confidence intervals for the mean and the variance of each and compare your results. What implications do you draw?

10.49 In the folder Misc, data set Humandev.xls, are two variables: the under-five mortality rate in 1960 and in 1980. At a 99% confidence level, obtain confidence intervals for both the means and the variances. Compare your results, and comment on the change in mortality rates over the intervening 20 years.

10.50 "When Scientific Predictions Are So Good They're Bad" was an article in the *New York Times* (September 29th 1998). The article's main point was that the National Weather Service predicted a flood crest of 49 feet, but the actual flood crest was 54 feet. The claim was that the town of Red River had been lulled into a false sense of security by the weather service's providing a single number to represent its forecast. If you were advising the weather service about this matter, what would you tell them to do in the future? Do you see a need for the residents of Red River to learn some statistical concepts?

10.51 If you were asked to estimate the mean and variance of phone use by a telephone company's customers, what factors would you take into account in designing the sampling procedure? If you suspected that business and family usage varies greatly, how would this knowledge affect your procedures?

10.52 Case Study: Was There Age Discrimination in a Public Utility?

You have several alternative ways in which to estimate the difference in salaries that allows for age differences. Restrict your attention to those hired and not hired from within the firm. Separate the population into those below 50 and those 50 and over, and calculate the mean salaries for each group using confidence interval techniques. Alternatively, calculate the salary per unit age—that is, salary divided by age, for those hired and not hired from within the firm—and estimate the mean of this variable. Consider doing this to make greater allowance for the variation of salary by age.

a. Comment on the theoretical implications of these two different approaches to assessing the impact of discrimination.

b. Produce the relevant confidence intervals, justifying your choice of confidence level, and evaluate your results. Which procedure would you recommend to the court and why?

[**Computer hint:** In the Discdata.xls file, use only former employees (ext.appl = 0). Create a data frame using Data, Split.]

Hypothesis Testing: How to Discriminate between Two Alternatives

11.1   What You Will Learn in This Chapter

This chapter continues our development of inference to a new situation, one in which the objective is to choose between two alternatives. One alternative is thought to be most likely to apply and is labeled the "null hypothesis," and the other is labeled the "alternative hypothesis." We ask questions such as, "Does process A take longer than B?" "Is the probability of contracting polio more likely using live antibodies or dead ones?" "Do daddy longlegs learn from their mistakes in losing their legs?" or "Are sunspots a source of global warming?"

We restrict our attention to just two alternatives. This inference procedure is called "hypothesis testing." We demonstrate how one can devise a strategy to use observed data to choose between the two alternatives in an "optimal manner." In setting up the hypothesis test, we note that there are two states of the world, we have only two choices to make, and that in any situation we can make one of two errors. Either we incorrectly reject the null, or we incorrectly reject the alternative hypothesis. To choose an optimal test procedure, we need to assess the cost, or importance to us, of each of these errors. In the process, we clarify the importance and limitations of hypothesis testing.

We also introduce the idea of a P value as a measure of the likelihood of the observed value of the statistic under the "null," or the presumed, hypothesis. In this way, we can transfer information expeditiously to others.

11.2   Introduction

In Chapter 10 we discussed estimation. Our solution to that set of problems involved having some prior knowledge as well as having some data that have been obtained in a particular way. Our prior knowledge involved knowing the relevant probability distribution and that the data were collected in such a way that we could be sure that we had a random sample. A random sample was important because it simplified greatly the procedures needed to use the sample to extract information about the unknown parameter values. We saw that the limited objective that we could achieve was to provide a confidence interval for the estimate of the unknown parameter value. It is true that if we had a very, very large sample we could rely on consistency of the estimator to obtain a point estimate for the unknown parameter value, but having such a large sample is both very costly and very unusual.

Our objective in estimation is to identify the precise distribution that generated the observed data, at least up to the limits imposed by our uncertainty. We can now consider an alternative problem. Suppose that we have even more information, but that we want to answer a different question. We believe that we actually know the distribution that is generating the observed data, but we also recognize that sometimes the relevant distribution is not what we think it is. What are some examples of this situation?

Suppose that you are the chief purchasing agent for a computer manufacturer and that part of your job is to order chips for the computers your firm manufactures. You have been doing this job for a while, so you have some very useful experience and knowledge of the situation. Let us suppose that your problem can be described as follows.

Usually, your supplier sends you chips that have a power usage rate of 90 milliamps, but on occasion when she has orders that exceed her firm's capacity, she will substitute a competitor's product for her own. The competitor's product has a power usage rate of 120 milliamps. Your firm is in heavy competition with the Japanese, so if you use these inferior chips, your firm will have to use special procedures to lower the overall power usage, and that is expensive. Over the past several months you have run a series of tests to verify that the mean power usage rates are indeed 90 and 120, respectively; that the variances are the same; and that the relevant probability distribution is the normal density function. Every few months your firm receives a large order of chips. Your task is to determine whether the delivered chips have mean power usage rates of 90 or of 120. Because your test procedure destroys the tested chips, you will wish to limit the total number of chips tested. The question that you want to answer is whether a particular batch of chips is from your regular supplier. Another way to express the matter is to ask how likely it is that your sample came from the distribution of power usage rates defined by your regular supplier's chips. So how do we solve this problem?

11.3 The Basic Idea of Hypotheses Tests

By now we have learned that it is always a good idea to plot a figure or a diagram to see the situation more clearly. Let us plot the two alternative distributions in the same diagram, as shown in Figure 11.1. In this figure, we see that the two distributions overlap, so that an observation from somewhere in the region of the overlap could as easily come from either distribution. Our problem can be reformulated as that of trying to devise a "decision rule" that will enable us to make, at least on average, reasonable decisions using a modest amount of data that we can obtain from the unknown distribution.

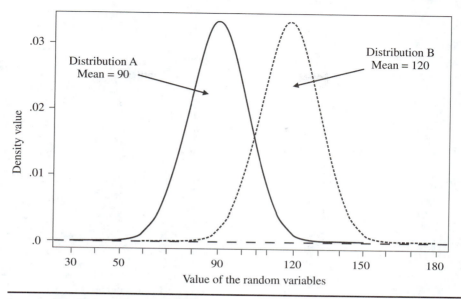

Figure 11.1   A comparison of two alternative distributions

An obvious initial solution is to pick some point between the two distributions, say the *critical bound* in Figure 11.2. The **critical bound** is a value that bounds the *critical region*. If an observation from the observed batch lies below the critical bound, then we declare that we have the distribution with the smaller power usage rate; but if the observed power usage rate from a test is greater than the critical bound, then we declare that we have the distribution with the larger power usage rate. This procedure sounds reasonable in this simple set of circumstances, but perhaps we should be a little cautious before we embark on extensive use of this naive idea.

We already know from our work in estimation that any results that we obtain from a sample of observations will involve considerable uncertainty about the precise values of the parameters of the distributions involved. Consequently, we cannot expect that we can ever be sure that we will be able to detect the actual distribution. What sort of errors can we make? There are two "states of the world"; the 90 mean power usage rate distribution applies, or the 120 mean power usage distribution applies. There are two decisions that we can make; we can choose the 90 mean power rate or the 120 mean power rate. Let us write these possibilities down as a two-by-two table.

Table 11.1 summarizes the situation. There are four possible outcomes: First, the state of the world is the 90 mean, and our decision rule leads us to pick either the 90 mean or the 120 mean. If we pick the 90 mean we happen to be correct, but we are unlikely to know that fact until it is too late to do us any good. But we could also pick the 120 mean, in which case we are wrong. Let us call this our first error, an "error of the first kind." Or, the state of the world is the 120 mean, and we could pick the 120 mean and be right, or we could pick the 90 mean and be wrong; but, as before we

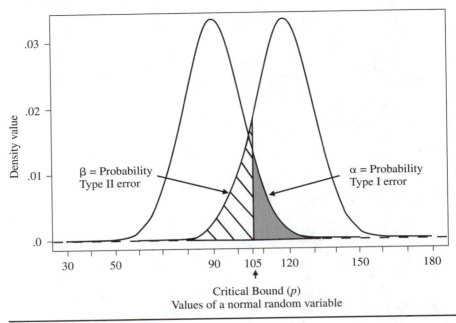

Figure 11.2   Illustrating probabilities of Type I and II errors

will never know whether we are right until it is too late to do us any good. Let us call our second error an "error of the second kind."

Talking about 90 milliamps and 120 milliamps is all very well, but it is a little clumsy. If we are to discuss alternative decision rules intelligently, we should develop some more useful terms. Let us call our statements about the alternative states of the world, our **hypotheses.** We began this discussion with an example in which we were fairly sure that we knew that the actual mean was 90, but that we needed to check that assumption. So let us label our hypothesis that the state of the world is the 90 mean distribution, the **null hypothesis;** the alternative assumption about the state of the world, we can call **the alternative hypothesis.** So we have in our modest problem two hypotheses about the actual state of the world—the null hypothesis, which is that hypothesis in which we have the greatest confidence, and the alternative hypothesis, the alternative state of the world that we must consider and against which we must guard ourselves.

Table 11.1   **Computer chip decision: Types of decision error**

		Decision	
		Mean 90	Mean 120
State of the World	Mean 90	✓	I
	Mean 120	II	✓

The actual state of the world is a fact, but a fact that we do not know. We hypothesize about the possible states of the world and seek a decision rule that will enable us to talk about the probable state of the world. We can make two types of errors using any decision rule that forces us to choose one, and only one, state of the world. We can incorrectly reject the null hypothesis, a **Type I error.** We can incorrectly reject the alternative hypothesis, a **Type II error.**

To get a better idea of these terms, let's try another example. In a court trial, the accused is either innocent or she is guilty; the actual situation that is known only to the accused is the state of the world. The jury hypothesizes two states, innocent or guilty; they are in fact asked to declare guilty, or "not guilty." (We will not make any subtle distinctions between not guilty and innocent.) Actually, given the circumstances, what jurors are asked to do is to declare: "guilt has been demonstrated to our satisfaction" versus "guilt has not been demonstrated to our satisfaction."

Whatever the jury declares, the state of the world, the "truth," is still unknown to all but the accused. Further, we have restricted our discussion to the existence of two exhaustive and mutually exclusive alternatives, both in terms of the state of the world and in terms of the allowed decisions. If one chooses alternative A, one necessarily rejects B—and vice versa.

Let the null hypothesis be innocent, or "not guilty" and the alternative hypothesis be guilty. However the jury decides, they run the risk of two types of error; an innocent person can be convicted, a Type I error; or a guilty person can be declared not guilty and let off, a Type II error.

Is there another alternative? Indeed there is. The courts in Scotland have the added choice of declaring that the prosecutor's case is "not proven." The "not proven" alternative is an appealing one, to statisticians, not to the accused. Choosing this alternative allows us to continue to collect data to be able to decide with more confidence. Although this approach has a lot to recommend it, the analysis of the implications of such a procedure is not at all easy; so we will continue with the simpler, but still challenging, task of trying to figure out the implications of having to choose between just two alternatives. We will make the issue even easier by sticking to situations in which there are two, and only two, alternatives; nothing else besides the null hypothesis and the alternative hypothesis can possibly occur.

These two hypotheses are usually labeled

- H_0: for the null hypothesis
- H_a, or H_1: for the alternative hypothesis

We can now explore the implications of our simple rule: pick a point, p, between the two hypothesized means and declare that the lower mean is the "correct" one if an observation lies below p and that the larger mean applies if an observation lies above p. But how do we decide on the value of p? And do we really want only one observation?

Look at Figure 11.1, which shows the two distributions involved in our computer chip example. The two distributions overlap. But what if we looked at the distribution of the sample mean, say $\bar{X}$, for each of the theoretical distributions? From our previous work, we know that the variance of the mean is given by σ^2/n, where σ^2 is the variance of the distribution of power usage and n is the sample size. Now it is

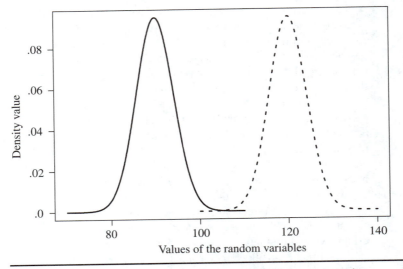

Figure 11.3   Testing hypotheses when the distributions are widely separated

clear that if n is large enough, the distributions of the estimator, $\bar{X}$, when applied to both of the hypothesized distributions will produce distributions of the estimator $\bar{X}$ that are clearly separated. This result follows because as n increases, the size of the variance decreases and if the variance of each distribution decreases enough, it is easy to distinguish the two distributions. Pick any point p that lies between the two distributions of the means and follow our rule; the situation is illustrated in Figure 11.3. This approach would seem to be a very easy way out of our problem; all we have to do is to choose a large enough sample.

If we could do this in all circumstances, we would indeed have solved our problem. But there is always a difficulty. In our case, the main difficulty is that the testing is both expensive and destructive, so that we want to keep the required sample size as small as possible. We are back to our original problem but this time with a better understanding of the situation. The difficulty that we really face is that we cannot easily and cheaply obtain a large enough sample to be able to distinguish with near certainty the two hypothesized distributions. Further, we now recognize that we will have to trade off our uncertainty about the outcome with the cost of sampling. A bigger sample will lower our uncertainty about our choice but only at a price.

Now we know how to proceed; we have to figure out the costs and benefits of our decision rule as a function of the sample size, n, and our choice of a critical bound p. The region to the right of the critical bound p in Figure 11.2 is called the **critical** or **rejection region,** and the region below the critical bound p is sometimes called the **acceptance region.** These two regions together contain all the possible values of the estimator, $\bar{X}$ in our case, that are consistent with the alternative hypothesis and the null hypothesis, respectively. The *critical region* is that region of the possible values of the estimator that are declared to be consistent with the alternative hypothesis; that is, these are the values that will lead us to state that we will reject the null hypothesis. Note that because we have two, and only two, alternative hypotheses, the statement that we reject the null hypothesis necessarily implies that we accept the alternative hypothesis. Alternatively, if we reject the alternative hypothesis, we necessarily must accept the null hypothesis.

A Digression on the Interpretation of Rejection Regions

We should be very careful with our use of language here. The terms *acceptance* and *rejection* refer only to our *decisions,* to our *chosen course of action* based on incomplete information and knowing that we could be wrong. Even after our decision we still do not *know* what the true state of the world is, but we will have taken action based on our estimate about the probable state of the world.

There is a philosophical distinction buried in this discussion. As we argued in Chapter 10, when we are trying to infer information about the state of the world we can never be absolutely sure that we are right. There is the old saying that "you can reject a hypothesis, but you can never accept a hypothesis"; that is, you cannot prove by logical deduction that something exists, although you can show that the existence of something is logically inconsistent with your observations. For example, we cannot build a "perpetual motion" machine, or a machine that will produce more energy output than is put into it. We cannot "prove by logical deduction" that you or I exist, but all our evidence indicates that our joint existence is very, very probable.

In the realm of statistics and of random variables, the situation is even worse, because usually we cannot even prove that something is logically impossible, only that it is very, very improbable. I am willing to go with the really big odds. So that when something is very, very probable I am prepared to act as if it were "proven"; and when something is extremely improbable, I am willing to act as if it were impossible. I suspect that you agree and are prepared to act in the same way. If so, we will have no further philosophical difficulties and can get on with the practical task of trying to decide the closer and more interesting cases.

How to Choose an Optimal Decision Rule

Now we can get back to the real problem: How do we trade off costs and benefits in deciding how big our sample size should be, and how do we choose a suitable decision rule? Examine Figure 11.2, but let us interpret this figure as representing the alternative distributions of a statistic, say $\bar{X}$, the sample mean, that could be drawn from one of two alternative distributions: one with a theoretical mean of 90 and one with a theoretical mean of 120 milliamps. Both have a variance of σ_o^2/n, where σ_o^2 is the known variance for the power usage rate distribution with either mean and n is the chosen sample size. For now let us not worry how we chose n. Also, let us pick any critical bound, p, between the two means; p may not necessarily be a very good choice, but at least we can see what the implications are and then we will be able to devise a better way of picking the "best p." At the moment, we do not know what a best p might be.

With the information that we have at the moment we can certainly calculate the probabilities of our two errors under the two alternative states of the world. As you read the discussion, keep an eye on Figures 11.2 and 11.3 to see clearly what is happening. Under each assumed state of the world, we can calculate the probabilities of making each of our decisions:

Mean $= 90$

pr $\{$Accept $H_0|H_0$ is true$\}$
$=$ pr $\{\bar{X}$ belongs to acceptance region *given* H_0 is true$\}$
$=$ pr $\{\bar{X} \leq p|H_0$ is true$\}$
$=$ pr $\{$Correctly accepting $H_0\}$

pr $\{$Reject $H_0|H_0$ is true$\}$
$=$ pr $\{\bar{X}$ belongs to critical region *given* H_0 is true$\}$
$=$ pr $\{\bar{X} > p|H_0$ is true$\}$
$=$ pr $\{$Type I error$\}$

Mean $= 120$

pr $\{$Accept $H_0|H_1$ is true$\}$
$=$ pr $\{\bar{X}$ belongs to acceptance region *given* H_1 is true$\}$
$=$ pr $\{\bar{X} \leq p|H_1$ is true$\}$
$=$ pr $\{$Type II error$\}$

pr $\{$Reject $H_0|H_1$ is true$\}$
$=$ pr $\{\bar{X}$ belongs to critical region *given* H_1 is true$\}$
$=$ pr $\{\bar{X} > p|H_1$ is true$\}$
$=$ pr $\{$Correctly rejecting $H_0\}$

The symbol "$|$" means that the expression that follows conditions the probability of the event defined by the expression before the symbol; that is, pr $\{$Reject $H_1 \mid H_0$ is true$\}$ means, "This is the probability that hypothesis H_1 is rejected given that the true state of the world is H_0." Further, the phrase "H_0 is true" is short for "under the assumption that the actual state of the world is such that the distribution has a mean of 90." Also notice that the probabilities of both Type I and Type II errors depend on the conditioning event—that is, on the *true* and *unknown* state of the world. The probabilities under the state of the world H_0 add to one; the probabilities under state of the world H_1 add to one; but you cannot add the probabilities under both H_0 and H_1. The probability of Type I error is evaluated under the null hypothesis, and the probability of Type II error is evaluated under the alternative hypothesis.

Let us work out an example with specific numbers. Suppose that σ_0^2/n has the value 144 when $n = 25$, so that the value of the standard deviation is 12 and the mean of $\bar{X}$ is either 90 or 120. A reasonable choice for p might be halfway between the two means, or 105. So our decision rule is just to "accept H_0" if an observed value of $\bar{x}$ is less than 105; otherwise, accept the hypothesis H_1.

What you do now is simple; obtain a sample of size 25 by randomly picking 25 computer chips, so that each has an equal chance of being selected. Calculate the sample mean, $\bar{x}$, and observe its value. If the observed $\bar{x}$ is less than 105 milliamps, you declare the received batch of computer chips to be acceptable with a mean of 90 milliamps instead of a mean of 120 milliamps.

But you could be wrong! To see how wrong let us compute the probabilities of Type I and Type II errors. The probability of Type I error is given by the probability that under the hypothesis H_0 the estimator $\bar{X}$ is greater than 105 when the variance is 144; that probability is .106:

$$\text{pr(Type I Error)} = \text{pr}(\bar{X} \geq 105 \mid \text{Mean} = 90, \text{Var} = 144)$$

$$= \text{pr}\left(\frac{\bar{X} - 90}{12} \geq \frac{105 - 90}{12} \mid \text{Mean} = 90, \text{Var} = 144\right)$$

$$= \text{pr}\left(Z \geq \frac{15}{12}\right); Z \text{ is distributed as } N(0, 1)$$

$$= .106$$

Correspondingly, the probability of Type II error is the probability under the hypothesis H_1 that $\bar{X}$ is less than 105 when the variance is 144; that probability in this example is also .106:

$$\text{pr(Type II Error)} = \text{pr}(\bar{X} \leq 105 \mid \text{Mean} = 120, \text{Var} = 144)$$

$$= \text{pr}\left(\frac{\bar{X} - 120}{12} \leq \frac{105 - 120}{12} \mid \text{Mean} = 120, \text{Var} = 144\right)$$

$$= \text{pr}\left(Z \leq -\frac{15}{12}\right); Z \text{ is distributed as } N(0, 1)$$

$$= .106$$

Both these probabilities were obtained by integrating the normal density function between the indicated bounds using the procedures discussed in Chapter 8 and summarized in Appendix A.

It has become conventional to label these two important probabilities α and β, respectively; that is, α is the probability of Type I error, β is the probability of Type II error. Correspondingly, the probability of not making an error under the null hypothesis is given by $(1 - \alpha)$, and the probability of not making an error under the alternative hypothesis is $(1 - \beta)$. This last probability, $(1 - \beta)$, is the probability of rejecting the null hypothesis (equivalently, accepting the alternative hypothesis) when the alternative hypothesis is true. The probability $(1 - \beta)$ is called the **power of the test.**

Now we have an interesting question. What is the effect of moving the position of p a little bit? Let us try this by moving p to the right toward the higher mean value. A glance at Figure 11.2, or even Figure 11.3, soon convinces us that moving p toward the right will decrease α but increase β. Correspondingly, moving p left, toward the lower mean, will increase α but decrease β. If then, we are to be able to choose between different values for p, that choice will have to reflect the trade-off between the values of α and β.

Clearly, a minimum requirement is that $(1 - \beta)$, the power of the test, the probability that the null hypothesis is rejected when the alternative hypothesis is true, should be greater than the probability that the null hypothesis is rejected when the null hypothesis is true. This complicated-sounding statement is merely the idea that the probability of convicting someone who is in fact guilty should be greater than convicting a person who is in fact innocent.

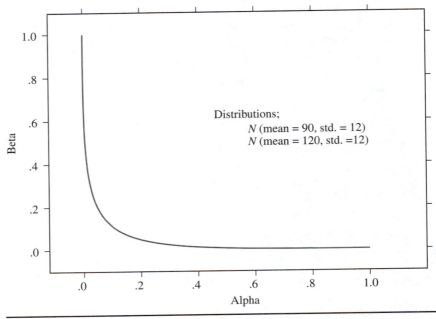

Figure 11.4   The beta–alpha curve for the hypothesis test illustrated in Figure 11.2

This requirement is a useful start, but there are still a lot of choices left for the value of the critical bound p. It is also clear that provided we hold n fixed, we cannot minimize both α and β.

We might take two approaches to this problem. First, if we have a rule for fixing α, then our procedure is quite easy, for the given α minimize β or, equivalently, maximize $(1 - \beta)$. In our very simple problem, fixing α necessarily fixes β at the same time. This is not always the case as we shall soon see; but it is a solution for our current problem, provided we can get a rule to fix α.

But suppose that we do not have a rule for assigning α, how might we find an optimal pair of values for α and β? To answer this question, it would help to explore the relationship between β and α—that is, between the probabilities of Type I and Type II errors and the distributions that are involved. For now, let us restrict ourselves to the normal distribution and to a given fixed sample size.

Figure 11.4 shows the trade-off between α and β as p is varied between a mean of 90 and a mean of 120; the shape and position of the curve depend on the two alternative distributions. For any problem of this type, the slope of the curve will always be downward from left to right as is demonstrated in Figures 11.4 to 11.7. Figure 11.4 shows the value of α and β for each possible value of p as it is varied from the lower to the higher mean. For a value of p near 90 we get large values of α and small values of β; for a value of p near 120, we get small values of α and large values of β.

Two pairs of distributions are represented in Figure 11.5. One pair has a common variance of 1, and the means differ by 2. For the other pair, the two distributions have

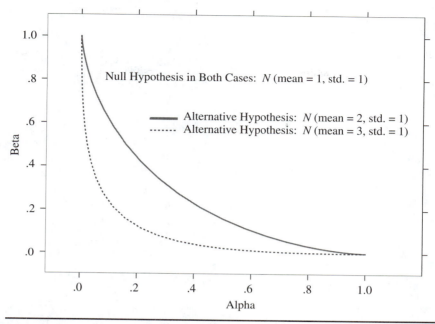

Figure 11.5 A Comparison of beta–alpha curves for different means, same variances

the same variance, 1, but the difference in the means is only 1. We see that the distance of the $\beta - \alpha$ curve moves out from the origin and the line becomes straighter when the difference in the means is less relative to the given variances. Alternatively, if, relative to the variance, the difference in the means is very large, then there is very little trade-off between α and β; both can be very small, see Figure 11.3. But if the difference is small, as in Figure 11.2, then there is a lot of potential for trade-off between the two probabilities and the curve lies farther from the origin.

As our next experiment, let us try to see what difference it makes to have a given fixed difference in the means but a difference in the variances. Consider Figure 11.6. When the null hypothesis variance is small relative to that of the alternative hypothesis, we obtain the dashed curve shown in Figure 11.6. But when the variance of the null hypothesis is large relative to that of the alternative hypothesis, the smooth curve applies. In the former case, small variations in the choice of α will induce small changes in β, whereas in the latter case small changes in α will induce large changes in β. For lowering both α and β, it is better to have the variance under the alternative hypothesis greater than that under the null. But it is better still to have both variances small.

Our last experiment can be illustrated in Figure 11.7. Here we are trying to see the effect of varying the sample size, n, as we increase it from that portrayed in the plot "Graph for Smaller n" to that portrayed in the plot "Graph for Larger n." We see that as sample size is increased, the $\alpha - \beta$ plot shifts in toward the origin; in short, we can lower both α and β! But remember that we can do this only by incurring the cost of a

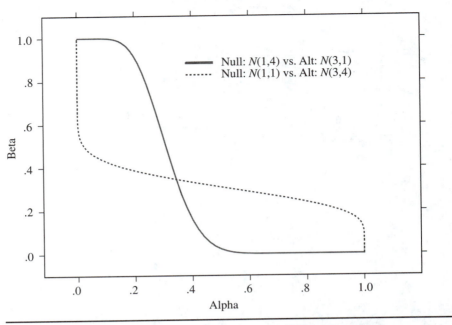

Figure 11.6   A comparison of beta–alpha curves: Same means, different variances

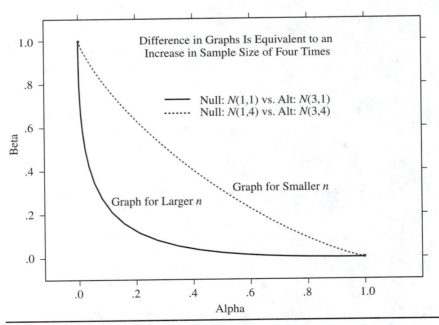

Figure 11.7   The beta–alpha curves to illustrate effect on increasing sample size

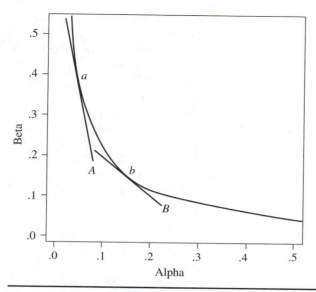

Figure 11.8   Illustrates how to choose optimal alpha and beta values

bigger sample size. The reason an increase in sample size leads to a lowering of both α and β is that the variance of $\bar{X}$ decreases. But this effect is just like increasing the distance between the means with a fixed size of variance for the parent distributions; compare Figures 11.2 and 11.3 and Figures 11.5 and 11.7. So we can conclude that it is easy to distinguish two means if they are wide apart, or we can get a big enough sample to make the variance so small that the difference in the means seems to be very large.

With all this preparation we can begin to tackle the main question: How do we choose the appropriate values for α and β? We have explored the relationship between the two probabilities of Type I and II error extensively. What we need now is a criterion to choose. What we have so far is the trade-off imposed by factors largely beyond our control.

Recall the example of the court trial. The jury has to declare an accused guilty or innocent. We saw that we have both types of error in this choice. Suppose that we can evaluate the probabilities of these errors. Our decision about how to pick our critical bound, our boundary for the critical region, depends on how we value these two types of error.

You may remember the old adage that "it is better that ten guilty men go free, than that one innocent man be hung." This statement indicates clearly someone's preferred relative price between the error of Type I and that of Type II. Let the null hypothesis be innocent and the alternative hypothesis be guilty; then Type I error is hanging an innocent man, whereas Type II error is letting the guilty go free. The cost to the unknown author of the adage of Type I error relative to that of Type II error is one-tenth, or the cost of Type II in terms of Type I is 10.

Look at Figure 11.8. The curved line is the trade-off between α and β that is determined by the shapes of the distributions. The straight line marked A is a line with slope 10 and represents the cost, or relative price, of Type II error in terms of Type I—that is, the price of β as a function of the price of α. We minimize our cost across both states of the world by finding the point of tangency between the straight line with slope 10 and the curve showing the trade-off in probabilities; that point is marked a in Figure 11.8. For a student of economics the last statement is one that is well recognized, but for others the logic may not be so clear. You can easily see that setting your choice of α and β in accordance with our rule minimizes cost by considering a different pair of values for α and β that are close to the supposed "optimal values." If you decrease β, you must increase α in accord with the curve indicating the trade-off between α and β, but the value to you of the change, as indicated by the straight line A, is worth less to you than the cost. Consequently, the cost per dollar spent is greater. The same type of argument indicates that the cost will rise if you consider increasing β.

What if our jury takes the view that for them the cost, or relative price, of Type I error in terms of Type II is one for one? This relative price is shown in Figure 11.8 as the line marked B, and the point of tangency that indicates the minimum cost across both states of the world is marked as b. The relative costs of the trade-offs between α and β and the fact that b indicates a cost minimum is even clearer than was true in the previous example.

By comparing these two cost-minimizing points we can evaluate the implications of the difference in attitudes toward Types I and II errors. For the former jury type, the optimum point is to have a very large value for β, .4, and a very small value for α, .04; whereas for the latter jury type, the optimum values for α and β are equal at a modest probability level of .16. The former jury is willing to trade a probability of nearly one-half of letting the guilty go free in exchange for a probability of only .04 of convicting an innocent person. The "eye for an eye" jury has an equal probability of convicting the innocent and of letting the guilty go free of .16. The "eye for an eye" jury lowers the probability of letting the guilty go free by a factor of less than four, but they raise the probability of convicting the innocent by a factor of four.

Under two different opinions about the trade-off between α and β, we have calculated the optimum values for both α and β. But what are the corresponding values for p_α, the critical bound? We can calculate both α and the corresponding value of p_α in the more explicit example of testing the computer chips. Suppose by using a similar argument we derive that the alternative optimal values for α are also .04 and .4 for the two types of computer chips.

To find p_α in these two cases we need to solve two probability statements. We require

$$\text{pr}\{\bar{X} \geq p_\alpha | H_0\} = .04$$

or

$$\text{pr}\{\bar{X} \geq p_\alpha | H_0\} = .4$$

To solve these equations we need to standardize the variable to be able to use the standard normal integrals in S-Plus (see Appendix A). The mean is by hypothesis 90 and the variance, $\bar{X}$, is known to be 144, so that the standard deviation is 12. We have either

$$\text{pr}\left\{ \frac{(\bar{X} - 90)}{12} \geq \frac{(p_\alpha - 90)}{12} \right\}$$
$$= .04$$

or

$$\text{pr}\left\{ \frac{(\bar{X} - 90)}{12} \geq \frac{(p_\alpha - 90)}{12} \right\}$$
$$= .4$$

We can solve in each case for p_α by recognizing that $Z = (x - 90)/12$ is distributed as $N(0, 1)$ and therefore involves no unknown parameters. The normal critical bound for $\alpha = .04$ is 1.75, and the critical bound for $\alpha = .4$ is 0.253. We solve

$$\frac{(p_\alpha - 90)}{12} = 1.75$$

or

$$\frac{(p_\alpha - 90)}{12} = 0.253$$

so that we have

$$p_\alpha = 111$$

or

$$p_\alpha = 93$$

Why Type I Error Is Usually Small

If you were to look at any table of standard probabilities for hypothesis tests, you would discover that the tabled α levels presented are all small; usually you see values of .1, .05, and .01. We might guess that the writers of the tables had, or thought their readers would have, high costs of Type I errors relative to those of Type II. The tables were originally created long before the advent of computers, when tables were a necessity for practical statistical work, not just a convenience as today. The choice of α values cited in the tables reflect the preferences of the statisticians writing them at that time.

The first use was in agricultural experiments to test for the effectiveness of new types of seed, fertilizer, and crop rotation, given the null hypothesis that the new procedures have no effect. Type I error in this situation is to decide that there is an effect, when in fact there is none; Type II error is to decide that there is no effect from some treatment, when there is. The early researchers clearly placed much greater emphasis on the Type I effects than on the Type II effects. The prejudice was to leave well enough alone unless there was overwhelming evidence to the contrary. Better not to introduce a new product that might be effective than to introduce a product that might not be effective. The FDA seems to use the same reasoning.

Recall our jury analogy. This discussion of Type I and II errors is reflected in the difference between the "standards of proof" between criminal trials and civil trials. In the former, the standard is "beyond a reasonable doubt"; for the latter, it is the "preponderance of the evidence." Presumably, the rationale is that the costs of Type I error are much greater in the former situation and less in the latter. Further, the cost of Type II errors, the wrongful release of a guilty party, is usually given little weight. As an aside, recent economic debates about the costs of crime that attempt to evaluate the social costs imposed by lowering the penalties for crime provide the factual basis for reassessing the costs of both Types I and II errors that might lead to a different trade-off between the two.

Recall the problem with the computer chips; you were to decide whether a given batch of chips from your supplier was, or was not, of the desired top quality of 90 milliamps of power. We had taken a sample of size 25 to obtain a known standard deviation of 12. The two theoretical distributions so defined were shown in Figure 11.1, and the corresponding $\beta - \alpha$ trade-off was shown in Figure 11.4. From what we now know, we could have carefully chosen our preferred level of sample size by determining, for example, the desired minimum $\beta - \alpha$ curve and then choosing the appropriate sample size to achieve that curve. Leaving this issue aside for the moment, let us concentrate on the choice of α and β levels.

We now realize that the choice depends on our assessment of the relative costs of Type I and II errors. If we agree that we place a high relative price on Type I error, then we might get lazy and use the standard tables with probabilities of Type I error of .1, .05, and .01, but if we do that, we will do so in full knowledge of the implications of what we are doing. If we pick an α level of .1 the corresponding level of β is approximately .1; for an α level of .05, the β value is about .2; and for an α level of .01, the β level is .4. So if you choose an α level of .01—that is, if you choose a probability of .01 of rejecting a perfectly good batch of chips—then the implied probability of accepting a bad batch of chips is very high, about 40%! Perhaps slavishly using the standard tables is not such a good idea. Clearly, from your point of view you want to guard against the acceptance of bad chips. Given our current discussion, the ways to do this are to

■ increase sample size to lower both α and β; but this may mean a big increase in the cost of testing
■ increase α to, say .2, in which case β is about .045, or about 4.5 percent

Look back at Figure 11.2. The two distributions are both symmetric with different means; we are merely trying to discriminate between them. So why is there this startling difference between the probabilities of Types I and II errors? If in Figure 11.2 we set α to a value of .01, we will see the problem immediately; p, the critical bound, is just below the mean of 120, so almost half of the entire distribution under the alternative hypothesis lies to the left of the implicitly chosen value of p. But why did we choose the mean of 90 to be the null hypothesis? Because, at the time we believed 90 to be the mean and would have been surprised to find it was not—it fit the definition of the null hypothesis. This sounded fine enough at the time, but maybe we should reexamine the issue.

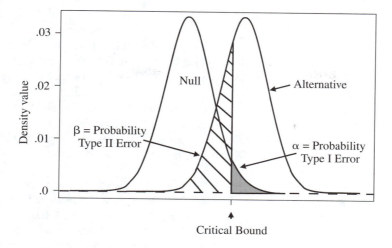

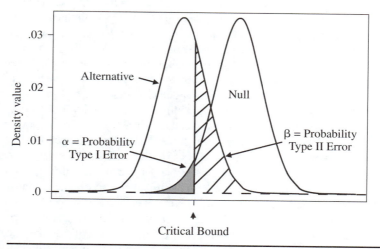

Figure 11.9   Illustrates the effect of exchanging null and alternative hypotheses

The Special Role of the Null Hypothesis

What if we reversed the roles of the null and alternative hypotheses? Examine Figure 11.9 carefully as you read this paragraph. If the 120 mean takes on the role of the null hypothesis, the 90 mean takes on the role of the alternative hypothesis, and we choose a low value for the probability of Type I error, say .01, then the probability of β is about .4; the numbers are the same as in the original example, but the interpretations have been reversed. Now the probability of incorrectly accepting a batch of bad chips is only .01; this is the probability of accepting a mean of 90 when the true mean is 120. And the probability of incorrectly rejecting a batch of good chips is .40; this is the probability of accepting 120 when 90 is the true mean. We might be safe from accepting bad chips, but we are going to send back an awful lot of good chips; it is likely that our supplier would soon refuse to do business with us any more. When the distributions are not so symmetrically placed relative to each other, the implications from choosing which distribution is null and which alternative are even more important.

The main lesson from all this is that we must be careful how we formulate our problem. We must not mechanically set up a hypothesis test and rush to the standard tables in the back of our favorite statistics book to look up the critical bound for a low value of α. We need to think the problem through and be sure we understand what it is that we are trying to do. You will get lots of practice at this in the Exercises at the end of this chapter.

Let us consider an example from our data directories. The folder Testscor contains the file Psatsat.xls, which contains in four columns the mathematics and verbal test scores for both the PSAT and the SAT. Using just the PSAT scores for now, we calculate the mean values for mathematics and verbal scores as 46.25 and 42.59, respectively. Consider testing the simple hypotheses that the means of the distributions for the mathematics and verbal scores are 46.3 and 42.6, respectively, against the alternative that they are each 50. We retain the assumption that the parent distributions for both mathematics and verbal scores are Gaussian in both cases. We do not know the variances for these data, but let us suppose for the sake of the exercise that the true variances are 124.96 for the mathematics and 115.41 for the verbal scores.

Under the null hypothesis that the mathematics mean is 46.3, we can derive the critical bound after assigning an α level. We recognize that we have a one-sided test that is "simple versus simple" and that "large values reject as the alternative is greater than the null." Let us suppose that we are willing to exchange level of confidence for narrowness of the acceptance region, so we pick an α of .2; the confidence level is only 80%. From the calculations under "Statistical Tables" in S-Plus, we obtain for a standard Gaussian distribution the critical bound, $d_\alpha = .84$; that is, for the standard Gaussian we agree to accept the null hypothesis if $Z \leq .84$ and agree to reject if $Z \geq .84$. Our observed statistic, the sample mean of the PSAT mathematics scores, has a Gaussian distribution with a variance of 124.96/520, where 520 is the sample size. The statistic has a mean under the null hypothesis of 46.3 and a mean under the alternative of 50; compare the situation that is illustrated in Figure 11.2. To get the critical bound for our statistic we need to use the equation that relates our statistic to the standard Gaussian distribution; under the null hypothesis, the unknown mean is 46.3:

$$Z = \frac{\bar{X} - 46.3}{\sqrt{124.96}} \sqrt{520} \tag{11.1}$$

We have chosen an α of .2 and a corresponding critical bound of 0.84, so that

$$\text{pr}(Z \leq .84) = .8$$

or

$$\text{pr}\left(\frac{\bar{X} - 46.3}{\sqrt{124.96}} \sqrt{520} \leq .84\right) = .8$$

Recall what we are looking for: a bound on $\bar{X}$ that satisfies our probability statement. We need only rewrite the last expression in terms of $\bar{X}$:

$$\text{pr}\left(\frac{\bar{X} - 46.3}{\sqrt{124.96}}\sqrt{520} \leq .84\right) = .8 \tag{11.2}$$

or

$$\text{pr}\left(\bar{X} \leq \frac{\sqrt{124.96}}{\sqrt{520}} \times .84 + 46.3\right) = .8$$

$$\text{pr}(\bar{X} \leq 46.71) = .8$$

Our derived critical bound on $\bar{X}$ is 46.71 and our observed $\bar{x}$ is 46.25, so we accept the null hypothesis. Note that the standard deviation of the mean in this example is $\sqrt{124.96}/\sqrt{520} = .490$. Given an alternative of a mean of 50, what is the power of this test; that is, what is the probability that the alternative hypothesis will be accepted when true and when the chosen critical bound is 46.71? This is the probability that the observed $\bar{x}$ will be greater than 46.71 when the mean of the parent distribution is 50. We have

$$\text{pr}(\bar{X} \geq 46.71 | H_1: \mu = 50)$$

$$= \text{pr}\left(\frac{\bar{X} - 50}{\sqrt{124.96}}\sqrt{520} \geq \frac{46.71 - 50}{\sqrt{124.96}}\sqrt{520} | H_1: \mu = 50\right)$$

$$= \text{pr}(Z \geq -6.71) = 1.0, approximately$$

Similarly, we could test the verbal scores for choosing between the two hypotheses, the verbal mean is 42.59 or the mean is 50. In this situation, given the information that we already have and the close similarity between the moments of the two sets of test scores, we can without calculation state that at any reasonable α level the null hypothesis that the mean is 42.59 versus it is 50 would be accepted. You can see this result by considering what would happen to our calculations when we substitute the values for the verbal scores. As a check, you should do the calculations. However, the example is useful in helping you to obtain a better feel for the procedure, so you should often be able to make the appropriate inference without actually having to do all the calculations.

11.4   Simple and Composite Hypotheses Tests

The procedure that we have followed so far is called a test of a **simple hypothesis versus a simple hypothesis**. *Simple* refers to the fact that under the hypothesis the distribution in question is completely specified; there are no parameters involved in the distribution that do not have either known or specified values. In the previous example, under the null hypothesis the mean was specified by the hypothesis and the variance was presumed known by the conditions of the problem. Consequently, under the null hypothesis the distribution is completely specified; the hypothesis is said to be simple.

Under the alternative hypothesis the hypothesis was also simple because we knew that we were dealing with a normal distribution, the variance was known, and the mean was specified by the hypothesis.

The procedure for testing hypotheses in the case of simple versus simple is to

- choose an appropriate estimator for the unknown parameter in the problem ($\bar{X}$ in our previous example)
- choose an appropriate sample size using our criteria
- specify a critical bound, say p_α, where p_α is chosen in accordance with the ideas we elaborated
- evaluate the probabilities of both Types I and II errors
- collect a sample in accordance with the principles elucidated in Chapter 9, calculate the estimate, say $\bar{x}_0$, and compare its value with that of p_α
- if $\bar{x}_0 < p_\alpha$, declare the alternative hypothesis rejected; so the null hypothesis is "accepted"
- if $\bar{x}_0 \geq p_\alpha$, declare the alternative hypothesis "accepted," because the null hypothesis is rejected

Now let us suppose that the alternative hypothesis is not completely specified. We can do this in several ways, but for now let us concentrate on what are called **one-sided** tests. The null hypothesis is still completely specified, but the alternative hypothesis is now that the alternative mean is merely bigger than that under the null. We no longer have a single alternative hypothesis, but a whole set of them—one for each possible value of the alternative mean. Consequently, we also have not just one alternative distribution, but a whole set of them—one for each alternative mean value.

Imagine that in Figure 11.2 the one alternative distribution shown is merely one example of an infinite number of alternative distributions—one distribution for each alternative mean, each of which can be any value that is greater than 90. Such a hypothesis is called a **composite hypothesis**. The hypothesis is "composite" because the alternative hypothesis is composed of a set of alternatives, not just a single alternative. Two alternatives are illustrated in Figure 11.10.

What difference will this make? It is clear from looking at Figure 11.10 that the choice of critical bound is basically the same. Before, we chose a value between the two alternative means—that is, between the null mean and some alternative mean that was to the right of the null mean. But in this case we have a range of means from 90 to infinity; we cannot choose a p_α that lies between the null mean of 90 and an alternative mean, because the alternative mean can be anything bigger than 90. However, if we pick some p_α to the right of 90, we can still calculate the probability of Type I error; α depends only on the specification of the null hypothesis and our choice of the critical bound, p_α.

What is different is that we cannot calculate the probability of Type II error, because there is now not just one Type II error but a range of Type II errors that corresponds to the range of alternative means. For each possible alternative distribution, we could calculate β as we did before.

This line of reasoning means that we should now treat β as a function of the value of the alternative mean. Let the set of alternative means be indicated by μ_a, which represents the values taken by the means under the range of the alternative hypotheses—so that β is given by some function of μ_a, $\beta = \beta(\mu_a)$. β is also a function of

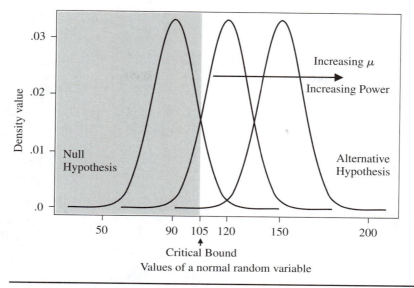

Figure 11.10   Simple versus composite hypotheses

the choice of critical bound p_α. This is summarized in Figure 11.10. For each μ_a, β is the probability under μ_a that $\bar{X}$ is less than the critical bound p_α.

If we have to specify β as a function of μ_a and our choice of p_α, how do we choose α, p_α, and what can we understand by the probability of Type II error? Let us try to answer the last question first. Recall the power of a test; the power was given by $(1 - \beta)$ in the simple versus simple case. We can generalize this by defining the power as $(1 - \beta)$, just as before, except that now the β involved is a function of both p_α and μ_a. Look at Figures 11.10 and 11.11. If we fix μ_a, the variation in power to changes in p_α is just like our first case. If we fix p_α, then we can plot the variation in power as a function of μ_a (see Figure 11.11). All of this sounds complicated, but it is in fact quite easy. If we increase p_α for fixed μ_a, power declines. If we increase μ_a for fixed p_α, then power increases.

The minimum value for the power in our easy example is α, the probability of Type I error, and that value is approached when the alternative hypothesis approaches the null hypothesis. In Figure 11.10, imagine sliding the alternative mean along toward the null mean; as you do this you will see that the power, $(1 - \beta)$, decreases toward α, the probability of Type I error. Indeed, when the alternative mean is equal to the null mean, the two probabilities are also equal. However, this last statement is not very meaningful in that if the null and alternative hypotheses were equal, then not only could we not distinguish the two hypotheses, there would be no point in trying to do so; they would be the same hypothesis! Nevertheless, the idea of looking at the limit is useful in trying to understand this analysis of power and its relationship to our choice of p_α.

Trying to choose the optimal value for p_α in this situation is much more difficult than in our first example. Usually, we pick an arbitrary value for α that approximately

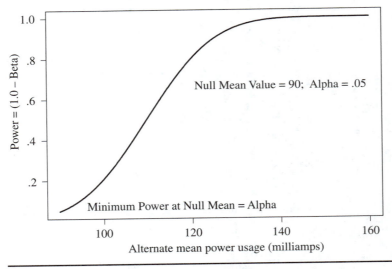

Figure 11.11   A power curve for simple versus composite hypothesis tests

represents our feelings about the cost of Type I error; that is, we decide whether we want a very low, a low, or a moderately high value for α, usually restricting ourselves to the standard values found in the tables. Or, we concentrate on the value we desire for p_α. In either case, we calculate the value of the "nonchosen" parameter, given our choice for the chosen parameter. To understand more fully the implications of our decisions, we can then calculate the power as a function of the values of the alternative means given our choice of p_α.

Having done all this, the next steps are exactly the same as in the first example: Collect a sample, observe the value of the estimate, and choose a hypothesis based on whether the observed estimate is less or greater than the chosen value of p_α.

Let us reevaluate our first example, in which you are the manager in charge of purchasing computer chips. Now, however, we are assuming that you are not as knowledgeable as before. You do know that the mean from your regular supplier is 90, that the relevant distribution is the normal, and that the variance for both the regular supplier's and the occasional supplier's distributions have the same value, $\sigma_X^2 = 144$. What you do not know now, that you knew before, is the value of the alternative mean, other than that it will be bigger; that is, the alternative supplier's chips use more power.

Let us suppose that we have chosen a value for α to be .05; that is, we want a probability of Type I error to be 5%. We can calculate the value of p_α needed to achieve an α of .05:

$$\mathrm{pr}\{\bar{X} \geq p_\alpha\} = .05$$

We do this by standardizing the probability statement

$$\mathrm{pr}\left\{\frac{(\bar{X} - 90)}{12} \geq \frac{(p_\alpha - 90)}{12}\right\} = .05$$

The required critical bound for an $N(0, 1)$ random variable can be obtained from the S-Plus menus <u>Labs</u>, <u>Z, t, Chi-square, F</u>, <u>Critical Values</u>. The value obtained is 1.645, so in solving for p_α,

$$\frac{(p_\alpha - 90)}{12} = 1.645$$

we get 109.7. Figure 11.11 shows the power curve for this choice of p_α. The probability of rejecting the null hypothesis when it is false, that is $(1 - \beta)$, is small for alternative means that are close to 90, but they soon increase quite rapidly.

But what if our worry in this example had been the critical value itself, not the level of α? Let us suppose that for technical reasons the critical bound should be 100 milliamps of power. The question now is, What is the value of α, and what does the power curve look like? Solving for α is easy; we merely substitute 100 for p in the previous expressions and solve for α instead:

$$\frac{(100 - 90)}{12} = .8333$$
$$\text{pr}\{Z \geq .8333\} = .202$$

where Z is an $N(0, 1)$ random variable, and α is .202, or the probability of rejecting the null hypothesis when it is true is about 20 percent. This value for α is quite high, but if we are constrained to use a p_α of 100, then the only way to reduce the value of α is to increase the sample size. Simultaneously, we will lower the corresponding value for β.

11.5   Two-Sided Hypotheses Tests

We have been very successful so far, so let us try another problem. Imagine that we have even less information now and that our requirements are also less strict; now we do not even know whether the alternative mean is bigger or smaller than that under the null hypothesis. This sort of situation shows up a lot in scientific work. For example, the null hypothesis might be that average water temperature has no effect on the density of fish in a pond, against the alternative hypothesis that it has some effect, either positive or negative (see Figure 11.12).

The basic approach that we follow here is the same, but this example has a novel feature—the critical region lies in two parts. In short, what we need to do is to accept the null hypothesis if the observed test statistic is close to the null parameter but to reject it otherwise. But this means that we have to specify two critical bounds this time, one for large positive differences and one for large negative differences.

However, as soon as we contemplate this new feature, we see a possible problem; how do we calculate α and β? α is the probability that the statistic, $\bar{x}$, lies in the critical region when the null hypothesis is true—Type I error. This implies that we have to figure out how to allocate the probability of Type I error between the two "subregions." First we need to discover how altering the choices for the pair of critical bounds changes the probability of Type I error.

Look at Figure 11.12. Let $p_{\alpha l}$ be the critical bound on the left and $p_{\alpha r}$ that on the right. If we try moving $p_{\alpha l}$ in a little bit so as to increase the probability in the

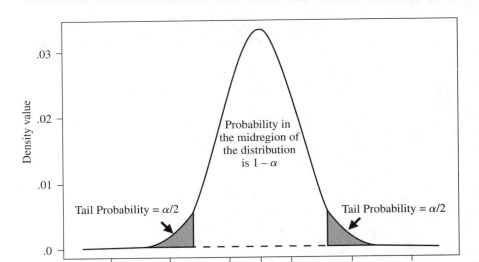

Figure 11.12   Critical Regions for a two-sided composite hypothesis

left critical region, we will have to move $p_{\alpha r}$ to the right to maintain a fixed value for α, where α is the sum of the probabilities in the two subregions. If we continue to move around $p_{\alpha l}$ and $p_{\alpha r}$, we will soon discover that for a given value of α, we can get different lengths of $(p_{\alpha r} - p_{\alpha l})$. Do we want to have a short or a long length for $(p_{\alpha r} - p_{\alpha l})$? A short interval would give us more information about the parameter whose value we are testing; that is, smaller deviations about the parameter would signal that the null hypothesis is wrong. So we need to chose $p_{\alpha l}$ and $p_{\alpha r}$ in such a way as to minimize the difference $(p_{\alpha r} - p_{\alpha l})$.

At this point you should begin to suspect that we have had this discussion before. Indeed, we have. Remember the discussion in Chapter 10 about the appropriate choice for the length of the confidence interval? If not, now is a very good time to review it. Our definition of the " acceptance region" in our current problem is reminiscent of our definition of the confidence interval, but our objectives are different. We choose $p_{\alpha l}$ and $p_{\alpha r}$, so that the values of the density function at those points are equal.

If we choose in this way, then we can easily see by experimenting, if need be, that we have the shortest interval for a given α, or that for a given length of acceptance region, we have the smallest value for α. Similarly, if we look back at Figure 10.5, we can conclude that our rule for choosing critical regions to minimize their length for a given value of α means that for an asymmetric distribution we will choose the critical bounds in an asymmetric manner.

Let us return to our computer chips example. If the null hypothesis is that the mean is 90, and it is known that the standard deviation is 12 for a distribution that is known to be normal, then to test that the mean is 90 against the alternative hypothesis that the mean is not 90, we choose the critical region as shown in Figure 11.12. Because the normal distribution is symmetric about the mean, the optimal choice for $p_{\alpha l}$ and $p_{\alpha r}$ is to pick them so that there is $\alpha/2$ probability to the left and $\alpha/2$ probability to the right. The equality of tail probabilities only implies symmetry in the values of $p_{\alpha r}$, $p_{\alpha l}$ when the distribution is symmetric.

Let α be .05, then by standardizing $p_{\alpha r}$ and $p_{\alpha l}$ in S-plus, we can use the <u>Labs</u>, <u>Inverse Statistical Tables</u>, <u>Normal</u> to solve for $p_{\alpha r}$ and $p_{\alpha l}$:

$$\text{pr}\{Z \geq Z_{\alpha/2}\} = .025$$

for the upper tail and

$$\text{pr}\{Z \leq -Z_{\alpha/2}\} = .025$$

for the lower tail gives the critical bounds $\pm Z_{\alpha/2} = \pm 1.96$. We can solve for

$$\frac{(p_{\alpha l} - 90)}{12} = -1.96$$

$$\frac{(p_{\alpha r} - 90)}{12} = 1.96$$

to obtain

$$p_{\alpha l} = 66.48$$

$$p_{\alpha r} = 113.52$$

If we had chosen the same α level but had chosen a single (upper) tail for the critical region for the alternative hypothesis, the 5% upper critical bound would have been $Z_\alpha = 1.645$. So for a one-tailed test for our computer chips example, we would obtain $p_{\alpha r} = 109.74$ by solving

$$\frac{(p_{\alpha r} - 90)}{12} = 1.645$$

Remember that one of the major distinguishing characteristics in all these tests and even for the estimation problem is that of how much information is assumed to be known. In the two-tailed test, we presume that we have less information than if we were to perform a one-tailed test; the values for the critical bounds reflect these differences in information, 113.52 versus 109.74. Alternatively, we could state that for the same chosen critical bound in the one-tailed test, we could have a smaller probability of Type I error. Clearly, to know that the alternative is on one specific side of the null is to know more than that the alternative is merely different.

11.6 Tests of Proportions

We began this chapter by stating that tests of hypotheses presumed more information than was true in the estimation case. The effect of this claim is strikingly clear when we consider testing hypotheses about proportions. Let us consider an experiment testing whether rocking had an effect on the crying of babies.

We have a random sample of babies; a random selection were rocked and the rest were not rocked. We can consider various forms of hypothesis tests. If you were a grandmother, you would probably have a firm hypothesis that rocking reduces crying; if you are an unmarried scientist you may be very skeptical of the benefits of rocking. The former would chose a one-tailed test—rocking has no effect versus that it reduces crying. The latter would chose a two-tailed test—a null of no effect versus some effect but of uncertain direction. Let us assume that "no effect" means that the probability of crying for the rocked babies is 50%; that is, rocked babies will cry at random and the probability of crying is .5. Define our estimator by $\hat{\pi} = K/n$, where K is the random variable measuring the number of babies that cried and n is the sample size. We have 126 observations, so it is reasonable to assume that the distribution of $\hat{\pi}$ is normal. We now need to determine the variance of the distribution to perform a test, either one- or two-tailed. Recall that in Chapter 10 when we were discussing the estimation of a proportion, we ran into a difficulty in that the variance of the chosen estimator was a function of the very parameter that we were trying to estimate. It is in this connection that the added information that we presume in hypothesis testing reveals its benefits.

Under the null hypothesis, the probability of a baby crying is .5. In which case, the variance for $\hat{\pi}$ *under the null hypothesis* is given by

$$\sigma_{\hat{\pi}}^2 = \frac{\pi_0(1 - \pi_0)}{n}$$
$$= \frac{.5 \times .5}{126}$$
$$= .00198$$
$$\sigma_{\hat{\pi}} = .044$$

The observed value of the test statistic is .38. The test statistic that is assumed to be distributed as normal is given by

$$\frac{.38 - .5}{.044} = -2.73$$

The critical bound for a probability of Type I error for a one-tailed test (lower bound) at a level of .01 is -2.33, so we reject the null hypothesis of no effect against the alternative that rocking reduces the proportion of babies crying.

This completes our development of the basic ideas of hypothesis tests. Any remaining questions will involve elaborations of the basic idea and techniques to handle special difficulties, such as, what to do if you do not know the variance. To this problem we now turn.

11.7   Hypotheses Tests when the Variance Is Unknown

We could borrow a leaf from our efforts in Chapter 10, for if we have a very large sample we can use the estimated value of σ^2 as if it were the true value of σ^2. Our justification you will recall is that our estimator for the variance is consistent. But that approach is not terribly useful, because most of our efforts have been directed to economizing on the amount of data that we use for making decisions; data collection is expensive and time consuming. What we need is a procedure that is useful when we have only relatively small amounts of data.

We have a solution from Chapter 10. Remember the statistic T defined by

$$T = \frac{\sqrt{n}(\bar{X} - \mu)}{S},$$

(11.3)

where $\bar{X}$ is a sample mean from a normal distribution with theoretical mean μ and a variance σ^2 estimated without bias by the estimator S^2. In Equation 10.6, we defined S^2 as m_2 multiplied by $n/(n - 1)$. We know that the Student's T distribution depends on the number of degrees of freedom, $(n - 1)$ in our case, and most importantly, the distribution of T does not depend on any unknown parameters.

Now how do we convert this information into a useful approach to a test of a hypothesis on μ that is the mean of a normal distribution? The null hypothesis is $\mu = \mu_0$, for some specified value μ_0. The alternative hypothesis can be μ_1, $\mu_1 \neq \mu_0$ or $\mu_1 > \mu_0$. Let us consider the easiest alternative first, the alternative mean is μ_1. We suppose that the specified value for μ_1 is greater than μ_0; this is merely to keep the discussion restricted to the elementary basics.

If we want to test two simple hypotheses, simple versus simple, then under the null hypothesis, the distribution of T, where T is defined by

$$T = \frac{\sqrt{n}(\bar{X} - \mu_0)}{S}$$

(11.4)

is a Student's T distribution with $(n - 1)$ degrees of freedom, where n is the sample size used to calculate $\bar{X}$ and μ_0 is the hypothesized mean for the theoretical distribution. We can either set a desired α level, or we can set a chosen critical bound and calculate the probability of Type I error. To illustrate, let us choose α to be .05. Our next task is to determine the value of the critical bound, p_α. We do this by solving the following equation:

$$\text{pr}\{T \geq p_\alpha\} = .05$$

for p_α. Note that in S-Plus the distribution is listed as Student's t, because they are observing statistics, not the random variable.

For example, let us return to our computer chip problem, where the hypothesized mean is 90, and now let us assume that we do not know the value of the variance, but that we have an estimate of 13.5 for S based on 24 degrees of freedom, where $n = 25$. From the Inverse Statistical Tables with degrees of freedom equal to 24 and α set to .05 we get a critical bound of 1.71, or $p_\alpha = 1.71$. A corresponding critical bound can be obtained for $\bar{X}$ by substituting for T in Equation 11.4:

$$\bar{X} \geq \mu_0 + \frac{p_\alpha S}{\sqrt{n}} = 90 + \frac{(1.71 \times 13.5)}{5}$$

$$= 94.62$$

(11.5)

To complete the test, we need only observe the value of $\bar{x}$; if $\bar{x} > 94.62$, then we reject the null hypothesis; but if $\bar{x} < 94.62$, then we accept the null hypothesis and reject the alternative hypothesis that $\mu_1 > \mu_0$. We did not need to state exactly what the specified alternative value of μ_1 is to derive the critical bound and its associated critical region. The actual value of μ_1 could be 95, or 130, neither value will affect our choice of critical region. To set up the critical bound, we merely need to know that we have a one-sided test and that the one side is above the null hypothesized value. The actual value of μ_1 in a test of simple versus simple affects the power of the test, or equivalently the probability of Type II error.

Let us return to our investigation of the PSAT mathematics and verbal scores. In Section 11.3, we discussed testing the hypotheses that the means of the parent distributions were 46.3 and 42.6, respectively, for mathematics and verbal scores against the alternative that the means were 50. There we assumed that the observed variances were equal to the unknown actual variances. Now we can remove that unwarranted assumption. To test the hypothesis that the mathematics mean for the parent distribution is 46.3 versus 50, we need to create a Student's T distribution under the null of 46.3 to derive the critical bound at our chosen α level. The sample size is 520, or 519 degrees of freedom; so the degrees of freedom are essentially infinite for our purposes. Consequently, the Student's T distribution and the Gaussian curve are as close to each other in assigning probabilities as we can ever expect to see. Therefore, we can use the Gaussian curve to determine the critical bound. Both the normal and the Student's T distributions under <u>Labs, Inverse Statistical Tables</u> in S-Plus yield the same critical bound. Our test is one-sided, simple versus simple, and "large values will reject." To obtain the critical bound on our observed statistic, we can begin with

$$\text{pr}(T \leq d_\alpha) = 1 - \alpha \tag{11.6}$$

or

$$\text{pr}(T \leq 0.84) = .8$$

Our definition of the statistic T under the null hypothesis is

$$T = \frac{\bar{X} - \mu}{S}\sqrt{n} = \frac{\bar{X} - 46.3}{\sqrt{124.96}}\sqrt{520}$$

so that we can derive the critical bound from

$$
\begin{aligned}
\text{pr}(T \leq 0.84) &= .8 \\
&= \text{pr}\left(\frac{X - 46.3}{\sqrt{124.96}}\sqrt{520} \leq 0.84\right) \\
&= \text{pr}\left(\bar{X} \leq 0.84 \times \frac{\sqrt{124.96}}{\sqrt{520}}\right) \\
&= \text{pr}(\bar{X} \leq 46.71) = .8
\end{aligned}
\tag{11.7}
$$

This is, of course, the same value for the critical bound that we obtained in Section 11.3. However, our *interpretation* of the results has changed. In particular, when using the Student's T distribution, the critical bound on the observed statistic is a function of the observed sample standard deviation, s, and this value will vary from sample to sample. Consequently, the actual value for the critical bound will also vary from sample to sample. This variation will be relatively greater at small sample sizes and virtually insignificant at sample sizes in the thousands.

Other hypothesis tests of the mean can be handled in a similar way.

Testing the Difference between Two Means

To demonstrate the power of this approach to our decision making needs, let us try another example. Suppose that you wish to compare the power usage rates of two new firms that are trying to compete with your regular supplier. One of your first questions is whether there is any difference between the means of the two new potential suppliers; if there is, you may have to handle each firm separately, but if not, then you can pool the results for the two firms and thereby save considerably on testing costs.

Your problem is to test whether the two means are the same or different. To keep this problem simple, let us continue to expect that the variances of both firms are the same, but we do not know what that variance is. The normal distribution is still the parent distribution. Testing whether two means are the same is like testing whether a random variable defined by the *difference* of the two random variables has a mean of *zero*. So instead of trying to devise a test for the "difference between two means," let us define a new random variable, D, where $D = Cm_1 - Cm_2$. Cm_1 and Cm_2 are the random variables indicating the mean power usage of the two rival firms that you are trying to evaluate.

First, we need to identify the probability distribution function of the random variable D. Because the normal distribution is still relevant for Cm_1 and Cm_2, and because we know that the distribution of the difference between two normal random variables is also normal, we know that the distribution of D is normal with mean zero under the null hypothesis of no difference between the means of Cm_1 and Cm_2. The only problem left is to figure out the variance of D, or how to estimate it.

Let us consider this problem in two stages. First, what if we knew the variances of the test outcomes in the two firms? We need to discover the variance of $D = Cm_1 - Cm_2$, where Cm_1 and Cm_2 are mean values using n_1 and n_2 observations, respectively. The answer to this question depends on a simpler question: What is the variance of a difference between two Gaussian random variables? Recall from the Exercises in Chapter 8 that the variance of a difference, when the two variables are independently distributed, is the sum of the constituent variances. Thus, if Y_1 and Y_2 are any two random variables, the variance of the difference is given by

$$E\{(Y_1 - Y_2) - [E\{Y_1\} - E\{Y_2\}]\}^2$$
$$= E\{[(Y_1 - E\{Y_1\}) + (Y_2 - E\{Y_2\})]\}^2$$
$$= E\{(Y_1 - E\{Y_1\})\}^2 + E\{(Y_2 - E\{Y_2\})\}^2 - 2E\{(Y_1 - E\{Y_1\})(Y_2 - E\{Y_2\})\}$$
$$= \sigma_1^2 + \sigma_2^2 - 0$$

The cross-product term is zero because the variables are independent, so we can calculate the expectation of each component separately. The variance of each mean, given that the variances of the parent distributions are σ_1^2 and σ_2^2 and that the respective sample sizes are n_1 and n_2, are σ_1^2/n_1 and σ_2^2/n_2. Consequently, the variance of the difference is

$$\sigma_D^2 = E\{(D - E\{D\})\}^2$$
$$= \frac{\sigma_1^2}{n_1} + \frac{\sigma_2^2}{n_2} \tag{11.8}$$

If we knew the variance of the difference, we could easily develop a test that the difference, D, was zero by recognizing that the statistic

$$\frac{D}{\sqrt{\sigma_1^2/n_1 + \sigma_2^2/n_2}} \tag{11.9}$$

is distributed under the null hypothesis of no difference—that is, that $D = 0$, as Gaussian with mean 0 and variance 1. Consequently, we can use the standard normal tables to define a critical region at a chosen α level. And if the variances are in fact the same, Equation 11.9 reduces to

$$\frac{D}{\sigma\sqrt{1/n_1 + 1/n_2}} \tag{11.10}$$

Suppose that you have the test results from two laboratories. One laboratory used a sample of size 30 to determine that an estimate for the variance of chip firm Outel was 141. Another laboratory tested the other chip firm and used a sample size of 15 to get an estimate of 148 for firm Chipco. The respective estimated means by the two laboratories for the two firms were 95 and 113 milliamps. Your job is to decide for your own firm whether there is any difference in the two theoretical means of the distributions of power usage between the two firms, Outel and Chipco.

We have concluded so far that the random variable D that we have just defined has a normal distribution—the mean is zero under the null hypothesis and nonzero under the alternative hypothesis. The variances of the parent distributions for the individual firm's test results are the same, but we do not know what the common value is. However, we can estimate the value of the variance from the information provided by the two laboratories. There is one unknown variance, but we have two estimates, one from each of the two laboratories. Which one should we use?

Why not both, at least if we can figure out how to do it? Each laboratory has given us a value of S^2, let us call them S_1^2 and S_2^2; S_1^2 has 29 degrees of freedom and S_2^2 has 14 degrees of freedom, say $n_1 - 1$ and $n_2 - 1$ degrees of freedom each. (Recall that "degrees of freedom" are the number of independent bits of data that we have, the number of observations minus the number of constraints that we place on the data.)

If we look at $(n_1 - 1)S_1^2$ and $(n_2 - 1)S_2^2$, we see that these two products are merely the sums of squares of the deviations of each variable about its sample mean. So if we add them, we will get a sum of squared deviations about each of the two means. In either event, each element of the sum is an estimator for the common unknown variance, σ^2. But we are trying to find an "average" estimator for the variance. We will maintain the assumption, which in this case is very plausible, that the two firm's samples are distributed independently of each other. If we knew the number of degrees of freedom, then we would be able to divide our sum by that number and obtain our average. Each laboratory calculated its customer's sample variance as a deviation about the mean, so that the sum of deviations about the mean for each laboratory is identically zero. In short, we have two constraints and we have lost 2 degrees of freedom. We conclude that the number of degrees of freedom is $(n_1 - 1) + (n_2 - 1) = n_1 + n_2 - 2$.

Now we have our desired estimator of the variance that uses both the laboratory's data and the knowledge that the variances for both chip firms are the same. Let us call it S_p^2 for the pooled sample variance. S_p^2 is defined by

$$S_p^2 = \frac{(n_1 - 1)S_1^2 + (n_2 - 1)S_2^2}{n_1 + n_2 - 2} \tag{11.11}$$

Now, at last, we have finished our preparations and can devise our test of whether or not the two firms have the same mean.

Just as in the previous case where we did not know the variance, we define the statistic T by

$$T = \frac{(D - 0)}{S_p \sqrt{\frac{1}{n_1} + \frac{1}{n_2}}} \tag{11.12}$$

which is distributed as Student's T with $(n_1 + n_2 - 2)$ degrees of freedom under the null hypothesis of no difference. Note that what we have derived is an exact analog to our first derivation of the Student's T distribution. The statistic $(D - 0)/\sigma \sqrt{\frac{1}{n_1} + \frac{1}{n_2}}$ is distributed as Gaussian with mean zero under the null hypothesis that the mean difference is 0 with a variance of 1. The statistic S_p^2/σ^2 is distributed independently of D as a chi-square distribution, so that the ratio is distributed as Student's T; recall Equation 10.20 and the discussion in Chapter 10. So what's the answer to our question as to whether the difference is statistically significant at our chosen level of confidence?

Let us substitute the actual numbers into the expressions and find out:

$$D = 113 - 95 = 18$$

$$n_1 + n_2 - 2 = 43, \quad \frac{1}{n_1} + \frac{1}{n_2} = \frac{1}{30} + \frac{1}{15} = \frac{1}{10}$$

$$S_p = \sqrt{\frac{(n_1 - 1)S_1^2 + (n_2 - 1)S_2^2}{n_1 + n_2 - 2}}$$

$$S_p = \sqrt{\left[\frac{((29 \times 141) + (14 \times 148))}{43}\right]} \tag{11.13}$$

$$= \sqrt{\left[\frac{(4089 + 2072)}{43}\right]}$$

$$= \sqrt{143.28} = 11.97$$

$$t = \frac{18 - 0}{11.97 \times \sqrt{0.1}} = 4.76$$

The S_p estimate of 11.97 is very close to the actual variance for our own firm, so perhaps we can have some confidence in the result and in our understanding that the two variances for the two competing firms are the same.

At the chosen α level our test for the difference between means has been converted to a test for a mean of zero for a Student's T distribution. Because we are testing whether the difference between the two firms is nonzero, we will need a two-sided test and the critical region will be for large negative or positive values of the difference. If we choose a 95% confidence level, 2.5% in each tail, the bounds for the Student's T distribution with 43 degrees of freedom will be approximately ± 2.02. The estimated value of the Student's T is 4.46, so we can claim with 95% confidence that the null hypothesis of no difference in the means is rejected; indeed, this hypothesis is rejected at any reasonable level of confidence.

Suppose that the observed differences in the means had been only 8, instead of 18. The observed Student's T statistic with all other observations the same and at the same confidence level would yield

$$t = \frac{8 - 0}{11.97 \times \sqrt{0.1}} = 2.11$$

At the same 95% level of confidence, the critical bounds are as before, ± 2.02 and the null hypothesis of no difference is rejected as before—but only marginally.

However, if we had chosen an α level of .02, that is, a confidence level of 98%, 1% in each tail, the Student's T critical bound with 43 degrees of freedom would have been 2.42, and with this bound we would have accepted the null hypothesis and decided to accept no difference in the means.

This example reminds us that we are making decisions without actually knowing what the true state of the world is. The actual difference, whatever it is, is a constant number, even if we do not know what that number is. Our decision changed in this last example, merely because we chose to weight the probabilities of Type I and II errors differently; that is, we chose a different confidence level. We thereby have a different decision, but the state of the world stays the same, no matter what we think!

An interesting question that we might want to ask about the PSAT scores is whether the means for the mathematics and verbal scores are the same. We can use the procedure for testing for the significance of a difference that we have just developed, but we need to be very careful as it is likely that the mathematics and verbal scores are correlated; they are not independent, as we need to maintain for the validity of the procedure that we just used. What we could do is to take two subsamples from the data and use one for estimating mathematical scores and the other for verbal scores. By this stratagem, we should be able to avoid the worst of the correlation problems. We still need to be careful that our subsamples have the same statistical properties as in the original sample. For example, if we picked a subsample of all people who scored less than 20 on the examination, we would clearly not have a random sample (as defined in Chapter 9). Other difficulties may not be so obvious. For example, let us consider calculating the mean and the sample variance for the PSAT mathematics scores for the first and last 650 students (using data not available in Xfiles). Our presumption is that the order of the students in the data file is random with respect to the score received on the examination. The overall mathematics mean was 44.4, but for the first 650 (nonzero) entries the mean is 41.8 and for the next 650 the mean is 46.4. The corresponding variance estimates are 127.4, 106.5, and 136.8. So apparently, we suspect that for the first group of students the mean and variance are substantially less than for the second group of students. One modest assumption is that the variations in performance across the two groups are independently distributed. Consequently, we can consider testing whether the means are the same using the pooled estimate of the variance.

However, here also we run into trouble because the variances seem to be different across the two groups. Let us ignore this further difficulty and evaluate the evidence in favor of the two means being the same. The pooled estimate of the variance we have already, the value of $S_p^2 = 127.4$; the number of observations is 1300. The observed difference is $d = (41.8 - 46.4) = -4.6$. The hypothesized difference under the null hypothesis is zero. Let us choose a confidence level of 95%. The null hypothesis is that the difference is zero, and the alternative is that it is nonzero; so this is a two-sided test with 2.5% probability of rejection on either side of the acceptance region. Using the Student's T distribution with 1298 degrees of freedom, we have the critical bounds $[-1.96, 1.96]$. Within the specified interval lies the acceptance region for a null hypothesis of a zero mean; that is:

$$\text{pr}(-1.96 \leq T \leq 1.96 | H_0)$$

$$= \text{pr}\left(-1.96 \leq \frac{d - 0}{\sqrt{127.4}}\sqrt{1300} \leq 1.96 | H_0\right) = .95 \tag{11.14}$$

or

$$\text{pr}\left(-1.96 \times \frac{\sqrt{127.4}}{\sqrt{1300}} \leq d \leq 1.96 \times \frac{\sqrt{127.4}}{\sqrt{1300}} | H_0\right)$$

$$= \text{pr}(-0.61 \leq d \leq 0.61) = .95$$

The observed statistic, -4.6, lies well outside this confidence interval, so we reject the null hypothesis of no difference in favor of there being a difference between the first and second groups of students as recorded in their PSAT scores. Given that the degrees of freedom are essentially infinite for our purposes, we would expect that the bounds obtained would be the same as those for the normal distribution, and indeed that is the case. Further, our result would hold even if we had used as an estimate of the variance the largest value of 136.8. Thus, we can be fairly certain that the difference in means is nonzero and indeed is quite large, about 10% of the larger mean.

An Aside on Statistical Significance

In many examples our tests of hypotheses are about whether a certain parameter is zero. Is a difference between two means nonzero? Is the effect of a new drug significantly different from zero? Does burning coal cause global warming? And so on. These questions are characterized by asking whether an effect exists—whether a parameter value is zero. We discuss whether the result is **statistically significant**; that is, at the assigned confidence level, the null hypothesis of "no effect," or of zero effect, is rejected in favor of there being an effect. We considered, for example, two firms producing computer chips in which we tested whether the difference in the means was nonzero. If we accept the null hypothesis of no effect, we say that the effect is statistically insignificant at the assigned significance level. And if we reject the null hypothesis of no effect, we say that the effect is statistically significant at the assigned significance level. Unfortunately, it is all too common for people to state that some tested effect is "significant" without reminding the reader that they are talking about *statistical* significance and without indicating the *associated significance level*.

But the potential confusion with people claiming statistical significance for some effect is worse. Statistical significance is really about the *detectability* of an effect. Consider, if there were no random variation, then one could measure the effect and declare it nonzero, or not. But there is always random variation and frequently some effects may be very small relative to the accuracy of the measuring instrument. So detecting a significant difference, or a significant effect, in the statistical sense involves two aspects of the problem—the actual size of the effect, if any, and the random variation about the effect. To say that an effect is statistically significant at an assigned significance level is to say that the effect is sufficiently large relative to the ambient noise so as to be *detectable* at the given confidence level. Detectability may be because the effect itself is large, or because the variation of the ambient noise is small. Thus, one might have a very large effect that is not detected, because the variation in the noise masks the effect; or one might have a very small effect that is detectable, because the variation in the ambient noise is even less.

Often a user of statistics, or a reader of statistical analysis, is not interested in detectability, but in the size of the effect itself. People want to say that an effect is "operationally significant"; by that they mean that the effect is pronounced and has consequences whether or not some given recording mechanism enables one to detect the difference. Significance in this sense is a synonym for "important effect." Consequently, it is important to distinguish whether one is talking about statistical significance—that is detectability—or about the importance of the effect—operational significance.

An example will help. Suppose that one is evaluating the effects on the fish population from dredging a river. Dredging the river will harm 15% of the fish in the river, but this important effect may, or may not, be detectable. Alternatively, dredging the river may affect only .01% of the fish population, but this effect can be declared statistically significant at the 99% level or even higher. In the former case, we have an important effect, an operationally significant effect, as measured by the consequences of the action, that may not be detectable. Whereas in the latter case, we have an unimportant effect as measured by its consequences, but that unimportant effect is easily detected and precisely measured as represented by the statistical significance at very high significance levels.

Try not to confuse these two equally useful, but very different concepts: statistical significance on the one hand and operational significance on the other.

P Values

The calculation of "*P* values" is a very important extension of the ideas developed in this chapter. The **P value** for any statistic is the probability under the null hypothesis of drawing an observation on the statistic that is at least as extreme as the actual value of the statistic. We can link this idea to α levels. The P value is the largest value of α for which the null hypothesis is "accepted" given the observed statistics.

We can clarify this definition by describing some specific alternatives. If we had a situation in which we were testing H_0: $\mu = \mu_0$ against the one-sided alternative $\mu > \mu_0$, we could calculate, under the assumption of the null hypothesis, H_0: $\mu = \mu_0$, the probability that any other random drawing of the statistic *under exactly the same experimental conditions* would yield a value that would be greater than the actually observed value of the statistic, $\bar{x}_0$. Similarly, if we were testing H_0: $\mu = \mu_0$ against the one-sided alternative $\mu < \mu_0$, we could calculate, under the assumption of the null hypothesis, H_0: $\mu = \mu_0$, the probability that any other random drawing of the statistic *under exactly the same experimental conditions* would yield a value that would be less than the actually observed value of the statistic $\bar{x}_0$. And for two-sided alternatives, if we were testing H_0: $\mu = \mu_0$ against the two-sided alternative $\mu \neq \mu_0$, we could calculate, under the assumption of the null hypothesis, H_0: $\mu = \mu_0$, the probability that any other random drawing of the statistic *under exactly the same experimental conditions* would yield an *absolute* value of a difference between $\bar{x}$ and μ_0 that is greater than the actual absolute difference observed.

Let us begin with the simplest example of a one-sided test using the normal distribution and Equation 11.1. The data involved are PSAT mathematics scores of 520 students. The observed sample mean is 44.38 and the observed sample variance is 127.4, so the variance of the mean is 127.4/520. Under the null hypothesis that $\mu = 45$, we can calculate the observed statistic z_0:

$$z_0 = \frac{44.38 - 45}{\sqrt{\frac{127.4}{520}}} = -1.35 \tag{11.15}$$

We might choose the alternative hypothesis that μ is less than 45; then we need to consider small values for the statistic. Under our assumptions z_0 is a drawing from a standard normal distribution, so the probability of obtaining a value less than or equal to that obtained, -1.35, is given by

$$P(z_0) = \int_{-\infty}^{z_0} \phi(z)dz \tag{11.16}$$

$$= \int_{-\infty}^{-1.35} \phi(z)dz = .089 \tag{11.17}$$

where $\phi(z)$ represents the standard normal density function and $\int_{-\infty}^{z_0} \phi(z)dz$ represents the area under the standard normal density function up to the observed value of z_0. This is the required P value. In S-Plus, the P values can be obtained directly from the Labs, Tests of Significance menu (see Appendix B). We conclude that the probability of getting a value of z_0 less than -1.35 is only .089, and, correspondingly, the probability of getting an $\bar{X}$ of 44.38 or less when the mean is 45 is also only .089. As a related example, suppose that the null hypothesis had been that the mean PSAT mathematics score is 50, what would have been our one-sided P values then? The observed z_0 value would be -11.35, and the corresponding calculation in Equation

11.16 would be a tiny 4×10^{-30}; such an event is extremely unlikely. One thing that this pair of examples clearly illustrates is that the P value depends on the value of the parameter in the null hypothesis. For example, suppose that the hypothesized mean is 43, what is the P value? Equation 11.16 in this case is

$$P(z_0) = \int_{-\infty}^{z_0} \phi(z)dz$$
$$= \int_{-\infty}^{2.79} \phi(z)dz = .997$$

since z_0 is 2.79; to see this merely substitute the value 43 for 45 in Equation 11.15. The P value indicates that drawing a value of 44.38 or less when the mean is 43 is virtually certain.

We can, of course, calculate P values even when we do not know the variance by using the Student's T distribution instead of the normal. The corresponding example using the PSAT scores was discussed in Equation 11.7, and because the degrees of freedom are essentially infinite for our purposes, the numbers will be the same notwithstanding the formal difference in the statement of the problem. Only when the degrees of freedom are less than 30 will the difference in value of P_α be noticeable.

In Equation 11.14, we discussed a two-sided test of a hypothesis—whether the difference between the PSAT mean scores for two subsets of students was significantly different from zero. We can calculate these P values as well. Utilizing the information in Equation 11.14, we observe a drawing from the Student's T distribution with infinite degrees of freedom with a value given by

$$t_0 = \frac{-4.6 - 0}{\sqrt{\frac{127.4}{520}}} = -9.29$$

and all we have to do is to evaluate the area under the Student's T density function between the limits $[-\infty, -9.29]$ and $[9.29, \infty]$.

$$P(t_0) = \int_{-\infty}^{-9.29} g(t)dt + \int_{9.29}^{\infty} g(t)dt$$
$$= 2 \times \int_{-\infty}^{-9.29} g(t)dt$$
$$\cong 0$$

where $g(t)$ is the Student's T density function. The observed values are so far out in the tails that the P value is effectively zero.

11.8 Some Practical Examples

Our discussion has covered in some depth the more mechanical aspects of hypothesis testing. This brief section explores some examples more closely related to the types of situations that you will actually face. We want to illustrate the thinking involved in setting up the problem. First, we must identify the statistical question; once that is known the rest is relatively easy. The main lesson in this section is how to think about inference problems.

Let us begin with a simple question. Is it true that the United States' use of energy is greater than that of Australia? Immediately, we see that we have to refine the question. The United States has a much larger population than Australia, so, at the very least, we should compare per-capita use of energy. Further, the U.S. produces a very large share of the total worldwide goods and services, a percentage far higher than the U.S. percentage of world population, so perhaps the U.S consumption of energy per dollar of output is a more useful measure. A simple alternative is output per dollar of Gross National Product (GNP), or Gross Domestic Product (GDP). In all of this discussion the important underlying question is, What is the relevance of the answer to one's main purpose? If you are interested merely in comparing the absolute size of the consumption levels, irrespective of population, or fuel efficiency, then the raw numbers may be relevant. But if you are more interested in the efficiency with which the United States uses energy resources, one of the ratio measures will be more relevant. Let us suppose that we are interested in the energy use per dollar of output, as we are interested in a measure of the "efficiency" of energy use. This measure abstracts from the size of the population and from the "size" of the economy given the population.

What data do we have? In Xfiles we have data on energy use by various countries for 21 years. For each country and for each year we can calculate the ratio of energy use to total production, where total production is defined as the sum of agricultural and industrial production. Using the variable names in the folder Energy, we can calculate

$$\frac{\text{energpc} \times \text{popmil}}{\text{agrprod} + \text{indprod}} = \text{energy per \$prod.} = E_{\$P}$$

These data have been collected for you in the folder Misc, under the file name, Energgdp.xls.

You can get an immediate impression of the comparisons between the data by plotting box-and-whisker plots of the variable "energdp," which is the S-Plus variable name for $E_{\$P}$. For each country we can calculate the moments of our variable $E_{\$P}$; the units of measurement are kilograms of oil per dollar of output. However, the individual observations for each country are over time. It is unlikely that the variations in energy use over the years are independent of each other; that is, if energy use is very high one year, it may well be true that energy use is high the subsequent year, or years. Let us leave this problem as we have not yet learned how to deal with it. One task would be to "test" whether the individual observations over time are mutually uncorrelated. So, let us assume that the individual observations are uncorrelated.

We have another "correlation problem." Are the U.S. and Australian data uncorrelated? One can make a case that it would be wise to check this assumption; but as we have not yet discovered how to deal with the situation in the case that there is correlation, we will very conveniently assume the problem away for now. However, recognize that these are important questions that will affect your analytical results and your interpretation of them.

Key questions now are, What is the relevant distribution for the variable $E_{\$P}$? and Is the distribution the same for the two countries? This is another matter for which you do not yet have the tools, so for *purely pedagogical reasons* we will continue to assume our difficulties away and assume that normality holds in both countries. However, this is something that we can get some handle on by calculating the first four moments. The standardized third and fourth moments should be approximately 0 and 3, as we have repeatedly noted. We are still at some disadvantage in that while we recognize that we are observing estimates of the third and fourth moments, we do not have any idea of the sample variation of these higher moments. The first four moments for the U.S. figures are (in kilograms per $ of output) 2.26, 0.80, 0.59, and 1.73, and the corresponding Australian figures are 1.28, 0.22, 1.49, and 4.59. Actually, the large sample standard errors for the third and fourth standardized moments under the assumption of Gaussianity are 0.6 and 1.2 for the United States and 0.53 and 1.07 for Australia. Allowing an approximate error band of about 2 standard deviations, we see that in both cases the assumptions of 0 and 3 for the third and fourth moments are not far out of bounds, so perhaps the assumption of normality is not such a bad approximation. Using some advanced procedures, we can confirm that the empirical evidence, scanty as it is, is consistent with the assumption of normality.

There is another good reason for plotting the box-and-whisker plots: checking the data. When one first uses any data set it is very good practice to plot the data to get a feel for what is there and query the presence of outliers (observations that are very extreme in value). Outliers may well be perfectly good observations and provide important evidence on the process under examination, but they may also indicate errors in recording or calculating the observed variables. In any event, you should know if there are any outliers, or indeed any observations that are for any reason "suspicious," and investigate further. You might be surprised how often with seemingly well used data there are serious errors. It is always wise to check.

What is immediately apparent from the box-and-whisker plots and the sample moments is that both the sample mean and the sample variance of energy use for Australia are substantially less than the corresponding figures for the United States: 2.26 versus 1.28 for the means and 0.80 versus 0.22 for the variances. So now we can ask whether the U.S. mean energy use per dollar of output is substantially greater than the value for Australia. We have already noted that the variances are not the same. Fortunately, the respective sample sizes are approximately the same; they would be exactly the same except for some missing data. Further, although the sample sizes are not very small, they are not very big either. The net result of these ruminations is to conclude that it is a reasonable choice that we use the Student's T distribution for the statistic:

$$\frac{\bar{x}_{US} - \bar{x}_A}{\sqrt{s_{US}^2/n_{US} + s_A^2/n_A}}$$

where $\bar{x}_{US}, \bar{x}_A$ are the respective means using n_{US} and n_A observations and s_{US}^2 and s_A^2 are the respective sample variances. If we plug in the numbers we obtained, we get

$$\frac{2.26 - 1.28}{\sqrt{0.80/17 + 0.22/21}} = 4.09$$

This statistic is under our assumptions distributed approximately as Student's T, with $21 + 17 - 2 = 36$ degrees of freedom. We can well conclude at any reasonable confidence level that the null hypothesis is rejected.

However, let us return to our earlier assumption that the Australian and U.S. data are uncorrelated. From Chapter 5 (Equation 5.8), we do know how to calculate a correlation coefficient. If we calculate the correlation coefficient between the U.S. and Australian data we obtain .91; that is, they are very highly correlated and the correlation is positive. Now using some of the relationships that we explored in Chapter 4, we can conclude that if the two series are correlated the variance of the difference is given by

$$\text{var}(\bar{x}_{US} - \bar{x}_A) = \frac{\sigma^2_{US}}{n_{US}} + \frac{\sigma^2_A}{n_A} - 2 \times \text{cov}(\bar{x}_{US}, \bar{x}_A) \tag{11.18}$$

We can estimate the covariance by the sample correlation times the product of the standard deviations. If ρ is the correlation between $\bar{x}_{US}$ and $\bar{x}_A$, then we can rewrite Equation 11.18 as

$$\text{var}(\bar{x}_{US} - \bar{x}_A) = \frac{\sigma^2_{US}}{n_{US}} + \frac{\sigma^2_A}{n_A} - 2 \times \rho \frac{\sigma_{US}}{\sqrt{n_{US}}} \frac{\sigma_A}{\sqrt{n_A}} \tag{11.19}$$

We estimate this variance by substituting the estimates of all the components into the expression. Although the distribution of the resulting statistic is very complicated, our use of the Student's T distribution will not be too different from the actual distribution. Our recalculated ratio of the difference $\bar{x}_{US} - \bar{x}_A$ relative to our estimate of its standard deviation—that is, to our estimate of the square root of the expression in Equation 11.19—is given by

$$(\bar{x}_{US} - \bar{x}_A) / \sqrt{s^2_{US}/n_{US} + s^2_A/n_A - 2 \times \hat{\rho} \sqrt{s^2_{US}/n_{US}} \sqrt{s^2_A/n_A}}$$
$$= (2.26 - 1.28) / \sqrt{0.80/17 + 0.22/21 - 2 \times 0.91 \sqrt{0.80/17} \sqrt{0.22/21}}$$
$$= 7.48$$

In this case, we conclude that any attempt to allow for the correlation between the two series leads to an even stronger rejection of the null hypothesis. Recall that our "rejection of the null hypothesis of no difference in the means" is not a statement of fact about the actual state of the world, but that given these empirical results a reasonable decision to make is that the U.S. energy figures are larger than those for Australia.

You may have been disturbed to note how "messy" the whole process of analysis was. In real life we would have been able to use a number of tools that you have not yet mastered and would therefore have been able to check our assumptions for their relevance. The idea that real analysis involves having to settle on compromises—to say that an assumption is approximately correct, to conclude that the results are reasonable under the circumstances—is the essence of statistical analysis in actual situations. The statistics provide a guide to reasonable decisions and actions. Given our numbers, it is reasonable to conclude on the evidence that the U.S. per-capita energy use figures are substantially greater than those for Australia. Our next step would be to determine why, by narrowing the source of the difference between the rates of energy usage. For example, we might speculate that the relatively greater U.S. usage reflects the relatively lower average cost of energy in the United States, so the United States specializes in "energy intensive" products. We would then try to obtain data to test that hypothesis.

Let us consider another instructive example. In the *Wall Street Journal* (November 11, 1996), there was a report about a religious seminar called Discovery that "purports to offer scientific proof that God exists." The Discovery teachers claimed that computer analysis of the Torah, the first five books of the Old Testament, "proves that God hid codes in the text to foretell later events." The article also stated that some statisticians examined the process, which involves picking algorithms that process the text as one might do to find a secret code. Now in any large book there is a reasonable probability that by chance alone such an analysis will yield names of people and events that the reader recognizes. The claim, however, is that the rate of occurrence of such discoveries is much higher than would be obtained by chance. The article noted that the statisticians indicated that the occurrence of the observed codes was greater in the Bible than in Tolstoy's *War and Peace*.

Let us examine this issue purely from the point of view of assessing the extent to which such a process does, or does not, support evidence of God's existence. To be clear about our objective, we will ignore the distinction between finding messages and being able to ascribe such messages to a supreme being.

Our sole objective is to assess this way of providing evidence for, or against, anything. A first thought along these lines is that using statistics we cannot *prove* anything, we merely adduce evidence in favor of or against a hypothesis; statisticians are, we recall, not in the business of proof but in the realm of *inference*. We recognize that we can cite seemingly overwhelming evidence in favor of, or against, a hypothesis and yet our conclusions can be quite wrong.

Our first thought is that there is no clearly and precisely stated hypothesis, and there is no clear statement of the choices that we are to make. In all our analyses, we examined how to choose between two mutually exclusive hypotheses. We played the game that we had narrowed down our options to just two alternatives. However, notice such a clean dichotomy does not exist in this case. Our first difficulty is to assess what we might expect from observations "by chance." Usually, statisticians assume the independence of events under the hypothesis that there is no effect; in this case, there is no message. But the words of a book, any book, are not written at random and that observation carries over to the letters used. It is most likely that there are groups of words and phrases that are repeated far more frequently than other words and phrases. It is also likely that there are many incidences of correlation between blocks of text, and often this will be the case for blocks of text widely separated within the book. After all, writers of a text, even a complicated and multiauthored text such as the Bible, are writing with an objective in mind and will usually have a definite style of writing that is maintained throughout the text. By "style of writing," we mean that the author's choice of words and phrases has a pattern and that some words and phrases appear far more often than others. Indeed, the very concept of textual comparisons rests on this notion that each author has a style that can be recognized by a descriptive statistical analysis. This means that the choice of words and phrases is not random, and so we cannot calculate the probability of occurrence of any given word, phrase, or group of phrases under the assumption of randomness. A possible line of attack to obtain a benchmark might be to calculate the observed frequency of occurrence of those words discovered in the Bible in a random selection of large texts or in a group of texts with an equivalent number of words. There are difficulties in making even this comparison, but at least we recognize that without such an approach we do not have a well-formulated null hypothesis.

The alternative hypothesis is equally vague. What constitutes a message? No one has claimed that there are sequences of *sentences* that give instructions or warnings—merely that there are words that are recognizable and, in the analyst's view, that are of religious relevance. Merely writing this sentence indicates how imprecise the statement of the alternative hypothesis is. Vague hypotheses, especially those that are *formulated after seeing the outcomes*, are not only misleading but intellectually dangerous. The alternatives are *formulated after seeing the data*, because the analyst's procedure is to try all sorts of "decoding schemes" and then list the names that are thereby discovered. These names then become the messages that were to be found. In all that we have done, we were careful to formulate our alternative hypotheses *before* we confronted the data and were careful to pose the problem in such a way that the demarcation between the alternatives was precisely indicated. However, such precision of definition of the problem is lacking in this situation.

The reader might well counter these arguments by pointing out that cryptographers use the same and many more techniques that are even more clever to discover messages sent by intelligence agents of other countries. True, but there is a fundamental difference. In a cryptographer's discovery of a message within a seemingly innocuous text, the message is composed of sentences, at least several phrases, within a relatively short text that contains confirmable details and has a specific interpretation. Further, the message is usually supported by corroborating evidence.

If nothing else, the discussion of this example has indicated to you some of the limits of statistical analysis and has reemphasized the distinction between deductive proof and inference.

11.9 Summary

This chapter has as its sole focus the problem of how to choose between two alternative hypotheses. In Chapter 10, we were concerned with inferring the parameter values, or values of the moments, of specific distributions. There we assumed that we knew the relevant distribution but not the values of its parameters. In this chapter, we presume to know even more; but more important, our focus is different. We move from asking what the value of a parameter is to presuming we know the value but want to test whether our presumption is correct. Our test is even more constrained in that we want to check our presumed knowledge against specified alternatives, even in the more complex case of simple versus composite alternatives.

Basically, we face two alternative states of the world, A or B, and want to make a decision about which is more likely to apply to our situation. We have two decision outcomes, A or B. Note that the outcome of our hypothesis test is definitely *not* to declare which of the two states of the world holds; it is only to provide a "reasonable" course of action, a decision. Whatever choice we make, there is some probability of error. We can commit *Type I* and *II errors*. Type I errors are *rejecting the null hypothesis* when it is true, and Type II are rejecting the *alternative hypothesis* when it is true. We noted that the procedure is "biased" in favor of the null, given the usual choices of α, the probability of Type I error. This is because the originators of the procedure did not want to abandon the null hypothesis unless under that hypothesis an extraordinary event were to occur. This is the "conservative" approach to testing hypotheses.

Only when the distance between the alternative hypotheses is large, which is equivalent to having a very small variance for the distributions, can we unambiguously choose with confidence and little probability of Type II error. The usual case is the two distributions overlap, so we really need a theory to be able to make a useful decision. In these situations, we have a choice between the level of Type I and II errors; decreasing one inevitably increases the other, so this decision is a real one. The choice of α level depends on your own assessment of the costs associated with Type I and II errors.

When we move to *simple* versus *composite hypotheses tests*, we can no longer talk about trading off α and β; now we have to consider a set of β values, one for each value of the alternative hypothesis. Our solution is to examine the power curve, where *power* is $1 - \beta$; power is the probability that the alternative hypothesis will be accepted when it is in fact true.

We ended our discussion of testing hypotheses by distinguishing between *statistical significance* of an effect and the importance, often confusingly termed, the "significance" of an effect. The latter is concerned with the degree of the effect, or its strength; whereas the former is really more concerned with the detectability of an effect. Very large effects may not be detectable because the variation in noise is too large; alternatively very small and unimportant effects may be easily detectable because the variation in the noise is even less. The former would at reasonable confidence levels be statistically insignificant and the latter statistically significant. However, from a practical perspective, the former situation needs to be recognized and the latter can be ignored.

We introduced a very useful way of summarizing "hypothesis test situations"—calculating *P values*, or significance probabilities. *P* values state the probability under the null hypothesis of observing in a repeated sample using exactly the same experimental conditions as in the original experiment a value of the statistic that is more extreme than that actually observed. Very small *P* values indicate that the observed value of the statistic is in a range that is improbable under the null hypothesis, and large values indicate that the observed value of the statistic is in a range of values that are very probable under the null hypothesis.

We presented two examples to give the reader a better understanding of the practicality of statistical analysis and the limits of inference. Our objective was to show the various questions that must be answered before beginning any analysis. We have not yet developed the tools to deal with all of these questions, but recognizing the need to answer such questions will help the reader gain a more sophisticated understanding of statistical tools.

Case Study

Was There Age Discrimination in a Public Utility?

In Chapter 10, we estimated a number of parameters from the distributions for the relevant variables; in this chapter, we will test hypotheses about those parameters. The first parameter was the mean salary of the employees in the original firm. One hypothesis we might consider is that the theoretical mean of the salaries of the original employees is $53,250 against the hypothesis that it is greater than $53,250. Do these two salary distributions have the same theoretical mean? Did the mean salary of former employees seeking to be rehired match those in the outside market or was it less? This is clearly a one-sided test with large values rejecting. We are reasonably sure that the Gaussian distribution is a suitable approximation, and we know that we do not know the variance. Consequently, our test is based on the Student's T distribution, with 254 degrees of freedom, and the statistic is 8.68. The critical bounds for $\alpha =$ .01, .001, .0001, are 2.34, 3.12, and 3.76. Consequently, we conclude that at almost any α level the null hypothesis is rejected in favor of the alternative. The firm's old employees earned far more than the average salaries of those applying from the outside, but this comparison does not allow for skill level, managerial responsibility, or even age.

We can also test hypotheses about other probabilities as well. We have an estimate of the percentage of employees that are female. If the industry average is 0.18 and the estimated proportion of females in this firm is .16, we can test the hypothesis that the mean of the proportion of employees that is female is .18 versus the alternative that it is different—in this case, a two-sided test. The binomial distribution is rel-

evant with 375 degrees of freedom. We use the Gausssian approximation for this test at a variety of α levels. The calculated statistic is -1.31 and at a 5% test level the lower critical bound is -1.96. We fail to reject the null hypothesis. The corresponding P value is .19; that is, the probability of getting a value as or more extreme under the null hypothesis is 19%. If we raise the probability of the test error, the probability of incorrectly accepting the null to .1, we still accept; but at an α level of .2 the critical bound is -1.28, and at this point we reject the null hypothesis. Recall that as we raise the probability of Type I error, we reduced the probability of Type II; we increased the power of the test. This example stresses the importance of specifying an appropriate α level; the conclusions drawn depend very much on your choice.

Our main interest is in the proportion of former employees 40 and over that were hired; we want to test the hypothesis that this proportion is the same as the proportion of the former employees who were 40 and over, or the same as the proportion of former employees who applied and who were 40 and over. Given that we have reduced all our choices to simple {0,1} choices, the relevant distribution is the binomial with varying degrees of freedom, depending on the number of "N/As" contained in the data. The proportion of former employees hired that are over 40 is .50 with 314 degrees of freedom. The proportion of former employees that are 40 and over and applied is .76; for the population of all former employees 40 and over the proportion is .84. We test the hypothesis that the estimated proportion .50 has a mean of .76 against the alternative that the proportion is less. Because we have so many degrees of freedom, let us choose a very small size of test; that is, let $\alpha = .01$.

continues on next page

(Continued)

The estimated statistic is -10.97, and the corresponding critical bound at $\alpha = .01$ is -2.33, so the null hypothesis is rejected. Indeed, even if we reduce α to $.001$, the null hypothesis is still rejected.

We conclude that there is no doubt that proportionately fewer people over 40 were hired than were in the population of all employees, or even within the proportion that applied. It is also true that the average salary of the employees was greater than the estimated market mean salary, so

that by hiring from the outside the average wage bill would be reduced.

However, we have not allowed sufficiently for the effect of "self-selection" on the outcome. As we mentioned previously, it is likely given the circumstances that older people within the firm who are near retirement (recall the average age, 46, and the average level of years of service, 21) will not be as aggressive in the rehiring process, they have less to gain, so that we would expect for these reasons alone fewer would be hired.

Exercises

Calculation Practice

11.1 Using the verbal and mathematics scores for the PSAT examination described in the chapter, perform one-tailed and two-tailed hypotheses tests, where appropriate, at the 7% significance level for the following hypotheses. Assume normality for the distributions, but do not assume that you know the variances.

a. The mean SAT math score is 450 against the alternative that it is higher.

b. The mean SAT verbal score is 450 against the alternative that it is lower.

c. The mean PSAT math score is 50 against the alternative that it is not.

d. The mean PSAT verbal score is 35 against the alternative that it is not.

11.2 A random sample of 10 observations is drawn from a normal distribution with unknown mean and variance. The sample variance is $S^2 = 160$, and the null hypothesis is $H_0: \mu = 150$. The alternative hypothesis is $H_0: \mu = 200$.

a. Determine the rejection region, and illustrate it with a diagram for $\alpha = .1$; $\alpha = .05$; and $\alpha = .01$.

b. Would you reject or accept the null hypothesis if the observed sample mean, $\bar{x}$, had a value of 158 at each of the following significance levels: $\alpha = .1$; $\alpha = .05$; and $\alpha = .01$?

c. Given the alternative hypothesis, calculate the power of this test and illustrate for the difference significance levels: $\alpha = .1$; $\alpha = .05$; and $\alpha = .01$.

d. Suppose that the alternative hypothesis is $H_1: \mu = 160$. How would your decisions to reject or accept the null at the three different significance levels specified change? Note that $\bar{x} = 158$.

e. Given this different alternative hypothesis, recalculate the power of the test for the three different significance levels: $\alpha = .1$; $\alpha = .05$; and $\alpha = .01$.

f. Compute and show in a diagram the P values for the following observed sample means: $\bar{x} = 158$; $\bar{x} = 160$; and $\bar{x} = 162$.

11.3 A random sample of 25 observations is drawn from a normal distribution with unknown mean and variance. The sample variance is

$S^2 = 400$, and we want to test the null hypothesis H_0: $\mu = 15$ against the alternative H_1: $\mu \neq 15$.

a. Determine and illustrate in a diagram the rejection region for $\alpha = .1$; $\alpha = .05$; and $\alpha = .01$.

b. Would you reject or accept the null hypothesis of the observed sample mean $\bar{x} = 32$ at a significance level of $\alpha = .1$; $\alpha = .05$; and $\alpha = .01$.

c. If the sample mean was $\bar{x} = 25$ instead 32, how would your results differ?

d. Suppose the sample variance was much lower, $S^2 = 25$. Recalculate the rejection region for the same significance levels.

11.4 Large introductory college courses are often split into smaller recitation sections, with each led by a different teaching assistant. Imagine you are an instructor for one of these large courses and one of your teaching assistants comes to you and asks for a pay raise for doing an above-average job. Her basis for this is as follows. There are 250 students enrolled in the course. Each recitation section contains 25 students. The final grades for the course have a mean of 70 and a standard deviation of 15. The average for her recitation section is 80, and the standard deviation is 14. Your assistant argues that it is unlikely than any 25 randomly selected students would average above 80 for their final grades. Therefore, she did an outstanding job of instructing the students and should receive a pay raise. Perform a hypothesis test to evaluate the teaching assistant's claim. Assume normality for the distributions, but you do not know the variance.

11.5 (Refer to Exercise 11.4.) You are evaluating your teaching assistants' performance. Two of your teaching assistants (Susan and Mary) are arguing over who did a better job of instructing her students. Each of the two recitations contains 25 students. The final course average for Susan's students is 75, with a standard deviation of 10. The final course average for Mary's students is 80 with a standard deviation of 5. Perform a hypothesis test on the difference of the two means to determine if there is in fact a difference in performance be-

tween the two recitation sections. Use the same assumptions as in the previous exercise.

11.6 The average values of arms transferred from the United States and the U.S.S.R. between 1981 and 1985 to 36 randomly selected countries are summarized in the table:

	U.S.	U.S.S.R.
Average Arms Transfers (in U.S.$ millions)	866.81	1,322.36
Sample Standard Deviation	1,471.70	2,082.07

Based on this information, can you conclude that, on average, the U.S.S.R. transferred a higher value of arms than the United States in the given period? Specify the test that you will use and your significance level.

11.7 In a random sample of 20 coffee drinkers (defined as those that have more than 200 mg of coffee a day), the average number of finger taps during a fixed interval of time was 248.3, with a standard deviation of 2.2. Similarly, in a random sample of 10 noncoffee drinkers, the average number of finger taps was 245.6, and the standard deviation was 2.3. Can you conclude that, on average, coffee drinkers make more finger taps than non-drinkers? Specify your test and the significance level.

Exploring the Tools

11.8 You want to choose between two simple alternatives, μ_1 and μ_2. The parent distribution is $N(\mu, \sigma_0^2)$, and you know the value of σ_0^2. Your information is based on a random sample of size 64, and σ_0^2 is 9. Pick a confidence level of 90%.

a. Compare your tests when μ_1 is the null, μ_2 is the alternative, and

(1) $\mu_1 = 0$, $\mu_2 = 1$

(2) $\mu_1 = 0$, $\mu_2 = 4$

(3) $\mu_1 = 0$, $\mu_2 = 10$

b. Let μ_2 be the null in each case and μ_1 the alternative, and compare your results.

Table 11.2   **Joint probabilities for "states of the world" and decisions**

		Decision		Marginal
		a	b	Probability of A, B
State of	A	$(1 - \text{pr}[\text{II}|p_\alpha])P_A$	$(\text{pr}[\text{II}|p_\alpha])P_A$	P_A
the World	B	$\text{pr}[\text{III } p_\alpha] (1 - P_A)$	$(1 - \text{pr}[\text{III } p_\alpha])(1 - P_A)$	$1 - P_A$
Marginal Probability of Decision a, b		$\text{pr}(a)$	$\text{pr}(b)$	

The objectives in this exercise are to help you evaluate the role of the alternative hypothesis in a "simple versus simple" setting and to understand the special role played by the null.

11.9 *Objective: To illustrate the sampling properties of hypothesis tests.* In this exercise, 500 random drawings of samples of size $n1 = 10$ are drawn, and the proportion of times the test rejects is recorded and plotted as a histogram overlaid on a plot of the theoretical distribution of rejections for each choice made in the dialogue.

[*Computer directions:* Start S-Plus. Click on Labs, Level of Significance of a Test. Accept the default values in the dialog; click Apply. Examine the output in the Graph window. Repeat the experiment by making various choices for the dialog alternatives.]

This exercise gives you practice in examining the statistical properties of hypothesis tests in a variety of circumstances; be bold and experiment!

11.10 **Worked.** *Objective: To illustrate the formal determination of optimal values for α and β (for the student with calculus).* Consider a choice between two states of the world. Let us label them A and B. Label the corresponding decisions a and b, to take decision a is to act in accordance with state of the world A and to take decision b is to act in accordance with state of the world B. The novel element in our development here is to presume that we have information on the probabilities of occurrence of states A and B; let the probability of A occurring be P_A and that of state B, be $P_B = 1 - P_A$.

As a first step we create for this problem a decision/state of the world table as we did in Table

11.1, but this time we add in the probabilities of occurrence for each state of the world. (See Table 11.2.)

The probability under the chosen decision rule that decision b will be taken conditional that the state of the world is A is $\text{pr}[\text{I}|p_\alpha]$, and $(1 - \text{pr}[\text{I}|p_\alpha])$ is the probability under the same decision rule and condition that decision a will be taken. Each entry in the body of the table is the joint probability of taking a given action for a given state of the world; that is, $\text{pr}[\text{II}|p_\alpha](1 - P_A)$ is the joint probability that with critical bound p_α action a will be taken and the state of the world is B; $\text{pr}[a]$ and $\text{pr}[b]$ are the marginal probabilities of taking actions a and b.

We need to specify how probabilities such as $\text{pr}[\text{II}|p_\alpha]$ are calculated. We will presume that the situation is similar to that found in Figure 11.2. State A is the lower mean value, and state B is the higher mean value; by our previous discussion the choice of p_α was somewhere between the lower and upper mean values. We see that as we increase p_α; that is, if we shift p_α to the right, the probability of Type I error will decrease and that of Type II will increase. For simplicity, let us assume that both distributions are Gaussian with the same variance $\sigma^2 = 1$ and means μ_A, μ_B. Letting $\phi(x_0|\mu_A)$, $\phi(x_0|\mu_B)$ represent the Gaussian cumulative distribution functions and $\phi(X|\mu_A)$, $\phi(X|\mu_B)$ the corresponding density functions, the probabilities are:

$$\text{pr}[I|p_\alpha] = \int_{p_\alpha}^{\infty} \phi(X|\mu_A)dX$$
$$= 1 - \phi(p_\alpha|\mu_A)$$

Table 11.3   **Loss table for the decision problem**

		Decision	
		a	b
State of the	A	$0	$L_1
World	B	$L_2	$0

$$\text{pr}[II|p_\alpha] = \int_{-\infty}^{p_\alpha} \phi(X|\mu_B)dX$$

$$= \phi(p_\alpha|\mu_B)$$

We now consider a corresponding loss table; each entry indicates the loss or gain to the decision maker from taking a given action given a specific state of the world.

We have assumed that correct decisions have zero cost, but that the two incorrect decisions have costs of $L_1 and $L_2, respectively (see Table 11.3).

What now is our task? We seek to find that value of p_α, and hence a value for α and β, such that the expected loss is minimal. Given our simplifying assumptions, the expected loss for this decision setting is

$$E\{Loss\} =$$

$$\$L_1 \times \text{pr}[I|p_\alpha]P_A + \$L_2 \times \text{pr}[II|p_\alpha](1 - P_A)$$

We minimize expected loss by setting the first derivative of this function with respect to p_α to zero. We obtain the equation

$$-L_1 \times \phi(p_\alpha|\mu_A)P_A +$$
$$L_2 \times \phi(p_\alpha|\mu_B)(1 - P_A) = 0$$

where $\phi(p_\alpha|\mu_A)$ and $\phi(p_\alpha|\mu_B)$ are the Gaussian density functions. The solution is given by

$$\frac{L_1}{L_2} = \frac{\phi(p_\alpha|\mu_B)(1 - P_A)}{\phi(p_\alpha|\mu_A)P_A}$$

If L_1, the cost of Type I error, is increased relative to L_2, then to retain the equality we need to increase the ratio on the right side. We can do this by

increasing p_α. If P_A is large relative to $(1 - P_A)$, then given a specific ratio for L_1/L_2, we require $\phi(p_\alpha|\mu_B)/\phi(p_\alpha|\mu_A)$ to be large, and that implies a large value for p_α. These results indicate that if the probability of state A occurring is large, or the cost of Type I error is large relative to that of Type II, we pick a small value of α and a large value of β.

Let us consider a numerical example. We are observing one of two distributions of temperatures on a Pacific atoll; both are distributed as Gaussian and both have a unit variance, but A has a mean of 23.5 and B has a mean of 25 degrees Celsius. If distribution A is true, a hypothesis of "no change" in the environment is accepted, but if distribution B is applicable, there will be flooding. Flooding will necessitate putting all the houses on stilts, and that will cost $10,000. If, however, the houses are not put onto stilts, and there is flooding, the cost is $20,000. With these assumptions $L_1 = \$20,000$ and $L_2 = \$10,000$. We assume that correct decisions have zero cost implications; for example, if houses are put onto stilts and there is flooding, the benefit from no flooding of the houses is $10,000. Lastly, we assume that the probability of the "no flooding" state A occurring is .8.

We now calculate the optimal p_α and the optimal values of α and β. $L_1/L_2 = 2$, $(1 - P_A)/P_A = 1/4$. We need to solve for $\phi(p_\alpha|\mu_B)/\phi(p_\alpha|\mu_A) = 8$, where $\mu_A = 23.5$ and $\mu_B = 25$. By substituting $\mu_A = 23.5$ and $\mu_B = 25$ in the Gaussian densities, we obtain the equation

$$\frac{\phi(p_\alpha|\mu_B)}{\phi(p_\alpha|\mu_A)} = \frac{e^{-1/2(p_\alpha - \mu_B)^2}}{e^{-1/2(p_\alpha - \mu_A)^2}} = 8$$

Solving this equation for p_α, we obtain

$$p_\alpha = \frac{2\ln(8) + (\mu_B)^2 - (\mu_A)^2}{2(\mu_B - \mu_A)}$$
$$= 25.64$$

Notice immediately that in this instance p_α is greater than both means. We can obtain the corresponding values of α and β by standardizing the value of p_α (in this instance we need merely subtract 23.5 and 25, respectively, from p_α) and evaluate the corresponding integrals from the Statistical Tables. We obtain the values $\alpha = .016$ and $\beta = .74$. These may seem like surprising results, but they are the outcome of our assumptions and indicate very clearly that a simple reliance on traditional α levels and expecting correspondingly small β values is misguided.

You might experiment by making the difference in mean temperatures larger, the probability of the normal weather lower, the difference in costs less, and the variance less, and by examining the effect on the resulting values for Types I and II errors. For example, consider the results if you set temperature to 28 degrees Celsius; next let the ratio of costs be 1/2 with $\mu_B = 28$. You might notice that it is not difficult to allow for different variances and to include nonzero returns from correct decisions. Experiment.

11.11 For each of the following situations, specify a two-by-two table of alternative states of the world and the alternative decisions to be made. Specify the two types of errors, and indicate how you would base your decision on observable outcomes in each case. Reverse the roles of null and alternative hypotheses, and comment on the implications.

a. The number of defective components is higher, or is lower, than before.

b. Mean shares fall more, or less, in this year than last year.

c. There is global warming or global cooling.

d. Under the Bush administration average real incomes rose or fell.

e. There is more, or less, violence shown on television.

11.12 In Exercise 11.8, if σ_0^2 were 1, or if it were 100, what would be the difference in your conclusions?

11.13 Suppose you want to choose between two hypotheses, μ_1 and μ_2, the parent distribution is $N(\mu, \sigma_0^2)$, and you know the value of σ_0^2. For any sample size, explain and illustrate what happens to your test result as you lower the assigned size of the test, α, from .10 to .001. Illustrate with an example, where $\mu_1 = 0$, $\mu_2 = 2$, $\sigma_0^2 = 9$, $n = 100$.

11.14 Compare two situations. You want to test whether $\mu_1 = 0$ against $\mu_2 = 2$, where the parent distribution is $N(\mu, \sigma^2)$. Let us agree to use the usual 95% confidence level and that your sample size is 100. The two situations are that (1) you know that $\sigma^2 = 4$, and in (2) you have only an estimate $s^2 = 3.4$.

a. Set up the hypothesis tests in the two cases, and compare the implications for your inferences.

b. Using the statistical tables (see Appendix B) obtain a 95% confidence level on σ^2 given the observed $s^2 = 3.4$. Using the bounds as possible (extreme) values for the unknown σ^2, evaluate what the test results might be if these bound values were equal to the unknown σ^2.

11.15 You want to test the hypothesis that $\mu = 3$ against the alternative that $\mu = 6$ for a normal distribution with known variance $\sigma^2 = 36$. You want a probability of Type I error of only .01 and a power of .99 (probability of Type II error is also .01). What sample size do you need to achieve this result?

11.16 Repeat your answer to Exercise 11.15 when you choose an α level of .01 and are willing to accept a probability of Type II error of .04.

11.17 *Worked.* *Objective: To demonstrate how to test for the equality of two variances using independent samples. If the estimators for the two vari-*

ances are independently distributed, we can use the F distribution by creating the random variable given by the ratio of the sample sums of squares about the mean. If the variances are equal, and there are n_1 and n_2 observations for each sample variance, the ratio is distributed as F with $n_1 - 1$ and $n_2 - 1$ degrees of freedom under the null hypothesis of equality of the variances σ_1^2 and σ_2^2. If σ_1^2 is the larger under the alternative hypothesis, large values of the F statistic will indicate rejection of the null hypothesis. Consider the variable "age" for the internal applicants that were not selected and the external applicants for the age discrimination data. Our null hypothesis is that the variances are the same; the alternative is that the variance for external applicants is greater, so that we have a single-sided test using the F distribution. The summary statistics for the age variable for the internal and external applicants are $\hat{\sigma}_{int}^2 = 32.5$, with $n_{int} = 52$, and $\sigma_{ext}^2 = 69.5$ with $n_{ext} = 58$.

[**Computer directions:** Start S-Plus. Click on Labs, Calculating Tests of Hypotheses. Click "sig1^2/sig2^2," and enter $\boxed{58}$ and $\boxed{52}$ in "n1" and "n2"; $\boxed{69.5}$ in s1^2 and $\boxed{32.5}$ in s2^2. Set Hyp. Value to "1"; click Apply.] At the default alpha level of 5% confidence the results are that the null hypothesis is very strongly rejected in favor of the alternative; the F statistic value is 2.14 with 57 and 51 degrees of freedom and a P value of .0061.

11.18 The data set, Film.xls, with revenues for various studios, is in folder Misc, in the Xfiles. When we discussed the sample moments of these data, we considered the return risk trade-off, so that the potential equality of the underlying variances is of interest. In particular, consider testing the hypothesis that the variances of returns for studios O and W are the same. Comment on the implications for choosing between the two studios.

11.19 We have examined the variation in the mean values of the energy use per capita for various countries in the folder Energy. However, we have not considered the variance of that use. Test the hypothesis that the variances for Norway and

Korea are the same. If true, what are the implications?

11.20 In the folder Misc, in the Xfiles, use the file Coles. It includes measurements on prefat and postfat for a group of volunteers in a fitness program. The differences in the mean values do not appear to be very large, so we might well consider whether there is a significant difference in the respective variances. Why can we not use the F distribution in this case?

11.21 *Objective: To illustrate the calculation of P values in a variety of situations.*

[**Computer directions:** Start S-Plus. Click on Labs, Tests of Significance. Accept the default values in the dialog; click on Apply. Examine the output in the Report window. Repeat the experiment by making various choices for the dialog alternatives.]

This exercise gives you practice in examining the calculation of P values; be bold and experiment!

11.22 *Objective: To illustrate the power of a test and how it depends on sample size and the extent of the difference between the null and alternative hypotheses for a fixed size of variance.* In this exercise, the histograms from the outcome of 500 trials of a hypothesis test are plotted against the theoretical predictions for the percentage of times the null hypothesis will be rejected. The key is to observe how the relative frequency of rejection under the alternative hypothesis varies with the size of the difference between null and alternative, the sample size, and the α level.

[**Computer directions:** Start S-Plus. Click on Labs, Power of a Test. Accept the default values in the dialog; click Apply. Repeat the experiment several times altering the settings in the dialog to explore the role of power in hypothesis tests. "D" represents the difference between the null and alternative hypotheses; all tests are right-sided.]

11.23 *Objective: To illustrate the power of a test and how it depends on sample size and the extent of the difference between the null and alternative*

hypotheses for a fixed size of variance. This exercise elaborates on the outcome of the previous exercise. In this exercise you will be able to alter the α levels; the difference, delta, between null and alternative hypotheses; the sample size; and power. You have the choice of fixing all but one of these variables and solving for the one not set; that is, you can calculate power given sample size, delta, and the α level; or you can calculate the sample size needed to achieve a given power for a given delta and α level, and so on.

[*Computer directions:* Start S-Plus. Click on <u>Labs, Sample Size, Level, and Power</u>. Accept the default entries in the dialog to begin. Click on the + and − buttons in "Buttons to change values" to see the graphs. You will create a series of graphs by incrementing/decrementing any one of the variables *alpha*, *power*, *delta*, or *n*. Experiment with different settings in Choose Which Value to Calculate. Each click on "Buttons to change values" creates a new overlaid set of graphs. The graphs show how power varies with each of the other values, alpha, delta, or Sample Size.]

11.24 *Objective: To explore the trade-off between Type I and Type II errors.* You are head of a medical research unit that is undertaking an investigation of the efficacy of a new cancer treatment. If the treatment is effective, patients enter into a complete and permanent remission. If the treatment is ineffective, it stimulates cancerous cells to reproduce even faster, thereby hastening each patient's death. Your unit is provided with some statistical data from a clinical trial. Based on these data, your unit is to make a recommendation to the FDA whether to approve this new treatment. Given the null hypothesis that the treatment "cures" cancer and the alternative hypothesis that the treatment does not cure, but rather kills, what value of alpha would you choose for your hypothesis test? Justify your selection.

As an alternative you can choose the desired value for Type II error and solve for Type I given some fixed sample size. How and why would you do this? Finally, if you have a large budget, consider that you could control the experimental sample size. Explain how you would choose the optimum sample size and the values for Types I and II errors.

11.25 Using graphical techniques, illustrate the optimal choice between Type I and II errors as the cost of I in terms of II falls from a very high value to a very low value. When the relative cost of Type I is high, what are your choices for α and β? When the relative cost of II is very high, what are your choices?

11.26 What is the implication of your results in Exercise 11.25 on the choice of which error type is null and which is alternative, if you use only the conventional α levels to be found in the tables?

11.27 Use the *P* values obtained in Exercise 11.21 to comment on the choice of null and alternative hypotheses for the situations discussed in Exercise 11.8.

11.28 The minimum power of a test involving a simple versus a composite, but one-sided alternative, is never less than the assigned α level. Explain and illustrate this claim.

11.29 If your sample size is large enough, then for any assigned α level and any given difference between the null and alternative hypotheses, both simple, the power will be approximately 1. On the basis of this observation, some people claim hypothesis tests are useless, because you can always reject any difference with enough data. What crucial aspect of this situation does that analysis miss, and what is the sensible resolution of this problem? (*Hint:* Think carefully about the trade-off between α and β, size of difference between hypothesis, and sample size.)

11.30 In the text, we discussed testing for the difference between two means where it was assumed that the parent distribution variances were the same. Suppose we have four independent random samples, each with its own mean that may, or may not, differ from the others, but that the variances are known to be the same in each of the four cases, even though the value of that variance is unknown.

Devise a test that $\mu_2 = \mu_3$ versus the alternative that the means are different that best uses all your information.

11.31 (Reference: *Judgement under Uncertainty: Heuristics and Biases*, Cambridge, 1998.) Tversky and Kahneman indicate that people's subjective assessments of probability are conditioned on the retrievability of instances; that is, if it is easy for you to remember something, you will tend to exaggerate the probability of the occurrence of such events. If you were to poll people's assessments of the probability of a fire in a large building before and after such a fire, the assessments of the probability of fire in such buildings would be much higher in the latter case; even though we all know that, by definition, rare events do occur, just with small probability.

Using your knowledge of inference obtained so far, discuss how you would proceed to test for the validity of the assertions made in the previous paragraph.

11.32 Experiment. (Reference: *Judgement under Uncertainty: Heuristics and Biases,* Cambridge, 1998.) Use the computer to generate 20 random sequences of the numbers {0,1}, sample size of 10.

[*Computer directions:* Start S-Plus. On the menu bar, select Data, Random Numbers. In Sample Size key in $\boxed{10}$. In Distribution select Binomial. In the Parameters box, in Probability, key in $\boxed{.5}$. In Sample Size, key in $\boxed{1}$. Click Apply 20 times. Twenty random samples will be in the Report window. Print the Report window.]

a. For each sequence so obtained, ask five fellow students if there is an approximate pattern in the sequence presented; label the sequence "patterned" if at least three of your evaluators agree that there is a pattern in the data.

b. You know that the sequences were generated "at random," but if you did not know this, how would you test the hypothesis that the data sequences are random using this experiment? (*Hint:* Although the probability of a specific pattern being obtained by chance is very low, the probability of some pattern being observed is very high; how might you estimate this probability?)

Applications

The objective of the first few exercises to follow is to explore the precise formulation of tests of hypotheses.

11.33 Using the data files for energy consumption for South Korea (Koreng.xls) and the Philippines (Phileng.xls) contained in the Energy folder, explain how you would test the hypothesis that energy consumption per capita in South Korea is higher than in the Philippines. State clearly your null and alternative hypotheses. Indicate which probability for Type I error you would select, and explain why. You could as easily select the probability of Type II errors and solve for the corresponding value for Type I. Why might you consider doing that in this case?

11.34 The data file Psatsat.xls in folder Testscor contains 520 observations for SAT and PSAT math and verbal scores. Explain how you would attempt to test the hypothesis that the PSAT is an easier examination than the SAT. Specify how you would organize your data set, state your null and alternative hypotheses, and indicate the relevant distribution for your test statistic.

11.35 Explain how you would test the hypothesis that PSAT math scores are higher than PSAT verbal scores. If you were to refine the statement that PSAT math scores are 4 points higher, how would you test this hypothesis? By being more specific in your statement of the null hypothesis, evaluate what, if anything, you have gained and lost.

11.36 In Chapter 7, Exercise 7.63, we discussed the daddy longlegs experiment and queried whether the data on lost legs were distributed as Poisson. In this exercise, test the hypothesis that daddy longlegs do not learn from their experiences. Identify at least two ways in which you can carry out this test. Discuss the plausibility of the assumptions that underlie your analysis.

11.37 The effects of diet and exercise are an often studied question that generates ambiguous results. Data obtained from a diet and exercise program are provided in the file Coles.xls. Use these data to construct tests for the following hypotheses. Provide an interpretation of your hypothesis testing results in each case.

a. Are men more responsive to exercise programs than women, in terms of body fat lost? in terms of weight lost?

b. Was this diet and exercise program successful? How do you measure "success"? Can you think of at least two ways to measure success for this program?

[**Computer hint:** Create two new variables *lossfat* and *losswt*. In S-Plus, on the menu bar, click on Data, Transform. In New Column Name, key in lossfat. In Expression, key in prefat-postfat. Click Apply. Repeat for losswt.]

11.38 Many firms in the late 1980s experienced "downsizing"— the elimination of jobs, mostly in middle management. Downsizing created a significant unemployment problem. Critics of downsizing argued that the unemployment effects outweighed any cost reduction enjoyed by firms, so that overall downsizing was harmful for the aggregate economy. Supporters of downsizing made the argument that the employees terminated were less productive so that firms were able to reduce costs without reducing aggregate output. One could surmise that smaller firms, which face greater pressures to adapt, are more productive. Use the data contained in the file Cosize.xls to explore the hypothesis that smaller firms are more productive (in terms of sales per employee). How do you formulate the hypotheses, and what criteria do you use to select the size of Type I error? Does your result depend on how you measure "small firms"?

11.39 The theory of liquidity preference tells us that people prefer to consume now rather than in the future. To entice individuals to save their money and delay consumption, they must be offered a reward for waiting, a rate of interest on their savings. The longer an individual delays consumption, the greater the risk faced, so a higher rate of return will be expected. From this, we might conclude that long-term interest rates should theoretically be higher than short-term interest rates. Use the data in the file Intrate.xls to assess the validity of this assertion. Explain carefully how you would formulate your specific hypotheses. Do your results vary depending on which interest rate pairings you select? Can you explain these results?

11.40 Pick two books, for example, a volume of Shakespeare's plays and a Faulkner novel. Select a sequence of five pages at random in each book, and count the number of prepositions used by each author. Also, count the total number of words, and obtain the percentage of the total words that are prepositions. Discuss how you would test the hypothesis that Shakespeare used more prepositions than Faulkner. After doing the calculations comment on your results.

11.41 Worked. *Objective: To explore the formulation of tests of hypotheses. Note:* This discussion is far more elaborate than you would be expected to produce. However, it is important that you recognize the limitations of the procedures and the true depth of the analysis that underlies these tools.

The data that we will discuss are in the folder Misc under the file Husbands.xls; the file contains observations on husbands' and wives' heights in centimeters.

"Are husbands taller than their wives?" is an apparently simple question. In this exercise, we will explore how to formulate the corresponding statistical question. In the process, we will have to recognize the facts we observe and the information we need in addition to the observed data, and finally we have to decide how to bring our statistical theory to bear on the problem.

Note first that the question asked is, "Are husbands taller than their wives?" not "Are men taller than women?" The corresponding statistical question would seem to be equally simple. Is the mean of the height distribution of "husbands" greater than the mean of the distribution of "wives"? Notice that these could differ even in a population where the mean height of men equaled the mean height of women because tall men select short women for wives and short men do not marry, or vice versa.

There are at least two concerns before we begin. Because we are dealing with husbands and wives, not men and women, we should be concerned about the effect of mutual selection on the outcomes. It is likely that the distributions of heights of husbands and wives are not independent of each other so that when comparing differences, we may not have independent samples. Second, are we concerned about the distribution of the difference in heights between each spousal pair, or are husbands on average taller than wives on average?

The latter question implies something a little different from the former. The latter merely says that there is a difference between the means of the distributions of husbands and wives who might select each other at random. The former says that men choose shorter women, correspondingly women choose taller men.

Let us investigate both questions in turn. But we will need to be clever to answer the latter.

What are the observable facts—the heights of husbands and wives. But do we have a random sample of husbands and a random sample of wives, or do we have a random sample of pairs of husbands and wives? In the data set "Husbands.xls," we have pairs of observations, so that we have a random sample of pairs. Given this joint distribution of heights, we could estimate the sample correlation between them using the procedures of Chapter 5. If we do that the answer is a correlation coefficient of .36.

What is the applicable distribution for heights? Earlier, we speculated that the distribution of heights might be approximately normal. As a very rough check on this issue, plot the histograms of heights for husbands and wives, and calculate the standardized third and fourth moments. The assumption of normality in both cases seems reasonable. This is a preliminary examination of the data, but we are forewarned by our theory to question the equality of the variances. In our case, the sample estimates are 4727 and 3906 centimeters squared for husbands and wives, respectively. These results mean that it is unlikely that the variances are equal.

If we address the former question, "Are husbands taller than their wives?" we can now do so using a procedure known as *testing paired differences*.

To do so, we create a new variable, *Difhw*, defined by

$$Difhw = heighth - heightw$$

Under the null hypothesis of no difference, the mean of *Difhw* is zero. The variance of *Difhw* is given by

$$var(Difhw) = var(heighth) + var(heightw) - 2cov(heighth, heigthw)$$

where we recall that the correlation between husbands' and wives' heights is .36. Remember that the covariance can either be obtained directly as the first cross-product moment between the variables, or we can obtain the sample covariance from the sample correlation by multiplying the correlation by $\sqrt{(var(heighth) \times var(heightw))}$.

We can estimate this variance directly merely by calculating the sample variance, s^2, of the new variable, *Difhw*, with sample mean, $\bar{D}$:

$$\bar{D} = \sum_{i=1}^{n} \frac{Difhw_i}{n}$$

$$s_D^2 = \sum_{i=1}^{n} \frac{(Difhw_i - \bar{D})^2}{(n-1)}$$

Given our prior assumptions concerning the distribution, we now have the same situation as discussed in the text. We have a variable *Difhw* that is distributed independently as Gaussian with unknown mean and variance, where the variance estimate is given by s^2. As in the text, we can easily form the Student's t statistic and base our calculations of the appropriate α level for the test that the mean of *Difhw* is zero on the Student's T distribution with $n-1$ degrees of freedom.

Our choice of α will depend on our assessment of the value of the trade-off between the costs of Types I and II errors. The actual value of the Student's t statistic is

$$t = \frac{(\bar{D} - 0) \times \sqrt{n}}{s_{\bar{D}}}$$

$$= \frac{(130.5 - 0) \times \sqrt{198}}{74.14}$$

$$= 24.8$$

Given this result, we would reject the null hypothesis of a difference in pairs of zero at very small α levels and still have power nearly one. The Student's T distribution at 198 degrees of freedom is essentially Gaussian.

Now let us consider the alternative question: "Are husbands taller than wives?" Our first task is to obtain a suitable sample. The question is, How do we obtain two sample distributions that are at least approximately uncorrelated? We can achieve this by taking two independent random subsamples from our existing data, say, of size

120. This was done in S-Plus by using the sample function. My results produced samples for husbands' heights and those of wives that had a correlation of $-.005$; let us agree that $-.005$ is as close to zero as we need.

Using our independent subsamples, our estimates for mean heights for husbands and wives separately are $\bar{x}_h = 172.00$ cm, and $\bar{x}_w = 159.36$ cm. The variance of this difference in means when the underlying variances are the same is given by

$$\sigma_{\bar{x}_h - \bar{x}_w}^2 = \left(\frac{\sigma_h^2}{n_h} + \frac{\sigma_w^2}{n_w} \right)$$

where n_h and n_w are both equal to 120, say n. The pooled estimate of the variance, $\sigma_{\bar{x}_h - \bar{x}_w}^2$, s_p^2, is given by

$$s_p^2 = \frac{1}{(2n-2)} ((n-1)s_h^2 + (n-1)s_w^2)$$

so that

$$s_p^2 = \frac{1}{2} \left(s_h^2 + s_w^2 \right)$$

$$s_h^2 = \sum \frac{(xh_i - \bar{x}_h)^2}{(n_h - 1)}$$

$$s_w^2 = \sum \frac{(xw_i - \bar{x}_w)^2}{(n_w - 1)}$$

where s_h^2, s_w^2 are the sample variances for husbands and wives; $s_h^2 = 4198.8$, and $s_w^2 = 3718.2$ with a sample size $n = 120$.

From this information we know that we can formulate an estimator for the difference in heights for which we know the distribution. Thus, using $\bar{X}_h - \bar{X}_w$ as an estimator for $\mu_h - \mu_w$, we can create a Student's T random variable with $(2n-2)$ degrees of freedom in which the common value of the variance, $\sigma_{\bar{x}_h - \bar{x}_w}^2$, is canceled:

$$T = \frac{[\bar{X}_h - \bar{X}_w - (\mu_h - \mu_w)]\sqrt{n/2}}{S_p}$$

Our null hypothesis H_0 is that $\mu_h - \mu_w = 0$ versus the alternative hypothesis, H_a that $\mu_h - \mu_w > 0$. We are choosing a one-tailed test because we are presuming that we suspect that husbands are taller than wives. Under H_0, the estimator

$$T = \frac{(\bar{X}_h - \bar{X}_w)\sqrt{n/2}}{S_p}$$

is distributed as Student's T with $(2n - 2)$ degrees of freedom. The analysis can proceed in precisely the same manner as discussed in the text.

We now have to pick an appropriate alpha level, or size of test. If we agree that we are interested in the difference purely from a scientific viewpoint, and we are only willing to reject if a very low probability event occurs under the null, let us choose $\alpha = .01$, or $(1 - \alpha) = .99$.

We can at last plug in our numbers and obtain our numerical answer. The observed difference in means is 126.4, the observed value of s_p is 8.12, and the sample sizes are 120 each. We obtain a Student's t statistic of 120.6, with 238 degrees of freedom; this indicates a very significant rejection of the null hypothesis and the P value is virtually zero. A Student's T distribution with 238 degrees of freedom is to all intents and purposes Gaussian.

Our conclusion is that husbands are taller than wives. Note, this conclusion, even though based on the evidence and with extremely low probability of being wrong by chance, does not make it so; wives on average could in fact be taller than husbands.

We can reconcile this with our data by noting that either a very low probability event did occur by chance, or that the various assumptions that we made to carry out the test were inapplicable and gave rise to an anomalous result. However, in part the lesson here is that in practice, many such assumptions have to be made to carry out any test so that the interpretation of one's results will depend on the relevance and importance of these assumptions for one's conclusions.

Although this evidence is plausible, and we would be advised to act as if it were true, we will never know with certainty whether it is true or not.

11.42 The file Husbands.xls also contains information on the ages of husbands and wives. With the previous worked question as a guide, discuss how you would formulate a hypothesis, and perform the calculations to answer the question, "Are husbands older than their wives?" Contrast this with the question, "Are married men older than married women?" Using the available data, how would you test this hypothesis?

This exercise shows you how much judgment is involved in the formulation of a hypothesis test, so the results of the test will provide useful information. It reminds us of the assumptions that are involved in analysis and indicates clearly the limits of the conclusions that we can draw from any data set.

11.43 Case Study: Was There Age Discrimination in a Public Utility?

Your Forensic Economic Consulting firm has been asked to develop the case for the plaintiffs. Indicate in detail the hypotheses that you would seek to test and assess their relevance to the case at hand. If you feel that new information would be useful, specify very carefully what it is, how it would contribute to your case, and how you would obtain it.

11.44 Case Study: Was There Age Discrimination in a Public Utility?

You are a member of a competing consulting firm, and you have been hired by the defendants. Through the process of discovery, you know the arguments and the strategy espoused by the Forensic Economics Consulting firm. Evaluate their arguments and either provide a rebuttal to them, or provide a strategy for analyzing the data yourself.

PART FIVE

Bivariate Distributions, Regression, and ANOVA

CHAPTER

12

The Generation of Bivariate and Conditional
Probability Distributions

12.1 What You Will Learn in This Chapter

Chapters 7 and 8 provided the theory for univariate distributions for discrete and continuous random variables, respectively. This chapter performs the same service for bivariate distributions. As such, it provides a link between Chapter 9 on sampling theory and Chapter 13 on regression. We reintroduce the ideas about the relationship between joint, conditional, and marginal distributions. This chapter provides the essential distribution theory that underlies the calculations we performed on bivariate data in Chapter 5. We indicate how joint and conditional distributions are generated and related.

We also note that the joint and conditional distributions are functions of parameters and that the theoretical moments of the distribution, which determine the shape, are also functions of the parameters (as was true in the case of the univariate distributions). We recognize that the sampling procedure is critical to our interpretation of any inferences that we might make. Further, our analysis of joint and conditional distributions will convince us that we should not confuse correlation with causality.

12.2 Introduction

In Chapters 7 and 8, we discussed mechanisms that generate probability distributions for discrete random variables and density functions for continuous random variables. Probability distributions or density functions are theoretical constructs that enable us to discuss characteristics of data in a precise way.

We recognized that a particular experiment generates, or implies, a particular type of distribution. Different experiments generate different distributions of random variables. The different types of distribution are characterized by their shapes. The idea of shape is made more mathematically rigorous by moments and parameters of a distribution. In Chapters 7 and 8, we saw how distributions can be generated and how to relate the theoretical moments of a distribution to its parameters. Using univariate, single-variable distributions, we were able to tie together moments, parameters, classes of distributions, and "shape" to characterize the properties of any experiment that produces random variables. Further, in Chapters 10 and 11, we demonstrated how to draw inferences about the values of parameters and moments based on observed data obtained from experimental, or survey, outcomes. Now we need to extend these insights to distributions of multiple variables.

In this chapter, we will see how to generate probability distributions and density functions for pairs of random variables. Introducing another variable means that we will have to rethink our procedures, but it will enable us to deal with more interesting problems. This chapter is a precursor to the next, in which we will develop the theory of the relationship between random variables. In these two chapters we develop the theory that underlies the development of the bivariate descriptive statistics we developed in Chapter 5. This approach is very similar to that followed in Chapters 7 and 8, where we developed a theory of univariate distributions to provide a theory for univariate histograms. In essence, the material discussed in this chapter and the next provides the development of a theory for "bivariate histograms" and correlation. It also will provide an explanation for the shape of the three-dimensional histogram that we plotted in Chapter 5. (The reader is advised to review Chapter 5 before proceeding.)

Once we begin to handle multiple random variables, we have to consider how they might be "related"; we use the quotation marks to remind ourselves that we are not talking about functional, or causal, relationships, but about a more subtle concept of "association," reflected in the shape of the joint distributions of the random variables. We want to be able to parametrize that aspect of the shape of the joint distribution caused by the association between the random variables and to relate these characteristics to the theoretical moments of the distribution.

We will consider both discrete and continuous random variables; however, with bivariate data we can also consider mixed distributions, in which one variable is discrete and one is continuous. Let us consider some examples of possible bivariate pairs for which we might want to find the joint distributions.

Examining bivariate distributions is a special case of examining multivariate joint distributions—two variables as opposed to n variables, $n > 2$. In special situations in which the variables are independently and identically distributed, we have run into examples of multivariate joint distributions frequently in the previous chapters. In Chapter 6, we referred repeatedly to joint distributions in different contexts; for example, in Sections 6.4, through 6.6, we made clear in the context of a single pair of discrete random variables the relationship between joint, marginal, and conditional distributions. This chapter will develop and extend that analysis to continuous random variables and to mixtures of continuous and discrete random variables. However, recognize that the basic principles enunciated in Chapter 6 remain the same. One last example is provided by the discussion in Chapter 7, Section 7.4, where we derived the distribution of getting K successes in n identical trials—in short, the binomial distribution. We began the derivation by writing down Equation 7.6 for the joint distribution of n independent and identically distributed random variables that can have only two outcomes.

These examples indicate that we have met and used the ideas of joint distributions many, many times in the past and have also related the joint distribution to the conditional and the marginal distributions. It would be useful to restate the relationship in the context of pairs of continuous random variables and probability density functions at this juncture. Keep in mind that the density function is the rate of change in probability. For a univariate density defined with respect to random variable X, the marginal density of X indicates the rate of change in probability to a unit change in X. For a joint density function, say $f(X,Y)$, the value of the density function indicates the rate of change in probability to unit variations in X *and* in Y.

The conditional density, say $f(Y|X)$, shows the change in probability to a unit change in Y at a given level for the variable X. Recall that we initiated the discussion about conditional probability by defining the conditional probability of a random variable Y, given a value x_0 for another random variable X

$$pr(Y|x_0) = \frac{pr(Y, x_0)}{pr(x_0)}$$

Our interpretation of the conditional probability was that we were redefining the probabilities of Y "restricted" to the space of pairs of points (Y,X) defined by setting $X = x_0$. Similarly, in terms of density functions, we extended the idea by defining the conditional density function by

$$f_{1|2}(X_1|X_2 = x_2^0) = \frac{f_j(X_1, X_2 = x_2^0)}{f_2(X_2 = x_2^0)}$$

where $f_{1|2}(X_1|X_2 = x_2^0)$ is the conditional density function, $f_j(X_1, X_2 = x_2^0)$ is the joint density function evaluated at $X_2 = x_2^0$, and $f_2(X_2 = x_2^0)$ is the marginal density function, also evaluated at $X_2 = x_2^0$. The interpretation is similar to that for the probability distributions; we are defining a new density function for X_1 that is restricted by the values set for X_2. From this definition it is easy to rearrange terms to obtain the relationship between the joint distribution and the conditional and marginal distributions shown in Equation 12.1. One way of thinking about conditional densities is that the conditional density of X given Y is "indexed" by the values of Y, and as the "index Y" is changed so is the conditional density and, so therefore, the rate of change between changes in X and in the probability of X.

Let us agree that when we write $f_{1|2}(X_1|X_2)$ we are considering the conditional distribution of X_1 conditional on X_2 for any possible value of X_2. Similarly, when we write $f_2(X_2)$ in the definition of a conditional distribution we are defining the conditional distribution for any value of X_2. Hereafter, we will be able to drop the repeated references to the actual value taken by the conditioning event in particular circumstances.

Consider X_1 and X_2, two continuous random variables. Let $f_j(X_1, X_2)$ represent the joint density function of X_1 and X_2, let $f_{1|2}(X_1|X_2)$ denote the conditional density of X_1 given values of X_2, and finally let $f_2(X_2)$ denote the marginal density function of X_2. Reexamine Equations 6.5 and 6.6. The relationship between the types of density is

$$f_j(X_1, X_2) = f_{1|2}(X_1|X_2)f_2(X_2) \tag{12.1}$$

Let us recall what this equation implies. First, we note that the joint density is the product of a conditional and a marginal density; this result follows immediately from the definition of the conditional density function. We will use this concept repeatedly in the discussion to follow to illustrate the empirical generation of joint distributions. But recognize that we can observe realizations on each component in turn. We may observe the joint densities, the conditional, or the marginal, or any two, or all of them. The procedures that we follow to make inferences about the parameters of these distributions depend on what precisely it is that we observe. We will elaborate on this matter later in the chapter. Also, recall that Equation 12.1 can be rewritten as

$$f_j(X_1, X_2) = f_{2|1}(X_2|X_1)f_1(X_1) \tag{12.2}$$

This is the general expression. However, recall from Chapter 6, Equations 6.12 and 6.13, that if the random variables are independent, then the marginal and conditional probability functions and the marginal and conditional density functions are the same for all values of the conditioning variable. Consequently, when the variables are independent, the joint density is given by

$$f_j(X_1, X_2) = f_2(X_2)f_1(X_1) \tag{12.3}$$

a simple product of the marginal density functions.

The corresponding joint *probability* distribution is obtained from the density function by integration—that is, by adding up the volume under the curve defined by $f_j(X_1, X_2)$. In Chapter 8, we demonstrated that if $f(X)$ is the univariate density function, then the corresponding probability distribution is given by

$$\text{pr}(X \le x_0) = \int_{-\infty}^{x_0} f(X)dX$$

which can be interpreted geometrically as an area. The same principle applies with the conditional distribution and the corresponding conditional density function. If $f(X|Y = y_0)$ is the conditional density function, the corresponding conditional probability distribution function is given by the area under the conditional density:

$$\text{pr}(X \le x_0|Y = y_0) = \int_{-\infty}^{x_0} f(X|Y = y_0)dX$$

We note that unlike the marginal distribution, the probability that X is less than any value, x_0, will vary depending on the value taken by y_0.

The situation with the bivariate distribution is very similar except that we must now deal with *volumes* under the curve defined by the joint density function $f(X,Y)$. The corresponding probability is given by

$$\text{pr}(X \le x_0, Y \le y_0) = \int_{-\infty}^{y_0} \int_{-\infty}^{x_0} f(X, Y)dXdY \tag{12.4}$$

As you will observe by examining the graphs later, all Equation 12.4 says is that the required probability is obtained from the joint density function by "adding up" the volume under the surface given by the density function $f(X,Y)$ from "$-\infty$" to the prescribed limits on each of X and Y.

Also, recall from Chapter 6 that we obtained the marginal distributions from the joint distributions by adding up the probabilities across the other variable:

$$\text{pr}(Y) = \sum_X \text{pr}(Y, X)$$

or

$$\text{pr}(X) = \sum_Y \text{pr}(Y, X)$$

and that a similar result holds for density functions. In this case, we have to integrate, a form of "adding up," when the variable changes continuously. If $h(Y,X)$ is the joint density function and $f(Y)$ is the marginal for Y and $g(X)$ is the marginal for X, we have

$$f(Y) = \int_X h(Y, X)dX \tag{12.5}$$

or

$$g(X) = \int_Y h(Y, X)dY$$

which expresses symbolically the idea of adding up the joint density with respect to one variable to obtain the marginal density of the other. If we examine Equations 12.1 and 12.5, we obtain another interpretation. Obtaining the marginal density from the joint is equivalent to obtaining the *expectation* of the conditional density with respect to the marginal density of the conditioning variable; that is, if the joint density function $h(Y, X) = h_X(Y|X)g(X) = h_Y(X|Y)f(Y)$, then

$$f(Y) = \int_X h_X(Y|X)g(X)dX$$

and

$$g(X) = \int_Y h_Y(X|Y)f(Y)dY$$

In each case, the marginal density is recognized as the *expected value of the conditional density,* the expectation with respect to the marginal distribution of the other variable.

12.3   Some Pragmatic Examples

Before we embark on a detailed development of joint and conditional distributions paralleling the arguments in Chapters 7 and 8, it would be helpful to consider some pragmatic examples that give rise either to joint or to conditional distributions.

Imagine first the outcome of measuring the size of a rectangular plate with coordinates labeled X and Y, where X and Y are continuous random variables. Along either coordinate, the measurement may be in error and we may be justified in believing that the errors along the X-axis are distributed independently of the errors along the Y-axis, and we might well reasonably assume that the densities involved are the same in both cases. So, if $g(X)$ is the density for the X measurements, the distribution for the joint

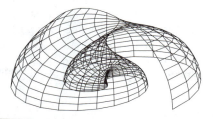

Figure 12.1   Illustration of the effect of curvature on the independence assumption of measurement errors

measurement errors is given by $f(X,Y) = g(X)g(Y)$, where $f(X,Y)$ is the joint density and $g(X)$, $g(Y)$ are the marginal densities for the measurement errors on each side (recall Equation 12.3). Given our observations in Chapter 3, it is likely that the probability density function $g(.)$ is the uniform density.

However, suppose now that we are measuring a curved plate, so that the degree of curvature of the plate varies over the plate (see the accompanying Figure 12.1). It may well be true that the errors of measurement along one axis are no longer independent of measurements along the other. This lack of independence may be due to the variations in curvature leading to variations in the density of measurement errors; a very curved section of the plate is liable to have bigger errors than a straight section of the plate. In this case the joint density is not given by the product of the marginal densities as in the previous case. For each measurement, the density of errors along any axis depends on the measurement along the other axis.

Many buy and sell decisions can be represented by two variables: one whether to buy or to sell and the other how much to pay or offer, given the decision to buy or sell. For example, suppose that we want to consider a buy decision. In this example, we have one discrete random variable, the binary decision to buy, and one continuous random variable, the amount to pay. The binary variable takes the values of 0 or 1 only—1 if the individual buys, 0 if she does not. The other variable can take on any positive value, at least theoretically! This is an example of a mixed distribution, one variable is discrete and one is continuous.

Another example might be given by considering the distribution of incomes and ages of a random selection of people. In this case, both variables are continuous, and it is likely that these variables are not independent. An example we will discuss later is provided by the joint densities of heights and weights for a specified group of people; this is another example of continuous nonindependent random variables.

Consider a different type of example: the number of traders who want to buy a specific stock in the stock market is itself a random variable having the Poisson distribution (Chapter 7). The distribution of the number of shares that each of the traders wants to buy is given by another distribution, the lognormal (Chapter 3). The distribution of the total number of shares to be bought in each period is a "compound random variable." Each period, the total number of shares is given by the sum of a random number of random variables. The difference from our previous examples in earlier chapters is that the probability distribution function for the random sum of random variables depends both on the distribution of the individual numbers of shares and on the distribution of the random number of traders who want to trade. The joint distribution, say $F_j(N_T, N_S)$, is given by the product of the marginal and conditional distributions; the marginal distribution for N_T, the number of traders; and the conditional distribution of N_S, the number of shares demanded. We reexpress this by

$$F_j(N_T, N_S) = G(N_S|N_T)H(N_T)$$

where $G(N_S|N_T)$ is the lognormal distribution whose *parameters* are functions of N_T and $H(N_T)$ is the Poisson distribution of the random variable N_T. $H(N_T)$ is given by

$$H(N_T) = \frac{e^{-\lambda}\lambda^{N_T}}{N_T!} \tag{12.6}$$

and $G(N_S|N_T)$ is given by

$$G(N_S|N_T) = \frac{\exp\{-\frac{1}{2}\{\log N_S - \mu_{N_T}\}^2\}/\sigma^2}{(N_S - \mu_{N_T})\sigma\sqrt{2\pi}} \tag{12.7}$$

where μ_{N_T} is a function of N_T, the number of traders. This equation looks quite formidable, but understanding it is easier when you recognize that the lognormal distribution is the normal distribution of the logarithm of a variable; that is, the logarithm of the variable N_S is distributed as normal.

Another experiment that generates an interesting joint distribution is provided by the following circumstance. Suppose that we are considering a rocket with many components, but to keep the discussion manageable, let us restrict attention to just two components. Designate by X and Y the life times of the two components that interact with each other in a particular way. For each component by itself we can describe the probability of failure at life span X, which is the same as the probability of survival up to the time X and failure at that moment. The probability of failure at time X is given by $\mathrm{pr}_X = \int_0^X \alpha e^{-\alpha u}\,du$. Similarly, for the component Y, the probability of survival to a life span of Y is given by $\mathrm{pr}_Y = \int_0^Y \beta e^{-\beta u}\,du$. Now, consider the effect of allowing the parameters α and β to depend on the survival of the other component. If X fails, the new parameter for probability of survival of Y is β^*; and if Y fails the parameter for the probability of survival of X is α^*. Clearly, we are assuming that the failure of either component is not critical to the survival of the entire rocket. I will not write down the joint distribution, called the "bivariate exponential" that Freund derived in 1961 to solve this problem; but you should note the process involved in creating this distribution. Freund derived the distribution by considering in detail the nature of the hypothetical experiment that provides an abstraction for the main circumstances involved in the interaction of components in complex systems.

These examples are meant to give you some notion of the various ways in which joint and conditional distributions are created by the operation of actual experiments. Further, these examples indicate that a careful exposition of the circumstances describing the characteristics of a hypothetical experiment will enable a statistician to derive the corresponding joint or conditional probability distribution. The principal ideas presented in this chapter are the same as those underlying the discussion in Chapters 6, 7, and 8. After discussing two particular examples in some detail, I will introduce yet another way in which joint and conditional distributions are observed. In the process, we will discover some important lessons concerning the need for careful control over our sampling procedures.

12.4 The Generation of a Bivariate Discrete Distribution

Recall that when we discussed the basics of probability theory in Chapter 6, we examined a simple joint probability distribution of two random variables $X1$ and $X2$; $X1$ took the values $-1, 0, 1$, and $X2$ took the values $0, 1$. The body of Table 6.6 gave the joint probability distribution. From it, we calculated the marginal probability distributions and conditional probability distributions. That joint probability distribution was merely a figment of our imagination; we made it up purely for the purpose of explaining the basic ideas involved in probability. Our task this time is to see how such probability distributions do arise.

Imagine that you are the manager of a real estate firm that handles two types of clients, buyers and renters, and that you have to allocate your staff between these two types of business. You do not want to waste staff by having them sit idle, but you do not want to lose business to your competitors. During your peak period the number of clients that arrive at your firm is most likely the Poisson distribution (Chapter 7).

But each client is either a buyer or a renter; we may agree that the relevant distribution for buyers and renters is the binomial probability distribution; that is, there is a constant probability as to whether each arrival at the firm is a buyer or a renter and that the arrival of buyers and renters is independent. Whatever is the status of the last arrival, we cannot infer from that information the status of the next arrival. From these two distributions we can derive the joint distribution for buyers and renters as follows.

In this example, we have a Poisson distributed sum of binomial probabilities. The distribution of the number of arrivals can be written:

$$\frac{e^{-\lambda}\lambda^N}{N!} \tag{12.8}$$

where λ is the mean number of arrivals in any hour during the peak period and N is the random variable for the number of arrivals, $N = 0, 1, 2, \ldots$.

Recall that the binomial distribution is

$$\binom{N}{B}\pi^B(1-\pi)^{N-B} \tag{12.9}$$

where N is the number of arrivals in a peak hour and B is the number of buyers; R, the number of renters is given by $N - B$. The definition of the binomial probability distribution depends on the outcome of the Poisson distribution in that the N is the N generated by the Poisson distribution. The Poisson distribution is the marginal distribution in this case, and the binomial distribution is the conditional distribution. The binomial depends on the outcome of the Poisson through the observed value of N, the total number of clients entering your firm.

To get the distribution of B, the number of buyers, and of R, the number of renters, all we have to do is to realize for any value of N, the number of arrivals, that

$R + B = N$. By replacing N with $R + B$ we can reexpress the conditioning Poisson distribution in terms of R and B and the conditional binomial probability distribution in terms of R and B alone. As we know, the joint distribution is the product of the conditional and the marginal distributions. Performing the required substitutions and multiplying the conditional and the marginal distributions, we get

$$\left[\frac{e^{-\lambda}\lambda^{R+B}}{(R+B)!} \right] \left[\binom{R+B}{B} \pi^{B}(1-\pi)^{R} \right] \tag{12.10}$$

$$= \frac{e^{-\lambda}\lambda^{R+B}}{B!R!} \pi^{B}(1-\pi)^{R} \tag{12.11}$$

which is the required joint probability distribution for the number of buyers, B, and renters, R, that will enter your firm during the peak period. The symbol λ represents the mean number of arrivals of both types, and π is the probability that a random arrival will be a buyer. The range of the variables is obtained by noting that the range for N, the variable in the Poisson distribution, was $0, 1, 2, \ldots$, and given N the range for B was $0, 1, 2, \ldots, N$ and that for R is $0, 1, 2, \ldots, N - B$. We redefined N as $R + B$, so that the range for $R + B$ is $0, 1, 2, \ldots$ and that for R, or B, is also $0, 1, 2, \ldots$.

This distribution is not like any other that you have seen so far, but nevertheless it is not only a valid probability distribution function, in that its entries are all positive and add to one, but it is a useful distribution for our purposes. Let us examine it for a moment to get the idea.

Suppose during the peak period that the mean number of arrivals per hour, λ, is 8 and that the probability of an arrival being a buyer, π, is .2. We could have estimated these parameter values, but let us not worry about estimation for now and accept the fact that we do have the values stated.

Our first question might be to decide how many staff we need to handle these arrivals. Suppose that it takes on average 15 minutes to deal with a renter and that it takes about 30 minutes to deal with a buyer. How many staff of each speciality do you need? A first easy answer is to recognize that per hour on average 1.6 (.2 times 8) arrivals are buyers who will take up 1.6 times 30 minutes, or 48 minutes. The per-hour average number of renters is 6.4 (.8 times 8) and the time needed is 6.4 times 15 minutes, or 96 minutes. This means that we need only 1 staff member dedicated to buyers, but that we will need to have two staff members to handle the renters. We could modify this result by figuring out what it would cost us in terms of lost revenues to have only one staff member to handle renters during the peak hours and then decide whether we want one or two. We could get even more sophisticated and allow for the variance of arrivals of buyers and renters. Nonetheless, we have illustrated the generation and use of a simple joint distribution using discrete random variables.

12.5 The Generation of a Bivariate Continuous Distribution

In Chapter 3, we discussed various examples that give rise to a univariate Gaussian distribution. For example, one might regard weight in mature individuals within a given age bracket as the result of many individual factors impinging on each individual so that the outcome is that weight is normally distributed about the mean weight for the given age. One might also, for similar reasons, anticipate that height is distributed as normal for a given age. If we now consider a random sample of people and measure their heights and their weights, we might expect that both variables are jointly distributed such that they are not independent, but that each marginal distribution is Gaussian. Such a distribution is known as the bivariate normal (Gaussian) distribution.

As another example, consider the data in the file Food.xls and the two pairs of variables {food consumption per capita and food prices}, {food production per capita and prices received by farmers}. It is reasonable to consider that there are random fluctuations in each variable due to a myriad of small forces acting on each component and that food consumption and food prices are associated in some way. Similarly, it is reasonable to assume that food production and prices received by farmers are associated in some way. We might guess that food consumption per capita and food prices are jointly normally distributed and that food production per capita and prices received by farmers are also jointly normally distributed. We now need to discover what the joint normal distribution looks like in each of these two cases and how the joint density function can be expressed as a function of two variables.

First recall that if two Gaussian variables are distributed *independently* of each other so that the joint density is simply the product of the marginals, the joint density that we obtain is

$$
\phi(X, Y) = \phi(X)\phi(Y) = \frac{\exp\left\{-\frac{1}{2}\left(\frac{X-\mu_x}{\sigma_x}\right)^2\right\}}{\sqrt{2\pi}\sigma_X} \frac{\exp\left\{-\frac{1}{2}\left(\frac{Y-\mu_y}{\sigma_y}\right)^2\right\}}{\sqrt{2\pi}\sigma_Y}
$$

$$
= \frac{\exp\left\{-\frac{1}{2}\left[\left(\frac{X-\mu_x}{\sigma_x}\right)^2 + \left(\frac{Y-\mu_y}{\sigma_y}\right)^2\right]\right\}}{2\pi\sigma_X\sigma_Y}
$$

(12.12)

The joint density shown in Equation 12.12 is merely the product of two independent normal densities with parameters $\{\mu_X, \sigma_X^2\}$, $\{\mu_Y, \sigma_Y^2\}$, respectively (refer to Equation 8.45).

Now let us consider the modification that we might observe if the joint normal density were not merely the product of the marginals; that is, there is some *association* between the variables. The argument that follows is not a proof but follows our intuition and what we have learned so far.

Recognize that whatever modification we make to Equation 12.12, the result should be reducible to the independent case when the parameter that characterizes the nonindependence is zero. Two thoughts come to mind in examining Equation 12.12 and recalling our work in Chapter 5 when we calculated the correlation coefficient: (1) the correlation coefficient was calculated as the average *product* of the variables and (2) the exponent in Equation 12.12 is a quadratic but *without the cross-product term*. Recall that the cross-product term was chosen to represent the interaction between two variables (discussed in Section 5.6). So one way to consider trying to obtain the joint nonindependent version of the bivariate normal is to add the cross-product term to the exponent with some coefficient to be determined. The cross-product term in the exponent of the Gaussian density will reflect the impact of the joint variation of X and of Y, and the magnitude of the coefficient will determine the strength of the effect.

If X and Y are of the same sign and both are large, one expects a big effect on the size of the exponent, and if the associated coefficient is positive that effect will increase the density. Correspondingly, if X and Y are of opposite signs and the coefficient is positive, the effect will reduce the magnitude of the density.

Let us consider what this implies, but first let us also simplify the problem by setting both means to zero and both variances to 1. In the exponent, the only important part at the moment, we have a quadratic with a cross-product term. Under these simplifying conditions we contemplate

$$\phi(X, Y) = \frac{\exp\left\{-\frac{1}{2}[X^2 + Y^2 + ?XY]\right\}}{2\pi?} \tag{12.13}$$

where the "?" indicates that we do not yet know what parameter should be entered. If X and Y are positively associated, then we would expect that the density would be relatively large for both X and Y of the same sign and absolutely large. Correspondingly, if X and Y are of opposite signs, we would expect the density to be small. In Equation 12.13, if we replace "?" by a positive parameter ρ, and if X and Y are positively associated, the sign in front of ρ should be negative because the sign of the exponent outside the square brackets [ ] is itself negative. If X and Y are of the same sign and large and we want to reflect positive association when our indicator, ρ, positive, we can do so by adding the term $-\rho XY$ to the squared terms. The term in square brackets will be less, so the whole exponent will be *greater* as will the density. In contrast, if X and Y have differing signs and we are still trying to represent a positive association, then adding the term $-\rho XY$ to the squared terms, the term in square brackets will be *larger*, so the exponent will be smaller and thus the *density will be less* as desired.

If we have a negative association between the variables X and Y we would expect the opposite results, and it should be easy for you to verify that all we need to do to achieve the correct pattern of densities is to make ρ negative.

We anticipate the notation in the next chapter and rewrite the exponent as

$$\exp\left\{-\frac{1}{2(1-\rho^2)}[X^2 + Y^2 - 2\rho XY]\right\}$$

where ρ summarizes the linear association between the random variables X and Y. At this moment, the extra term $1/(1 - \rho^2)$ is mysterious. As it turns out, this term is needed to make sure that the variance term for the correlated variables is correctly stated. Right now, we need not concern ourselves, except to verify, as we will, that we have managed to obtain a valid density function—that is, one that integrates to one. If our intuitive reasoning is correct, then we have obtained the bivariate standardized normal density—that density with both means set to 0 and the variances equal to 1.

As we will discover in the next chapter, the parameter ρ that we have chosen to represent the introduction of the cross-product terms in the density function is in fact the theoretical correlation coefficient. That is, ρ is the correlation coefficient that measures the degree of linear association between the two random variables; ρ is the theoretical analog to the sample correlation coefficient labeled r (Chapter 5). Many of the properties that we derived for the sample correlation coefficient also hold for the theoretical analog ρ. We will postpone our discussion of this until the next chapter.

The equation for the standardized bivariate normal with nonzero correlation coefficient is in fact

$$\phi(X, Y) = \frac{\exp\left\{-\frac{1}{2(1-\rho^2)}[X^2 + Y^2 - 2\rho XY]\right\}}{2\pi\sqrt{1-\rho^2}} \tag{12.14}$$

If ρ in Equation 12.14 is zero, then we have, as we wanted, the same joint density we obtained for the independent variable case; compare Equation 12.12. The most complete formulation is given by allowing the variances to take values other than one and the means to be nonzero. We have

$$\phi(X, Y) = \frac{\exp\left\{-\frac{1}{2(1-\rho^2)}\left[\left(\frac{X-\mu_x}{\sigma_X}\right)^2 + \left(\frac{Y-\mu_Y}{\sigma_Y}\right)^2 - 2\rho\left(\frac{X-\mu_x}{\sigma_X}\right)\left(\frac{Y-\mu_Y}{\sigma_Y}\right)\right]\right\}}{2\pi\sigma_X\sigma_Y\sqrt{1-\rho^2}} \tag{12.15}$$

This formula at first sight appears to be quite formidable, but if you keep in mind the steps that we took to derive the equation, albeit very informally, you will have less trouble. Equation 12.15 is the bivariate Gaussian, or normal, density function. It is described by five parameters: μ_X, μ_Y, σ_X, σ_Y, and ρ. These parameters are the means and standard deviations of the respective random variables included in the bivariate density, and ρ is the measure of covariation between the two variables.

The joint bivariate *probability function* is given by integrating, calculating the volume under the surface $\phi(X, Y)$, with respect to both arguments, X and Y. Formally, we write

$$\text{pr}(X \leq x_0, \ Y \leq y_0) = \tag{12.16}$$

$$\int_{-\infty}^{y_0}\int_{-\infty}^{x_0} \frac{\exp\left\{-\frac{1}{2(1-\rho^2)}\left[\left(\frac{X-\mu_x}{\sigma_X}\right)^2 + \left(\frac{Y-\mu_Y}{\sigma_Y}\right)^2 - 2\rho\left(\frac{X-\mu_x}{\sigma_X}\right)\left(\frac{Y-\mu_Y}{\sigma_Y}\right)\right]\right\}}{2\pi\sigma_X\sigma_Y\sqrt{1-\rho^2}} dXdY$$

By examining the diagrams to follow, you will gain further insight into the nature of this very important distribution. Let us examine first the three-dimensional plot of the standardized bivariate normal density for independently distributed random variables; this is the formula expressed in Equation 12.12, but we set the means to 0, the two variances to 1, and by choice $\rho = 0$ (Figure 12.2).

Notice that the density is largest in the middle; that is, the largest rate of change in probability with respect to changes in either variable occurs under the largest values for the density. All around the edges of the graph of the bivariate density the probability volume under the graph is small, but it increases rapidly as the values of X and Y move toward the middle, the area of large variation in the density. If we take a large sample of pairs of values from this joint distribution, we would expect to see a distribution of points that looks something like Figure 5.1 from Chapter 5.

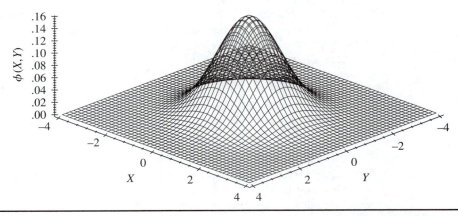

Figure 12.2   Plot of the standard bivariate normal density function with zero correlation coefficient

A useful way of looking at these bivariate functions is to examine the contour plots. Each contour plot is a plot of all values of X and Y that produce the *same value* for the density function. Contour plots, as their name implies, are like the contour plots of hills on a map where each contour is a line connecting points of equal height. So in this case, the contour plots of the density functions are lines connecting points of X and Y that produce equal values for the density. In all the graphs to follow, it is important that you relate the shape of the contour plots to the shape of the density function. The small ellipses in the middle correspond to the areas of highest density, and the ellipses on the extremes represent areas of low density. If the density function is more complicated—for example, if it looks like several hills—then one would have to label each contour with its corresponding density value to get a clear picture of the density. However, in all the simple cases that we will examine we need not add the density values to each contour line.

We can relate our contour plots to the scatter diagrams that we examined at length in Chapter 5. The scatter diagrams are visual representations of sampled values from the joint density function. Given our discussion in this section, we expect to see thinly distributed points in the scatter plots in those areas where the density function has low values and thickly (densely) distributed points where the density function is large; re-examine Figures 5.2 to 5.7 from Chapter 5.

In contour plots, the orientation of the graphs is particularly clear. The "orientation" is the angle made by the slope of the major axis of the contour plot. Further, if you look back to the scatter diagrams of Chapter 5, you will recognize that each contour level relates to the relative frequency of observations drawn from such a density; the highest contour levels correspond to the greatest density of points. The orientation of the graphs corresponds to the orientation of points obtained from a drawing from the density. Consider the contour plots in Figure 12.3 that correspond to the graph of the bivariate density in Figure 12.2.

To see the effect of altering the means to nonzero values and changing the variances to nonunitary values, consider the next two plots of the bivariate normal density

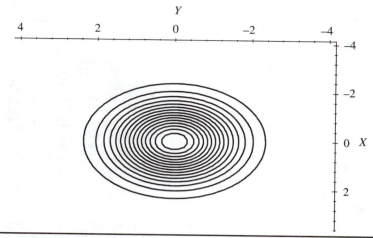

Figure 12.3　Contour plot of the standard bivariate normal density function with zero correlation coefficient (maximum density in the center of the ellipses)

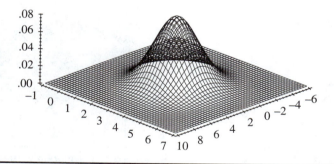

Figure 12.4　Plot of bivariate normal density function with nonzero means and nonunitary variance for X (correlation coefficient $= 0$)

function for independent variables. Using Equation 12.12, consider setting the values of μ_X, μ_Y to 2 and 3, respectively, and σ_X^2, σ_Y^2 to 4 and 1, respectively. Figure 12.4 plots the density function, and Figure 12.5 plots the corresponding contours. In particular, compare the scales on the axes of the two contour plots to see the effect of the change in assumptions.

Notice that in both of the previous situations the orientation of the contour plots is the same because ρ is zero in both cases. The only differences are where the contour ellipses are centered and the scaling of the axes. The ellipses are in fact centered at the means, $(0, 0)$ in the former case, and at $(2, 3)$ in the latter case. The magnitudes of the variances determine the scales on the two axes; compare the scales for the two sets of density plots.

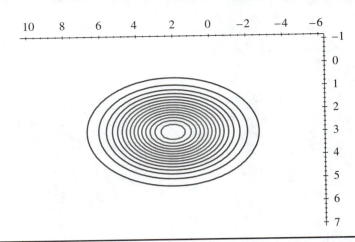

Figure 12.5   Contour plot of bivariate normal density function with nonzero means and nonunitary variance (correlation coefficient = 0)

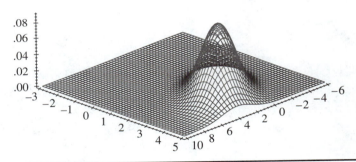

Figure 12.6   Joint density of the bivariate normal distribution with nonzero means and nonunitary variances (correlation coefficient = .5)

The next pair of graphs will illustrate what happens when there is a nonzero value for ρ; in this case ρ equals .5. A ρ of .5 means that the two variables are positively associated, and that concept is clearly illustrated in the contour plot (see Figures 12.6 and 12.7).

We now consider the effect of a negative value for ρ. Examine the next two graphs, which have the same means and variances for X and Y, but the value of ρ has been changed from .5 to −.5. Now we expect a negative orientation to the contour plots, and that is what we observe (see Figures 12.8 and 12.9).

Lastly, let us consider the effect of a large value of ρ on the density and the contour plots (see Figures 12.10 and 12.11).

We have examined the bivariate normal density function in some detail. Probabilities are obtained by integrating over each variable as we showed in Equation 12.17;

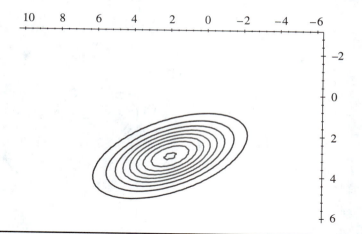

Figure 12.7   Contour plot of bivariate normal density with correlation coefficient = .5

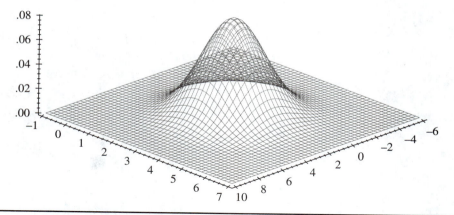

Figure 12.8   Plot of bivariate normal density function (correlation coefficient = −.5)

the probability can be represented by the volume under the surface of the density plot. As a practical example, consider the probability for the standardized normal when x_0 and y_0 are both 0.25. We have

$$\text{pr}(X \le 0.25,\ Y \le 0.25) = \int_{-\infty}^{0.25} \int_{-\infty}^{0.25} \frac{\exp\left(-\frac{1}{2}(X^2 + Y^2)\right)}{2\pi} dX\,dY$$

$$= .358$$

If you look back to the density and contour plot for the standardized normal density (see Figures 12.2 and 12.3), the volume covered by the integral is that region lying in the upper left corner of the contour plot bounded by the values of $X = 0.25$,

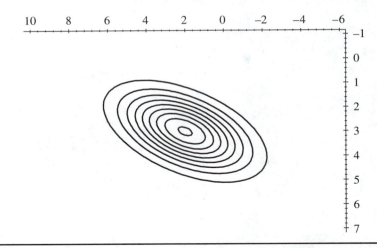

Figure 12.9   Contour plot of bivariate normal density (correlation coefficient $= -.5$)

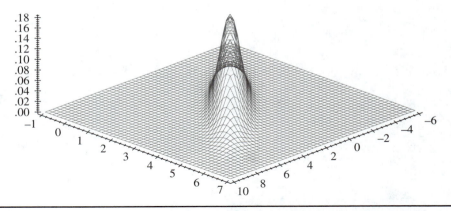

Figure 12.10   Density plot of a bivariate normal density function (correlation coefficient $= .9$)

$Y = 0.25$, $X = -\infty$, and $Y = -\infty$. And if you look at the density itself, you can see here as well that it is the volume under the graph bounded by lines $X = 0.25$, $Y = 0.25$, $X = -\infty$, and $Y = -\infty$.

As an alternative, consider the probability over the same interval but for the density with nonzero means and nonunitary variances (see Figures 12.4 and 12.5). The calculation is

$$\text{pr}(X \leq 0.25, \ Y \leq 0.25) = \int_{-\infty}^{0.25} \int_{-\infty}^{0.25} \frac{\exp(-\frac{1}{2}((\frac{X-2}{2})^2 + (\frac{Y-3}{1})^2))}{4\pi} dX \, dY$$

$$= 5.6448 \times 10^{-4}$$

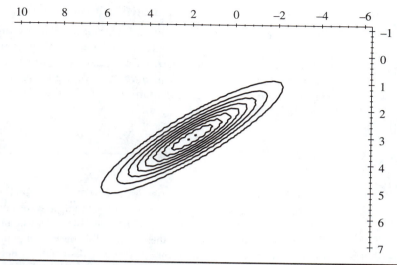

Figure 12.11   Contour plot of bivariate normal density (correlation coefficient = .9)

The considerable difference is because with the change in means and in values of σ_X and σ_Y the volume under the density that the integral covers is much less (see Figure 12.5).

Now let us consider a more interesting calculation. First, recognize that for the distribution that we just examined the probability of getting X *and* Y values less than or equal to their respective means is .25. You can see this intuitively; if you are integrating under the density between $(-\infty, \mu_X)$ and $(-\infty, \mu_Y)$ for each variable and given the symmetry of the bivariate normal density for *independent variables,* one would have covered only one-quarter of the whole distribution. But, if one had calculated the probability for the variable X to lie in the interval $(-\infty, \mu_X')$ for *any* value of Y, the result would be .5 as in the case of a single random variable. Consider now the situation in which X and Y are correlated, and the correlation coefficient, $\rho = .9$. We calculate the probability that both variables are less than their means:

$$\mathrm{pr}(X \leq 2, \ Y \leq 3) =$$

$$\int_{-\infty}^{2} \int_{-\infty}^{3} \frac{\exp(-\frac{1}{2(1-.81)}((\frac{X-2}{2})^2 - 1.8(\frac{X-2}{2})(\frac{Y-3}{1}) + (\frac{Y-3}{1})^2))}{4\pi\sqrt{1-.81}} dY \, dX$$

$$= .428$$

And we might speculate that, as the correlation becomes increasingly greater the integral of the density up to the means will approach .5, the same value that one obtains for the univariate case. But what of the result when the two variables have a negative correlation coefficient? The answer as you might suspect is a much smaller number than .25; when $\rho = -.9$ the calculated probability is 7.1783×10^{-2}.

The Conditional Normal Density Function

So far in our development of the joint Gaussian density function, we have not examined the conditional density function and the relationship between the joint, conditional, and marginal distributions. Let us do so now, but to keep the notation as simple as possible let us agree that both means are zero and that both variances are unity. Thus, the joint normal distribution for two random variables X and Y is

$$\phi(X, Y) = \frac{\exp\left\{-\frac{1}{2(1-\rho^2)}\right\}[X^2 + Y^2 - 2\rho XY]}{2\pi\sqrt{1-\rho^2}} \tag{12.17}$$

The first step is to consider obtaining one of the marginal distributions from the joint distribution. Let us consider obtaining a marginal distribution from $\phi(X, Y)$, say $\phi(X)$. We do so by "integrating out" the variable Y. Physically, the interpretation of this process of integrating out the variable Y is the continuous counterpart to adding up probabilities to get a marginal probability distribution; here we are adding up densities to get the marginal density. To demonstrate this operation we rewrite the integral of Equation 12.17 as follows:

$$\int \phi(X, Y)dY = \int \frac{\exp\left\{-\frac{X^2}{2(1-\rho^2)}\right\}}{\sqrt{2\pi}} \frac{\exp\left\{-\frac{1}{2(1-\rho^2)}\right\}[Y^2 - 2\rho XY]dY}{\sqrt{2\pi}\sqrt{1-\rho^2}} \tag{12.18}$$

where we have extracted the X^2 term from the integral with respect to Y. We have also allocated the term 2π between the two products in the expression. Now if in the remaining part of the quadratic expression $[Y^2 - 2\rho XY]$, we "complete the square" by adding in $(\rho X)^2$ and subtracting the same quantity outside the integral, we will have added nothing overall and the bracketed term would now be

$$[Y^2 - 2\rho XY + \rho^2 X^2] = [Y - \rho X]^2$$

Consequently, the expression in Equation 12.18 has been rewritten as

$$\int \phi(X, Y)dY = \int \frac{\exp\left\{-\frac{X^2-\rho^2 X^2}{2(1-\rho^2)}\right\}}{\sqrt{2\pi}} \frac{\exp\left\{-\frac{1}{2(1-\rho^2)}\right\}[Y - \rho X]^2 dY}{\sqrt{2\pi}\sqrt{1-\rho^2}}$$

and the integral is now one involving a normal variable with a mean of ρX and a variance of $(1 - \rho^2)$. Thus, by the definition of a density function, the integral with respect to the variable Y is 1. What is left over, is

$$\frac{\exp\left\{-\frac{X^2-\rho^2 X^2}{2(1-\rho^2)}\right\}}{\sqrt{2\pi}}$$

After dividing out the common factor, $(1 - \rho^2)$, we obtain

$$\phi(X) = \frac{\exp\{-\frac{1}{2}X^2\}}{\sqrt{2\pi}}$$

and this expression is nothing more than a univariate standard Gaussian density.

Our last demonstration using the normal density function is to derive the conditional normal density from the joint density. As we know, the conditional density can be formally expressed as the ratio of the joint density and the marginal density. We derive

$$
\begin{aligned}
\phi(Y|X) &= \frac{\phi(X, Y)}{\phi(X)} \\[2ex]
&= \frac{\dfrac{\exp\left\{-\frac{1}{2(1-\rho^2)}\right\}[X^2+Y^2-2\rho XY]}{2\pi\sqrt{1-\rho^2}}}{\dfrac{\exp\{-\frac{1}{2}X^2\}}{\sqrt{2\pi}}} \\[3ex]
&= \frac{\exp\left\{-\frac{1}{2(1-\rho^2)}\right\}[Y^2 + \rho^2 X^2 - 2\rho XY]}{\sqrt{2\pi}\sqrt{1-\rho^2}} \\[3ex]
&= \frac{\exp\left\{-\frac{1}{2(1-\rho^2)}\right\}[Y - \rho X]^2}{\sqrt{2\pi}\sqrt{1-\rho^2}}
\end{aligned}
\tag{12.19}
$$

What this last equation tells us is that the conditional distribution of a standard normal variable Y on a variable X can be expressed as a normal distribution itself with a mean of ρX and a variance of $(1 - \rho^2)$. The most important part of this derivation is that the conditional mean of Y given X is ρX. We see immediately that the conditional mean of Y is a linear function of X and the slope coefficient is ρ.

The general case is not much more complicated. We could allow for the individual means to be nonzero and the variances to be other than unity in value. If μ_Y is the unconditional mean of the variable Y, μ_X is the unconditional mean of X, and σ_Y^2, σ_X^2 are the respective variances, then the conditional mean of Y given $X = x_0$ is

$$E\{Y|X = x_0\} = \mu_Y + \rho\frac{\sigma_Y}{\sigma_X}(x_0 - \mu_X) \tag{12.20}$$

This last equation is very important as it indicates clearly that the conditional mean obtained from a bivariate normal distribution is linear in the conditioning variable, that the constant term in the expression is the unconditional mean, and that the slope parameter is $\rho\frac{\sigma_Y}{\sigma_X}$.

By a similar line of argument, one can easily show that the conditional variance of the variable Y, given $X = x_0$ is

$$\sigma_{Y|x_0}^2 = (1 - \rho^2)\sigma_Y^2 \tag{12.21}$$

and that the conditional variance for X given $Y = y_0$ is

$$\sigma_{X|y_0}^2 = (1 - \rho^2)\sigma_X^2$$

Moments of Joint and Conditional Density Functions

Now that we have indicated how bivariate distributions can be generated and have demonstrated the relationship between joint and conditional density functions, we can derive the moments of these distributions. This analysis generalizes that in Chapters 7 and 8 for the univariate distributions and density functions. Recall that theoretical moments are nothing more than the expected values of powers of the random variables, or powers of the deviations of the variables from their respective means, either sample, or theoretical. We will examine the moments only up to the second power in this chapter, but as with the univariate case, we could go to as high a power as we might wish.

We can deal with the conditional probability distributions and conditional density functions quite quickly because they are in fact univariate distributions and density functions that happen to depend on the values taken by the conditioning variable. The main point to remember is that the rth moment of a variable Y conditional on a variable X is merely the rth moment of Y using the *conditional distribution* or *conditional density* of the variable Y, conditioned on the variable X.

To begin, let us consider the simpler example of a discrete joint distribution. Let $F(X, Y)$ denote any of the discrete bivariate distributions we discussed, or indeed, any discrete bivariate distribution. We defined the expectations of X and of Y—that is, the first moments about the origin—as

$$
\begin{aligned}
E\{X\} &= \sum_{X,Y} X F(X, Y) \\
&= \sum_{X} X F_X(X) = \mu'_X
\end{aligned}
\tag{12.22}
$$

$$
\begin{aligned}
E\{Y\} &= \sum_{X,Y} Y F(X, Y) \\
&= \sum_{Y} Y F_Y(Y) = \mu'_Y
\end{aligned}
\tag{12.23}
$$

In these two equations, μ'_X and μ'_Y are the first moments about the origin for X and for Y; $F_X(X)$ and $F_Y(Y)$ denote the marginal distributions of X and of Y, respectively; and the notation $\sum_{X,Y}$ denotes summation over all values of both X and Y. Consequently, one obtains the first moments about the origin by obtaining the appropriate marginal distribution—that of X in the first case and that of Y in the second. The variances, the second moments about the mean, are obtained in a similar manner as follows:

$$
\begin{aligned}
E\{(X - \mu'_X)^2\} &= \sum_{X,Y} (X - \mu'_X)^2 F(X, Y) \\
&= \sum_{X} (X - \mu'_X)^2 F_X(X) = \sigma_X^2
\end{aligned}
\tag{12.24}
$$

$$E\{(Y - \mu'_Y)^2\} = \sum_{X,Y}(Y - \mu'_Y)^2 F(X, Y)$$

$$= \sum_{Y}(Y - \mu'_Y)^2 F_Y(Y) = \sigma^2_Y \qquad (12.25)$$

Essentially, each of these moments is the corresponding moment of the relevant *marginal distribution*.

So far we have not really addressed the association, if any, between the two variables. We now do so. Consider the first cross-product moment, σ_{XY}, defined by

$$E\{(X - \mu'_X)(Y - \mu'_Y)\} = \sum_{X,Y}(X - \mu'_X)(Y - \mu'_Y)F(X, Y) \qquad (12.26)$$

$$= E\{XY\} - 2\mu'_X\mu'_Y + \mu'_X\mu'_Y \qquad (12.27)$$

$$= E\{XY\} - \mu'_X\mu'_Y \qquad (12.28)$$

The first cross-product moment is also known as the *covariance*.

Now we have to take into account the nature of the relationship between the variables as defined by the properties of the joint distribution, $F(X, Y)$. For example, if X and Y are independent so that the joint distribution is merely the product of the marginal distributions, then Equation 12.26 yields $E\{(X - \mu'_X)(Y - \mu'_Y)\} = 0$.

This result follows because with X and Y independent, we can calculate the expectation of $(X - \mu'_X)$ independently of $(Y - \mu'_Y)$, or vice versa, and each of those calculations yields zero; that is, by definition,

$$E\{(X - \mu'_X)\} = 0$$

and

$$E\{(Y - \mu'_Y)\} = 0$$

As an example, consider the discrete distribution in Equation 12.10 when we set $\lambda = 8$ and $\pi = .2$; λ is the mean rate of arrival of either buyers or renters and π is the probability that an arrival will be a buyer. In this case, $E\{R\} = 6.4$ and $E\{B\} = 1.6$; that is, the expected number of renters per hour is 6.4 and the expected number of buyers is 1.6. But is the arrival of buyers and renters uncorrelated? Evaluating Equation 12.26 yields a value of zero, $E\{XY\} = 10.24$ and $\mu'_X\mu'_Y = 10.24$, so we can conclude that the arrivals of buyers and renters are uncorrelated.

But if X and Y are not independent of each other, the situation is more complex. We can gain a glimpse of what is happening by rewriting Equation 12.26 in the following manner:

$$\sigma_{XY} = E\{(X - \mu'_X)(Y - \mu'_Y)\} \qquad (12.29)$$

$$= \sum_{X}(X - \mu'_X)\left[\sum_{Y}(Y - \mu'_Y)F(Y|X)\right]F_X(X) = \sum_{X}(X - \mu'_X)G(X)F_X(X)$$

where

$$G(X) = \left[\sum_Y (Y - \mu_Y') F(Y|X) \right]$$

The actual result depends on the specific formulation of the conditional distribution, equivalently on the form of the function $G(X)$.

To illustrate, let us consider a very simple example. Suppose that the operation of an electronic device depends on the state of each of two components that are either working or not. The state of one component, X, has a probability of .5 of working, $\text{pr}(X = 1) = .5$, and a probability of .5 of not working, $\text{pr}(X = 0) = .5$. The state of the other component, Y, depends on the state of X. If $X = 1$, the probability that $Y = 1$—that Y is also working is .8—and if $X = 0$ the probability that Y is working, that $Y = 1$, is .6. The joint discrete distribution is

$$F(X, Y) = \pi(X)^Y (1 - \pi(X))^{1-Y} \left(\frac{1}{2} \right)^X \left(\frac{1}{2} \right)^{1-X}$$

where

$$\pi(X) = \begin{cases} \pi_1 = .8 & \text{for } X = 1 \\ \pi_2 = .6 & \text{for } X = 0 \end{cases}$$

and

$$X = \{0, 1\}, \ Y = \{0, 1\}$$

By substituting the alternative values for X and for Y in this expression, it is easy to verify by hand that $E\{X\} = .5$, $E\{Y\} = \frac{1}{2}(\pi_1 + \pi_2)$ and that $E\{XY\} = \pi_1$; note that the only nonzero value for XY is when both X and Y are 1. Using our relationship in Equation 12.26, we see that $\sigma_{XY} = \pi_1 - (\frac{1}{2})(\frac{1}{2}(\pi_1 + \pi_2)) = \frac{3}{4}\pi_1 - \frac{1}{4}\pi_2$. Clearly, X and Y are correlated.

For continuous random variables, we have very similar results, except that "integration of density functions" replaces "summation of probabilities." Formally, for a bivariate density function $f(X,Y)$ with marginal densities $g(X)$ and $h(Y)$, we define

$$E\{X\} = \int_X \int_Y X f(X, Y) dY dX \tag{12.30}$$

$$= \int_X X g(X) dX$$

$$E\{Y\} = \int_Y \int_X Y f(X, Y) dX dY$$

$$= \int_Y Y h(Y) dY$$

Note that the formulation illustrated in Equations 12.30 and 12.31 parallels that in Equation 12.22. As in the discrete case, it is still true that the expectation of means and variances involves integrating the joint density function to get the appropriate marginal density function.

We define the variances by

$$E\{(X - \mu'_X)^2\} = \int_X \int_Y (X - \mu'_X)^2 f(X, Y) dY dX \qquad (12.31)$$

$$= \int_X (X - \mu'_X)^2 g(X) dX$$

$$E\{(Y - \mu'_Y)^2\} = \int_Y \int_X (Y - \mu'_Y)^2 f(X, Y) dX dY$$

$$= \int_Y (Y - \mu'_Y)^2 h(Y) dY$$

And last we define the first cross-product moment, or covariance, by

$$E\{(X - \mu'_X)(Y - \mu'_Y)\} = \int_X \int_Y (X - \mu'_X)(Y - \mu'_Y) f(X, Y) dY dX \qquad (12.32)$$

As with the discrete case, if the variables are independent so that the joint density function is the product of the marginals, we have

$$E\{(X - \mu'_X)(Y - \mu'_Y)\} = 0$$

because

$$E\{(X - \mu'_X)\} = 0$$

and

$$E\{(Y - \mu'_Y)\} = 0$$

Let us consider the covariance of the standard bivariate normal distribution as an example; that is, we assume that $\mu_X = \mu_Y = 0$ and $\sigma_X = \sigma_Y = 1$. We define

$$\sigma_{X,Y} = E\{XY\} \qquad (12.33)$$

$$= \int_X \int_Y XY \frac{\exp\{-\frac{1}{2(1-\rho^2)}\}[X^2 + Y^2 - 2\rho XY]}{2\pi\sqrt{1 - \rho^2}} dX dY$$

At first sight, this appears to be a formidable calculation. But, if we rearrange terms so that the joint density is rewritten as the product of the conditional and the marginal densities, the calculation can be quickly reduced to expressions that we recognize. Consider:

$$E\{XY\} = \int_X X \left\{ \int_Y Y \frac{\exp\{-\frac{1}{2(1-\rho^2)}\}[Y - \rho X]^2}{\sqrt{2\pi}\sqrt{1-\rho^2}} dY \right\} \frac{\exp\{-\frac{1}{2}X^2\}}{\sqrt{2\pi}} dX$$

$$= \int_X \rho X^2 \frac{\exp\{-\frac{1}{2}X^2\}}{\sqrt{2\pi}} dX$$

$$= \rho$$

(12.34)

The expression in { } in the first line of equation 12.34 is the expectation of Y with respect to the conditional density function of Y given X; the conditional density of Y has a mean of ρX. In the second line, ρX times X yields ρX^2, so the last integral is the expectation of ρX^2, which in turn is simply ρ. This result follows because the variance of X is by the statement of the problem, 1. We conclude that the covariance between two standard normal random variables is given by ρ. In the more general case in which the normal variables have variances, σ_X^2, σ_Y^2 the covariance between X and Y is given by $\rho\sigma_X\sigma_Y$.

12.6 Bivariate and Conditional Distributions Obtained by Sampling

Suppose that we are interested in the heights and weights of people because we want to explore the relationship between height and weight, perhaps after allowing for other effects such as the amount of smoking, or the extent of drug use, or the benefits of exercise. If we take a random sample of individuals and measure heights and weights, we obtain a sample from the bivariate density of heights and weights. If we presume that there is a specific theoretical probability distribution function that models the heights and weights of a given class of people at some point in time, then the random sampling of individuals in that class at that time will produce a sample from the specific bivariate density. We suspect that the two random variables, height and weight, are not independent. Although we expect to see that taller people are heavier on average, we still expect to see both short, fat people, and tall, skinny people.

Another example that we could have used is to sample individuals randomly, but instead of recording their heights and weights, we could record their incomes and their expenditures. This procedure would provide us with a sample from a joint distribution of incomes and consumption, and it is also most plausible that incomes and consumption are not independent of each other.

However, in both situations, we could have considered a different way of collecting the sample. Imagine that we take our sample not by randomly sampling individuals but by first taking a sample of people's weights, or people's incomes, and given each weight, or each income, we obtain a random sample of the heights, or a random sample of consumption. This seemingly minor change in the way in which we carry out the sampling makes a substantial difference in what it is that we have observed. First, we note that the sampling is in two stages. The first stage is to sample randomly the weights or the incomes of people. This is exactly the procedure that we have used before, so that we would expect to get the marginal distribution of weights, or incomes; the theoretical distribution for the former we have already agreed is the normal distribution. For the latter, we have a reasonable consensus that the best overall theoretical distribution is what is called the lognormal distribution. In any event, we have at the first stage a sample from a single univariate distribution.

The real difference comes at the second stage, where we sample heights, or consumption, *given values* for weights or incomes. The idea is that for each value of weight that we obtain in the first stage, we sample for the heights in the second stage only among individuals with that specific weight. The situation is similar for the sampling of consumption. The sample distributions that we obtain in this second stage are always from the *conditional distributions,* not the joint. In our current examples, we will get samples from the conditional distribution of heights given weights and from the conditional distribution of consumption given incomes. Alternatively, we can begin with a joint distribution and subsample from it by sampling one variable having conditioned the samples by the values of the other variable. Practical examples of sub-sampling from the joint density were illustrated in Chapter 5 in Figures 5.8 to 5.12. In those figures we also showed the box-and-whisker plots for one variable conditional on the value specified for the other variable. Each box-and-whisker plot represents a "sample" from a conditional distribution.

If all that we get to observe is this second distribution, then any statistical analysis that we carry out must be with the conditional distributions and not with the joint distributions. We will explore this idea extensively in the next chapter. If, however, we know the marginal distributions as well, then we can recapture the joint distributions by obtaining the product of the conditional and the marginal distributions.

The major lesson in this discussion is that *how we sample* bivariate data is very important for understanding what the corresponding theoretical distribution should be. If we sample individuals at random and for each individual we record the variable values of interest, we have sampled from the joint distribution. But, if we sample on one characteristic first and then conditional on the observed characteristic, we sample for another characteristic, the relevant distribution for the second characteristic is a conditional one, conditioned on the value obtained on the first characteristic. As an extreme case, to clarify this important difference, consider two alternatives. One, you specify a very low income value and then conditional on that income value, you obtain a random sample of consumption expenditures; that is, you sample randomly among the subpopulation that have the specified income level. Now carry out the same procedure, but having first chosen a very high income level. A moment's reflection will indicate that the distributions of consumption in the two cases will be very different.

There is, of course, one case in which this procedure will not alter the distribution that you observe. If the two variables are independent of each other, then sampling on one variable first will make no difference to the distribution that you will observe. For example, consider sampling first on height and then for each height, sample randomly for IQ levels. The observed distributions of IQ levels should not differ, except for random variations, across the subsamples determined by heights.

12.7   Summary

In this chapter, we reintroduced the concepts of joint and conditional density and probability distribution functions for pairs of random variables. On many previous occasions, we have talked about joint, conditional, and marginal distributions, but we have not until now considered how conditional and joint distributions could be generated.

The most important joint distribution we discussed was the bivariate Gaussian (normal). The difference between the joint distribution of independent and dependent Gaussian distributions can be seen by adding a cross-product term in the exponent with a coefficient. The coefficient ρ is the correlation coefficient and, therefore, is the theoretical analog of the sample correlation coefficient r defined in Chapter 5.

We defined the moments for bivariate distributions and for bivariate density functions. The most important moment we obtained was the covariance between two variables. In the case of the Gaussian distribution, the covariance is $\rho \sigma_X \sigma_Y$.

As in Chapters 7 and 8, where we derived a sequence of univariate distributions, we noted in this chapter that unique joint distributions are generated by unique experiments. Further, we noted that the process of sampling for more than one variable at a time must be done with caution; one must note whether the sampling is from a joint or a conditional distribution.

Case Study

Was There Age Discrimination in a Public Utility?

There are only two continuous cardinal variables involved in this case, age and salary. In Chapter 9, we discussed the sampling issue and concluded that we should regard our observations as a random drawing from a joint distribution of employee characteristics that is conditional on the fact that we have a single firm at a precise moment in time. This "master" joint distribution is multivariate (there are many variables involved) and is mixed continuous and discrete. In this section, let us concentrate on the joint distribution of age and salary.

In Chapter 4, we calculated the moments of the marginal distributions of age and salary and of the distributions conditional on various factors such as sex or hire status. In this discussion, let us restrict attention to the joint distribution of age and salary conditional on only the firm's characteristics. In Chapter 4, we discovered that the standardized third and fourth moments were approximately 0 and 3, respectively, but this is only an approximation. Indeed, there is some evidence that the age distribution is skewed to the left and that the salary distribution is skewed to the right. Further, we suspect that the two distributions are not independent because in Chapter 5 we discovered small, but noticeable, correlations between the variables (see Figure 5.14).

We can conclude that, although the joint distribution of age and salary is not bivariate normal, that assumption is nevertheless a reasonable approximation. We leave to Chapter 13 the decision as to whether they are independent.

Exercises

Calculation Practice

12.1 Worked. *Objective: To enable you to see how the scatter plot of observations on two variables generated by a pair of random variables changes as you alter the correlation between them.* The exercise also indicates how the scatter plots vary from sample to sample. Experiment with various values of n; especially when n is small, note the variability of the points within each graph.

[*Computer directions:* Start S-Plus. On the menu bar, click Labs, Bivariate Descriptive Statistics, Scatterplots I. Click Apply.]

12.2 Worked. *Objective: To let you experiment with generating bivariate data with different choices for n and for ρ (rho), the correlation coefficient.* For the values of $n = 10, 20, 50, 100$; for values of ρ from $-.99$ to $.99$ examine the scatterplots. Notice the difficulty in detecting "by eye" the correlation when the value of ρ is between $-.4$ and $.4$ approximately, and n is small.

[*Computer directions:* Start S-Plus. On the menu bar, click Labs, Bivariate Descriptive Statistics, Scatterplots II. In the dialog box, set "n" and "rho" to desired values; click Apply. Each click of Apply gives you a different sample.]

12.3 If X_1 and X_2 have the following joint distribution:

		X_1				
		−2	−1	0	1	2
	1	.10	.10	.08	.05	.04
X_2	2	.10	.05	.08	.05	.05
	3	.05	.08	.05	.08	.04

a. What are the marginal distributions of X_1 and X_2?

b. What is the conditional distribution of $X_2|X_1 = -1$; of $X_1|X_2 = 3$?

c. Are X_1 and X_2 independent?

d. If X_1^* and X_2^* have the same marginal distributions as X_1 and X_2, but are independent, what would the joint distribution of X_1^* and X_2^* look like? Summarize the difference between the two joint distributions.

12.4 Using the distribution of paired heights of men and women in the file Husbands.xls, plot the sample contour plots for this joint distribution. Using this graph, how might you infer the distribution of wives' heights if the height of husbands is 170 cms?

[*Computer directions:* In S-Plus, import the file Husbands.xls, in folder Misc, in the folder Xfiles. Highlight both height variables. Click on Graph, 2D Plot. Scroll to Contour Plot. Highlight and click OK. As an alternative, you can examine the color-filled plots by choosing Contour-Filled as the plot type.]

12.5 Using the same data set, examine the joint distribution of husbands' and wives' ages. Compare the two sets of graphs.

12.6 Using the file Psatsat.xls in folder Testscor, examine the contour plots for psatmath and psatverb; what do you conclude? Compare this result with that obtained using the satmath and satverb scores.

Exploring the Tools

12.7 If $X_1 = \{A, B, C, D\}$, $X_2 = \{M, F\}$, X_1, X_2 are distributed independently of each other, and each is distributed according to the equally likely principle, write the joint distribution of X_1 and X_2.

12.8 If X_1 is distributed uniformly over the numbers $\{1, 2, \ldots, 10\}$ and $X_2 = 2 + (1/2)X_1$, write

a. the joint distribution of X_1 and X_2. What is peculiar about this distribution?

b. the conditional distribution of X_2 given X_1.

c. the conditional distribution of X_1 given X_2.

12.9 *Objective: To distinguish between marginal, joint, and conditional probabilities.*

For each of the following scenarios, indicate whether you would be calculating a marginal probability, a joint probability, or a conditional probability.

a. the probability that an individual has lung cancer

b. the probability that an individual is a smoker and has lung cancer

c. the probability that an individual has lung cancer, given she is a smoker

d. the probability that a student's grade in economics will be an *A*, given that she earns an *A* in her calculus class

e. the probability that a student's grade in economics will be an *A*, and that she earns an *A* in her calculus class

f. the probability that a student's grade in economics will be an *A*

12.10 Imagine the following situation. You are interested in the relationship between weight and fat measurement; see for example, the file Coles.xls in folder Misc. Potentially, you can observe people attending a health clinic, or you can sample people at some firm or university.

a. Explain how you would obtain:

(1) a sample of the joint distribution of weight and fat

(2) a sample of conditional distributions of weight, conditional on specified fat measurements

(3) conditional distributions of fat for specified weight levels

(4) a joint distribution of weight and fat, conditional on height

b. How would you obtain the relevant marginal distributions from these sampled distributions? What further information might you need in each case?

12.11 *Objective: To show the relationship between joint, conditional, and marginal distributions.* The data set Htwtkest.xls in the folder Misc contains a table of cells of heights and weights of 4995 women in the United Kingdom. This data set represents a joint distribution of heights and weights. If the individual cell entries, the counts for each cell, are divided by the total 4995, the entries are estimates of the joint probability in each cell.

a. Sum across rows and divide the row totals by the sum of all the rows to obtain the marginal probability distribution for weight.

[*Computer hint:* Import Htwtkest. On the menu bar, click on Data, Transform. Select Data Frame Htwtkest. In New Column Name, key in margdistwt. In Expression, key in apply(Htwtkest[,2:12],1,sum) /4995. Click on Apply.]

Plot the marginal probability distribution for weight. [Highlight column margdistwt, and select Graph, 2D Plot, High Density Line Plot.]

Produce the summary statistics (the moments) for the marginal probability distribution. [To calculate the mean, click on Data, Transform. In New Column Name, key in mean. In Expression, key in sum(margdistwt*weight). Click Apply.] (*Note:* The expression, apply(Htwtkest[,2:12],etc.), is an S-Plus command to sum all the rows selecting only columns 2 to 12.)

b. To produce the distribution of weight conditional on height equal to 58 inches, divide each entry in column ht58 by the column total. Plot the High Density Line Plot for the distribution of weight conditional on height 58 inches.

[*Computer hint:* To calculate the conditional distribution, on the menu bar, click on Data, Transform. In New Column Name, key in condht58. In Expression, key in ht58/sum(ht58). Click Apply.]

c. To produce the distribution of height conditional on a weight of 176.5 pounds, divide each entry in the row for 176.5 by the total of the row for 176.5. Plot the High Density Line Plot for the distribution of height conditional on a weight of 176.5 pounds.

[**Computer hint:** Re-import Htwtkest (to remove columns added in 1 and 2 above). On the menu bar, click on <u>Data</u>, <u>Transpose</u>; click Apply. Open the Object Browser and double click on Data Frame "last.transpose." Highlight row 1 of last.transpose, and double click on the Remove Row button on the toolbar. Repeat the directions in (b) substituting X18 (which is the 176.5 pound column) for ht58 and naming the new column condht176.5.]

d. If you multiplied the marginal probability that a woman's height is 60 inches by the conditional probability that a woman's weight is 176.5 pounds given that the corresponding height was 60 inches, what probability would you have?

e. If you divided each entry in the row for a weight of 200 pounds by the corresponding row total, what would you have? Explain.

Applications

12.12 *Objective: To investigate the construction and analysis of contour plots.*

The data file Cosize.xls in folder Misc provides information on sales and employment for 138 firms. Using your intuition, what would you hypothesize about the sign and magnitude of the correlation between sales (sales) and employment (empl)? Can you assert something about the direction of causality? What can you hypothesize about the shape of the contour plot? Record your hypotheses, and then calculate the correlation. Construct the contour plot using S-Plus. Are your hypotheses confirmed or rejected?

12.13 Explain how the use of ranked data, instead of actual data, would affect the construction and analysis of a contour plot. Illustrate by plotting the contour plots for heights of men and women in the file Husbands.xls, in the folder Misc.

12.14 In the folder Testscor, in file Psatsat.xls are the variables psatmath and psatverb. Examine the contour plots of these two variables.

[**Computer directions:** In S-Plus, import Psatsat.xls. On the menu bar, click <u>Graph</u>, <u>2D Plot</u>, <u>Contour Plot</u>. Click OK. In the dialog box, select *psatmath* for the "x Column(s)" and *psatverb* for the "y Column(s)." Click OK.] You may want to try the Contour-Filled plot. If you were to randomize the order of psatverb and plot the contour plot, what would you expect to see? Try it and check your supposition.

[**Computer hint:** To randomize psatverb, on the menu bar, click on <u>Data</u>, <u>Random Sample</u>. In Sampling Prob., select "psatverb." Click Apply. Open the Object Browser and double click on Data Frame "last.sample." Copy the newly randomized psatverb column to the Psatsat data frame. Do the Contour graph using the randomized psatverb.]

12.15 (Refer to Exercise 12.14.) Repeat the first part of the experiment, for satmath and satverb. Except for differences of scale are there any noticeable differences in the contour plots? Can you explain these results?

12.16 Compare the results obtained if you examine the contour plots for *psatmath* and *satmath*. Similarly, examine *psatverb* and *satverb*. What impressions do you get? What conclusions about the relationship between PSAT and SAT do you draw?

12.17 In the folder Intrate, use the file Monyld.xls, which contains the variables representing the three-month and six-month bill rates (*bill3mo* and *bill6mo*, respectively). Regarding these data as representing a sample from the joint distribution of three- and six-month bill rates, plot the contours and comment. Examine next the three-month bill rate and the five-year note rate (*note5yr*). Comment on the observed difference. Can you explain the differences that you observe?

12.18 Using the data in the Energy folder, compare the contour plots for agricultural and industrial production across countries. For example, can you explain the differences between Argentina and the United States, between Korea and Norway?

12.19 In the folder Firmdata, use the files Avon.xls and Campbell.xls. In each file are recorded the variables for long-term debt (*ltdebt*) and sales. If you do a contour plot of these two variables for each of these firms, what conclusions can you draw about the relationship between long-term debt and sales and how it varies by type of firm?

12.20 Using the data in Exercise 12.19, if the data observed are drawings from a joint distribution of long-term debt and sales, how would you obtain an approximation to a conditional distribution of sales conditional on long-term debt?

12.21 Re-examine the folder Testscor, file Psatsat.xls. How would you obtain an approximation to the conditional distribution of satmath scores conditional on satverb scores?

12.22 Case Study: Was There Age Discrimination in a Public Utility?

Much has been made of conditional distributions in this chapter. Clearly, conditioning of the variables age and salary are critical in this case. Viewing the data that you have available as a series of conditional distributions, show in some detail how the insights obtained in this chapter and in Chapter 9 help you to understand the statistical aspects of the problem. Explore in some depth the various types of conditional distributions involved. In the process, summarize for a potential jury the relevance to this one case of any analysis using such data.

CHAPTER

13

The Theory and Practice of Regression Analysis

13.1 What You Will Learn in This Chapter

Chapter 5 provided the initial mechanics and basic concepts for analyzing linear structural relationships; this chapter completes that analysis by building on the theory developed in Chapter 12. In this chapter we analyze in depth the relationship between the conditional mean of a variable and its conditioning event. This provides the basis for analyzing linear structural relationships used to a great extent in every science and in most decision problems. We will relate the idea of the slope of a regression function to the idea of correlation; in the process, we will distinguish correlation from causality. In this connection, a careful reading of Chapter 12 is most useful in providing the theoretical basis for the analysis in this chapter.

All of the inference theory that we learned in Chapters 10 and 11 carries over to this chapter. In previous chapters, we discussed using estimation and hypothesis testing for parameters and moments of a univariate marginal distribution. In this chapter, we will discuss using inference for parameters and theoretical moments of a *conditional distribution*. The details may differ, but the principles are the same. As an aside we explain the origin of the word *regression*.

13.2 Introduction

This chapter pulls together two areas of interest: the description of bivariate distributions and structural relationships between pairs of random variables. One area is the description of bivariate distributions and the relationship between observed bivariate histograms and bivariate density functions. Chapter 12 provided the theory for the bivariate histograms that were discussed in Chapter 5. This discussion was similar to that in Chapters 7 and 8, which provided the theoretical analysis of univariate histograms and empirical probability distributions. We introduced the idea of a structural relationship in Chapters 2 and 5. This chapter will provide the theory underlying the calculation of the sample correlation coefficient and the inferences that we might make on the basis of observing some value for that coefficient. Thus, this chapter

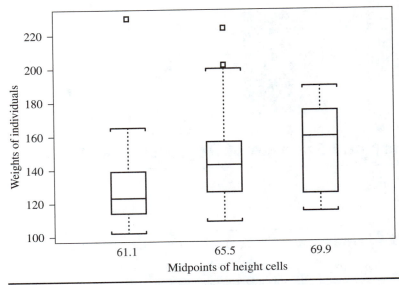

Figure 13.1   Box-and-whisker plots of women's weights given their heights

plays the same role for the calculations in Chapter 5 as the analysis in Chapters 10 and 11 did for the calculations in Chapter 4.

In Chapter 12 we saw that a bivariate joint distribution can be reexpressed as the product of the marginal and the conditional distributions, so the key to the relationship between any two random variables is contained in the properties of the conditional distribution. When we obtained the correlation coefficient, ρ, in that chapter, we were in effect using this implicit connection between the variables. Recall the scatter plot diagrams in Chapter 5 (see Figures 5.2 to 5.7). We calculated sequences of box-and-whisker plots for each pair of variables (see for example, Figure 5.9), which we reproduce in this chapter for ease of reference as Figure 13.1. For each selected value of women's heights we presented the box-and-whisker plots for the corresponding weights. In terms of the discussion in Chapter 12, our box-and-whisker plots were "samples" from the corresponding conditional probability density functions—in this case, observations on the conditional distribution of weights given specified values for the heights. In prior figures in Chapter 5, we illustrated observations on the conditional distributions of final scores given midterm scores, car fuel consumption given weight of car, and the conditional level of IQ given height (see Figures 5.4 to 5.6).

What we observed in those graphs was that we could consider fitting an approximate straight line through the medians of the box-and-whisker plots to summarize the connection between the variables and hence to indicate the shape of the joint distribution. The slope of the line that we implicitly fitted in Chapter 5 depended on the value of the sample correlation coefficient; if positive the line sloped upward, and if negative the line sloped downward. The larger the size of the correlation coefficient, the greater the degree of association between the variables. There are two polar cases, where the correlation is unity and where it is zero. The former case indicates that the two variables are functions of each other; that is,

$$Y = \beta_0 + \beta_1 X$$

where Y and X are the two variables involved. This equation implies that we have in effect only one random variable, X, and a linear transformation of that random variable, which we label Y.

The other extreme case involved a coefficient of zero, in which case there is no linear relationship between the two variables. As we saw in Chapter 5, a zero correlation coefficient means either that there is no relationship between the two variables—they are independently distributed; or the relationship is nonlinear in such a manner that the correlation is zero, even though the variables are related. Examples were given in the exercises.

The objective of this chapter is to link the analysis in Chapters 5 and 12 and in so doing to provide the theory that underlies the calculations that we performed in Chapter 5. The theory that we will develop in this chapter will also give us the tools to interpret the results of our calculations in a manner similar to that achieved in Chapters 10 and 11 for univariate distributions. In the next section, we examine the relationship between two variables, X and Y, wherein we fix values of X and observe samples of Y given the fixed values of X. We relate these results to the underlying joint density functions.

13.3   The Regression Model

One major lesson from Chapter 12 is that any joint distribution is the product of a conditional and of a marginal distribution (recall Equations 12.1 and 12.2). We also saw in Chapter 12 that we could obtain observations on the conditional distribution directly. Consequently, the key to the shape of the joint distribution lies in the properties of the conditional distribution—that is, in the way in which the distribution of one variable changes as values of the conditioning variable change. One particular way in which this dependence between the two variables can be expressed is in terms of the conditional mean, or in terms of the first moment of the conditional distribution. A specific example of this was illustrated by the normal distribution in Equation 12.20.

Some of the practical examples of these joint distributions from our previous studies are the grades of NYU students; measures of heights and weights; car mileage and car weight; consumption and income, either for individuals or for geographic regions; and salary and years of service for our case study. In each case, we can consider the joint distribution of the two variables. Further, from our work in Chapter 12, we can also consider the conditional distribution of final grades on midterm grades, car mileage on car weight, salary on years of service, and consumption on income.

In general, the conditioning relationship between any two variables X and Y might be expressed in terms of any one or more of the moments of the conditional distribution, not just the first. However, one of the convenient properties of the conditional Gaussian distribution is that the relationship between one of the variables, Y, and the conditioning variable, X, is that the relationship can be completely expressed in terms of the conditional mean (as we showed in Equation 12.20). We do not need to investigate any other moments of the conditional Gaussian distribution. Although this result does not hold for all other distributions, it is a sufficiently common result that we can usually and safely ignore the other moments. Consequently, in all that follows in this chapter we will concentrate our attention on the conditional mean, which is the first moment about the origin of the conditional distribution. The conditional properties of the conditional distribution can be completely determined by specifying the conditional mean. We want to evaluate the conditional mean of consumption on income, of final grades on midterm grades, of GNP levels on the aggregate money supply, and so on.

For a pair of continuous random variables X and Y with conditional density function $f(Y|X)$, the general expression is given by

$$E\{Y|X = x_0\} = \int Yf(Y|X = x_0)dY$$

$$= g(x_0)$$

(13.1)

where $g(x_0)$ is some function of the conditioning value $X = x_0$. Recall Figures 5.8 to 5.12, in which we illustrated the relationship between the pairs of variables by plotting a line of box-and-whisker plots. The line of median points indicates approximately the line of the conditional mean as we have defined it in Equation 13.1.

In these examples, we see that in some cases the assumption of a relationship between one variable and the conditioning variable is approximately linear—for example, midterm and final grades, consumption and income. But that for some variables, such as the conditional relationship between mileage and car weight, the relationship might be nonlinear. Indeed, in this example, we see evidence that the relationship might involve the second moment as well.

To further simplify matters, let us restrict $g(.)$ to be a linear function of X. Whether or not we can restrict our attention to linear functions $g(.)$ depends on the functional form of $f(Y|X)$; our decision to use only linear functions $g(.)$ is in fact a restriction on the conditional densities that we choose to observe and analyze. We have therefore

$$E\{Y|X = x_0\} = \int Yf(Y|X = x_0)dY$$

$$= \beta_0 + \beta_1 x_0$$

(13.2)

This equation tells us that the conditional mean of Y given the observation of a value x_0 on a variable X is a linear function of the observed value of X. In the case of the Gaussian distribution examined in Chapter 12, β_0 in Equation 13.2 is in fact the unconditional mean of the variable Y—namely μ'_Y—and β_1 is given by $\rho \frac{\sigma_Y}{\sigma_X}$ (see Equation 12.20).

It is convenient to reexpress the relationship between Y and X utilizing the conditional mean. Equation 13.2 indicates that, conditional on observing $X = x_0$, the vari-

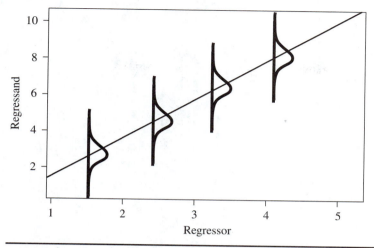

Figure 13.2   Illustration of the conditional distribution of the regressand given values of the regressor

able Y varies randomly about the conditional mean, $\beta_0 + \beta_1 x_0$. We can restate this by defining a new random variable ϵ in the following way:

$$\epsilon \equiv Y - (\beta_0 + \beta_1 x_0) \tag{13.3}$$

or

$$Y = \beta_0 + \beta_1 x_0 + \epsilon$$

where ϵ has the same distribution, or density function as Y, except for the mean; the symbol "$\equiv$" stresses that the equation is a definition for the variable ϵ. Y has a conditional mean of $\beta_0 + \beta_1 x_0$, and ϵ by definition in Equation 13.3 has a mean of zero. It is also assumed that the distribution of ϵ is independent of the regressor variable X. Equation 13.3 is known as the **regression equation.** For obvious reasons Y is known as the **dependent variable,** or the **regressand,** and the X variable is called the **independent variable,** or the **regressor.** This relationship between the conditional mean and the *distribution* of the regressand for each value of the conditional mean is shown in Figure 13.2.

We can provide a representative plot of this relationship (see Figure 13.3). In this plot, the individual points represent the observed values of Y for the given value of X indicated on the X-axis. The straight line that runs through the "middle of" the points is the line of the conditional mean as we have defined it in Equation 13.2. Each point represents a single drawing from the conditional distribution indicated by the specified value for the regressor. In this example, $\beta_0 = 4$ and $\beta_1 = 2$; the added "error term" is ϵ, and its distribution is Gaussian with a mean of 0 and a variance of 1. This implies that the conditional distribution of the variable Y is also Gaussian with a variance of 1 but a conditional mean of $4 + 2 \times X$. The relationships among observations on Y; its conditional mean, $E\{Y|X\}$; and the term ϵ are further illustrated in Figure 13.3.

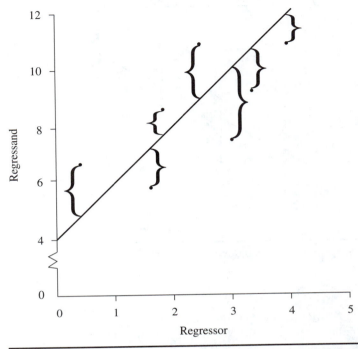

Figure 13.3   Illustration of the relationship between individual observations and the line of conditional means

In most textbooks, the line in Equation 13.3 is the usual statement of the "regression model." Y is represented by a deterministic mean, $\beta_0 + \beta_1 x_0$, plus a random component represented by the "random variable" ϵ. All we are saying in Equation 13.3 is that we can reexpress the conditional variation of Y into the sum of two components: the conditional mean, $\beta_0 + \beta_1 x_0$, and a zero mean random variable with the same density function as that of Y, except for the mean. Keep this definition of ϵ in mind when interpreting regression models.

The second line in Equation 13.3 is called the regression equation for reasons that we will explore later. The regression line can be interpreted in a different manner that is most useful for both science and policy implementations of social science research. Consider a simple version of the relationship between consumption and income, the so-called permanent income hypothesis. This hypothesis says that over the long run, say a decade or more, and given constant interest rates, the relationship between consumption and disposable income is

$$C = \beta_1 Y + \epsilon \tag{13.4}$$

in which C is consumption per annum, Y is income per annum, and ϵ represents the fact that for any one year the equation will not hold exactly, but that there will be some random deviations. We are presuming that for a given value of income, $Y = y_0$, we will observe some consumption value c_0; C is in fact a random variable with a mean of $\beta_1 Y$. The variation of C about its mean $\beta_1 Y$ is represented by the random variable ϵ. Given a value y_0 for Y and an observation ϵ_0 on ϵ, Equation 13.4 determines an observed value for C, c_0, that is given by

$$c_0 = \beta_1 y_0 + \epsilon_0$$

Equation 13.4 has to be completed by specifying the *distribution* of the term ϵ. Because the difference between the observed value of C and that given by the term $\beta_1 Y$ is often due to "errors of observation," or "errors of measurement," the added term ϵ is called an "error term." To keep the analysis as uncomplicated as possible in the discussion to follow we will always presume that ϵ is distributed as Gaussian.

The regression model is very common in science, engineering, biology, economics, and all disciplines that try to explain observable events in terms of a theoretical structure or that attempt to use theory to implement some policy proposal. In Chapter 5, we had many examples: the relationship between fuel consumption and weight of car, between midterm and final grades, between income and money, between investment and profits, between years of service and salary, and so on. Almost all of the discussion of policy in the current media will at some stage inevitably involve the properties of some regression. For example, if we increase government expenditures per pupil on education, will educational standards improve? This question requires a regression of educational standards on expenditure. Yet another example involves the effect of fertilizer on crop yields. Predicting the effect of adding a particular type of fertilizer requires a regression equation between fertilizer and crop yields. Adding scrubbers to industrial smoke stacks to reduce particulate pollution requires a regression of the reduction of particulate emissions on the size and extent of scrubbers installed in the stacks. And so on.

The model that we have just proposed together with its examples is a typical regression model that purports to describe a causal relationship between two variables. The causal relationship is between the *conditional mean of C* and values taken by the conditioning variable Y. The *observed* relationship is between the *observed C* and Y and is a called a structural relationship; that is, there is no functional relationship between the observed C and Y, there is only a relationship that has to be described in terms of random variables. Although there is no functional relationship between the observed C and the observed Y, there is between the *unobserved conditional mean of C* and the conditioning variable Y (see Chapter 2).

We now see that to propose a structural relationship between two variables, say W and X, is to define a random variable ϵ, $\epsilon \equiv W - \beta_0 + \beta_1 x_0$, and to specify the conditional mean of W given X. In short, we are specifying the conditional distribution for W as a function of X. Further, if we know the distribution of X itself, then by using the relationship between conditional and marginal distributions, we obtain the joint distribution for W and X. Hence, to propose a structural relationship is also to propose a joint distribution if one can postulate a marginal distribution for the conditioning variable.

Less abstractly, if W represents consumption and X represents income, then we are postulating a conditional relationship between consumption and the "conditioning event" income. This provides us with the conditional distribution of consumption given income. If we have a marginal distribution for income, we can determine the joint distribution between consumption and income.

At this point in the discussion we discover an important limitation to the analysis. Imagine that we have obtained the joint distribution of W and X by using this approach. However, from Equation 12.2, we know that we can rewrite the joint distribution of W and X as

$$f(W, X) = f_{X|W}(X|W)g(W) \tag{13.5}$$

where $g(W)$ is the marginal distribution of W and $f_{X|W}(X|W)$ is the conditional distribution of X given W. From our discussion, we know that we can determine the conditional mean of X given W by an operation similar to that shown in Equation 13.1. But if we are trying to interpret the equation, $W = \beta_0 + \beta_1 \times X + \epsilon$ as a *causal relationship* observed with error, the simultaneous existence of a conditional relationship of

$$X = \gamma + \delta \times W + u \tag{13.6}$$

seems to be an embarrassment.

There is in fact nothing wrong with the theory. Once we have obtained the joint distribution of W and X, we can, in principle, examine either the conditional distribution of W given X, or the conditional distribution of X given W. From the statistical point of view, either conditional distribution is equally valid. If we are looking at a sample drawing from the joint distribution—for example, the sample of women's heights and weights as discussed in Chapter 5—we can consider either the conditional distribution of heights given weights or of weights given heights. Similarly, we can consider the conditional distribution of consumption given income or derive the conditional distribution of income given consumption. Indeed, we know how to sample from such a distribution. We collect a random sample of individual consumption levels, and then, in a second stage sample, we collect a sample of income levels for each observed consumption level. This might be an unusual way to sample income and consumption, but theoretically there is nothing to prevent us from doing just that.

But if individual income "causes" individual consumption in some sense, as seems likely from economic theory, what is the meaning to the conditional mean of income on consumption? The answer is that statistics is essentially about *acausal relationships*. Statistics is about random variables, and we began by noting that we had to develop our ideas about probability and the shapes of distributions for variables that had no causal relationships. Concepts of "causality" can be defined *only* in the context of the discipline under examination, not in terms of statistics. Causality is a concept that has meaning only in economics, physics, psychology, biology, or other fields. Causality implies a direction for the relationship between two variables—that is, either from X to Y, or from Y to X. But correlations as properties of joint distributions merely indicate the *association* between X and Y; there is no sense of X leading or "causing" Y, or vice versa. If X is correlated with Y, then Y is correlated with X. "Correlation is not causality."

We can conceive of situations in which variables are causally related, but the correlations are zero; we gave an example in the Exercises in Chapter 5. Alternatively, we can conceive of situations in which two variables are not related causally but have nonzero correlations. One way in which this can occur is that both variables are associated with a third variable, and the third variable may be the one that is causally related. However, variables can be associated in even more tenuous ways. Examples here are the famous ones provided by Yule of what he called "nonsense correlations"; his most famous example was that there was a correlation of 0.95 between the proportion of marriages in the Church of England to all marriages and the mortality rate for data collected between 1866 and 1911. As Yule stated, this result, like any other result, can be rationalized by anyone of some ingenuity and goodwill.

Another amusing statement of this problem is given by G. B. Shaw in the Preface to the *Doctor's Dilemma*, where he states:

> Even trained statisticians often fail to appreciate the extent to which statistics are vitiated by the unrecorded assumptions of their interpreters. . . . It is easy to prove that the wearing of tall hats and the carrying of umbrellas enlarges the chest, prolongs life, and confers comparative immunity from disease . . . anything, in short, that implies more means and better nurture . . . can be statistically palmed off as a magic-spell conferring all sorts of privileges.

Consequently, we must conclude that a nonzero correlation between two variables is neither necessary nor sufficient for causality. This is not to deny that if, as we postulated for income and consumption, two variables are causally related in a linear fashion, they have a nonzero correlation. Consequently, although nonzero correlations cannot be used to prove causality, they are a useful guide to possible linear causal relationships. What we can say, that is accurate and more general, is that if X "causes" Y—that is, one has a tested theory that demonstrates a causal connection between values of the variable X and that of Y—then one can determine a conditional distribution for Y that is a function of the variable X. In such a conditional distribution, the conditional mean of Y given X may, or may not, be a linear function of X. Further, there is the possibility that other moments are also functions of the conditioning variable. Certainly, it is true that the conditional distribution of Y given X is not equal to the marginal distribution of Y, at least for some values, or ranges of values, of the conditioning variable X. But we are still left with the conundrum that once we have obtained the joint distribution of Y and X, we can always obtain the conditional distribution of X given Y.

At this stage, you might well ask of what use are correlations if what you are interested in is causality. The answer is that we have to start somewhere, and the discovery of a strong correlation, especially where such correlations were indicated by some theory, is an excellent beginning. The results warrant further study to determine the lines of causality. A medical researcher recently stated the matter very well, when he said that the observation of a correlation between the incidence of a disease and the presence of a defective gene was gratifying, but what that result really meant to him was that the hard clinical work of trying to determine the nature of any causality that might exist should now begin.

13.4   Estimation and Inference: The Basics

We are at last ready to discuss the problem of estimation and inference. This section merely extends the ideas discussed fully in Chapters 10 and 11. We are assuming that we have obtained a sample from the conditional distribution of Y given

X. In subsequent discussions, we will restrict our attention to the given set of X values observed, $\{x_i\}_{i=1,n}$. The practical problems that we will address involve the relationship between grades, consumption and income, the logarithms of money and GNP, interest rates and housing starts, car mileage and car weights, and so on.

Let us review and summarize our notation. We assume that we have n observations on a variable that we will generically label X, $\{x_i\}_{i=1,n}$. The model that we assume is further described by

$$Y_i = \beta_0 + \beta_1 x_i + \epsilon_i$$

where

$$\epsilon_i \equiv Y_i - (\beta_0 + \beta_1 x_i)$$

(13.7)

and the distribution of $\{\epsilon_i\}_{i=1,n}$ is that of n independently and identically distributed Gaussian random variables with zero means and a common variance of σ_ϵ^2. The ϵ_i are assumed to be distributed independently of the $\{x_i\}$. In particular, the variance of the ϵ_i is assumed to be a constant. This statement is just another way of saying that we have n drawings from the conditional distribution of Y given the observed conditioning values $\{x_i\}_{i=1,n}$. All that we have added beyond our discussion is to specify the variance as σ_ϵ^2 and to restrict our attention to cases where the underlying conditional distribution is the same Gaussian distribution for all n observations.

Notice that for whatever units of measurement of Y and X, the parameter β_1 must have the units of measurement of Y per unit of X. For example, when X represents height in inches and Y represents weight in pounds, then β_1 must have the units of pounds per inch. In the example relating car weight, X, to fuel consumption, Y, car weight might be measured in kilograms and fuel consumption in kilometers per liter; β_1 would have the units kilometers per liter per kilogram. In each case, β_0 will have the same units of measurement as that of the dependent variable Y.

Before continuing with our development of the regression problem, let us discuss the joint distribution. Recall that we can summarize the linear association between X and Y in terms of a parameter without units of measurement. The dimensionless measure is ρ, the covariation between the standardized variables X^{st} and Y^{st}, where X^{st} and Y^{st} are defined by

$$X^{st} = \frac{X - \mu'_X}{\sigma_X}$$

and

$$Y^{st} = \frac{Y - \mu'_Y}{\sigma_Y}$$

For both standardized variables the means are zero and the variances are 1. If we define $\phi(Y^{st}|X^{st})$ to be the conditional normal density function and $\phi(X^{st})$ to be the marginal normal density function, then we can derive ρ (reexamine Equation 12.34):

$$\text{cov}(Y^{st}, X^{st}) \tag{13.8}$$
$$= E\{Y^{st}X^{st}\}$$
$$= \int Y^{st}X^{st}\phi(Y^{st}|X^{st})dY^{st}\phi(X^{st})dX^{st}$$
$$= \rho \int (X^{st})^2\phi(X^{st})dX^{st}$$
$$= \rho$$

We have now defined all the parameters that we need to estimate and about which we might test hypotheses: β_0, β_1, μ'_X, μ'_Y, ρ, σ_ϵ^2, σ_X^2, and σ_Y^2. For example, we could calculate the means of income and consumption, the variances of consumption and of income, the correlation between consumption and income, and the regression parameters relating the conditional mean of consumption and income. Similar remarks apply to our other examples, such as weights and heights, the logarithms of the money supply and GNP, and car mileage and car weight.

Consider Table 13.1, which provides the basic estimates for the parameters for each of the data sets. Notice the importance of determining the units of measurement and recognizing when the parameter is a nondimensional number. The logarithms of the GNP and money supply data are logarithms of dollar values times 10^6 for GNP and dollar values times 10^9 for the money supply.

There is a simple relationship between the three variances:

$$\sigma_Y^2 = \beta_1^2 \sigma_X^2 + \sigma_\epsilon^2$$

which is easily confirmed by squaring both sides of Equation 13.7 and taking expectations, recognizing that ϵ_i is distributed independently of X. The regression parameters and the means are related as we recall from the development in Chapter 12:

$$E\{Y|X = x_0\} = \beta_0 + \beta_1 x_0$$
$$= \mu'_Y + \rho \frac{\sigma_Y}{\sigma_X} x_0$$

We have just stated that ρ, the correlation coefficient, is the covariance between the standardized variables. The covariation between any two normal random variables was written as $\sigma_{X,Y}$ and from what we have shown here we have the relationship

$$\sigma_{X,Y} = E\{(Y - \mu'_Y)(X - \mu'_X)\} = \rho\sigma_X\sigma_Y \tag{13.9}$$

However, it is convenient to rewrite this result in yet another way. $E\{(Y - \mu'_Y)(X - \mu'_X)\}$ can be regarded as a theoretical moment and is in fact the first cross-product moment of the joint distribution of X and Y. Formally, we can state

$$\mu_{11}(X, Y) \equiv E\{(Y - \mu'_Y)(X - \mu'_X)\} \tag{13.10}$$

And now we immediately have an idea of an estimator for $\mu_{11}(X, Y)$. Following our practice in Chapter 10—for example, $E\{M'_1\} = \mu'_1$; but $E\{M_2(X)\} = \frac{n-1}{n}\mu_2(X)$—we can guess that a useful estimator might be the random variable that is defined by the product of the random variables X and Y. So an obvious way to begin is to consider the expectation of $M_{11}(X, Y)$, where $M_{11}(X, Y)$ is defined by

$$M_{11}(X, Y) = \frac{1}{n} \sum_i ((X_i - \bar{X})(Y_i - \bar{Y})) \qquad (13.11)$$

As usual it is easier to begin with the standardized bivariate normal distribution. In Equation 13.8, we calculated the expected value of each of the n terms in the sum in Equation 13.11; $\bar{X}$ and $\bar{Y}$ are zero by assumption here, so we have

$$
\begin{aligned}
E\{M_{11}(X^{st}, Y^{st})\} &= \frac{1}{n} \sum E\{Y_i X_i\} \\
&= \frac{1}{n} \sum \rho \\
&= \rho
\end{aligned}
\qquad (13.12)
$$

By following the development we used to show that the theoretical covariance between two *arbitrary* joint normal variables is $\sigma_{X,Y} = E\{(Y - \mu'_Y)(X - \mu'_X)\} = \rho \sigma_X \sigma_Y$, we can show that

$$
\begin{aligned}
E\{M_{11}(X, Y)\} &= \frac{1}{n} \sum E\{(Y_i - \bar{Y})(X_i - \bar{X})\} \\
&= \frac{n-2}{n} \rho \sigma_X \sigma_Y \\
&\cong \rho \sigma_X \sigma_Y
\end{aligned}
\qquad (13.13)
$$

We lost 2 degrees of freedom because we had to estimate μ'_X and μ'_Y by $\bar{X}$ and $\bar{Y}$.

We will not derive the result here, but if we accept as true for a moment that the corresponding variance for $M_{11}(X, Y)$ is

$$\text{var}(M_{11}(X, Y)) = \frac{1}{n}(1 - \rho^2)^2 \qquad (13.14)$$

we notice immediately that we have run into a problem that is very similar to one we have already faced; the variance of our estimator depends on the value of the very parameter that we are trying to estimate. Remember the problem of estimating a probability for a binomial distribution (see Equation 10.17). If we add the observation that the distribution of the statistic $M_{11}(X, Y)$ converges very slowly to the Gaussian (a fact that is illustrated in the exercises), we can agree that we ought to try another avenue of attack for this problem. Our first approach, although it has not produced a very useful estimator, has been informative.

If estimating ρ seems to be somewhat awkward, might we do better by estimating β_1? If we take this route, we will also have to estimate β_0. Reconsider the regression equation for the observed data:

$$y_i = \beta_0 + \beta_1 x_i + \epsilon_i$$

and calculate the average $\{y_i\}$ and the average $\{x_i.\}$ We obtain

$$\bar{y} = \beta_0 + \beta_1 \bar{x} + \bar{\epsilon}$$

Because the means of the random variables $\{\epsilon_i\}$ are zero, the observed $\bar{\epsilon}$ will be very small, except with very low probability, so we have approximately

$$\beta_0 \doteq \bar{y} - \beta_1 \bar{x} \tag{13.15}$$

and the symbol "$\doteq$" indicates that the right side approximates the left side. However, we now see how we could obtain an estimator for β_0 once we have an estimator for β_1. If $\hat{\beta}_1$ is an estimator for β_1, then we can easily define an estimator for β_0 by

$$\hat{\beta}_0 = \bar{Y} - \hat{\beta}_1 \bar{x} \tag{13.16}$$

and the properties of the estimator, $\hat{\beta}_0$, depend on the properties of $\hat{\beta}_1$ and on $\bar{Y}$ and $\bar{x}$. We need therefore to concentrate only on finding an estimator for β_1. Consequently, let us simplify the model by setting β_0 to zero, so we observe that

$$y_i = \beta_1 x_i + \epsilon_i \tag{13.17}$$

This can easily be done for any model with nonzero β_0 by redefining the variables in terms of deviations about the means—that is, in terms of $\{y_i - \bar{y}\}$ and $\{x_i - \bar{x}\}$. In terms of the model described in Equation 13.17, we now want to find an estimator for the parameter β_1.

Review the two figures that we have used to illustrate the regression equation, Figures 13.2, 13.3. One way of finding an estimator for β_1 is to use the principle that the line to be fitted should be as close to the points on average as we can manage; but we need to decide how to measure "close, on average." Recall how we defined ϵ_i initially. In our current version, we have

$$\epsilon_i \equiv Y_i - \beta_1 x_i \tag{13.18}$$

and we interpret ϵ_i as an "error term. If ϵ_i represents an "error," or a deviation of the observed y_i about the regression line given by $\beta_1 x_i$, then it would seem reasonable as a first choice to pick our estimator, $\hat{\beta}_1$, so that we minimize the squared errors. For each choice of $\hat{\beta}_1$ we determine a set of residuals for the regression fit. Let us define the **residuals**, or unexplained deviations, by

$$\hat{\epsilon}_i = y_i - \hat{\beta}_1 x_i,$$
$$i = 1, \ldots, n$$

We seek to minimize the sum of squared residuals by the appropriate choice of $\hat{\beta}_1$:

$$\min_{\hat{\beta}_1} \sum_i \hat{\epsilon}_i^2 = \min_{\hat{\beta}_1} \sum_i (y_i - \hat{\beta}_1 x_i)^2 \tag{13.19}$$

The expression "$\min_{\hat{\beta}_1} \sum_i$" means find that value of $\hat{\beta}_1$ that will minimize the summation of the squared terms. It is important that you recognize that we have carefully distinguished between the actual parameter value as represented by β_1 and the values that we will obtain by solving Equation 13.19 as represented by $\hat{\beta}_1$. The two will be equal only under very special circumstances and with a probability approaching zero.

Our task now is to find the minimum of the expression in Equation 13.19. The expression $\sum_i (y_i - \hat{\beta}_1 x_i)^2$ as a function of $\hat{\beta}_1$ varies continuously with respect to the value of $\hat{\beta}_1$ and clearly has a minimum possible value of zero. Consequently, we should

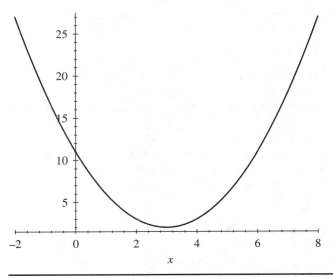

Figure 13.4   Illustrating the minimum of a squared error function (first derivative is the slope of the curve)

be able to find that value of $\hat{\beta}_1$ that minimizes the expression (see Figure 13.4). Note that the slope of the function that gives the sum of squares as a function of $\hat{\beta}_1$ decreases to zero and then increases as we pass through the minimum point. Formally, we know that we minimize a function when its rate of change is zero. The rate of change of the expression with respect to $\hat{\beta}_1$ is given by the first derivative. We calculate the first derivative and then choose that value of $\hat{\beta}_1$ that sets the derivative to zero. As we approach the minimum value the rate of change decreases to zero and as we pass through the minimum point, the derivative changes sign and the rate of change begins to increase.

All we need to do now is to calculate formally the first derivative of the squared error function with respect to $\hat{\beta}_1$. The derivative is given by

$$\frac{d\sum_i (y_i - \hat{\beta}_1 x_i)^2}{d\hat{\beta}_1} = 2\sum_i (y_i - \hat{\beta}_1 x_i)(-x_i) \tag{13.20}$$

$$0 = -\sum_i y_i x_i + \hat{\beta}_1 \sum_i x_i^2$$

or

$$\hat{\beta}_1 = \frac{\sum_i y_i x_i}{\sum_i x_i^2}$$

The first line in Equation 13.20 formally expresses the derivative of the expression, the second line indicates how we solve for $\hat{\beta}_1$ by choosing $\hat{\beta}_1$ such that the second line is zero, and the third line gives the result. This procedure is called **least squares;** that is, we find the optimum value for the regression slope parameter by finding that value that produces the "least sum of squares." In Equation 13.20, we derived an estimate of β_1 that depends on the observed values for the $\{y_i\}$ as well as those of the $\{x_i\}$. The formula for the estimator would be

$$\hat{\beta}_1 = \frac{\sum_i Y_i x_i}{\sum_i x_i^2}$$

to stress that $\hat{\beta}_1$ is an estimator depending on the random variables $\{Y_i\}$. Recall that all the analysis in this chapter is conditional on the *observed* values for the $\{x_i\}$.

Now that we have obtained an estimator for β_1, we can go back to the slightly more complicated model with a nonzero intercept and settle on an estimator for β_0 as well. We use Equation 13.16 to obtain

$$\hat{\beta}_0 = \bar{Y} - \hat{\beta}_1 \bar{x} \tag{13.21}$$

Our last task is to examine the distributional properties of these estimators. Remember that because each of $\hat{\beta}_0$ and $\hat{\beta}_1$ is a function of a random variable, Y, each is a random variable and therefore has a distribution of its own.

A first question is whether the estimators are biased. Because we can easily obtain the estimator $\hat{\beta}_0$ from Equation 13.21, it will be convenient to reexpress our regression equation in terms of deviations about the mean; this initial step will simplify the algebraic details that we have to handle. Let us define new observed variables by

$$y_{di} = y_i - \bar{y}$$
$$\bar{y} = \beta_0 + \beta_1 \bar{x} + \bar{\epsilon}$$
$$\bar{x}_{di} = x_i - \bar{x}$$
$$\epsilon_{di} = \epsilon_i - \bar{\epsilon}$$

so that

$$y_{di} = \beta_1 x_{di} + \epsilon_{di}$$

Consider the estimator for β_1 in this simpler model:

$$
\begin{aligned}
E\{\hat{\beta}_1\} &= E\left\{\frac{\sum_i Y_{di} x_{di}}{\sum_i x_{di}^2}\right\} \\
&= \frac{E\left\{\sum_i Y_{di} x_{di}\right\}}{\sum_i x_{di}^2} \\
&= \frac{E\left\{\sum_i (\beta_1 x_{di} + \epsilon_{di}) x_{di}\right\}}{\sum_i x_{di}^2} \\
&= \beta_1 \frac{\sum_i x_{di}^2}{\sum_i x_{di}^2} + \frac{E\left\{\sum_i \epsilon_{di} x_{di}\right\}}{\sum_i x_{di}^2} \\
&= \beta_1
\end{aligned}
\tag{13.22}
$$

Remember that all the analysis is conditional on the observed values of the $\{x_i\}$, so that for the purposes of the analysis in this section we can treat the $\{x_i\}$ as given numbers. We also recall that the $\{\epsilon_i\}$ have a zero mean by design and that the $\{\epsilon_i\}$ are distributed independently of the $\{x_i\}$. Our first conclusion is that the estimator that we derived is unbiased for β_1.

We also note that $\hat{\beta}_1$ is a linear estimator in that it is a linear function of the random variable Y (review Equation 13.22). Linear functions of normal random variables are themselves normally distributed; consequently, we conclude under the prescribed conditions of the problem that $\hat{\beta}_1$ has a normal distribution with a mean of β_1. All that is left to do is to discover the value of its variance. Fortunately, given our current stripped down model that task is not difficult. We define from Equation 13.22, line 4:

$$
\begin{aligned}
E\left\{(\hat{\beta}_1 - \beta_1)^2\right\} &= E\left\{\left(\frac{\sum_i \epsilon_{di} x_{di}}{\sum_i x_{di}^2}\right)^2\right\} \\
&= \frac{E\left\{\sum_i \epsilon_{di}^2 x_{di}^2 + \sum_i \sum_{j \neq i} \epsilon_{di} x_{di} \epsilon_{dj} x_{dj}\right\}}{\left(\sum_i x_{di}^2\right)^2} \\
&= \frac{\sigma_\epsilon^2 \left(\sum_i x_{di}^2\right)}{\left(\sum_i x_{di}^2\right)^2} = \frac{\sigma_\epsilon^2}{\left(\sum_i x_{di}^2\right)}
\end{aligned}
\tag{13.23}
$$

The calculation that leads from the second to the third line in Equation 13.23 depends on the fact that the $\{\epsilon_i\}$ are independent of the $\{x_i\}$ with a zero mean, so that the second term in the second line has a zero expectation; and the expectation of $\epsilon_{di}^2 x_{di}^2$ is simply $\sigma_\epsilon^2 x_{di}^2$. We summarize for convenience:

$$
\hat{\beta}_1 \sim N\left(\beta_1, \frac{\sigma_\epsilon^2}{\left(\sum_i x_{di}^2\right)}\right)
\tag{13.24}
$$

Our next task is to determine the distributional properties of the estimator $\hat{\beta}_0$; look back at Equation 13.21. First, we obtain the expectation of $\hat{\beta}_0$:

$$
\begin{aligned}
E\{\hat{\beta}_0\} &= E\{\bar{Y} - \hat{\beta}_1 \bar{x}\} \\
&= E\{\beta_0 + \beta_1 \bar{x} + \bar{\epsilon} - \hat{\beta}_1 \bar{x}\} \\
&= \beta_0 - E\{(\hat{\beta}_1 - \beta_1)\bar{x}\} \\
&= \beta_0
\end{aligned}
\tag{13.25}
$$

so that $\hat{\beta}_0$ is also unbiased. $\hat{\beta}_0$ is also a linear estimator in that it is a linear function of the random variable Y. We can conclude that the distribution of $\hat{\beta}_0$ is normal. Our next step is to determine the variance. From line 2 in Equation 13.25, we observe that

$$E\{(\hat{\beta}_0 - \beta_0)^2\} = E\{(\bar{\epsilon} - (\hat{\beta}_1 - \beta_1)\bar{x})^2\}$$

$$= E\{\bar{\epsilon}^2 + [(\hat{\beta}_1 - \beta_1)\bar{x}]^2 - 2\bar{\epsilon}(\hat{\beta}_1 - \beta_1)\bar{x}\}$$

$$= \frac{\sigma_\epsilon^2}{n} + \frac{\sigma_\epsilon^2 \bar{x}^2}{(\sum_i x_{di}^2)} - 0 \tag{13.26}$$

$$= \sigma_\epsilon^2 \left(\frac{1}{n} + \frac{\bar{x}^2}{(\sum_i x_{di}^2)} \right)$$

The calculation involving $\bar{\epsilon}^2$ should be familiar from our extensive use of this result in Chapters 7 and 8. The last term in line two of Equation 13.26 is zero because $E\{\bar{\epsilon}(\hat{\beta}_1 - \beta_1)\bar{x}\} = 0$ (see Exercise 13.13).

Finally, we have not yet allowed for the two estimators to be correlated. This is a new problem for us in our investigation of the distributional properties of estimators. We already know that each of $\hat{\beta}_0$ and $\hat{\beta}_1$ is normally distributed, so that we can conclude that they are jointly normally distributed, but we have yet to determine the nature of the correlation between them. We do so now:

$$E\{(\hat{\beta}_0 - \beta_0)(\hat{\beta}_1 - \beta_1)\} = E\left\{ (\bar{\epsilon} - (\hat{\beta}_1 - \beta_1)\bar{x}) \left(\frac{\sum_i \epsilon_{di} x_{di}}{\sum_i x_{di}^2} \right) \right\}$$

$$= -\sigma_\epsilon^2 \frac{\bar{x}}{\sum_i x_{di}^2} \tag{13.27}$$

Confirm these results by substituting into Equation 13.27 and simplifying the algebra. It is easy to show that

$$E\left\{ \bar{\epsilon} \left(\frac{\sum_i \epsilon_{di} x_{di}}{\sum_i x_{di}^2} \right) \right\} = 0$$

because $\sum_i x_{di} = 0$; this result is worked out in detail in Exercise 13.13.

In Equation 13.27, we see that the correlation between the two parameter estimators is a linear function of the mean of the $\{x_i\}$ and that the slope of the relationship is negative for positive $\bar{x}$; a high estimate for β_1 implies a low estimate for β_0, and the strength of the relationship depends on the ratio of the error term variance to the variation in the $\{x_i\}$. If the error term variance is small relative to the variation in the $\{x_i\}$, then the degree of correlation between $\hat{\beta}_0$ and $\hat{\beta}_1$ is low. Intuitively, one can easily understand the negative relationship between the estimates for positive $\bar{x}$. Plot a few points with positive x values to be explained by a linear regression line. Now by eye fit a straight line to the data. As one increases the slope to obtain a better fit the intercept term is reduced, and vice versa. Similar results hold if $\bar{x}$ is negative, except the sign of the relationship changes.

We can interpret these results in terms of actual data. For example, suppose that our regression was between the logarithms of the money supply and levels of GNP, or between weight and height. Small errors in estimating the slope parameter can cause large changes in the estimates of the intercept term. If we overestimate the relationship between weight and height, we will tend to underestimate the overall weight at a height of "zero." If we underestimate the slope parameter between the money supply

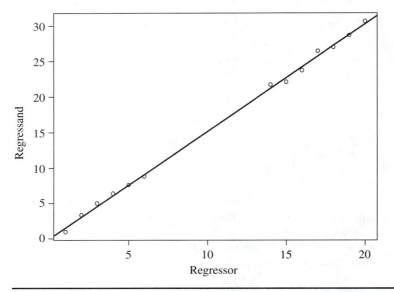

Figure 13.5   Illustration of the effect on estimator variance of the distribution of the regressor values: Alternative I

___

and GNP, we will overestimate the level of GNP associated with a "zero" money supply. Our errors in estimating the relationship between changes in the variables lead us to make compensating errors in the level of the dependent variable that is not a function of changes in the conditioning event.

These comments are illustrated in Figures 13.5 and 13.6. In these figures, note that when the regressor values are spread out the variance of the estimator for β_1 is less than when the regressor values are distributed tightly about the mean of the observed $\{x_i\}$. Further, it is clear that in the former situation the covariance between the estimates will be less than in the second case. In the second case, it is clear from the graph that if there are small variations in the error terms at the extremes of the range of the regression values their impact on the variation in the estimator for β_0 is substantial.

All of the variance and covariance terms we discussed involve the term σ_ϵ^2. So to proceed, we will need an estimator for this parameter as well. Because σ_ϵ^2 is the error term variance, it is natural to consider that an estimator of that variance would be given by the average squared error:

$$\hat{\sigma}_\epsilon^2 = \frac{1}{n} \sum_i \hat{\epsilon}_i^2 \tag{13.28}$$

where

$$\hat{\epsilon}_i = Y_i - \hat{\beta}_0 - \hat{\beta}_1 x_i$$

The symbol $\hat{\epsilon}_i$ is a predictor for the unknown ϵ_i that is determined by the model and the estimators that we have already derived, and it is also normally distributed with

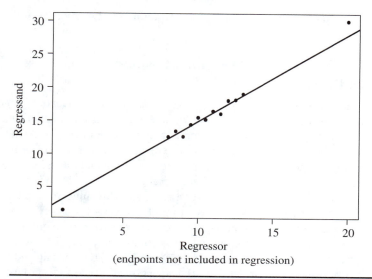

Figure 13.6 Illustration of the effect on estimator variance of the distribution of regressor values: Alternative II

zero mean. Certainly, if we were able to observe the actual model, the expression $\frac{1}{n} \sum_i \epsilon_i^2$ would clearly provide an unbiased estimate of the term, σ_ϵ^2. But we have lost information in having to estimate the two parameters, β_0 and β_1. This difficulty is just like the one we faced when we were obtaining the estimator S^2 for σ^2 in Chapter 10 (Equation 10.6). We discovered that having to estimate the mean, $\bar{x}$, cost us a degree of freedom in that the estimate added a constraint to the distribution of the differences, $(x_i - \bar{x})$. So here as well, by having to estimate two parameters we have lost 2 degrees of freedom. Consequently, an unbiased estimator of the variance of the error terms would be

$$\hat{\sigma}_\epsilon^2 = \frac{1}{n-2} \sum_i \hat{\epsilon}_i^2 \tag{13.29}$$

In the Exercises, you will be asked to prove that $E\{\hat{\sigma}_\epsilon^2\} = \sigma_\epsilon^2$, or $\hat{\sigma}_\epsilon^2$ is unbiased for the parameter σ_ϵ^2.

In Chapter 10, we derived the chi-squared distribution as the distribution for a sum of squared independently distributed Gaussian random variables. Given that $\hat{\epsilon}_i$ is distributed as Gaussian with zero mean and a variance of σ_ϵ^2, we would expect the expression

$$\frac{\sum_i \hat{\epsilon}_i^2}{\sigma_\epsilon^2} \tag{13.30}$$

to be distributed as chi-square as well; this is because each term, $\hat{\epsilon}_i/\sigma_\epsilon$, is distributed as Gaussian with zero mean and unit variance. However, we know from our discussion in Section 10.4 that the chi-square distribution also depends on the degrees of freedom involved. The degrees of freedom in this situation are $(n-2)$, so we may conclude that the distribution of the expression in Equation 13.30 is chi-square with $(n - 2)$ degrees of freedom. It is.

The Coefficient of Determination and the Degree of Fit

A key aspect of running any regression analysis is to evaluate how good the fit is. We need to pose the question as to how much of the variation in consumption is actually explained by the variation in income, or how much of the variation in weight is explained by height. It is all very well to claim that there is a linear relationship between the value of the conditional mean of consumption and the values of the conditioning event income, or between the conditional mean of weight and the conditioning event of height. The question is how good is the fit? How much of the total variation is accounted for by the model? Does our model account for nearly all of the variation, or only some insignificant amount? We can now answer these questions.

In Chapter 5, when we discussed the correlation coefficient, we noted that a correlation coefficient near ± 1 indicated a near functional relationship and hence a "very good fit" of the model to the data; recall that a correlation coefficient of exactly ± 1 indicates an exact functional relationship between the variables. Even though we have extended our ideas about structural relationships to regression analysis and have related our notions about correlation to questions concerning causal mechanisms, the need to summarize our findings in terms of a "measure of the degree of fit" is still important. The fitting of a regression model is a matter of accounting for variation in the data. If there were no variation in the original data, there would be nothing to explain. Throughout the text, we have represented variation in data by the second moment. So the thought naturally occurs that a measure of the degree of fit of a regression model might be the proportion of the total variation in the original data that is accounted for by the model.

The total variation in the data is given by the observed sum of squares:

$$\sum y_i^2 \tag{13.31}$$

which is called the *total sum of squares*. The model is $y_i = \beta_0 + \beta_1 x_i + \epsilon_i$, so the coefficient β_0 merely adds a constant to the values of $\{y_i\}$. We can simplify our problem immediately by rewriting $\{y_i\}$ as

$$y_i = y_{di} + \bar{y}$$

where

$$y_{di} \equiv y_i - \bar{y}$$

With this definition, the total sum of squares of $\{y_i\}$ can be reexpressed as

$$\sum y_i^2 = \sum y_{di}^2 + n\bar{y}^2$$

because

$$\bar{y} \sum y_{di} = 0$$

This expression indicates that the total sum of squares can be separated into the total sum of squares for the y_{di} plus n times the square of $\bar{y}$. The benefit of this reexpression is that we can now simplify the algebra needed to analyze the distribution of the total sum of squares into that part that is due to the model and that part that is due to the presence of errors. We have in fact the following very useful result:

$$\sum y_{di}^2 = \sum \hat{y}_{di}^2 + \sum \hat{\epsilon}_{di}^2 \tag{13.32}$$

where

$$\hat{y}_{di} = \hat{\beta}_1 x_{di}$$

and

$$\hat{\epsilon}_{di} = y_{di} - \hat{y}_{di}$$

We now need to demonstrate this simple, but useful, fact. Consider the square of both sides of the equation:

$$y_{di} = \hat{y}_{di} + \hat{\epsilon}_{di}$$

and if we add over the n observations, we have formally:

$$\sum y_{di}^2 = \sum \hat{y}_{di}^2 + \sum \hat{\epsilon}_{di}^2 + 2 \sum \hat{y}_{di} \hat{\epsilon}_{di} \tag{13.33}$$

We want to show that when the last term in Equation 13.33 reduces to zero, Equation 13.33 reduces to Equation 13.32. Let us rewrite that part of the expression by substituting for the definitions of $\hat{\epsilon}_{di}$ and $\hat{y}_{di}$:

$$\sum \hat{y}_{di} \hat{\epsilon}_{di} = \sum \hat{y}_{di} y_i - \sum \hat{y}_{di} \hat{y}_{di} = 0 \tag{13.34}$$

We accomplish our objective by showing that the two parts of the right side of Equation 13.34 are equal:

$$\sum \hat{y}_{di} y_i = \hat{\beta}_1 \beta_1 \sum x_{di}^2 + \hat{\beta}_1 \sum x_{di} \epsilon_{di}$$

$$= \hat{\beta}_1 \left[\beta_1 \sum x_{di}^2 + \sum x_{di} \epsilon_{di} \right]$$

for the first part, and

$$\sum \hat{y}_{di} \hat{y}_{di} = \hat{\beta}_1^2 \sum x_{di}^2$$

$$= \hat{\beta}_1 \frac{\beta_1 \sum x_{di}^2 + \sum x_{di} \epsilon_{di}}{\sum x_{di}^2} \sum x_{di}^2$$

$$= \hat{\beta}_1 \left[\beta_1 \sum x_{di}^2 + \sum x_{di} \epsilon_{di} \right]$$

for the second part. Given that the two statements are equal, we have the result that was stated in Equation 13.32. Our conclusion is very important, for it says that the **total sum of squares, TSS,** of the original data can be separated into the sum of three parts: (1) the square of the part "accounted for by the model," (2) the squared mean, and (3) the square of the error terms. Symbolically, we have:

$$\sum y_i^2 = \overset{(1)}{\sum} \bar{y}^2 + \overset{(2)}{\sum} \hat{y}_{di}^2 + \overset{(3)}{\sum} \hat{\epsilon}_{di}^2 \tag{13.35}$$

The component $n\bar{y}^2 + \Sigma \hat{y}_{di}^2$ is called the **regression sum of squares, RSS** (about the origin), the component $\Sigma \hat{y}_{di}^2$ is the regression sum of squares, RSS (about the mean), and the component $\Sigma \hat{\epsilon}_{di}^2$, is the **error sum of squares, ESS.** Note that a clear distinction between the regression sum of squares about the mean and about the origin is often not made, so that you have to be careful when interpreting other peoples' work. Because there is usually little theoretical interest in the constant term, β_0, most researchers restrict their analysis to the regression sum of squares about the mean.

We can reexpress Equation 13.35 in a very succinct manner:

$$TSS = RSS + ESS$$

where TSS and RSS have to be interpreted as either about the origin or about the mean. The only restriction is that both TSS and RSS have to be in the same terms. If TSS is about the mean, then so must be RSS, if the equation is to work; and if TSS is about the origin, then so must be RSS.

Now we can answer the question about the degree of fit of any regression. We define R^2, the *multiple coefficient of determination,* by

$$R^2 = \frac{n\bar{y}^2 + \sum \hat{y}_{di}^2}{\sum y_i^2} \tag{13.36}$$

R^2 shows the *proportion* of the total variation in $\{y_i\}$ that is accounted for by the model; R^2 is nothing more than the ratio of RSS to TSS. The **multiple coefficient of determination** quantifies the degree of association between more than two variables. Often, we are not very concerned about the constant term, β_0, and hence we restrict attention to the regression model in terms of deviations about the mean; in short, we have

$$R_d^2 = \frac{\sum \hat{y}_{di}^2}{\sum y_{di}^2} \tag{13.37}$$

The interpretation of R_d^2 is that it shows the proportion of the total variance about the mean that is accounted for by the regression equation; and R_d^2 also is simply the ratio of RSS to TSS. From Equation 13.35, it is clear that both R^2 and R_d^2 are bounded by the limits of 0 and 1, respectively. If the model explains nothing so that $\Sigma \hat{y}_{di}^2 = 0$, or even $n\bar{y}^2 + \Sigma \hat{y}_{di}^2 = 0$, then the appropriate version of R^2 is zero. On the other extreme, if $\Sigma \hat{\epsilon}_{di}^2$ is identically 0, then R^2 and R_d^2 are both 1.

Suppose for a moment, merely to simplify notation, that $\bar{y}^2$ is zero. We can rewrite R_d^2 in the following manner:

$$R_d^2 = \frac{\sum \hat{y}_{di}^2}{\sum y_{di}^2} = \frac{\hat{\beta}_1^2 \sum x_{di}^2}{\sum y_{di}^2}$$

$$= \frac{\left(\sum y_{di} x_{di} / \sum x_{di}^2\right)^2 \sum x_{di}^2}{\sum y_{di}^2}$$

(13.38)

$$= \frac{\left(\sum y_{di} x_{di}\right)^2}{\sum x_{di}^2 \sum y_{di}^2}$$

$$= r^2$$

Equation 13.38 demonstrates, in this simple situation using the model $y_i = \beta_1 x_i + \epsilon_i$, that the multiple coefficient of determination is nothing more than the squared correlation coefficient. We qualified this with "in this simple situation," for the result does not carry over to the case in which there is more than one regressor on the right side in addition to the constant term. For example, we could easily propose a regression equation of the following form:

$$y_i = \beta_0 + \beta_1 x_{1i} + \beta_2 x_{2i} + \beta_3 x_{3i} + \epsilon_i$$

(13.39)

This equation represents a **multiple regression** involving one regressand, y_i, three regressors, $\{x_{1i}, x_{2i}, x_{3i}\}$, a constant term, and an error term. In this situation, the coefficient of determination is still defined by Equations 13.36 or 13.37; but there are now several correlation coefficients, one for each pair of variables.

We can conclude this section by summarizing the calculations for the regressions on the data sets in Table 13.1. These results are presented in Table 13.2; the corresponding units of measurement are in Table 13.1. Ignore for the moment the entry for "F statistic."

In each case, observe that the regression coefficients are estimated with values that are many times greater than their estimated standard deviations. In all cases, the estimated correlation between the two regression parameters is negative and sizable, and the estimated coefficient of determination for the proportion of the variation of the dependent variable accounted for by the model is very large.

Notice that consumption increases with income, but for the measures used only about one-half of each increment of income increases consumption. GNP also increases

Table 13.1 **Estimates for the Basic Parameters for a Selection of Pairs of Variables**

Parameter	Consumption/Income	logGNP/logM	Car mpg/Weight
$\hat{\mu}_Y$	115.2 in $\$10^6$	11.97 in log$\$$	28.7 mpg
$\hat{\mu}_X$	185.7 in $\$10^6$	4.30 in log$\$$	2676.2 lb.
$\hat{\sigma}_Y^2$	6,014 in $\$10^{12}$	0.999 in log$\$^2$	54.3 mpg^2
$\hat{\sigma}_X^2$	24,309 in $\$10^{12}$	1.068 in log$\$^2$	366,592 lb.^{2}
$\hat{\rho}$	0.995	0.989	−0.83
$\hat{\beta}_0$	23.2 in $\$10^6$	7.74 in log$\$$	55.6 mpg
$\hat{\beta}_1$	0.495	0.985	−0.010 mpg/lb.

Table 13.2 **Summary of the Regression Estimates**

Parameters	Consumption/Income	logGNP/logM	Car mpg/Weight
$\hat{\beta}_0$	23.22	7.74	55.64
$\hat{\beta}_1$	0.495	0.985	−0.01
Std($\hat{\beta}_0$)	1.19	0.083	1.55
Std($\hat{\beta}_1$)	0.005	0.019	0.0006
Cor($\hat{\beta}_0$, $\hat{\beta}_1$)	−0.77	−0.97	−0.98
R_d^2	0.99	0.979	0.68
F statistic	$10050_{1,93}$	$2759_{1,60}$	$317.2_{1,148}$

with the money supply. But mileage decreases with car weight. For the latter, for every 10 pounds of weight, the estimated reduction in mileage is 0.1 mile per gallon. Compare the graphs of the observed data with the fitted regression line for these two cases (see Figures 13.7 and 13.8). In particular, the graph for car mileage and car weight indicates that the appropriate regression line may well not be linear, and that the second moments may also be functions of the conditioning variable car weight.

We can have a lot of confidence in the values of the regression coefficients obtained, and our models have clearly accounted for a significant proportion of the total variation; our results are operationally significant. However, we are still dealing with observed statistics, so we recognize that not only might the true values of the coefficients differ substantially from those we have presented, but that we must be very cautious in assigning any idea of causality to these results. Indeed, even for the mileage regression for which we might well guess that "weight" *causes* a reduction in mileage, we should recognize that these regression results were obtained from historical data. Our results are very much dependent on the sample of cars chosen. Our

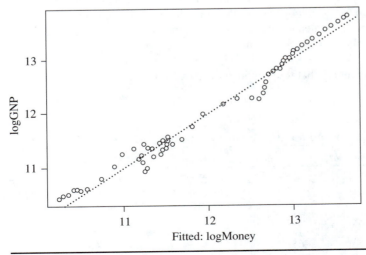

Figure 13.7   Plot of logGNP on logMoney supply with fitted model

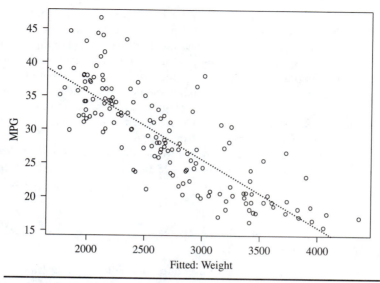

Figure 13.8   Plot of the observed car mpg on car weight with fitted model

results represent "history," but by no means anything that we would label "causal." Further, we have already noted that the model that we used for the regression analysis of the car mileage data might not be correct, even though we obtained very strong fits to the data. In addition, notwithstanding the seemingly very good regression results for the relationship between logGNP and logMoney supply, we should note that there is much controversy in economics over the proper relationship between money and GNP. In particular, we must recognize that the results obtained are quite definitely influenced by the historical events that generated the data; we would expect to see different coefficient values if we analyzed data from a different country or from the same country over a different time period. "Causality" is a very difficult concept to pin down in a nonexperimental discipline and is not very easy even within an experimental discipline that has great control over experimental conditions.

13.5   Estimation and Inference: Confidence Intervals and Hypotheses Tests

We are now prepared to determine confidence intervals and set up tests of hypotheses in the context of regression analysis, just as we did in Chapters 10 and 11 for the univariate models. The principles that we learned in Chapters 10 and 11 apply here as well, even though occasionally some of the algebra may seem a bit more complicated. We shall set up confidence intervals for the parameters of the regression and will indicate how to test hypotheses on their values.

Some of the questions that we can now pose are to query whether the slope coefficient in the regression of logGNP on logMoney supply is unity or whether the slope relationship between car mileage and weight is .01 or more. Sometimes we want to ask whether the intercept is zero, for if it is we have a relationship that is proportional; this is a claim for the relationship between long-term consumption and "permanent" income. Further, if we have confidence in the continued relevance of our model and its estimates, we may want to forecast the values of the dependent variable given some possibly unobserved values for the regressor. For example, in the car mileage case we may want to predict the mileage of either very heavy or very light cars, using the same engine technology. In all these examples, we are interested in using our results to infer more general statements and to be able to test meaningful hypotheses that are of pragmatic interest.

We begin with the case in which we do not know the variance of the error terms. We presume to know the model as we have outlined it, including the distribution of the error terms, but we do not know the values of any of the parameters. Before continuing, a quick review of the principles developed in Chapters 10 and 11 would be helpful.

Confidence Intervals for the Regression Parameters

In Section 4, Chapter 10, we introduced the Student's T distribution to be used when the unknown variance of a normally distributed variable was involved. With respect to $\hat{\beta}_0$ and $\hat{\beta}_1$, we have a similar problem in that the value of σ_ϵ^2 is unknown. Following our development in Section 10.4 and using the statistical properties summarized in Equations 13.24, 13.26, and 13.29, we define for each parameter:

$$\frac{\hat{\beta}_0 - \beta_0}{\hat{\sigma}_\epsilon \sqrt{1/n + \bar{x}^2/\sum x_{di}^2}} \tag{13.40}$$

$$\frac{(\hat{\beta}_1 - \beta_1)\sqrt{\sum x_{di}^2}}{\hat{\sigma}_\epsilon} \tag{13.41}$$

These are the Student's T statistics. In each case, we have written the ratio of a standard Gaussian variable to the square root of a random variable that is distributed as chi-square with $(n - 2)$ degrees of freedom. Recall from Chapter 10 that such a ratio is distributed as Student's T with $(n - 2)$ degrees of freedom.

For example, in Equation 13.41, the result is obtained by taking the ratio of

$$\frac{(\hat{\beta}_1 - \beta_1)\sqrt{\sum x_{di}^2}}{\sigma_\epsilon} \tag{13.42}$$

and

$$\frac{\hat{\sigma}_\epsilon}{\sigma_\epsilon} \tag{13.43}$$

so that the common unknown σ_ϵ is canceled. The expression in Equation 13.42 is that of a random variable that is distributed as normal with zero mean and unit variance; the expression in Equation 13.43 is that of a random variable that is distributed proportional to the square root of a chi-squared variable with $(n - 2)$ degrees of freedom. The ratio of 13.42 to 13.43 yields the expression in Equation 13.41. A similar analysis holds for the derivation of the expression in Equation 13.40.

To illustrate the use of these results, consider the case in which one wants to obtain a 90% confidence interval for an estimated value of $\hat{\beta}_1$ of .8, using 20 observations, the estimated standard deviation is 1.2, and the observed value for $\sqrt{\Sigma x_{di}^2}$ is 4.3. What are the lower and upper bounds for a 90% confidence interval for the estimated β_1? Recall Equation 10.27. Let T represent the statistic defined in Equation 13.41. We have, following the procedure in Chapter 10,

$$\text{pr}[-d_\alpha \leq T \leq d_\alpha] = (1 - \alpha)$$

or

$$\text{pr}[-1.70 \leq T \leq 1.70] = .90 \tag{13.44}$$

This interval was calculated using a Student's T distribution with $(20 - 2) = 18$ degrees of freedom and assigning an α level of .1, so that $(1 - \alpha) = .9$. We can obtain these bounds as in Chapter 10 by integrating the Student's T distribution over the appropriate interval using <u>Labs, Statistical Tables</u>. We proceed by substituting into Equation 13.44 the expression that is distributed as T and is defined in Equation 13.41. We obtain

$$\text{pr}[-1.70 \leq T \leq 1.70] = \text{pr}\left[-1.70 \leq \frac{(\hat{\beta}_1 - \beta_1)\sqrt{\Sigma x_{di}^2}}{\hat{\sigma}_\epsilon} \leq 1.70\right]$$

$$= \text{pr}\left[\hat{\beta}_1 - \frac{1.70\hat{\sigma}_\epsilon}{\sqrt{\Sigma x_{di}^2}} \leq \beta_1 \leq \hat{\beta}_1 + \frac{1.70\hat{\sigma}_\epsilon}{\sqrt{\Sigma x_{di}^2}}\right]$$

$$= \text{pr}\left[.8 - \frac{1.70 \times 1.2}{4.3} \leq \beta_1 \leq .8 + \frac{1.70 \times 1.2}{4.3}\right]$$

$$= \text{pr}[.33 \leq \beta_1 \leq 1.27] = .90$$

We conclude that a 90% confidence interval using the Student's T distribution with 18 degrees of freedom for an estimated $\hat{\beta}_1$ of .8 is [0.33, 1.27].

An interesting question is whether it is plausible that the slope coefficient relating logGNP to logMoney supply is unity. By using these procedures, we can easily provide a confidence interval for the appropriate coefficient. Let us choose a relatively large alpha level, say .2, to examine a fairly short confidence interval given that we are most interested in the region around unity.

From our results, we have

$$\text{pr}[-d_\alpha \leq T \leq d_\alpha] = (1 - \alpha)$$

or

$$\text{pr}[-1.296 \leq T \leq 1.296] = .80$$

where the observed statistic t is defined by

$$t = \frac{(\hat{\beta}_1 - \beta_1)\sqrt{\sum x_{di}^2}}{\hat{\sigma}_\epsilon}$$

$$\hat{\beta}_1 = .985$$

$$\frac{\hat{\sigma}_\epsilon}{\sqrt{\sum x_{di}^2}} = .0188$$

From these results we derive the 80% confidence interval as

$$\text{pr}\left[\hat{\beta}_1 - \frac{1.296\hat{\sigma}_\epsilon}{\sqrt{\sum x_{di}^2}} \le \beta_1 \le \hat{\beta}_1 + \frac{1.296\hat{\sigma}_\epsilon}{\sqrt{\sum x_{di}^2}} \right] =$$

$$\text{pr}[.985 - 1.296 \times .0188 \le \beta_1 \le .985 + 1.296 \times .0188] =$$

$$\text{pr}[.961 \le \beta_1 \le 1.009]$$

We conclude that even at a relatively low level of confidence, to achieve a narrow confidence interval, the observed interval does cover unity. We can tentatively conclude that the unknown coefficient is at least close to unity. In short, a unit increase in the logMoney supply is apparently associated with a unit increase in logGNP, after allowing for the differences in the original units of measurement that were specified in Table 13.1.

Predicting the Dependent Variable

A special and important example of estimation is called *prediction;* if the sequences of data are consecutive points in time (time series), the process is called *forecasting.* **Predicting** is the process of estimating the response of the dependent variable to a specified occurrence of the independent, or regressor, variable. Recall the basic regression equation:

$$y_i = \beta_0 + \beta_1 x_i + \epsilon_i$$

Let us define a predicted value of the random variable Y conditional on observing $X = x_0, \check{Y}_0$. The specified value of X, x_0, is some value of X and need not be contained in the set of values of X that were used in estimating the parameters β_0 and β_1. Indeed, this is often the case in that the prediction of Y depends on a value of x_0 that is not even contained in the range of values of $\{x_i\}$. We define the *predictor* of the conditional mean of Y by

$$\check{Y}_0 = \hat{\beta}_0 + \hat{\beta}_1 x_0 \tag{13.45}$$

where $\hat{\beta}_0$ and $\hat{\beta}_1$ are the least squares estimators. We distinguish between $\check{Y}_0$, the predictor of the conditional mean of Y given a specified value for X, from the results obtained from regressing $\{y_i\}$ on the model and the observed values $\{x_i\}$ to obtain the fitted values $\{\hat{y}_i\}$. The choice of such an estimator seems to be natural enough. But we should check that the estimator has reasonable statistical properties. This is easily done:

$$E\{\check{Y}_0\} = E\{\hat{\beta}_0 + \hat{\beta}_1 x_0\}$$
$$= \beta_0 + \beta_1 x_0$$

(13.46)

so that our predictor, $\check{Y}_0$, is unbiased for the conditional mean of Y given $X = x_0$. Further, given that $\check{Y}_0$ is a linear sum of $\hat{\beta}_0$ and $\hat{\beta}_1$, and these variables are themselves normally distributed variables, we conclude that so is $\check{Y}_0$. Our last task is to determine the variance of our prediction:

$$\text{var}(\check{Y}_0) = E\{(\check{Y}_0 - (\beta_0 + \beta_1 x_0))^2\}$$
$$= E\{[(\hat{\beta}_0 - \beta_0) + (\hat{\beta}_1 - \beta_1)x_0]^2\}$$
$$= E\{(\hat{\beta}_0 - \beta_0)^2 + [(\hat{\beta}_1 - \beta_1)x_0]^2 + 2(\hat{\beta}_0 - \beta_0)(\hat{\beta}_1 - \beta_1)x_0\}$$

(13.47)

From this equation we see that the variance of $\check{Y}_0$ is a weighted sum of the variances and covariances of the estimators of the regression parameters. Using our results, we can immediately write down the variance for the predictor of the conditional mean.

$$\text{var}(\check{Y}_0) = \sigma_\epsilon^2 \left(\frac{1}{n} + \frac{\bar{x}^2}{(\sum_i x_{di}^2)} \right) + \frac{\sigma_\epsilon^2 x_0^2}{(\sum_i x_{di}^2)} - 2\sigma_\epsilon^2 \frac{\bar{x} x_0}{\sum_i x_{di}^2}$$

$$= \sigma_\epsilon^2 \left[\frac{1}{n} + \frac{\bar{x}^2}{(\sum_i x_{di}^2)} + \frac{x_0^2}{(\sum_i x_{di}^2)} - \frac{2\bar{x} x_0}{\sum_i x_{di}^2} \right]$$

$$= \sigma_\epsilon^2 \left[\frac{1}{n} + \frac{(x_0 - \bar{x})^2}{(\sum_i x_{di}^2)} \right]$$

(13.48)

The variance indicated in the last line is interesting. There are two components: The first term reflects the variance involved in estimating the unknown value of σ_ϵ^2; the second term involves the variance induced by estimating the slope parameter, β_1. Note that the prediction error is least for values of X in the neighborhood of $\bar{x}$; the further x_0 is from $\bar{x}$ the greater is the variance. This implication will be illustrated in the Exercises. Our first and perhaps most important lesson in prediction is that the predictions that are the most accurate are those closest to the mean of X. The farther the specified value of X is from the mean, the greater is the variance, and the increase in variance is proportional to the square of the difference between x_0 and $\bar{x}$. Notice further, that the bigger $\Sigma_i x_{di}^2$, the less is the impact of this effect. So that if one can control the values of $\{x_i\}$ used to estimate the parameters, one's optimal choice is as large a variation as can be accomplished. Notice further, that while the first term in the variance of the prediction declines as the number of observations, n, increases, the increase in n does not necessarily imply an increase in the size of $\Sigma_i x_{di}^2$.

We might also be interested in predicting the value of the dependent variable itself; that is, we want to predict, conditional on $X = x_0$, the value of y_0. This is the sum of the conditional mean and a *new realization* of the error term:

$$y_0 = \beta_0 + \beta_1 x_0 + \epsilon_0$$

(13.49)

The unbiased predictor is just $Y_0 = \hat{\beta}_0 + \hat{\beta}_1 x_0$ as before. The expected difference between the predictor and the variable is zero, so that the estimator is unbiased:

$$E\{Y_0 - \hat{\beta}_0 + \hat{\beta}_1 x_0\} = 0 \tag{13.50}$$

or

$$E\{Y_0 - \check{Y}_0\} = 0$$

The difference in the two cases arises when we assess the variance of the estimator in that we now have an extra term. Because the new, as yet unobserved error term, ϵ_0, is distributed independently of the disturbance terms in the calculation of $\hat{\beta}_0$ and $\hat{\beta}_1$, we can simply add the variance of the disturbance term to Equation 13.48:

$$\text{var}(Y_0) = \sigma_\epsilon^2 \left[1 + \frac{1}{n} + \frac{(x_0 - \bar{x})^2}{\left(\sum_i x_{di}^2 \right)} \right] \tag{13.51}$$

Note that the only difference between this variance calculation and that in Equation 13.48 is the "1" inside the bracket.

Now that we have the variances stated precisely, it is a simple extension of our previous work to determine a confidence interval for either the conditional mean, $\check{y}_0$, or y_0 itself. In the equation for the variance, either Equation 13.48 or 13.51, we need only substitute an estimate for σ_ϵ^2, which has already been given by Equation 13.29. We can proceed in exactly the same manner we used to create a confidence interval for the regression parameters, using the Student's T distribution. Because a prediction is simply a linear combination of the regression parameters, we can use all the previously derived theory in this case as well. Recall Equations 13.40 and 13.41. Thus, the estimator

$$T = \frac{(\check{Y}_0 - Y_0)}{\hat{\sigma}_\epsilon \sqrt{\left[\frac{1}{n} + \frac{(x_0 - \bar{x})^2}{\left(\sum_i x_{di}^2 \right)} \right]}}$$

$$\hat{\sigma}_\epsilon = \sqrt{\frac{1}{n-2} \sum \hat{\epsilon}_i^2}$$

$$Y_0 = \beta_0 + \beta_1 x_0 \tag{13.52}$$

is distributed as Student's T with $(n - 2)$ degrees of freedom. We can therefore choose a confidence level, say α_0, and calculate from the Student's T distribution with $(n - 2)$ degrees of freedom the $\alpha_0/2$ critical bounds, say $t_{\alpha_0/2}$, and immediately write the $(1 - \alpha_0)$ confidence interval. If we write

$$\hat{\sigma}_f = \hat{\sigma}_\epsilon \sqrt{\left[\frac{1}{n} + \frac{(x_0 - \bar{x})^2}{\left(\sum_i x_{di}^2 \right)} \right]} \tag{13.53}$$

the $(1 - \alpha_0)$ confidence interval for Y_0 is

$$[\check{y}_0 - t_{\alpha_0/2} \times \hat{\sigma}_f, \check{y}_0 + t_{\alpha_0/2} \times \hat{\sigma}_f] \tag{13.54}$$

Table 13.3 **Table of Predictions for Car Mileage**

Weight	Forecast	Standard Error	90% Lower	90% Upper
1000	45.6	1.01	44.30	46.88
2500	30.5	0.35	30.06	30.97
5000	5.40	1.35	3.66	7.14

where $\check{y}_0$ is the sample estimate obtained from the estimator $\check{Y}_0$. To provide a confidence interval for y_0, where $y_0 = \check{y}_0 + \epsilon_0$, the only change needed is to add a "1" inside the bracket in Equation 13.53. I will provide an example later, but for now you recognize that although the formula for $\hat{\sigma}_f$ is complicated relative to that for the individual regression coefficients, the principles are exactly the same as those we have used repeatedly in Chapter 10 (recall Section 10.4).

Consider as an example the problem of determining a confidence interval for car mileage, if the corresponding car weight is only 1000 pounds and when it is 5000 pounds; the minimum observed weight was 1755 pounds and the maximum was only 4360 pounds. For comparison, consider a weight of 2500 pounds that is close to the median weight. The predictions with their 90% confidence level bounds are presented in Table 13.3

The entries in Table 13.3 were obtained from the regression routines in S-Plus using the "Predict" options. We substituted estimates for the parameters in Equation 13.52, and set the value for x_0 to 1000, 2500, and 5000. We observe that the standard error of estimate for the forecasts is least at a weight of 2500, which is near the mean weight of 2676 pounds. Further, we see that lowering or raising the weight significantly beyond the values used in the regression yields substantial and startling results.

In the examples in the next subsection, I will further illustrate the variation in confidence widths that is due to the contribution to the standard error arising from the component $(x_0 - \bar{x})^2$ of Equation 13.53.

More Examples   Xfiles contains a folder called Firmdata, which records various financial and operational data on an annual basis for a selection of firms over the period 1975 to 1994. One of these firms is Digital Equipment Corporation. We examine a simple regression of sales on inventory to focus on the relationship between these two variables; the data are plotted in Figure 13.9. The R^2 value obtained from this regression was .659, a reasonably large value.

The coefficient estimates and standard errors for the regression parameters are

$$\hat{\beta}_0 = -1304.03, \ \text{Std.Er.} = 1782.9$$
$$\hat{\beta}_1 = 16.06, \quad \ \text{Std.Er.} = 2.891$$

The value "2.891" is obtained by dividing the residual standard error, $\hat{\sigma}_\epsilon = 3007$, by the square root of the sum of squares of the inventory variable, $\sqrt{\Sigma x_{di}^2} = 1040.1$ (see Equations 13.23 and 13.29). The standard error of the estimate of $\hat{\beta}_0$ is obtained similarly. With 16 degrees of freedom on 18 observations, the critical bound for a Student's T

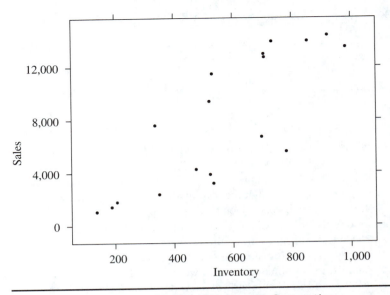

Figure 13.9   Plot of sales on inventory for Digital Equipment Corporation

distribution at a confidence of $(1 - \alpha) = .90$ is 1.75. Consequently, 90% confidence intervals for $\hat{\beta}_0$ and $\hat{\beta}_1$ are

$$\hat{\beta}_0 : [-1304.3 - 1.75 \times 1782.9, -1304.3 + 1.75 \times 1782.9]$$

or

$$[-4424.4, 1815.8]$$

$$\hat{\beta}_1 : [16.06 - 1.75 \times 2.89, 16.06 + 1.75 \times 2.89]$$

or

$$[11.00, 21.12]$$

What have we learned from these results? First, we can reasonably conclude that there is a positive relationship between sales and inventory levels, but we know to be very cautious about imputing any idea of causality to these regression results. Further, it would appear that the constant term is very likely zero; we could obtain an interval including zero with much higher confidence levels than that used earlier. The estimated degree of association between sales and inventory levels is between 11 and 21 units of sales to a unit change in inventory levels. Note very carefully, this does *not* mean that if one were to increase inventory levels that sales would increase; indeed, this is a palpably false statement. What the result does say is that, *historically,* we observe higher sales levels associated with higher inventory levels; this result is probably the outcome of a complex decision-making process used by management. If management were to alter their decision-making procedures, the observed historical relationship would no longer hold.

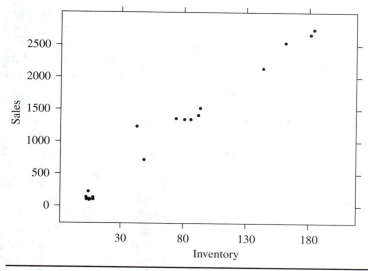

Figure 13.10   Plot of sales on inventory for Hasbro

Let us consider a related example. In the same folder, there are 20 observations on the same variables for the firm Hasbro, the toy manufacturer (see Figure 13.10). The coefficient estimates are

$$\hat{\beta}_0 = 97.23, \ \text{Std.Er.} = 44.95$$
$$\hat{\beta}_1 = 14.76, \ \text{Std.Er.} = 0.51$$

the R^2 value was 0.98, and the estimated standard error of the disturbance terms was 143.2. If we calculate a 90% confidence interval for Hasbro data, the results are

$$\hat{\beta}_0 : [97.23 - 1.33 \times 44.95, 97.23 + 1.33 \times 44.95]$$

or

$$[37.4, 157.0]$$

$$\hat{\beta}_1 : [14.76 - 1.33 \times 0.51, 14.76 + 1.33 \times 0.51]$$

or

$$[14.08, 15.44]$$

Notice, there are both differences and similarities. Even though we have chosen the same confidence level, the calculated critical bound for the Student's T distribution is now only 1.33 instead of 1.75; the reason is that there are 20 observations in the Hasbro data, whereas there are only 18 observations in the Digital data. Consequently, the Hasbro intervals are narrower than those for Digital at the same confidence level and for the same estimated standard error of estimate.

Notice also that the standard errors for both coefficients in the Hasbro data are much smaller than for Digital. The Hasbro intercept term would seem to be greater than zero for any reasonable confidence level, whereas the constant term for Digital seemed to be zero. The estimated slope coefficients for the two firms are remarkably similar, 16.1 versus 14.8; we might speculate whether or not they are the same, and we will return to this question later.

We now have the results from two regressions between the same variables over the same time period but involving different firms. What speculative conclusions might we draw that we might test with additional data using different firms and possibly different time periods? It would seem that there is a positive relationship observed between sales and inventory and that the degree of relationship, if not the same across firms, is very similar. We know that we have merely observed an "association" between these variables, but our results indicate that we might well be rewarded by trying to discover why and how these variables are so closely related. Presumably, the answer lies in analyzing the decision-making process of the firms' management. One might speculate that firms facing a projected increase in sales would arrange to increase inventory levels accordingly, so that a regression between contemporaneous observations on sales and inventories would yield the results observed.

Here we have an example of statistical analysis leading to theoretical speculations and to more detailed research. This is one of the best examples of the benefits of this type of empirical research.

Let us consider one more example. In the folder Energy, the subfolder auseng.xls contains annual data from 1971 to 1991 on various GDP statistics, energy use, exports, and imports. Let us consider Australia as an agricultural country that is rapidly industrializing. In this connection, what is the association, if any, between industrial production (indprod) and agricultural production (agprod)? We have 21 observations. Let us consider only the value of the estimated slope coefficient, because the intercept term is of no great interest. The estimated R^2 is a respectable .80. The estimated value for β_1 is .097 and its corresponding standard error is .011, with an observed Student's T statistic of 8.71, a result that is significant at any reasonable confidence level. We conclude that agricultural and industrial production, at least in these levels, are positively correlated. The reason for this is most likely that both are the outcome of growth in the overall economy; agricultural production rises for the same reasons that industrial production rises. A more careful analysis might discover that after allowing for the overall drift up in the Australian GDP—that is, after allowing for factors that are common to the growth in both subsectors—there may well be a very different relationship between these two important sectors of the Australian economy.

As a final illustration in this section, let us consider the estimated widths of the confidence intervals for predicting the conditional mean of the regressand. Our example uses the data from Hasbro in the folder Firmdata. One of the outputs from the regression routine that I used to provide the earlier calculations is a set of columns that represent the fitted values, the estimated standard error of the fit given the observed value for the regressor, and the lower and upper confidence interval bounds for each observation (see Figure 13.11). One thing that we observe very clearly in this figure is that in the vicinity of the means of the regressor and the regressand, the confidence interval width is minimal, whereas on the tails, the interval is largest as was indicated by the term $(x_0 - \bar{x})^2$ in Equation 13.53. For values of the regressor in the vicinity of

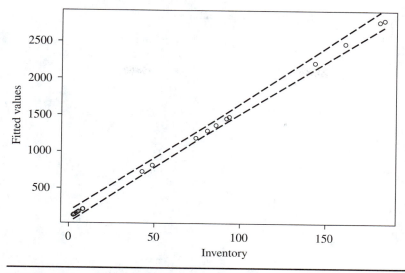

Figure 13.11   95% Confidence intervals for Hasbro forecasts

the mean the forecast interval is minimum; for example, for the fitted value 1189 the standard error of fit is 32.6, whereas for fitted values of 173 and 2811, the standard errors of fit are, respectively, approximately 43 and 70.

Confidence Intervals for the Error Term Standard Deviation

Recall from Chapter 10, Section 10.4, that we can obtain a confidence interval for the error term standard deviation σ_ϵ by noting that Equation 13.30 is distributed as chi-square with $(n - 2)$ degrees of freedom. The procedure that we follow here is almost exactly the same as that we used in Chapter 10 (Equation 10.30). Let us use a confidence level of 95% and let W represent the expression in Equation 13.31. Suppose that the observed value for $\sum_i \hat{\epsilon}_i^2$ is 21.6; this was obtained from our earlier values by multiplying 1.2, the estimate for σ_ϵ^2, by 18, the degrees of freedom. We have

$$\text{pr}[d_{\alpha 1} \leq W \leq d_{\alpha 2}] = (1 - \alpha)$$

$$= \text{pr}\left[d_{\alpha 1} \leq \frac{\sum_i \hat{\epsilon}_i^2}{\sigma_\epsilon^2} \leq d_{\alpha 2}\right]$$

$$= \text{pr}\left[\frac{d_{\alpha 1}}{\sum_i \hat{\epsilon}_i^2} \leq \frac{1}{\sigma_\epsilon^2} \leq \frac{d_{\alpha 2}}{\sum_i \hat{\epsilon}_i^2}\right]$$

$$= \text{pr}\left[\frac{\sum_i \hat{\epsilon}_i^2}{d_{\alpha 2}} \leq \sigma_\epsilon^2 \leq \frac{\sum_i \hat{\epsilon}_i^2}{d_{\alpha 1}}\right] \qquad (13.55)$$

$$= \text{pr}\left[\sqrt{\frac{\sum_i \hat{\epsilon}_i^2}{d_{\alpha 2}}} \leq \sigma_\epsilon \leq \sqrt{\frac{\sum_i \hat{\epsilon}_i^2}{d_{\alpha 1}}}\right]$$

$$= (1 - \alpha)$$

Choose values for $d_{\alpha 1}, d_{\alpha 2}$, such that

$$\text{pr}[W \leq d_{\alpha 1}] = \frac{\alpha}{2}$$

$$\text{pr}[W \geq d_{\alpha 2}] = \frac{\alpha}{2}$$

We now have, using $S^2 = \sum_i \hat{\epsilon}_i^2 / \nu = 1.2$, where $\nu = 18$ degrees of freedom:

$$(1 - \alpha) = \text{pr}\left[\sqrt{\frac{\sum_i \hat{\epsilon}_i^2}{d_{\alpha 2}}} \leq \sigma_\epsilon \leq \sqrt{\frac{\sum_i \hat{\epsilon}_i^2}{d_{\alpha 1}}} \right]$$

$$= \text{pr}\left[\sqrt{\frac{S^2 \nu}{d_{\alpha 2}}} \leq \sigma_\epsilon \leq \sqrt{\frac{S^2 \nu}{d_{\alpha 1}}} \right]$$

$$= \text{pr}\left[S\sqrt{\frac{\nu}{d_{\alpha 2}}} \leq \sigma_\epsilon \leq S\sqrt{\frac{\nu}{d_{\alpha 1}}} \right]$$

$$= \text{pr}\left[1.095 \times 0.756 \leq \sigma_\epsilon \leq 1.095 \times 1.48 \right]$$

$$= \text{pr}\left[0.83 \leq \sigma_\epsilon \leq 1.62 \right] = 0.95$$

And we have a 95% confidence interval for the error term standard deviation when the estimated standard deviation is $1.095 = \sqrt{1.2}$.

The *F* Distribution and Measuring the Goodness of Fit

Earlier, we defined R^2 and R_d^2 as measures of the degree of fit of the model to the data. In principle, if R^2, or R_d^2, is approximately 1, then we can reasonably claim that we have obtained a good fit to the data. But if we obtain quite a small value for R^2 it is not clear whether we are observing a low level of fit, or there is really no explanatory power in the model and our nonzero value for R^2 is purely due to chance.

This puzzle is even more important when we recognize that when we add a regressor to the list of regressors, the value of R^2 cannot decrease. More precisely, if the correct model were

$$y_i = \beta_0 + \beta_1 x_i + \epsilon_i$$

but we were to consider the extended model

$$y_i = \beta_0 + \beta_1 x_i + \beta_2 z_i + \epsilon_i$$

where the variable $\{z_i\}$ is any variable, then the worst that can happen is that the value of R^2 will not decrease and could even increase. An exercise is provided to explore this issue.

We need a confidence interval for R^2, or R_d^2. Unfortunately, because the components of R^2, RSS, and TSS are correlated, deriving the appropriate distribution is very difficult, and the result is not simple. However, our research has shown us that the correlation between the estimated residuals and the estimated conditional means is always zero (see Equation 13.34). We have also said that the error terms are distributed independently of the $\{x_i\}$ and are Gaussian. Consequently, RSS and ESS are independently distributed. We have already seen that ESS/σ_ϵ^2 is distributed as chi-square with $(n-2)$ degrees of freedom.

We need to do a bit more thinking to examine the situation with respect to RSS. Let us keep life very simple to begin and agree to examine the regression only in terms of deviations about the mean, so that both TSS and RSS are defined in terms of sums of squares about the mean; we do not care about the effect of $\bar{y}$ on the results. Now, if the model had no relevance—that is, if β_1 were zero—and we were to estimate β_1 in any case using our procedures, our estimator for $\beta_1 = 0$ is

$$
\begin{aligned}
\hat{\beta}_1 &= \frac{\sum_i Y_{di} x_{di}}{\sum_i x_{di}^2} \\
&= 0 + \frac{\sum_i \epsilon_{di} x_{di}}{\sum_i x_{di}^2}
\end{aligned}
\tag{13.56}
$$

which from our assumptions is distributed as normal with zero mean and from Equation 13.24 has a variance of $\sigma_\epsilon^2/(\Sigma_i x_{di}^2)$. Given that we are continuing the analysis conditional on the observed values for the $\{x_i\}$, we can immediately conclude that $\hat{\beta}_1 x_{di}$ also has a mean of zero, is distributed as Gaussian, and that its variance is $\sigma_\epsilon^2 x_{di}^2/(\sum_i x_{di}^2)$. Consequently, if we now consider the corresponding standardized variable, say $\{\tilde{Y}_i\}$—that is:

$$
\tilde{Y}_i = \frac{\hat{\beta}_1 x_{di}}{\sigma_\epsilon \sqrt{\frac{x_{di}^2}{\left(\sum_i x_{di}^2\right)}}}
\tag{13.57}
$$

we see that $\tilde{Y}_i$ is distributed as normal with zero mean and unit variance. Following our previous line of reasoning we would suspect that the sum of the $\{\tilde{Y}_i^2\}$ would be distributed as chi-square. There is, however, one last difficulty and that is to determine the degrees of freedom, but this turns out to be very simple. The sum of the $\{\tilde{Y}_i^2\}$ actually involves only the one random variable, $\hat{\beta}_1$, so the degree of freedom is only 1. We can see this in another way. The total degrees of freedom for the total sum of squares is n, the degrees of freedom associated with the mean, $\bar{y}$, is 1, and the degrees of freedom associated with ESS are $(n-2)$. By definition, the sum of the degrees of freedom on the right side must add up to the total degrees of freedom. So, we conclude by this approach as well, that the degree of freedom for RSS is also 1; $n = 1 + 1 + (n-2)$. We can simplify the expression shown in Equation 13.57:

$$
\sum \tilde{Y}_i^2 = \frac{\hat{\beta}_1^2 (\sum_i x_{di}^2)}{\sigma_\epsilon^2}
\tag{13.58}
$$

which is distributed as chi-square with 1 degree of freedom.

What would be the difference if β_1 in the original model were nonzero? Going back to Equation 13.57, we note that $\tilde{Y}_i$ would then be distributed as normal, with the same variance, but a mean of $\beta_1 x_{di}$. When we square $\tilde{Y}_i$, we are going to obtain on average from one sample to another larger values than we would if β_1 were 0. Just to see the point, suppose that β_1 is 10 and the variance is as we specified it. Let $x_{di} = 1$ for the sake of the argument. Then $\hat{\beta}_1 x_{di}$ will be distributed about 10 and not about 0, so that the squared terms will be very much larger than the squared terms when $\beta_1 = 0$.

Let us return to our assumption that $\beta_1 = 0$. We now have two chi-square distributions that are independent of each other, and both involve division by the unknown parameter σ_ϵ. Our difficulty is that we do not know σ_ϵ and so far our determination of the relevant distributions depends on that knowledge. We have met this difficulty before, when we discovered the Student's T distribution; there, we examined the ratio of standardized Gaussian to a chi-square distribution so that the common unknown value of σ was canceled. Could we not try the same device here?

The answer is yes. The distribution of the *ratio* RSS to ESS no longer depends on the unknown value of σ_ϵ. We cannot prove this assertion here, but as you will see this result ties in very neatly with our previous findings, so that the result is at least plausible. After an inessential division of both numerator and denominator by their respective degrees of freedom, we create a new random variable with a distribution that is known as the F distribution. Our new variable is defined by

$$F = \frac{\text{RSS}/1}{\text{ESS}/(n-2)} = \frac{\text{RSS}(n-2)}{\text{ESS}} \tag{13.59}$$

You might find it a little strange that we have indicated the division by 1 in the equation. This is because our current example is so simple. If we had a regression equation like that in Equation 13.39, which involves three regressors and a constant term, then the degrees of freedom for RSS_d would be 3; that for ESS would be $n - 4$; and in the previous expression for the variable F, we would have divided RSS_d by 3 and ESS by $n - 4$.

The F distribution involves 2 degrees of freedom, v_1, v_2, but by design does not depend on the unknown σ_ϵ^2. The symbol v_1 represents the numerator degrees of freedom, and v_2 represents the denominator degrees of freedom; in our current example, v_1 is 1 and $v_2 = (n-2)$. The F distribution is also available in S-Plus under the <u>Labs</u>, <u>Statistical Tables</u> and is accessed the same as the normal and Student's T distributions. The F distribution is also known as the "variance ratio distribution," which is a more informative name.

The F random variable is always positive and may be "infinite." The distribution is skewed to the right. Comparative plots of the F distribution for a variety of values for the degrees of freedom are presented in Figure 13.12. The first two moments are

$$\mu_1' = \frac{v_2}{v_2 - 2}, \text{ for } v_2 > 2$$

$$\mu_2 = \frac{2v_2^2(v_1 + v_2 - 2)}{v_1(v_2 - 2)^2(v_2 - 4)}, \text{ for } v_2 > 4$$

As with the Student's T distribution, for certain values of the degrees of freedom, no moments exist. Note that the constraints are all on the denominator degrees of freedom.

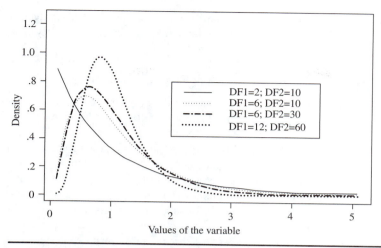

Figure 13.12   Plots of the density function for the F distribution with different degrees of freedom

This is because for low values of the denominator degrees of freedom the division by very small terms dominates the distribution so that it has "very fat tails." The existence of the third and fourth moments depends on there being enough degrees of freedom; one needs at least 6 to have a third moment, and at least 8 to have a fourth. Remember from our discussion about the Student's T distribution what the nonexistence of a moment means. Under the curve defining the moment there is no finite area over the whole range of the variable (see Figure 10.8), so the limits of the approximating sums defining the moments do not converge to the corresponding integrals.

If you think back to how we derived the F distribution, you will quickly see that when the numerator degree of freedom is 1, the F distribution is the distribution of a squared Student's T distribution. Recall how we obtained the Student's T; it was the ratio of standard normal to the square root of a variable divided by its degrees of freedom, and the variable had a chi-square distribution. If we square this ratio, we get exactly what we have just obtained. The advantage of the F distribution over the Student's T is that one can deal with many more degrees of freedom in the numerator; that is, one can allow for more than one regressor in defining the RSS.

We have already cited the F statistics for the examples that we have examined in this chapter. If you recall Table 13.2, the F statistic for consumption/income regression was 10,050, with 1 and 93 degrees of freedom; that for the log of GNP on log of the money supply was 2759, with 1 and 60 degrees of freedom; and the F statistic for the mileage example was 317.2, with 1 and 148 degrees of freedom. All these F statistics are huge, so the corresponding P values are essentially zero. These results are all overwhelmingly statistically significant. But, as we have stated repeatedly, these regression results that were obtained from a given set of historical data do not necessarily reflect causality. That there is a very strong degree of association cannot be denied, but ascribing causality from the regressor to the regressand is problematic at best.

Testing Hypotheses in Regression Equations

We have shown how to estimate and how to provide confidence intervals for the regression coefficients, β_0 and β_1. We consider extending the analysis to tests of hypotheses about the values of the coefficients, β_0 and β_1. Before examining an example in detail think about the general idea that is involved. If we hypothesize a value for β_1, say that it has the value, β_{10}, we know that our first task is to obtain the probability distribution for an estimator of β_1; this distribution may unfortunately depend on the value of some unknown parameter and usually the unknown value of σ_ϵ^2 is the culprit. But if we can find a modified distribution of the estimator $\hat{\beta}_1$, so that the only unknown parameter is β_{10}, then we can easily obtain a critical bound such that the probability of exceeding that bound is very low under the null hypothesis. This is exactly what we did in each example in Chapter 11. And this is exactly what we shall do here as well.

Let us derive the test procedure in the context of a simple example. Afterward, we will do the actual calculations. Suppose that we have carried out a linear regression and have an estimate for β_1 that is 0.8 with an estimated variance of $\hat{\sigma}_\epsilon / \sqrt{\Sigma_i x_{di}^2} = 1.2/4.3 = 0.28$ as we discussed in Equation 13.44. By the analysis and the assumptions that we made there, we presume that the distribution of the estimator, $\hat{\beta}_1$, is Gaussian with mean β_{10} and variance 0.28. Recall that the distribution of the error sum of squares was proportional to a chi-square distribution, so the ratio of the Gaussian distribution of $\hat{\beta}_1 - \beta_{10}$ to the chi-square distribution is distributed as Student's T. Also, recall that Student's T distribution depended only on the degrees of freedom, so no unknown parameters are involved (see Equation 13.41). We have therefore that

$$\frac{(\hat{\beta}_1 - \beta_{10})\sqrt{\sum x_{di}^2}}{\hat{\sigma}_\epsilon} \tag{13.60}$$

is distributed as Student's T with $20 - 2 = 18$ degrees of freedom under the null hypothesis that the true value of β_1 is β_{10}. If we pick a probability of Type I error, α, of .1 and we choose a two-sided alternative hypothesis, $\beta_1 \neq \beta_{10}$, the two-sided critical bounds are ± 1.70. Substituting these numbers into Equation 13.60, we obtain for a β_{10} value of 1.0, the observed statistic,

$$\frac{(0.8 - 1.0) \times 4.3}{1.2} = -0.72$$

We would conclude that the null hypothesis is accepted at an α level of 0.1. But if β_{10} were 2.0, the numbers are

$$\frac{(0.8 - 2.0) \times 4.3}{1.2} = -4.3$$

which is very strongly rejected. As we have just seen, the testing of hypotheses in the context of linear regression is the same as the testing of hypotheses about moments or parameters of distributions.

In the More Examples section, we noted that we should consider testing whether the estimated slope coefficients for the relationship between sales and inventories for the two firms considered were the same. Let us do that here recalling first our discussion on the comparison of two means in Chapter 11. We may well assume that the distributions of the estimates for regression parameters for Digital and Hasbro are independent of each other. We have two estimators, one for each firm, that are individually distributed as normal. To test that the difference in means is zero, we create a new random variable, $\hat{\delta}$, defined by

$$\hat{\delta} = \hat{\mu}_1 - \hat{\mu}_2 \tag{13.61}$$

The distribution of the estimator $\hat{\delta}$ is under the assumptions of this problem normal with mean

$$\delta = \mu_1 - \mu_2$$

and variance

$$\sigma_{\hat{\delta}}^2 = \sigma_{\hat{\mu}_1}^2 + \sigma_{\hat{\mu}_2}^2$$

We estimate the variance of the difference by

$$\hat{\sigma}_{\hat{\delta}}^2 = \hat{\sigma}_{\hat{\mu}_1}^2 + \hat{\sigma}_{\hat{\mu}_2}^2$$

$$= \frac{\hat{\sigma}_{\epsilon_1}^2}{\sum x_{1di}^2} + \frac{\hat{\sigma}_{\epsilon_2}^2}{\sum x_{2di}^2} \tag{13.62}$$

where the subscripts refer to each firm's estimates, and we do not assume that the error term variances for each firm are the same. Clearly, the variances of the regressors will differ across firms. Substituting the empirical results obtained into Equations 13.61 and 13.62, we have

$$\hat{\delta} = 16.06 - 14.76$$
$$= 1.30$$

and

$$\hat{\sigma}_{\hat{\delta}}^2 = 8.357 + 0.262$$

or

$$\hat{\sigma}_{\hat{\delta}} = \sqrt{8.357 + 0.262}$$
$$= 2.94$$

We see immediately that the observed difference is less than one-half of a standard deviation, so that at any reasonable level for Type I error we would accept the null hypothesis of no difference in the means.

Let us be careful about what this result means. First, the actual means despite our conclusion may well differ substantially, but our estimates have not revealed that state because of sampling error. However, we may face a more subtle error in that the two means may differ by a very small amount so that, given the size of the estimated standard deviations, the actual difference is undetectable at any reasonable level of Type I error. Note that the reason that we cannot detect any difference is due entirely to the very large size of the standard deviation for Digital. It may be the case that on reexamining their data, we discover there are errors in the recording of the data, or that special circumstances prevailed, and that once these circumstances are allowed for, these results would yield a standard error that is much, much smaller. Under these circumstances, the observed difference in slope coefficients could be significantly different from zero.

Calculations

We have discussed a very large number of calculations in developing regression analysis. Anyone could easily get the impression that the calculations are very complex and impossible to keep straight, much less remember. In fact, all the calculations we have performed are based on a relatively few numbers. The objective of this very short section is to illustrate this fact and to show you that everything we have done reduces to rearranging just six numbers. Let us use the numbers from the Digital Equipment Corporation example.

The six numbers that we need are

- n, the sample size
- $\bar{x}$, the sample mean of the regressor
- $\bar{y}$, the sample mean of the regressand
- $\sum_i x_{di}^2$, the sum of squared deviations of the regressor about its mean
- $\sum_i y_{di}^2$, the sum of squared deviations of the regressand about its mean
- $\sum_i x_{di} y_{di}$, the sum of the product of the deviations of x and of y about their means

In the Digital example, these six numbers are

$$
\begin{aligned}
n &= 18 \\
\bar{x} &= 566 \\
\bar{y} &= 7783 \\
\sum_i x_{di}^2 &= 1{,}081{,}795.0 \\
\sum_i y_{di}^2 &= 4.2352 \times 10^8 \\
\sum_i x_{di} y_{di} &= 1.73691 \times 10^7
\end{aligned}
\tag{13.63}
$$

From these six numbers we can obtain every calculation that we discussed. Note carefully that in the following results, the calculated numbers may differ slightly from the numbers obtained through the regression routine because of the rounding off of large numbers.

We have immediately the equations for the estimates:

$$\hat{\beta}_1 = \frac{\sum_i x_{di} y_{di}}{\sum_i x_{di}^2} = \frac{1.73691 \times 10^7}{1{,}081{,}795.0} = 16.06$$

$$\hat{\beta}_0 = \bar{y} - \hat{\beta}_1 \bar{x} = 7783 - 16.06 \times 566 = -1304.03$$

$$\hat{\sigma}_\epsilon^2 = \frac{1}{n-2} \sum \hat{\epsilon}_i^2 = \frac{1}{16} \sum_i \{y_{di} - \hat{\beta}_1 x_{di}\}^2$$

$$= \frac{1}{16} \left[\sum_i y_{di}^2 + \hat{\beta}_1^2 \sum_i x_{di}^2 - 2\hat{\beta}_1 \sum_i x_{di} y_{di} \right] \qquad (13.64)$$

$$= \frac{1}{16} \left[\sum_i y_{di}^2 - \frac{\left(\sum_i x_{di} y_{di}\right)^2}{\sum_i x_{di}^2} \right]$$

$$= \frac{1}{16} \times 1.4464 \times 10^8 = 9.04205 \times 10^6$$

$$\hat{\sigma}_\epsilon = 3007$$

The corresponding standard errors and the R_d^2 values are also easily obtained:

$$R_d^2 = \frac{\text{RSS}}{\text{TSS}} = \frac{\hat{\beta}_1^2 \sum_i x_{di}^2}{\sum_i y_{di}^2}$$

$$= \frac{\left(\sum_i x_{di} y_{di}\right)^2}{\sum_i x_{di}^2 \times \sum_i y_{di}^2} = 0.6585$$

$$\text{Est. Std. Er. } \hat{\beta}_1 = \frac{\hat{\sigma}_\epsilon}{\sqrt{\sum_i x_{di}^2}} = \frac{3007}{1040.1} = 2.89$$

$$\text{Est. Std. Er. } \hat{\beta}_0 = \hat{\sigma}_\epsilon \sqrt{\frac{1}{n} + \frac{\bar{x}^2}{\sum_i x_{di}^2}}$$

$$= 3007 \times 0.5929 = 1782.9 \qquad (13.65)$$

$$F = \frac{\text{RSS} \times (n-2)}{\text{ESS}} = \frac{\hat{\beta}_1^2 \sum_i x_{di}^2 \times 16}{\sum_i \hat{\epsilon}_i^2}$$

$$= \frac{\left[\left(\sum_i x_{di} y_{di}\right)^2 / \sum_i x_{di}^2\right] \times 16}{\sum_i y_{di}^2 - \left(\sum_i x_{di} y_{di}\right)^2 / \sum_i x_{di}^2}$$

$$= \frac{\left(\sum_i x_{di} y_{di}\right)^2 \times 16}{\sum_i x_{di}^2 \times \sum_i y_{di}^2 - \left(\sum_i x_{di} y_{di}\right)^2}$$

$$= 30.85$$

We could add other computations, but you now see that all the calculations that we require for any aspect of regression analysis can be obtained by manipulating the six numbers listed in Equation 13.63. This summary is also to give you a clearer perspective of the links between the various calculations.

13.6　The "Regression" in Regression Analysis

Why is regression analysis called "regression analysis"? What is the origin of the word "regression"? The idea goes back to Sir Francis Galton (1822–1911), who was interested in the association between parents' and offspring's physical characteristics. He was particularly interested in the relationship between the heights of fathers and sons. But before we discuss Galton's work, consider the following scenarios.

New York City often experiments with new teaching methods or procedures. A typical outcome is that the lowest scoring students before the change do better after the change, but the best scoring students do worse. As another example, consider a basketball coach who congratulates his best scorers and harangues his worst performers, only to discover that the best scorers do worse next game, but his worst performers improve on average. A vice-president of a firm has an annual dinner at which the top managers are feted. Inevitably, the average performance of the best managers falters the next year. The stock advisors with the best investment record are featured in the *Wall Street Journal;* very seldom do they appear again the next year.

The question is whether there is some psychological effect involved in these examples, or are these results merely an artifact of statistical calculations? It has been claimed that giving praise leads the praised to "slack off," to "rest on their laurels," whereas those who are criticized for their performance see the need to improve and try harder. This is certainly plausible, and there is even some experimental evidence that supports the basic concept. But a knowledge of statistics will dampen one's enthusiasm for such explanations.

Let us consider a very simple situation in which we can measure performance by a test. Let us repeat the test on large numbers of subjects many times. In short, we collect a large number of histograms. From this information, we conclude that the outcome of the test on a *randomly selected* group of people has a normal distribution. The assumption of normality is not necessary, but it is helpful to focus on a familiar distribution. Selecting someone at random and giving them a test can then be regarded as a drawing from this distribution. Now let us add the idea that there are errors of observation, or random errors in "test taking," so that if an individual is tested repeatedly, his or her test results will vary about some mean value. To keep life very very simple, assume that the error distribution is also normal. Thus, a test observation, y_{it}, where i represents the ith individual and t represents the tth trial, or test, is given by

$$y_{it} = A_i + \epsilon_{it}$$

where A_i indicates the ith person's native ability, the A_i are drawn from a normal distribution, and ϵ_{it} is the error for the ith individual in taking the tth test.

Now consider collecting a random sample of individuals for a test and testing them twice. The first test can be regarded as a random sample from the distribution of $\{y_{it}\}$, which is normal with mean μ_A, the mean of the distribution of the $\{A_i\}$. The variance of y_{it} is $\sigma_A^2 + \sigma_\epsilon^2$; as usual we assume that the error term has a zero mean. But the second test is different in that we are testing exactly the same individuals again. Although we may well have a random sample drawn from the distribution of $\{\epsilon_{it}\}$, the distribution of $\{y_{it}\}$ in the second test is conditional on the values of $\{A_i\}$ observed in the first test.

Suppose that we observe someone who has a very low score in the first test. This result may be due to the fact that he has a very low value for A_i or that he has drawn a very low (negative) value for $\{\epsilon_{it}\}$. Alternatively, if we observe someone who has a very large value for y_{it}, that result may be because that person has a very large value for A_i or a very large value for ϵ_{it}. Let us select two groups; one contains subjects that have a very low value for y_{it}, and one contains subjects that have a very high value for y_{it}. In the former group, we will have selected a disproportionate share of low (negative) ϵ_{it}. Similarly, we will have selected a disproportionate share of high ϵ_{it} in the high values for y_{it}. The average value for ϵ_{it} in the low scorers' group will be negative, and the average value for ϵ_{it} in the high scorers will be positive. The more extreme we choose the low scorers, the lower the average value of ϵ_{it} in that group. Similarly, the more extreme we choose the high scorers, the higher the average value of ϵ_{it} in that group.

We now retest the original population of subjects. This means that the observed sample of $\{A_i\}$ is kept and we merely get a new drawing from the ϵ_{it}. But, because the second sample from ϵ_{it} is independent of the first, conditional on the existing $\{A_i\}$, the new random draws on ϵ_{it} are as likely to be positive as to be negative. From the subjects in the lower group of test scores from the first test, the average value for ϵ_{it} on the second draw will be much higher, zero. Similarly, for the subjects in the upper group of test scores in the first test, the average value of the ϵ_{it} on the second draw will be much lower, zero.

We now have our explanation for our results. They may well be due to the way in which we sample our data from one test to another and not to the psychology of peoples' reactions to praise or blame. However, do note that these explanations are not mutually exclusive; both effects could be operating. But, it is clear in many circumstances that the statistical explanation is the dominant one.

To see this result even more clearly, consider the problem of trying to distinguish between the two explanations. One way to think about the matter is to split each of the two groups into two subgroups by selecting members at random. Let us suppose that the mean values for y_{it} in the two subgroups for the lower scores are approximately the same and similarly for the two subgroups of the high scorers. Blame, or praise, as appropriate only one of each of the subgroups; do nothing with the other subgroups. Using the second test results, you will want to test whether the mean of blamed low scorers have significantly higher scores in the second test than the unblamed low scorers. Similarly, compare the means in the second test of the praised and the unpraised high scorers from the first test.

Now we can learn what this discussion has to do with providing an explanation for the word "regression." Galton observed precisely what we have just discussed while comparing the heights of fathers and of sons. Even though the overall average of the heights of sons tends to be slightly taller than for parents because the average height of the population is increasing due to better nutrition and infant health, the statistical effect we have demonstrated still dominates the outcomes. The average height of sons (second test) from short parents (first test) is taller than the general increase would indicate. The average height of sons (second test) from tall parents (first test) is shorter than the general increase would indicate.

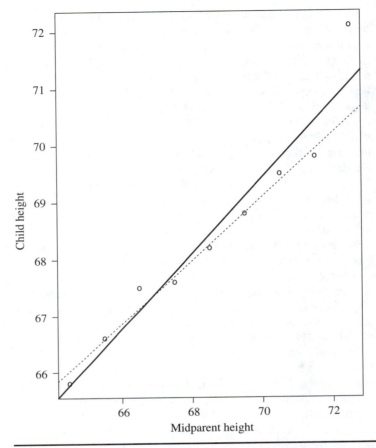

Figure 13.13   Illustration of Galton's demonstration of "regression to mediocrity" between parents and children

A simpler example was provided by Galton, using a comparison of the heights of parents, termed the "Midparent height" to the heights of their children, termed "Child." Galton's graph is summarized in Figure 13.13, and the data were extracted from the figure he produced.* If we plot the scatter diagram of average parents' heights, Midparent height, on the X-axis and the average heights of children, "Child height," on the Y-axis, we will observe a regression line that tilts up for small values of parents' heights and down for the large values of parents' heights. Notice the two regression lines: the solid line shows the result using all the data points and the dashed line that obtained if we drop the very last observation that seems to be an "outlier" in the series. In short, we can say, as did Galton, that children's heights

---

* Sir Francis Galton, "Regression towards mediocrity in hereditary stature," *Journal of the Royal Anthropological Institute,* 15: 135–145.

"regress" to the mean of parents' heights. Since then lines representing the mean scatter of points between two variables have been termed "regression lines," even if the statistical situation is completely different.

13.7 Summary

This chapter introduced the concept of *regression analysis.* We may view regression from two different, but related, perspectives. The first is that the regression line, defined in Equation 13.3, is a statement about the conditional distribution of the random variable Y given observations on the random variable X. In particular, Equation 13.3 describes the conditional mean of Y given X. Y is known as the *regressand,* or as the *dependent variable.* The conditioning variable X is known as the *regressor,* or the *independent variable.* In principle, we could consider many other ways to describe the conditional distribution—for example, by expressing the variance of Y in terms of variations in X—but we decide for the sake of simplicity to restrict our attention to the conditional mean. The description of the conditional distribution is completed by defining the distributional properties of Y in addition to the form of the conditional mean. One way to express this notion is to define an "error term," ϵ, as in Equation 13.3. If we were to add information about the marginal distribution of X, then we could recapture the joint distribution of both Y and X. However, once we have the joint distribution of Y and X, then we can derive the conditional distribution of X given Y, and therefore we can define the regression of X on Y in a similar manner. The existence in this framework of two equally valid regression equations, one for Y on X and one for X on Y, indicates clearly that we are dealing with measures of association rather than with causal relationships, which are unidirectional.

The other way we can generate a regression model is by postulating a causal mechanism that is expected to hold between two variables Y and X. Further, by recognizing that there will be errors of observation of Y, one can create a regression relationship as summarized in Equation 13.3. Formally, the statistical statement is the same as that we used in the previous paragraph. However, there is a difference in the interpretation; in this case, we are restricting our attention to a regression in one direction only—that indicated by our theory of the relationship between the variables. But we have seen in this chapter that the statistical procedures we have available to us cannot distinguish between the two interpretations.

We linked the development of this chapter and the last to that in Chapter 5 on correlation coefficients by showing that the correlation coefficient measured the association between two variables and is a property of both the conditional distribution and the joint distribution. Further, we showed that the correlation coefficient can be regarded as the "slope" coefficient in a regression between two variables in standardized form; that is, β_1 in Equation 13.3 has units of measurement associated with it, units of Y per unit of X, whereas the correlation coefficient is dimensionless.

Next, we obtained estimators for the parameters of the conditional distribution. Our criterion for obtaining estimators of the regression parameters was to "minimize the *error sum of squares,*" or the sum of the *residuals* squared (see Equation 13.19). Given the assumption of normality for the distribution of the error terms, we derived that the joint distribution of the estimators of β_0 and β_1 were jointly normal and both unbiased, and the variances and covariance given in Equations 13.23, 13.26, and 13.27. We also obtained an estimator for σ_ϵ^2 and saw how to obtain a confidence interval for it using the chi-square distribution (see Equation 13.55).

We recognized that the *total sum of squares* (see Equation 13.35) could be factored into two, or three, components, depending on whether one is measuring the total sum of squares about the mean or about the origin. Using the former, we obtained the very important result that

$$TSS = RSS + ESS$$

where TSS is the total sum of squares (about the mean), RSS is the *regression sum of squares* (about the mean), and ESS is the error sum of squares.

Having obtained the distributions of the regression parameters and of the appropriate variances, our next task was to obtain confidence intervals for the regression parameters. Further, as a special case of this exercise, we obtained confidence intervals for the estimator for the conditional mean for any chosen value of X; this process is known as *prediction,* or when the data are ordered in time, as *forecasting.*

As a measure of overall goodness of fit we defined the (multiple) *coefficient of determination,* R^2, or R_d^2, which in the simplest case of only two variables is the same as the square of the correlation coefficient (see Equation 13.38). While the coefficient of determination is bounded by 0 and 1, 0 if there is no explanation for the dependent variable from the independent variable and 1 if the model is exact and the error terms are identically zero, its own distributional properties are difficult. Consequently, we defined instead the ratio of RSS to ESS and discovered that this ratio after division by the corresponding degrees of freedom is distributed as F_{ν_1,ν_2} with ν_1 and ν_2 degrees of freedom. We also discovered that an F distribution with $\nu_1 = 1$, ν_2 arbitrary is in fact the square of a Student's T distribution with ν_2 degrees of freedom.

We completed this chapter by explaining the origin of the use of the word *regression* in regression analysis. The explanation was useful because it gave us considerable insight into the use of regression analysis. The regression problem is present whenever one is evaluating performance in a test–retest situation. The observed regression to the mean is due to bias in the sampling in the second test, given the outcomes of the first.

Case Study

Was There Age Discrimination in a Public Utility?

In Chapter 5, we discussed the correlation between age and salaries over all former employees and by subgroups. In this chapter, we can extend that analysis to the regression framework and in the process provide more information about the relationship between age and salaries as well as test hypotheses about the regression coefficients. Recall Figure 5.14 from Chapter 5.

The output from the S-Plus regression routine is

continues on next page

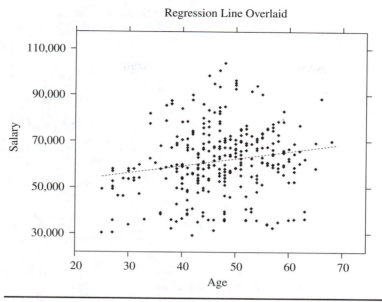

Figure 13.14   Discrimination study: Regression of salary on age

(Continued)
*** Linear Model ***
Call: lm(formula = salary ~age, data = Ext.appl.0, na.action = na.omit)

Residuals:

Min	1Q	Median	3Q	Max
−32079	−7542	49.62	8380	42104

Coefficients:

	Value	Std.Error	t value	Pr(> $|t|$)
(Intercept)	46950.64	4551.36	10.32	0.0000
age	309.27	95.10	3.25	0.0013

Residual standard error: 14460 on 310 degrees of freedom

Multiple R-Squared: 0.033

F-statistic: 10.58 on 1 and 310 degrees of freedom, the p-value is 0.001272

This output statement informs us that we have regressed salary on age. The data set Ext.appl.0, which includes all the former (internal) employees in the Discdata.xls data set, has been used (where variable ext.appl is 0). In addition, we have omitted observations with NA from the regression. The basic statistical properties of the residuals are listed in the next line. The values of the estimates of the regression coefficients follow. We see from the results cited that the mean level of salary independent of the age effect—that is, the estimated value for the coefficient on the constant term—is about $46,950 and that for every year's difference in age, income increases by an estimated $309.27. These regression results are graphed in Figure 13.14. Note that these results are, of course, only estimates; the estimated values will not be exactly equal to the actual parameter values and may indeed be quite different. Further, the regression results indicate the level of association between income and age; the results do not claim that if an individual ages by one year his income will, even on average, increase by $309.27. Indeed, this is a reminder that regression measures degrees of association,

continues on next page

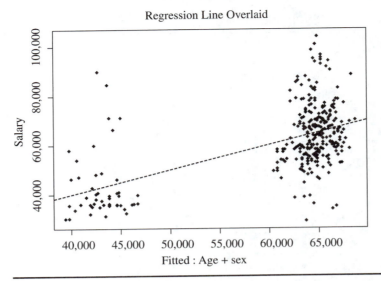

Figure 13.15   Discrimination study: Regression of salary on age and sex

(Continued)

not necessarily the effects of causal mechanisms.

Examining the Student's t statistics and the P values and the P value for the F statistic, we see for this regression that the estimated coefficient values are individually and jointly very highly significant. But we also see from the quoted R^2 value of 0.033 that only 3.3% of the total variation in salaries is explained by age. Recall our discussion about the difference between statistically significant and operationally significant that we had in Chapter 11. Clearly in this instance, the age variable is statistically significant— that is, its estimate is considerably greater than its standard deviation—but the operational significance is very slight indeed.

Although it is not of direct relevance to our major concern about age discrimination, it is of interest to consider the effect of allowing for differences in salary levels by sex as well as age. This regression procedure introduces a topic that we have alluded to but have not developed. However, you should by now have no great difficulty in obtaining an

intuitive feel for the extended results. They are meant to provide a point of contrast and an extension of the analysis presented; these procedures anticipate the material in your next regression course.

The results of this regression follow, and Figure 13.15 illustrates the regression fit.

*** Linear Model ***

Call:

lm(formula = salary ~age + factor(sex), data = Ext.appl.0, na.action = na.omit)

Residuals:

Min	1Q	Median	3Q	Max
−34610	−7887	−2381	5709	47312

Coefficients:

	Value	Std.Error	tvalue	pr(> |t|)
(Intercept)	45388.58	3886.49	11.68	0.0000
age	187.15	81.94	2.28	0.0230
sex -	−10560.93	977.50	−10.80	0.0000

Residual standard error: 12340 on 309 degrees of freedom

Multiple R-Squared: 0.2981

F-statistic: 65.62 on 2 and 309 degrees of freedom, the p-value is 0

continues on next page

(Continued)

The overall layout of the results is the same except the addition of factor (sex), which treats sex as a code rather than a numeric value. A comparison of the graphs is very revealing. The effect of introducing a sex category in addition to age as a regressor is to reduce the estimated effect of age on salaries from $309.27 per year to $187.15 per year. There is also an estimated $10,561 discount for being female given the age difference. All estimated coefficient values are highly statistically significant and the degree of regression fit is much higher, up to 29.8% from 3.3%, but both variables are still not very operationally significant.

Figure 13.15 plots observed salary values with a regression line overlaid. Clearly, allowing for differences due to sex indicates that there are two salary regions—one for men, the upper, and one for women, the lower.

Exercises

Calculation Practice

These exercises are to give you practice in the calculations needed in regression analysis and to help you to recognize the numerous connections between the various statistics. Further, for you to be able to understand the output from computer regression packages, you need to know exactly what it is that the computer is actually doing; for this understanding you need to have performed similar calculations yourself.

13.1 You are provided with 44 observations on sales and airplay rankings of popular music singles in the file named Rock.xls, folder Misc. You are investigating the influence of radio airplay on record sales. Specifically, you hypothesize that the more someone hears a song on the radio, the more likely they will come to like the song and buy the album (the greater the airplay time last week (airlstwk), the higher the sales volume will be this week (slsrank)). Construct the relevant scatter diagram, and indicate whether preliminary visual examination of the data confirms or refutes your hypothesis.

13.2 Using the file Rock.xls, calculate the first two moments of airplay last week and sales this week, as well as the covariance and correlation between these two variables. Are the results consistent with your expectations? Do your computations confirm or refute your hypothesis in Exercise 13.1?

13.3 Using the file Rock.xls and your hypothesis from Exercise 13.1, write out the regression equation you would use to investigate your hypothesis. Then, obtain by hand estimates for β_0 and β_1. You may use the computer to obtain all the sums, squares, and cross-product terms, but use the equations in the text to calculate the actual coefficients. Are the signs of the estimated β_0 and β_1 what you had expected?

13.4 Using the regression equation and your parameter estimates from Exercise 13.3, calculate by hand the F statistic for the equation as a whole, together with its degrees of freedom. Compute the coefficient of determination, R^2. What can you infer from these summary statistics about the validity of your original hypothesis regarding airplay last week and sales this week?

13.5 Repeat Exercises 13.3 and 13.4 using the Regression routine in S-Plus.

[***Computer directions:*** On the menu bar, click on Statistics, Regression, Linear.] Are the statistics obtained the same?

**13.6 *Worked. Objective: To practice the mechanics of regression and learn exactly what is produced by the Regression algorithm in S-Plus.* The data have been kept very simple to facilitate your learning how to do regression calculations. Let $\{x_i\} = -2, -1, 0, 1, 2$, and $\{\epsilon_i\} = .1, -.2, .3, -.4, .2$:

$$y_i = -2 + 2x_i + \epsilon_i, \quad i = 1, 2, ..., 5$$

These data have been stored for your convenience in the folder Misc, file name Varreg1.xls.

a. Examine the data. Plot y_i on x_i, using the Scatterplot function in S-Plus.

[***Computer directions:*** Start S-Plus. Import the file Varreg1.xls in folder Misc. Click on column xreg1, hold down the CTRL key, and click on column yreg1. On the menu bar, click Graph, 2D Plot, Scatterplots, OK.]

Before doing any further calculations, examine the plot carefully and try to identify the basic properties of the data.

b. Calculate the first two moments of the three variables and their standard deviations. Next, calculate the covariances between $\{x_i\}$ and $\{y_i\}$ and between $\{x_i\}$ and $\{\epsilon_i\}$. In this first exercise, the means of the $\{x_i\}$ and the $\{\epsilon_i\}$ are zero, and the relationship between the regressor variable $\{x_i\}$ and the error term $\{\epsilon_i\}$ is also special; $\Sigma x_i \epsilon_i = 0$. Note how these special relationships simplify your calculations.

[***Computer directions:*** With file Varreg1.xls open, (1) calculate moments and the standard deviations. Open the menu bar, click on Text Routines, Moments. In the dialog, select Data Frame, Varreg1. In Variables, select "xreg1." Click OK.

(2) Calculate the covariance between $\{x_i\}$ and $\{y_i\}$: Click on Data, Transform. In New Column Name, key in $\boxed{\text{cov}}$ and in Expression, key in $\boxed{\text{sum(yreg1*xreg1)/5}}$. Click Apply. (The answer = 4 and will be in the cov column in the Varreg1 data frame.)]

Recall that $\bar{x}$ and $\bar{\epsilon} = 0$ in this exercise. Why was it correct here to ignore the mean of yreg1 when calculating the covariance between yreg1 and xreg1?

If you were to calculate the covariance by clicking on Statistics, Data Summaries, Correlation, and covariance, you would get an answer of 5.0. This is because the computer covariance routine divides the sum of the cross products by the degrees of freedom, which in this instance are 4. Earlier, we divided by 5, the number of observations. Use the latter, rather than the former, in your calculations.

c. Calculate the correlation coefficient between $\{y_i\}$ and $\{x_i\}$. Note, there are two ways in which you can do this. Comment on the relationship between them. There are also two second moment calculations that you could use here; which should you use? Do you divide the sum of squares by 5 or by 4? Try using both to examine the difference. If you divide the sums of squares by 5 in each case as well as the covariance, the common factor of 5 will cancel from the calculations; alternatively, you could divide both variance estimates by $(n - 1)$ as well as the covariance and that term will cancel from the calculations. Your best strategy is to be consistent, so that you obtain cancellation.

From the visual aid provided by the scatter plot and the calculations that you have just made, what conclusions can you draw about the regression that you will calculate next?

d. When $\bar{x}$ is zero as in this case, the estimator for β_1 is very simple:

$$\hat{\beta}_1 = \frac{\sum x_i y_i}{\sum x_i^2}$$

Calculate $\hat{\beta}_1$ using this definition.

[***Computer directions:*** With the file Varreg1.xls open, click on Data, Transform. In New Column Name, key in $\boxed{\text{bhat}}$. In the Expression box, key in $\boxed{\text{sum(yreg1*xreg1)/sum(xreg1^2)}}$. Click Apply. The answer, 2.0, will be in the column bhat in the Varreg1 data frame.]

Calculate $\hat{\beta}_0$ using $\hat{\beta}_0 = \bar{y} - \hat{\beta}_1 \bar{x}$; $\bar{y} = -2$ and recall $\bar{x} = 0$.

e. The variances for $\hat{\beta}_0$ and $\hat{\beta}_1$ are given in Equations 13.23 and 13.26. Recall the simplification in the calculations that is implied by $\bar{x} = 0$. To get an estimator for these variance terms, we need an estimator for the error variance, σ_ϵ^2, which is provided in Equation 13.29.

[**Computer directions:** With file Varreg1.xls open, calculate $\hat{\sigma}_\epsilon^2$ using the value of $\bar{\epsilon}$, which in this case is zero. On the menu bar, click on Data, Transform. In New Column Name, key in $\boxed{\text{evarhat}}$. In Expression, key in $\boxed{\text{sum}(((\text{yreg1}+2)-(\text{bhat*}}$ $\boxed{\text{xreg1}))^2)/3}$. Click Apply. The answer, 0.11, will be in the column evarhat in the data frame.]

In the previous expression, why did we write: "(yreg1 + 2)?" Recall the value of $\hat{\beta}_0$. Using these definitions, obtain the estimates for the standard errors of $\hat{\beta}_0$ and $\hat{\beta}_1$ by substituting the values you have just calculated into the noted equations. In passing, you might also obtain an estimate for the covariance between the estimators $\hat{\beta}_0$ and $\hat{\beta}_1$ using Equation 13.27.

f. Finally, we will obtain an estimate for the F statistic and for the coefficient of determination, R^2, using both Equations 13.59 and 13.36, 13.37. Explain the difference between them.

[**Computer directions:** With the file Varreg1.xls open, calculate y_{di} and y_{di}^2. On the menu bar, click on Data, Transform. In New Column Name, key in $\boxed{\text{ydi}}$. In Expression, using the calculated value for $\bar{y}$, key in $\boxed{\text{yreg1}+2}$. Click Apply. For Column Name, key in $\boxed{\text{ydisq}}$ and in Expression, key in $\boxed{\text{ydi}^2}$. Click Apply.

Calculate the regression sum of squares about the mean, $\Sigma \hat{y}_{di}^2$. In Column Name, key in $\boxed{\text{RSS}}$. In Expression, key in $\boxed{\text{sum}((\text{bhat*xreg1})^2)}$. Click Apply. The answer = 40.

Calculate the error sum of squares $\Sigma \hat{\epsilon}_{di}^2$. In Column Name, key in $\boxed{\text{ESS}}$. In Expression, key in $\boxed{\text{sum}((\text{ydi-bhat*xreg1})^2)}$. Click Apply. The answer = 0.34.

To calculate the TSS about the mean, click on Data, Transform. Key in $\boxed{\text{sum(ydisq)}}$. To calculate the TSS about the origin, key in $\boxed{\text{sum(yreg1}^2)}$. The answers = 40.34, 60.34.]

The F statistic, together with its degrees of freedom (Equation 13.59), is now easily calculated.

So far you have done regression by hand. You will now discover that you can use the S-Plus regression routine to do these calculations.

g. Repeat (f) using the regression routine in S-Plus.

[**Computer directions:** On the menu bar, click on Statistics, Regression, Linear. The Data Frame should read "Varreg1." In Formula, key in $\boxed{\text{yreg1~xreg1}}$. (The first variable listed is the dependent variable.) Click the Plot tab; in Plots uncheck all boxes except Residuals vs Fit. Click the Results tab, and check Long Output and Correlation Matrix of Estimates. Click Apply.]

The output in the Report window will be as follows:

Linear Model
Call: lm(formula = yreg1~xreg1,
data = Varreg1, na.action = na.omit)

Residuals:

	1	2	3	4	5
	0.1	−0.2	0.3	−0.4	0.2

Coefficients:

	Value	Std. Error	t value	pr(> |t|)
(Intercept)	−2.0000	0.1506	−13.2842	0.0009
xreg1	2.0000	0.1065	18.7867	0.0003

Residual standard error: 0.3367 on 3 degrees of freedom
Multiple R-Squared: 0.9916
F-statistic: 352.9 on 1 and 3 degrees of freedom, the p-value is 0.0003292
Correlation of Coefficients:
(Intercept)
xreg1 0

Following is a description of the Report window output. The first line indicates you have chosen the Linear (Regression) Model. The next line, "Call," confirms that you are regressing yreg1 on xreg1, that the data used are in the file Varreg1, and that you are omitting rows with missing observations. The next line lists the residuals, $\hat{\epsilon}_i$, the estimated error terms. If there are more than a few observations, instead of listing the residuals, you will see their summary statistics.

The next set of lines give you in turn: the estimated values of the coefficients, here $\widehat{\beta}_0$ is -2.00 and $\widehat{\beta}_1$ is 2.00. The next column shows the standard errors for each estimated coefficient—that is $\hat{\sigma}_{\beta_0}$ and $\hat{\sigma}_{\beta_1}$. The next column shows the t statistics, $\widehat{\beta}_0/\sigma_{\widehat{\beta}_0}$, $\widehat{\beta}_1/\sigma_{\widehat{\beta}_1}$, and the final column is the P value —that is, the probability of obtaining the observed t statistic or greater under the null hypothesis that $\widehat{\beta}_0$, respectively $\widehat{\beta}_1$, is zero.

The following line gives the square root of the error variance, $\hat{\sigma}_\epsilon$, 0.3367 with its degrees of freedom 3. The next line shows the value of R^2, about the mean. The F statistic, with its degrees of freedom, follows. The last entry is the P value for this statistic; 0.0003292 is the probability of getting an F statistic of this size or greater under the null hypothesis that $\widehat{\beta}_1$ (in this example) is zero.

The F statistic is most important when there is more than one regressor. The very last entry shows the correlation between the regression coefficients, in this case, between $\widehat{\beta}_0$ and $\widehat{\beta}_1$; and they are uncorrelated.

Confirm that in each case the numbers you obtained by hand match those produced by the computer algorithm; your numbers should agree to the second and often to the third decimal place. Differences will be due to accumulated errors from rounding off the numbers. This effect is very striking in the calculations for the standard deviations for $\hat{\beta}_0$ and $\hat{\beta}_1$. By using the value for $\hat{\sigma}_\epsilon^2$ of 0.11, instead of 0.113333, you will calculate for $\hat{\beta}_0$ a standard deviation of 0.148 and for $\hat{\beta}_1$ a value of 0.235. This shows the necessity of keeping more digits during your calculations than the accuracy of the original data would normally warrant.

13.7 In Exercise 13.6 we calculated, both by hand and by computer, a simple regression problem that had three important special characteristics: the means of the regressor x and the actual error terms, ϵ, which are not normally observed, were both zero. Also, the covariation between x and ϵ was zero by design. In this exercise, you will remove these special properties and reassess your calcula-

tions. Note that the equation for y, the regressand, is exactly as it was in Exercise 13.6. The data follow and are in folder Misc, file Varreg2.xls:

$$y_i = -2 + 2x_i + \epsilon_i$$
$$x_i = 1, 2, 4, 8, 12$$
$$\epsilon_i = 0.1, 0, 0.3, -0.3, 0.1$$

a. Import the file Varreg2.xls. Repeat the calculations exactly as performed in Exercise 13.6 to facilitate comparisons. When calculating $\hat{\beta}_1$ with Varreg2 data, note the extra steps needed to obtain the estimate. The simplest way to calculate $\hat{\beta}_1$ is to rewrite the variables $\{y_i\}$ and $\{x_i\}$ in terms of deviations about their respective means as explained in the text.

If $y_i = \beta_0 + \beta_1 x_i + \epsilon_i$, then

$$y_i - \bar{y} = \beta_0 + \beta_1 x_i - \beta_0 - \beta_1 \bar{x} + (\epsilon_i - \bar{\epsilon})$$
$$= \beta_1(x_i - \bar{x}) + (\epsilon_i - \bar{\epsilon})$$

or

$$y_{di} = \beta_1 x_{di} + \epsilon_{di}$$

In the previous exercise you calculated y_{di}, and you will do so again here. But in addition you will calculate x_{di}. The idea is to estimate β_1 with respect to the covariation between y_{di} and x_{di}. $\hat{\beta}_0$ is then easily obtained from

$$\hat{\beta}_0 = \bar{y} - \hat{\beta}_1 \bar{x}$$

Because most interest is in the variation about the mean and not in the mean itself, analysis is usually restricted to terms that are expressed in terms of deviations about the mean—that is, to TSS, RSS, R^2, and F statistic values, that are in terms of deviations about the mean only.

Begin by repeating (a), (b), and (c) in Exercise 13.6.

[**Computer directions:** Generate the new variables x_{di}, y_{di}, and ϵ_{di}. Using Varreg2.xls, on the menu bar, click on Data, Transform. In the dialog box, in New Column Name, key in $\boxed{\text{xdi}}$. In Expression, key in $\boxed{\text{xreg2}-5.4}$. Click Apply. For New Column Name, key in $\boxed{\text{edi}}$. In Expression, key in $\boxed{\text{ereg2}-.04}$. Click Apply. For New Column Name, key in $\boxed{\text{ydi}}$

. In Expression, key in $\boxed{\text{yreg2}-8.84}$. Click Apply. Using <u>Statistics</u>, <u>Data Summaries</u>, <u>Summary Statistics</u>, for xreg2, yreg2, and ereg2, we have $\bar{x} = 5.4$, $\bar{y} = 8.84$, $\bar{e} = .04$.]

With this transformation, calculate $\hat{\beta}_1$ and $\hat{\beta}_0$ as in Exercise 13.6. Calculate the estimated variances for the regression coefficients using the equations in the text; calculate TSS, ESS, RSS, R^2 (about the mean), and the F statistic with 1 and 3 degrees of freedom.

b. Repeat the call to S-Plus's regression routine; follow the instructions in Exercise 13.6. Compare your results with those obtained by the computer algorithm and those obtained in Exercise 13.6. Be careful in your comparisons; the results will differ if you have carried too few digits in your calculations.

Comment on the difference in your results in light of the fact that the regression equation was the same using Varreg1 and Varreg2 and only the data differed between the two cases.

13.8 (Refer to Exercises 13.6 and 13.7.) To gain further insight, try the same exercise using a third data set. In this case, the data are stored in the folder Misc, file Varreg3.xls. The $\{x_i\}$ are the same as in Exercise 13.6, but the error terms, $\{\epsilon_i\}$, are the same as in Exercise 13.7. Consequently, what we have here is the simplification that comes from the regressor having a zero mean, but where the covariation between the regressor and the error term is nonzero.

Compare your results with 13.6 and 13.7 results. In particular, note how the changes in the statistical properties of the variables $\{x_i\}$ and $\{\epsilon_i\}$ among the three cases not only affect the ease of calculation but alter the values of the estimates.

After these three exercises, you should have a firm grasp of the mechanics of regression calculations and be familiar with the output from the computer algorithms. Hereafter, you can use the S-Plus regression routine to run regression analyses of real data.

Exploring the Tools

13.9 In the text, the estimators for the coefficients were derived by minimizing a squared function of the errors between the observed dependent variable and the fitted model (see Equation 13.19 and the following). In this exercise, you will be able to evaluate this claim in detail.

Using the three data sets Varreg1, Varreg2, and Varreg3, in the folder Misc, calculate the value of $\Sigma\hat{\epsilon}_i^2$ as a function of $\hat{\beta}_0$ and of $\hat{\beta}_1$. Actually, because $\hat{\beta}_0 = \bar{y} - \hat{\beta}_1\bar{x}$, minimizing $\Sigma\hat{\epsilon}_i^2$ only involves adjusting the value of $\hat{\beta}_1$.

The expression for $\Sigma\hat{\epsilon}_i^2$ is

$$\sum(\hat{\epsilon}_i^2) = \sum(y_i - \hat{\beta}_0 - \hat{\beta}_1 x_i)^2$$
$$= \sum(y_i - \bar{y} - \hat{\beta}_1(x_i - \bar{x}))^2$$

Calculate $\Sigma(\hat{\epsilon}_i^2)$ for each value of $\hat{\beta}_1$ in the range $\{1.7, 1.8, 1.9, 2.0, 2.1, 2.2, 2.3\}$. Can you determine the value of $\hat{\beta}_1$ that produces the minimum of $\Sigma(\hat{\epsilon}_i^2)$ for each of the data sets? You may well have to interpolate for values of $\hat{\beta}_1$ to find the true minimum. Explain the differences in the estimated values for $\hat{\beta}_1$ and why they differ from the value that was used to produce the observed values of $\{y_i\}$—namely, $\beta_1 = 2$.

13.10 (Refer to Exercise 13.9.) The expression for $\hat{\beta}_0$ indicates that the regression line goes through the means, $\{\bar{x}, \bar{y}\}$. Use your results and the plots provided in S-Plus's regression algorithm to confirm this statement for each of the three data sets used in Exercise 13.9.

13.11 In the exercises in Calculation Practice, you calculated the estimated sample variances and standard deviations of the two estimators, $\hat{\beta}_0$ and $\hat{\beta}_1$. Because we actually know the value of β_1 used to generate the observed data, we can calculate the value of $(\hat{\beta}_1 - \beta_1)^2$, and we can calculate the value of the variation in the error terms $\{\epsilon_i\}$ directly. Using each of the three data sets Varreg1, Varreg2, and Varreg3, calculate $(\hat{\beta}_1 - \beta_1)^2$, $\sigma_\epsilon^2/\Sigma x_{di}^2$, where

$\sigma_\epsilon^2 = \frac{1}{5}\sum \epsilon_i^2$; and $\hat{\sigma}_\epsilon^2 / \sum x_{di}^2$, where $\hat{\sigma}_\epsilon^2 = \frac{1}{3}\sum \hat{\epsilon}_i^2$. Explain the differences observed between these expressions in light of the differences in the three data sets.

13.12 (Refer to Exercise 13.11.) Perform the same checks by comparing $(\hat{\beta}_0 - \beta_0)^2$; $\sigma_\epsilon^2(\frac{1}{n} + \bar{x}^2 / \sum x_{di}^2)$, where $\sigma_\epsilon^2 = \frac{1}{5}\sum \epsilon_i^2$; and $\hat{\sigma}_\epsilon^2(\frac{1}{n} + \bar{x}^2 / \sum x_{di}^2)$, where $\hat{\sigma}_\epsilon^2 = \frac{1}{3}\sum \hat{\epsilon}_i^2$. Compare the results for the three data sets, Varreg1, Varreg2, and Varreg3.

13.13 **Worked.** *Objective: To demonstrate that $\hat{\beta}_1$ and $\bar{\epsilon}$ are uncorrelated.* In deriving the variance for the estimator $\hat{\beta}_0$ and the covariance between $\hat{\beta}_0$ and $\hat{\beta}_1$ in the text, we claimed that

$$E\{\bar{\epsilon}(\hat{\beta}_1 - \beta_1)\} = 0$$

in which case, the proofs of Equations 13.26 and 13.27 are complete. An easy way to see this is as follows:

$$\hat{\beta}_1 - \beta_1 = \frac{\sum \epsilon_{di} x_{di}}{\sum x_{di}^2} = \frac{\sum (\epsilon_i - \bar{\epsilon}) x_{di}}{\sum x_{di}^2}$$

$$E\{\bar{\epsilon}(\hat{\beta}_1 - \beta_1)\} = E\left\{\frac{\bar{\epsilon}\sum \epsilon_{di} x_{di}}{\sum x_{di}^2}\right\}$$

$$= E\left\{\frac{\bar{\epsilon}\sum (\epsilon_i - \bar{\epsilon}) x_{di}}{\sum x_{di}^2}\right\}$$

$$= E\left\{\frac{\bar{\epsilon}\sum \epsilon_i x_{di}}{\sum x_{di}^2} - \frac{\bar{\epsilon}^2 \sum x_{di}}{\sum x_{di}^2}\right\}$$

The second term in the last expression is zero by construction; $\sum x_{di} = 0$. The expectation of the first term is given by

$$E\left\{\frac{\bar{\epsilon}\sum \epsilon_i x_{di}}{\sum x_{di}^2}\right\} = E\left\{\frac{\frac{1}{n}\sum \epsilon_i \sum \epsilon_i x_{di}}{\sum x_{di}^2}\right\}$$

$$= E\left\{\frac{\frac{1}{n}\sum \epsilon_i^2 x_{di}}{\sum x_{di}^2} + \frac{\sum_{i \neq j} \epsilon_i x_{di} \epsilon_j x_{dj}}{\sum x_{di}^2}\right\}$$

$$= \sigma^2 \frac{\sum x_{di}}{\sum x_{di}^2} + 0 = 0$$

because the ϵ_i are independent and $\sum x_{di} = 0$. The result is proven.

13.14 **Worked.** *Objective: To show that the estimator $\hat{\sigma}_\epsilon^2$ is unbiased.* In Equation 13.29, we defined the estimator $\hat{\sigma}_\epsilon^2$ as an estimator for σ_ϵ^2 and claimed that the estimator is unbiased. This exercise is the proof:

$$\hat{\sigma}_\epsilon^2 = \frac{1}{n-2}\sum \hat{\epsilon}_i^2$$

$$\hat{\epsilon}_i = (y_i - \hat{\beta}_0 - \hat{\beta}_1 x_i)$$

$$\hat{\beta}_0 = \bar{y} - \hat{\beta}_1 \bar{x}, \quad \hat{\beta}_1 = \frac{\sum y_{di} x_{di}}{\sum x_{di}^2}$$

$$y_{di} = y_i - \bar{y}, \quad x_{di} = x_i - \bar{x}$$

As we can always redefine the regression so that $\bar{x}$ is zero, we will not lose any generality by assuming that $\bar{x}$ is zero, and we thereby save a lot of algebraic complications in the following development.

Under this assumption, we have

$$\hat{\beta}_0 = \beta_0 + \bar{\epsilon}, \quad \hat{\beta}_1 = \frac{\sum x_i y_i}{\sum x_i^2} = \beta_1 + \frac{\sum x_i \epsilon_i}{\sum x_i^2}$$

Using these relationships we can write

$$\sum \hat{\epsilon}_i^2 = \sum (y_i - \hat{\beta}_0 - \hat{\beta}_1 x_i)^2$$

$$= \sum (\beta_0 + \beta_1 x_i + \epsilon_i - \beta_0 - \bar{\epsilon} - \hat{\beta}_1 x_i)^2$$

$$= \sum [(\epsilon_i - \bar{\epsilon}) + (\beta_1 - \hat{\beta}_1) x_i]^2$$

$$= \sum [(\epsilon_i - \bar{\epsilon})^2 + (\beta_1 - \hat{\beta}_1)^2 x_i^2$$

$$+ 2(\epsilon_i - \bar{\epsilon})(\beta_1 - \hat{\beta}_1) x_i]$$

We take expectations term by term to obtain

$$E\left\{\sum (\epsilon_i - \bar{\epsilon})^2\right\} = E\left\{\sum \epsilon_i^2 - n\bar{\epsilon}^2\right\}$$

$$= n\sigma_\epsilon^2 - \frac{n}{n}\sigma_\epsilon^2$$

$$= (n-1)\sigma_\epsilon^2$$

$$E\left\{(\beta_1 - \hat{\beta}_1)^2 \sum x_i^2\right\} = \sigma_\epsilon^2$$

$$E\left\{2(\beta_1 - \hat{\beta}_1)\sum(\epsilon_i - \bar{\epsilon})x_i\right\}$$

$$= E\left\{2(\beta_1 - \hat{\beta}_1)\left[\sum \epsilon_i x_i - \bar{\epsilon}\sum x_i\right]\right\}$$

$$= 2E\left\{-\frac{\sum x_i \epsilon_i}{\sum x_i^2}\left[\sum \epsilon_i x_i - \bar{\epsilon}\sum x_i\right]\right\}$$

And using the fact that $\sum x_i = 0$, we can simplify the expression to

$$2E\left\{-\frac{\left[\sum x_i \epsilon_i\right]^2}{\sum x_i^2}\right\} = -2\sigma_\epsilon^2$$

Adding the three terms together, we obtain

$$(n-1)\sigma_\epsilon^2 + \sigma_\epsilon^2 - 2\sigma_\epsilon^2 = (n-2)\sigma_\epsilon^2$$

or

$$E\left\{\frac{1}{n-2}\sum \hat{\epsilon}_i^2\right\} = \sigma_\epsilon^2$$

13.15   Worked. *Objective: To discover the properties of the F distribution and its dependence on the degrees of freedom.* The F distribution introduced a distribution for the ratio of variance estimators. This exercise is designed to let you experiment with this distribution and examine its shape for various values of the two degrees of freedom parameters, $df1$ for the numerator and $df2$ for the denominator. It is important to remember that the F distribution is a distribution for the ratio of squared Gaussian random variables; the degrees of freedom indicate the number of terms in the summations. When $df1 = 1$, the F distribution can be regarded as the distribution of the square of a random variable distributed as Student's T.

Pay attention to the cases in which $df1 = df2$.

[**Computer directions:** Start S-Plus. On the menu bar, click Labs, Z, t, Chi-square, F, F curves. In the dialog box, vary values of $df1$ and $df2$ by clicking on the buttons.]

13.16   Worked. *Objective: To visualize the relationship between regression lines and scatter plots.*

In Chapter 5, we explored the mechanics of linear regression and in this chapter we have explored the theory. This exercise will give you experience in visualizing the relationship between the fitted regression line and the sample points. It will also help you visualize the distribution of the regression line from one sample draw to the next. In particular, you should pay attention to the relationship between the slope coefficient, the desired R^2, and the number of observations (n).

a. For various values of sample size n, experiment with varying R^2 (expressed as a %) for a given choice of slope parameter. What conclusion do you draw?

b. Experiment with varying the number of sample regressions to get a better idea of the variability of the regression line.

c. As you vary R^2 for a given slope, notice the variation in dispersion of the sample points about the regression line. How is this reflected in the variance of the error term?

[**Computer directions:** Start S-Plus. On the menu bar, click Labs, Bivariate Descriptive Statistics, Least Squares. In the dialog box, vary Sample Size, Slope of True Line, and Desired R-square to desired values. Click Apply.] (*Note:* The samples are fixed Xs that are n equally spaced points from -1 to $+1$. All graphs produced during the lab are on the same scale of X from -1 to $+1$ and Y from -6 to $+6$. This allows the results in any one graph to be comparable to any other. [Individual sample points show only if the number of sample regressions is 1.])

Write up an evaluation of your experimental results indicating what general principles you have observed. In particular, what is the relationship between slope, R^2, and the size of error term?

Applications

13.17   Worked. *Objective: To illustrate use of the regression routines and provide practice in* *interpreting the results.* In the folder Firmdata, we have some times series on firm performance for seven firms. It will be interesting to explore some financial relationships and examine the extent to which they differ across firms.

a. Do sales generate income, in that there is an approximate linear relationship between income (dependent variable) and sales? How does the slope coefficient vary across firms? What conclusions can you draw from a close examination of the data?

[**Computer directions:** Start S-Plus. Import file Xfiles\Firmdata\Avon.xls. On the menu bar, click Statistics, Regression, Linear. In the dialog, set Data Frame to "Avon." In Formula, key in income ~sales. Click on the Plot tab; in Plots check only Residuals vs Fit. Click Apply. The results are in the Graph window and the Report window. Repeat for each company.]

b. Research provides the products that lead to income; but income provides the cash needed to finance research. Try checking the latter notion by regressing the research expense variable *rdexp* on the variable *income*. What differences do you notice across the representative terms?

[**Computer directions:** Repeat instructions from (*a*), using *rdexp* as the dependent variable and *income* as the independent variable for all the firms.]

Commentary: [This discussion presumes that you have performed the calculations; they are not reproduced here to save space.] (1) With one exception, Digital, the estimated slope coefficients between income and sales are positive, and Digital's negative coefficient is not statistically significant at any reasonable level. Most of the estimated coefficients are statistically significant at reasonable confidence levels. Nevertheless, these fairly consistent regression results across six different firms do not in any way *prove* causality from sales to income. However, the close relationship observed in most cases indicates that there is something here to be investigated further. If we view the matter as economists, not as statisticians, we recognize that increased sales will increase income provided costs do not rise more than com-

mensurately. As a counterexample, Amazon's sales have been increasing dramatically but not its "income," because costs of expansion and the development of new systems have consumed more resources than were provided by the firm's own sales. A regression of Amazon's sales and income over this period would definitely not conform to the qualitative conclusions reached here.

The range of estimated coefficient values is from 0.01 to 0.14, so that given the estimated standard errors it is reasonable to conclude that although there seem to be similar forces at work leading to a positive relationship between sales and income, there are substantial differences in the relationship across firms. On close examination of the residual plots, it is clear that there are more factors at play in this regression than just the effect of sales on income; similar comments apply to Johnson but not as strongly. The residual plots for Campbell, Digital, and Johnson indicate that in each case there is evidence of some other factor that impinges on the relationship in that the residuals are clearly highly positively correlated, although there appears to be some evidence that the "tightness" of the relationship declines toward the end of the period.

(2) Four firms, Campbell, Hasbro, Johnson, and Three.m, show a strong positive relationship between contemporaneous research expenditures and income. The estimated coefficients are in all but one case very strongly statistically significant. With the exception of Johnson, there is no clear evidence in the residual plots that there are factors not considered in the analysis that are affecting research expenditures. To an economist, these results are puzzling in that one would not expect contemporaneous research expenditures to be very closely linked, except by chance, to contemporaneous income; rather research expenditures should be linked to the firm's expectations of future income growth arising from that research. However, there is a school of thought that in industries where obtaining outside financing is difficult, leading firms depend on their own internally generated resources, high incomes are needed to finance research expenditures. A quibble with this argument is that

this is at best a necessary, but not a sufficient, condition. The firm will still want to be assured that its research expenditures have a high probability of a sizable positive payoff.

Of more interest, is that the estimated slope coefficients are remarkably close to each other for the firms with very significant coefficients; contrast this result with that in (a). This is another result that requires further analysis as to why we have apparently achieved such a remarkable uniformity of result.

13.18 As industrial production rises and falls, so does employment given some fixed level of technology and capital stock. If we examine the statistical results for a regression of employment level (dependent variable) on industrial production (independent variable), what if anything can we conclude? The data are contained in the folder Gnp, subfolder Domgnp, Domgnp.xls. Run a Linear Regression following the computer directions in Exercise 13.17, using variables *emp* and *indprod* for the employment level and industrial production, respectively.

13.19 A question long debated by economists involves the relationship between the change in money wages (dependent variable) and the unemployment level (independent variable); this is a version of the famous Phillips curve. Run a Simple Regression, using the computer directions in Exercise 13.17. Use the file folder Gnp, subfolder Domgnp, Domgnp.xls, and variables *dwage* and *unemp* for change in money wages and unemployment level, respectively. What, if anything, can you conclude from this regression?

13.20 The idea of "wage driven" price increases is that an increase in wages leads to inflation. However, the problem is trying to distinguish between inflation in final goods prices leading to a demand for higher money wages and whether higher money wages lead to inflation. This problem we will ignore.

Statistically, what we observe is the relationship between the *cpi* and *money wages* (see the variable *wage*). Consider the regression of "cpi" on "wage."

Using the file folder Gnp, subfolder Domgnp, Domgnp.xls, follow the computer directions in Exercise 13.17. Comment on the relevance of your results to the issue of the relationship between the cpi and money wages.

13.21 *Worked. Objective: To illustrate use of the regression routine.* In a weight reduction program at NYU, a number of students of both sexes were enrolled. It is reasonable to presume that weight and height are positively correlated, but the relationship between height and fat is not so obvious. In the folder Misc, file Coles.xls are the variables *ht* for height, the regressor variable, and the variables *prewt* and *prefat*, the preprogram weight and fat measurements. Regress each of these latter two variables on height, and comment on the differences between the regressions.

[*Computer directions:* Start S-Plus. Import file Xfiles\Misc\Coles.xls. On the menu bar, click Statistics, Regression, Linear. In the dialog Data Frame select Coles. In Formula, key in prewt~ht. Click on the Plot tab; in Plots check only Residuals vs Fit. Click Apply. The results are in the Graph window and the Report window. Repeat for prefat.]

It is as plausible to regress ht on prewt as the other way around. Try regressing ht on prewt, using the same linear regression computer instructions. Once again the temptation to label a significant regression result as "causal" is potentially misleading. Does height "cause" preprogram weight, or preprogram weight "cause" height? The tools that you have so far do not enable you to decide this issue.

13.22 Economic theory tells us that as your income rises, consumption of (normal) commodities increases. The intuition is that the more income you have, the greater quantities of all commodities you consume. Use the data contained in the file Food.xls in the Misc folder to explore the hypothesis that as your income (*y*) rises, the quantity of food you consume (*qd*) rises. See the computer directions in Exercise 13.21. Can you relate the result of your hypothesis test to common sense? What difficulties do you anticipate from your statistical analysis?

13.23 The file Psychol.xls in folder Misc contains data on Intelligence Quotient measures and height (measured in inches) for 50 individuals. Explore the hypothesis that shorter people are smarter than taller people. How does this hypothesis differ from the hypothesis that smarter people are shorter than less-intelligent people? Would your testing procedure differ between the two hypotheses? Test both of these hypotheses, and explain any differences in the results you obtain.

13.24 (Refer to Exercise 13.21.) Consider whether the effects of the exercise program, if any, were greater or less for weight or fat. We might speculate that with large values for prewt we would have high values for postwt, but that a regression of the latter on the former would indicate a slope coefficient with a value less than one; that is, even though heavier people are still heavier after the program, they are less so.

Run a regression of postwt on prewt and comment on the apparent effectiveness of the exercise program. See the computer directions in Exercise 13.21. Compare these results with those obtained by regressing postfat on prefat. Is the program more effective for fat or weight reduction? How would you decide this issue? (*Hint:* Remember that regression coefficients have units of measurement attached.)

13.25 Among the members of your class, ask the students to provide a measure of arm length, height, or shoe size. Be very specific about what you want measured and how. Ask them to acquire the same information from their parents. For each pair of mothers and daughters and fathers and sons, repeat the calculations that gave rise to the "regression fallacy" that was discussed in the text. Compare the box-and-whisker plots of the two sets of measurements. Comment.

13.26 Consider the following experiment. Pick a course with multiple sections. In each section, have the students play a fair game; that is, the probability of losing is .5 and the probability of winning is .5. In one section, praise the winners and criticize the losers; and in the other section, do the opposite; and in a third section, do neither. Replay the game in each section. Compare the outcomes in the three cases. What comments can you make about the efficacy of praise and blame in affecting performance in these situations and the relevance of the statistics that you calculate?

13.27 Consider this a companion experiment to Exercise 13.26. Randomly select half the students to play a game that is biased in their favor; that is, their probability of winning is .6, so that the probability of the opponent winning is only .4. These probabilities represent the "innate capabilities" of the two types of students. Play a sequence of games for each pair of students, and record the number of wins for each. Do this twice; you need not, but you may, praise and blame the students on their performance in the first round. Repeat the analysis that gave rise to the regression fallacy, and confirm that the conclusions you came to hold in this case as well. Now, select the good students and calculate their average performance in both trials, and select the poor students and calculate their performance in the two trials. Test whether the mean scores are the same for each group across the two trials. Comment on your results.

13.28 Case Study: Was There Age Discrimination in a Public Utility?

Your firm, Forensic Economics Consulting, has been asked to represent the defendants in this case. You have been asked to explain to your colleagues the benefits from using regression analysis.

Explain in detail with examples your strategy for using regression analysis to address the issues in this case. Your task is to convince your colleagues of the benefits of regression analysis so that resources will be provided for its use.

13.29 Case Study: Was There Age Discrimination in a Public Utility?

Implement the regression strategy you espoused in Exercise 13.28. Assess the outcome, and recommend to your company president the presentation that should be made to the defendants' lawyers.

CHAPTER
14

Comparing Populations through the Analysis of Variance

14.1   What You Will Learn in This Chapter

The topic of this chapter is the *analysis of variance,* or ANOVA as it is known. We consider a series of observations on the outcomes from a variety of treatments, or experimental conditions. Analysis of variance asks the question, Is there more variation in output across treatments relative to the variation within treatments? In essence we ask, given the usual variation in output from any treatment, or experimental condition, does an increase in the level of the treatment, or does a difference in the conditions of the experiment, lead to a recognizable difference in the output? The answer is obtained through the procedure called ANOVA.

14.2   Introduction

Much of our interest in using statistics lies in comparing effects. We treat subjects for diseases, design ways to improve production, improve teaching methods, rearrange schedules for greater efficiency, compare performance across state and national boundaries, and so on. In each case, underlying our question is the concern whether the differences between the mean values are detectable. The major factor impeding the detectability of any difference is the inherent variability of the data. As an example look again at Figures 11.1 and 11.3 in Chapter 11, which represent the differences between two means. In the second graph, the difference in means is very large relative to the size of the respective variances, so that detecting a difference is almost trivial. In Chapter 11, we showed how to compare two mean values and test the hypothesis that the difference was zero when the situation was not so obvious. As we saw there, the efficiency of that comparison depends critically on the sizes of the variances of the two distributions that are involved. For example, consider Figure 14.1, and compare it with Figure 14.2. In the former case, the degree of difference between the means is small relative to the variability of the data; whereas in the second figure the difference in the means is large relative to the variability of the data, so we can easily determine that the means differ.

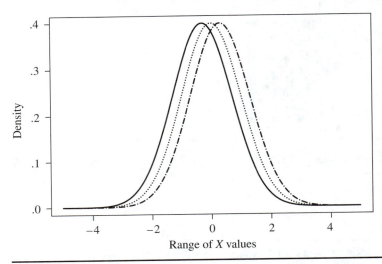

Figure 14.1   Comparison of three distributions with different means and large variances

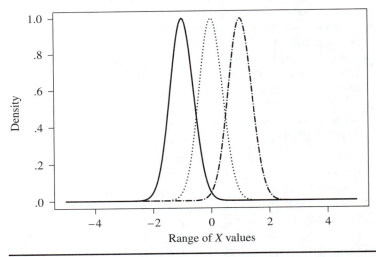

Figure 14.2   Comparison of three distributions with large differences in the means relative to the variances

In this chapter, we will investigate the idea of comparing means more extensively and will show how to compare many means at once. More generally, we will set up the mechanism that will allow us to answer a variety of questions of the type just discussed. Further, we will be able to do this with a very simple framework. Consequently, as you will discover, the tool of analysis of variance is one of the major workhorses of statistical analysis. Before proceeding, let us review from our data sets some questions that are typical of those amenable to the analysis of variance.

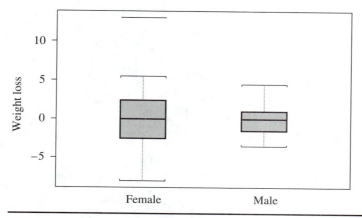

Figure 14.3   Box-and-whisker plot of weight loss by categories: Male and female

In the data set, Energy, we could query whether fuel per capita, or energy use per capita, differs significantly across countries. Whether we will be able to detect any differences depends on the degree of variability of the data. In the folder Misc, we might be interested in whether there are significant differences in blood pressure across age groups (see file Coles.xls). We might also ask whether the relative weight, or relative fat loss, varies by sex or by age. Other questions are whether the fuel consumption of cars differs significantly across make and model and whether housing starts differ by interest rate level.

This last question indicates an advantage to the approach that we are taking here. One way for us to formulate this question is to propose a model of the relationship between volume of housing starts and the interest rate; this relationship may, or may not, be linear. If the relationship is linear, we can use regression analysis (discussed in Chapter 13), but if not we may be at a loss as to how to proceed. Indeed, we may have no idea of what the nonlinear mechanism looks like. With the approach that we will take in this chapter, we do not need to specify a precise relationship between housing starts and interest rates but merely ask whether there is a detectable difference between the means of housing starts for low, medium, and high interest rates.

14.3   An Introduction to One-Way Analysis of Variance

Let us develop the model for analysis of variance in the context of a simple example. Suppose that we are interested in the difference between males and females with respect to the amount of weight gained or lost after participating in a fitness program. Our question is whether the gain or loss differs significantly between males and females. A box-and-whisker plot of the two data series is in Figure 14.3. To contrast this example, consider the difference in height between the sexes (see Figure 14.4). In either case, our initial objective is to calculate the mean values for each sex and then to see if the differences are significant given the degree of variation of the data.

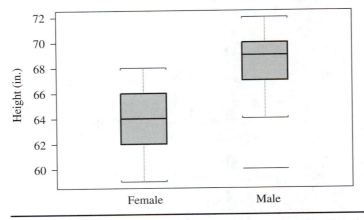

Figure 14.4   Box-and-whisker plots for heights by categories: Male and female

Let us write down a model for this type of situation. Let y_{ij} denote the observed weight loss by individual j of sex $i = \{M, F\}$. We recognize that for each sex there will be many factors impinging on the weight gain or loss, so we expect that the distribution about the mean is Gaussian. Our observed model is therefore

$$
\begin{aligned}
y_{ij} &= \mu_i + \epsilon_{ij} \\
&j = 1, 2, \ldots, n_i \\
&i = 1, 2
\end{aligned}
\tag{14.1}
$$

The theoretical model statement is

$$
\begin{aligned}
Y_{ij} &= \mu_i + \epsilon_{ij} \\
&j = 1, 2, \ldots, n_i \\
&i = 1, 2
\end{aligned}
\tag{14.2}
$$

There are n_i observations of each sex. The error terms are assumed to be distributed as Gaussian with zero mean and constant variance, σ_ϵ^2, across the two sexes. Equations 14.1 and 14.2 summarize our model for the analysis of variance. The basic idea is that we are going to compare the variation within groups, in our case that is within the sexes, to the variation across the groups, or in our case, across the sexes. The former variation depends on σ_ϵ^2, and the latter depends on the square of the difference between the means. Our null hypothesis is that

$$
H_0 : \mu_1 = \mu_2
\tag{14.3}
$$

The alternative hypothesis is that the μ_i are different. We can simplify the situation by extracting the common mean value in the following manner:

$$
Y_{ij} = \mu + \delta_i + \epsilon_{ij}
$$

where

$$
\delta_i = \mu_i - \mu
\tag{14.4}
$$

Mean μ is the average of the μ_i, so the null hypothesis becomes

$$H_0 : \delta_i = 0 \tag{14.5}$$

and the alternative hypothesis is $\delta_i \neq 0$. This approach makes sense because we are almost always interested in the differences between the groups, not the overall level of the responses. Because we are interested in differences from overall means, it seems reasonable to obtain estimators of these differences. We can stress the differences by rewriting Equation 14.4 as

$$Y_{ij} - \mu = \delta_i + \epsilon_{ij} \tag{14.6}$$

This equation suggests that we calculate the various means and take differences. Define n by $n = n_1 + n_2$; n is the total number of observations on the two groups combined. A first guess as to useful estimators is

$$\hat{\mu} = \frac{1}{n} \sum_{i,j} Y_{ij}$$

$$\hat{\mu}_i = \frac{1}{n_i} \sum_{j} Y_{ij} \tag{14.7}$$

$$\hat{\delta}_i = \hat{\mu}_i - \hat{\mu}$$

The overall sample mean is $\hat{\mu}$, $\hat{\mu}_i$ is the sample mean for the ith group, and $\hat{\delta}_i$ is the estimate of the difference between the overall mean and the ith group mean.

Using these definitions of the estimators, we can reexpress the components of the model in terms of the observed estimates as follows:

$$\begin{aligned} y_{ij} - \hat{\mu} &= (y_{ij} - \hat{\mu}_i) + (\hat{\mu}_i - \hat{\mu}) \\ &= (y_{ij} - \hat{\mu}_i) + \hat{\delta}_i \end{aligned} \tag{14.8}$$

Equation 14.8 states that the total variation of the observed y_{ij} about the overall estimated mean, $\hat{\mu}$, can be separated into two components: the variation of the observed y_{ij} about the estimated individual group means plus the variation of the group means about the overall mean. Given all the technical expertise that we have mastered by now, it is simple for us to show that all the estimators in Equation 14.7 are unbiased for their respective parameters. Further, given our assumptions about the distribution of ϵ_{ij}, we can also show that the distribution of each estimator in Equation 14.7 is Gaussian. If you do not see these results right away, then spend a few moments convincing yourself that these statements are true.

Now let us consider squaring and summing the terms in Equation 14.8. We have

$$\begin{aligned} \sum_i \sum_j (y_{ij} - \hat{\mu})^2 &= \sum_i \sum_j \left[(y_{ij} - \hat{\mu}_i)^2 + \hat{\delta}_i^2 + 2(y_{ij} - \hat{\mu}_i)\hat{\delta}_i \right] \\ &= \sum_i \left[\sum_j (y_{ij} - \hat{\mu}_i)^2 + n_i \hat{\delta}_i^2 \right] \end{aligned} \tag{14.9}$$

The cross-product term drops out because if we sum over the index j first, we get zero; that is,

$$\sum_j (y_{ij} - \hat{\mu}_i)\hat{\delta}_i = 0$$

because $\hat{\mu}_i$ is the estimated mean of the observed y_{ij} for each index i. We have, in a manner similar to that in the last chapter, a decomposition of the total sum of squares. The total sum of squares equals the sum of the within group sum of squares and the between group sum of squares. Symbolically, we have for the observed data:

$$\text{TSS} = \text{WSS} + \text{BSS}$$
$$\text{TSS} = \sum_i \sum_j (y_{ij} - \hat{\mu})^2$$
$$\text{WSS} = \sum_i \sum_j (y_{ij} - \hat{\mu}_i)^2 \qquad (14.10)$$
$$\text{BSS} = \sum_i n_i \hat{\delta}_i^2$$

In terms of the random variables and the estimators defined above, we have:

$$\text{TSS} = \text{WSS} + \text{BSS}$$
$$\text{TSS} = \sum_i \sum_j (Y_{ij} - \hat{\mu})^2$$
$$\text{WSS} = \sum_i \sum_j (Y_{ij} - \hat{\mu}_i)^2 \qquad (14.11)$$
$$\text{BSS} = \sum_i n_i \hat{\delta}_i^2$$

BSS is the **between group sum of squares,** and **WSS** is the **within group sum of squares.** WSS measures the variability of the data within each group about the individual group means, whereas BSS measures the sum of squares generated by the variation between the individual group means and the overall mean.

By this stage in the analysis you can almost guess what is to come next. Because the components that enter Equation 14.9 are the squares of the observed Gaussian variables with zero means under the null hypothesis that $\mu_1 = \mu_2$, we can surmise that the squares that we have in Equation 14.11 will be distributed as chi-square. We face two small difficulties. One has to do with the unknown scale involved in the equation because we do not know the error variance, σ_ϵ^2. The other problem is that we need to figure out the degrees of freedom.

We can eliminate the first problem by taking ratios of the sums of squares, each divided by its unknown scale factor, σ_ϵ^2. We remove the second difficulty by noting that the degrees of freedom for TSS are $(n - 1)$, the total number of observations less 1 degree of freedom for having to estimate the overall mean. Calculating the degrees of freedom for the BSS is a little more subtle. One way to view the matter is that we have only a single, independent difference to estimate because $\Sigma_{i=1}^2 \delta_i = 0$, so we have 1

Table 14.1   **Analysis of Variance Table for *k* Groups**

Source of Variation	Sum of Squares	Degrees of Freedom	Mean Sum of Squares	$F_{\nu_1 \nu_2}$
Between	BSS	$k-1$	$MBS = BSS/(k-1)$	$\nu_1 = k-1$
Within	WSS	$(n-1)-(k-1)$	$MWS = WSS/(n-k)$	$\nu_2 = n-k$
Total	TSS	$n-1$		$F = MBS/MWS$

Table 14.2   **Analysis of Variance Table for NYU Weight Loss by Sex**

Source of Variation	Sum of Squares	Degrees of Freedom	Mean Sum of Squares	$F_{\nu_1 \nu_2}$
Between	0.007	$k-1=1$	$MBS = 0.007$	$\nu_1 = 1$
Within	431.98	$(n-1)-(k-1)$	$MWS = 13.1$	$\nu_2 = 33$
Total	431.99	$n-1=34$		$F = MBS/MWS$
				$= 0.007/13.1$
				$= 0.0005$

degree of freedom. To calculate the WSS degrees of freedom, we can subtract the degrees of freedom for BSS from those for TSS. Alternatively, we can think of the WSS as having $(n-2)$ degrees of freedom, as we have n observations and two group means to calculate. Under the null hypothesis that $\mu_1 = \mu_2$, equivalently that $\delta_i = 0$, we note that BSS/σ_ϵ^2 is distributed as chi-square with 1 degree of freedom. Under the alternative hypothesis that $\delta_i \neq 0$ we would have to add to the distribution the sum of the squares of the δ_i. Under both hypotheses, WSS/σ_ϵ^2 is distributed as chi-square with $n-2$ degrees of freedom. Following similar arguments as indicated in Chapter 13, we can show that the within and between sums of squares are independently distributed.

In Chapter 13, we discovered that when we have a pair of independent chi-square variables scaled by an unknown parameter, σ^2, we create an F distribution by taking the ratio of BSS to WSS after dividing each by its corresponding degrees of freedom (recall Equation 13.59). Under the null hypothesis that $\delta_i = 0$, we have

$$F_{1,n-2} = \frac{BSS/1}{WSS/(n-2)} = \frac{BSS \times (n-2)}{WSS \times 1} \tag{14.12}$$

Observing a large value of $F_{1,n-2}$ indicates rejection of the null hypothesis. Recall that the F_{1,ν_2} distribution is the square of the Student's T distribution with ν_2 degrees of freedom.

This analysis is known as ANOVA, the analysis of variance. It is very common to summarize the operations in terms of a table that shows the breakdown of the total variance into its component parts (see Table 14.1). In this table, we have allowed for k groups, and so k means, and therefore $k-1$ degrees of freedom for BSS.

Having derived the theory, let us consider the actual calculations for the problem of weight loss for the NYU students and ask whether there is any difference between the sexes. Referring to Equation 14.1, the y_{ij} values represent weight loss by both sexes and the i index indicates "Male" and "Female." We reproduce Table 14.1 as Table 14.2 but include in it the entries for our specific problem on weight loss: $k = 2$,

Table 14.3 **Analysis of Variance Table for NYU Students' Heights by Sex**

Source of Variation	Sum of Squares	Degrees of Freedom	Mean Sum of Squares	$F_{\nu_1 \nu_2}$
Between	127.9	$k - 1 = 1$	MBS = 127.9	$\nu_1 = 1$
Within	411.5	$(n - 1) - (k - 1)$	MWS = 8.75	$\nu_2 = 47$
Total	539.4	$n - 1 = 48$		$F = 127.9/8.75$
				$= 14.6$

$n = 35$. An examination of Table 14.2 indicates that the probability of rejecting any difference in weight loss is very small indeed given an observed F value of 0.0005 with 1 and 33 degrees of freedom. An examination of the box-and-whisker plots in Figure 14.3 illustrates our formal analysis of the observed weight loss separated into the two categories Male and Female.

To contrast, let us examine whether for these same NYU students there is a detectable difference in heights. Examine Table 14.3, in which the ANOVA figures for student heights are given for a breakdown by sex; $k = 2$ as before, but n is 49. And now we see that with 1 and 47 degrees of freedom, an observed F value of 14.6 indicates rejection of the null hypothesis of no difference in height at a probability of more than 99.96%; that is, the probability under the null hypothesis of getting a value of F that is this large is less than 0.1%. Recall that you can calculate the probability of getting an F value this large by using the routines in S-Plus [click Labs, Statistical Tables, F, select 14.6 for the F statistic, 1 for the numerator degrees of freedom, and 47 for the denominator degrees of freedom. The output is in the S-Plus Results window.] Once again it pays to examine the box-and-whisker plots of the data to interpret these results more efficiently (see Figure 14.4).

For a more complicated example, suppose that we are interested in whether average fuel consumption differs significantly across different weights of cars. Using the file Cardata.xls in the folder Misc, let us plot the box-and-whisker plots for the mpg, having created four equal intervals for the weight of the cars observed (see Figure 14.5). The ANOVA results that we obtain are shown in Table 14.4. There is very strong evidence that mpg differs by car weight. By using the integral of the F distribution contained in the "F tables," you can calculate the values of the critical bounds for any confidence level or determine the P value.

Let us consider a very different example; examine the scatter diagram in Figure 14.6, which shows the number of damaged O-rings in the space shuttle *Challenger* as a function of temperature. These data clearly indicate the presence of a nonlinear relationship

Table 14.4 **Analysis of Variance Table for MPG by Car Weight**

Source of Variation	Sum of Squares	Degrees of Freedom	Mean Sum of Squares	$F_{\nu_1 \nu_2}$
Between	5719	$k - 1 = 3$	MBS = 1906	$\nu_1 = 3$
Within	2607	$(n - 1) - (k - 1)$	MWS = 17.4	$\nu_2 = 150$
Total	8326	$n - 1 = 154$		$F = 1906/17.4$
				$= 109.7$

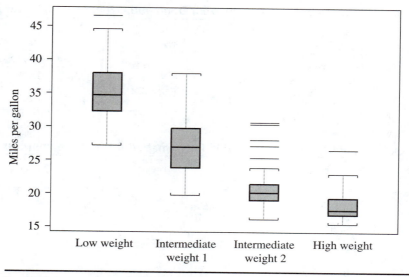

Figure 14.5   Box-and-whisker plots for mpg by categories by weight

between temperature and the number of damaged O-rings. Below about 68 degrees Fahrenheit the occurrence is highly probable and above that temperature the results are unlikely but do occur. What if we do an ANOVA on these data and separate them by temperature into two ranges, below and above 67°. The results are shown in Table 14.5. What we see in this table is that the *formal* ANOVA procedures do not give a very clear

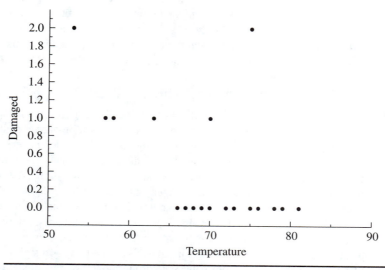

Figure 14.6   Scatter plot of damaged O-rings by temperature for the shuttle *Challenger*

Table 14.5

Analysis of Variance Table for Damaged O-Rings: Temperature Break at 67

Source of Variation	Sum of Squares	Degrees of Freedom	Mean Sum of Squares	$F_{\nu_1 \nu_2}$
Between	0.67	$k - 1 = 1$	MBS = 0.67	$\nu_1 = 1$
Within	8.81	$(n - 1) - (k - 1)$	MWS = 0.42	$\nu_2 = 21$
Total	9.48	$n - 1 = 22$		$F = .067/.042$
				$= 1.60$

Table 14.6

Analysis of Variance Table for Damaged O-Rings: Temperature Break at 65

Source of Variation	Sum of Squares	Degrees of Freedom	Mean Sum of Squares	$F_{\nu_1 \nu_2}$
Between	3.57	$k - 1 = 1$	MBS = 3.57	$\nu_1 = 1$
Within	5.91	$(n - 1) - (k - 1)$	MWS = 0.28	$\nu_2 = 21$
Total	9.48	$n - 1 = 22$		$F = 3.57/0.28$
				$= 12.7$

picture of what is happening. This is because the within group variation given the dividing temperature of 67° is large relative to the differences in numbers of damaged O-rings, which must be in single units. The P value for the F statistic observed is 0.2, which is quite high; that is, the probability under the null hypothesis of no difference in numbers of damaged O-rings of getting a value this large or larger is 0.2.

If we divide the range of temperature into two new groups, below 65° degrees and above that temperature, a seemingly small change, we obtain the results shown in Table 14.6. Now we see very clear evidence that the means of the two groups are very different. The observed F statistic is now much larger and the corresponding P value has fallen to 0.0018! If the NASA engineers had only carried out this analysis of these data, the loss of the *Challenger* might have been prevented. Certainly, this example indicates that these analyses—indeed, all statistical analysis—must be done with understanding of the problem and with care. This example also indicates that often there is no substitute for a clear graph of the data.

For Multiple Treatments, Which Is Best?

In Table 14.4 we examined the effect of car weight on gasoline mileage by defining four levels of weight and estimating mean consumption within each weight category. Our F statistic with 3 and 150 degrees of freedom was 109.7, which is very highly significant. Now the inevitable question arises: Which effect is the greatest? In this particular problem we think the answer is obvious; the largest car weight will experience the lowest miles per gallon. But if we were comparing the effects of different treatments in a production process, we would want to know which had the greatest impact, and that answer might not be so obvious. For example, we might be comparing alternative analgesics and investigating which had the greatest impact on reducing migraine headaches. So far, all we are able to conclude from our analysis is that there is a significant difference over all the cell means; we cannot yet say anything more. We cannot state which treatment has the largest effect, how large the largest difference is, or whether it is significant. However, solving these problems is not as simple as you might at first guess. We will deal with these issues step by step.

Let us extract a little more information from our current procedure when the number of treatments, or the number of cells, k, is only two. If we obtain a statistically significant value for the F statistic, we are justified in drawing the inference that with high probability there is a sizable difference between the two means. But, which is greater and how large is the difference? Observing a significant F statistic merely indicates that there is a significant *difference* between the means; it provides summary information about the entire set of means without distinction. If however, we reject the null of no difference and $k = 2$, we still need to *describe* the difference in terms of direction and magnitude; in short are we claiming μ_1 is greater than μ_2, or is it the other way around? And by how much does one mean exceed the other?

The simplest solution to this problem is to look at the estimated difference; this can be expressed in terms of either $\hat{\mu}_1 - \hat{\mu}_2$, or $\hat{\delta}_i$, as discussed in Equation 14.7. Your choice is based purely on your interest and the question posed. In the former case, one is interested in the actual difference between the two means—the usual case; and in the second case, one is interested in the difference between the largest cell mean and the overall mean.

In some circumstances, the units of measurement of the observed dependent variable may be unfamiliar to the reader. For example we might be considering prices in U.S. dollars, pounds sterling (£), or Euros, so we would prefer a measure that is invariant to scale effects. We can achieve this by describing the difference in means relative to the size of the pooled standard deviation, which is nothing more than WSS divided by the appropriate degrees of freedom and multiplied by the "inverse of the pooled sample size," (Section 11.7). Define s_p by

$$s_p = \sqrt{\frac{\text{WSS}}{(n-k)}} \times \sqrt{\frac{1}{n_1} + \frac{1}{n_2}}$$

$$\text{WSS} = \sum_i \sum_j (y_{ij} - \hat{\mu}_i)^2 \tag{14.13}$$

to obtain

$$\frac{\hat{\mu}_1 - \hat{\mu}_2}{s_p}$$

$$\hat{\mu}_1 = \frac{1}{n_1} \sum_j y_{1j}$$

$$\hat{\mu}_2 = \frac{1}{n_2} \sum_j y_{2j}$$

We may describe the result by saying that the difference between the means is "so many standard deviations away from zero." For example, we may say something like, "The price of a Mercedes in Euros is 1.6 standard deviations greater in Germany than in the Canary Islands."

For example, in the analysis of O-ring damage, we obtained a very significant F statistic for a temperature break at 65° F, (Table 14.6). The estimated mean number of damaged O-rings in the two cases, below 65° and above 65°, are

$$\hat{\mu}_1 = 1.25$$
$$\hat{\mu}_2 = 0.21$$

$$s_p = \sqrt{0.28} \times \sqrt{\frac{1}{4} + \frac{1}{19}} = 0.291$$

$$\frac{\hat{\mu}_1 - \hat{\mu}_2}{s_p} = \frac{1.25 - 0.21}{0.291}$$

$$= 3.57$$

We complete our analysis of the *Challenger* data by noting that the difference in means is 3.57 standard deviations and that the low temperature cell has the greater number of O-ring failures. You can now appreciate that if the *Challenger* management team had only examined the data in this very simple manner, they might have saved the loss of the *Challenger,* not to mention the many lives that were lost. It is truly amazing that even in the twentieth century, such well known and easily implemented procedures were ignored, when the benefit from their implementation was so enormous.

Recall the case of the investigation of car mileage as a function of car weight, where $k = 4$. We have already noted from the calculation of the F statistic that the differences are very significant; the F statistic was 109.7 with 3 and 150 degrees of freedom. And now we have a problem, in fact two problems, as we ask which weight has the greatest effect on car mileage. In principle, we can compare $\hat{\mu}_1$ with $\hat{\mu}_2$, or $\hat{\mu}_3$, or $\hat{\mu}_4$, or $\hat{\mu}_2$ with $\hat{\mu}_3$, and so on. With k cells, or treatments, there are in principle $k \times (k - 1)/2$ individual comparisons; when $k = 4$, that yields 6 comparisons to be made. If $k = 8$, not an unrealistic value, the number of comparisons becomes 28.

If we merely follow the example where $k = 2$ and contemplate making all these pairwise comparisons by testing the null hypotheses of zero difference against the alternative of a nonzero difference, then we can define a statistic that is distributed as Student's T with $(n - k)$ degrees of freedom (Section 11.7). To test a hypothesis about a specific difference, we define

$$H_o : T = \frac{\hat{\mu}_i - \hat{\mu}_j}{s_p} = 0, i \neq j$$

$$H_a : T = \frac{\hat{\mu}_i - \hat{\mu}_j}{s_p} \neq 0,$$

(14.14)

or

$$H_a : T = \frac{\hat{\mu}_i - \hat{\mu}_j}{s_p} > 0$$

The first alternative hypothesis is two-sided and the second is one-sided, representing different levels of information that we might have. If we proceed in this manner, we will run into a difficulty, for if we assign the same α level to each test, the probability of Type I error for *all six comparisons* will be greater than α! Imagine for a moment that we are making 100 comparisons, and we continue to assume that all the differences are distributed independently of each other. If the chosen α level for each test is 0.05, then purely by chance under the joint null hypothesis of no difference in any of the means, we would expect on average five significant rejections of the null hypothesis, and the probability of getting at least one such rejection is a huge 0.994. Clearly, we need to rethink our approach. The crude, but workable, solution is to use what is called the **Bonferroni inequality,** which states, assuming the statistical independence of comparisons, that the probability of making at least one Type I error from a given set of comparisons is less than or equal to the sum of the α values used for each individual comparison. So if we set a single α level for q comparisons, the probability of Type I error for the family is no greater than $q\alpha$. Alternatively, if we set an overall Type I error level of α, the individual probabilities of Type I error should be set to α/q. The overall probability of Type I error is known as the **familywise Type I error rate.** In our example using car weights and mileage, if we want a familywise error rate of only 0.12, the individual α levels must be set to 0.02.

We now come to our second problem, *pretesting bias*. **Pretesting bias** is incurred when a hypothesis test is carried out conditional on the outcome of a prior test. The source of the bias is easy to see. Suppose that we use the F test to test that there is a significant difference between some one or more means. Given that we reject the null hypothesis, we then test for the significance of individual pairwise comparisons at some specified α level. Because we only implement the second test given a rejection of the null hypothesis in the prior F test, we can see that the assignment of the probability of Type I error in the second test will be incorrect, even after allowing for the Bonferroni inequality effect.

The way out of this box is that either we can use a general test for some mean(s) to be significantly different, not caring which, or we can perform a sequence of tests on the individual comparisons. But what we should not do is to perform the F test and *subsequently* on the basis of a significant rejection of the joint null hypothesis, perform individual tests on each of the comparisons. The difficulty in this two-stage procedure is that we can no longer claim that the assigned probabilities of Type I error are correct. An easy way to see this is to consider the case where $k = 2$. If we have rejected the null hypothesis using the F test, then an "individual" comparison test using the same assigned α level will reject with probability 1.0!

Let us consider another example. Data on the coagulation times in response to four alternative diets are cited in one of the S-Plus manuals. They are listed only as A, B, C, and D. Which diet has the highest coagulation time? Note that people with arterial blockages are aided by "thinning of the blood." Figure 14.7 is a box-and-whisker plot of the coagulation times for the four diets. The more specific question is whether diet C is significantly greater than A, B, or D. Given the question posed, we will choose the path of testing a set of individual comparisons and eschew using the general F test. For the record, if we were to use the general F test the F statistic would be 13.57 with 3 and 20 degrees of freedom; the corresponding P value would be 0.000047!

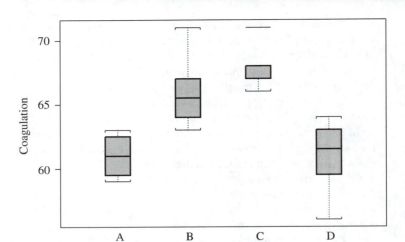

Figure 14.7   Box-and-whisker plots of blood coagulation times for four diets

We have agreed to test whether the mean of diet C has a longer coagulation time than the means for diets A, B, and D. We need first an estimate for the residual standard deviation; that is given by the square root of the MWS, the mean within sum of squares. The value obtained is 2.37 with 20 degrees of freedom. The individual estimated means are A, 61; B, 66; C, 68; D, 61, with, respectively, 4, 6, 6, and 8 observations each. Recalling Equations 14.13 and 14.15, we can calculate the corresponding Student t statistics:

$$t = \frac{\hat{\mu}_C - \hat{\mu}_A}{s_p}$$

$$= \frac{68 - 61}{2.37 \times \sqrt{\frac{1}{4} + \frac{1}{6}}}$$

$$= 4.58$$

$$t = \frac{\hat{\mu}_C - \hat{\mu}_B}{s_p}$$

$$= \frac{68 - 66}{2.37 \times \sqrt{\frac{1}{6} + \frac{1}{6}}}$$

$$= 1.46$$

$$t = \frac{\hat{\mu}_C - \hat{\mu}_D}{s_p}$$

$$= \frac{68 - 61}{2.37 \times \sqrt{\frac{1}{8} + \frac{1}{6}}}$$

$$= 5.47$$

We have chosen to examine three comparisons, so that if we choose a familywise α level of 0.06, the individual α levels must be 0.02; a Student's T distribution with 20 degrees of freedom for a one-tailed test has a corresponding critical bound of 2.20. We conclude that diet C's coagulation rate is significantly greater than that for diets A and D but not significantly greater than that for diet B. The probability of Type I error for this multiple comparison is less than or equal to 0.06.

Given these results, one would be justified in recommending diet C. If there were some other reason to consider the other diets, for example differences in cost, one might well extend the analysis to include the comparisons between diet B and the other two. With the difference between diets B and C so small, 1.46 standard deviations, if diet B were cheaper, or otherwise more desirable, one might well recommend it instead of diet C.

The Link to Regression Analysis

It is easy to show that, formally, ANOVA is a special case of regression analysis. To see this connection, at least in principle, we will rewrite our regression equations. Recall Section 13.5, on the F distribution, in which we introduced a more general regression equation. We repeat that statement in slightly different notation:

$$y_j = \beta_0 + \beta_1 x_{1j} + \beta_2 x_{2j} + \beta_3 x_{3j} + \epsilon_j \tag{14.15}$$

where we are considering three regressor variables in addition to the constant term. There are n observations on the $\{y_j\}$ and each of the $\{x_{ij}\}_{i=1,3}$. Vectors will assist us in rewriting our equations. A **vector** is merely a column of observations on a variable. Thus, if we had only four observations the vectors would be

$$\tilde{y} = \begin{Bmatrix} y_1 \\ y_2 \\ y_3 \\ y_4 \end{Bmatrix}$$

and

$$\tilde{x}_i = \begin{Bmatrix} x_{i1} \\ x_{i2} \\ x_{i3} \\ x_{i4} \end{Bmatrix}$$

$$i = 1, 3$$

and

$$\tilde{\epsilon} = \begin{Bmatrix} \epsilon_1 \\ \epsilon_2 \\ \epsilon_3 \\ \epsilon_4 \end{Bmatrix}$$

and to complete matters, we define the constant vector, CV, by

$$C\tilde{V} = \begin{Bmatrix} 1 \\ 1 \\ 1 \\ 1 \end{Bmatrix}$$

We can now rewrite Equation 14.15 to represent the relationship between all the observations as

$$\tilde{y} = C\tilde{V}\beta_0 + \tilde{x}_1\beta_1 + \tilde{x}_2\beta_2 + \tilde{x}_3\beta_3 + \tilde{\epsilon} \tag{14.16}$$

The notation in Equation 14.16 means that each element in the vector $C\tilde{V}$ is multiplied by β_0 and added to the multiplication of each element of the vector $\tilde{x}_1$ by β_1, and that is added to the multiplication of each element of the vector $\tilde{x}_2$ by β_2, and so on. Each row in this big "vector" equation is given by Equation 14.15.

Now that we have our more general expression for a regression model, we can easily show that ANOVA is a special case of regression. We will use an example. Suppose that we have three groups to compare with group means $\mu_i, i = 1, 2, 3$. The model can be written as we did in Equation 14.1 as

$$y_{ij} = \mu_i + \epsilon_{ij}$$
$$j = 1, 2, \ldots, n_i$$
$$i = 1, 2, 3$$

But, if we use our "vector" formulation, we will see the connection between ANOVA and regression. We begin by stacking the y_{ij} in one long vector that has $n = \Sigma_i n_i$ elements; the first n_1 elements contain all the observations on the first group, the next n_2 elements contain all the observations for the second group, and so on. We have, therefore,

$$\tilde{y} = \left\{ \begin{array}{c} y_{11} \\ y_{12} \\ \vdots \\ y_{1n_1} \\ y_{21} \\ y_{22} \\ \vdots \\ y_{2n_2} \\ y_{31} \\ \vdots \\ y_{3n_3} \end{array} \right.$$

A vector for the error terms can be created in exactly the same manner. We next define a "regressor" vector for each group; that for the first group is

$$\tilde{x}_1 = \left\{ \begin{array}{lll} 1 & & \\ 1 & & \\ \vdots & & \\ 1 & n_1 & \text{observations} \\ 0 & & \\ 0 & & \\ \vdots & & \\ 0 & n_2 & \text{observations} \\ 0 & & \\ \vdots & & \\ 0 & n_3 & \text{observations} \end{array} \right.$$

and the regressor vector for the second group is

$$\tilde{x}_2 = \begin{cases} 0 \\ 0 \\ \vdots \\ 0 \quad n_1 \quad \text{observations} \\ 1 \\ 1 \\ \vdots \\ 1 \quad n_2 \quad \text{observations} \\ 0 \\ \vdots \\ 0 \quad n_3 \quad \text{observations} \end{cases}$$

and so on. We can now pull this all together in terms of a "vector" equation; we have

$$\tilde{y} = \tilde{x}_1 \mu_1 + \tilde{x}_2 \mu_2 + \tilde{x}_3 \mu_3 + \epsilon \tag{14.17}$$

We complete our specification of the model by stating that the error terms are distributed as Gaussian independently of the "regressors" with zero mean and variance, σ_ϵ^2. The constant vector is not needed in this discussion because we have rewritten the model in terms of individual means, instead of an overall mean and the deviations from it. Recall that this approach implies there are only 2 degrees of freedom in the model, as the sum of the differences between the individual means and the overall mean must be zero.

The analogy is now complete. If we compare the model defined in Equation 14.16 with that defined in Equation 14.17, we see that ANOVA is, indeed, a special case of regression analysis with a special type of regressor vector; each is composed of only 1's and 0's. Actually, the special nature of the ANOVA regressors leads to some particularly simple mathematical properties that we need not investigate at this time.

However, you should recognize that the effect of a single variable on the regressand can be captured approximately by dividing the range of the regressor up into a series of intervals, say low, medium, and high. By doing so, we convert a regression between a single regressor and a regressand into an ANOVA problem where the total variation of the regressand is subdivided into the "cells" determined by the individual means for the low, medium, and high values for the regressor; in short, one regressor is represented by three blocks, or groups, of data, each corresponding to one division of the regressor.

The implication of this is that all the analysis we used in the previous chapter carries over to this one. More important, recognizing the link between the two procedures enables you to gain an enhanced understanding of both and to be able to assess the advantages and disadvantages of each. A major advantage of using ANOVA, instead of linear regression, is that the conditional mean relationship between Y and X need not be linear and one need not know what the nonlinear relationship is to be able to pose some pertinent questions and obtain useful answers. For example, recall the analysis of the "tent function" in the Exercises in Chapter 5. Recall that the tent function, when plotted, looked like a "tent," or a pyramid. We saw that correlation analysis, and so regression analysis as well, is not a very useful tool in this example. This is because the slope of the function over the upper half of X values offsets the slope of the function over the lower half, thereby producing a correlation, or average slope over all the X values, of approximately zero. However, if you

Table 14.7   **Analysis of Variance Table for Simulated Problem: _Y_ Depends on _X_ Squared**

Source of Variation	Sum of Squares	Degrees of Freedom	Mean Sum of Squares	$F_{\nu_1 \nu_2}$
Between	4.73	$k - 1 = 2$	MBS $= 2.37$	$\nu_1 = 2$
Within	3.97	$(n-1) - (k-1)$	MWS $= 0.04$	$\nu_2 = 97$
Total	8.71	$n - 1 = 99$		$F = 2.37/0.04$
				$= 57.8$

were to carry out an analysis of variance on the Y values split into three groups for the X values, one low, one high, and one in the middle, you would easily reject the null hypothesis that the mean values of the Y for all three groups are the same. The means for the high and low values of X would be approximately equal and low, whereas the mean of Y for the middle values of X would be larger.

Suppose the relationship between a variable Y and a variable X is $Y = 2 - X^2$, where the range of X is $[-1, 1]$.

Imagine now that we have a large number of observations taken at random from the values of X and that we have recorded the corresponding values of Y. We know, because we have created the data, that Y is a function of X, but if we calculate the correlation for a random sample of 100 observations we observe that the mean value is only 0.04. If however, we separate the Xs into three categories, of low, medium, and high values, and relative to these three categories for the values of X calculate the ANOVA, we obtain the results shown in Table 14.7. We see immediately that the null hypothesis of no differences among the means for each of the three categories of X values is rejected very, very, strongly.

The analysis cited in Table 14.3 also illustrates, although in less striking fashion, this advantage of ANOVA over regression analysis. Examine the box-and-whisker plots shown in Figure 14.5. Observe that for the very largest group by car weight the decrease in mpg seems to be less than would be predicted by a simple extrapolation of the results for the first three groups. This observation may be a useful insight, or it may merely be an artifact of how we calculated the group means. In either event, our observation deserves further exploration.

14.4   Summary

In this chapter, we have introduced one of the most useful tools of statistical analysis, _analysis of variance, ANOVA_. The model for the analysis of variance was presented in Equations 14.1 to 14.7. The basic idea of ANOVA is that we compare the variation within groups to the variation across groups. We create groups either by grouping the values of the variable of interest by the levels of some category or by breaking up the range of a continuous variable into a series of disjoint segments. For example, we may be interested in comparing the variation in SAT scores across the category "Sex," which has two levels, or across the category "type of high school," which may have several levels. Alternatively, we may be interested in comparing the variation in numbers of housing starts across ranges of interest rates. In the former example, we are interested in the question whether the mean score for "Males" is significantly different from that for

"Females," or whether different types of high schools have significantly different test scores. In the latter example, we are interested in whether the average number of housing starts differs significantly by the range of interest rates that prevail at purchase.

In both cases, the answer depends on the degree of variation inherent in the observations relative to the differences between the group means. The bigger the inherent variation as indicated by σ_ϵ^2 in Equation 14.11, the less our ability to discriminate between differences in group means as we illustrated in Figures 14.1 and 14.2. A major advantage of ANOVA is that we do not have to formulate a very specific model of the relationship between the values of the variable of interest and the values of the conditioning event. All we need do is to speculate that there are differences by groups and then to compare group means relative to the inherent noise of the model as measured by σ_ϵ^2. We illustrated the advantages of this when there was a nonlinear relationship between the values of the variable of interest and the values of the conditioning, or "grouping" variable; recall Figure 14.5 and the analysis of the quadratic function's values as illustrated in the results cited in Table 14.7.

If we reject the joint null hypothesis that none of the mean treatment effects are different, we are faced with the question as to which specific individual comparison is the greatest. This raises two problems. The first is *pretesting bias,* which is the effect on the probabilities of Types I and II errors for a subsequent test that is performed on the basis of the outcome of a prior test. A related issue is the *Bonferroni inequality,* which states that the probability of at least one Type I error in a family of comparisons is less than or equal to the sum of the individual assigned α values to each individual comparison. We avoid pretesting bias by deciding which procedure to use; apply the F statistic to test for some difference, or perform a sequence of tests on individual comparisons after allowing for the Bonferroni inequality.

Finally, we saw that ANOVA is in fact a special case of linear regression, so all the procedures and statistics that we developed for linear regression can be applied to ANOVA examples as well. Both in formal ANOVA and in the analysis of multivariate regressions—that is, regressions involving more than one regressor and a constant term—the presentation of the ANOVA tables that we have illustrated is a very common procedure.

Case Study

Was There Age Discrimination in a Public Utility?

This is the most important chapter in the book for this case study in that the tools developed here are directly relevant to our purposes. We begin with the central question, Is there a significant relationship between age and hire status? Let us recall the proportions of individuals in each level of the hire status category: 29% were not hired, 46% were hired, and 25% retired or did not apply. If we perform an analysis of variance for age by the levels of the hire status category, we obtain the results that the BSS, the sum of squared differences stemming from the differences in effect on age by hire status, has a value of 5548.4 with 2 degrees of freedom, and the WSS, the within sum of squares stemming from the random variation within cells, is 31821 with 476 degrees of freedom. These numbers yield an $\underline{F}$ statistic with a value of 41.5 with 2 and 476 degrees of freedom; the corresponding $\underline{P}$ value is approximately zero.

However, this is an unfair comparison for our purposes, because the results are heavily dependent on the role played by the retirees. If we redo the analysis of variance by restricting hire status to either 0 or 1—that is, by eliminating the effect of retirees—we obtain 165.3 with 1 degree of freedom for the BSS and 21776.3 for the WSS with 356 degrees of freedom. These numbers produce an $\underline{F}$ statistic of 2.7 with 1 and 356 degrees of freedom; the corresponding $\underline{P}$ value is .1. We may well conclude with high probability that age and hire status are related and that this result is independent of the role played by those who chose to retire.

Examine the values of the estimated coefficients, the estimates of the cell means. For the hire status with levels, 0, 1, and 9, the overall mean is 46.95 (very close to the unrestricted mean), and the differential for being hired is –0.69 and that for being in the "did not apply" group is 2.52. If we ignore the retirees, we get a hired differential of –0.69 as well. So, although these results are very highly statistically significant, the operational impact is minor.

We can explore another, but similar, approach to this problem. Consider using a contingency table (recall Chapter 5) for hire status and age divided into three categories, 24 to 37, 38 to 54, and 55 to 69. We obtain the following table of results; table entries are the observed relative frequencies based on 479 observations:

Hire.stat	Age Groups 24–37	38–54	55–69	Row Total
0	.061	.200	.029	.29
1	.094	.336	.027	.46
9	.021	.094	.138	.25
Column Total	.18	.63	.19	1.0

And if we perform a chi-square test for independence—that is, for a test on the difference between the relative frequencies and those that would be obtained if hire status and age group were independent—we get a value of 129.0 with 4 degrees of freedom, and the corresponding $\underline{P}$ value is approximately zero. But as indicated, these results are to be expected because they include the effect of the retirees. The corresponding table without the "did not apply" group follows:

Hire.stat	Age Groups 24–37	38–54	55–69	Row Total
0	.061	.173	.154	.39
1	.089	.366	.156	.61
Column Total	.15	.54	.31	1.0

The chi-square test for the independence of the factors hire status and age group is again rejected with a chi-square value of 9.1 with 2 degrees of freedom and a corresponding $\underline{P}$ value of .01. But as we have already seen by examining the estimated cell coefficients in the analysis of variance and as would also be confirmed by examining the differences between the observed relative frequencies and those that would be obtained under independence, the statistically significant results are not operationally significant. See the following table, which lists the relative frequencies under the assumption of independence.

Hire.stat	Age Groups 24–37	38–54	55–69	Row Total
0	.0585	.211	.121	.39
1	.092	.33	.189	.61
Column Total	.15	.54	.31	1.0

Our final conclusion from the analysis of this chapter is that there is evidence of an association between "hired status" and "age," but that the relationship though detectable, does not seem to be a very impor-

continues on next page

(Continued)

tant one. However, we have also noted on several occasions in previous chapters that there are many explanations for the limited results that we have found. More evidence is required to explore and to be able to state more precisely the explanation for these results; that analysis may well conclude that "age discrimination" was not an issue in this case.

Exercises

Calculation Practice

In ANOVA calculations, the most difficult part is to separate the data into the various cells as determined by the "grouping" variable. Once that is done we merely need to calculate the variance within each group and the variance of the group means about the overall mean of the entire sample. In the calculations that follow we will use S-Plus to calculate the ANOVA output, but we will begin with Worked examples to illustrate the process.

14.1 Worked. *Objective: To give you practice in using the ANOVA routine.* In the folder Misc, use the file Housing.xls, which contains information on the number of housing starts by quarter of the year. First, we want to know whether there are statistically significant differences in housing starts across quarters. We will answer this by comparing the variation in mean housing starts by quarter to the variation in housing starts within quarters, using the S-Plus ANOVA routine.

[**Computer directions:** Import file Housing.xls. On the menu bar, click on <u>Statistics</u>, <u>Analysis of Variance</u>, <u>Fixed Effects</u>. In Data Frame select Housing. In Formula key in $\boxed{\text{hsestrts}\sim\text{factor(qtr)}}$. Click the Results tab, and check the Means box. Click Apply. The results are in the Report window. A copy of the report from the Analysis of Variance follows:

*** Analysis of Variance Model ***
Short Output:
Call:

aov(formula = hsestrts ~ factor(qtr), data = Housing, na.action = na.omit)

Terms:

	factor(qtr)	Residuals
Sum of Squares	12.38	19645.53
Deg. of Freedom	3	109

Residual standard error: 13.42513

Estimated effects may be unbalanced

	Df	Sum of Sq	Mean Sq
factor(qtr)	3	12.38	4.1269
Residuals	109	19645.53	180.2342

	Fvalue	pr(F)
factor(qtr)	0.02289763	0.9952796
Residuals		

Tables of means

Grand mean

43.012

factor(qtr)

	1	2	3	4
	43.085	43.399	43.09	42.491
rep.	28.000	28.000	28.00	29.000

The "Call" line reproduces the formula used to calculate the ANOVA and confirms that the data frame is Housing. The reason for the use of the function factor(.) is to be sure that the quarters that are designated by numbers are treated as factors; that is, the designations "1," "2," and so on, are to be treated as an identifying symbol to separate the response variable, *hsestrts,* into its four groups of quarters. If you do not use factor(qtr), it will treat qtr as a variable with four numeric values 1, 2, 3, 4. In the former case, the degrees of freedom are 3, (4 − 1), and in the latter case 1, for a single cardinally measured variable.

The BSS (Sum of Sq.) is 12.38 with 3 degrees of freedom. The WSS (Residuals) is 19645.5 with 109 degrees of freedom. TSS can be obtained by adding these two together. The TSS has 112 degrees of freedom (why 112?).

The F statistic (F value) is 0.0229, with 3 and 109 degrees of freedom. Last is the P value for the F statistic, in this case the probability of getting a value this large, or larger, under the null hypothesis of no difference between the means is 0.995; that is, nearly certain.

The "Table of means" includes the "Grand mean" for the 113 observations and the means for each quarter. We modify Equation 14.10, in this case, as follows:

$$F_{3,109} = \frac{\frac{BSS}{3}}{\frac{WSS}{109}} = \frac{BSS \times 109}{WSS \times 3} = \frac{12.38 \times 109}{19645.53 \times 3}$$
$$= 0.023$$

In this expression, 3 = number of cells, or groups, minus 1 and 109 is the total number of observations minus the number of cells as is illustrated in Table 14.1. *Note:* Ignore warning messages.

14.2 Worked. *Objective: To review the calculations required by the ANOVA procedure.* In the folder Misc, use the file Cars93.xls, which contains observations on the price (midprice) of a sample of cars together with the number of cylinders (cylindrs) in the engine. Follow the computer directions in Exercise 14.1, using *midprice* for the data variable and *cylindrs* for the grouping variable. As in the previous exercise, the Report window has tables for the analysis of variance followed by a listing of the means. The value for BSS is 1843.1, with 2 degrees of freedom, and WSS is 1028.8, with 45 degrees of freedom. The corresponding F statistic is 40.31, and not surprisingly the probability of getting a larger value under the hypothesis of there being no difference in the means across cylinder groups is virtually zero. The expression for the F statistic is

$$F_{2,45} = \frac{\frac{BSS}{2}}{\frac{WSS}{45}} = \frac{BSS \times 45}{WSS \times 2} = \frac{1843.1 \times 45}{1028.8 \times 2}$$
$$= 40.31$$

The three means for 4, 6, and 8 cylinders are, respectively, 12.8, 21.0, and 31.4. It is almost immediately clear that the means are significantly different.

14.3 In the folder Misc, use the file Cryanova.xls, which contains a variable that counts the number of babies that cried on a given experimental day and another variable that indicates whether or not the baby involved was rocked. On your own and following the guidance of the previous worked examples, determine whether rocked babies cried less than unrocked babies.

Exploring the Tools

14.4 Worked. *Objective: To help you explore the importance of the assumptions of Gaussianity.* A key assumption in ANOVA is the Gaussianity of the error terms. In this exercise, we explore the effect of variations in the distribution of the error terms on the ANOVA results. Recall Equation 14.2. Let us set $\mu_1 = -.5$, $\mu_2 = .5$, so that $\mu = 0$. Also $k = 2$ and $n = 60$.

Three variables have been created, *ygaus, ystdt,* and *ychisq,* and put in the dataset Anovastat.xls in the folder Misc. In each case the dependent variable is the sum of a grouping variable, *dg;* that is, $-.5$ for 30 observations and $.5$ for 30 observations plus an error term. For ygaus the error term is $N(0, 1)$; for ystdt, the error term is a Student's T distribution with 5 degrees of freedom. For ychisq, the error term is a chi-square variable with 10 degrees of freedom with the mean of 10 subtracted; the result is divided by $\sqrt{20}$, the theoretical standard deviation for a chi-square with 10 degrees of freedom. This yields a variable with a theoretical mean of 0 and a theoretical standard deviation of 1. Following the computer directions in Exercise 14.1, calculate the analysis of variance for each of ygaus, ystdt, and ychisq, using dg as the "grouping variable." In the Report window, compare your results in the three cases, and comment on the effect that the lack of normality for the error distribution has on the outcomes.

Refer to Table 14.1 in the text.

14.5 This exercise is designed to give you practice in examining ANOVA's ability to detect differences in the means. To accomplish this, you will vary the size of the variance of the disturbance terms, ϵ_{ij} (see Equation 14.3). Experiment with various choices for the variance and n, the sample size. Comment on your results. Examine the trade-off among the ability to detect differences in the means for various values of n, the sample size, and the size of the variance for the error terms.

[**Computer directions:** Start S-Plus, on the menu Bar, click on Labs, Between and Within Variation. In the dialog box, click Sample to see the results of your changes to n and sigma.] *Note:* There are 4 graphs. The top set of graphs are for unequal means, and the bottom set of graphs are for equal means. The graphs to the left portray the distribution of points sampled. The graphs to the right are box-and-whisker plots for the data portrayed in the left graphs.

Applications

14.6 *Objective: To give you experience in using the ANOVA routines and practice in drawing conclusions from your results.* In the folder Misc, use the file Energgdp.xls, which contains data on energy per capita and energy use per GDP (in U.S. dollars) for six countries. Use the ANOVA procedure as described in Exercise 14.1 to investigate whether there are significant differences between the countries in terms of their energy use per capita (energpc), and the energy use per GDP (energdp).What policy conclusions can you draw?

14.7 In the folder Misc, use the file Cosize.xls which contains data on the sales per employee for six companies. The firms are grouped as large or small based on the number of employees. "Small" is less than 50,000 employees, and "large" is greater than 50,000 employees; the variable name is *sizeco*. The question is whether sales per employee (saleemp) is greater or less for small firms than for large firms (efficiency vs. scale). Are large firms less efficient?

[**Computer note:** Because the company size is alphanumeric (its entries are "small" and "large"),

there can be no confusion as to whether a factor designates subsets of sales per employee or a cardinal measurement of a variable. As a result, after clicking on Statistics, Analysis of Variance, Fixed Effects, in Formula, key in |saleemp~sizeco| without the word *factor*.]

14.8 The EPA wants to know the difference between makes of cars' estimated gas mileage. Car manufacturers produce both low- and high-gas-mileage cars but have to keep the averages down by adjusting the relative number of cars produced.

In the folder Misc, use the file Cardata.xls, which contains the variables *mpg* and *make*. Using make as a grouping variable, investigate whether there are significant differences between the makes with respect to miles per gallon of gas. This procedure implicitly averages over the firms' mix of cars by weight. Use the computer directions in Exercise 14.1. Repeat the calculations to examine the differences with respect to gas mileage *mpg* and the country of origin of the car, using the variable *origin* as the grouping variable. Origin codes 1 for US cars, 2 for European, and 3 for Japanese. What conclusions do you draw from your calculations?

14.9 We want to know whether an exercise program does or does not lower weight, one's fat levels, or one's blood pressure. In the folder Misc, use the file Coles.xls, which contains preprogram and postprogram weight figures, and prefat and postfat levels for both males and females.

You could use ANOVA procedures to determine whether women or men lose more weight, or more fat. You might also be tempted to use ANOVA to ask whether postweights, or postfat levels, were lower than preweights and prefat. But this is not a good idea. Explain why not.

What other procedures might you use to compare the difference between preconditions and postconditions? (*Hint:* Recognize that in comparing preweights and postweights, you are looking at the same people in both cases, not people who have and have not taken the weight loss program and who were selected at random.)

14.10 We want to know whether and how much the basal rate, a measure of oxygen consumption (see variable *basalrat*) differs across flighted and nonflighted birds (see the variable *flight*.) A corollary question is the difference in basal rate between herbivorous and carnivorous birds (see the variable *foodhab*). Use the computer instructions in Exercise 14.1 and file Birds.xls in the Misc folder. Use the data variable basalrat and group variables flight and foodhab to examine these questions. Do herbivorous birds have a higher basal rate than carnivorous birds? What about flighted versus nonflighted birds?

14.11 In the text, it was pointed out that ANOVA procedures are particularly useful when the nature of the relationship between two (or more) variables is unknown in the beginning. The data file Caffeine.xls, in the Misc folder, has a measure of nervousness, number of finger taps per minute (see variable *taps*), and the level of caffeine consumed (see variable *group1*). Use the computer instructions in Exercise 14.1. Is there a significant difference across varying caffeine levels, and if so, what is the nature of the variation? Is it linear? nonlinear? How do you answer these questions? Plot by hand the means against the caffeine levels 0 mg, 100 mg, 200 mg (coded 1, 2, and 3, respectively, in group1).

14.12 A frequently debated issue in the press is whether there is racial discrimination for people who receive the death penalty. A prior question is whether there is a statistically detectable difference. The file Capital.xls, in the Misc folder, contains the dependent variable *death,* indicating whether the convicted murderer received the death penalty (yes $= 1$, no $= 0$) and two grouping variables indicating race of killer (*rk*), and race of victim (*rv*), each with only two categories, black and white. Perform two ANOVA experiments. Use the computer directions in Exercise 14.1 to evaluate this claim by looking at the possible difference in rates by race of killer and by race of victim.

Because the dependent variable is a discrete (0, 1) variable, the conditions for analyzing the ANOVA

test are not met. Discuss this problem and its potential implications for your analysis. Discuss the implications of the difference in your results between race of killer and race of victim.

Finally, even if you discover statistically significant differences, state very precisely the limits to the inferences that you can draw. (*Hint:* Reconsider the arguments on "causality" in Chapter 13.)

14.13 High levels for both life expectancy and literacy are common measures of the "state of advancement" of a country. Data on such measures for 130 countries are provided in the file Humandev.xls, in the folder Misc. The dependent variables of interest are *literacy* and *life*. Two potential "grouping" variables of interest are *urbpop88,* the percentage of the population that lived in cities in 1988, and *gnpcap87,* the GNP per capita in 1987 in US dollars. Are there any significant differences across countries by urban population and by GNP per capita in literacy (variable name, literacy) and in life expectancy (variable name, life)? Use the computer directions in Exercise 14.1. You will carry out altogether four ANOVA experiments. One might expect a highly significant outcome for these experiments. However, use ideas from previous chapters to try to refine this notion and be more specific about the way in which countries differ in literacy and life expectancy when grouped by urbanization and level of GNP. Are there any surprises?

14.14 (A team exercise) Pick three books, for example, a volume of Shakespeare's plays, a Faulkner novel, and an Agatha Christie mystery. Select a sequence of five pages at random in each book, and calculate the mean percentage use of prepositions in each sample; you may want to restrict the definition of "prepositions." Indicate how you would test the hypothesis that all the authors used the same percentage of prepositions against the hypothesis that each is different. If the percentages are different, do you see any explanation? How might your results have differed if you had selected only modern mystery writers?

14.15 You are given a coin, and it is claimed that it is a "fair" coin. You realize that no coin can be strictly fair; there must be some imperfections in the coin, so you interpret fair to mean that the probability of a head is within the range .495 to .505. Indicate how you would test this proposition and what sample size you would pick. Defend your choice.

14.16 Try this example of ESP (extra sensory perception) testing. Show a candidate a sequence of simple pictures, and ask him or her to concentrate for a few moments on the figure shown. Ask another candidate in another room to write down what he or she thinks the first candidate saw. The order of selecting the cards should be done at random. Run several trials, and then test whether there are significant differences between the pairs of candidates. If any pair of candidates is selected as providing superior ESP performance, rerun the experiment to see if on a subsequent occasion they still have superior performance. Comment on your findings.

14.17 There is a famous experiment in the United Kingdom that is designed to test whether people can tell the difference as to whether tea is added to the milk, or milk is added to the tea. Using either tea or coffee, run an experiment to test whether people can tell the difference in the order in which the milk is incorporated. Justify your analytical procedures.

14.18 Case Study: Was There Age Discrimination in a Public Utility?

In the text, we claimed that ANOVA techniques were especially useful in those cases where the exact nature of the relationship between "treatment" and "outcome" is not known. The ANOVA approach is to specify treatment levels and then to investigate whether the difference between means is statistically significant given the natural variation in the data.

Indicate, with at least one example, how you would apply this principle to the case study.

Perform the recommended analysis, and evaluate the results in terms of the support the procedure does, or does not, provide for the plaintiffs. In particular, assess whether there are benefits of using ANOVA instead of regression analysis.

PART SIX

Retrospective

CHAPTER
15

Retrospective

15.1 What You Will Learn in This Chapter

This chapter summarizes all that you have learned in this text. While reading this chapter, you should review your notes from the previous chapters. In particular, try to discover how much you have learned and how your view of the world has been changed. The key to statistical analysis is in the *interpretation* of facts that are observable to everyone; this is the main lesson that you should acquire in this chapter. Recognizing the central role of probability and distributional theory is critical to your mastery of statistical reasoning.

15.2 Introduction

The objective of this short chapter is to provide a review of all that you have learned on your intellectual journey through statistics. We will do so without details so that you can concentrate on the main lessons that have been acquired. This review will enable you to see very clearly the essential role that statistics plays in the formulation and implementation of public policy, the operation of a business, or the ordering of your own life. Another section explores the intricate relationship between the formulation of scientific theories and statistics. These results were initially discussed in Chapters 1 and 2, but now you have the knowledge to understand what we could only hint at in those first two chapters.

The outline of this very short chapter is straightforward. In the next section, we will review the fundamentals of what you have learned in this text. That review is followed by an evaluation of the role of statistics in everyday life. The third section clarifies the relationship between science and statistics. The last section indicates where you might go from here in your study of statistics.

15.3 A Schematic Review of What You Have Learned

To appreciate what you have learned in this text, recall what we agreed that we knew when we started. We began by recognizing that in many cases we could observe data and have no idea of any causal connection between the observations themselves or between the observations and anything else. The former notion can be restated that we could observe no pattern in the data. The latter idea is that we could not relate our given observations to any other observables; there are no apparent causal connections. Examples of this "lack of structure" involved everything from the outcomes of tossing coins and dice and the rolling of a roulette wheel, to the breakdown of machinery, the incidence of diseases, changes in the weather, the firing of neurons, radioactive decay, the occurrence of accidents, the operation of the stock market, genetic inheritance, and so on. Sometimes, as in some of these examples, what we did not know was a *residual* of what it is that we think we know. For example, we might well have a theory about genetic inheritance, but when we have used our knowledge to the fullest extent, we will still face a component of the outcome that contains no pattern. People have been trying to find patterns in stock market data for decades to little avail; we still can say little about the spread of diseases, much less predict who is going to succumb and who is not. A further example involves the relationship between fuel consumption and car weight. Even after allowing for all our engineering calculations, there is still some variation left in the data that seems to have no causal explanation, no discernible pattern. Other examples are provided by economic analysis and policy evaluation. Even after we have used our best models of the economy or of the behavior of economic agents and institutions, there is a lot of variation left in the data for which we have no explanation; there is no pattern. Even in engineering, after all the calculations have been completed and all the models run and processes simulated, there is still much that is unexplained for which allowance must be made.

Thus, we may justifiably say that a key aspect of all life is the presence of variation in events for which we have no causal explanations. Whether or not this is due to our ignorance does not matter; we are still faced with the problem that there is variation in the data for which we have no explanation. The only difference between fields of study is the extent of our ignorance relative to what we do know; in some cases the presence of unexplained variation is minimal, such as in certain areas of physics or chemistry, and in other cases the presence of unexplained phenomena dominates what it is we think we know, for example, in sociology and political science. Every other field of study lies somewhere in between these extremes. In this text and in the study of statistics itself, we have concentrated on these unexplained components of phenomena. Either we have no explanation at all, or we are looking at the variation after allowing for all our understanding of the events under examination.

We concluded that unexplained variation in observed phenomena is ubiquitous and that we did not know what to do about the matter. This is where we began; we knew nothing.

Our first task was to describe the phenomena as a preliminary step toward acquiring some insight about random variation. At this early stage, we defined *random* in a very intuitive manner as "variation without explanation." We began our description of the data with measures of location and spread using the box-and-whisker plots and then progressed to examining histograms. We soon realized after looking at many, many histogram plots that we were really talking about shapes of histograms. Indeed, at least when restricted to very large data sets, our major discovery was that the same experiment repeated produced the same shape of histogram and that different experiments produced different shapes of histograms. You may not have recognized it at the time, but this was a monumental discovery. In fact, the whole of statistical analysis can be said to be based on this notion.

To proceed, we decided that we would be better served by translating visual ideas of shape into mathematical measures of shape so that we could capture various aspects of shape in terms of numbers. This notion led to the concept of moments. The first four moments were especially useful in describing the shape of histograms. We explored this idea of relating the shape of histograms produced by various experiments to the values of the first four moments at some length.

Our next step in this exploration was to extend the idea of shape to bivariate distributions, and this in turn led us to define the idea of correlation. In particular, we saw that by examining the box-and-whisker plots of one variable, Y, given some small range of values for the other variable, X, we might fit an approximate straight line through the medians of the box-and-whisker plots. These "lines of medians" gave a good indication of the shape of the bivariate distribution in so far as they related to the overall association between the two variables. We showed that the *correlation coefficient,* which is defined as the measure of linear association between two standardized variables, is a scaled version of the slope coefficient relating variations in one of the variables to variation in the other.

By this stage in our development of statistics, we recognized that we had a lot of regularities in random phenomena to be explained. Why is it that as the number of observations gets to be very large, we see ever-more smooth histograms? Why does the same experiment produce the same shape of histograms? Given that different experiments produce different shapes, how can we relate the conditions of the experiment to the observed shape? If we knew enough about the experiment that generated the data, would we be able to predict the shape of the histogram and the values of its moments? The setting was right to produce a theory of histograms, and that is what we proceeded to do in terms of our development of probability theory.

We developed probability theory to explain empirical distributions of relative frequencies and histograms. We began by developing a theory for random data that had only a finite number of discrete outcomes. After defining a number of important concepts in probability, we extended the analysis to continuous random data and began to develop the theory that underlies histograms of continuous data. An important lesson was to learn the relationship between conditional, marginal, and joint distribution functions But the most important lesson was to realize that the theory that we had developed provided models for understanding data. Probability theory is to observing the statistics of random events as economic theory is to observing consumer behavior, or the theory of physics is to observing the behavior of gases. Our development of probability theory was completed in the chapters in which we derived the probability distributions of discrete variables and in those in which we derived density functions for continuous variables.

A key element of this development was to recognize that the shape of probability and density functions depends on the values of their parameters. We saw that as we changed the values of the parameters that determine the specific form of the distribution function, we changed the shape of the distribution and the values of the theoretical moments. Recall that we defined theoretical moments in analogy to the moments of sample distributions; *theoret-*

ical moments measure aspects of the shape of probability and density functions in a similar manner to that in which *sample moments* measure the shape of sample distributions. This innovation created a "triangle" of relationships between the shape of the distribution, the values of the parameters, and the values of the moments.

In the process, we developed a very important tool, expectation. The *expectation* of any function of a discrete random variable is the probability weighted sum of the function, or for continuous variables, the integral of the function of the variable with respect to the density function. This operation yields the mean value of the function. Recall that the expectation, like the definition of the first moment about the origin that it generalizes, is that value of the function such that averaged differences from that value are zero. The expectation of powers of the variable yields moments and these, in turn, measure aspects of the shape of the distribution. The importance of expectation is that for every estimator that we define— that is, for every function of the random variables that we wish to examine—we will need to consider the expectation as our first step in assessing the statistical properties of that estimator. But to talk of estimators at this juncture is premature. Before proceeding, we needed to introduce the notion of *sampling*.

Sampling is the crucial link between our theory and the calculations that we made using the observed data. The theory of sampling that we introduced enabled us to interpret our calculations in a general way. In the first section of the text when we calculated sample moments as descriptive measures of the histograms, the results were bound in time and space to the here and now. We were merely describing the actual data observed where and when it was observed. We had no rationalization to extend our results beyond relevance to what we had actually observed. But, by introducing sampling theory and conceiving of hypothetical populations, we discovered that we could *interpret* our observations as a sample, or drawing, from a parent theoretical distribution. This was another leap, not just a step, in the usefulness of our procedures. We discovered that we could generalize our empirical findings far beyond the particularities involved in our specific sample; we could interpret our results. The base for inference had been created.

Inference, as its name implies, is the process of drawing general conclusions from specific observations. The technical tools that we use to do that involve the theory of distributions of random variables, the creation of functions of the data called *estimators,* and the derivation of the statistical properties of the estimators. Our interpretations of our calculations and all our generalizations arise from our statistical theory. For example, we observe on June 23, 1996, at 4.00 P.M., the blood pressures of a specific group of students at New York University in Coles Sports Center. Using the sample moments that we developed in Chapters 4 and 5, all we can say about these data is to cite the numbers calculated and define the data as specifically as possible. The benefit of the theory that we have developed is to be able from these same numbers to *infer* something like, "A 90% confidence interval for the weight of New York University male undergraduate students is between 124 and 160 pounds, and the distribution of such weights is Gaussian." Notice that our interpretation is to infer from the specific numbers obtained a wealth of information that generalizes our statements from the very specific group actually measured to the class of New York University male undergraduates at anytime and that we claim to know the theoretical distribution that underlies the generation of these data. This interpretation of the actual numbers comes from the theory that we developed and from nothing else.

In the last few chapters, we elaborated on this broad theme. We moved from inferring distributions for estimators to testing hypotheses about unobserved parameter values. We extended the analysis to regression and to the comparison of means in general. A major point is that the inferences to be drawn in regression analysis and ANOVA generalize the work in Chapters 10 and 11 in a very simple manner. No matter how complicated the regression problem may be, once we have obtained the distributions of the various estimators, then all the procedures that were used in the two chapters on inference carry over exactly as in the earlier chapters.

Regression analysis can be interpreted from two alternative perspectives. We began with the need to summarize the relationship between two jointly distributed random variables, when that relationship was reflected in a linear conditional mean. We also discovered the link between causal models and the statistical procedures that we use to discover them when such relationships can only be observed with error. Finally, we noted that ANOVA is a special case of regression that has its own advantages over regular regression analysis, especially when we can reduce our problem to the comparison of group means.

15.4 The Role of Statistics in Everyday Life

One way you can recognize the progress you have made in understanding random data is to think back to your first reading of this text. Recall Chapter 1, in which we noted many examples for which a knowledge of statistics and probability theory was claimed to be needed. As a first example, consider choosing a money manager for an inheritance that your favorite aunt just bequeathed to you.

Recall how you might have thought about the matter before you began to read this book. After reading all the experts and talking to a few more, you would have soon become convinced that neither you nor anyone else can pick a money management firm with guaranteed performance. Not only performance, but performance relative to other money management firms, varies by month, year, and certainly over any five-year period; sometimes the results are great, sometimes they are terrible, and most of the time they are passable, but not exciting. In your old state of knowledge, you really would be at a loss as to how to proceed. Give up and put the money in the bank, but you are soon told that practice is just as risky as investing, probably more so. Pick whichever firm your parents use, that of a friend, one that has a pleasing name perhaps; if one of them did all right last year, decide to go for it anyway, but that still leaves a choice of hundreds. A rational decision seems to be beyond your grasp, and you could be forgiven for feeling totally depressed. You have inherited all this money, and you do not know what to do with it; your last option is to spend profligately.

Now let us consider how you could approach the problem using the lessons learned in this book. To begin the process, you would recognize the benefit of getting some idea of the data themselves. You collect as much data as you can on the performance measures of different money managers over several years. To keep the discussion uncluttered, let us concentrate on only two firms. And now you begin your journey of statistical exploration.

As a preliminary step, let us plot the histograms and box-and-whisker plots of the data for each firm; this operation gives you some idea of the distribution of the data for the two firms. To formalize your visual inspection, you calculate the first four moments and begin to recognize that the sample distributions have "fat tails," are skewed to the right, and that the means differ between the two sample distributions, but that the variances seem to be very close.

You recognize that the data that you are dealing with are random, implying that you should ask which probability distribution, or in this case, density function is likely to be relevant. But the real question is what is the appropriate experiment that would generate these data. An important corollary question to ask is how the data were sampled. At this stage, you are trying to determine the appropriate theoretical distribution that is involved and to decide whether the implicit sampling mechanism used in generating the observed data will enable you to make inferences about the theoretical moments and distributional parameters.

Let us suppose to keep our discussion uncomplicated that you decide that the sampling procedure can usefully be regarded as simple random and that the underlying theoretical distribution is Gaussian. Part of your reasoning here is that the outcomes you are observing are the result of very many random and seemingly independent "shocks" to the firm's performance. The stage is now set for more formal procedures to be used.

You decide that the decision you want to make is to choose the firm with the larger mean value for its performance, provided there is no difference in the variances. So your first task is to settle the issue of whether the variances are the same. That is a question that we did not directly address. However, you do know that you have two independent samples and that the estimator of the variance is distributed as chi-square with the corresponding degrees of freedom. What you do not know is the distribution of a difference between two variance estimators. However, you do know enough to be able to go to a more advanced textbook and discover the answer for yourself. Meanwhile, if you think about the matter a solution may occur to you. Given the independence of the samples, the distribution of the ratio of the variance estimators will be distributed as F and under the alternative hypothesis that the numerator variance is larger, you will likely observe bigger values for the F distribution than would be the case under the null hypothesis. So here you have a potential solution to your problem.

Let us agree that you have solved your difference in the variances problem, and that you are convinced that the variances are as far as you can determine the same. The next step is to test the hypothesis that the two means are the same against the hypothesis that they are different, given that the variances are the same. At this stage, you might be a little more adventurous in that you would really like to know whether the difference is greater than δ_0, your minimum difference for agreeing to distinguish the performance of the two firms. Under the conditions of the problem as you have defined it, the estimator for the actual difference, δ, is simply the difference between the sample means. Further, you know from the theory that you have mastered that the distribution of the difference estimator is also Gausssian with the corresponding variance. You have two choices here. Either you can calculate a confidence interval for δ, or you can test the null hypothesis that $\delta \leq \delta_0$ against the alternative hypothesis that $\delta > \delta_0$, where δ_0 is the minimum difference that you will accept to distinguish the performances of the two firms. In the former case, you know to decide on a confidence level that is suitable for your purposes;

you have to choose between high confidence and a relatively wide interval and lower confidence and a relatively narrower interval. An alternative is to examine the P value for the estimate obtained and decide what to do on the basis of the indicated probability of observing a larger value of the statistic. If you choose to test the hypothesis that $\delta \leq \delta_0$, you know to decide on a probability of Type I error by trading off your cost of Type I to Type II errors against the cost indicated by the trade-off in probabilities implied by the problem. Having observed your results you will make the appropriate decision, and yet you will be aware of the risks that you are incurring in making this decision.

If you compare the two scenarios that we have just illustrated you will recognize quite vividly the substantial amount of information and skill in decision making that you have acquired. Note that you have gained on two fronts. First, you have a lot more information. Second, you have very much more insight into the nature of the decision problem that you are solving and its relevance to your needs. However, also realize that the actual data that you had to begin with, the "raw information" that you faced before reading this text, is exactly the same as the amount of "raw information" that you have now. The difference is in the theory and the analytical procedures that you have learned in this text.

Case Study

Was There Age Discrimination in a Public Utility?

We can now summarize what we learned about the discrimination suit from the data provided. What we have learned falls into two categories: those facts that enable us to interpret the data and our various calculations and the facts that we want to adduce that are germane to the suit.

In the former category, we have concluded that we are examining the outcomes of a joint distribution on the ages, salaries, and demographic characteristics of the employees of the firm under question. Further, conditional on the particularities of the firm itself and the particular time at which the events occurred, we have a random sample. Further, we conclude that although the distributions of age and salary are not Gaussian—the former has negative skewness, the latter positive skewness—the Gaussian is a useful approximation. The variables are not independent but are weakly and positively correlated, and this holds true even for the separation of the data into male and female components.

In the latter category, we have made the following tentative conclusions. There is a statistically significant relationship between age and hire status in that those retained were on average younger than those in the work force originally. However, although this result is statistically significant, the very low R^2 values obtained and the small size of the estimated coefficients that we calculated indicates clearly that the effect is operationally insignificant.

Even the weak positive correlations linking salary to age and the weak negative effect between age and hire status ignore the issue of self-selection that could not be further investigated with the data on hand; that is, there are plausible alternative explanations that these data cannot address.

The final conclusion is, subject to the usual provisos of statistical analysis, that there is no strong evidence for the union position.

15.5   The Relationship between Science and Statistics

You are by this stage in your statistical development better able to appreciate the unique roles that statistics and probability theory play in the development of science. You have seen that inevitably all sciences involve errors in observation and in measurement. As a consequence, the effect of such errors on one's evaluation of the data requires knowing how and to what extent one can separate out the "actual" observations from the mixture of actual data and error. In choosing between any two hypotheses in the context of any science, the effect of such errors on one's conclusions must always be considered. More important, you have now seen that statistics provides not only the basic tools, but also the very language, needed to evaluate scientific hypotheses. The basic paradigm for the mature scientific discipline is one of proposing hypotheses that are then "tested" against the observed data. But as we have seen, the very process of collecting the data is guided by statistical principles.

Although we have not explored the matter at all, a very important branch of statistical theory is concerned with the "design of experiments." In designing experiments, the designer tries to determine useful ways of setting up an experiment and of recording the data so that the most information can be obtained. For example, one requirement for experiments using live subjects is that to assess the effects of a treatment, one should ensure before analyzing the data that neither the experimenter, nor the experimental subjects, knows which subjects got the treatment and which did not. Such a practice inhibits such effects as the "Hawthorne Effect," named after the site, the Hawthorne Works, of the Western Electric Company, which initiated experiments on the effects of different lighting levels on factory productivity. As reported by Mr. C. E. Snow, Western Electric discovered that both raising and lowering the lights raised productivity. What was happening in fact was that the workers on the factory floor were responding to what they perceived as increased attention. The presence of the Hawthorne Effect vitiated the results of the original experiment. For a fascinating early study involving complex issues of experimental design, read *Management and the Worker.** Once again we see that statistics is involved in the evaluation of scientific theories.

Statistics and probability theory are also involved in the formulation of the sciences. You may be accustomed to the idea of functional relationships to express physical theories—for example, the relationship between weight and the extension of springs, Hooke's law of proportionality—this is by no means the only way to express even physical theories and is certainly not the only way to express theories in the social sciences. A much more realistic and useful way to express relationships is between events and probability distributions. For example, in thermodynamics, one determines the pressure of a gas at a given temperature in terms of an "average" over all possible assemblies of the molecules involved; the distribution of the

---

*F. J. Roethisberger & W. J. Dickson. (1946). *Management and the Worker*. Harvard University Press.

molecules of a gas at any point in time must be given in terms of a probability distribution. Similarly in economics, the reaction by consumers to a change in relative prices has to be expressed in terms of a change in the distribution of consumption over the affected population. To investigate the effect of an increase in income for a group of consumers requires that we understand the effect of the income increase on the group's distribution of income. In short, you have seen that merely to express theories in modern science requires the language of statistics and of probability theory.

The key concept in all this discussion is the idea of a probability distribution, or its continuous variable equivalent, the density function. The formulation of theories in modern science requires these concepts. Further, the only thing that we can observe is best described as drawings from probability or density functions. Consequently, statistical and probability concepts are required at the very heart of all science. The concepts are also at the very heart of all policy decisions, which are nothing more than the practical *implementation* of scientific concepts.

15.6   What Might You Learn Next in Statistics?

Your next course in statistics might be a formal course at the university, or it might be the result of "on the job training." In either event, I hope that what you have learned in this text will provide you with the basic understanding to proceed either with instruction or even on your own. As you proceed, the same principles that you mastered in this text will be used many, many times. There are two broad areas in which you can progress, "on the extensive margin, or on the intensive margin," as economists like to term the situation.

Your progress on the extensive margin will involve learning many new statistics, how to estimate, and how to test hypotheses in a bewildering variety of circumstances. However, it is useful for you to realize that throughout your mastery of new techniques you will still be using the principles learned in this text. Some of the tasks that you will learn to handle will involve regression with several regressors and ANOVA problems where there are two treatment effects whose effects have to be estimated separately. In both cases, you will learn how to extract the individual effects of the separate regressors or treatments. You will also learn how to estimate parameters and how to test hypotheses when the relevant distribution is not Gaussian. More important, you will learn how to test whether a hypothesized probability distribution, or density function, is the appropriate one for your circumstances.

On the intensive margin you will review the material that we covered in the text, especially the material on probability and on the theory of probability distributions and density functions with much greater rigor, and concomitantly, more use of mathematics. You will learn how to derive all the distributions that we have discussed and how to prove all the ideas that we discovered by intuition and by experiment. In this learning environment you will discover many subtleties that we have missed in our first attempt. And with some luck, you will gain even more insight into the mysterious, but fascinating, world of random events.

Exercises

Applications

15.1 There is considerable controversy in the educational establishment about the effectiveness of assigning homework to elementary school students. For example, studies have been cited that purport to claim there is a negative relationship between the amount of homework assigned to elementary school students and their grades. Some have claimed that this shows that assigning homework is deleterious to effective learning for such students. Given that the cited studies have not made any mistakes in calculating the statistics from the observed data, use your understanding of statistical methodology to debate this issue. Can you provide plausible explanations for this outcome that are not due to homework lowering student achievement? If you were to test your hypotheses, how would you proceed?

15.2 Explain why assessing causal relationships in the context of economic and financial relationships is so difficult. Be as specific and insightful as you can. What suggestions do you have for improving the extent to which observers can learn from economic and financial data?

15.3 "One can never prove a hypothesis, only disprove it." Debate this issue. In the process, tell why this statement in the context of stochastic variation is at best a half-truth. In your answer, discuss the limits to "knowing" engendered by living within a stochastic environment.

15.4 From the *New York Times* (January 31, 1999): "Every time a disease cluster turns up, communities worry, scientists scramble for a cause and. . . lawyers start suing. Yet over and over again despite years—sometimes decades—of effort to link the disease with a cause, scientists usually come up empty handed."

A "disease cluster" is the occurrence of a sequence of outbreaks of a disease over a small geographical region within a short period of time that is higher than would be expected by chance at some small preassigned probability level.

Given what you have learned in this text, discuss this issue both from the perspective of the statistical reasoning involved and the relationship between statistics and causality. Can you recommend a research strategy to investigate this issue? Can you make a plausible argument for the random occurrence of clusters? Can you create a computer algorithm to simulate such an occurrence?

15.5 Both estimation and hypothesis testing are aspects of inference. Summarize briefly, but clearly, the extent to which this is true, and discuss the fundamental differences between these two aspects of inference.

15.6 (Reference: *Judgement under Uncertainty: Heuristics and Biases,* Cambridge, 1998.) Tversky and Kahneman discuss the notion of anchoring, whereby initial estimates of probability tend to be maintained despite evidence to the contrary.

Consider the following experiment. Fill a small clear glass jar with small coins, say pennies, or shells or anything suitable. Run three trials on three selections of students, but keep the numbers of students in each group the same. For the first trial, ask the group of students to estimate the number of coins in the jar without discussing the issue among themselves. On the second trial, write on the blackboard in large numbers a number that is much larger than the actual number of coins in the jar; write only the number, and make no reference to the jar of pennies. Finally, repeat the experiment, except write a much smaller number on the blackboard than the number of pennies in the jar. Examine carefully the distribution of estimates in the three trials. Before seeing the results state your anticipation of the outcomes. What practical implications do you draw from this experiment?

15.7 (Reference: *Judgement under Uncertainty: Heuristics and Biases,* Cambridge, 1998.) Consider an experiment with three situations to be compared:

- Drawing a red marble from a bag containing 50% red marbles

- Drawing a red marble, with replacement, seven times in succession from a bag that contains 90% red marbles

- Drawing a red marble at least once in seven successive tries, with replacement, from a bag containing 10% red marbles

a. Without actually calculating the outcomes, make an informed guess about the respective probabilities of these three events and order them according to probability. Next, calculate the probability of each experiment and assess the accuracy of your guess.

b. If, instead of estimating the probability of drawing red balls, you had been assessing the profitability of a firm's returns, what implications for investing in the stock market could you draw?

15.8 Random number generators are computer algorithms, so the sequence of numbers they generate are in fact related to each other in a very precise manner. How can these numbers be regarded as random? Does declaring a variable to be "stochastic," or random, merely indicate our ignorance about the causes that generate its values?

15.9 In Chapter 1, several questions were posed on the need for information and a procedure for processing it to devise strategies for making useful decisions and evaluating scientific hypotheses. Review those questions, and answer them using the insights that you have gained in this text. If you kept your answers from the time you first read Chapter 1, review your old answers in light of your latest efforts.

15.10 Pick any example of the relevance of statistics that was discussed in Chapter 1 and evaluate the extent to which you now understand the role played by statistical reasoning in decision making and in science. Try to indicate the extent to which the sophistication of your insight into these matters has been enhanced by your mastery of the material in this text.

15.11 (Reference: *Judgement under Uncertainty: Heuristics and Biases,* Cambridge, 1998, p.28.) "An investigator has reported a result that you consider implausible. He ran 15 subjects, and reported a significant [Student's *t* statistic] value, *t* = 2.46. Another investigator has attempted to duplicate his procedures, and he obtained a nonsignificant value of *t* with the same number of subjects. The direction was the same in both sets of data."

You are reviewing the literature. What is the highest value of *t* in the second set of data that you would describe as a failure to replicate? What can you say about the value of the Student's *t* statistic for a joint sample obtained by pooling the two independent sets of results if the second result produced a *t* value of 1.5?

What conclusions do you draw about the evaluation of scientific experiments? If you were to design a replication experiment to determine whether a prior outcome was valid, what would be your recommendations about choice of sample size? Suppose that the original sample size was 15 and the *t* statistic was 2.0.

15.12 (Reference: *Judgement under Uncertainty: Heuristics and Biases,* Cambridge, 1998, p.26.) Suppose that a doctoral student investigated an experiment using 40 animals and with respect to one measurement, she obtained a Student's *t* statistic of 2.70—a theoretically surprising result.

The student replicated the experiment with an additional 20 subjects and obtained a Student's *t* statistic of 1.24 with the effect in the same direction. Provide arguments for or against each of the alternative research strategies below.

a. She should pool the results and publish the results as "fact."

b. She should report the results as a tentative finding.

c. She should run another experiment with a different group of subjects.

d. She should try to find an explanation for the difference between the two sets of results.

15.13 "States with No Death Penalty Share Lower Homicide Rates" read a September 22, 2000, *New York Times* lead article. The *New York Times* examined homicide rates categorized by whether the state was one of the early 12 without capital punishment, or one of the 36 states that passed new legislation allowing capital punishment after the 1972 Supreme Court's *Furman v. Georgia* decision. The *New York Times* also examined some demographic variables that seemed to be similar across the categories, and plotting a time series of homicide rates by state over the time period 1982 to 1996 revealed little difference between states with and without the death penalty.

Before answering the following questions, recall the calculations you did on capital punishment statistics in the file Capital, in the Misc folder. Also, recall that from the economist's perspective what counts is not the "severity" of punishment itself but the expectation of punishment—that is, weighted average of the penalties times the probability of actually incurring those penalties. Further, recall that when many factors affect an observable outcome, but the researcher only observes some of the factors, great care is needed in drawing any conclusions. In general, one cannot draw any conclusions from observing only part of the data-generating mechanism within a nonexperimental setup in which the uncontrolled variables are expected to change substantially.

Use your training to assess the validity and usefulness of the following procedures and the justification provided for the inferences drawn. Indicate what, if anything, can be concluded from the statistics quoted, and where possible, indicate how you could have improved the relevance of the analysis. Note carefully that you are being asked to comment exclusively as a "statistician," and your personal feelings and moral stance are irrelevant to answering the questions. The questions are, Does the evidence support the inference? Could the analytical procedures have been improved to shed more light on the questions posed? Could the statistical questions have been asked more precisely? and What is the central question?

a. States with the death penalty had more homicides per year per 100,000 population than states without the penalty; no confidence intervals were provided; approximate average number of homicides was 5 for states without and about 9 for states with.

b. North Dakota does not have a death penalty, South Dakota does; the corresponding homicide rates were 1.1 and 1.4 per 100,000 population.

c. "Those who have labored long in the criminal justice system know that . . . blacks get the harsher hand in criminal justice and particularly in capital punishment cases." Recall your analysis of the Capital data in Misc.

d. "The death penalty also has been employed much more often when the victim was white—82 percent of the victims of death row inmates were white, while only 50 percent of homicide victims were white." Comment in light of the statistics in the file Capital and in light of the fact that most crime is "local."

e. "I do not think the death penalty is a deterrent of any consequence in preventing murders. . . . Most homicides . . . are impulsive actions, crimes of passion, in which the killers do not consider the consequences of what they are doing." If this is correct, of what deterrent value is lifetime imprisonment? Following the argument to its logical conclusion, what policy implications do you see?

15.14 Case Study: Was There Age Discrimination in a Public Utility? "The use of statistics has been a major feature in the evolution of employment discrimination law in the United States. Both Federal and state courts have relied on statistical proof mainly because direct evidence of discrimination is seldom available. Although statistics can be an important source of proof in employment discrimination cases, some defendants and plaintiffs try to use statistics as a drunken man uses a lamppost—for support and not illumination." Elias Grivoyanis, Statistical Consultant, 1999

Using this quote as a starting point, discuss the usefulness and relevance and the strengths and weaknesses of statistical analyses in court cases of this type. What recommendations would you make to improve the use of statistical reasoning in court trials?

15.15 Case Study: Was There Age Discrimination in a Public Utility? Two major topics of debate are the impact of "junk science" in court cases and the difference between the way science and the courts look at what constitutes evidence and proof. *Junk science* refers to scientific claims by persons whose scientific credentials are suspect, if not actually nonexistent.

Using this case as an example, discuss these two related issues. What recommendations can you give to the courts to improve their operation and the incidence of "just" outcomes?

PART SEVEN

Appendixes

APPENDIX

A

Mathematical Appendix: Review of Concepts and Conventions

This appendix is meant to give you a review of the mathematics that will be used in the text. A quick look at its contents will indicate to you whether there is any material that you need to relearn, or perhaps learn for the first time, before reading the text. The appendix also is meant to provide a convenient summary of the terms and notational conventions that are used in the text. The notational conventions, in particular, have been chosen to facilitate following the material. By examining the appendix, you can obtain a reasonable notion of the level of mathematical sophistication used in the text.

This review is not intended to teach you the mathematics required in the course. If you do need to learn some of the mathematics reviewed here, you are advised to obtain a suitable book. I have found that the Schaum "Outline Series" are excellent for an in-depth review of mathematical material, and they always provide numerous examples and exercises with detailed answers. The Schaum series is published by McGraw-Hill.

Formal calculus will not be required, but some of the concepts involved in calculus will be used. Concepts such as continuity and limits are very important. Although everything that will be used in the text is reviewed in this appendix, some prior exposure to these concepts would be of great value to the student. High-school level algebra is the mathematical tool used most in the course. Spend some time making sure that you are very comfortable with algebraic concepts and operations.

It is very important for your mastery of the material that you practice obtaining an approximation to a solution before working out the detailed answer, or you try to visualize the problem and its solution in terms of graphs or pictures; the idea is to gain an intuitive feel for the nature of the problem and of its solution. There are many reasons for taking the time to do this. First, if you have an intuitive grasp of the problem and its solution, you will protect yourself from obvious gross errors. More important, being able to visualize the problem enhances immeasurably your understanding of the problem and its solution. Think the problem through, rather than merely manipulating symbols.

This last statement is very important. Many students "learn" mathematics, or mathematically based subjects, by memorizing rules and simply manipulating symbols that are essentially meaningless to the student. If approached this way, the study of mathematics and statistics remains a mystery. This text has been designed to help you deal with this issue. One technique is to bring together both detailed calculations and more intuitive insights obtained by postulating approximations and reformulating the problem and its solution in terms of pictures and graphs.

As you read the text, especially as you do the Exercises, always try first to obtain a visual picture of the problem or at least to consider an approximate solution. Your objective each time is to hone your intuition about the concepts in this text.

A.1   Notational Conventions

Lowercase letters at the end of the alphabet, such as x, y, z, are used to represent the observed values of variables. For example, the observed level of consumer income might be represented by y, the height of police recruits by x, and so on. Sometimes, it is useful to emphasize the idea of observation, so an o subscript is used; for example, x_o, y_o, and z_o, might represent the eye colors of three students. Exceptions to this general rule involve letters that represent well-known variables, especially with GNP statistics—that is, statistics involving aggregate measures of economic performance such as national income, saving, consumption, and so on.

Random variables are always represented by uppercase letters, such as X, Y, Z, and so on. Usually random variables are represented by letters at the end of the alphabet. Uppercase letters are used to distinguish random variables from other variables because they are theoretical concepts and are not directly observed.

Chapters 3 and 4 will introduce various calculations of the observed data; some of these are known as sample moments. They are designated by lowercase letters, usually from the middle of the alphabet, such as md, m_1, m_2, m_{11}. Lowercase letters are used because the numbers represented by md, m_2, and so on, are calculated from observed data, and we are following the convention that observed variables are written as lowercase.

Chapters 6 through 8 will introduce probability distributions and density functions, which are functions of random variables. Probability distributions and density functions are theoretical concepts and as such are not directly observed. Individual distributions, unless given a specific name, such as Gaussian, are labeled as $f, g,$ and h. Although this part of the notational scheme does not agree with our convention that random variables and thus functions of random variables should be represented by uppercase letters, the custom is so well established, I have acquiesced to standard practice. The shape and properties of distributions depend on certain parameters contained in the formulation of the distributions; these have Greek symbols, such as $\alpha, \beta, \theta,$ and π. Distributions can be described by "moments," and these also have Greek symbols to represent them: $\mu_1, \mu_2, \mu_3,$ or μ_{11}.

As a general rule, the appearance of a Greek letter indicates a theoretical quantity, and often these will be the unknown parameters of theoretical distributions.

Linear Equations

Sometimes, we will need to discuss linear equations, such as

$$y = a + bx$$

or

$$z = c + dw$$

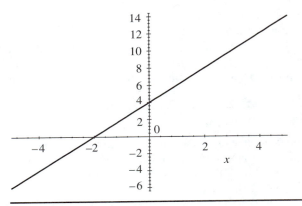

Figure A.1   Plot of $y = a + bx$: $a = 4$, $b = 2$

where w, y, z, x are variables and a, b, c, d are the coefficients of the equation. Figure A.1 shows an example where the intercept term, a, takes the value 4 and the slope coefficient b is 2. The intercept indicates the value of the response, y, when the argument of the function, x, takes the value zero. The slope coefficient, b, indicates the change in y to a unit change in the argument, x; or, more simply, $\Delta y = b\Delta x$. The change in y equals b times the change in x.

In this particular example, $y = 4$ when $x = 0$, because $a = 4$; and $\Delta y = b\Delta x$; given that $b = 2$, y increases by two units for each unit increase in x.

Often the equations that we will consider will also involve adding an *unobserved* term u, or v. The idea is that y is not given *exactly* by the linear equation but only approximately; u and v are usually interpreted as "noise terms." The noise term in an equation is always placed last. For example,

$$y = a + bx + u$$

This last equation implies that y is only approximately equal to $a + bx$ and differs from that result by a perturbation that is expressed by the addition of the term u.

In this text, linear equations involving more than one argument will be used frequently. As an example,

$$y = \alpha + \beta_1 x_1 + \beta_2 x_2 + \beta_3 x_3$$

In this equation, the intercept term is α and the rates of change to variations in x_i, $i = 1, 2, 3$ are given by the values of the coefficients β_i. The change in y, Δy, to a unit change in x_i *holding all other variables constant,* is given by $\beta_i \Delta x_i$. Figure A.2 shows the plane that is generated by the equation $y = 3 + 2x_1 + (-1.5x_2)$.

Figure A.2, the dependent variable y is plotted on the vertical axis. Equations involving more than one argument can also be expressed as approximate expressions by adding an unobserved error term at the end:

$$y = \alpha + \beta_1 x_1 + \beta_2 x_2 + \beta_3 x_3 + u$$

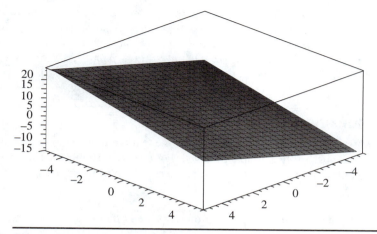

Figure A.2   Three-dimensional view of the plane

The addition of the error term, u, means that the equation relating y to variations in the x_i, $i = 1, 2, 3$ is only approximate. These are the "structural equations" that are discussed in Chapter 2.

Equations are often written in a more succinct form that indicates the idea of a function but without specifying the details of the relationship; this is especially true for relationships that are nonlinear. An example is

$$y = f(x; \theta)$$

$$y = \frac{e^{-\frac{1}{2}\{\frac{x-\mu}{\sigma}\}^2}}{\sigma \sqrt{2\pi}}$$

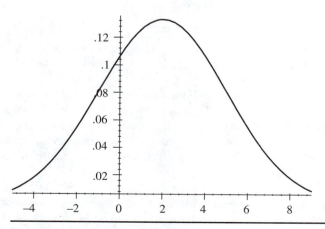

Figure A.3   Plot of the nonlinear function $f(x, \theta)$

In the first "schematic" expression, θ represents all the parameters of the function, μ and σ. Figure A.3, μ and σ take the values 2 and 3, respectively. In this expression, π is the number 3.1416. The expression "$f(.)$" represents the generic form of a function; the example listed below $f(.)$, $e^{-1/2}\{(x - \mu/)\sigma\}^2/\sigma\sqrt{2\pi}$, is a particular case of the generic formulation.

A.2 Indexing

Most of the variables you will see in the text are indexed to represent "cases" or "observations" of the variable involved. For example, suppose we use y to represent the incomes of physics professors, and there are ten of them. We can write this as

$$\{y_1, y_2, y_3, \ldots, y_9, y_{10}\}$$

where the incomes of the ten professors are in thousands of dollars:

32.0 35.7 41.2 44.3 45.3 48.8 49.1 51.0 52.1 55.7

Thus, y_1 takes the value \$32,000, y_2 takes the value \$35,700, ..., and y_{10} takes the value \$55,700.

The advantages of using indexed variables to represent actual observations is that we can more easily discuss operations on the data, such as summing the values or dividing them by some constant. More important, using indexed variables enables us to generalize what we are doing to a wide variety of data that can be expressed in the same way.

Indexed variables can also be used to represent cases with "categorical" data—data grouped into categories. For example, the eye colors of five students can be represented by

$$\{x_1, x_2, x_3, x_4, x_5\}$$

where x_1 takes the value "blue" for student number 1, x_2 takes the value "brown" for the second student, and so on.

We can write a set of indexed variables by

$$\{x_i\}, \text{ or } \{x_j\}, \text{ or } \{x_k\}_{k=1,K} \text{ or } \{x_l\}_{l=3,L-2}$$

for single-indexed data. In the last two examples, the number of observations has been emphasized; this is especially important when we may want to look at only a subset of all the cases.

Sometimes, we have many variables we want to treat as a block, in which case we will use a single letter with indexing to represent each variable in the block. For example, m might represent measures of the money supply, so that, m_1 represents the M_1 measure of the money supply, m_2 represents the M_2 measure of the money supply, and so on. An indexed variable y_1, y_2, y_3, could represent different sources of income, such as y_1 represents earned income, y_2 represents rental income, and y_3 represents dividend income.

Frequently, we need double indexing—one index for the particular item and one for the case or observation. With our money variable, we would also need a time index, t. So that $m_{t,2}$ represents the tth observation on the money supply M_2, and

$y_{i,2}$ represents the ith individual's receipt of income of type "2," or rental income. We might have data on individual car ownership by city, so that c might represent car ownership, the first (row) index might represent the individual and the second (column) index the city; thus, $c_{r,m}$ stands for car ownership by the rth individual in the mth city.

We write doubly indexed data by

$$\{x_{ij}\}, \text{ or } \{k_{m,n}\}_{m=1,M}^{n=1,N}$$

where the second index usually refers to the variable type, or class, and the first index to time or the case observed. The first index indicates the row of the two-dimensional array and the second index the column. For example, suppose that $\{x_{i,j}\}$ represents the incomes of five economics professors in three universities; we have five rows and three columns. In thousands of dollars, the entries might look like

$$\{x_{ij}\} = \begin{matrix} 32 & 37 & 30 \\ 45 & 47 & 50 \\ 49 & 51 & 53 \\ 56 & 61 & 70 \\ 70 & 80 & 95 \end{matrix}$$

Sometimes the data, or some calculations that we have made, produce a square data array—that is, as many rows as columns. The entries on the diagonal of the array are the entries $\{x_{i,i}\}$ and the entries that are below the diagonal are represented by $\{x_{i<j}\}$; that is, we keep the row elements that have row index less than the column index. Examples are given later.

For all the indexed variables, the choices of letters used to represent the indices are purely arbitrary and have no innate significance; we simply choose those that are convenient. The most common choices are i, j, k, and l.

A.3   Sigma Notation

In analyzing statistics, we have to do a lot of adding up. Consequently, we need a compact way of expressing this idea and its various ramifications. If we have a string of numbers that we want to add, say {24, 32, 15, 16, 21}, we can express this as

$$24 + 32 + 15 + 16 + 21 = 108$$

or

$$\text{sum}\{24, 32, 15, 16, 21\} = 108$$

However, when we are using variable names to represent our data or other types of variables, we will need a succinct way of describing the operation of "adding up." We do this by using the Greek letter Σ, which stands for summing up. Suppose that $\{x_i\}_{i=1,5}$ represents our five numbers—$x_1 = 24$, $x_2 = 32$, $x_3 = 15$, $x_4 = 16$, $x_5 = 21$—then an efficient way to represent the operation of adding up these numbers is

$$\sum x_i = 108$$

or

$$\sum_{i=1}^{5} x_i = 108$$

if we want to emphasize the range of the index over which we are adding up the numbers. For example, we might want to sum only the middle three numbers. We write that operation as

$$\sum_{i=2}^{4} x_i = 63$$

This last operation represents, of course, nothing more than

$$32 + 15 + 16 = 63$$

Usually, we are making general statements and the limits of summation are indicated by variable names as well. For example, to represent the addition of a variable from the kth to the nth values, we would write:

$$\sum_{i=k}^{n} x_i$$

When we have variables with double indices, we have a lot of flexibility to express a variety of useful operations in simple ways. The simplest case is where we merely want to add all the terms in the two-dimensional array, $\{x_{i,j}\}$. We write

$$\sum_{i} \sum_{j} x_{i,j}$$

or more simply

$$\sum_{i,j} x_{i,j}$$

Suppose now that we want to add all the elements of $\{x_{i,j}\}$, except for those cases where $i = j$, or the diagonal terms; we write

$$\sum_{i \neq j} x_{i,j}$$

and if we want to add all the terms of a doubly indexed variable for which i is less than j, for all values of the array $\{x_{i,j}\}$ that are below the diagonal, we write

$$\sum_{i < j} x_{i,j}$$

To be sure we have understood these statements, examine the following example:

$$\{x_{i,j}\}_{i=1,2;\ j=1,2,3} = \begin{array}{ccc} 1 & 3 & 5 \\ 4 & 6 & 3 \end{array}$$

where the array $\{x_{i,j}\}$ has two rows and three columns; i indexes the rows, j indexes the columns. Check for yourself the following statements:

$$\sum_{i \neq j} x_{i,j} = 15$$

or

$$3 + 5 + 4 + 3 = 15$$

$$\sum_{i<j} x_{i,j} = 3 + 5 + 3 = 11$$

$$\sum_{i \leq j} x_{i,j} = 18$$

or

$$1 + 3 + 5 + 6 + 3 = 18$$

A simpler result is that when summing over two indices, you can sum over either index first; that is,

$$\sum_i \sum_j x_{i,j} = \sum_i \left[\sum_j x_{i,j} \right] = \sum_j \sum_i x_{i,j} = \sum_j \left[\sum_i x_{i,j} \right]$$

In the example,

$$\sum_i \sum_j x_{i,j} = 22$$

Sum over whichever index is more convenient or simplifies calculation.

Summation obeys some useful rules. If a and c are constants:

$$\sum_{k=1}^{n} c = nc$$

$$\sum_l a x_l = a \left[\sum_l x_l \right]$$

$$\sum_{j=1}^{m} (y_j + / - z_j) = \left(\sum_{j=1}^{m} y_j \right) + / - \left(\sum_{j=1}^{m} z_j \right)$$

and the symbol "$+/-$" indicates either the operation of addition or subtraction. For example, if a equals 3, c equals 5, n equals 10, we have

$$\sum_{k=1}^{10} 5 = 10 \times 5 = 50$$

$$\sum_l 3 x_l = 3 \left[\sum_l x_l \right]$$

and if $\{y_j\} = \{2, 4, 7, 9\}$ and $\{z_j\} = \{3, 1, 6, 8\}$, we have

$$\sum_{j=1}^{m}(y_j + z_j) = 5 + 5 + 13 + 17 = 40$$

$$\left(\sum_{j=1}^{m} y_j\right) = 2 + 4 + 7 + 9 = 22$$

$$\left(\sum_{j=1}^{m} z_j\right) = 3 + 1 + 6 + 8 = 18$$

$$22 + 18 = 40$$

$$\sum_{j=1}^{m}(y_j - z_j) = (-1) + 3 + 1 + 1 = 4$$

$$\left(\sum_{j=1}^{m} y_j\right) = 2 + 4 + 7 + 9 = 22$$

$$\left(\sum_{j=1}^{m} z_j\right) = 3 + 1 + 6 + 8 = 18$$

$$22 - 18 = 4$$

Sometimes the variable that we add up is the index itself. For example,

$$\sum_{j=1}^{5} j = 1 + 2 + 3 + 4 + 5 = 15$$

or

$$\sum_{j=1}^{5} j^2 = 1^2 + 2^2 + 3^2 + 4^2 + 5^2 = 55$$

An example that will come up frequently is to evaluate sums of products. For $\{p_j\}$ equal $\{.2, .2, .3, .1, .2\}$ and $\{x_j\}$ equal $\{2, 3, 3, 4, 5\}$, we have

$$\sum_{j=1}^{5} p_j x_j = (.2)2 + (.2)3 + (.3)3 + (.1)4 + (.2)5 = 3.3$$

We also need to do a lot of algebraic manipulation of sums of powers and powers of sums of indexed variables. Some of these are simple to follow:

$$\sum_{k=1}^{m} x_k^2 \quad \text{or} \quad \sum_{k=1}^{m} x_k^4$$

The meaning should be clear, take the square, or fourth power, of each variable value as given by $x_k, k = 1, 2, \ldots, m$, and add up the powers.

Now consider a slightly more complex version:

$$\sum_{i=1}^{n}(x_i - a)^2$$

The operation is to subtract a from each variable value, x_i, square the result, and then add up the squares. It is convenient to consider the expansion of the quadratic and then add:

$$\sum_{i=1}^{n}(x_i - a)^2$$

$$= \sum_{i=1}^{n}[x_i^2 - 2x_i a + a^2]$$

$$= \sum_{i=1}^{n} x_i^2 - 2a \sum_{i=1}^{n} x_i + na^2$$

Suppose that $\{x_i\}$ has the values $\{2, 4, 6, 8, 10\}$ and a the value 6:

$$\sum_{i=1}^{n}(x_i - a)^2 = (2 - 6)^2 + (4 - 6)^2 + (6 - 6)^2 + (8 - 6)^2 + (10 - 6)^2$$

$$= (-4)^2 + (-2)^2 + (0)^2 + (2)^2 + (4)^2 = 40$$

This result is, of course, the same as

$$\sum_{i=1}^{n} x_i^2 - 2a \sum_{i=1}^{n} x_i + na^2$$

$$= 2^2 + 4^2 + 6^2 + 8^2 + 10^2 - 2 \times 6 \times [2 + 4 + 6 + 8 + 10] + 5 \times 6^2$$

$$= 180 - [12 \times 30] + 220 = 40$$

Involved in these calculations are terms like

$$(a + b)^n$$

where a and b are any numbers and n is an integer. We have just seen the result for $n = 2$. Consider the result for $n = 3, 4$ as well:

$$(a + b)^2 = a^2 + 2ab + b^2$$
$$(a + b)^3 = a^3 + 3a^2 b + 3ab^2 + b^3$$
$$(a + b)^4 = a^4 + 4a^3 b + 6a^2 b^2 + 4ab^3 + b^4$$

When Pascal looked at this result, he recognized an easy way to represent the coefficients for any value of n and created what we call **Pascal's triangle.**

n				1				
1			1		1			
2		1		2		1		
3	1		3		3		1	
4	1	4		6		4		1
5	1	5	10		10		5	1

Each row shows the coefficients for the expansion of $(a + b)^n$ for the values of n listed on the side. The student can easily extend the triangle to higher values of n. We will discover in the text another way of generating the terms in the expansion of $(a + b)^n$.

We can generalize these results in terms of our summation notation to the powers of sums of an indexed variable. Consider,

$$\left(\sum_{i=1}^{n} x_i\right)^2 = \sum x_i^2 + \sum_{i \neq j} x_i x_j$$

$$= \sum x_i^2 + 2 \sum_{i < j} x_i x_j$$

Note what the last two statements say: $\sum_{i \neq j} x_i x_j = 2 \sum_{i < j} x_i x_j$. For n equal to 3 or 4, verify this result for yourself. To see this result in terms of numbers, let $\{x_i\} = \{1, 3, 5, 6\}$.

$$\left(\sum_{i=1}^{n} x_i\right)^2 = (1 + 3 + 5 + 6)^2 = 15^2 = 225$$

$$\sum x_i^2 + \sum_{i \neq j} x_i x_j = (1^2 + 3^2 + 5^2 + 6^2) +$$

$$(1 \times 3 + 1 \times 5 + 1 \times 6 + 3 \times 1 + 3 \times 5 + 3 \times 6 +$$

$$5 \times 1 + 5 \times 3 + 5 \times 6 + 6 \times 1 + 6 \times 3 + 6 \times 5)$$

$$= 71 + 154 = 225$$

$$= \sum x_i^2 + 2 \sum_{i < j} x_i x_j =$$

$$(1^2 + 3^2 + 5^2 + 6^2) + 2 \times (1 \times 3 + 1 \times 5 + 1 \times$$

$$6 + 3 \times 5 + 3 \times 6 + 5 \times 6)$$

$$= 71 + 2 \times 77 = 71 + 154 = 225$$

Consider as well,

$$\left(\sum_{i=1}^{n} x_i\right)^3 = \sum_{i=1}^{n} x_i^3 + \sum_{i \neq j} x_i^2 x_j + \sum_{i \neq j \neq k} x_i x_j x_k$$

$$\left(\sum_{i=1}^{n} x_i\right)^4 = \sum_{i=1}^{n} x_i^4 + \sum_{i \neq j} x_i^3 x_j + \sum_{i \neq j} x_i^2 x_j^2 + \sum_{i \neq j \neq k} x_i^2 x_j x_k + \sum_{i \neq j \neq k \neq l} x_i x_j x_k x_k$$

Note that the expansions produce a series of terms for which the sums of the powers ALWAYS add up to the power in the original expansion; in the example for $n = 3$, all products have exponents that add up to three. We have individual terms with powers of three, x_i^3; terms with squares and single powers, $x_i^2 x_j$; and triples of terms in single powers, $x_i x_j x_k$. In the next example showing the expansion of a sum to the fourth power, we have terms all of whose exponents add to four.

If you have any difficulty in seeing any of these relationships, expand in terms of just two variables, then three at a time, and then four, in order to be sure that you understand the expansions.

A.4   Elementary Set Theory

The "elementary" in this heading is meant to convey that we will use the barest essential elements of set theory. The main area of relevance is in Chapter 6 on probability theory.

A *set* is merely a collection of elements, or objects, that are the designated members of the set. The economics professors in your university constitute a set; so do the teacups in your kitchen, the people signed up for tickets for a new play, the integers greater than 5, the feasible collection of initial conditions for a growth model, the words less than eight-letters long in this text, and the zeros in an nth-order polynomial. All that is needed is a rule for defining membership in the set. The only confusion comes from exercising the decision rule for inclusion in the set; for example, is a professor of economics in a political science department to be regarded as a member of the set of economics professors? Basically, any collection of objects with a precise rule for inclusion in the set constitutes a set.

What distinguishes the advantages of set theory is not the definition of a set but the tools for manipulating sets and their members. When we define probability in Chapter 6, we will require the flexibility to determine the probability of any collection of events that is feasible. Consequently, we will need definitions for the manipulation of the members of sets to create new sets that are themselves subsets of a collection of sets. If we can assign "probability," represented by a number between zero and one, to member A and to member B, we should also be able to define probabilities for "A and B," "A or B," "neither A nor B," and so on. In this section, we will develop the tools for manipulating and creating sets. In Chapter 6, we will use the tools developed here to build a theory of probability.

The first criterion is membership: for a set S, does x belong to S? To indicate that x belongs to the set S, we usually write

$$x \in S$$

and we write for an element that does not belong to S:

$$x \notin S$$

If we have a set S, the next most important matter is to define *subsets*, collections that are included within the original set S. For example, our set of economics professors could have as a subset those economics professors that are over 40 years of age, or the set of integers greater than 5 can have as a subset, those integers less than 20.

We define a subset by saying that A is a subset of S when every member of A is also a member of S; that is, if $s \in A$, then $s \in S$. This is expressed by

$$A \subset S$$

Consider a simple set S containing the elements $s_1, s_2, s_3, s_4, s_5, s_6, s_7$; $S = \{s_i\}$. Let us define the subsets, A_j, by

$$A_1 = \{s_1, s_3, s_5, s_7\}$$
$$A_2 = \{s_2, s_4, s_6\}$$
$$A_3 = \{s_1, s_2, s_3, s_4\}$$
$$A_4 = \{s_1, s_2, s_3, s_4, s_5, s_6, s_7\}$$
$$A_5 = \emptyset$$

With these subsets, let us see what we can discover about set manipulation. First, let us confirm that each A_j is a subset of S. A_j, $j = 1, 2, 3$ are clearly subsets of S, because every element of A_j belongs to S. Formally, if $s_i \in A_j$, $s_i \in S$; that is,

$$A_j \subset S$$

The last two sets are more interesting. A_4 contains all the elements that are in S, so that it is identical to S. A_5 is the set consisting of "no elements" it is called the "null set." You should distinguish the null set, which contains no elements from the set $\{0\}$, which contains a single element, "0."

The subsets A_4 and A_5 are related to each other in the following manner. Let us define the "complement set." The set A_j^c is the set that contains all elements that are in S and that are not in A_j. So it is not difficult to see that the complement of S is A_5, or $\emptyset$, and the complement of A_5, or $\emptyset^c$, is S. The complement of A_1 is A_2, and vice versa.

We can now define a series of operations on sets that enable us to create new sets out of old. Indeed, in Chapter 6 we will require that any set that can be defined by any number of the operations we discuss later is still a subset of S. The two new operations are called "union" and "intersection." The *union* of two sets is the set that contains any element in either of the two sets. More formally,

$$A = A_j \cup A_k$$

For example, using our sets A_j, we have

$$A_c = A_1 \cup A_2$$

or

$$A_c = \{s_1, s_2, s_3, s_4, s_5, s_6, s_7\}$$

because

$$A_1 = \{s_1, s_3, s_5, s_7\}$$

and

$$A_2 = \{s_2, s_4, s_6\}$$

More formally, we can say, "If $s_i \in A_1$ or $s_i \in A_2$, then $s_i \in A_c$."

Another example is

$$A_d = A_2 \cup A_3$$

or

$$A_d = \{s_1, s_2, s_3, s_4, s_6\}$$

because

$$A_2 = \{s_2, s_4, s_6\}$$

and

$$A_3 = \{s_1, s_2, s_3, s_4\}$$

Recall that the formal statement is, "If $s_i \in A_3$ or $s_i \in A_2$, then $s_i \in A_d$. Note carefully, that in defining A_d each element from A_2 and A_3 is included in A_d, but that is all; there are no "duplicates." What is $A_4 \cup A_5$? Obviously, it is simply A_4. Indeed, it is clear that $A_i \cup A_5$ is A_i.

We now consider intersection. The *intersection* of two sets is the set of all elements that are contained in both of the sets. For example,

$$A_e = A_2 \cap A_3$$
$$A_e = \{s_2, s_4\}$$

The formal statement is, "If $s_i \in A_2$ and $s_i \in A_3$, then $s_i \in A_e$."

Consider:

$$A_f = A_1 \cap A_2$$
$$A_f = \emptyset$$

because

$$A_1 = \{s_1, s_3, s_5, s_7\}$$

and

$$A_2 = \{s_2, s_4, s_6\}$$

The sets A_1, A_2 are said to have "null intersection"; that is, they have no elements in common. There are no s_i such that s_i belongs to both A_1 and A_2.

These operations on sets obey a number of useful rules. They are listed here for your review. For any sets A, B, C that are subsets of a set S:

$$A \cup \emptyset = A$$
$$A \cup B = B \cup A$$
$$A \cup A = A$$
$$A \cup (B \cup C) = (A \cup B) \cup C$$

The results for intersection are similar. Again for sets A, B, C that are subsets of a set S:

$$A \cap \emptyset = \emptyset$$
$$A \cap B = B \cap A$$
$$A \cap A = A$$
$$A \cap (B \cap C) = (A \cap B) \cap C$$

Similarly, we have a number of relationships for the operation of complementation:

$$(A^c)^c = A$$
$$S^c = \emptyset, \emptyset^c = S$$
$$A^c \cap A = \emptyset, A^c \cup A = S$$

The last operation that we need to define is called "difference." The difference between two sets A, B, often known as the *relative complement* of B in A, is the set $A - B$, which is defined by the set of elements that are in A, but not in B. It could well be true that $A \cap B = \emptyset$.

Given our verbal definition, we can immediately see that $A - B = A \cap B^c$, the difference contains only those elements that are in A and in the complement of B. Indeed, $A \cap B^c$ is a good way to define what we mean by the difference $A - B$.

As you can see already, the possibilities for creating new sets out of S are very rich. For example, we can ask how many subsets can be constructed from a set S with p members, a_i. The answer is easily obtained when we recognize that for each member of S, we create new subsets by declaring whether a_i is, or is not, a member of the postulated subset. We need only ask how many such choices there are. For each member, there are two choices, so that the total number of subsets of S is 2^p. For example, if $S = \{a_1, a_2, a_3\}$, we claim that there are $2^3 = 8$ subsets. Let us enumerate them:

$$\emptyset, \{a_1\}, \{a_2\}, \{a_3\}, \{a_1, a_2\}, \{a_1, a_3\}, \{a_2, a_3\}, \{a_1, a_2, a_3\}$$

In the Exercises, there are numerous examples of operations on sets that will enable you to gain some facility in manipulating sets and achieving a better understanding of what is involved. You will use this material extensively in Chapter 6.

A.5 Elements of Calculus

The material that follows cannot be construed as an attempt to teach you the formal elements of calculus for the first time. What it is intended to do is to present the basic notions and insights that Newton and Leibnitz had. For those of you who have had calculus, the following pages will provide a review of the basic concepts that you may have forgotten while mastering the algebraic formalism of modern calculus. These insights will be especially useful for our development of probability concepts when applied to continuous random variables, such as heights, income, temperature, and so on. The material in this section is used extensively in all chapters after the sixth.

The basic concepts that I want to explore with you are limits, continuity, differentiability, and integration. In part these notes have benefited from reading Gilbert Strang's *Calculus* (Wellesley-Cambridge Press, Wellesley, MA). This is an excellent book from which to learn calculus and an even better book from which to really learn calculus, if you have only had the standard "cookbook" approach. Because I want to be sure that the student masters the basic insights, I highly recommend Strang to anyone who wants to gain a better insight into what "calculus is really all about."

Limits and Continuity

We begin with limits and to do that we begin with sequences of terms. Consider the sequences:

$$\{a_n\} = \left\{\frac{1}{n}\right\}, \text{ or } \left\{\frac{n-1}{n}\right\}, \text{ or } \left\{\frac{n(n+1)}{n(n-1)}\right\}, \text{ or } \left\{\frac{n^2}{2^n}\right\}$$

The first and last of these have limits of 0 as $n \to \infty$. The middle two sequences have limits of 1 as $n \to \infty$. The first is easy to see, for as n gets bigger and bigger, the size of $1/n$ gets smaller and smaller. The second example is not much more difficult; it can be rewritten as $1 - (1/n)$, and the second component we have already seen goes to 0. The next two examples are not as easy to see, but the limits are, respectively, 1 and 0 (see Figure A.4).

In these examples, a "limit" means we can ignore what happens for the first few terms, even the first few million terms, as we are only interested in what happens as n goes to infinity. For example, the first few terms of the sequence $\{n^2/2^n\}$ are 1/2, 4/4, 9/8, 16/16, 25/32, and so on. The first few terms are *increasing* but thereafter are decreasing. The key to evaluating limits is that for *any small* number, ϵ, we can find an integer, N, so that for *all* terms of the sequence $\{a_n\}$ with $n > N$, $a_n < \epsilon$. Usually, the test is expressed in terms of the absolute value of a_n, $|a_n|$, because what counts is the size of a_n, not its sign. We would then seek a value for N, given an ϵ, such that $|a_n| < \epsilon$ for all values of $n > N$. A diagram should help; see Figure A.4.

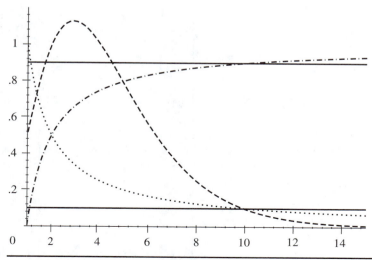

Figure A.4   Plots of $1/n$, $(n-1)/n$, and $n^2/2^n$

Two horizontal lines are shown, one at the value 0.1 for the sequences $1/n$ and $n^2/2^n$. One is at the value 0.9 {0.9 is within 0.1 of 1.0} for the sequence $(n-1)/n$. The reader can easily see that for $N = 10$, certainly for $N = 12$, all the terms of the sequences for $n > N$ are within ϵ of the limiting value; ϵ in this example is 0.1. The trick is that the test must hold for any choice of ϵ and that far enough out in the sequence *all* the terms in the subsequent sequence will meet the test.

Many sequences do not converge to zero or one but to more interesting numbers. In particular, consider the following situation. Suppose that I buy a bond for $1.00 that will pay me at the end of one year $(1 + R)$. I get my original dollar back and a return that reflects the interest earned. Presumably, R is something like ten cents. Now let us suppose that I now buy a bond that pays half as much twice a year, and that I immediately reinvest my first period's earnings for the second period. In the first period I receive $(1 + R/2)$. I promptly invest this amount and will receive $(1 + R/2) + $(1 + R/2)(R/2) = $(1 + R/2)^2$. I now arrange to be paid quarterly and have the money earned each quarter to be reinvested for me. I now receive per year $(1 + R/4)^4$. I can continue in this way at least in principle. The question is, Is there a limit to the amount that I will receive, and better still. What is it? I want to ask the question

$$\lim_{n \to \infty} \left(1 + \frac{R}{n}\right)^n = ?$$

The amount inside the parentheses tends to one, but we are multiplying more and more such terms. To see what is happening, let us examine the sequence for $R = 1$. We get

$$(1 + 1) = 2$$

$$\left(1 + \frac{1}{2}\right)^2 = 2.25$$

$$\left(1 + \frac{1}{10}\right)^{10} = 2.5937$$

$$\left(1 + \frac{1}{100}\right)^{100} = 2.7048$$

$$\left(1 + \frac{1}{10,000}\right)^{10,000} = 2.7181$$

We are in fact approaching the real number 2.7182818284590 . . .; for most cases 2.718 will do quite nicely. This limit is the real number e and it plays a central role in much of calculus. Our answer to our problem of the returns received from my investment is given by e^R; that is,

$$\lim_{n \to \infty} \left(1 + \frac{R}{n}\right)^n = e^R$$

And if R is 0.05, a nominal annual 5% rate of return, my actual compounded return is $e^{0.05} = 1.0513$, or subtracting my original investment of $1.00, my net return is $0.0513.

By compounding, I have gained 0.13 cent over a single year. This may not sound like a lot for a single dollar, but think of the gain if I had invested a million dollars.

Limits for Functions

The next step is to extend our current idea to functions and the behavior of $f(x)$ as x, the argument of $f(x)$, approaches some value. The question is, What is the value of $f(x)$ as $x \to a$, where a is some interesting point for the function $f(x)$. So instead of examining what happens to a sequence, a_n, as $n \to \infty$, we now ask what happens to $f(x)$ as $x \to a$. The concept is the same. For example, if $f(x)$ is the function x^3, we might want to consider the behavior of $f(x)$ in the neighborhood of 0. We have

$$\lim_{x \to 0} x^3 = 0$$

but if instead $f(x)$ is the function $1/x$, the $\lim_{x \to 0} x^{-1}$ does not exist. See Figure A.5.

The idea of "limit" involves a subtlety that may not be immediately apparent. For a limit of a function to exist, we need both the right and left limits to exist and to be the same. More formally,

$$\lim_{x \to a} f(x) = L$$

if and only if

$$\lim_{x \to a^-} f(x) = L$$

and

$$\lim_{x \to a^+} f(x) = L$$

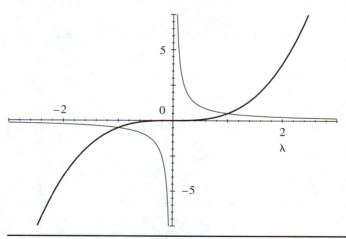

Figure A.5   Plot of the the functions x^3 and $1/x$

What this expression is saying is that the limit of $f(x)$ as x approaches *a from the left* is L and the limit as x approaches *a from the right* is also L. When this is true, the limit of $f(x)$ exists at $x = a$, and the value of the limit is L. In Figure A.5, the limit of x^3 from both the left and the right is zero. However, for the function $1/x$, the limits from the left and the right do not exist and are even farther apart in that as $x \to 0^+$—that is, from the right—$f(x)$ tends to $+\infty$, but that as $x \to 0^-$—that is, from the left—$f(x)$ tends to $-\infty$.

Continuity

We can now discuss the concept of continuity. A function is continuous if one can draw its graph without lifting the pen from the paper. More formally, a function is continuous if it is continuous at every point that is defined for the argument of the function. We are now left with determining the continuity of a function at a point. To do so, we need three conditions to be met:

1. If a is the point at which we are evaluating the continuity of $f(x)$, then $f(a)$ is defined at a.
2. The limit of $f(x)$ exists, and its value is L.
3. $f(a)$ equals the limit value L.

All of this is a rather pedantic way of saying that the limit and the value of the function agree at the designated point. We want to be very specific about the ways in which a function cannot be continuous. If $f(x) = x^2$, then at any point, say for $x = 2$, where $f(x) = 4$, the limit is

$$\lim_{x \to 2} x^2 = 4$$

or

$$\lim f(x) \to f(2), \text{ as } x \to 2$$

In this example, the point a is 2, $f(2)$ is defined, the limit of $f(x)$ exists at $x = 2$, and the limit equals $f(2)$. The importance of this definition is best seen by the cases where the function is not continuous.

The three functions plotted in Figure A.6 are

$$f(x) = \begin{cases} x & \text{if} & x < 0 \\ 1 & \text{if} & x = 0, \quad \text{dashed line} \\ x & \text{if} & x > 0 \end{cases}$$

$$g(x) = \begin{cases} -1 & \text{if} & x \le 0 \\ 1 & \text{if} & x > 0, \quad \text{dotted line} \end{cases}$$

$$h(x) = \frac{1}{x}, \text{ pair of thick black lines}$$

We have three examples of discontinuities in the neighborhood of 0. For $f(x)$, $f(0)$ exists and equals 1, but that value is not equal to the limit of $f(x)$ as $x \to 0$, which is 0. For $g(x)$, a step function, the limit from the right is not equal to the limit from the left, so that the limit (that is, the limit from both sides) does not exist. And for $h(x)$, the limit does not exist at all, even if restricted to either side.

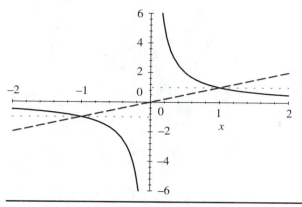

Figure A.6   Plots of three functions: $f(x)$, $g(x)$, and $h(x)$

A question that often arises in statistics is whether a function has high contact with the x-axis as $x \rightarrow \pm\infty$; that is, does the function rapidly approach 0 as $x \rightarrow \pm\infty$? By "high contact," we mean that for any choice of ϵ, ϵ small, there is a (small) value for the argument of the function such that for all argument values that are greater, the function value is within ϵ of 0. Consider the following two examples (see Figure A.7):

$$w = Kx^2 \left(1 + \frac{x^2}{2}\right)^{-3/2}$$

$$z = x^2 \frac{e^{-\frac{1}{2}x^2}}{\sqrt{2\pi}}$$

where K is a constant chosen so that the area under the curve $(1 + \frac{t^2}{2})^{-3/2}$ is 1.

In Figure A.7, the solid line is the plot for z, and the dashed line is the plot for w. Clearly, the z plot has high contact with the axis as $x \rightarrow \infty$, but that is certainly not true for the plot for the function w.

The Derivative

One very important example of limit involves rates of change:

$$\lim_{\Delta x \to 0} \left\{ \frac{f(x + \Delta x) - f(x)}{\Delta x} \right\}$$

If this limit exists, it is the "derivative" of the function $f(x)$. Examine Figure A.8.
Between the points $x = 1$ and $x = 2$, we have

$$\Delta f = f(x + \Delta x) - f(x)$$
$$= f(1 + 1) - f(1)$$
$$= 4 - 1 = 3$$

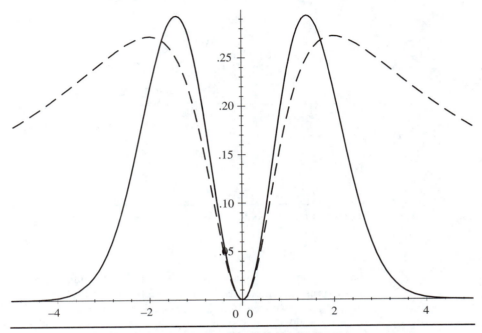

Figure A.7   Comparison of the support for the normal and *T* distributions

because

$$\Delta x = 1, \ \frac{\Delta f}{\Delta x} = 3$$

The smooth line is the function $f(x) = x^2$, the line of crosses is the approximation $\Delta f/\Delta x$ over the interval $[1, 2]$ for x, and the line of diamonds is df/dx evaluated at $x = 1$. We define df/dx by

$$\lim_{\Delta x \to 0} \frac{\Delta f}{\Delta x} = \lim_{\Delta x \to 0} \frac{f(x + \Delta x) - f(x)}{\Delta x}$$

or

$$\lim_{\Delta x \to 0} \frac{\Delta f}{\Delta x} = \lim_{\Delta x \to 0} \frac{(x + \Delta x)^2 - x^2}{\Delta x} = \lim_{\Delta x \to 0} \frac{x^2 + 2x\Delta x + \Delta x^2 - x^2}{\Delta x}$$

$$= \lim_{\Delta x \to 0} \frac{2x\Delta x + \Delta x^2}{\Delta x} = \left(\frac{df}{dx}\right)_{x=1} = 2$$

At $x = 1$, $df/dx = 2$, where df/dx is the limit of the ratio of differences. What this limit says is that as $\Delta x \to 0$, the *ratio* of Δf to Δx approaches the limiting value of $2x$, even though Δf and Δx are both approaching 0. The derivative gives the *relative* rate of change in Δf to that of Δx.

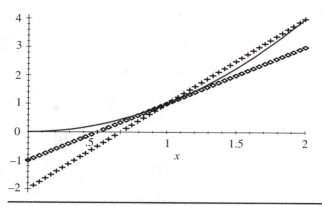

Figure A.8   Plot of $f(x) = x^2$; $\Delta f/\Delta x$: $x \in [1, 2]$; $(df/dx)_{x=1}$

As you can see from Figure A.8, we can approximate the change in the function x^2 at the point $x = 1$ by a *linear* equation with slope coefficient of 2; that is, we approximate the function $f(x) = x^2$, starting at $x = 1$, with the linear equation $y = a + [\lim_{\Delta x \to 0} \frac{\Delta f}{\Delta x}]x$, or $y = -1 + 2x$. Here a is the appropriate intercept term chosen, so that $y = f(x)$ at $x = 1$; $a = -1$ in this instance. This is the equation shown by the "diamonds." Our approximation using $\lim_{\Delta x \to 0} \Delta f/\Delta x$ is much more accurate than the slope coefficient of 3 that we obtained by the approximation $\Delta f/\Delta x$. The ratio $\Delta f/\Delta x$ also provides a linear approximation to the function over the interval $x \in [1, 2]$; this is the line given by the crosses in Figure A.8. The derivative provides a much better approximation than does $\Delta f/\Delta x$ near the point at which the derivative was calculated, $x = 1$; it provides a much worse approximation near $x = 2$. To get a good approximation at $x = 2$, we should calculate the derivative at the value $x = 2$.

The function x^2 is nonlinear, so we would expect that the derivative and the slope of the approximating linear equation would be different for different values of x. And so it is; if you were to repeat the argument at $x = 2$, you would derive that $\lim_{\Delta x \to 0} \Delta f/\Delta x = 4$, and at $x = 0$ the derivative is 0. Of course, this was clear from the fact that we derived the derivative above as the *function* $2x$, so that for any value of x we can easily calculate the "local slope."

Whenever the $\lim_{\Delta x \to 0} \Delta f/\Delta x$ exists, we say that the derivative exists, and writing it as a function of x is termed "taking the derivative." Symbolically, we have

$$D[f(x)]_{x=a} = \lim_{\Delta x \to 0} \frac{\Delta f}{\Delta x}_{x=a}$$

is the derivative of $f(x)$ at the point $x = a$.

Continuity of a function and the existence of its derivative need to be distinguished. For example, the function $y = |x|$ is continuous at $x = 0$, but it does not have a derivative there; $y = |x|$ is clearly continuous,—"I can draw the curve without lifting the pen from the paper"—and the limit conditions for continuity hold at $x = 0$. But let us plot the derivative of the function for $x \neq 0$ and see what happens as $x \to 0$. Note that

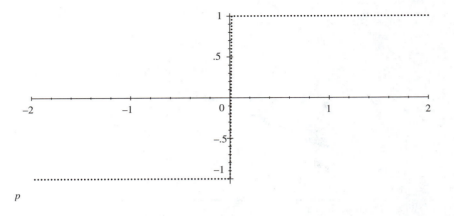

p

Figure A.9 Plot of the derivative of $y = |x|$; $x \neq 0$

$y = x$ for $x > 0$; but that $y = -x$ for $x < 0$. This means that $dy/dx = 1$, for positive x; and $dy/dx = -1$, for negative x. See Figure A.9.

The derivative does not exist at $x = 0$, because the limit from the left is -1 and the limit from the right is 1.

Consider as another example the function $y = \sqrt{x}$. The limit $\sqrt{x + \Delta x} - \sqrt{x}$ as $\Delta x \to 0$ is clearly 0 and $\sqrt{x}$ at $x = 0$ is zero, so the function is continuous. But if we try to evaluate the derivative, we face a difficulty. We can expand the function $\sqrt{x + \Delta x}$ in what is known as the binomial series, which in our case is

$$(x + \Delta x)^\alpha = x^\alpha \left(1 + \frac{\Delta x}{x} \right)^\alpha$$

$$= x^\alpha \left\{ 1 + \alpha \frac{\Delta x}{x} + \frac{\alpha(\alpha - 1)}{2!} \left(\frac{\Delta x}{x} \right)^2 + \right.$$

$$\left. \frac{\alpha(\alpha - 1)(\alpha - 2)}{3!} \left(\frac{\Delta x}{x} \right)^3 + \ldots \right.$$

$$= x^\alpha + \alpha x^{\alpha - 1} \Delta x + \frac{\alpha(\alpha - 1)}{2!} x^{\alpha - 2} \Delta x^2 + \ldots$$

By substituting $\frac{1}{2}$ for α, we obtain

$$\lim_{\Delta x \to 0} \frac{\sqrt{x + \Delta x} - \sqrt{x}}{\Delta x}$$

$$= \lim_{\Delta x \to 0} \frac{x^{1/2} + \frac{1}{2} x^{-1/2} \Delta x - \frac{1}{8} x^{-3/2} \Delta x^2 + \frac{3}{48} x^{-5/2} \Delta x^3 \ldots - x^{1/2}}{\Delta x}$$

$$= \frac{1}{2} x^{-1/2}$$

And the limit of $1/2x^{-1/2}$ as $x \to 0$ does not exist. So this function does not have a derivative at $x = 0$; in short, there is no linear approximation to the function at this point, even though it is continuous at zero. Although for this function $f(x + \Delta x) - f(x) \to 0$, the rate is slower than for Δx, so the derivative, which is the limit of a ratio, has no limit. The ratio of $f(x + \Delta x) - f(x)$ to Δx increases without limit as $\Delta x \to 0$.

The Integral as a Limit of Sums

There are two major ways of looking at the *idea* of an integral: as the limit relationship between adding and integration, which is similar to the limit relationship between taking differences and the derivative, or as the "inverse operation" of taking a derivative.

Let us begin with differences and adding and then relate that notion to the idea of differentials and integrating by taking limits as an interval, Δx, is allowed to go to zero. Suppose we have two series of numbers: $v_1 = 1$, $v_2 = 2$, $v_3 = 3$, $v_4 = 4$ and $f_0 = 0$, $f_1 = 1$, $f_2 = 3$, $f_3 = 6$, $f_4 = 10$. A moment or two playing with these two sequences will soon convince you that they are related in the following manner:

$$v_i = f_i - f_{i-1}$$
$$i = 1, 4$$

First, taking differences in the sequence $\{f_i\}$ as shown yields the sequence $\{v_i\}$. We can reverse the process; *adding the terms* of the sequence $\{v_i\}$ produces the sequence $\{f_i - f_0\}$, although at the moment it might be difficult to see the relevance of the f_0 term, given its value of zero:

$$\sum_{i=1}^{j} v_i = \sum_{i=1}^{j} (f_i - f^{i-1})$$
$$= f_j - f_0, j = 1, 4$$

In this sum, all the intervening terms f_i, $i = 1, 3$ cancel out in the summing process; f_0 can be interpreted as the sum of zero terms in the series $\{v_i\}$. So our first relationship to be generalized to the continuous argument case is the relationship between adding and differencing; they are in a sense inverse operations; "adding" is the anti-difference. The v_i are the differences of the f_i, and the f_i are the sums of the v_i.

An interesting problem arises if we observe only the differences, $\{v_i\}$. Assume that we have the same sequence $\{v_i\}$, but we are not given a sequence f_i. From our equations, we know that

$$\sum_{i=1}^{4} v_i = \sum_{i=1}^{4} (f_i - f_{i-1})$$
$$= f_4 - f_0$$

But the same numbers in the series $\{v_i\}$ can produce an infinite number of values for f_4 and f_0; we only require that the difference between f_4 and f_0 be equal to $\sum_{i=1}^{4} v_i$;

that is, for the sum of the differences to be 10, we could have $f_4 = 10$ and $f_0 = 0$, or $f_4 = 20$ and $f_0 = 10$, or $f_4 = 9$ and $f_0 = -1$. Merely listing the differences shows how the fs change, but cannot tie down the totals; these depend on the value of f_0, or f_4. Thus, adding up differences can tell us the "sum" only up to an additive constant. To tie down the sum, we need further information, such as the value of f_0, or the value of f_n. This problem of the "indeterminacy" of the sum of differences will also be apparent in the discussion on integrals that is to follow.

We are now going to consider adding up differences, but will investigate what happens as the number of terms that we add up increases as we decrease the size of the intervals over which we calculate the differences. Let me use an example from Strang's *Calculus* book. Suppose that in each of four years the income from your nascent firm is $\{\sqrt{1}, \sqrt{2}, \sqrt{3}, \sqrt{4}\}$ in thousands of dollars. What is the total income over the four years? The initial answer is merely to add up the four terms:

$$\{\sqrt{1} + \sqrt{2} + \sqrt{3} + \sqrt{4}\} = 6.1463$$

or

$$\sum_{i=1}^{j} v_i = f_j - f_0$$

Each term represents the rate of flow of income at the end of the year interval. We can plot what is happening here. In Figure A.10, recognize that $\{\sqrt{1}, \sqrt{2}, \sqrt{3}, \sqrt{4}\} = \{1, 1.4142, 1.7321, 2\}$.

The area under each "block" represents the income for that year, and the length of the base of each of the four blocks is 1. The income of your firm is a function of time, t, and the interval of time over which income was calculated was one year; time is in units of "one year." For example, during the third year, between year 2 and 3 on the

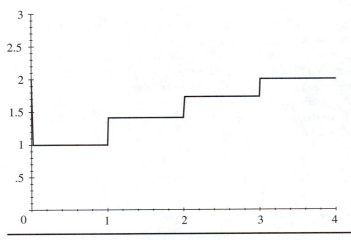

Figure A.10   Plot of annual increments to income

time axis, the income was 1.732, and the time interval, Δt, was 1. The area of the rectangle between year 2 and 3 is

$$1.732 \times 1$$

or

$$\text{height} \times \text{base} = \text{area}$$

As soon as you have to start paying quarterly tax payments, you realize that your income receipts are obtained at least in quarters of a year, so that you should really record your income each quarter. Now you have 16 income entries, 4 for each year, and the time interval, Δt, is now 1/4. Your income stream is now $\{\sqrt{1/4}, \sqrt{2/4}, \sqrt{3/4}, \ldots, \sqrt{16/4}\}$. Each of the 16 entries represents the flow of income at the end of the quarter. If we plot the new graph we will now have sixteen narrow rectangles, each with a base of 1/4 and a height given by $\sqrt{i/4}$, $i = 1, \ldots, 16$. Similar to our previous discussion, the income for the eighth quarter is

$$\sqrt{\frac{8}{4}} \times \frac{1}{4}$$

or

$$\text{height} \times \text{base} = \text{area}$$

The income for the third year calculated as a sum at the end of the year is given by $\sqrt{3} = 1.7321$. But the income for the third year is more accurately expressed in terms of quarters as

$$\sqrt{\frac{9}{4}} \times \frac{1}{4} + \sqrt{\frac{10}{4}} \times \frac{1}{4} + \sqrt{\frac{11}{4}} \times \frac{1}{4} + \sqrt{\frac{12}{4}} \times \frac{1}{4} = 1.6179$$

When we added up the four "annual" flows we got \$6,146.30. By adding up the quarterly rates of flow we obtain \$5,558.65. We can refine this procedure indefinitely, at least in principle! If we do so, we are trying to discover how to "add up" the income flows as we *continuously* refine our measurement of the rate of flow and reduce the size of the interval over which we calculate the rate. We now recognize that our previous annual measure was an amount that applied at the end of the quarter; $\sqrt{3} = \sqrt{12/4}$. If we measured in terms of weeks we would have 208 weekly entries; $\sqrt{i/52}$, $i = 1, 208$ for the four years. And if we measured in terms of days, we would have 1460 entries; $\sqrt{i/365}$, $i = 1, 1460$. Now Δt is only $1/365 = .00274$. Each rectangle has become narrower than in the previous approximation, and the approximation has become closer to the true rate of flow.

To visualize this process a bit better, in Figure A.11 we have plotted the quarterly rectangles for the third year together with an approximating smooth line.

In Figure A.12, we have plotted a line through the tops of the income rectangles, as we did in the previous figure. To get an ever better approximation to a continuous rate of flow, the interval, Δt, is much smaller. As in each approximation the total income for any period was given by the area of the rectangles, so the total income will be given by the area under the curve that we are constructing. As you look at the

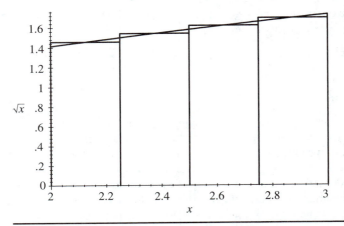

Figure A.11   Approximation by quarters for the third year

curve visualize it as the limit of adding together rectangles with narrower and narrower bases until we agree that we have a "smooth" curve.

The curve represents the rate of flow of income, and the area under the curve represents the total income for the four-year period. The curve that we have derived by increasing the accuracy of our approximation is given by $I = \sqrt{t}$; that is, income in our fictitious firm is flowing at the rate indicated by $\sqrt{t}$, so we are in the lucky situation of income growing as our firm matures. The total income for the four years is given by the area under the curve for $\sqrt{t}$ over the range 0 to 4 in years, and this area represents $5,333. In Figure A.13, the income flow is plotted as a continuous function of time (the dashed line), as is the corresponding accumulated total income from the flow (the thick line).

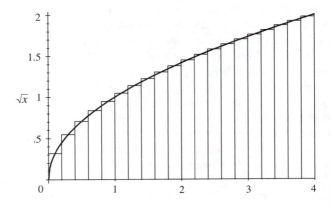

Figure A.12   An improved approximation to the function

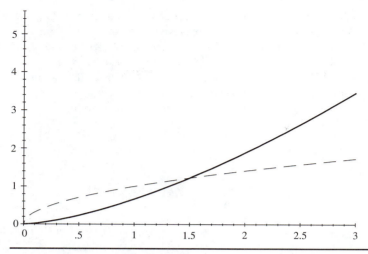

Figure A.13   Plot of accumulated income and flow of income

The height of the thick line indicates the area under the dashed line up to that point; for example, at 1.5 years the accumulated income is equal in magnitude to the current rate of flow of income.

This may at first sight be a puzzle. Consider turning on the tap in the bathtub at a rate of 10 gallons a minute, or 1/6 of a gallon a second. Note that in specifying the rate of flow, we state both an amount of water and the corresponding amount of time for the flow to pass; 10 gallons a minute and 1/6 gallons a second are the same rate of flow, merely expressed in terms of different units of measurement of time, t. To begin, the volume of flow is much bigger than the accumulated amount of water in the tub, which starts at zero. Soon the amount of water in the tub exceeds a minute's flow and thereafter the total is greater than the amount per minute. If we were to plot the water flow we would have a straight line at a level of 10 gallons per minute, if the time axis is measured in minutes; each minute adds 10 gallons; v_i in our previous notation is 10. Correspondingly, f_i is the accumulated flow from the beginning when we turned on the tap to the ith recorded minute. And as before, $v_i = f_i - f_{i-1}$, $f_i = \Sigma_{j=1}^{i} v_j$, and f_0 is zero.

The thick line is equal to the area under the rate curve. This curve shows the definite integral of the limiting process for the differences, v_i as $\Delta t \to 0$. The integral is definite because we had definite limits, we were adding up between 0 and 4.

Another way to interpret the integral is as an "antiderivative." If $v(x)$ is some function known to be a derivative, then what is the function, $f(x)$, for which $v(x)$ is the derivative: $v(x) = D[f(x)]$, where $D[.]$ indicates taking the derivative? $D[f(x)] = \lim_{\Delta x \to 0} \Delta f / \Delta x$. The analogy with the previous discrete version is clear; $v(x)$ is like the limit of v_i as $\Delta t \to 0$, so that v becomes a *continuous* function of time. An "antiderivative" is intuitively clear; $f(x)$ is the antiderivative of $v(x)$ if $v(x) = D[f(x)]$; $v(x)$ is the continuous version of taking the difference:

$$v(x) = \lim_{\Delta x \to 0} \frac{f(x + \Delta x) - f(x)}{\Delta x}$$

Much of the fascination and the heartache for students in studying calculus is in figuring out $f(x)$ from $v(x)$; sometimes we can do this analytically and sometimes only numerically. We recovered $f(t)$ here numerically, by calculating the area underneath the $v(t)$ curve. Now we will briefly consider the role of the integral as an "antiderivative." We emphasize the basic ideas. We do not provide algebraic formulae for the integral given a function for the rates of change. A simple example will illustrate the principles. Suppose that $f(x) = x^n$. We know that we can derive the difference function, or derivative, from $f(x)$ by

$$\lim_{\Delta x \to 0} \frac{f(x + \Delta x) - f(x)}{\Delta x}$$

$$= \lim_{\Delta x \to 0} \frac{(x + \Delta x)^n - (x)^n}{\Delta x}$$

$$= \lim_{\Delta x \to 0} \frac{x^n + nx^{n-1}\Delta x + \binom{n}{2} x^{n-2}\Delta x^2 + \left[\text{terms in } (\Delta x)^{k>2}\right] - (x)^n}{\Delta x}$$

$$= \lim_{\Delta x \to 0} \left\{ nx^{n-1} + \binom{n}{2} x^{n-2}\Delta x + \left[\text{terms in } (\Delta x)^{k>1}\right] \right\}$$

$$= nx^{n-1}$$

The steps involved in this expansion are

1. Expand $(x + \Delta x)^n$ using Pascal's triangle.
2. Cancel x^n and $-x^n$.
3. Divide out Δx.
4. Take the limit as $\Delta x \to 0$.

We can consider the inverse operation. Given nx^{n-1}, what is its integral, or antiderivative? Clearly, x^n, because the derivative of x^n is nx^{n-1}. A slightly more tricky question is, What is the antiderivative of x^{n-1}? As before the question is, What is the function of x such that its derivative is x^{n-1}? A moment's thought yields x^n/n.

Another important expression is e^{ax}. What is its derivative? Let us use our limit definition once again:

$$\lim_{\Delta x \to 0} \frac{f(x + \Delta x) - f(x)}{\Delta x} = \lim_{\Delta x \to 0} \frac{e^{a(x+\Delta x)} - e^{ax}}{\Delta x}$$

$$= \lim_{\Delta x \to 0} \frac{e^{ax}\left(e^{a\Delta x} - 1\right)}{\Delta x}$$

$$= \lim_{\Delta x \to 0} \frac{e^{ax}\left(1 + a\Delta x + \left[\text{terms in } (\Delta x)^{k\geq 2}\right] - 1\right)}{\Delta x}$$

$$= e^{ax} \lim_{\Delta x \to 0} \frac{a\Delta x + \left[\text{terms in } (\Delta x)^{k\geq 2}\right]}{\Delta x}$$

$$= ae^{ax}$$

The only piece of information that you need to derive this result is that

$$e^{a\Delta x} = 1 + a\Delta x + \frac{(a\Delta x)^2}{2!} + \frac{(a\Delta x)^3}{3!} + \cdots$$

The antiderivative of e^{ax} is also very simple, because, as we have just seen, the derivative of e^{ax} is proportional to e^{ax}. The solution is immediate; try $\frac{1}{a}e^{ax}$, the derivative of which is by analysis $\frac{1}{a}ae^{ax} = e^{ax}$. These are the easy examples, but even in the more complicated situations, the principles are the same and apply in the same manner. In the text, you will not be required to know the integrals of complicated functions nor will you have to derive complex derivatives. However, it is very important that you understand the ideas that have been discussed in these few pages.

Let us finish with one last observation. Our examples of antiderivatives are of what is called the "indefinite integral" as opposed to the definite integral that is defined as the area under a curve from initial point a to terminal point b. I will introduce one last piece of notation. We need a symbol for either "antiderivative" or for the limit result from adding up ever-smaller, but more numerous, rectangles. Let us define

$$\int_a^b v(t)dt = f(b) - f(a)$$

where

$$\frac{df(x)}{dx} = v(x)$$

Either we can take limits of the v_i terms to obtain $f(b) - f(a)$ to great accuracy, or we can take limits of $\Delta f(x)/\Delta x$ as $\Delta x \rightarrow 0$ to get $df(x)/dx$. In this formulation, we have a definite integral as we have precise limits to the summing up; we do so between a and b. An indefinite integral starts from a "difference function," $v(x)$, and we try to find the antiderivative, $f(x)$, given by

$$\int v(x)dx = f(x) + C$$

The addition of the $+C$ is the surprise. Recall that if we merely had the differences $\{v_i\}$, then we could not tie down the total; the sum of the v_i produced $f_n - f_0$, so that if we did not know f_0 we could not determine f_n. So here as well, if all we know is the difference function, then the antiderivative must be expressed by adding an arbitrary constant C. This is because the derivatives of both $f(x)$ and $f(x) + C$ are the same. The $+C$ does not occur in the definite integral because the limits of integration tie down the limits of the sums that are involved.

A major theme in this development is the relationship between "summing" and integrating; integration is best regarded as the limit of summing as the number of terms goes to infinity and the length of the interval over which the differences are defined goes to zero. Integration is "continuous summing up." Another major theme is the inverse relationship between differentials and integrals; the discrete analog is the inverse relationship between differencing and summing up. Almost all of mainstream calculus is concerned with the relationship between the rate of change and the accumulated change. If one begins with accumulated levels, one is interested in the rate of change; the rate is obtained from the levels by differentiation. If one begins with rates of change, one is interested in discovering the accumulated levels; the levels are obtained from the schedule of changes by integration. In one case we begin with $f(x)$ and seek $v(x)$, its derivative; in the other case we begin with $v(x)$ and seek its integral, $f(x)$.

A Worked Example   In Chapter 8, you will examine a particularly simple function used to define the "uniform distribution." In this worked example, we will use the ideas we developed to illustrate the main ideas in the context of a problem that you will need in the text. We consider the integrals of terms like x^n for any n, but we are particularly interested in very small values of n.

What is the integral of $x^0 = 1$ for all values of x? Let us suppose that we restrict the range of x to the interval $[0, 1]$; this is done merely to simplify our efforts and will have no effect on the generality of our results. Formally, we have

$$\int_0^1 dx$$

is given by the area under the curve $f(x) = x^0 = 1$ over the interval $[0, 1]$; see Figure A.14. This result is immediately obvious; the area is "base" times "height," or $(1 - 0) \times 1 = 1$. If we were to generalize to an interval $[a, b]$ the integral

$$\int_a^b dx = (b - a) \times 1 = b - a$$

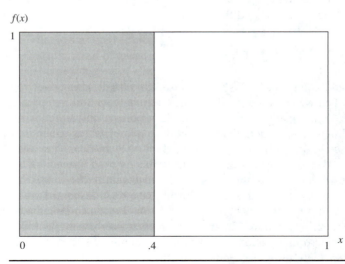

$f(x)$

Figure A.14   Illustration of an integral of a constant function: $f(x) = x^0 = 1$ from 0 to 0.4

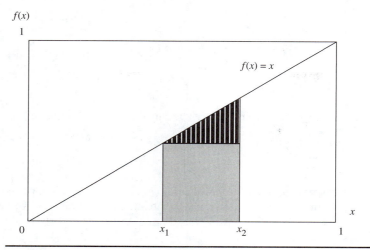

Figure A.15   Illustrating the integral of the function $f(x) = x$

is again given by the area under the constant curve; the base now is $(b - a)$ and the height is again 1, so that the area is $(b - a) \times 1$. Returning to the original problem where x was restricted to the interval $[0, 1]$, the integral

$$\int_0^{0.4} dx = 0.4$$

is illustrated by the shaded area in the graph in Figure A.14.

Now let us consider the integral of the function $f(x) = x$, and let us pretend that we do not know the formal algebraic statement that the integral of x is $1/2x^2$; we shall discover that fact directly. Consider specifically the integral that is illustrated in Figure A.15:

$$\int_{x_1}^{x_2} x \, dx$$

and we will use the idea that integrals represent the areas under curves. The area under this curve is represented in the graph by two components, a square, shaded area and a triangular area with parallel lines; the area required is the sum of the two.

The shaded area is given by

$$(x_2 - x_1) \times x_1$$

and the triangular area is given by

$$\frac{1}{2}(x_2 - x_1) \times (x_2 - x_1)$$

so the sum is

$$(x_2 - x_1) \times x_1 + \frac{1}{2}(x_2 - x_1) \times (x_2 - x_1)$$

$$= \frac{1}{2}(x_2^2 - x_1^2)$$

We conclude that the integral of the function $f(x) = x$ is given by

$$\int_{x_1}^{x_2} x\,dx = \frac{1}{2}(x_2^2 - x_1^2)$$

The demonstration for the function $f(x) = x^2$ is a little more complicated, but not by very much. We want to represent the integral of $f(x) = x^2$ by an area, where x is contained in the interval $[0, b]$ (see Figure A.16).

$$\int_0^b x^2\,dx$$

Let us divide the total range of x into n equal-sized intervals so that we can approximate the area under the graph by the sum of the areas of the n rectangles. The area of each rectangle is given by

$$\frac{b}{n} \times \left(r \times \frac{b}{n}\right)^2$$

$$r = 1, 2, \ldots n$$

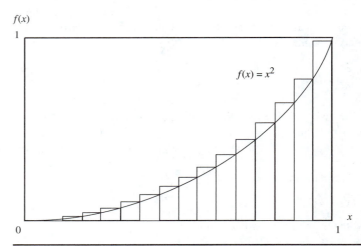

Figure A.16   Illustrating the integral of $f(x) = x^2$

where $\frac{b}{n}$ is the width of each rectangle and the height of the function, and hence the height of the rth rectangle is given by $\left(r \times \frac{b}{n}\right)^2$; $\left(r \times \frac{b}{n}\right)$, where $r = 1, 2, 3, \ldots, n$ are the n points at which the function $f(x) = x^2$ is evaluated. To get the integral, all we have to do is to add up the areas under the n rectangles.

We have

$$\sum_{r=1}^{n} \frac{b}{n} \times \left(r \times \frac{b}{n}\right)^2$$

$$= \left(\frac{b}{n}\right)^3 \sum_{r=1}^{n} r^2$$

And now all we have to do is to solve this last expression. By checking in the mathematical tables that provide such information, you can discover that

$$\sum_{r=1}^{n} r^2 = \frac{1}{6} n (n + 1) (2n + 1)$$

so we can determine that

$$\left(\frac{b}{n}\right)^3 \sum_{r=1}^{n} r^2$$

$$= b^3 \frac{\frac{1}{6} n (n + 1)(2n + 1)}{n \times n \times n}$$

$$= \frac{b^3}{6} \left(1 + \frac{1}{n}\right) \left(2 + \frac{1}{n}\right)$$

All that remains is to take limits of the last expression as n, the number of intervals, goes to infinity; the answer is $b^3/3$. We can conclude that, in general,

$$\int_{a}^{b} x^2 dx = \frac{1}{3}(b^3 - a^3)$$

Our development of the integrals of the sequence of functions, $f(x) = x^0$, or x, or x^2 would indicate the general result that

$$\int_{a}^{b} x^{r-1} dx = \frac{1}{r}(b^r - a^r)$$

or

$$\int x^{r-1} dx = \frac{1}{r} x^r$$

You can easily verify this generalization for yourself by taking the derivative of the integral for any value of r.

Exercises

These exercises are designed to give you practice in manipulating the expressions and in exploring the meaning and limitations of the relationships that were defined above. The exercises are grouped by topics.

Notation and Use of Indices

A.1 For each of the following equations specify which terms are variables, which are the coefficients or parameters of the expressions, and which are the error terms.

(a) $y = a + bx$

(b) $y = a + bx + u$

(c) $z = c - dw + v$

(d) $w = c + dx + ey + u$

(e) $y = f(x; \theta)$

(f) $z = g(y; \phi) + v$

(g) $z = \dfrac{e^{-\frac{1}{2}\left(\frac{x-\mu}{\sigma}\right)^2}}{\sigma\sqrt{2\pi}}$

(h) $p(z) = \dfrac{e^{-\lambda}\lambda^z}{z!}$

A.2 If $\{x_j\}$, $j = 1, 9$ represents the numbers {22, 31, 45, 62, 25, 33, 47, 13, 58}, perform the following calculations. Before formally carrying out the summations, try guessing the approximate values.

(a) $\displaystyle\sum_{j=1}^{9} x_j$

(b) $\displaystyle\sum_{j=1}^{6} x_j$

(c) $\displaystyle\sum_{j=3}^{9} x_j$

(d) $\displaystyle\sum_{j\geq 4}^{9} x_j$

(e) $\displaystyle\sum_{j\neq 4}^{9} x_j$

(f) $\displaystyle\sum_{j \text{ even}} x_j$

(g) $\displaystyle\sum_{j \text{ odd}} x_j$

(h) $\displaystyle\sum_{j=1}^{9} x_j^2$

(i) $\displaystyle\sum_{j=1}^{9} \sqrt{x_j}$

A.3 If the doubly indexed sequence $\{z_{j,k}\}$, $j = 1, 4$; $k = 1, 4$ represents the two-dimensional array

2	4	3	5
6	9	4	3
5	2	7	9
3	6	8	4

perform the following calculations, but first try to guess the result for each item.

(a) $\displaystyle\sum_{j,k} z_{j,k}$

(b) $\displaystyle\sum_{j\leq k} z_{j,k}$

(c) $\displaystyle\sum_{j} z_{j,k}$

(d) $\displaystyle\sum_{k} z_{j,k}$

(e) $\displaystyle\sum_{j\geq k} z_{j,k}$

(f) $\displaystyle\sum_{j=k} z_{j,k}$

(g) $\displaystyle\sum_{j<k} z_{j,k}$

A.4 If the sequence $\{x_i\}$ takes the values, $\{-3, -1, 0, 1, 2, 4\}$, evaluate the following expressions. As before, try to get an approximation to each term before evaluating it exactly.

(a) $\sum x_i^2$

(b) $\left(\sum x_i\right)^2$

(c) $\sum x_i^3$

(d) $\left(\sum x_i\right)^3$

(e) $10 \times \sum x_i$

(f) $\sum x_i - 5$

(g) $\sum [x_i - 5]$

(h) $\sum [x_i - 5]^2$

(i) $\left(\sum [x_i - 5]\right)^2$

A.5 Expand the following expressions algebraically, where $\{x_j\}$ is any array of length n and a, b are arbitrary constants. Try to visualize each operation before doing the formal calculation.

(a) $(a - b)^2$

(b) $(a - b)^3$

(c) $(a + b)^3$

(d) $(a - b)^4$

(e) $\sum x_j - a$

(f) $\sum [x_j - a]$

(g) $\sum [x_j - a]^2$

(h) $\sum [x_j - a]^3$

(i) $\sum [x_j + a]^3$

(j) $\sum [x_j - a]^4$

A.6 If $\{x_k\}$ takes the values $\{-2, -1, 2, 3, 5\}$, expand the following expressions algebraically and evaluate numerically each of the expressions, before and after algebraic expansion. Compare your results. Try to visualize each operation.

(a) $\sum x_k$

(b) $\sum x_k/5$

(c) $\sum x_k^2$

Substitute $\sum x_k/5$ for $\bar{x}$, when expanding the following expressions.

(d) $\sum [x_k - \bar{x}]$

(e) $\sum [x_k - \bar{x}]^2/5$

(f) $\sum [x_k - \bar{x}]^3/5$

(g) $\sum [x_k - \bar{x}]^4/5$

(h) $\sum |[x_k - \bar{x}]|$

A.7 If $y = 10 + 2x_1 + (-3)x_2 + x_3$,

(a) What is the value of y, when $x_1 = x_2 = x_3 = 0$?

(b) What is the value of y, when $x_1 = 2$, $x_2 = 3$, $x_3 = 4$?

(c) What is the change in the value of y, when $\Delta x_2 = -2$, and all other variables are constant?

(d) What is the change in the value of y, when $\Delta x_3 = -1$ and $\Delta x_1 = 3$, and all other variables are constant?

(e) What are some values of x_1, x_2, x_3 that satisfy $y = 0$?

(f) How does your last answer change if you keep $x_3 = 2$?

Set Theory

A.8 If $S = \{H, T, B, O\}$, list all the sets that can be generated from S. Before you begin, determine how many sets there are.

A.9   If $S = \{a_1, a_2, a_3, a_4, a_5, a_6, b_1, b_2, b_3, c_1, c_2, c_3, c_4, c_5\}$, how many sets can you create from S?

A.10   Using the set S defined in Exercise A.9, answer the following questions. For each term, express in words and in diagrams the operation being performed.

(a) Define $A = \{a_1, a_2, a_3, a_4, b_1, b_2, b_3\}$, $B = \{b_1, b_2, b_3, c_1, c_2, c_4, c_5\}$, $C = \{a_1, a_2, a_3, b_3, c_1, c_2\}$, $D = \{c_2, c_4, c_5\}$

(b) $A \cap B =$

(c) $A \cap D =$

(d) $B \cup C =$

(e) $(A \cap B) \cup C =$

(f) $(A \cup B) \cap C =$

(g) $A \cap (B \cup C) =$

(h) $A \cup (B \cap C) =$

(i) $A^c =$

(j) $D^c =$

(k) $A - B =$

(l) $B - D =$

(m) $C - D =$

(n) $D - A =$

(o) $D - C =$

(p) $(A \cup B)^c =$

(q) $(A \cap B)^c =$

(r) $S^c =$

(s) Show that $(B \cup D)^c = B^c \cap D^c$

(t) Show that $(B \cap D)^c = B^c \cup D^c$

(u) $C \cap S =$

(v) $C \cap S^c =$

A.11   Set operations reflect the logical concepts of "and" (conjunction), "or" (disjunction), and "not" (negation). Intersection is the set theoretic equivalent of "and"; union is the set theoretic equivalent of "or"; and complementation is the set theoretic equivalent of "not." Reexpress the operations in (A.10) in terms of conjunction, disjunction, and negation of events. Imagine that the $\{a_i\}$ represent height groupings, the $\{b_i\}$ represent eye colors, and the $\{c_i\}$ represent blood type. Describe the characteristics of the original sets in terms of the heights, eye colors, and blood types selected and of the sets that you created with the operations in (A.10).

A.12   Imagine that you have observations on income by level, education by years and by university, town or city of residence, sex, IQ, and occupation. By creating the appropriate sets show how you can define the following groups of people using your knowledge of set theory:

(a) income levels greater than $40,000 and education greater than high school

(b) living in Boston, did not go to Harvard, and IQ greater than 120

(c) income level less than $100,000, living in either the Northeast or the Southwest, and an engineer or a dentist

(d) born in Michigan; age less than 20, or greater than 50; and not living in Michigan

(e) IQ greater than 100, neither an engineer nor a dentist, and female

Limits and Continuity

In all of the exercises in this section, draw a diagram to illustrate the problem. Try to visualize the solution.

A.13   Determine the limits of each of the following sequences.

(a) $\{1, 1/2, 1/3, 1/4, \ldots\}$

(b) $\{1, 0, 1/2, 0, 1/3, 0, 1/4, \ldots\}$

(c) Compare the last result to $\{1, 1/2, 1, 1/3, 1, 1/4, \ldots\}$

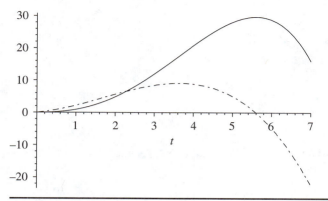

Figure A.17   Plot of a derivative and an anti-derivative

(d) $\{1, -1/2, 1/3, -1/4, 1/5, \ldots\}$

(e) $\{1, 3/2, 5/4, 7/6, 9/8, \ldots\}$

(f) $\{(n-1)/(n-k)\}$, for some fixed value of k, n an integer

(g) $\{n^{-2}\}$, for n a positive integer

(h) x^2 for some value of x in the interval $(0, 1)$

(i) $\frac{n \times (n-1) \times (n-2) \ldots (n-k)}{n \times n \ldots \times n(k \text{ times})}$, as $n \to \infty$

(j) $(ax^3 + bx^2 + cx + d)/(ex^4 + fx^2 + g)$, as $x \to \infty$

(k) $(ax^3 + bx^2 + cx + d)/(ex^3 + fx^2 + g)$, as $x \to \infty$

(l) The asymptotic behavior of a ratio of polynomials, such as those in A.13 **(j)** and **(k)**, is determined solely by the leading terms—that is, the terms with the highest powers. Explain.

(k) What governs the limiting behavior of a ratio of polynomials as $x \to 0$?

Derivatives and Antiderivatives

A.14   For the pair of graphs in Figure A.17, indicate which is the derivative of the other and which is the integral. Where is the inflection point for the integral, and with what property of the derivative curve is it associated? (An inflection point is a point at which the rate of change of a curve changes; it is where the second derivative passes through zero.) Relate the values of the integral curve to the area under the derivative curve. What is the significance of the two zeros of the derivative curve? Indicate how the derivative curve reflects the rates of change of the integral curve. When the derivative curve is greater than the integral, what does this indicate?

APPENDIX

B

Directions for Using the Student Version of S-Plus 4.5

Following are directions for installing and using S-Plus 4.5 Student Version for Windows. These instructions assume a familiarity with MS Windows operations.

B.1 Installing, Starting, and Closing S-Plus

1. Installation

- Minimum system requirements: 486 IBM-compatible PC (Pentium recommended), 66 MHz, 32-MB memory, math coprocessor, 40-MB hard disk space, CD-ROM drive (local or networked).
- Operating system requirements: Microsoft Windows 3.1, 95, 98, 2000, or NT.
- Insert the S-Plus CD into the CD-ROM drive. Installation may begin automatically. If not, run setup.exe in the root directory of the CD-ROM. Use the default settings for installation. Install the StatConcepts Labs and the Text Routines.
- The data files used in this text will be installed in a folder called Xfiles in the root directory of the drive where you install S-Plus.

2. Starting S-Plus

- To start S-Plus: In Windows 95 and above, click on Start, Programs, S-Plus Student Edition 4.5. In Windows 3.x, click on the S-Plus Student Edition 4.5 icon on the desktop. When you start S-Plus, you will see a Select Data dialog; click on Cancel or, if you wish to import a file, click on Import File and OK.

3. Closing S-Plus

- To close S-Plus: Click Exit in the File menu, or click the Close button in the top right corner of the window. A dialog box, "Commit Changes to Objects," will appear, highlighting objects that are to be retained as modified or created in your current session. If you do not want to keep these changes, click on any individual object, or click the "Deselect All" button. Click OK. See directions in the dialog.

B.2   Using S-Plus in This Text

- The Exercises at the end of each chapter include work with S-Plus. They include computer directions for each type of application as it is introduced. Some of the exercises will reference the computer data files and will not have computer directions with them. For these exercises, refer to the computer directions in the previous worked examples plus the explanations in this appendix (especially Section F).
- The Labs are self-contained illustrations of the statistical ideas used in the text. They should be used as directed in the Exercises, but feel free to experiment with them.

B.3   General Notes about S-Plus

1. Certain conventions have been followed in the computer directions in the Exercises.

- Menu bar and drop-down menu items have been underlined.
- "Enter" indicates that the Enter key on the keyboard should be pressed.
- The names of dialogs and boxes in a dialog begin with a capital letter.
- Information to be keyed into the computer is enclosed in boxes, for example, sum(mpg).
- The term *folder* is used predominantly in the text. Folder is synonymous with *directory* used in MS Windows 3.x.

2. Terminology:

- Data frames. The data files used in this text and imported into or created in S-Plus are called data frames. S-Plus also recognizes other data types such as vectors and matrices; however, the exercises in this text do not work with these data types.
- Objects. Data files, graphs, functions, and so on, are all identified as *objects* in S-Plus.
- Object names must start with an alphabetic character. Any combination of alphanumeric characters may be used. The only special character permitted in object names is the period (.).

3. **S-Plus is case-sensitive.** When you key in the name of a data frame, column of data, and so on, the case must match exactly the actual name. (Data, data, daTa are all different names.) Folder names and file names (data frames) in the Xfiles begin with a capital letter followed by lowercase letters; for example, Xfiles and Misc are folders; Domgnp and Coles are file names. The names of columns of data in the Xfiles are all lowercase (gnp, wages, age). S-Plus assigns default column names to data created in the program (V1, V2, note the capital V). In addition, S-Plus uses capital letters for new data frame names, such as SDF1. In general, functions keyed into the Commands window and in Expression are

lowercase. **Ignoring the case is a major source of errors in processing; check all names carefully for use of the correct case.**

4. To highlight more than one column of data or more than one variable, click on the top of the first column, hold down the CTRL key, and click on the top of the second column. More than one variable in a list can be selected in the same fashion, by holding down the CTRL key and clicking on the second variable, third variable, and so on.

5. Only a small number of the features and functions of S-Plus will be used in this text. In the dialogs and drop-down menus, you will see many selections that will not be referred to because this is a first text in statistics. Feel free to investigate and use the Help command to learn about other features.

B.4 Data Files

1. The data for this text are in the Xfiles folder, which has nine subfolders. Eight of the folders contain data in the .xls format: Agedisc, Energy, Firmdata, Gnp, Intrate, Misc, Testscor, and Wheatpr. The ninth folder, Readme, contains .txt format text files describing the variables in the data files and one file, Readindx.txt, with an index of the data files. To read the text files, open MS Explorer or File Manager; find Xfiles, Readme, and the file relating to the data. For example, Readeng.txt has descriptions of all the files in the Energy folder. Double click on the file name, and the text will display in MS Notepad.

2. To read the .xls data files in S-Plus, on the S-Plus menu bar click on <u>File</u>, <u>Import Data</u>, <u>From File</u>. Navigate to find the folder Xfiles. Click on Xfiles. Click on the subfolder desired (e.g., Energy). **Select the "Files of type" Microsoft Excel .xls or All Files *.*.** Highlight the desired file, and click OK. The data will display in the Data window. *Note:* When you import data files, if you have imported the file before you will get a dialog "Duplicate Name." Click OK to replace the file.

B.5 Windows in S-Plus

1. **Data window.** All imported and created data will be placed into this window. The name of the data will be in the top left corner of the Data window. The column names will be listed across the top. Create a new data frame by clicking <u>Data</u>, <u>New Data Object</u>, data.frame, OK, or by clicking the New Data Frame button on the Standard toolbar. The new data frame will be named SDF#. SDF1 will be assigned to the first data frame created. Data can be keyed into any area in the Data window. Entire columns and rows can be added, deleted, and moved around in the Data window by using the buttons on the Data toolbar that appear when the Data window is highlighted or by using the clipboard Copy and Paste buttons. A right mouse click while in the Data window will bring up several data actions. A double click on a column name permits you to key in a new name. In Section F, see the <u>Data</u> menu bar options.

2. **Report window.** The results from using the <u>Statistics</u> command on the menu bar will be placed in the Report window. The Report window can be printed by highlighting the window and clicking on the Print button on the Standard toolbar or by clicking <u>File</u>, <u>Print Report</u> on the menu bar. Information in the Report window can be highlighted, cut, copied, pasted, deleted, and so on. A right mouse click will bring up several options.

3. **Graph Sheet window.** Graphs created in S-Plus are displayed in the Graph window. New graph windows will appear as new graphs are created. The Graph window can be printed by highlighting the window and clicking on the Print button on the Standard toolbar or by clicking <u>File</u>, <u>Print Graph Sheet</u>. Graphs can be created from the menu bar <u>Graph</u> command or from the Commands window. The former graphs are named GS#, and the latter are GSD#. See the Commands window in this section for more graphs created in the Commands window. Also refer to Section F for <u>Graph</u> menu bar options.

4. **Message window.** The Message window will appear toward the bottom of your S-Plus window displaying any error, warning, or informational messages generated when using the menu bar <u>Data</u>, <u>Statistics</u>, or <u>Graph</u> commands. **Note: If the menu bar command does not create a result after clicking OK or Apply, look for the Message window to determine why. Perhaps a variable name was entered incorrectly or a function or operation was incorrectly used.**

5. **Object Browser.** Everything in S-Plus is defined as some type of object; for example, an object might be a vector, a data frame, or a graph. The Object Browser is similar to MS Explorer. S-Plus maintains the data frames you have imported or created with any modifications you make. In the Object Browser, click on data.frame in the left pane; the names of data frames appear in the right pane. Objects can be deleted by highlighting the object and clicking the DEL key on the keyboard. See Object Browser in S-Plus Help for more information.

6. **Commands window.** The Commands window permits entering more specialized commands than those supported by the menu bar in S-Plus.

- To open the Commands window click <u>Window</u>, <u>Commands Window</u> on the menu bar, or click the Commands window button on the Standard toolbar. The command line begins with a ">"prompt where you begin keying your command.

- The $< -$ means "gets" as in $x < -10 + 4$; the variable x "gets" the value of $10 + 4$. To see the contents of x, at the > prompt key in $\boxed{x}$. Enter.

- Make reference to a variable name within a data frame by using the data frame name plus a $ and the variable name. For example, in Domgnp$gnp, "Domgnp" is the data frame, and "gnp" is the variable name.

- The results of the Commands window instructions are in the Commands window following the command, or in the Graph window if the output is a graph. If a data frame was created, open the Object Browser and double click on the data frame name to see the contents of the data frame.

- Error messages are displayed in the line after the command. If a "+" appears, an error has occurred in the number of () in the immediately preceding command line. Other messages will describe the error that has occurred.

- Clicking the up arrow key on the keyboard will copy previous commands in the command window to the current line. The command can then be edited and re-executed by clicking on the Enter key.

- If a function is applied to a variable, the variable referenced must be enclosed in parentheses (). For example, boxplot (Domgnp$gnp) will create the box-and-whisker plot for the variable "gnp" in the data frame "Domgnp."
- A graph created in the Commands window will replace a previous graph created from the Commands window. The graphs created in the Commands window are named GSD#.
- To list the arguments used in a function, key in args(function name). Enter. For example, args(boxplot).
- Boxplot is a function that creates box-and-whisker plots. To key in this function at the Command window prompt >, the format is boxplot(variable name(s)). Multiple variable names will create more than one plot per graph sheet. For example, with file Cardata open, key in boxplot(Cardata$mpg, Cardata$hp). Enter.

B.6 Menu Bar Commands

Following is a description of the menu bar commands used in this text.

1. Data:

(a) New Data Object. (The New Data Frame button on the toolbar can be used also.) This menu command creates an empty data frame. When data sets need to be created or changed in size or orientation, such as creating a subset of data by quarters from another data frame, begin by clicking on New Data Object. Then data can be copied and pasted using the clipboard as necessary.

(b) Split. This menu command creates two or more new data frames based on the values in the column selected. In the dialog box in Data Frame, select the data. In Group Column, select the column to be split on. In Result Type, click on Separate D.F.'s. In Save As, enter the name of the data frames to be created. (The value being split on will be appended to the new data frame names.) Check Show in Data Window. Click Apply. For example, with the Discdata.xls data frame highlighted, select column "ext.appl." Click on Separate D.F.'s. In Save As, key in ext.int . Check Show in Data Window. Click Apply. Two new data frames will appear on the screen. Data frame "ext.int.0" with only data for ext.appl = 0, and data frame "ext.int.1"with data for ext.appl =1.

(c) Subset. This menu command creates a new data frame based on data characteristics in the selected column of data. In the dialog box in Data Frame, select the data. In "Subset Rows with," key in a formula referring to a column of data (in this case "age") in the data frame such as age<40. In Result Type, select Data Frame. In Save As, enter a data frame name. Check Show in Data Window. Click Apply. A data frame will be created with the data that satisfy the formula.

(d) Transform. This menu command changes data, depending on the expressions keyed into the Expression dialog box. In the dialog box, in Data Frame, select the data to be transformed. In New Column, key in a new column name or leave the box blank and V# will be assigned as a name. In Expression, key in the equation that transforms the data. Click Apply. The answer will be placed in the column named in the data frame selected. If the answer is a scalar, it will be repeated throughout the column.

Following is a glossary of functions used in the Expression box in the <u>Transform</u> dialog.

- **Length** counts the number of occurrences of a given variable. For example, with the Coles.xls data frame highlighted, keying length (age) will give the number of occurrences of the variable "age" in the data set Coles.xls. The result will be placed in a column of the Coles data frame.
- **Log** calculates the log to the base *e* for the variable following the function. For example, with Geyserl .xls highlighted, key in log (interval). The logs of the variable interval will be placed in the first available column in the Geyserl data frame.
- **Rank** creates a new column of data in the highlighted data frame indicating the sequential ranking of the data specified, low to high. For example: rank(mpg) will create a new column with a rank for each instance of the variable mpg.
- **Seq** generates a sequence of numbers in the highlighted data frame. The function format is seq (beginning number, last number, interval). For example, to generate a sequence of numbers beginning with −2, ending with l0, with intervals of 2, key in seq(−2, 10, 2). The sequence of numbers will be placed in a new column in the highlighted data frame.
- **Sqrt** calculates the square root of the variable named and can be used any place in equations. For example, key in mpg + sqrt(hp).
- **Sum** adds all the values of the variable(s) that follow the command. Using the proper parentheses, other arithmetic operations can be performed on the variables, such as subtract, multiply (*), divide (/), raise to a power (^), and take the square root (sqrt). For example, in S-Plus, with the file Psatcell.xls highlighted, key in sum(pmmark*pmobs)/520. Each instance of pmmark and pmobs will be multiplied; and the sum will be calculated and divided by 520. The answer will be displayed in a column of the data frame Psatcell.xls. See Chapter 4 Worked Exercises for more illustrations of how "sum" works. Note an alternative method for transforming data. With a data frame highlighted, right click on the mouse, and select Insert Column. A dialog appears with a Fill Expression box. All the function commands can be used in this box. A column name can also be specified. The position of the column within the data frame can be specified.

(e)   <u>Random Numbers</u>. This menu command generates random numbers from a specified distribution. In the dialog, the Sample Size and the Distribution must be entered. Depending on the distribution selected, other parameters may need to be specified. The resulting random numbers will be placed in the data frame specified in Save As. The default data frame is last.rdist. If the Print Results box is checked the random numbers generated will be listed in the Report window. Click Apply when the dialog selections are complete. To view the data frame created, open the Object Browser and double click on the data frame name specified in Save As.

(f)   <u>Random Sample</u>. The Random Sample menu command generates random samples of the observations in the highlighted or selected data frame. In the dialog, in Data select the data frame name. In Sampling Prob. select the column name of the variable to be randomized. The Save As file name will be the location of the randomized data. The default name is last.sample. Click Apply. To view the data frame created, open the Object Browser and double click on the data frame name specified in Save As.

2. <u>Statistics</u>: The results of the statistics calculations are displayed in the Report window when the Print Results box is checked.

   (a) <u>Data Summaries</u>, <u>Summary Statistics</u>. In the dialog, in Data Frame, select the data frame to be used. In Variables, select the variable(s) on which the statistics are to be calculated. For more than one variable, hold down the CTRL key and click on the variable. Under Statistics, select the statistics you want to calculate. Click on Apply when the dialog is complete.

   (b) <u>Data Summaries</u>, <u>Correlation</u>. In the dialog, in Data Frame, select the data frame to be used. In Variables, select the variables to be correlated. Select the second variable by holding down the CTRL key and clicking the variable name. In the Method to Handle Missing Values, you may need to select "omit" for data frames that have some missing values. Click Apply.

   (c) <u>Regression</u>, <u>Linear</u>. In the dialog, in Data Frame, select the data frame to be used. In the Formula box, key in the name of the dependent variable, a tilde (~), and the independent variable. Select the Plot tab, uncheck all but Residuals vs Fit. Click Apply. The answer will be in the Graph window and the Report window. For an explanation of the output see Exercise 13.6.

   (d) <u>Analysis of Variance</u>, <u>Fixed Effects</u>. In the dialog, in Data Frame, select the data frame to be used. In the Formula box, key in the name of the dependent variable, a tilde (~), and the independent variable. For example, saleemp~salesco. Click the Results tab, and select the Means box. Click Apply. The results are described in Exercise 14.1. Note: If the independent variable is a number that should be treated as a factor, such as "qtr" when it is 1,2,3,4, use the function "factor." For example, hsestrts~factor(qtr).

3. <u>Graph</u>: A graph created by this menu command will be placed in a new Graph Sheet window.

   (a) General Graph Directions: (1) In the data frame, highlight the column to be graphed by clicking the top of the column. If two columns are to be graphed, hold down the CTRL key as you click on the top of the second column. The first column clicked will be on the x-axis, the second on the y-axis. (2) On the menu bar, click on <u>Graph</u>, <u>2D Plot</u>. In the dialog, select the Plot Type you want. Click OK. If a dialog box appears, complete the information needed.

   (b) Labels and titles can be placed on graphs by highlighting the Graph window, clicking on <u>Insert</u>, <u>Titles</u>, <u>Main</u> and keying in the title on the box that appears on the graph. Use the S-Plus Help commands if you want to enhance the graphs further.

   (c) Print graphs by highlighting the Graph Sheet window, then click either on the Print button on the Standard toolbar or on <u>File</u>, <u>Print Graph Sheet</u> on the menu bar.

   (d) Types of graphs used in this text:

- Histogram. Follow the "General Graph Directions," highlighting one column of data and select Histogram. If you want to control the number of cells in a Histogram, *do not highlight the column* to be graphed. Highlight the Data window with the data, go to step (2) of the "General Graph Directions," and select Histogram as Plot Type. In the dialog box, in "*x* Column(s)," scroll to the column to be plotted; click on the Options tab; in Bars, Number of Bars, key in the number you want. Click OK.
- Scatter plot. Follow the "General Graph Directions" highlighting one or two columns of data, and select Scatter Plot.
- Scatter plot with trend line. Follow the "General Graph Directions," highlighting one or two columns of data to be plotted, and select Fit-Linear Least Squares.
- Box-and-whisker plot. (1) One per Graph Sheet. Highlight the column to be graphed and follow the "General Graph Directions," selecting Box Plot. Or when the dialog appears, leave "*x* Column(s)" blank, and key in the column name to be plotted in "*y* Column(s)." Click OK. (2) More than one boxplot per Graph Sheet. To put more than one boxplot on a graph for comparison purposes, you must use the Commands window. See Boxplot in B.5, "Commands Window."
- Contour plot. Follow the "General Graph Directions." Select Contour as Plot Type.
- High-density line plot. Highlight the column of data you want to plot and follow the "General Graph Directions." Select High Density Line Plot as the Plot Type.

4. Text Routines:

(a) Contingency Tables.

- Cell 2x2. This menu command calculates the number of variables in the cells of data that have been split into a two-by-two matrix. In the dialog, in Data Frame, select the data. In First Variable, select a variable. In Cut Point, key in the point where the first variable will be split. In Second Variable, select a variable. In Cut Point, key in the point where the second variable will be split. The number of observations in each cell is displayed in the Report window. In the output matrix, the number of observations in the left-hand cells is less than the first cut point. The number of observations in the right-hand cells is greater than or equal to the second cut point.
- Cell 3x3. This menu command calculates the number of variables in the cells of data that have been split into a three-by-three matrix. In the dialog, in Data Frame, select the data. In First Variable, select a variable. In "Cut Point 1," key in the point where the first variable will be split between the first and second third. In "Cut Point 2," key in the point where the first variable will be split between the second and last third. In Second Variable, select a variable. In "Cut Point 1," key in the point where the second variable will be split between the first and second third. In "Cut Point 2," key in the point where the second variable will be split between the second and last third. The Cut Point 1 boundary is less than the number entered and the Cut Point 2 boundary is

greater than or equal to the number entered. The number of observations in each cell is displayed in the Report window.

(b) Central Limit Theorem. This menu command generates 100 random samples of five different sizes from the raw data. The means of each sample are calculated. The first four moments and two standardized moments are then calculated for the means of each sample and displayed in the Report window. A histogram of the means of the five samples is created. In the dialog, in Data Frame, select the data. In Variable, select the variable to be sampled. In Sizes of Sub-samples, the default setting is 5, 10, 20, 40, 60. Other sample sizes can be keyed in if desired.

(c) Moments. This menu command calculates the number of observations, the four moments, the standard deviation, and the standardized variables for the variable specified. The results are diplayed in the Report window. In the dialog, in Data Frame, select the data. In Variable, select the variable. Several boxes are set to default values, but you can change them if you wish.

(d) Wald-Wolfowitz Runs Test. This menu command calculates the Wald-Wolfowitz Runs Test. In the dialog, in Data Frame, select the data. In Variable, select the variable to be tested. The Runs Test assumes the data have only two values, for example 0,1. If your data have more than two values, click the Create Two Categories box, and the routine will change your data to the two-value format. If the data have strong trends click the Difference Data box. Adjust the Critical Bound as desired.

B.7 Probability and Density Calculations

This section gathers together all the S-Plus computer routines needed to produce the probability and density calculations that are required in the text and that are usually found in statistical tables in the appendices of textbooks. Because we have used the computer so extensively in this text, it is not necessary to include the usual tables in the text itself. However, in Section I, "Statistical Tables," for the convenience of the reader we have listed examples of the types of tables normally seen. Students can create their own results using the routines. Further, by these means, the student can produce "table entries" that are not available in the regular tables.

Some of the probability calculations are done using S-Plus Labs, Statistical Tables or Labs, Inverse Statistical Tables; other calculations use the S-Plus Commands window. In addition, by using Labs, Statistical Tables and selecting Extended Tables, you can generate probability tables.

Binomial Coefficients

To produce the binomial coefficients, use

$$C_k^n = \frac{n!}{k!(n-k)!}$$

The binomial coefficients can be calculated in S-Plus. In the Commands window at the > prompt, key in choose(n,k). Enter. Where n and k represent integer numbers, $k \leq n$, representing n things taken k at a time. If you want to produce all the binomial coefficients, key in choose(n, 0:n). Enter.

Example: At the Commands prompt >, key in

choose(5, 3). Enter.
[1] 10.
key in
choose(5, 0:5). Enter.
[1] 1 5 10 10 5 1
key in
choose(5, 2:4). Enter.
[1] 10 10 5

Binomial Probabilities

To obtain the probabilities for the binomial distribution for k successes over n independent trials with a probability on each trial of p, in S-Plus click <u>Labs</u>, <u>Statistical Tables</u>, <u>Binomial</u>. In the dialog, click on Single Value. Enter your value of n into No. of trials, p into the Prob. of success, and k into the No. of successes. Click Apply.

Example: To calculate the probabilities that $B = 3$, or $B \leq 3$, or $B \geq 3$ when $\pi = 0.4$, set n to 8, p to 0.4, and k to 3 in the Lab. The output in the Report window is as follows:

n = 8 and pi = 0.4
P(B = 3) = 0.278692
P(B <= 3) = 0.594086
P(B >= 3) = 0.405914

Multiple probabilities can be calculated. For example, setting n to 8, p to 0.4, and k to 3:5 produces in the Report window:

n = 8 and pi = 0.4
P(B = 3 4 5) = 0.278692 0.232243 0.123863
P(B <= 3 4 5) = 0.594086 0.826330 0.950193
P(B >= 3 4 5) = 0.405914 0.173670 0.049807

Poisson Probabilities

Poisson probabilities can be calculated from the <u>Labs</u>, <u>Statistical Tables</u>, <u>Poisson</u>. Click on Single Value. Set Count to k, the number of successes, and the parameter "lambda," to λ.

Example: To calculate the probabilities that $P = 3$, or $P \leq 3$, or $P \geq 3$, when $\lambda = 4$, set $k = 3$, lambda = 4. The output in the Report window is as follows:

lambda = 4.000000
P(P = 3) = 0.195367
P(P <= 3) = 0.433470
P(P >= 3) = 0.566530

And setting $k = 3:6$, lambda $= 4$, produces in the Report window:

lambda $= 4.000000$

P(P = 3 4 5 6) = 0.195367 0.195367 0.156293 0.104196
P(P <= 3 4 5 6) = 0.433470 0.628837 0.785130 0.889326
P(P >= 3 4 5 6) = 0.566530 0.371163 0.214870 0.110674

Gaussian Density and Probabilities

Using the standard Gaussian, or standard normal, distribution, we may want to calculate the density value for any value of the variable, Z, called a "quantile" value; we may want to calculate the probability of the variable being contained between two quantile values; we may merely want to calculate the tail probabilities for any quantile value; or we may want to find the quantile value that corresponds to a stated probability. We can answer all these questions in this section. Recall that the standard Gaussian distribution has a mean of 0 and a variance of 1.

1. Density calculation for any quantile value:
   What is the value of the normal density at $Z = 0$? In the Commands window, key dnorm(0) . Enter.
   [1] 0.3989423. This is the maximum value for the density.
   What are the values of the normal density for a range of Z values from -3 to 3? In the Commands window, key in
   dnorm($-3:3$) . Enter.
   [1] 0.004431848 0.053990967 0.241970725 0.398942280
   [5] 0.241970725 0.053990967 0.004431848
2. Probability calculation for any quantile:
   To calculate the probability that $Z \leq Z_0$, in the Commands window, key in pnorm(Z_0) .
   To calculate the probability that $Z_0 \leq Z \leq Z_1$, in the Commands window, key in pnorm(Z_1) $-$ pnorm(Z_0) .
   Examples: What is the probability that Z is < 1.96? Key into the Commands window, pnorm(1.96) . Enter.
   [1] 0.9750021
   What is the probability that $-1.96 \leq Z \leq 1.96$? Key into the Commands window, pnorm(1.96) $-$ pnorm(-1.96) . Enter.
   [1] 0.9500042
3. To obtain the "tail probabilities," on the menu bar click on <u>Labs</u>, <u>Statistical Tables</u>, <u>Normal</u>. Select Single Value, and enter a quantile into Normal Statistic. Example: To calculate the probabilities that $Z \leq 1.96$, or $Z \geq 1.96$, or that $|Z| \geq 1.96$, set the quantile to 1.96 in the Lab. Click Apply. The output in the Report window is
   P(Z <= 1.96) = 0.975002
   P(Z >= 1.96) = 0.0249979
   P(|Z| >= 1.96) = 0.0499958
4. If you want to calculate the quantile value, Z_0, associated with a probability of p_0, solve for Z_0 in the equation:

$$\text{pr}(Z \le Z_0) = p_0$$

On the menu bar click on <u>Labs</u>, <u>Inverse Statistical Tables</u>, <u>Normal</u>. Select Single Value, and enter a desired probability value in the box "P($Z \le z$) =."
Example: What is the quantile that is associated with the probability of 0.8?
Key in $\boxed{.8}$ into "P($Z \le z$) =" in the Lab.
Click Apply. The output in the Report window is
P(Z <= z) = 0.8
Quantile (z) = 0.841621

Uniform Density and Probabilities

Using the uniform distribution, we may want to calculate the density value for any value of the variable, U, called a "quantile" value; we may want to calculate the probability of the variable being contained between two quantile values; we may merely want to calculate the tail probabilities for any quantile value; or we may want to find the quantile value that corresponds to a stated probability. We can answer all these questions in this section. The "standard" uniform distribution—that is, the uniform distribution that is defined over the range [0, 1]—does not require any calculations. So we illustrate the calculations using a uniform distribution over the range $[-1, 2]$; the reader can choose any limits she desires.

1. Density calculation for any quantile value, for example, 0.2: To calculate the uniform density defined over the range $[-1, 2]$ for $U_0 = 0.2$, at the > prompt in the Commands window, key in $\boxed{\text{dunif}(0.2, \text{min} = -1, \text{max} = 2)}$. Enter.
   [1] 0.3333333
2. Probability calculation for any quantile:
   To calculate the probability that $U \le U_0$, in the Commands window, key in $\boxed{\text{punif}(U_0, \text{min} = -1, \text{max} = 2)}$.
   To calculate the probability that $U_0 \le U \le U_1$, in the Commands window, key in $\boxed{\text{punif}(U_1, \text{min} = -1, \text{max} = 2) - \text{punif}(U_0, \text{min} = -1, \text{max} = 2)}$.
   Examples: Set U_0 to 0.2, U_1 to 0.7; in the Commands window, key in $\boxed{\text{punif}(.2, \text{min} = -1, \text{max} = 2)}$. Enter.
   [1] 0.4
   $\boxed{\text{punif}(.7, \text{min} = -1, \text{max} = 2) - \text{punif}(.2, \text{min} = -1, \text{max} = 2)}$. Enter.
   [1] 0.1666667
3. To obtain the "tail probabilities," on the menu bar click on <u>Labs</u>, <u>Statistical</u> <u>Tables</u>, <u>Uniform</u>. Enter in "Uniform minimum," and "Uniform maximum," which indicates the range of the uniform distribution. Enter "x minimum" and "x maximum" to obtain the range for which the tail probability is to be calculated. Click Apply.
   Example: To calculate the probability $1.2 \le U \le 2.0$ for a uniform distribution with range $[-1, 2]$, set "Uniform minimum" = -1, "Uniform maximum" = 2, "x minimum" = 1.2, and "x maximum" = 2. The output in the Report window is
   a = -1.000000 b = 2.000000
   P(1.200000 <= U <= 2.000000) = 0.266667
4. If you want to calculate the quantile value, U_0, that is associated with a probability of p_0, solve for U_0 in the equation

$pr(U \leq U_0) = p_0$

Example: For $P_0 = 0.8$, uniform over the range $[-1, 2]$, solve for U_0. In the Commands window, key in

$\boxed{\text{qunif}(0.8, \min = -1, \max = 2)}$. Enter.

[1]1.4

Student's T Density and Probabilities

Recall that the Student's T distribution depends on a degree-of-freedom (d.f.) parameter. For any given value for the degrees of freedom, we may want to calculate the density value for any value of the variable, T, called a "quantile" value; we may want to calculate the probability of the variable being contained between two quantile values; or we may merely want to calculate the tail probabilities for any quantile value; or we may want to find the quantile value that corresponds to a stated probability.

1. Density calculation for any quantile value:
   Example: If $T_0 = 0$ for Student's T distribution with 6 d.f., to calculate the density, key into the Commands window at the > prompt
   $\boxed{\text{dt}(0, \text{df} = 6)}$. Enter.
   [1] 0.3827328. This is the maximum value for the density.
   To get the density for a range of values from -3 to 3, key in
   $\boxed{\text{dt}(-3:3, \text{df} = 6)}$. Enter.
   [1] 0.01549193 0.06403612 0.22314229 0.38273277
   [5] 0.22314229 0.06403612 0.01549193

2. Probability calculation for any quantile:
   To calculate the probability that $T \leq T_0$, enter into the Commands window
   $\boxed{\text{pt}(T_0, \text{df} = \text{df}_0)}$. To calculate the probability that $T_0 \leq T \leq T_1$, enter into the Commands window $\boxed{\text{pt}(T_1, \text{df} = \text{df}_0) - \text{pt}(T_0, \text{df} = \text{df}_0)}$.
   Examples: To get the probability $t \leq 1.96$ for 6 d.f., in the Commands window at the > prompt, key in
   $\boxed{\text{pt}(1.96, \text{df} = 6)}$. Enter.
   [1] 0.9511524
   To get the probability for a Student's T distribution with 6 d.f. and probability $-1.96 \leq t \leq 1.96$, key in
   $\boxed{\text{pt}(1.96, \text{df} = 6) - \text{pt}(-1.96, \text{df} = 6)}$. Enter.
   [1] 0.9023048

3. To obtain the "tail probabilities," enter <u>Labs</u>, <u>Statistical Tables</u>, <u>Students t</u>.
   Select Single Value. Enter the degrees of freedom in the box "Deg. of Freedom" and quantile into "t Statistic."
   Example: To calculate the probabilities that $T \leq 1.68$, or $T \geq 1.68$, or $|T| \geq 1.68$ with 6 d.f., set degrees of freedom to 6 and the quantile to 1.68. Click Apply. The output in the Report window is
   Degrees of freedom = 6
   P(T <= 1.68) = 0.928021
   P(T >= 1.68) = 0.0719792
   P(|T| >= 1.68) = 0.143958

4. If you want to calculate the quantile value, T_0, associated with a probability of

p_0, for T_0 in the equation:

$$\text{pr}(T \leq T_0) = p_0$$

Click on <u>Labs</u>, <u>Inverse Statistical Tables</u>, <u>Students t</u>. Select Single Value. Enter a desired probability value in the box "P(T $\leq$ t) =" and the degrees of freedom. Example: What is the quantile that is associated with the probability of 0.8 for a Student's T distribution with 6 degrees of freedom? Set degrees of freedom to 6 and the probability to .8. Click Apply. In the Report window is

Degrees of freedom = 6
P(T <= t) = 0.8
Quantile(t) = 0.905703

Chi-Square Density and Probabilities

Recall that the chi-square distribution depends on a degrees-of-freedom parameter. For any given value for the degrees of freedom, we may want to calculate the density value for any value of the variable, $X2$, called a "quantile" value; we may want to calculate the probability of the variable being contained between two quantile values; we may merely want to calculate the tail probabilities for any quantile value; or we may want to find the quantile value that corresponds to a stated probability.

1. Density calculation for any quantile value:
   To calculate for a chi-square distribution with 6 d.f. and the density for $X2 = 3$. In the Commands window at the > prompt, key in dchisq(3, df =6). Enter.
   [1] 0.1255107
   To get a range of densities for $X2$ from 1 to 3, key in dchisq(1:3, df = 6). Enter.
   [1] 0.03790817 0.09196986 0.12551072

2. Probability calculation for any quantile:
   To calculate the probability that $X2 \leq X2_0$, enter in the Commands window pchisq(X2_0, df = df_0). To calculate the probability that $X2_0 \leq X2 \leq X2_1$, enter in the Command window pchisq(X2_1, df = df_0) − pchisq(X2_0, df = df_0). Enter.
   Examples: To calculate the probability $X2 \leq 1.96$ with 6 d.f., at the Commands prompt >, key in pchisq(1.96, df = 6). Enter.
   [1] 0.07665963
   To calculate the probability that $X2$ is between 0.6 and 1.96, key in pchisq(1.96, df = 6) − pchisq(0.6, df = 6). Enter.
   [1] 0.07306014

3. To obtain the "tail probabilities," on the menu bar click on <u>Labs</u>, <u>Statistical Tables</u>, <u>Chi-square</u>. Select Single Value. Enter the degrees of freedom in "Deg. of Freedom" and a quantile into "Chi-square Statistic."
   Example: To calculate the probabilities that $X2 \leq 1.68$, or $X2 \geq 1.68$ for a chi-square distribution with 6 d.f., set the quantile to 1.68 and the degrees of freedom to 6. Click Apply. The output in the Report window is

Degrees of freedom $= 6$

$P(X2 <= 1.68) = 0.0533452$

$P(X2 >= 1.68) = 0.946655$

4 If you want to calculate the quantile value, $X2_0$, associated with a probability of P_0, solve for $X2_0$ in the equation:

$$pr(X2 \leq X2_0) = p_0$$

We enter <u>Labs</u>, <u>Inverse Statistical Tables</u>, <u>Chi-square</u>. Select Single Value. Enter the degrees of freedom and a desired probability value in the box "$P(X2 \leq x2) =$"

Example: What is the quantile that is associated with the probability of 0.8 for a chi-squared distribution with 6 degrees of freedom? To solve for $X2_0$ in the equation $pr(X2 \leq X2_0) = P_0$ when d.f. $= 6$, $P_0 = 0.8$, key in probability and d.f. in the Lab. Click Apply. In the Report Window is

Degrees of freedom $= 6$

$P(X2 <= x2) = 0.8$

$Quantile(x2) = 8.558060$

F Density and Probabilities

Recall that the F distribution depends on two degrees-of-freedom parameters, a numerator and a denominator degrees of freedom. For any given values for the degrees of freedom, we may want to calculate the density value for any value of the variable, F, called a "quantile" value; we may want to calculate the probability of the variable being contained between two quantile values; we may merely want to calculate the tail probabilities for any quantile value; or we may want to find the quantile value that corresponds to a stated probability.

1. Density calculation for any quantile value:
    To calculate the density for an F distribution with 6 and 12 d.f. at $F_0 = 3$, in the Commands window at the > prompt, key in
    $\boxed{df(3, df1 = 6, df2=12)}$. Enter.
    [1] 0.04954522
    To calculate the densities for a range of values $F_0 = 1$ to 3, key in
    $\boxed{df(1:3, df1 = 6, df2 = 12)}$. Enter.
    [1] 0.54625819 0.16406250 0.04954522

2. Probability calculation for any quantile:
    To calculate the probability that $F \leq F_0$, enter in the Commands window
    $\boxed{pf(F_0, df1 = df1_0, df2 = df2_0)}$. To calculate the probability that $F_0 \leq F \leq F_1$, enter in the Commands window
    $\boxed{pf(F_1, df1 = df1_0, df2 = df2_0) - pf(F_0, df1 = df1_0, df2 = df2_0)}$.
    Examples: At the Commands prompt >, key in
    $\boxed{pf(1.96, df1 = 6, df2 = 12)}$. Enter.
    [1] 0.8487393
    $\boxed{pf(1.96, df1 = 6, df2 = 12) - pf(0.6, df1 = 6, df2 = 12)}$. Enter.
    [1] 0.574469

3. To obtain the "tail probabilities," enter <u>Labs</u>, <u>Statistical Tables</u>, <u>F</u>. Select Single Value. Enter the degrees of freedom in the boxes "Numerator df" and

"Denominator df," and a quantile into "F statistic."
Example: What are the tail probabilities when the degrees of freedom are 6 and 12 and the quantile is 1.68? Key in the variables in the Lab. Click Apply. The output in the Report window is
Numerator degrees of freedom = 6
Denominator degrees of freedom = 12
P(F <= 1.68) = 0.790867
P(F >= 1.68) = 0.209133

4. If you want to calculate the quantile value, F_0, associated with a probability of P_0, solve for F_0 in the equation:

$$\text{pr}(F \leq F_0) = p_0$$

Click on Labs, Inverse Statistical Tables, F. Enter a desired probability value in "P(F ≤ f) = " and the numerator and denominator degrees of freedom.
Example: What is the quantile associated with the probability of 0.8 for an F distribution with 6 and 12 degrees of freedom? Key in the variables in the Lab. Click Apply. In the Report window is
Numerator degrees of freedom = 6
Denominator degrees of freedom = 12
P(F <= f) = 0.8
Quantile(f) = 1.718150

B.8 Statistical Tables

The following tables are produced in S-Plus by clicking <u>Labs</u>, <u>Statistical Tables</u>, selecting a distribution, and choosing the dialog entry Extended Tables. Choose the remaining settings in the dialog to create a table for the range of data desired. The output will be in the Report window.

Table B.1 **Probabilities from Binomial Distribution Function**

n = 4

	0.00	0.01	0.02	0.03	0.04	0.05	0.06	0.07	0.08	0.09	0.10
0	1	0.9606	0.9224	0.8853	0.8493	0.8145	0.7807	0.7481	0.7164	0.6857	0.6561
1	0	0.0388	0.0753	0.1095	0.1416	0.1715	0.1993	0.2252	0.2492	0.2713	0.2916
2	0	0.0006	0.0023	0.0051	0.0088	0.0135	0.0191	0.0254	0.0325	0.0402	0.0486
3	0	0.0000	0.0000	0.0001	0.0002	0.0005	0.0008	0.0013	0.0019	0.0027	0.0036
4	0	0.0000	0.0000	0.0000	0.0000	0.0000	0.0000	0.0000	0.0000	0.0001	0.0001

	0.11	0.12	0.13	0.14	0.15	0.16	0.17	0.18	0.19	0.20	0.21
0	0.6274	0.5997	0.5729	0.5470	0.5220	0.4979	0.4746	0.4521	0.4305	0.4096	0.3895
1	0.3102	0.3271	0.3424	0.3562	0.3685	0.3793	0.3888	0.3970	0.4039	0.4096	0.4142
2	0.0575	0.0669	0.0767	0.0870	0.0975	0.1084	0.1195	0.1307	0.1421	0.1536	0.1651
3	0.0047	0.0061	0.0076	0.0094	0.0115	0.0138	0.0163	0.0191	0.0222	0.0256	0.0293
4	0.0001	0.0002	0.0003	0.0004	0.0005	0.0007	0.0008	0.0010	0.0013	0.0016	0.0019

	0.22	0.23	0.24	0.25	0.26	0.27	0.28	0.29	0.30	0.31	0.32
0	0.3702	0.3515	0.3336	0.3164	0.2999	0.2840	0.2687	0.2541	0.2401	0.2267	0.2138
1	0.4176	0.4200	0.4214	0.4219	0.4214	0.4201	0.4180	0.4152	0.4116	0.4074	0.4025
2	0.1767	0.1882	0.1996	0.2109	0.2221	0.2331	0.2439	0.2544	0.2646	0.2745	0.2841
3	0.0332	0.0375	0.0420	0.0469	0.0520	0.0575	0.0632	0.0693	0.0756	0.0822	0.0891
4	0.0023	0.0028	0.0033	0.0039	0.0046	0.0053	0.0061	0.0071	0.0081	0.0092	0.0105

	0.33	0.34	0.35	0.36	0.37	0.38	0.39	0.40	0.41	0.42	0.43
0	0.2015	0.1897	0.1785	0.1678	0.1575	0.1478	0.1385	0.1296	0.1212	0.1132	0.1056
1	0.3970	0.3910	0.3845	0.3775	0.3701	0.3623	0.3541	0.3456	0.3368	0.3278	0.3185
2	0.2933	0.3021	0.3105	0.3185	0.3260	0.3330	0.3396	0.3456	0.3511	0.3560	0.3604
3	0.0963	0.1038	0.1115	0.1194	0.1276	0.1361	0.1447	0.1536	0.1627	0.1719	0.1813
4	0.0119	0.0134	0.0150	0.0168	0.0187	0.0209	0.0231	0.0256	0.0283	0.0311	0.0342

	0.44	0.45	0.46	0.47	0.48	0.49	0.50
0	0.0983	0.0915	0.0850	0.0789	0.0731	0.0677	0.0625
1	0.3091	0.2995	0.2897	0.2799	0.2700	0.2600	0.2500
2	0.3643	0.3675	0.3702	0.3723	0.3738	0.3747	0.3750
3	0.1908	0.2005	0.2102	0.2201	0.2300	0.2400	0.2500
4	0.0375	0.0410	0.0448	0.0488	0.0531	0.0576	0.0625

Values in table represent $P(X = x)$ for specified value of n.

Values of p across columns, values of x down rows.

Table B.2   **Probabilities from Poisson Cumulative Distribution Function**

	8.1	8.2	8.3	8.4	8.5	8.6	8.7	8.8	8.9	9.0
0	0.0003	0.0003	0.0002	0.0002	0.0002	0.0002	0.0002	0.0002	0.0001	0.0001
1	0.0025	0.0023	0.0021	0.0019	0.0017	0.0016	0.0014	0.0013	0.0012	0.0011
2	0.0100	0.0092	0.0086	0.0079	0.0074	0.0068	0.0063	0.0058	0.0054	0.0050
3	0.0269	0.0252	0.0237	0.0222	0.0208	0.0195	0.0183	0.0171	0.0160	0.0150
4	0.0544	0.0517	0.0491	0.0466	0.0443	0.0420	0.0398	0.0377	0.0357	0.0337
5	0.0882	0.0849	0.0816	0.0784	0.0752	0.0722	0.0692	0.0663	0.0635	0.0607
6	0.1191	0.1160	0.1128	0.1097	0.1066	0.1034	0.1003	0.0972	0.0941	0.0911
7	0.1378	0.1358	0.1338	0.1317	0.1294	0.1271	0.1247	0.1222	0.1197	0.1171
8	0.1395	0.1392	0.1388	0.1382	0.1375	0.1366	0.1356	0.1344	0.1332	0.1318
9	0.1256	0.1269	0.1280	0.1290	0.1299	0.1306	0.1311	0.1315	0.1317	0.1318
10	0.1017	0.1040	0.1063	0.1084	0.1104	0.1123	0.1140	0.1157	0.1172	0.1186
11	0.0749	0.0776	0.0802	0.0828	0.0853	0.0878	0.0902	0.0925	0.0948	0.0970
12	0.0505	0.0530	0.0555	0.0579	0.0604	0.0629	0.0654	0.0679	0.0703	0.0728
13	0.0315	0.0334	0.0354	0.0374	0.0395	0.0416	0.0438	0.0459	0.0481	0.0504
14	0.0182	0.0196	0.0210	0.0225	0.0240	0.0256	0.0272	0.0289	0.0306	0.0324
15	0.0098	0.0107	0.0116	0.0126	0.0136	0.0147	0.0158	0.0169	0.0182	0.0194
16	0.0050	0.0055	0.0060	0.0066	0.0072	0.0079	0.0086	0.0093	0.0101	0.0109
17	0.0024	0.0026	0.0029	0.0033	0.0036	0.0040	0.0044	0.0048	0.0053	0.0058
18	0.0011	0.0012	0.0014	0.0015	0.0017	0.0019	0.0021	0.0024	0.0026	0.0029
19	0.0005	0.0005	0.0006	0.0007	0.0008	0.0009	0.0010	0.0011	0.0012	0.0014
20	0.0002	0.0002	0.0002	0.0003	0.0003	0.0004	0.0004	0.0005	0.0005	0.0006
21	0.0001	0.0001	0.0001	0.0001	0.0001	0.0002	0.0002	0.0002	0.0002	0.0003
22	0.0000	0.0000	0.0000	0.0000	0.0001	0.0001	0.0001	0.0001	0.0001	0.0001
23	0.0000	0.0000	0.0000	0.0000	0.0000	0.0000	0.0000	0.0000	0.0000	0.0000
24	0.0000	0.0000	0.0000	0.0000	0.0000	0.0000	0.0000	0.0000	0.0000	0.0000

	9.1	9.2	9.3	9.4	9.5	9.6	9.7	9.8	9.9	10.0
0	0.0001	0.0001	0.0001	0.0001	0.0001	0.0001	0.0001	0.0001	0.0001	0.0000
1	0.0010	0.0009	0.0009	0.0008	0.0007	0.0007	0.0006	0.0005	0.0005	0.0005
2	0.0046	0.0043	0.0040	0.0037	0.0034	0.0031	0.0029	0.0027	0.0025	0.0023
3	0.0140	0.0131	0.0123	0.0115	0.0107	0.0100	0.0093	0.0087	0.0081	0.0076
4	0.0319	0.0302	0.0285	0.0269	0.0254	0.0240	0.0226	0.0213	0.0201	0.0189
5	0.0581	0.0555	0.0530	0.0506	0.0483	0.0460	0.0439	0.0418	0.0398	0.0378
6	0.0881	0.0851	0.0822	0.0793	0.0764	0.0736	0.0709	0.0682	0.0656	0.0631

Values in table represent $P(X = x)$.

Values of lambda across columns, values of x down rows.

Table B.3 **Probabilities from Standard Normal Cumulative Distribution Function**

	0.00	0.01	0.02	0.03	0.04	0.05	0.06	0.07	0.08	0.09
0.0	0.5000	0.5040	0.5080	0.5120	0.5160	0.5199	0.5239	0.5279	0.5319	0.5359
0.1	0.5398	0.5438	0.5478	0.5517	0.5557	0.5596	0.5636	0.5675	0.5714	0.5753
0.2	0.5793	0.5832	0.5871	0.5910	0.5948	0.5987	0.6026	0.6064	0.6103	0.6141
0.3	0.6179	0.6217	0.6255	0.6293	0.6331	0.6368	0.6406	0.6443	0.6480	0.6517
0.4	0.6554	0.6591	0.6628	0.6664	0.6700	0.6736	0.6772	0.6808	0.6844	0.6879
0.5	0.6915	0.6950	0.6985	0.7019	0.7054	0.7088	0.7123	0.7157	0.7190	0.7224
0.6	0.7257	0.7291	0.7324	0.7357	0.7389	0.7422	0.7454	0.7486	0.7517	0.7549
0.7	0.7580	0.7611	0.7642	0.7673	0.7704	0.7734	0.7764	0.7794	0.7823	0.7852
0.8	0.7881	0.7910	0.7939	0.7967	0.7995	0.8023	0.8051	0.8078	0.8106	0.8133
0.9	0.8159	0.8186	0.8212	0.8238	0.8264	0.8289	0.8315	0.8340	0.8365	0.8389
1.0	0.8413	0.8438	0.8461	0.8485	0.8508	0.8531	0.8554	0.8577	0.8599	0.8621
1.1	0.8643	0.8665	0.8686	0.8708	0.8729	0.8749	0.8770	0.8790	0.8810	0.8830
1.2	0.8849	0.8869	0.8888	0.8907	0.8925	0.8944	0.8962	0.8980	0.8997	0.9015
1.3	0.9032	0.9049	0.9066	0.9082	0.9099	0.9115	0.9131	0.9147	0.9162	0.9177
1.4	0.9192	0.9207	0.9222	0.9236	0.9251	0.9265	0.9279	0.9292	0.9306	0.9319
1.5	0.9332	0.9345	0.9357	0.9370	0.9382	0.9394	0.9406	0.9418	0.9429	0.9441
1.6	0.9452	0.9463	0.9474	0.9484	0.9495	0.9505	0.9515	0.9525	0.9535	0.9545
1.7	0.9554	0.9564	0.9573	0.9582	0.9591	0.9599	0.9608	0.9616	0.9625	0.9633
1.8	0.9641	0.9649	0.9656	0.9664	0.9671	0.9678	0.9686	0.9693	0.9699	0.9706
1.9	0.9713	0.9719	0.9726	0.9732	0.9738	0.9744	0.9750	0.9756	0.9761	0.9767
2.0	0.9772	0.9778	0.9783	0.9788	0.9793	0.9798	0.9803	0.9808	0.9812	0.9817
2.1	0.9821	0.9826	0.9830	0.9834	0.9838	0.9842	0.9846	0.9850	0.9854	0.9857
2.2	0.9861	0.9864	0.9868	0.9871	0.9875	0.9878	0.9881	0.9884	0.9887	0.9890
2.3	0.9893	0.9896	0.9898	0.9901	0.9904	0.9906	0.9909	0.9911	0.9913	0.9916
2.4	0.9918	0.9920	0.9922	0.9925	0.9927	0.9929	0.9931	0.9932	0.9934	0.9936
2.5	0.9938	0.9940	0.9941	0.9943	0.9945	0.9946	0.9948	0.9949	0.9951	0.9952
2.6	0.9953	0.9955	0.9956	0.9957	0.9959	0.9960	0.9961	0.9962	0.9963	0.9964
2.7	0.9965	0.9966	0.9967	0.9968	0.9969	0.9970	0.9971	0.9972	0.9973	0.9974
2.8	0.9974	0.9975	0.9976	0.9977	0.9977	0.9978	0.9979	0.9979	0.9980	0.9981
2.9	0.9981	0.9982	0.9982	0.9983	0.9984	0.9984	0.9985	0.9985	0.9986	0.9986
3.0	0.9987	0.9987	0.9987	0.9988	0.9988	0.9989	0.9989	0.9989	0.9990	0.9990
3.1	0.9990	0.9991	0.9991	0.9991	0.9992	0.9992	0.9992	0.9992	0.9993	0.9993
3.2	0.9993	0.9993	0.9994	0.9994	0.9994	0.9994	0.9994	0.9995	0.9995	0.9995
3.3	0.9995	0.9995	0.9995	0.9996	0.9996	0.9996	0.9996	0.9996	0.9996	0.9997
3.4	0.9997	0.9997	0.9997	0.9997	0.9997	0.9997	0.9997	0.9997	09997	0.9998
3.5	0.9998	0.9998	0.9998	0.9998	0.9998	0.9998	0.9998	0.9998	0.9998	0.9998

Values in table represent $P(Z <= z)$.

Table B.4   **Probabilities from _t_ Cumulative Distribution Function with 5 Degrees of Freedom**

	0.00	0.01	0.02	0.03	004	0.05	0.06	0.07	0.08	0.09
0.0	0.5000	0.5038	0.5076	0.5114	0.5152	0.5190	0.5228	0.5265	0.5303	0.5341
0.1	0.5379	0.5417	0.5454	0.5492	0.5529	0.5567	0.5604	0.5642	0.5679	0.5716
0.2	0.5753	0.5790	0.5827	0.5864	0.5901	0.5937	0.5974	0.6010	0.6047	0.6083
0.3	0.6119	0.6155	0.6190	0.6226	0.6262	0.6297	0.6332	0.6367	0.6402	0.6437
0.4	0.6472	0.6506	0.6540	0.6575	0.6608	0.6642	0.6676	0.6709	0.6743	0.6776
0.5	0.6809	0.6841	0.6874	0.6906	0.6938	0.6970	0.7002	0.7033	0.7065	0.7096
0.6	0.7127	0.7157	0.7188	0.7218	0.7248	0.7278	0.7308	0.7337	0.7366	0.7395
0.7	0.7424	0.7453	0.7481	0.7509	0.7537	0.7565	0.7592	0.7620	0.7647	0.7673
0.8	0.7700	0.7726	0.7752	0.7778	0.7804	0.7829	0.7855	0.7880	0.7904	0.7929
0.9	0.7953	0.7977	0.8001	0.8025	0.8048	0.8071	0.8094	0.8117	0.8140	0.8162
1.0	0.8184	0.8206	0.8227	0.8249	0.8270	0.8291	0.8312	0.8332	0.8353	0.8373
1.1	0.8393	0.8412	0.8432	0.8451	0.8470	0.8489	0.8508	0.8526	0.8545	0.8563
1.2	0.8581	0.8598	0.8616	0.8633	0.8650	0.8667	0.8684	0.8700	0.8716	0.8733
1.3	0.8748	0.8764	0.8780	0.8795	0.8810	0.8825	0.8840	0.8855	0.8869	0.8884
1.4	0.8898	0.8912	0.8926	0.8939	0.8953	0.8966	0.8979	0.8992	0.9005	0.9018
1.5	0.9030	0.9043	0.9055	0.9067	0.9079	0.9091	0.9102	0.9114	0.9125	0.9136
1.6	0.9148	0.9158	0.9169	0.9180	0.9190	0.9201	0.9211	0.9221	0.9231	0.9241
1.7	0.9251	0.9260	0.9270	0.9279	0.9288	0.9297	0.9306	0.9315	0.9324	0.9333
1.8	0.9341	0.9350	0.9358	0.9366	0.9374	0.9382	0.9390	0.9398	0.9406	0.9413
1.9	0.9421	0.9428	0.9435	0.9443	0.9450	0.9457	0.9464	0.9470	0.9477	0.9484
2.0	0.9490	0.9497	0.9503	0.9509	0.9516	0.9522	0.9528	0.9534	0.9540	0.9546
2.1	0.9551	0.9557	0.9562	0.9568	0.9573	0.9579	0.9584	0.9589	0.9594	0.9600
2.2	0.9605	0.9609	0.9614	0.9619	0.9624	0.9629	0.9633	0.9638	0.9642	0.9647
2.3	0.9651	0.9655	0.9660	0.9664	0.9668	0.9672	0.9676	0.9680	0.9684	0.9688
2.4	0.9692	0.9696	0.9699	0.9703	0.9707	0.9710	0.9714	0.9717	0.9721	0.9724
2.5	0.9728	0.9731	0.9734	0.9737	0.9741	0.9744	0.9747	0.9750	0.9753	0.9756
2.6	0.9759	0.9762	0.9765	0.9767	0.9770	0.9773	0.9776	0.9778	0.9781	0.9784
2.7	0.9786	0.9789	0.9791	0.9794	0.9796	0.9798	0.9801	0.9803	0.9805	0.9808
2.8	0.9810	0.9812	0.9814	0.9817	0.9819	0.9821	0.9823	0.9825	0.9827	0.9829
2.9	0.9831	0.9833	0.9835	0.9837	0.9839	0.9841	0.9842	0.9844	0.9846	0.9848
3.0	0.9850	0.9851	0.9853	0.9855	0.9856	0.9858	0.9859	0.9861	0.9863	0.9864

Values in table represent $P(T <= t)$.

Table B.5 **Probabilities from Chi-Square Cumulative Distribution Function with 6 Degrees of Freedom**

	0.00	0.01	0.02	0.03	0.04	0.05	0.06	0.07	0.08	0.09
0.0	0.0000	0.0000	0.0000	0.0000	0.0000	0.0000	0.0000	0.0000	0.0000	0.0000
0.1	0.0000	0.0000	0.0000	0.0000	0.0001	0.0001	0.0001	0.0001	0.0001	0.0001
0.2	0.0002	0.0002	0.0002	0.0002	0.0003	0.0003	0.0003	0.0004	0.0004	0.0005
0.3	0.0005	0.0006	0.0006	0.0007	0.0007	0.0008	0.0008	0.0009	0.0010	0.0011
0.4	0.0011	0.0012	0.0013	0.0014	0.0015	0.0016	0.0017	0.0018	0.0019	0.0020
0.5	0.0022	0.0023	0.0024	0.0025	0.0027	0.0028	0.0030	0.0031	0.0033	0.0034
0.6	0.0036	0.0038	0.0039	0.0041	0.0043	0.0045	0.0047	0.0049	0.0051	0.0053
0.7	0.0055	0.0057	0.0060	0.0062	0.0064	0.0067	0.0069	0.0071	0.0074	0.0077
0.8	0.0079	0.0082	0.0085	0.0088	0.0090	0.0093	0.0096	0.0099	0.0102	0.0106
0.9	0.0109	0.0112	0.0115	0.0119	0.0122	0.0126	0.0129	0.0133	0.0136	0.0140
1.0	0.0144	0.0148	0.0152	0.0156	0.0159	0.0164	0.0168	0.0172	0.0176	0.0180
1.1	0.0185	0.0189	0.0193	0.0198	0.0203	0.0207	0.0212	0.0217	0.0221	0.0226
1.2	0.0231	0.0236	0.0241	0.0246	0.0251	0.0257	0.0262	0.0267	0.0273	0.0278
1.3	0.0283	0.0289	0.0295	0.0300	0.0306	0.0312	0.0318	0.0323	0.0329	0.0335
1.4	0.0341	0.0348	0.0354	0.0360	0.0366	0.0373	0.0379	0.0385	0.0392	0.0398
1.5	0.0405	0.0412	0.0418	0.0425	0.0432	0.0439	0.0446	0.0453	0.0460	0.0467
1.6	0.0474	0.0481	0.0489	0.0496	0.0503	0.0511	0.0518	0.0526	0.0533	0.0541
1.7	0.0549	0.0557	0.0564	0.0572	0.0580	0.0588	0.0596	0.0604	0.0612	0.0620
1.8	0.0629	0.0637	0.0645	0.0653	0.0662	0.0670	0.0679	0.0687	0.0696	0.0705
1.9	0.0713	0.0722	0.0731	0.0740	0.0749	0.0758	0.0767	0.0776	0.0785	0.0794
2.0	0.0803	0.0812	0.0821	0.0831	0.0840	0.0850	0.0859	0.0869	0.0878	0.0888
2.1	0.0897	0.0907	0.0917	0.0926	0.0936	0.0946	0.0956	0.0966	0.0976	0.0986
2.2	0.0996	0.1006	0.1016	0.1026	0.1036	0.1047	0.1057	0.1067	0.1078	0.1088
2.3	0.1099	0.1109	0.1120	0.1130	0.1141	0.1151	0.1162	0.1173	0.1184	0.1194
2.4	0.1205	0.1216	0.1227	0.1238	0.1249	0.1260	0.1271	0.1282	0.1293	0.1304
2.5	0.1315	0.1327	0.1338	0.1349	0.1360	0.1372	0.1383	0.1394	0.1406	0.1417
2.6	0.1429	0.1440	0.1452	0.1464	0.1475	0.1487	0.1499	0.1510	0.1522	0.1534
2.7	0.1546	0.1557	0.1569	0.1581	0.1593	0.1605	0.1617	0.1629	0.1641	0.1653
2.8	0.1665	0.1677	0.1689	0.1701	0.1714	0.1726	0.1738	0.1750	0.1762	0.1775
2.9	0.1787	0.1799	0.1812	0.1824	0.1837	0.1849	0.1861	0.1874	0.1886	0.1899
3.0	0.1912	0.1924	0.1937	0.1949	0.1962	0.1975	0.1987	0.2000	0.2013	0.2025

Values in table represent $P(X2 <= x2)$.

Table B.6 | **Probabilities from *F* Cumulative Distribution Function**

	0.00	0.01	0.02	0.03	0.04	0.05	0.06	0.07	0.08	0.09
0.0	0.0000	0.0099	0.0198	0.0295	0.0391	0.0486	0.0580	0.0673	0.0765	0.0856
0.1	0.0946	0.1034	0.1122	0.1209	0.1295	0.1380	0.1464	0.1547	0.1630	0.1711
0.2	0.1791	0.1871	0.1949	0.2027	0.2104	0.2180	0.2255	0.2330	0.2404	0.2476
0.3	0.2548	0.2620	0.2690	0.2760	0.2829	0.2897	0.2965	0.3031	0.3097	0.3163
0.4	0.3227	0.3291	0.3355	0.3417	0.3479	0.3540	0.3601	0.3661	0.3720	0.3779
0.5	0.3837	0.3895	0.3951	0.4008	0.4063	0.4118	0.4173	0.4227	0.4280	0.4333
0.6	0.4385	0.4437	0.4488	0.4539	0.4589	0.4639	0.4688	0.4736	0.4784	0.4832
0.7	0.4879	0.4926	0.4972	0.5017	0.5063	0.5107	0.5151	0.5195	0.5239	0.5282
0.8	0.5324	0.5366	0.5408	0.5449	0.5490	0.5530	0.5570	0.5609	0.5649	0.5687
0.9	0.5726	0.5764	0.5801	0.5838	0.5875	0.5912	0.5948	0.5984	0.6019	0.6054
1.0	0.6089	0.6123	0.6157	0.6191	0.6224	0.6257	0.6290	0.6322	0.6354	0.6386
1.1	0.6417	0.6448	0.6479	0.6510	0.6540	0.6570	0.6599	0.6629	0.6658	0.6686
1.2	0.6715	0.6743	0.6771	0.6799	0.6826	0.6853	0.6880	0.6906	0.6933	0.6959
1.3	0.6985	0.7010	0.7036	0.7061	0.7085	0.7110	0.7134	0.7159	0.7183	0.7206
1.4	0.7230	0.7253	0.7276	0.7299	0.7321	0.7344	0.7366	0.7388	0.7409	0.7431
1.5	0.7452	0.7473	0.7494	0.7515	0.7536	0.7556	0.7576	0.7596	0.7616	0.7636
1.6	0.7655	0.7674	0.7693	0.7712	0.7731	0.7749	0.7768	0.7786	0.7804	0.7822
1.7	0.7840	0.7857	0.7874	0.7892	0.7909	0.7926	0.7942	0.7959	0.7975	0.7992
1.8	0.8008	0.8024	0.8040	0.8055	0.8071	0.8086	0.8102	0.8117	0.8132	0.8147
1.9	0.8161	0.8176	0.8190	0.8205	0.8219	0.8233	0.8247	0.8261	0.8275	0.8288
2.0	0.8302	0.8315	0.8328	0.8341	0.8354	0.8367	0.8380	0.8393	0.8405	0.8418
2.1	0.8430	0.8442	0.8454	0.8466	0.8478	0.8490	0.8502	0.8513	0.8525	0.8536
2.2	0.8547	0.8558	0.8570	0.8581	0.8591	0.8602	0.8613	0.8624	0.8634	0.8645
2.3	0.8655	0.8665	0.8675	0.8685	0.8695	0.8705	0.8715	0.8725	0.8734	0.8744
2.4	0.8753	0.8763	0.8772	0.8781	0.8791	0.8800	0.8809	0.8818	0.8827	0.8835
2.5	0.8844	0.8853	0.8861	0.8870	0.8878	0.8886	0.8895	0.8903	0.8911	0.8919
2.6	0.8927	0.8935	0.8943	0.8951	0.8958	0.8966	0.8974	0.8981	0.8989	0.8996
2.7	0.9004	0.9011	0.9018	0.9025	0.9032	0.9039	0.9046	0.9053	0.9060	0.9067
2.8	0.9074	0.9081	0.9087	0.9094	0.9100	0.9107	0.9113	0.9120	0.9126	0.9132
2.9	0.9139	0.9145	0.9151	0.9157	0.9163	0.9169	0.9175	0.9181	0.9187	0.9192
3.0	0.9198	0.9204	0.9210	0.9215	0.9221	0.9226	0.9232	0.9237	0.9243	0.9248

Numerator and Denominator Degrees of Freedom $= 2$ and 15.

Values in table represent $P(F <= f)$.

Index

Bold page numbers indicate a major reference, usually a definition.